KU-341-870

Contents

List of Abbreviations   vii

Maps   ix

Introduction: Up the Republic! Republicanism in Ireland   xiii

1 The Imagined State: 1918–1919   1

2 Two Governments: 1920   111

3 War and Peace – Trials of the Counter-state: 1921   221

4 The Republic Fractured: 1922–1923   345

Conclusion   449

Appendix: Biographical Glossary   457

Notes   465

Bibliography   505

Acknowledgments   515

Index   517

Northamptonshire Libraries & Information Services	
Askews & Holts	

List of Abbreviations

IN TEXT

ADRIC	Auxiliary Division, RIC
ASU	active service unit
CDB	Congested Districts Board
CI	County Inspector (RIC)
C-in-C	Commander-in-Chief
DI	District Inspector
DMP	Dublin Metropolitan Police
DORA	Defence of the Realm Act
GAA	Gaelic Athletic Association
GHQ	General Headquarters
GOC	General Officer Commanding
IG	Inspector General (RIC)
IRA	Irish Republican Army
IRB	Irish Republican Brotherhood
ILP/TUC	Irish Labour party and Trades Union Congress
ITGWU	Irish Transport and General Workers' Union
IV	Irish Volunteers
LGB	Local Government Board (UK)
MLA	Martial Law Area
OC	Officer Commanding
PR	proportional representation
RIC	Royal Irish Constabulary
ROIA	Restoration of Order in Ireland Act
SF	Sinn Féin
TD	Teachta Dála (deputy, Dáil Éireann)
UIL	United Irish League
USC	Ulster Special Constabulary
UVF	Ulster Volunteer Force

PENGUIN BOOKS

THE REPUBLIC

Charles Townshend is the author of the highly praised *Easter 1916: The Irish Rebellion*. His other books include *The British Campaigns in Ireland, 1919–21* and *When God Made Hell: The British Invasion of Mesopotamia and the Making of Iraq, 1914–21*.

CHARLES TOWNSHEND

The Republic

The Fight for Irish Independence,
1918–1923

8000335O763

PENGUIN BOOKS

Published by the Penguin Group
Penguin Books Ltd, 80 Strand, London WC2R ORL, England
Penguin Group (USA) Inc., 375 Hudson Street, New York, New York 10014, USA
Penguin Group (Canada), 90 Eglinton Avenue East, Suite 700, Toronto, Ontario, Canada M4P 2Y3
(a division of Pearson Penguin Canada Inc.)
Penguin Ireland, 25 St Stephen's Green, Dublin 2, Ireland (a division of Penguin Books Ltd)
Penguin Group (Australia), 707 Collins Street, Melbourne, Victoria 3008, Australia
(a division of Pearson Australia Group Pty Ltd)
Penguin Books India Pvt Ltd, 11 Community Centre, Panchsheel Park, New Delhi – 110 017, India
Penguin Group (NZ), 67 Apollo Drive, Rosedale, Auckland 0632, New Zealand
(a division of Pearson New Zealand Ltd)
Penguin Books (South Africa) (Pty) Ltd, Block D, Rosebank Office Park,
181 Jan Smuts Avenue, Parktown North, Gauteng 2193, South Africa

Penguin Books Ltd, Registered Offices: 80 Strand, London WC2R ORL, England

www.penguin.com

First published by Allen Lane 2013
Published by Penguin Books 2014
001

Copyright © Charles Townshend, 2013
All rights reserved

The moral right of the author has been asserted

Images 3, 4, 5, 7, 11, 15, 21, 23 © Getty Images;
Images 12, 26, 30 © Corbis Image; Images 9, 13, 14 © Imperial
War Museum; Images 1, 17, 18, 19 © Military Archives; Image 2 © Cork
Public Museum; Image 16 © Davison & Associates Ltd;
Images 6, 8, 10, 20, 22, 24, 25 © George Morrison;
Images 27, 28 © National Library of Ireland.

Typeset by Jouve (UK) Milton Keynes
Printed in England by Clays Ltd, St Ives plc

Except in the United States of America, this book is sold subject
to the condition that it shall not, by way of trade or otherwise, be lent,
re-sold, hired out, or otherwise circulated without the publisher's
prior consent in any form of binding or cover other than that in
which it is published and without a similar condition including this
condition being imposed on the subsequent purchaser

ISBN: 978–0–141–03004–3

www.greenpenguin.co.uk

MIX
Paper from
responsible sources
FSC **FSC™ C018179**
www.fsc.org

Penguin Books is committed to a sustainable
future for our business, our readers and our planet.
This book is made from Forest Stewardship
Council™ certified paper.

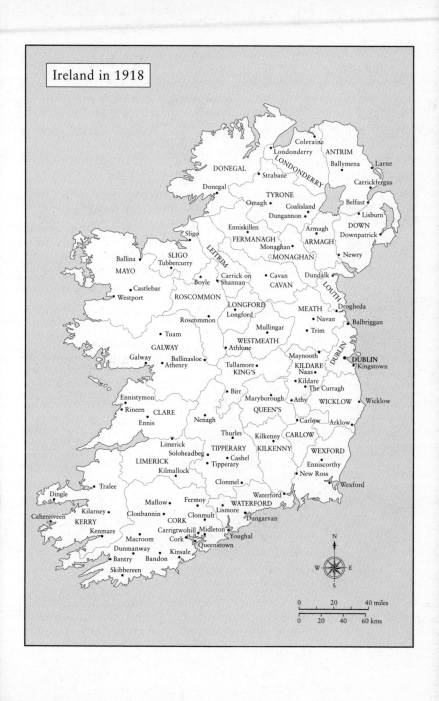

Ireland in 1918

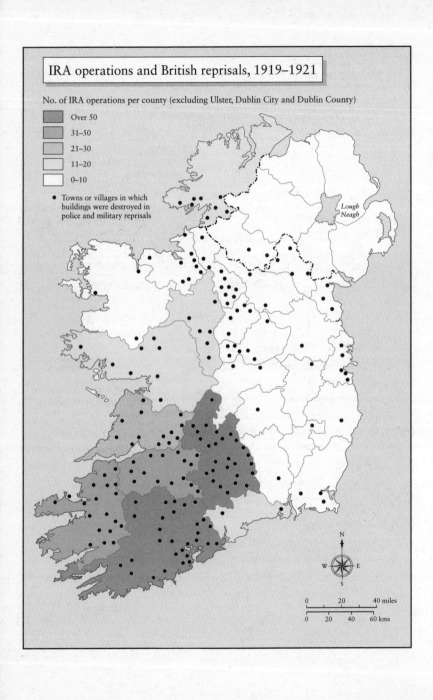

IRA operations and British reprisals, 1919–1921

No. of IRA operations per county (excluding Ulster, Dublin City and Dublin County)

Over 50
31–50
21–30
11–20
0–10

• Towns or villages in which buildings were destroyed in police and military reprisals

Lough Neagh

N
W — E
S

0   20   40 miles
0   20   40   60 kms

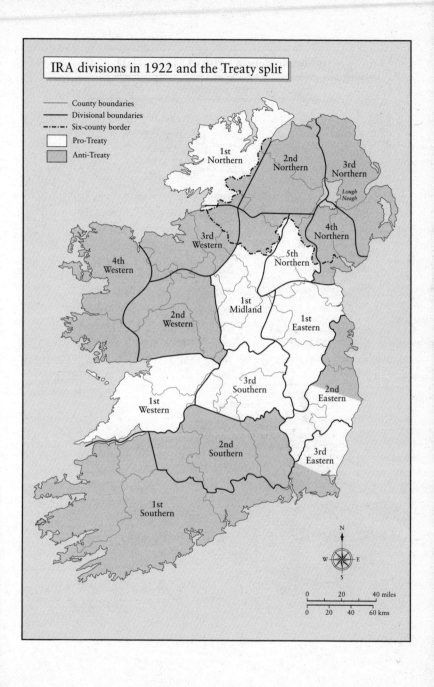

IRA divisions in 1922 and the Treaty split

County boundaries
Divisional boundaries
Six-county border
Pro-Treaty
Anti-Treaty

1st Northern
2nd Northern
3rd Northern
Lough Neagh
3rd Western
4th Northern
5th Northern
4th Western
1st Midland
2nd Western
1st Eastern
3rd Southern
2nd Eastern
1st Western
2nd Southern
3rd Eastern
1st Southern

N
W E
S

0   20   40 miles
0   20   40   60 kms

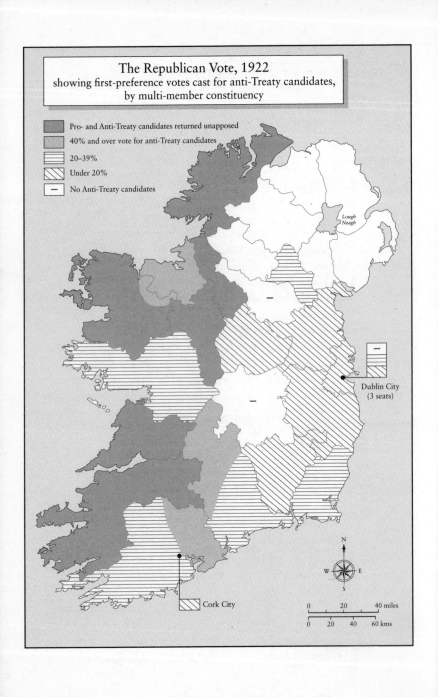

The Republican Vote, 1922

showing first-preference votes cast for anti-Treaty candidates, by multi-member constituency

Pro- and Anti-Treaty candidates returned unopposed
40% and over vote for anti-Treaty candidates
20–39%
Under 20%
No Anti-Treaty candidates

Lough Neagh

Dublin City (3 seats)

Cork City

N
W   E
S

0   20   40 miles
0   20   40   60 kms

Introduction: Up the Republic!
Republicanism in Ireland

'MILLIONS OF IRISHMEN WERE AND ARE SEPARATISTS IN CONVICTION'

On 21 January 1919 an independent Irish Republic was unilaterally declared by an assembly of Sinn Féin MPs, elected to the United Kingdom parliament in the general election of December 1918 on a platform of refusing to take their seats at Westminster. Ten years earlier, such an event would have seemed all but fantastic. Before the First World War, republicanism in Ireland was a marginal political movement. The political mainstream was dominated by the 'Irish party', a parliamentary nationalist group aiming to secure Home Rule, devolved government within the United Kingdom, rather than an independent Irish republic. At the peak of its power, under the leadership of Charles Stewart Parnell in the mid-1880s, it had sent eighty-six MPs to Westminster, where they briefly held the balance of political power. With Parnell also heading the Land League, an anti-landlord movement which effectively controlled much of the country, the party represented a formidable challenge to British rule. Two Irish Home Rule bills were introduced by their Liberal allies, in 1886 and 1893. By the time the second was voted down by the House of Lords after passing the Commons, Parnell's public career had been wrecked by his private life, and his party was split by bitter internal divisions. 'Parnellites' railed against the clerical forces that had helped English hypocrisy destroy their leader. The rift lasted nearly a decade, but in 1901 the party reunited as the United Irish League (UIL) under the leadership of the Parnellite John Redmond. Home Rule was back on track when the Liberals won a landslide victory in the 1906 general election. The UIL, commonly known as the nationalist, or Irish, party, with eighty-four seats, almost matched Parnell's 1886 total. Even though the unionists won seventeen seats, and the British political landscape was itself changing – with Labour taking forty-two seats – the party seemed beyond doubt to represent the voice of Irish nationalism.

By contrast, the voices of republicans seemed muted. The longest-established republican organization was a small oathbound secret society which rejected constitutional politics, and was committed to securing Irish independence by physical force. Its founder, James Stephens, never intended that it should have a title: it was to be an invisible presence, known merely as 'the organization'. Like the European secret societies Stephens studied, it was modelled on Freemasonry, and it was to be invisible not just to the authorities but to most of its own members. Its branches – 'Circles' – were headed by 'Centres' whose identity was known only to the higher District and County 'Head Centres', who in turn were known only to the Supreme Council. The organization's anonymity did not last. The title 'Irish Revolutionary Brotherhood' appeared early on, and when the organization adopted a formal constitution in 1873 it became the Irish Republican Brotherhood. Its members were popularly known as Fenians, and 'Fenianism' indicated an attitude of defiance as much as an organization.[1]

Though it never managed to launch its war against England, the IRB proved highly resilient. Its dynamic was well described by a Cork man who joined it in 1917. 'It was a close-knit, practical, hard-headed body, and it evoked an extraordinary spirit of loyalty and brotherhood amongst its members. It was not propagandist; it sought rather to find and bind together men of good character who had reached the conclusion that there was no solution to the problem of achieving national freedom except through the use of physical force.'[2] But after the failure of their one attempted insurrection, in 1867, Fenians were aware that the use of force was not as straightforward as they would have liked. Their greatest political impact was achieved, in fact, by accidental terrorism, when London tenements were destroyed during an attempted prison rescue in 1867 – bringing Ireland fleetingly to the top of the English political agenda. The Irish-American Fenian organization, Clan na Gael, went on to adopt terrorist methods, but the IRB held fast to its belief in open insurrection. Its 1873 constitution seemed to recognize, though, that insurrection could not succeed unless the mass of the people were ready to join it. How a small secret society could mobilize the masses and credibly challenge the military power of the state was a problem that the Fenians never resolved. Though IRB propaganda was marked by a populist spirit, the Fenian relationship with public opinion remained ambivalent. What if the people never supported military action, or if they voted for something less than independence? Would democracy prevail, and how?

By the time Stephens created his revolutionary organization, republican ideas had been etched in Irish political thought for over half a century. Every June republicans made a pilgrimage to the grave of Theobald Wolfe Tone at Bodenstown in Kildare, to assert their descent from the United Irish movement of the 1790s, allies of the first French Republic. Tone had believed that, by establishing a republic on the French model, Ireland's denominational or sectarian divisions could be transcended. The 'common name of Irishman' would replace the labels Catholic, Protestant and Dissenter. Fenians held on unswervingly to Tone's conviction that only through 'breaking the connection' with England, 'the never-failing source of all our political evils', could Ireland prosper. They were less sure, perhaps, how Tone's republic was actually to be constituted. Shortly after the foundation of the IRB a Fenian writer had published a republican constitution, but its details (such as a two-chamber assembly, with a life presidency elected by an upper house) do not seem to have preoccupied later republicans. The idea of a French-republican-style administrative reorganization, replacing the old counties and provinces with departments, for instance, did not make much impression.[3] 'Fenian propagandist work', as the celebrated IRB veteran John O'Leary recalled, 'was entirely separatist with practically no reference to Republicanism.'

Republicanism, for most of its adherents, was about achieving separation – sovereign independence – rather than implementing any concrete political programme. Michael Collins, who became president of the IRB Supreme Council in 1919, was at one with previous republican thinking in publicly insisting that 'the cause was not the Irish Republic' – 'our real want was ... liberation from English occupation.'[4] Subsequent writing about republicanism has likewise resisted the temptation to discuss the concept of the republic in any detail. Fenians became effectively defined not by their ends but by their means: they were 'physical-force men'. This virtual elevation of a method into an end in itself was attacked by a republican grouping more ideologically sophisticated than the IRB, the Irish Socialist Republican party founded by James Connolly in 1896. Connolly's newspaper the *Workers' Republic* insisted that sovereign independence by itself was an empty concept.

National freedom must bring social change: an independent Ireland run by capitalists would be no improvement for the people.

The IRB preferred not to explore the social content of independence, but early in the twentieth century the organization began to be revitalized. One of the prime movers in this, Bulmer Hobson, was from the same Protestant republican background as Wolfe Tone and several of the outstanding United Irish and Young Ireland leaders of the nineteenth century. The Protestant republican tradition had withered in face of the Home Rule threat, though Hobson hoped it could be revived. He predicted in 1905 that 'Protestant Ulster is awakening to the fact that its grandfathers dreamed a dream, and its fathers tried to forget it – but the call of it is in their ears.' As a seer he was proved wrong: the call would go unanswered. But as an organizer his achievements were real. The Dungannon Club, founded in Belfast late in 1905 and carrying a title designed to appeal to Protestant memories, launched a movement that quickly spread – even if its appeal to Protestants remained limited. The title of its newspaper, the *Republic*, nailed its colours firmly to the mast.

Hobson's republicanism drew on many sources – European revolutionary activists like Giuseppe Mazzini as well as Tone and the Young Ireland writer John Mitchel. Within the IRB he always stressed the constitution's emphasis on mobilizing the mass of the people. His most fertile concept, 'moral insurrection', originated with the Young Irelander James Fintan Lalor. Hobson saw that this could offer a kind of third way between constitutionalism (which conceded the legitimacy of the Union) and open rebellion (which was doomed to failure). In his 1909 pamphlet *Defensive Warfare* he adapted Lalor's recipe for the twentieth century. It provided a complete programme of passive resistance – economic boycott, tax strikes, civil disobedience – designed to paralyse the working of the modern state without exposing the resisters to violent repression.

Hobson's pathbreaking pamphlet was published under the banner of Sinn Féin, an umbrella group of separatists committed to electoral politics (unlike the IRB), but also (unlike the Irish party) to abstention from Westminster. The Dungannon Clubs merged with it in 1907, and Hobson himself might have challenged the man often seen as Sinn Féin's founder, Arthur Griffith, for the leadership of the party. Griffith, a natural polemicist rather than an organizer like Hobson, puzzled some separatists by arguing that Ireland should follow the example of Hungary. After the defeat of their armed rebellion in 1848–9, Hungarian nationalists had altered their strategy and secured equality with Austria by unilaterally seceding from the Austrian state. In the 'dual monarchy' that followed, two autonomous states shared a monarch, an army and a foreign policy. Though Griffith was an IRB man, his republicanism resembled that of the great Italian revolutionary leader Garibaldi, who accepted constitutional monarchy as essentially republican. (Garibaldi regarded Britain as a republic because its monarch was popular.) Like that of the great 'Liberator', Daniel O'Connell, who had led the mass movement for Catholic emancipation in the 1820s, Griffith's primary aim was the repeal of the 1801 Act of Union that had created the United Kingdom. The British parliament might conceivably be impelled to reverse what it had then done, whereas – he believed – it could not realistically be brought to recognize an Irish republic.

Though republican organizations might look marginal, separatist attitudes were certainly widespread in Ireland. The Land League founder and lapsed IRB man Michael Davitt argued in his 1904 tract on the land war, *The Fall of Feudalism in Ireland*, that 'the numerical strength of the strongest revolutionary organisation by no means measured the strength of the feeling for complete independence. Millions of Irishmen were and are separatists in conviction and aspiration who would on no account become members of a secret society.' The separatist urge was intensified by the 'Irish-Ireland' movement that blossomed from the 1890s on – embracing literature, language and sport, as well as the production and consumption of goods. The movement to revive the Irish language was in theory unpolitical: the founder of the Gaelic League, Douglas Hyde, could call for the 'de-Anglicization' of Ireland even while remaining a political unionist. He simply wanted to change the 'most anomalous position' of Ireland – 'imitating England and yet apparently hating it' – by minimizing the imitation. The movement to revive, or reinvent, Irish sports, led by the Gaelic Athletic Association (GAA), was more directly confrontational, and, as time passed, the inherent separatism of the whole cultural-nationalist project became ever clearer.[5]

The third Home Rule Bill, introduced in 1911, seemed to be the final triumph of constitutionalism. But as it passed slowly through parliament under the terms of the new Parliament Act, it triggered a crisis that would set Irish republicanism on a new course. As the bill rolled forward, resistance to Home Rule – previously focused in the House of Lords – became much more widespread. Its leader, the high-profile lawyer Sir Edward Carson, was ready to push it to the brink of open defiance of government, and had the charisma to make the threat credible. There had been sporadic instances of quasi-military activity – drilling and shooting – in Ulster during the Home Rule crises of 1886 and 1893, but the unionist mobilization that began in 1911 was on an entirely different scale. In 1912, as the Ulster Covenant, pledging resistance to the 'conspiracy to set up a Home Rule parliament' by 'all means which may be found necessary', was signed by almost half a million people, it took increasingly military shape. A craze for public drilling – which turned out to be not quite so illegal as most people had assumed – swept the province.[6] In 1913 a formally organized citizen militia, the Ulster Volunteer Force, approached a strength of 100,000.

When nationalists in turn mobilized to support Home Rule, forming the Irish Volunteers in December 1913, republican activists could move from the sidelines to the centre of events. Though it was less well funded and supported than the UVF, the IV organization also grew dramatically, with its membership touching a six-figure total in 1914. Most of the rank and file were probably home rulers rather than separatists, and certainly never imagined really going into battle, but a command structure developed with very different ideas. The Volunteer Executive was dominated by IRB men, who were also plentiful among IV officers generally. For the first time since 1867, the Fenians had their hands on something like an army. The socialist republicans also began to march down the path of military action, when in the wake of industrial conflict in Dublin in 1913 Connolly formed the Irish Citizen Army. This was ostensibly a small force set up to protect strikers from the police and the employers' paid strikebreakers, but once the First World War began Connolly – following the Bolshevik rather than the Menshevik line – aimed to give history a push by initiating direct armed action.

If there was any doubt about the seriousness of the Ulster crisis, it was removed by the action of British army officers at the Curragh in March 1914, declaring that they would resign their commissions rather than confront the UVF. When the UVF ran some 20,000 rifles into Larne in April, it doubled its armament. By July, with two (or three) armed militias aiming to put pressure on the government for and against Home Rule, and the army's reliability in question, there were real fears of imminent civil war. One of these militias was at least partially controlled by republicans. The rank and file of the Irish Volunteers might have joined to support Home Rule, but many of their leaders were separatists. When European war broke out in August, the physical-force men were at last in a position to act on the old Fenian belief that 'England's difficulty' would be 'Ireland's opportunity'. The old and new guards of the IRB, Tom Clarke and Seán MacDermott, were pushed on towards insurrection by a visionary and charismatic figure, Patrick Pearse. Probably the most influential republican after Wolfe Tone, Pearse did not actually join the IRB until long after he had already secured national significance as a Gaelic League leader and writer. Like many, he 'came to nationalism through the Gaelic League';[7] his belief that the loss of language was fatal made him a dedicated educator. He was probably sworn into the IRB shortly after he became director of organization of the newly formed Irish Volunteers: within months he had been co-opted on to the Supreme Council. Pearse's rhetoric made a crucial connection between Fenian insurrectionism and the new, culturally defined sense of Irish national identity.

Easter Week 1916 projected the republic to the political centre stage. The Irish Volunteers and the Citizen Army came out to fight together as the Army of the Irish Republic. Pearse's historic proclamation asserting the Irish people's inalienable right to 'national freedom and sovereignty' was issued under the heading 'Poblacht na hEireann, Provisional Government of the Irish Republic'. The Gaelic title was a new coinage – literally 'Republic of Ireland' – because there was no Gaelic adjective for 'Irish'. So a republic was nominally established, but while Pearse's proclamation spelt out its social aspirations more clearly than Fenian thinking had, its political form was still left to the imagination. The fact that its members expected to come under overwhelming military assault within hours may explain this. As the days passed they might possibly have set out some kind of programme for the intended political structure of the 'sovereign independent Irish state', had they seen it as an important issue. But even Connolly seems to have shared the view of the famous insurrectionist Auguste Blanqui that the important thing was to get across the river, not discuss what might be on the other side. Subsequent republican writers have mostly agreed, and though the 1916 Republic has been claimed as a pioneering 'People's Republic', it remains a shadowy entity – a gesture not a blueprint.[8] The Provisional Government's members who were in the GPO (five of the seven signatories of the proclamation) do not seem to have met or tried to act as an executive. Pearse took a joint civil–military post as president of the Provisional Government and commander-in-chief of the Army of the Republic, but the term 'President of the Irish Republic' seems to have rested – by IRB tradition – with Tom Clarke as president of the Supreme Council. This IRB tradition would continue after the suppression of the 1916 rebellion. Beyond that, not much happened to suggest that the Republic was seen as anything other than a symbol. Only one of the leaders adopted the French revolutionary style of dating his diary entries and memoranda.[9] Pearse dated his surrender order 29 April, not 'day 6 of the Republic'.

In the repressive backwash following the Easter rebellion, republicanism appeared to have been condemned by yet another failure. But the British reaction, above all the execution of the republican leaders, ensured that it would survive. Ironically, General Sir John Maxwell, the military commander responsible for the executions, saw their effect more quickly than most politicians. He had spent several years commanding in Egypt, and that experience had certainly alerted him to the threat of nationalism. Just a fortnight after Pearse's surrender, he warned the Prime Minister, H. H. Asquith, that 'the younger generation is likely to be more revolutionary than their predecessors,' and that 'though the rebellion was condemned, it is now being used as a lever to bring on Home Rule,' or even 'an Irish Republic'. A month later he told Asquith that it was 'becoming increasingly difficult to differentiate between a Nationalist and a Sinn Feiner'. In the event of a general election, 'very few, if any, of existing Nationalist MPs would be re-elected'.[10] He no doubt had little liking for the Home Rulers, but could see that they were preferable to any group that was likely to replace them.

Whether Asquith could have responded to this unexpectedly perceptive advice we cannot know: at the end of the year he was forced out of office and replaced by David Lloyd George. After the rebellion, Lloyd George had led a further round of Home Rule negotiations, which merely forced the nationalist party to acknowledge that some form of partition was inevitable, and accelerated its loss of prestige. The brief flurry of interest in Ireland that the British government had been forced to take was soon replaced by its traditional inattentiveness. The war that had justified Britain's crushing reaction to the rebellion remained to be won. Only then might Home Rule, pushed through by the Liberals under the party truce after the outbreak of the world war, but suspended for the duration, finally come into force.

PART ONE

The Imagined State:
1918–1919

Ireland in 1918 hung, like the rest of Europe, on the edge of an epoch. The tide of regime change that would transform the postwar world had already started to run with the collapse of the Tsarist empire in Russia. In January 1918 President Woodrow Wilson unveiled the 'fourteen points' on which the new world order was to be based. Their most resonant concept was national self-determination. This had profound implications for empires like the British, and even for the multinational state that was the United Kingdom itself. The Union of 1801 between Great Britain and Ireland had never been accepted as legitimate by Irish nationalists. The governing structure that it had created had never worked, as even its supporters admitted. Ireland sent 105 MPs to the Imperial Parliament at Westminster, the sole source of Irish legislation. British statutes formed the corpus of Irish law, yet the hundred years of the Union were littered with exceptional legislation that recognized that Ireland was indeed different. The Westminster parliament was notoriously uninterested in Irish affairs, and British governments seldom put together a coherent Irish policy. The government of Ireland was exercised through an awkward arrangement in which a lord lieutenant (colloquially called the viceroy) in Dublin and a chief secretary in London shared power. The Irish administration, 'Dublin Castle', was famously dysfunctional. The attempt, such as it had been, to integrate Ireland into the UK had undoubtedly failed.

Yet Britain's strategic interest in Ireland was intense and dominating. The force that had originally brought Norman-English rule to the sister island had only increased in the following eight centuries. In an age of global commerce and naval contestation Ireland, 'the Heligoland of the Atlantic', was regarded as the keystone in the arch of British world power. 'The channel forbids union, the ocean forbids separation' as even the Irish Patriot leader Henry Grattan accepted. Losing control of Ireland was unthinkable. The Home Rule project was the attempt to give Ireland autonomy while preserving the UK state in its vital sphere of security. Yet even Home Rule, designed to placate unionist fears of Irish nationalism, had created the most severe crisis in the history of the modern British state. Unionists had dismissed it as a sham, an unworkable compromise which could never prevent Ireland from moving on to independence. After the war broke out in 1914 it had been enacted, and placed on ice for the duration of hostilities. Whether it could ultimately square the circle of Anglo-Irish relations was perhaps the greatest question to face Britain at the end of the war.

As the world war entered its fourth, climactic year, Ireland was superficially at peace. The eruption of Easter Week 1916, decisively crushed in physical terms, had been widely dismissed in political terms as a crazy aberration. Indeed, if the British government had possessed the composure to consign its leaders to an asylum rather than putting them in front of a firing squad, what followed might have been very different. Many Irish people, especially the families of the 100,000 or more Irishmen serving in the British army, remained as committed to the war effort as the British were.[1] Recruitment, which had fallen away, seemed (to police eyes at least) to be improving again. The Irish nationalist party, supporters of the British government's Home Rule policy, had lost a handful of elections to Sinn Féin, but still appeared dominant. The Irish Convention, set up by Prime Minister David Lloyd George to work out a form of Home Rule that would be acceptable to unionists as well as nationalists, offered optimists the prospect of a final political settlement.

The long protraction of its discussions – it met in July 1917, and went on until April 1918 – at first seemed encouraging rather than depressing. At least the unionists went on talking, even if they showed remarkably little inclination to compromise. Very few people could imagine that Sinn Féin's exclusion would mean that any eventual agreement would be nugatory. Sinn Féin, a party with just three MPs, had demanded that the Convention's terms of reference should allow it to recommend complete Irish independence, and that 'political prisoners' should be treated as prisoners of war. It was assumed, though, that once a settlement was reached, Sinn Féin would fade away.

Patrick Pearse's revolution seemed to have ground to a halt, and republicanism seemed to remain as marginal as it had ever been. Many people saw the 1916 insurrection as the last nail in the coffin of the physical-force doctrine. But the calm was illusory. Revolutionaries may still have been few, but they were oddly undismayed by the failure of the rising. They had been energized by the heady experience of Easter Week, and still more by its repressive aftermath. Those who might have identified themselves as 'United Kingdomers', united against the Germans, as one 1914 cartoon had optimistically suggested, were in decline. It is hard not to see the death of Thomas Kettle – the home ruler with the deepest commitment to the war – on the western front in September 1916 as a symbolic moment in this process. Although recruitment trickled on, opposition to it was becoming ever firmer. Anti-recruitment activity, even – perhaps especially – where it was unpopular, brought together a range of more or less radical nationalists and bound them into a cohesive grouping under the Sinn Féin banner. Literally, indeed – the green-white-orange tricolour devised by the Young Ireland movement in the 1840s sprang up everywhere now as the 'Sinn Féin flag'. Three Sixteeners fought and won by-elections under the SF banner in 1917, the first of them while still in prison.

The death of the 1916 leader Thomas Ashe on hunger strike (imprisoned for anti-recruitment campaigning) in Dublin's Mountjoy gaol in September unleashed an emotional tsunami. The 'outburst of popular sympathy created the greatest possible stir throughout the country', as the Chief Secretary lamented. Ashe's funeral, carefully stage-managed to take its place in a succession of intensely emotive manifestations of 'separatism', also demonstrated a new practical capacity among the state's opponents. The Irish Volunteers took temporary control of the capital city as the cortège passed through to Glasnevin cemetery, impressing the British military commander in Ireland. Sinn Féin, General Mahon noted, was 'exhibiting discipline to a degree which is perhaps the most dangerous sign of the times'. The simple, single-sentence funeral oration by Michael Collins, in deliberate contrast to earlier, highly wrought nationalist rhetoric, pithily projected a new spirit of no-nonsense activism.

The quickening of separatist mobilization was apparent at the first Sinn Féin national convention (Ard-fheis) on 26 October. This demonstrated not just the growing scale of the organization, but also its increasing radicalism. In the election to its presidency, Arthur Griffith – a famous national figure since the time of the Boer War, and the organization's chief inspirer – stood aside in favour of Eamon de Valera, who had been virtually unknown until he commanded a Volunteer battalion during the 1916 rebellion. Fighting the by-election in East Clare in July

1917, he had said that 'although we fought once and lost, it is only a lesson for the second time.' The organization set out its aim as being to secure an independent Irish republic, with the proviso – a concession to Griffith, who was not a convinced republican – that after achieving independence the people could choose their own form of government.

Less public, but still more important, was the convention of the semi-underground militia, the Irish Volunteers, held the following day. Temporarily paralysed by the large-scale arrests that had followed Easter Week, the Volunteers had been rebuilding locally even before the majority of the arrested Sixteeners were released in mid-1917. At the October convention, de Valera's election as president of the Volunteers signalled the fusion of the military with the political organization, while elections to the Executive projected 1916 men such as Cathal Brugha, its chairman, and Michael Collins, its director of organization, into key roles. Richard Mulcahy, who had planned Thomas Ashe's funeral (and had been Ashe's deputy in 1916), and now became director of training, had exactly the kind of methodical administrative capacity that worried General Mahon. The twin organization had shown itself able to survive an apparently major setback. By the second anniversary of the Easter rebellion it would have been a significant challenger to the dominant nationalist party. A few weeks before that anniversary, though, its standing was radically transformed, not by its own actions but by the decision of the British government to enforce compulsory military service in Ireland.

'THE COUNTRY IS THOROUGHLY ROUSED'

The venerable Fenian mantra of 'England's difficulty' – a deceptive idea in 1916, when Britain was armed to the teeth – fitted reality much better in the last years of the war. As British resources dwindled, the conscription issue became ever more pressing. Compulsory military service had been a highly contentious issue in Britain itself. The ingrained liberal tradition of anti-militarism had been strong enough to fend it off for a year and a half, and the eventual decision to impose conscription in 1916 split the Liberal government. In Ireland, the issue was dramatically more explosive. Resistance to even voluntary recruitment had been a keystone of separatist-nationalist activity ever since 1914.

Recruitment had caused the split in the Volunteer movement in 1914, and even though the constitutional nationalists of the Irish parliamentary party still supported voluntary enlistment, they knew that compulsion would never be accepted in Ireland. At first, the government (seemingly unconcerned to shore up its Irish nationalist allies) ignored this, but after the 1916 rebellion Ireland was hastily excluded from the new Military Service Act. For the next couple of years there was a tacit consensus that – quite apart from the likelihood of major long-term political alienation, a prospect the government was able to ignore – raising conscripts in Ireland would need more troops than it would produce.

This sleeping-dogs policy could not survive the shock of the 1918 German offensive on the western front. On 25 March, four days after the Germans broke through the British lines, David Lloyd George's coalition government finally took the decision to prepare a Military Service Bill for Ireland. Crisis on the western front begot crisis in Ireland, and both would test the resources of an already malfunctioning administration. Responsibility for implementing conscription would fall on the heads of the army and the police in Ireland. The British army appeared omnipresent in Ireland, but though the country was dotted with military barracks, which were particularly visible in the capital city, the main task of the Irish garrison was not so much to control Ireland as to prepare new drafts for the army overseas. The real control over Ireland, outside Dublin – which had its own unarmed force, the Dublin Metropolitan Police (DMP) – lay with the armed police of the Royal Irish Constabulary.

The RIC, given its royal title for its part in suppressing the 1867 Fenian rising, was known as 'the eyes and ears of Dublin Castle' – the pre-echo of Kafka was perhaps not wholly inappropriate. It was a centrally commanded, semi-military force, created as a primary line of defence against armed rebellion; in 1866 *The Times* had grumbled that it 'resembles, indeed, a continental *gendarmerie* far more nearly than is consistent with our habits of local self-government'. But it also accepted that it gave good value for money: 'no part of our expenditure yields a better return.' The government depended on the 10,000 men of the RIC, distributed in thousands of local stations, for the supply of all its information – not only political, but social as well. The RIC County Inspectors' monthly reports monitored almost every aspect of Irish life, paying close attention to agricultural yields and prices. Everything from the census through the inspection of weights and measures to the issue of dog licences and fishing permits was administered by the police, generally regarded as the most efficient of the thirty-odd departments forming the ramshackle Irish administration in Dublin Castle.[2]

The fact that RIC men were stationed outside their native counties, to shield their families from intimidation, gave some colour to the nationalist charge that the force was 'an army of occupation'. But the rank and file of the force were exclusively Irish. The great majority of recruits were farmers' sons, who joined for a secure job and a guaranteed pension. They were selected for their physique, intelligence and 'good character'.[3] They lived in stations grandly labelled 'barracks', and their admirers as well as their enemies saw these, as the conservative *Morning Post* put it, as 'those little barrack forts that are the block-houses of Imperial rule in Ireland'. Armed with cavalry carbines (though not generally carrying them on duty), RIC men were supposed to mix drill and target practice with study of the law. They shared their founder, Robert Peel, with the English police, but whereas English constables were 'bobbies', their Irish counterparts were 'peelers', reflecting their less amiable image. The long period of peace between 1867 and 1914 had allowed the force to become far more civilianized and integrated with local communities than its organizational ethos – and its nationalist critics – would suggest.[4] But the war pitched the RIC back into the front line of defending the state. Its military limits were sharply revealed by the 1916 rebellion, and years of low-level clashes with protesters at military recruitment meetings and anti-conscription demonstrations eroded the sense of consensual policing that had been slowly established. The paralysis of the police was alarmingly illustrated by the Clare County Inspector's rather helpless (and mistaken) complaint during the East Clare by-election in 1917 that 'almost every young man carries a revolver.'

The General Officer Commanding (GOC) in Ireland, Lieutenant General Bryan Mahon,[5] and the Inspector General of the RIC, Brigadier General Sir Joseph Byrne, now produced a sobering assessment of the prospects of applying the Military Service Bill. Conscription could be enforced, they said, 'but with [here the Inspector General inserted "the greatest"] difficulty. It would be *bitterly* opposed by the *united* Nationalists and Clergy.' They recognized the unique potential of the measure to provoke a mass national movement. Strikes would dislocate the life of the country, and railway, postal and telegraph communications would be cut. A key decision would be whether to attempt to impose conscription across the whole country simultaneously, or do it district by district. Either way, 'the country must be put under some kind of military control. Law would have to be dropped, because ordinarily, for the first fortnight at least, there would be bloodshed and a great deal of suffering to the civil population in every way.' At least two brigades of troops, in the GOC's opinion (the IG thought 'considerably more'), in addition to the existing garrison would be needed, for three months or more.[6]

This was a charmless scenario. How many men would conscription produce? A year earlier, Mahon had estimated 160,000 ('with very liberal exemptions'), so he thought that – since emigration remained suspended for the duration of the war – the total should be greater now. Exactly how much greater, he did not say. A more important question was probably what proportion of that total 'would make good and reliable soldiers'. The two chiefs evidently disagreed on this: Mahon considered that once enlisted the conscripts would be sound enough; the Inspector General, Byrne (who had been General Maxwell's chief of staff in 1916), thought that only 'some' of them would be; 'a considerable number would be likely to give trouble.' The first step must be 'to get all known leaders out of the way at once'; then 'everyone, irrespective of who he is', must be arrested 'on the first sign of giving trouble'. These were drastic measures, the GOC admitted, but the situation was serious – otherwise 'it would not be considered necessary to have conscription at this inopportune time.' The government was in a bind: it would consider imposing conscription only in desperate circumstances, but those very circumstances would make the policy even harder to carry out.

The division between the two chief Irish enforcers was echoed in the Irish government. The 'greening' of Dublin Castle, the remarkable increase in the number of Catholics in high office since the turn of the century, produced a disconcerting opposition to conscription. Most alarming was the refusal of the Lord Chief Justice to discipline local magistrates who passed anti-conscription resolutions.[7] The division was also mirrored among British ministers. The Chief Secretary for Ireland, Henry Duke, preferred the Inspector General's cautious assessment, warning that full conscription would 'be likely to end the whole chapter of effort to establish concord between the two countries'. It would 'consolidate into one mass of antagonism all the Nationalist elements in Ireland, politicians, priests, men and women'.[8] But Duke's fellow Conservative Walter Long, the First Lord of the Admiralty, took a much firmer line. Long, who had served as chief secretary ten years before, had (largely through lack of competition) established himself as the government's leading expert on Irish policy. In April 1918 he was given an unprecedented liaison role, 'responsible for Irish administration to the Cabinet'.[9] His confidence that though 'the Irish will talk, shout, perhaps get up a fight or two,' they 'will know when they are beaten', reflected his paternal take on Irish national character.

Curiously, at no point did the Cabinet seem to worry about the advisability of arming and training a vast number of potential dissidents. Duke's gloomy reflection in late March that 'we might almost as well recruit Germans' was ignored, and when the Cabinet discussed the issue at the beginning of April, even Duke had a bout of optimism. Although it would inevitably 'cause disturbances', he thought conscription could be carried through – perhaps by a Home Rule government. He even thought there was a chance of setting up 'a Conservative Parliament' if Home Rule was implemented alongside conscription. ('To support the introduction of Conscription and not to carry it through', however, would be disastrous, and create 'a state of suppressed rebellion'.)[10] Within a fortnight Duke had decided that in any scenario conscription 'will produce a disaster'.[11] He resigned on the day the Military Service Bill was rushed through parliament, 16 April. The Cabinet followed Long's line. The Prime Minister, David Lloyd George, belligerently dismissed Duke's fears of civil war with one of his favourite historical parallels: 'Lincoln had to face a similar situation.'[12] Like Lincoln, he implied, he would not flinch from fighting to vindicate the Union.

Seeing Duke as a broken reed, he had been casting around for a more robust replacement for several months, but the search was not an easy one. The Irish chief secretaryship was never the most coveted Cabinet post, and in this moment of crisis its appeal was especially limited. Two Liberals shied away, one because he did not want to enforce conscription, the other because he (sensibly) doubted that the government was 'firm on Home Rule'. In this fix, a remarkable new idea emerged. The Chief Secretary would be spared the task of enforcing conscription; he would stay in London, and the lord lieutenancy would be put 'in commission'. Ireland would be governed instead by three commissioners, military, civil and legal: Lord French, Lord Midleton and Sir James Campbell. This emergency scheme had at least the virtue of being a kind of structural reform of the Irish administration – something scarcely attempted since the 1801 Act of Union, even though the administration's flaws had always been obvious. Though it was stillborn, it had fateful consequences. Field Marshal French immediately crossed to Dublin and set up what he called 'Advanced General Headquarters' in Dublin Castle. A volunteer was eventually found to take on the job of chief secretary, the rather obscure Liberal Edward Shortt, and within a fortnight French was made lord lieutenant. In his own mind he went to Ireland as, in effect, military governor – he wanted it made clear that the plan was to set up 'a quasi-military government in Ireland' with a soldier at its head.[13]

French, who had been parked as commander-in-chief of home forces since being relieved of command of the expeditionary force in France, was spoiling for a fight. His immediate priority was to tighten controls on the press (which was 'very outspoken' and doing 'a good deal of harm'), arrest people who 'spread discontent and sedition', and make arrangements to place any of the large cities of Ireland 'in a state of siege [a concept not recognized in British law, which he may have borrowed from the French] at an hour's notice'. But the 'essence' of his project was to be air power, a weapon so far used only in open warfare. He planned to establish 'strongly entrenched "Air Camps"' in the centre of each of the four Irish provinces. With the range of military aircraft then available, the size of these areas should allow them at least one hour 'to play about with either bombs or machine guns'. This cheery view of the use of lethal force was echoed in French's darkly humorous assertion that air power 'ought to put the fear of God into these playful young Sinn Feiners'.[14]

French certainly did not downplay the challenge: he had 'no doubt that the country is thoroughly roused by a bitter animosity and resolution to oppose conscription'. The issue went critical on the day he wrote this to Lloyd George, 18 April. Meetings of nationalist leaders (including the Labour leader Thomas Johnson) at the Dublin Mansion House, and the Catholic Hierarchy at Maynooth, signalled an unprecedented fusion of Irish national opinion. Significantly, the Irish party withdrew from Westminster – not for the first time in its history, indeed, but this time seemingly proving that Sinn Féin's much mocked abstentionist strategy was better than its own. It was no surprise that

conscription was hugely unpopular; the question was whether opposition to it would shift into direct action, and maybe even to armed
resistance. Sinn Féin, whose consistent rejection of military service made
it the natural rallying point for anti-conscription activity, remained
studiedly ambiguous on this.

The Catholic Church was also, inevitably, ambivalent. Many of the
junior clergy were already engaged in the national movement – as early
as January 1917 the RIC had warned that 'practically all' the clergy
'showed open sympathy with the action taken by the rebels' in 1916.
This may have been an exaggeration, but the drift was unmistakable.
There had been patriot priests before 1916 – Ernest Blythe had been
curious to find one a member of the IRB – but they had kept a low
profile. The celebration of the piety of the rebels, led by the *Catholic
Bulletin*, created a new dynamic. From July 1916 the *Bulletin* published
a series of biographical notes under the heading 'The Events of Easter
Week', and by September over fifty 'martyrs' had been commemorated.
The listing went on through 1917. Martyrdom could not be in a mistaken cause. The 'identification of Catholic practice and republican
nationalism' was deliberate and sustained.[15] The long quarrel between
the Fenians and the Church was being composed. Between 1917 and
1921 something like half the priests working in Clare, for instance,
would publicly associate themselves with the separatist cause.[16] When
Sinn Féin began to contest elections in 1917, eighty-odd priests across
the country subscribed to an election fund. Fr Michael O'Flanagan, a
leading influence in the early Sinn Féin election campaigns (in the view
of Sinn Féin activist Kevin O'Shiel he was 'far and away the most powerful factor' in winning the North Roscommon election), became the
organization's vice-president in October 1917.

The bishops were naturally more cautious. Although one or two of
them had fiercely denounced the repression of the 1916 rebellion, the
Hierarchy's traditional endorsement of legitimately constituted order
kept it out of politics. In June 1917, it issued a letter of instruction repeating the long-standing ban on priests speaking on 'political or kindred
affairs' in church, but calling on them to 'exhort their people to beware
of dangerous associations', and 'sedulously shun all movements that are
not in accord with the principles of Catholic teaching'. Though it did not
precisely identify any of these, it hinted that some 'forms of government
that are popular at the moment' were associated with 'civil tyranny and

religious persecution'. The 'form' it had in mind was surely republican.[17] At the same time, the Church's support for the old parliamentary party was being eroded, especially in the north, because of John Redmond's acceptance of partition in the 1916 constitutional negotiations.

The conscription threat ended this political neutrality. Military intelligence reported that the Catholic clergy, who, 'except for some of the younger members', had so far been 'generally pro-British and anti-Sinn Fein', had now 'to a man declared against conscription and all their influence will be used against it'. The bishops had even discussed trying to persuade Catholic RIC men not to enforce it.[18] Crucially, the Hierarchy opposed compulsory military service not just on universal principle, but specifically for Ireland – on the basis that the Irish had not given their consent to the war. This was in one sense democracy in the abstract, but in identifying Ireland as outside the political community represented at Westminster it was also pure nationalism. As soon as the government announced its intention to introduce conscription, the Hierarchy labelled it in openly political terms 'a fatal mistake surpassing the worst blunders of the last four years', and warning that it might provoke 'desperate courses'. On 18 April 1918 it took two decisive actions. It issued a declaration that conscription was being forced on Ireland 'against the will of the Irish nation', and denouncing the Military Service Bill as 'an oppressive and inhuman law which the Irish people have a right to resist'. And it organized countrywide masses of intercession for the following Sunday, after which the anti-conscription pledge would be signed by the congregations. The bishops were clearly hoping to avert the threat of violent nationalist resistance, but both the forceful wording of their anathema and the national organizational framework provided by the Sunday masses accelerated the process of mobilization.

The pledge drafted by the Sinn Féin Executive, and agreed at an all-party meeting in the Dublin Mansion House a few hours before the bishops met, committed people to 'resist Conscription by the most effective means at our disposal'. It was accompanied by a statement starkly labelling the passage of the conscription bill 'a declaration of war on the Irish nation'. When the draft was taken to the meeting at Maynooth by Sinn Féin's President, Eamon de Valera, the Hierarchy's head, Cardinal Logue, balked at the phrase 'the most effective means', and the bishops' manifesto used the phrase 'every means that are consonant with the law of God'. There was another slight difference: where the Mansion House pledge denied the right of the British government to impose compulsory service, the bishops took a moral rather than political line, condemning enforced conscription as 'oppressive and inhuman'. But the crucial word in both was 'resist', and Logue's demand for a commitment to passive resistance failed. The Archbishop of Dublin, William Walsh, 'made short work of his passive resistance, for nobody could define what passive resistance meant'.[19] And even Logue himself made clear that it did not mean 'we are to lie down and let people walk over us.'[20]

The fusion of clerical and political leadership over the conscription issue in April 1918 transformed Irish politics. The Catholic Church provided a framework for mass mobilization that would probably have been beyond the resources of any political organization at that point. Archbishop Walsh became a trustee of the new Irish National Defence Fund, intended to support the families of those arrested for opposing military service. A branch was established in every parish and administered by the local priest. The local clergy also facilitated the Parish Defence Committees, which were seized on by the Irish Volunteers as an ideal vehicle for organizing resistance activity. The kind of resistance they planned was certainly active, and possibly armed. Though several people were reported by the police as having refused to sign the pledge because it was too restrictive, most seem to have interpreted it as setting few limits.[21]

The political atmosphere across the country was thunderous even before Sunday 21 April. In Tyrone, the local press reported with some awe that the speechmaking was 'most violent, bitter and seditious, and from start to finish breathed nothing but hatred of England'. In Longford the police reported not only a surge in Volunteer activity such as drilling, but a far more confrontational, 'extremely aggressive' Volunteer public posture.[22] 'A sort of Holy War against the British Army is being preached,' and priests were 'stating that they will themselves lead their people to death sooner than accept' conscription.[23] The actual day of the masses and pledge-signings was a truly dramatic one, felt by many to be nationalist Ireland's first real equivalent to the fevered mass commitment of the anti-Home Rule Ulster Covenanters' meetings at the height of the prewar crisis in 1912–14. Hundreds of thousands signed the pledge and subscribed to the Defence Fund, which amassed £250,000 over the next few weeks.

The final nail in the coffin of the conscription project was hammered in by the labour movement. A special meeting of the Irish Trades Union

Council on 20 April issued a call for a general strike on the 24th. No comparable shutdown had ever been seen in Ireland.[24] A week later Constance Markievicz and Agnes O'Farrelly arranged 'the Woman's Day' (Lá na mBan), bringing together the women's organizations Cumann na mBan and the Irish Women's Franchise League to endorse the pledge 'Irishwomen! Stand by your countrymen in resisting conscription.'[25] The veteran nationalist T. M. Healy, who had witnessed several, judged ' "Anti-conscription" ... the most remarkable movement that ever swept Ireland'. The Sinn Féin publicist Aodh de Blacam was to claim, with some justification, that in the conscription crisis 'the Irish republic came into its own.'[26]

'COMBATING GERMAN INTRIGUE'

Facing the storm of protest, the government pulled back, deciding in mid-May to put conscription on ice once again. Even Long eventually accepted that, since resistance would be led by 'priests and women', no government would be able to go on with repression 'after one or two priests and a few women have been shot by the soldiers'. But he warned that abandoning conscription altogether would be regarded as a triumph for the Hierarchy. This would 'have a very serious ... effect upon the stability and prestige of Government in Ireland', so he urged the Lord Lieutenant as late as October to make clear that conscription remained a possibility.[27] This semi-mystical sense of prestige led the authorities to keep the threat, and the resistance it provoked, alive right up to the end of the war.

On top of this, when the government decided to shelve conscription it also decided at the same moment to launch a new round of arrests of the nationalist leaders who had frustrated its plans. On the night of 17–18 May seventy-three prominent Sinn Feiners were picked up and immediately deported under the Defence of the Realm Act (DORA). More followed later. The justification was the allegation that Sinn Féin was still actively conspiring with the great enemy. The so-called 'German Plot' has generally been dismissed as a fabrication, and ironically it was also scouted by some of the British authorities themselves – French included. But the ghost of Roger Casement's abortive Irish Brigade still haunted Britain. Casement's idea of recruiting Irish prisoners of war in Germany to fight against Britain had seemed – not only to Casement himself – a dangerous one. Though a bare handful of men had joined the unit, and the Germans had treated it with ill-concealed contempt, it revived memories of the very real threat posed by French military expeditions to Ireland in the 1790s. Bizarrely, one of its members, Corporal Joseph Dowling, was found stranded on a small island off the Clare coast on 12 April, after landing in a dinghy from a German submarine. His reason for being there is still a mystery: the Germans may have sent him to set up a communication station, but nobody on the Irish side knew of this. His claim, after his arrest, to have been sent to negotiate with nationalist leaders (improbably enough, he specified the parliamentarians John Dillon and John Redmond) was dismissed even by Walter Long as 'incredible', and French too 'didn't believe a word' of it. Despite this, the strange intelligence officer at Dublin Castle, Major Price, seems to have convinced the head of the RIC to call for the arrest of the Sinn Féin leaders.[28]

French still thought that 'combating German intrigue' was just as important as 'restoring order' in Ireland. But while pro-German attitudes certainly existed, actual links with Germany were hard to identify. Chief Secretary Shortt soon had to admit to the Prime Minister that not all those arrested had been in direct contact with German agents, and none could be proved to have been. All he could say was 'we know that some one has, and each of the interned persons has said or done something which gives ground for the suspicion that he or she is in it.' The risks of failing to make sure of the evidence before acting had been pointed out to the Cabinet, but ignored. Within days of the arrests there was an 'outcry for the evidence' and it became clear that the Irish Executive had nothing but what the Cabinet Secretary dismissed as 'evidence of the most flimsy and ancient description'.

Ironically, there does seem to have been some kind of republican contact with Germany in 1918 – Michael Collins sent one of his trusted men to Ballina to get in touch with a German submarine supposed 'to be off the north coast of Mayo with arms', though without success.[29] (In Ballina it was believed that German rifles had actually been landed in a cave near Killalligan.)[30] But as with later 'dodgy dossiers', the real problem was not that the intelligence information was made up, or at least 'sexed up', but that ministers were ready to believe it. They assumed that Sinn Féin wanted to work with Germany (and vice versa). It was their underlying mindset that – as with most intelligence failures – shaped the misreading of evidence.

The affair further bruised the government's fragile credibility in Ireland. As against that, Sinn Féin was knocked off balance, at least temporarily, and the national agitation was visibly quietened. All but nine of the twenty-one members of Sinn Féin's Standing Committee were arrested, and the organization was 'harassed continually' for the rest of the year, 'its offices raided, its property confiscated and its members imprisoned'.[31] By the autumn the head of the RIC could attribute the becalming of Sinn Féin to 'the firm attitude of the government, the internment of the most prominent and mischievous leaders and organisers'. But in the longer term the arrests of May 1918 rebounded on the government. Most of those taken could, like Arthur Griffith himself, be described as 'moderates' (though at the time the British could not see this). The most visible leaders were not necessarily the most dangerous to Britain. Those who escaped arrest were more radical, the Irish Volunteer leaders in particular. Michael Collins, Cathal Brugha, Harry Boland and Richard Mulcahy, the Chief of the new General Headquarters (GHQ) Staff just established in March 1918, all remained at large.

The political result of the German Plot arrests was pithily assessed by one of the more 'extreme' of the arrestees, Constance Markievicz – a highly visible Citizen Army and women's movement pioneer, whose death sentence for her part in the 1916 rising (she was widely believed to have shot an unarmed policeman on St Stephen's Green) had been commuted. After Arthur Griffith had been elected for East Cavan in June, she wrote that 'putting us away cleared the issues for us so much better than our own speeches ever could'. When she was selected as a candidate for the 1918 general election, she observed that 'My present address alone [Holloway gaol] will make an excellent election address . . . Sending you to jail is like pulling out all the loud stops on all the speeches you ever made . . . our arrests carry so much further than speeches.'[32]

'THE MOVEMENT'

The 'almost inconceivable foolhardiness' of the government's 'pin-pricking coercion' has been widely condemned, then and since.[33] The senior parliamentarian nationalist John Dillon, baffled by the apparent determination of the British to 'manufacture Sinn Feiners', was eventually reduced to the conclusion that the government actually wanted to eliminate his party. This, if true, would at least have indicated some deliberate political strategy, however deluded. But simple incomprehension is a far more likely explanation of British reactions. At this critical juncture, when the Cabinet needed to work out how seriously to take the radical nationalist opposition in Ireland, it was not well served by the Irish Executive. Local police downplayed Sinn Féin's significance, because (as one officer noted) they tended not to see any organization 'as being of any real consequence unless it was led by what were termed "people of importance"'.[34] Governmental understanding of Sinn Féin was shaped by advisers like the Vice-President of the Local Government Board, Sir Henry Robinson, who assured ministers that 'if conscription was started and resolutely carried through, Sinn Féin would die at once.' He based this sanguine view on his belief that 'the farmers hated Sinn Féin and wanted to be quit of it.' He admitted that they had to appear to support it, 'otherwise no-one would deal with them'. (Ministers failed to ask him whether this might indicate that Sinn Féin had wider support than he suggested.) Robinson blamed the trouble on 'the young shopmen in the towns'. When ministers asked how much danger of 'outrage and anarchy' there would be, Robinson said it depended on how the policy was implemented. If the administration was weak, 'the people would fight to the death against it, but if they saw the administration was determined, they would accept it.'[35] This sort of mild Orientalist psychology would reappear in official views as the crisis evolved.

French, unsurprisingly, took a similar line. He was careful not to attribute Irish rejection of conscription to cowardice. 'I do not for one moment believe that "fear of bullets" is any greater deterrent to Irishmen than to any other nationality.' Anticipation of danger was not one of the 'weaknesses of the Irish', he told his Cabinet colleagues. But 'their race has one very marked characteristic' – they were 'peculiarly liable to be influenced by their immediate environment'. As he made clear, he meant this not in a physical but in a moral sense. In 'suitable surroundings' it was easy to rouse them to imperial enthusiasm, but they were just as easily 'filled with hatred and anger by a few crafty sedition mongers or young priestly fanatics, amongst whom alone they live'.

These experts seriously misread the new resistance. It may not have been a mass movement, but it was truly a movement. Many of its activists, indeed, talked simply of 'the movement' rather than any particular group labels. A wide range of people converged around a separatist programme so broad as to be an outlook, an attitude or an atmosphere, rather than a strategy. Patrick Pearse had analysed its dynamic even before the war – 'a multitudinous activity of freedom clubs, young republican parties, labour organisations, socialist groups and what not ... many of them seemingly contradictory, some mutually destructive, yet all tending towards a common objective'. The young Todd Andrews in Dublin experienced that revolutionary psychological dynamic. 'We ... had the universally satisfying feeling that comes from belonging to an exclusive club or to any group of conspirators.' He and his fellow activists 'were enthusiasts ... we had created for ourselves what was in effect a mystical view of Ireland'.

On the other side of the country, in the unionist-dominated Cork town of Bandon, Liam Deasy recalled (with undimmed intensity half a century later) 'the thrill of those early parades – the feeling of high adventure, the sense of dedicated service ... the secret rendezvous, and the gay comradeship'. All were 'like signs of the return of the Golden Age of Ireland's ancient chivalry'. Todd Andrews rejected the idea propounded by Eoin MacNeill and James Connolly that Ireland was not an abstraction but a population (an idea that would also become a crucial element of the argument for the Anglo-Irish Treaty of 1921). 'Our Ireland was an Ireland which had nothing to do with economics, property, or with how people lived or loved or prayed. It had in fact become a political abstraction'. For him, mythical symbols like the 'Dark Rose' and the poor old woman had immediate political meaning: 'from Caitlin Ni Uallachain, Roisin Dubh and the Sean Bhean Bhocht proceeded the Republic.'[36] In 1916, in fact, Eoin MacNeill had felt the need to remind his fellow Volunteer leaders precisely that 'what we call our country is not a political abstraction', and that 'there is no such person as Caitlin Ni Uallachain or Roisin Dubh or the Sean-bhean Bhocht, who is calling upon us to serve her'. He plainly recognized the psychological power of these personifications, even if his schoolmasterish realism was no match for it.[37]

Andrews knew well enough that not everyone in the movement was a republican. Sinn Féin emerged from disparate elements, and at first its structure was loose. When George Noble Plunkett, a papal count, whose son Joseph had signed the 1916 proclamation of the Republic, was elected as the first independent nationalist MP in January 1917 – with vociferous Sinn Féin support – he tried to create a party organization under his own control. He was persuaded to adopt the Sinn Féin policy of refusing to go to Westminster, and set up a 'Council of Nine' in April 1917 to bring all advanced nationalists together, but still went on building his own Liberty League. Not until the October convention were the groups fully merged. The turning point was the election of Eamon de Valera in East Clare in July. The most prominent Volunteer commander to survive the 1916 executions, he proved an adept navigator of Sinn Féin's diverse ideological currents. His declaration that though 'we want an Irish Republic', he would 'not put in a word against' another form of government, 'so long as it was an Irish government', paved the way for the formula adopted by the party in October.

Sinn Féin's flexibility allowed it to pick up many strands of nationalism. It could be vague about its ends, but it had a coherent and persuasive conception of its means. Before 1916 its founder, Arthur Griffith, had elaborated a political strategy – abstention and civil disobedience – shaped by his understanding of the Hungarian resistance to Austrian rule in the mid-nineteenth century. That resistance produced the 'compromise', the dual monarchy in which Hungary became an equal partner. For Griffith, that outcome was both effective and attainable – unlike the idea of a republic, which Britain could never accept. This condemned him, in the eyes of some republicans, as a 'monarchist'. Griffith's strategy was often called 'non-violent', though this negative label hardly captured its ambitious and challenging reach. The name Sinn Féin, routinely translated as 'ourselves alone', invoked the idea of self-reliance, and signified a process of recreating an autonomous Irish people from within. (There was a strong echo here of the famous slogan of the Italian Risorgimento, 'l'Italia fara da se'.) It offered a complete programme of resistance, psychological as much as physical. Part of its appeal was undoubtedly that it offered an alternative to violence, without descending into the flawed strategy of parliamentarianism, which (even in the hands of the most aggressive filibusterers) legitimized British authority. Its third way offered the attractive prospect of paralysing the British state by non-cooperation or passive resistance, and actually building a counter-state while the struggle was in progress.

A perceptive take on Sinn Féin was provided by an outsider, Roger Chauviré, Professor of French at University College Dublin. Fascinated by the phenomenon he saw taking shape around him, he published a series of articles in the *Revue de Paris* and *Le Correspondant* (under the pseudonym Sylvain Briollay) analysing 'The Psychology of Sinn Fein'. 'What strikes one most in Sinn Fein thought', he suggested, 'is its extremist character.' He knew well enough that 'the epithet "extremist" annoys the Sinn Feiners'; but he used it in a rather unconventional sense. 'I mean the clear and deliberate determination to ignore what is, and to take account, nay to admit the very existence, only of what ought to be.' If you tried to 'get to the bottom of these men', he asked, 'what do you find? Wholehearted faith in the power of ideas, in the irresistible superiority of right.' He saw this faith as uniquely Irish. The French might seem to have shown the same confidence in ideas, but with them this did not 'imply the abandonment of a positivism tinged on occasion with irony'. French people, like most others, expected ideas to work by eventually mobilizing superior force – not otherwise. For the Irish, 'there is between justice and might, not a harmony to be realised in the long run, but immediate and substantial identity'. Sinn Feiners were 'millenarians . . . as sure of their triumph as of the rise of to-morrow's sun'.[38]

Chauviré suggested that, 'in the idealism of Sinn Fein, and especially in its uncompromisingness', there was 'an enormous element of illusion'. (Its critics would say self-delusion.) The potency of the belief that Irish-America would ensure the liberation of Ireland, for instance, was not reduced by its being quite unrealistic. 'One must have lived in Ireland to understand the spell cast, in the long run, by the endless repetition of gratuitous statements.' Illusion was almost the foundation of activism: 'analysis and too clear a consciousness of things' would be 'dangerous . . . for the leaders', would 'cut at the root of their energy'. Realists who 'pride themselves on . . . lucid disillusionment' did nothing for the cause, he thought, just because 'they say there is nothing to do.' (Kevin O'Higgins made a similar point when he wrote that 'the whole history of the world is the triumph of mind over matter. We are backing our Idea against aeroplanes and armoured cars.')[39] Interestingly, though, Chauviré saw only a narrow division between the real objectives of the Sinn Feiners and those of their arch-opponent John Redmond. Redmond's demand for Irish units fighting under Irish flags in the war, for instance, was intended to produce 'an army of national defence, available *against any enemy*'. Redmond's 'supreme vision . . . was the very dream of Sinn Fein', and the only questions which separated them were questions of 'method and expediency'.[40]

The movement's dynamism was most obvious in the mushroom growth of local Sinn Féin clubs (*cumainn*) after the party's election victories in early 1917. In Sligo, which had not 'risen' in 1916, the police reported a virtual tripling between June (five Sinn Féin clubs with a total membership of 283) and July (fifteen clubs, 773 members). By September the total had more than doubled again to thirty-two clubs with 1,747 members. Even earlier, in some places at least, the shift of public opinion meant that 'it was only necessary for anyone with a bit of cheek to stand up after Mass in almost any place and make a speech about Easter Week to succeed in getting a Sinn Féin Cumann started.'[41] They took the names of legendary republicans like Wolfe Tone or Patrick Pearse; sometimes an increasingly radical stance was indicated by a change of patron saint – as when Frank Aiken's club in Camlough, Co. Armagh replaced Eoin MacNeill, the prewar Volunteer leader tarred by his infamous countermand of the Easter 1916 mobilization, by Thomas Ashe, the 1916 hero and 1917 martyr. Often they were the hub of a social network of groups – in this case a Gaelic League branch, a GAA club, a Cumann na mBan camogie league and the 'Thomas Ashe' cycling club.[42]

Still, radicalism was not rampant. Todd Andrews's Volunteer company in Rathfarnham helped to set up the 'Brothers Pearse' Sinn Féin Cumann that met in Pearse's old school building, St Enda's. 'The membership included some very old men, usually tradesmen and labourers, as well as women of various ages and conditions of life.' What Andrews found particularly noticeable was not just the age, but the 'astonishingly conservative' views of the male Sinn Feiners on the issue of women's suffrage, and indeed on 'all sorts of social questions'. 'Social questions such as housing, land division, public health, education, were seldom discussed and generally the subjects for debate were of the "England's difficulty, Ireland's opportunity" variety,' unless they debated the issue raised in a popular ballad of the time, 'Is it true the women are worse than the men?'[43] In Quilty, Co. Clare, 'frequently there was nothing to discuss at these Sunday meetings,' and the Sinn Féin organization was kept alive only by 'getting the Volunteers to attend' them.[44]

The movement's activism thrived on public defiance. At Easter 1917 in Carrick-on-Suir, a committee was formed to collect subscriptions for high mass to be offered for repose of the souls of the executed 1916 leaders. Schools were asked to allow their pupils to attend, shopkeepers to shut their shops on the mass morning. When one unionist refused, 'a few of us called on him and compelled him to close his doors.' This committee led directly to the establishment of both a Sinn Féin club and a Volunteer company in the town; 'invariably it was the same faces one saw at both.'[45] Non-violent Sinn Feiners could easily be radicalized by the reaction of the police, which often became physical. After putting up a Sinn Féin poster on the chapel gate at Fourmilewater, Waterford, Patrick Ryan and his comrades wrestled with the police to stop them taking it down.[46] After three members of the republican boy-scout movement, Fianna Eireann, got into a fight with police trying to pull down a tricolour from Blarney Castle, they joined the Irish Volunteers. One of them, Frank Busteed, would become a formidable gunman and later a flying-column commander.[47] In some places republican mani-festations soon became impressive. In June 1917 a group of speakers including Con Collins and Thomas Ashe were met at Rathkeale by a procession claimed to be three miles long, made up of several hundred horse-drawn cars, each adorned with a tricolour.[48] In Kanturk, in north Cork, well over a hundred marched to celebrate a Sinn Féin victory on the District Council in November 1917. 'They were in fours ... 16 boy scouts headed the procession followed by 64 girls and 120 men and boys. A Sinn Fein flag was carried in front and about 80 of the men carried pikes.' (The watching policemen seemed to count the girls more carefully than the pikemen.) 'Most of the houses along the route were illuminated with lighted candles. The streets were lined with a crowd of men, women and children, who raised cheers several times.' For Todd Andrews, the liking for demonstrations and torchlight processions was very much a Sinn Féin rather than a Volunteer tendency. Still, old fash-ioned as it might be, it gave colour to the new mobilization.

This was a 'movement' in the semi-mystical sense promoted by Ger-man nationalist thought, a *Bewegung* manifesting an underlying sense of community – a *Volksgemeinschaft*. British intelligence noted with some frustration that 'the whole movement is peculiarly well disciplined' (not-ably in regard to drink, which had been a fertile cause of information leakage in the past).[49] Its social profile was also unusually wide. Its breaching of gender boundaries, in particular, was one of the movement's most novel features. Young republicans 'caught up in the first wave of patriotic excitement' swept aside traditional gender roles. Kevin O'Shiel remembered the 'big percentage of youth' in the crowd welcoming Count Plunkett at Carrick railway station during the North Roscommon by-election campaign: not just 'large numbers of young men', but 'more curious still for those days, young women'.[50] Although the fact that Cumann na mBan went on as a separate organization preserved in part the 'separate sphere' of women's activity, the reality of common activism outweighed – at the time at least – this formal segregation.

The 'second Sinn Féin party', as the post-1916 grouping has been called, was a loose one. The tension between the party founders' commitment to passive resistance and the Sixteeners' belief in armed action was potentially unstable. The replacement of Arthur Griffith by Eamon de Valera as president of Sinn Féin in October 1917 symbolized the movement's reorientation. But, as Michael O'Flanagan pointed out, the balancing of old and new was evident all the way across the Executive elected at the 1917 Ard-fheis. Griffith and O'Flanagan himself became vice-presidents. Darrell Figgis and Austin Stack were elected secretaries, William T. Cosgrave and Laurence Ginnell became joint treasurers. The poll for the Standing Committee was headed by two men of opposite ideas, Eoin MacNeill and Cathal Brugha. Brugha, with Constance Markievicz, had urged that MacNeill should be kicked out of the organization, yet MacNeill topped the poll comfortably. O'Flanagan did not mince words in saying twenty years later that 'the split was there from the start.'[51] The coalition was held together by what may be called 'elective affinity' – the term borrowed by Max Weber from Goethe – rather than formal ideology. The fact that four out of the seven members of the new Executive (including de Valera and Griffith) were former pupils of Christian Brothers' schools testified as much to the power of common socialization as to formal ideas.[52] Griffith's decision to step back was just the most striking instance of a sense of unity that deflected personal differences – at least for what the republican publicity chief Frank Gallagher was to call the 'four glorious years'.

Sinn Féin's social conservatism was of a piece with the nationalist party – and indeed the IRB. The 'new' movement has been seen by some as largely a repackaging of the 'old' constitutional movement.[53] The rapidly growing membership of Sinn Féin in 1917–19 did not, on this view, come from nowhere; it came primarily from the old Irish party.[54] There was certainly a substantial haemorrhage of personnel from the United Irish League and Ancient Order of Hibernians, and a more or less direct transmission of the UIL's local organizational structure.[55] But the Sinn Féin leadership cohort was significantly different from that of the UIL – perhaps more like that of the IRB. At local level the difference was most obvious – 45 per cent of leading Sinn Feiners in Connacht were farmers, as against only 20 per cent of the national leadership. It seems likely that there was also a significant mobilization of new, especially younger participants – certainly in the west. In East Galway, in December 1918, 'the middle-aged businessmen, large farmers and shopkeeper-graziers who had dominated the UIL . . . were dramatically pushed aside by the young professionals, small farmers, artisans, and landless labourers of Sinn Féin.'[56]

'EVERY SOD OF RANCH LAND'

Sinn Féin's first move in conjuring up a counter-state was made even before the conscription crisis. Food shortages during the winter of 1917–18, though brought about not by crop failure but by exports to Britain, revived still-raw memories of famine. One leaflet issued by the Women's Delegates Committee specifically called on people to 'REMEMBER '47' and (invoking the 'Land War' of the 1880s for good measure) 'HOLD THE HARVEST' – urging farmers to 'stand by the townspeople now' as the townspeople had stood by the farmers in the 1880s. The Irish Food Council, part of the wartime food-control machinery, could not prevent Irish food supplies from being sent to Britain. Sinn Féin appointed its own food controller, Diarmuid Lynch, who used direct rather than bureaucratic action. On 21 February he intercepted a herd of thirty-four pigs on their way to the North Wall docks, had them slaughtered and distributed the meat to deprived households. This bit of Robin-Hood-style social banditry was dismissed as mere criminality by the authorities – Lynch himself was arrested, convicted and deported to the USA – but it demonstrated a canny awareness of publicity. 'It certainly greatly enhanced the prestige of Sinn Féin' as 'the party of action and not of talk'.[57] A new ballad, 'The Pig Push' – dedicated to the Sinn Féin Food Controller – notable for lumpen jollity ('We'll have pig's cheeks and pork chops enough for you and me / there'll be rashers for our breakfast and some sausages for tea') also contained a rather chilling prophecy, linking the noise of the doomed porkers to the future fate of the political police: 'they'll hear the "G" Division squeal as far off as Berlin'.[58]

This sort of exploit was uncomplicated in comparison with the challenge of the land issue – land hunger and hostility to 'landlordism' – that had inflamed the west of Ireland for more than a century. The Conservative government's land reforms of the early twentieth century, enabling tenants to buy their farms, had defused some of the issue's explosive potential, but plenty of pressure remained. For one thing, the land-purchase process had been slow, and at the end of the war as much as one-third of untenanted land remained unpurchased. The Congested Districts Board owned at least 70,000 acres in 1917, and instead of letting this land to 'uneconomic holders', it maximized its profits by leasing it to 'graziers' – farmers who used the land for cattle rather than crops. The CDB's motive – to reduce the eventual price paid by buyers – was sensible in principle, but in practice its policy racked up rural tensions. Graziers or 'ranchers', as the bigger graziers were exotically labelled, were fiercely and often violently resented; cattle-driving, the dispersal of herds by crowds of landless men, had flared up during the so-called Ranch War after 1906. Over a thousand cattle-drives took place in 1907–8, and though the agitation petered out, drives continued sporadically after that. By the last year of the war pressure on the land, aggravated by the suspension of emigration, was intense – above all in the west – and the sense of agrarian crisis was exacerbated by fears of famine, as exports of food to Britain went on rising.

Sinn Féin may have been short on social radicalism but it was drawn by the persistent power of agrarian agitation, with its huge political resonance. The Land War of the 1880s had been the most intense public conflict since Wolf Tone's 1798 rebellion, and the Land League had acquired quasi-governmental status by giving national leadership to a mass campaign to cut rents. By contrast, the Ranch War of the 1900s, led by the nationalist MP Laurence Ginnell, had been stifled, in part, by the Irish party's coolness towards it. Even so, the movement had shown the depth of hostility that persisted in the west. In 1914 land agitation had subsided to unusually low levels, but three years later it grew again, and the winter of 1917–18, the hardest of the war, saw a sharp upsurge. Some Sinn Féin leaders were deliberately arguing for a renewal of the Ranch War early in 1917. Ginnell, who had been expelled from the Irish party in 1909 (for demanding publication of its accounts) and now sat as an independent, joined Sinn Féin in 1917 and relaunched the movement. 'Young landless people can easily be ready . . . to clear cattle off every ranch, and keep them cleared until distributed,' he suggested. In a speech at Elphin in January that year (a resonant echo of his speech there in November 1907) he urged his listeners to 'seize the present opportunity to have every sod of ranch land broken up'. Eamon de Valera called on all Sinn Féin clubs 'to divide the land evenly'.[59]

Sinn Féin branches in the west weighed into the renewed Ranch War by passing resolutions setting rates for conacre – eleven-month – tenancies (£4 per acre for residential land in Ballymote, Co. Sligo, £2 an acre on 'ranches'). Early in 1918 the Sinn Féin Standing Committee endorsed the policy of breaking up grazing estates and replacing them by tillage. In East Galway, Sinn Féin declared that 'the land is a question of national and vital importance', and the people had 'a grievance in not getting the land they are able and willing to till'. There could be 'no peace until this economic hardship is removed by just and equitable distribution of the ranches'. In effect, Sinn Féin in Galway 'was an agrarian movement', and its dramatic expansion in the spring of 1918 was largely due to this. (Even before the conscription crisis, membership – as logged by the police – leapt from 4,742 to 6,343; nothing like a majority of these can have come from the old party.)[60]

In many places local Sinn Féin leaders headed mass occupations of farms whose owners refused to accept the rental rates determined by the organization. Crowds – often 500 strong – marched in military style under the Sinn Féin banner, and land was taken 'in the name of the Irish Republic'.[61] The posting of placards by fields occupied 'By Order of the Irish Republic' in February 1918, if not before, may represent the earliest public appearance of the counter-state.[62] In this agrarian guise, the Republic could quickly generate plenty of support, but it also risked unleashing forces beyond its control. Constable Jeremiah Mee of the RIC watched one such occupation – billed as a 'Monster Meeting' – at Ballintogher, where the Sinn Féin club had announced that a farm was to be divided among 'deserving small farmers'. Its secretary, faced with an impossibly large crowd of deserving individuals, played for time by taking a list of names and promising to announce a selection at a meeting a week later; the police obligingly arrested him before the deadline for the promised decision came.[63]

As cattle-drives and forcible occupations multiplied, Sinn Féin found itself running with an agitation that was far more socially divisive than earlier anti-landlord campaigns. The approach of auction day for the much disliked eleven-month leases threatened confrontation between landed and landless republicans. The fields targeted for redistribution were by no means all part of big estates: the term 'ranch' was distinctly flexible. The conservatives among the national leadership moved in February 1918 to limit cattle-driving to 'ranches strictly known as such' (a formula used by the UIL during the Ranch War), and protect 'land occupied by relatively small farmers'.[64] The Sinn Féin Executive ruled that local *cumainn* were not to become involved in land seizures without the approval of their constituency organization, while the Volunteer Executive (like the IRB Supreme Council during the Land War) pronounced the agitation 'neither of a national nor of a military character', ordering that Volunteers should not take part. In spite of this, local units – apparently with approval at brigade level – did just that. 'It was only natural', as one Clare Volunteer wrote, that the Volunteers were 'anxious to back up the popular agitation and . . . took the leading part in it'.[65] The Clare IV commander Michael Brennan noted that 'all over the county Volunteers took part in [cattle-drives] as organised units'. In West Cork, a number of Volunteer companies were involved in 'the ploughing of a grabbed farm' guarded by the RIC near Kinsale. They 'entered the lands in the early morning, the policeman was overpowered and his rifle seized. The Volunteers then proceeded to plough the entire farm.' Just as they finished, 400 troops with fixed bayonets allegedly arrived on the scene.[66]

Where Sinn Féin did try to stop them, it could run into difficulties. In Quilty, Co. Clare, the local priest rallied a group of Volunteers to stop a drive organized by the publican Michael Casey. 'The mob refused to listen to the appeals of Fr McKenna and actually attacked us with stones; the priest was struck . . . on the forehead and wounded. After that we retired.' This humiliation forced the battalion commandant to 'court-martial' Casey and fine him, and insist that the local company ensure that cattle-driving was prevented.[67] It was obvious that the 'tillage campaign' could produce acute social conflict. One local newspaper saw it unleashing 'a reign of terror similar to that of the Bolsheviks', while the police spoke of 'a state of utter lawlessness amounting to anarchy'.[68] Yet land hunger could – as the earlier Land League had shown – be viewed as having a national dimension, and agrarian incidents could easily be 'transformed into significant episodes of the national struggle'. They were linked not just by their own logic but by their common fate at the hands of the police (increasingly supported by troops).[69] The political potential lay in the identification of the authorities and the British legal system with the existing tenurial system. An attack on one might not necessarily be, but could easily be, seen to be an attack on the other.

'A BITTER AND AGGRESSIVE FEELING'

The land struggle could force Sinn Féin into awkward positions, but another of its leading strategies, the boycott of the police, was much less problematic. Boycotting was a classic mechanism of civil resistance: it had provided one of the headline weapons in the Land War. It was the ostracizing of land agents like Captain Boycott, indeed, that gave the technique its modern name. (Before that, Parnell had to use the distinctly unIrish phrase 'send to Coventry'.) Theoretically non-violent, the Land War boycotts had been sustained in practice by widespread intimidation. Sinn Féin aimed to use the boycotting of English products to assert Irish economic independence, but so far these had proved fairly ineffective – protracted, uneven in application and probably marginal in impact. The social war against the RIC was different: it was truly a knife to the heart of the British state's legitimacy in Ireland. It was also, just as importantly, a blow to its administrative credibility. Most people still repudiated the idea of violent resistance, partly on moral grounds, but also for pragmatic reasons. Common sense dictated (and the 1916 experience seemed to confirm) that armed rebellion was doomed to fail in face of British power. Many believed that its only result would be even heavier repression, once again setting back the national cause a generation. Before people would support or even tolerate armed attacks on the forces of the Crown, they needed to be psychologically mobilized to perceive them as legitimate targets – and also to grasp their vulnerability.

The idea of boycotting the RIC predated the reorganization of Sinn Féin, and some Irish Volunteer officers began to call for it almost as soon as they were released from prison at the end of 1916. Indeed de Valera, who is often credited with launching the strategy during the East Clare election, may not at that point have been a member of Sinn Féin. Volunteers at local level certainly played a leading part in pressing the policy – and quite possibly enforcing it by intimidation. In a speech in

December 1917, nominally under the banner of Sinn Féin, the IV leader Eamon O'Dwyer in Tipperary directly warned the RIC note-takers that if they were sensible men they would join their fellow countrymen's bid for freedom. The alternative might go beyond mere ostracism: 'at the present time there was a great movement afoot to secure the independence of Ireland by "passive resistance" which was all very well in its way, but it was necessary that this movement have the support of rifles and machine guns.' All young men should 'train and make themselves efficient and be ready to act their part when the time came – as surely it would come'.[70]

The process of levering the police apart from the community was decisively accelerated by the conscription crisis. Throughout the midlands and the south in March 1918 'a bitter and aggressive feeling' was 'gradually ... being manifested towards the police'.[71] The prospect of mass clashes in which they could be overwhelmed pushed the RIC on the defensive. In North Tipperary, police 'are practically always confined to their barracks fearing an attack'; the south was no less hostile, and Limerick was 'seething with hatred for the government'. The anti-conscription movement brought large-scale meetings, as at Castletownbere in Cork where Mary MacSwiney administered the women's pledge, and went on to declare that 'the police were worms – no decent girl would walk on the same side of the road with one of 'em.' An Englishman watching the event at Castletownbere noted that 'the police who had been listening with approval up to this point got a severe shock at this.'[72] Women's attitudes were vital, and Cumann na mBan organizers like Bridie O'Mullane in Sligo worked to solidify them, even urging mothers to pull their children in off the streets if policemen approached.[73] The conscription issue allowed priests as well as political leaders to target the police, pushing on the tilt of opinion against them; Father Dennehy of Eyeries declared that 'any Catholic policeman who assisted in conscription would be excommunicated and cursed ... the curse of God would follow them in every land.'

The RIC had always depended, in the last resort, on the use of firearms to quell serious disturbances; and its constables now clearly lost the confidence to confront crowds alone. In West Cork by April, 'the general unrest, the rancour versus the police, the probability of attacks on them and their barracks, the raids for arms' made it 'necessary to concentrate the police'. Already eight permanent stations and protection posts and one coast-watching post had been 'discontinued'.[74] Boycott actions became further-reaching as time went on: anyone who drove the RIC or provided them with supplies became liable to boycott or attack themselves.[75]

The confrontation with the RIC clearly provided a crucial basis for insurgent military action. While the boycott 'had not the success that it was hoped for', in that the vast majority of RIC men were not induced to resign, it did 'draw a distinct demarcation line between the people and the police'.[76] Surprisingly few Volunteers, though, seemed to recall the boycott as part of their activity, and historians of 'public defiance' have not seen it as part of that process. Boycotting was, in a sense, instinctive, and it worked in part because its enabling logic – that the armed RIC was an 'army of occupation' rather than a legitimate police force – had been widely propagated long before the war. (The unarmed Dublin Metropolitan Police, which was not subject to the boycott, was a different case.) The more deadly implication – that RIC men were traitors to the national cause – was probably not so widely accepted until after 1916. 'Now they would be treated as outcasts.' This would be crucial to the individuals who eventually took the decision to use lethal weapons against the police.

'AN IRISH REPUBLIC POSSESSING ITS OWN DISTINCT FLAG'

The revivalist atmosphere of the movement was vividly reflected in the explosion of tricolour flags in 1917–18. Kevin O'Shiel wryly noted the way it shifted the balance of public displays in his northern home town, Omagh, Co. Tyrone. Previously nationalist displays, mounted by the Ancient Order of Hibernians – 'Hibs' – had been a monochrome green. The 'inexorable laws of patriotism confined them to one colour – green – and forbade any display of "England's cruel red" . . . It took Sinn Féin to add orange to the depressing traditional green, thus giving nationalist processions a tiny touch more of colour and brightness' (even though the colours were still 'far from the dazzling, if somewhat barbaric splendour of those of their Orange rivals'). This may seem a mere cosmetic point, but it was not trivial. The tricolour was a revolutionary banner. The flag of Ireland, to which the 1916 proclamation summoned 'her children', was of course not the tricolour. Pearse and O'Rahilly had debated the issue of the precise symbols that should stand on the solid green ground – a harp, uncrowned and possibly winged.[77] Three different flags (only one a tricolour) seem to have been flown over the GPO during the rebellion, but tricolours had sprung up all across the city. They voiced a political message, even if it was often misread – as it seems to have been. The green and white caused no problems, but many saw the orange as gold. This perhaps reflected the gold and white sash worn by Robert Emmet in a portrait that adorned so many homes, or – less happily – the papal colours. One of Sinn Fein's early propagandists, the Clare priest Patrick Gaynor, repeatedly invoked the 'Green, White and Gold' tricolour as the flag of the Republic in his 1917 pamphlet *The Faith and Morals of Sinn Fein*. Some indeed saw it as yellow, an even more puzzling perception (unless deployed as it was by the veteran parliamentarian Joe Devlin, waving the old green flag during the South Longford by-election with the defiant boast that 'there is no yellow streak in it').

O'Shiel himself paid tribute to the tricolour's power when he first saw it some time in 1914, as a student at Trinity College (where, incidentally, he 'never met one who avowed himself a Sinn Feiner', and 'regarded such as being either idealistic idiots . . . or designing mischief-makers, paid and employed by the Castle to subvert and destroy the Home Rule movement'). He was intrigued by 'an arresting and attractive miniature flag . . . sticking out of an empty flower vase' in the rather depressing sitting room of his digs, and also – since he prided himself on knowing the 'flags of all the nations' – baffled. When he eventually found out what it was, he was astounded: 'Words can convey little idea of the effect' of realizing that it was the flag of the republicans of 1848. Almost half a century later he vividly recalled his 'emotional reaction to that significant bit of cloth'. 'So there was an Irish Republic possessing its own distinct flag proclaiming its sovereignty . . . And what a fine, bright flag it was – I thought – like a flame of hope. As I gazed on it, how dull and inanimate like a dead fish, Home Rule of any degree appeared vis-a-vis an independent republic.'[78]

Flying the tricolour – called the 'Easter Week flag' at first, then the 'Sinn Féin flag' – quickly became a craze. In Kerry in April 1917, the Volunteers hoisted one on the monument to the Earl of Kerry in Lixnaw. In Armagh, Frank Aiken's path to eventual high military command began with hoisting a flag opposite the RIC barrack in Camlough.[79] On 26 April a large 'republican flag' was raised over Sligo Town Hall. In Galway, 'flags were always very prominent at meetings, football matches and all national functions. They were flown high from telegraph poles, buildings and high trees.'[80] Altitude not only improved the flags' visibility, but helped to protect them from the police. The Anabla company in Kerry sent four men to Kenmare wood to cut an 18-foot pole to mount a 'Republican flag' outside the schoolhouse; the RIC tried and failed to remove it, and it stayed flying for a year.[81] In Abbeydorney, when they found that 'every time [national flags] were hoisted they were burned down by the RIC', they 'decided to paint the flag on a piece of sheet iron which we erected on the steeple of the Abbey'. This finally defeated the police efforts to get at it.[82] Some Volunteers claim even to have booby-trapped tricolours to protect them from destruction. This was a craze in which fun combined with real political point-making. When the journalist Sidney Czira 'introduced the flag to New York by flying it at the top of a Fifth Avenue bus', she was interested to see 'that the cops already recognised it as, at every intersection of the streets, they stood to attention in salute'.[83]

The flag was a banner both of passive resistance and of physical force. The distinction may have been blurring in 1918, though Seamus Robinson thought that 'the pacifism of Sinn Féin was gaining ground.' (It was, he admitted, 'a very vigorous sort of pacifism, if you like, but it was certainly not a military force'.) The Sinn Féin programme, resting primarily on the creation of the 'constituent assembly' advocated by Griffith – on the Hungarian model – and the projection of Ireland's case to the postwar peace congress – the Italian model – was perhaps increasingly persuasive. Robinson worried that the senior Sinn Feiners he knew in Reading gaol – men like Ernest Blythe, Arthur Griffith, Darrell Figgis, Seán Milroy and Seán T. O'Kelly – 'had their own good sound reasons for thinking that a united passive resistance policy was *all-sufficient* to win our independence' (or the kind of independence they wanted). But he concluded that, since Sinn Féin 'had such immense support from the people', the Volunteers did not need to 'waste their time on it'. For people of his outlook, Sinn Féin was 'the cloak for Volunteer meetings'.[84]

'JACK, THE FIGHT COULD LAST A HUNDRED YEARS, ONE HUNDRED YEARS'

The Irish Volunteer organization had been decapitated by the 1916 rebellion. Even where no arrests were made, as in Carrigaholt, Co. Clare – later the 5th Battalion area of the West Clare Brigade – local companies seldom met. 'Drilling resumed but only in remote places.' In some areas, such as Limerick, where serious disagreements over the Volunteers' action (or lack of it) in 1916 had paralysed the command, nothing would be done until separate new battalions had been built up.[85] But the release of prisoners quickened the pulse of the citizen militia and boosted its prestige; mere survival 'gave us an opportunity to show that the 1916 Rising was not another '67 failure'.[86] The men seem to have come out with no definite idea what to do next. Seamus Robinson insisted that 'nowhere in camps or gaols did anyone ever suggest how or when "a beginning must be made": it would have been foolish.' But it seems that even those Volunteers who had, before Easter 1916, been unsure about the need to fight no longer questioned it.

The internment camps, and big military prisons like Wandsworth, were, as J. J. ('Ginger') O'Connell – Chief of Inspection on the pre-1916 Volunteer Headquarters Staff – argued, a crucial factor in 'the "militarization" of the Volunteers'. He meant by this the development of a military ethos. 'The entire surroundings were absolutely non-civilian; the prisoners now became familiar with precisely the side of military life of which they had never had any previous experience – guard duties, escorts, interior economy, inspections, cooking, sanitation, and military routine generally.' This knowledge was acquired 'by the way, and very unwillingly', but 'it sank in nevertheless and left its mark.' It would produce 'a great homogeneity amongst the released Volunteers', an unconscious shaping that created far-reaching possibilities for the future.[87]

But even while hundreds of the organization's leading figures remained in gaols or internment camps in Britain, local initiatives to rebuild it began. The pattern set up then would reverberate over the years. A key role was played by junior Volunteers like Ernest Blythe, a Belfast journalist who had moved to Kerry to improve his Irish and become captain of the Lispole company. He had been an organizer in Clare before 1916, and now began to tour the whole area, equipped with nothing more than a list of possible names.[88] Another was Seán Treacy of Solohead, Co. Tipperary, who had tried to rouse his county to action but had not made enough of an impression on the police to merit arrest in the aftermath of Easter Week. The son of a small farmer (his widowed mother employed one labourer), he seems to have played soldiers with unusual professionalism as a child, before becoming an enthusiast for the language movement. The military failure of 1916 changed Treacy's priorities. His commitment to the Gaelic League was sidelined, and he threw all his energy into establishing Volunteer companies. He was a natural activist, who vitally combined personal charm with iron determination and a daunting work-rate. As his warning to his brother Jack that 'the fight could last a hundred years' showed, he was ready for the long haul.[89] The rebuilding of the Volunteers would depend heavily on men like these, and they were not found everywhere.

Another grassroots organizer was Eoin O'Duffy, a younger son who had had to leave the family farm to make a living, starting as a clerk in the county surveyor's office, and then by dint of hard study – and without engineering qualifications – being accepted as a surveyor. A 'true Gael', Gaelic Leaguer and Gaelic Athletic Association stalwart, he was twenty-six years old at the time of the rising, but took no part in it. Only in 1917 did he commit his energies to the Volunteer movement, recruited, on his own account, by a chance meeting with Michael Collins after a GAA match at Croke Park. Collins told him that the Volunteers were 'not so strong in Monaghan as they should be', and O'Duffy was provoked to do something about it. He became a section commander in the Clones company, then the only Volunteer unit in the county. Four months later, with its strength at twenty, the company held a 'new election of officers', and O'Duffy became captain. At that point, he 'got directly in touch with GHQ and acting on their instructions I succeeded in forming Companies at Newbliss and Scotstown . . . These Companies were formed into Battalions of which I was appointed Commandant. Early in 1918 I succeeded in forming outposts at Carrickmacross, Ballybay, Castleblayney and Monaghan . . . thus forming the nucleus of five Battalions.' At the beginning of August a Monaghan Brigade was established, and O'Duffy was 'unanimously elected Brigadier'. By the end of the First World War in November, his brigade boasted '56 Companies and 5 Battalion Councils, and a Brigade Council fully staffed' – every one of which had been 'organised by myself alone and unaided'.[90]

This bald account – O'Duffy was no stranger to self-promotion, but here was recounting simple fact – tells us a lot about the resurgence of the Volunteer organization in the last year of the Great War. Its formal structure was modelled on the regular armies of Europe, notably Britain's, but it was built from the bottom up. The core unit was the local company – the smallest viable piece of the jigsaw: smaller groupings did exist, called outposts, but these were originally regarded as too small to have any function. The underlying logic of the organization was steady expansion – sections would come together as a company, companies as a battalion, battalions as a brigade. Critics have sometimes mocked its pseudo-regular structure, as a kind of self-deception as much as a propaganda device. The reality was, though, usually more informal. G Company of the 7th Battalion of the Kilkenny Brigade, for instance, rarely used its formal title: the Volunteers 'usually referred to our Company as the Callan lads or the town lads'.[91]

A new organizational structure was drawn up by Michael Collins and approved at a Volunteer assembly in Dublin on 'the Sunday of the "black frost"' in spring 1917, well in advance of the national convention in the autumn. Though he had fought in the GPO in 1916, Collins had never belonged to any Volunteer unit, and was loosely attached to the Dublin Brigade after his release from prison. Before the meeting, at the Plaza Hotel not far from Parnell Square, Collins energetically lobbied the IRB in support of his scheme. According to Liam Archer (then a company commander in the Dublin Brigade) this led Cathal Brugha – who had been vice-commandant of the 4th Battalion in 1916, and had left the IRB because he believed that the movement no longer needed a secret organization – to oppose it. This, Archer thought, was the beginning of an antagonism that would become much more serious over time.[92] Brugha's opposition to the scheme appears to have had less to do with its technical merits than with the fact that its author was an enthusiastic IRB man. And the brotherhood, led by Thomas Ashe until his death in September, does seem to have been a fairly effective instrument in the reconstitution of the Volunteer structure – as well, of course, as a vehicle for Collins's personal power.[93]

After the Plaza Hotel meeting a new Volunteer Manifesto, launched on 22 May, declared their mission to be to 'complete by force of arms the work begun by the men of Easter Week'. It blamed the failure of 1916 on a 'misunderstanding' (an oblique reference to the 'countermanding order' issued by the Chief of Staff, Eoin MacNeill). To prevent any recurrence of such conflicting orders, 'Volunteers are notified that the only orders they are to obey are those of their own Executive.' It also, in a critical comment on the 1916 strategy that reflected Collins's own view, declared that the Executive 'would *not* issue an order to take the field until they consider that the force is in a position to wage war on the Enemy with reasonable hope of success'. Volunteers would not 'be called on to take part in any forlorn hope'.

Even so, the structure drawn up by Collins followed naturally from the model constructed by Patrick Pearse before 1916. The image of a regular military system was vital for those who wanted to infuse military values into the Volunteer ranks. The Volunteer General Headquarters Staff in Dublin, usually known as GHQ, reconstituted in March 1918 and filled with 1916 veterans like Richard Mulcahy, the Chief of Staff, naturally took this line. They did not follow Pearse further than this; they did not make the mistake attributed to his HQ staff of 'thinking in army corps' – believing the Volunteers could fight a conventional war. Their key aim was to cultivate the sense of being an army, no matter how thin were their ranks or how slender their resources. The sense of regularity they fostered was potent, though it was possibly misleading. The Volunteers were a viscerally territorial force. Only the local company could really function as a military unit: companies were natural local groupings, mostly surviving from the pre-1916 force, and more or less identically twinned with the Sinn Féin clubs. 'When a Sinn Fein Club has been established . . . the Irish Volunteers join it in large numbers and the connection between the two is very close,' at least as far as the Cork RIC could see. 'In most cases there is little to distinguish Irish Volunteer from Sinn Fein branches.' In Kerry they were thought 'practically synonymous', and that was certainly so in Sneem, where 'the Volunteers took over the Sinn Féin club.'[94] The symbiosis could flow in either direction: whereas in Co. Dublin 'most of the young Sinn Feiners consider themselves Irish Volunteers though not actually enrolled as such,' the Inspector General saw many Sinn Féin clubs as simply 'branches of the Volunteers'.[95]

Above this local level, structures became less visceral and more notional. Though the Volunteer battalion was modelled on the equivalent regular formation – usually around 500 men strong – the collection of companies that actually constituted one was somewhat arbitrary. Geography as well as numbers played a part in deciding the issue. By late 1918 Cork county contained eighteen battalions. When the Cork Brigade commandant, Tomás Mac Curtain, told one of his battalion commanders, Frank Hynes, that his battalion was 'too big for Scally and yourself . . . I'm thinking of splitting it up', Hynes 'thought that what he intended doing was to take a few of the companies and form another [battalion]'. Instead, 'he dissolved the whole Battalion and held an election for two Battalion staffs.'[96] Battalions of several hundred might possibly be assembled for occasional meetings, but could hardly hope to take the field as units. They, and still more brigades – the 'highest' organizational level of the IV – were, in a sense, imagined entities.[97] Brigades became, none the less, arguably the most crucial structural tier of the Volunteers. Brigade boundaries were 'sacrosanct', as one senior officer put it, with only slight exaggeration. They were rarely crossed or shifted. The recasting of the brigade structure by GHQ in 1918, dividing most counties into two and some, like Cork and Tipperary, into three, was probably its most influential intervention in local activity. A few adjustments were later made – as when southern County Dublin (where two new battalions were set up in 1920–21) separated from the Dublin Brigade to join with north County Wicklow shortly before the July 1921 Truce that halted the Anglo-Irish war. Some adaptations were strategic, like this, others were driven by local power relations rather than GHQ blueprinting. Clare was a well-known instance, divided into three via some painful negotiations to accommodate the three leading local families, Barretts, Brennans and O'Donnells.[98]

When the structure was established, its contents were still at the fluid stage but, as they gradually solidified, brigades came to represent the functional limit of the intense localism that animated the organization. The fixity of the brigade areas also reflected in part the slow pace of the organization's development in many places. Though the larger formations operated only at the staff level, they played a vital role in generating a sense of both identity and purpose. Battalions and brigades had commandants, vice-commandants, adjutants and signalling and engineering officers, and battalion and brigade councils met regularly to conduct administration. The localism of the citizen militia, in one sense a limiting factor, was also a source of great resilience and flexibility. What was needed was a military doctrine suited to these strengths.

No suitable doctrine was ready to hand. At the 1917 Volunteer Convention there was no mention of a 'renewal of hostilities', according to north Cork leader Seán Moylan, because no units bigger than companies existed. 'Hostilities' were still assumed to be large-scale actions. As brigades were formed (Moylan would command Cork No. 2), the first 'hypothetical plans' were mooted. Moylan – a schoolteacher by profession – believed that the Volunteers 'luckily escaped the direction of professional soldiers', and eventually 'reverted to the traditional guerrilla warfare of the locally organised clans'.[99] But the logic of action took time to emerge. 'One of the difficulties was that no one had any clear idea as to what form our activities would eventually take,' as Roger McCorley in Belfast wrote. 'There was a general idea that some day the signal for a rising would come and we would drive the enemy into the sea at one fell swoop.' Seán Moylan was still 'thinking in terms of a nationwide military effort on the lines of Easter Week, and from discussions I had with other Volunteers it seems to me that the same idea was widely held.' As Todd Andrews remembered it, 'to the extent that any of us thought about the future of the Volunteers, or what we were training for, it was to start another and perhaps bigger 1916 insurrection. But in fact I don't think we gave any thought at all to the future military objectives of the Volunteers.' He was clear that 'guerrilla tactics were never mentioned.' Things may have differed from place to place. One of the leading exponents of 'hedge-fighting' in the pre-1916 Volunteers, Ginger O'Connell, after his release in mid-1917 went to Sligo and started a series of lectures for local Volunteers. Though we do not know what he told them, it may well have followed his earlier thinking.

The Volunteer General Staff issued no operational orders during the conscription crisis, merely instructing Volunteers to try to avoid arrest. If an attempt was made to arrest them 'while in possession of arms ... the arms should be used' (to defend the weapons as much as the men).[100] In Westmeath, GHQ's policy was understood to be 'to display ... strength and determination ... as much as possible, knowing that the RIC would report' such things as parades and meetings. These were held daily. In Leitrim, 'apart from drilling, very little was done to meet the threat of conscription,' though the Volunteers made lists of all houses that had arms 'so that they could be easily got if the crisis came to a head', and also of local food stocks.[101] Other units did develop more ambitious plans, envisaging large-scale conventional action. In Beaufort, Co. Kerry, for instance, the local unit thought that 'being situate at the foot of the Gap of Dunloe, we held the entrance to what would have been the main hideout in South Kerry if the British had attempted to enforce conscription.'[102] The Dublin Brigade adopted the 'Block System' (worked out by Joseph O'Connor), in which battalion areas were divided into blocks in which Volunteers threatened with arrest would 'open fire or resist enemy activity by whatever means they possessed'.[103] In south

Roscommon 'we constructed several dugouts to accommodate our men should the thing come to a head.' In Ahane, Co. Limerick, 'we drilled three times a week and had lectures on our plan of battle under different circumstances.'[104] Cork Brigade orders indicated the scale of 'active service' operations envisaged: each company quartermaster was urged to 'look round his district, fix in his mind's eye the best place to billet men not on duty', and also 'fix mentally, central farmhouses to be used for cooking purposes'. Hot food and drink was 'an absolute necessity' for men 'on arduous military work'.[105]

There is some evidence that guerrilla thinking was in the air during the crisis. Interestingly, the nationalist MP Arthur Lynch, who had 'seen a good deal of the Sinn Feiners', told Lloyd George in May that 'they really thought that they could beat the British army, not by regular fighting, but by guerrilla methods . . . They did not intend to fight in the towns, but to withdraw at once to the country where they had lots of clever guerilla leaders.'[106] Whoever he had been talking with was more far-sighted than most. Seán Moylan thought it lucky that conscription was never imposed, because there would have been an orthodox 'textbook type of fighting', with disastrous results, whereas the averting of the conscription threat took the pressure off and 'permitted the development of an altogether different and more effective method of fighting'.

The most universal military idea of the Volunteers was the determination to hang on to their weapons, and get more wherever they could. Since the prewar crisis, Volunteers had come almost to fetishize the modern service rifle as the pre-eminent symbol of military credibility, and indeed of national manhood. The *Irish Volunteer* journal had intoned in 1914 that the 'man who has once handled a rifle and is not smitten with a desire to own one is not an Irishman'. The 1916 Volunteer who resigned when told by his commander to protect his rifle 'as he would the honour of his mother or his wife' seems to have been unusual.[107] Even the imposing single-shot 'Howth Mausers' acquired in 1914 had been discounted by some – not entirely without reason – as antiques. But, apart from a few survivals from Easter 1916, the prospects of securing magazine-loading rifles like the Lee-Enfield were limited to the occasional careless or co-operative soldier on leave. The first service rifle acquired by the Thurles company was bought for 50 shillings by the brigade quartermaster from a British soldier, who 'did not appear to be in any way concerned about what might happen to him when he reported back without his rifle'. Joseph Clancy of the Munster Fusiliers (who later became the training officer of the East Clare Brigade) came home on leave with his short Lee-Enfield, complete with bayonet and twenty rounds of ammunition. He arranged with his brother and the local Volunteers that 'they could have itself and the ammunition by holding me up as I was on my way to Sixmilebridge railway station returning to France.'[108] It took the British army a surprisingly long time to tumble to such ruses, but even so the pickings were nowhere near enough to equip more than a handful of men.

The Volunteer leadership worried at first that raiding private houses for arms would risk alienating the public. The conscription crisis changed this, and orders were issued by battalion commanders like Liam Deasy in West Cork that companies should collect all available firearms in their districts. The public reaction seems to have been co-operative – as one Volunteer recalled, it was often a misnomer to call them 'raids'. The result was a biggish haul of shotguns and a fair quantity of revolvers, though overall totals are impossible to estimate. Shotguns did not rank with rifles as symbols of military status, and it took time for their effectiveness to be understood. Volunteers were often conscious of lacking knowledge of firearms and their maintenance. In some places, where Volunteers 'had little knowledge of making dry dumps', guns were only taken from 'unfriendly' people: 'we left the arms with friendly people, on the understanding that they would keep them safe . . . in good order.'[109] This may have meant that the guns got taken away in one of the periodic police swoops. Certainly many 'unfriendly' guns were taken out of the picture early on: 20,800 had been surrendered to the police in Ulster by January 1919, and in all some 100,000 were handed in between 1918 and 1920.[110] The Volunteers might well have secured at least as many – which would certainly have provided some kind of gun for every man – but subsequent complaints of shortages suggest that they did not.

The most common substitute for guns in spring 1918 was pikes – half the blacksmiths across the country seemed to be turning them out. They were paid for by funds raised at dances. In Clare, 'money was very scarce at the time and many of the lads could not afford . . . the price of a shaft. We had some exercises with these pikes but I'm afraid they were more of a novelty than anything else.'[111] The notion of using such primitive weapons can hardly have fostered a belief in open combat, though some thought it 'most heartening to hear the young men . . . discuss the weapons they would use, such as sleans, pikes and pitchforks, as well as shotguns'. Michael Higgins in Galway remembered pike drill without much affection: he had a hazy recollection of commands like 'Left Parry', 'Right Parry' and 'Forward Thrust' but a strong memory 'that both the pikehead and the handle were very heavy and that I was always glad when the pike drill instruction was over'. In any event, 'no use was ever made of these pikes afterwards.'[112]

The supply of guns would never be sufficient; manpower was less of a problem. Enthusiasm was fuelled by the release of many internees at Christmas 1916, and though recruitment figures stayed quite low over-all, this was partly due to careful selection. Companies in strongly unionist areas seem to have been especially choosy about their member-ship. By late 1917, though, numbers were swelling. Patrick McKenna claims that a general mobilization of Volunteers at the Casement Fort – a prehistoric hill fort near Casement's landing-place in 1916 – in early August 1917 called forth no fewer than 5,000 men, some on horseback; a crowd of 10,000 people listened to addresses by Thomas Ashe, Austin Stack and Con Collins. The conscription crisis produced a dramatic surge. The Lixnaw company was not unusual in leaping from 84 to 260 strong. When James Keating returned from prison to Fethard during the crisis, he was impressed by the scale of change in the movement. 'Men were now drilling and training openly and it looked as if a Volunteer company had been established and put on a proper footing.' In Longford the surge led to the creation of a brigade organization for the county.

This rapid expansion was shortlived: the Lixnaw company fell back to 100, and like many others the Fethard company collapsed. Nearly two years passed before another serious effort was made to establish one in Fethard.[113] In some areas an effort was made to limit the surge. North Roscommon accepted no new members: 'We believed by now we had recruited any man who was any good in the area.' Others learnt a disagreeable lesson. The great influx 'imposed a heavy burden of work on . . . training officers'; since most of the recruits 'had not the same ideals or tradition of the original Volunteers', they had to be 'trained, disciplined, lessoned to an . . . understanding of the objective of the Vol-unteer movement'. Seán Moylan felt that the newcomers clung to the old preference for demonstrations, meetings, oratory and torchlight processions: they did not understand 'that an entirely different situation had arisen'.[114] (Though in Dublin Joe O'Connor charitably judged that the transient recruits 'were the better for the training they received during their connection with the Volunteers'.) In Tipperary, where 'we ... were swamped' initially, the roll plummeted – from 120 to 5 parading in 6th Battalion, 3rd Tipperary Brigade – and Seán Treacy concluded that if there was another conscription crisis they should refuse to accept recruits en masse.[115] GHQ instructed in June that 'at the present moment great care should be taken in recruiting'; in the cities of Dublin, Cork and Limerick, men should not be accepted until they had been confirmed by the Battalion Council, and in rural areas recruits should be vouched for by at least ten of the company they were to join.[116]

Who did join? Sir Henry Robinson, the Vice-President of the Local Government Board, blamed the anti-conscription agitation on 'the young shopmen in the towns', and this was not an entirely misleading social analysis of the Volunteer movement. Shop assistants and clerks, who made up only 4 per cent of the workforce outside Dublin, may have formed up to a fifth of active Volunteers. Skilled workers were also heavily over-represented in Volunteer ranks. By contrast, farmers and agricultural workers seem to have formed a minority, at least after 1919.[117] If so (the figures are still debated), this was sharply at variance with the belief of many Irish-Irelanders in the essentially rural identity of Ireland. It can be suggested that the social basis of the Sinn Féin– Volunteer movement was modern rather than traditional. Membership statistics would never be comprehensive, especially in respect of the occupational background of Volunteers, but again the dismissive perception of the authorities – that the movement did not include 'important' people – was certainly correct. The revolutionary generation was made up of mostly obscure people, whose most obvious common characteristic was their youth. Before 1919 the median age of rank-and-file Volunteers was twenty-three, and of officers twenty-five. After that the average age rose by about a year, but overall no more than 5 per cent of Volunteers were over forty, while an overwhelming majority were under thirty (82 per cent in 1917–19, rising to 88 per cent in 1920–21 and 92 per cent in 1922–3). More overwhelming still was their denominational homogeneity, far exceeding what might have been expected in a national movement with a history rich in iconic Protestant heroes. Though it would be impossible to compile accurate statistics, there can be no doubt that Protestants were significantly under-represented in the

Volunteers as a whole, more strikingly in Belfast than in the rural south. It has indeed been suggested that there were 'far more "pagans" – as atheists or non-practising Catholics were often known – than Protestants' in the Volunteers.[118]

'THE FIRST OFFICERS WERE ELECTED'

In one respect the Volunteers were a truly revolutionary army: they elected their officers. Many units started collectively, without any officers; then, as in Glendine (mid-Clare), a battalion staff officer arrived to organize elections. In many places, leaders emerged naturally: Liam Deasy recorded that when Charlie Hurley organized a new company in Castletownbere, 'the esteem in which he was held' led to 'his immediate election as Captain'. When Joe O'Connor reorganized the 3rd Battalion of the Dublin Brigade, he also ran the brigade – 'I had not been properly appointed but it was understood that being the senior officer, my orders were accepted.' He offered 'to resign command' of his battalion when de Valera got out of gaol, and de Valera in turn 'offered to confirm me in the command of the Dublin Brigade'.[119] In Miltown Malbay, 'for some months I don't think we had any officers,' but 'in the spring of 1918 Martin Devitt, afterwards Vice O C [Vice-Officer Commanding] of the Mid-Clare Brigade, came into the area and the first officers were elected under his direction.'[120] The 'first election of company officers by secret ballot' in the Cashel battalion (later the 2nd Battalion of Tipperary No. 3 Brigade) took place in early 1918. Elections became universal in 1918, and continued in many places right through into 1921. (When 2nd Southern Division was formed in 1921, and Ernie O'Malley was put in command of it, Moylan fretted that 'the nomination of officers was a new departure.')[121]

Election seemed so natural that many Volunteers appear to have been unaware of its significance – most of their recollections speak of election and appointment interchangeably. The Cork Brigade veteran Florrie O'Donoghue argued that the elective system 'proved itself sound, mainly because of the spirit in which men served'.[122] But the problems it could pose were clear to the central organizers from the start. The IRB, which still saw the Volunteers as its own army, made urgent efforts to ensure that 'no one will be elected an officer of the Volunteers who is not a member of the Organisation.' Seamus Robinson brushed off the urgings of 'young fellows with notebooks rushing round buttonholing individuals with anxious whispers' at a meeting in Parnell Square in 1917. 'That sort of thing', he snorted, 'would undermine the authority and efficiency of the whole Volunteer movement.' When Thomas Fitzpatrick, a former British army officer who had served at Gallipoli and Salonika, joined the Belfast battalion in 1919 he was told that he would have to join the IRB to 'be in any position of responsibility'. He duly took the oath, but was slightly surprised that 'they never bothered about me afterwards.'[123] Seamus McKenna was sworn into the Belfast IRB late in 1919, but found that 'little of importance was discussed' at its monthly meetings. 'Looking back I cannot recall any useful purpose served by our particular Circle.' He knew that the brotherhood's aim was to ensure that senior Volunteer officers were men 'who would see that the fight for the Republic was relentlessly pursued', but again could not 'recall that this was effective in Belfast'.[124]

The variable success of the IRB's bid to regain control of the Volunteers can be seen as a kind of quiet split. In some places it had no difficulty: in Meath, 'the brigade officers appear to have been appointed from among the members of the IRB,' and the selection process merely ratified decisions already made.[125] In north Roscommon, 'those of us who were in the IRB and who were organising the Volunteers automatically became Volunteers.' In Tyrone, 'the whole directional policy of the Volunteer movement was carried out through IRB channels.'[126] But the Head Centre of the Armagh IRB admitted that though the IRB 'attempted to take control of the newly formed Companies', it was 'a difficult job and the IRB lost control'. He thought it 'only natural that the Volunteers would break away from the control' of the small organization.[127] In South Tipperary, a breaking point arrived when the IRB Centre refused to approve a plan to kidnap the RIC sergeant who had arrested Seán Treacy (on the grounds that the brotherhood 'stood for something higher than the capture of "a bloody old policeman"'). Even the county's top IRB man, Eamon O'Dwyer, reached the conclusion that the old organization should be allowed to die a silent death.[128] Neither the first commander of the Belfast Brigade, Seán O'Neill, nor his successor, Roger McCorley, was an IRB man. McCorley, whom Seamus McKenna thought 'one of the most daring and active Volunteer officers in Ireland, ... could not be induced under any circumstances to join the IRB'.

The IRB was losing its grip, but the free election of officers was seen as a problem by others too. Charlie Hurley might be, as Liam Deasy said, 'a natural genius', but local prestige did not necessarily translate into military efficiency or energy – too often the reverse. One answer was to have secret ballots in the larger units. In Dundrum, three battalion staff were elected 'unanimously' and only one – the quartermaster, John Ryan – by secret ballot. When Seán Treacy came to a Battalion Council meeting as vice-OC of the brigade, he 'insisted on having the first three appointments made by secret ballot', so the election was repeated – though without any change in the result.[129] Sometimes officers recognized their own inadequacy: Frank Hynes's company captain 'saw that as such he was a failure and couldn't get the men to attend'. (At the meeting to elect his successor, one man apparently stood up and dismissed the need for an election – 'there's not a man here who will soldier under any man but Frank Hynes. We'll have him for Captain or no one.') In Kerry, 'when the Bealnadeega Company was first formed I was in charge,' James Daly recorded, 'but I stepped down in favour of Thomas O'Leary who had resigned from the RIC.'[130]

The quality of officers was highly variable at this stage. In Virginia, Co. Cavan, when the company captain was arrested the unit was taken over by Phil Wrett, 'a heavy boozer' who 'while in a drunken bout, would give military orders such as "halt" or "form fours" ... more often than not ... while the RIC were present'.[131] The supply of individuals capable of taking up senior posts was, and remained, limited. Even the legendary Tom and Seán Hales of Bandon were severely (though privately) judged by Ernie O'Malley – 'fond of themselves and of publicity', decent enough men but 'neither [was] fit to take charge of a Brigade or even of a Battalion.'[132] Not every officer wanted to take up staff posts, indeed (if anything the fledgling Volunteer officer corps was marked by a lack of confidence in its abilities), and they often fell vacant. Local battalions had to be taught that, as the Cork Brigade adjutant, Florrie O'Donoghue, told them, 'it is necessary always to keep the Battalion Staff complete, and men must be found for these positions.'[133] Ernie O'Malley, acting as commander of the Offaly Volunteers, had to round up local officers for a battalion election – 'see that your officers attend punctually, no excuse accepted.'[134]

'SENTIMENTALLY SEDITIOUS SHOPGIRLS'

Of all Irish separatist organizations, Cumann na mBan (always, unlike the Volunteers, known by the Irish version of its title)[135] was perhaps the least disrupted by 1916. It had mobilized for the rising alongside the Volunteers and played – where allowed – what may be called a semi-combat role, under fire with the fighters. One or two women had indeed fired rather than merely carried or loaded rifles, though they were in the Citizen Army, not Cumann na mBan. High-profile women of both organizations like Constance Markievicz and Kathleen Lynn had been visible among the rebel leadership. Some eighty women were arrested, and though nearly all were released, they caused real embarrassment to the authorities. The leadership of 1916 veterans like Helena Molony and remarkable widows like Aine Ceannt, Kathleen Clarke and Hanna Sheehy Skeffington (not to mention sisters like Sheila Humphreys) might have been expected to propel Cumann na mBan into the vanguard of militant separatism after 1916.

An impetus to gender equality was manifested in the League of Women Delegates, formed in 1917 to protest against the under-representation of women on Count Plunkett's Council of Nine. (The only woman on it was Countess Plunkett.) But though (after a series of rebuffs) they achieved the co-option of four 'ladies' on to the Sinn Féin Executive, the Sinn Féin Convention in October 1917 mustered a bare dozen women among over a thousand delegates.[136] Radical groupings such as the Women Delegates, Cumann na dTeachtaire, the Irish Women Workers' Union and the Irish Women's Franchise League indicated a coherent Irish feminist impulse, but it was only haltingly transmitted into Cumann na mBan as a whole. In fact much of Cumann na dTeachtaire's time was spent on non-political issues such as the prevention of venereal disease and the provision of public lavatories for women, and the group disappeared without trace early in 1919.[137]

But Cumann na mBan became more feminist after 1916, or at least 'its feminist members found it easier to present the organisation in a more progressive light.'[138] It also became more explicitly republican. By 1918 its constitution invoked the proclamation of the 1916 Republic as the basis for 'seeing that women take up their proper position in the life of the nation'. Members were urged to play a full part in local public life and 'assert their right as citizens to take part' in the nomination of parliamentary and local government elections. To make them more effective, branches were to set up lectures, debates and classes on civic education.

This progressive line was clear in the organization's highest-profile propaganda action, the delivery of a message to President Wilson in January 1918 (even though its bearer, Hanna Sheehy Skeffington, was not actually a member of the organization). The message invoked 'the generosity of the American administration on all things affecting women's lives and welfare', and appealed to it to 'recognise the political independence of Ireland in the form of an Irish Republic' – contending that 'from its inauguration' [in 1916] the Republic 'was prepared to give women their full place in the Councils of their Nation'.[139] By 1919 Cumann na mBan's constitution claimed that 'by taking their place in the firing line, and in every other way helping in the establishment of the Irish Republic', they had 'gained for the women of Ireland the rights that belonged to them under the old Gaelic civilisation, where sex was no bar to citizenship'. Since those rights had been 'stolen from them under English rule', it followed that an independent republic would restore them.

Women activists were assessed in sharply different ways, ranging from the *Times* correspondent's dismissive 'shop girls led away to sedition by sentimentalism'[140] to the idiosyncratic writer Shaw Desmond's weird invocation of 'Ireland's fierce virgins'. 'Hollow-cheeked women of parted lips whose souls under the drive of their passion seemed to be peering out from the staring eyes. Women as impossible to stop as running water or lambent flame ... ecstatic – but ruthless'. 'They were not "womanly" women, these Amazons of Sinn Féin, although they were "feminine" women – to the last hair on their fine, compact heads, and to the last nail on their slender, almost cruel hands ... ruthless, wonderful women.' 'These young girls, many of them of a curious physical beauty, had deliberately transformed all the love of life and potency of love which they had to the full, into another channel – the channel of country ... the religion of Nationalism.' 'All the ordinary attributes of woman had been either coerced or cajoled into a sort of suppressed fierceness.'[141]

Cumann na mBan was in the front line of the anti-recruitment campaign and the police boycott. In the 1918 conscription crisis it effectively took over the Woman's Day (Lá na mBan) on 9 June from its original organizers, an independent committee led by Alice Stopford Green and Agnes O'Farrelly. One of Cumann na mBan's founders, Nancy Wyse Power, rather unkindly dismissed this committee as 'odds and ends', and the organization's Executive feared that unless it took control 'the demonstration might ... prove inadequate.'[142] The Day itself saw Cumann na mBan leading processions in towns all across the country (albeit outnumbered in Dublin itself by the 2,400-strong Irish Women Workers' Union), and it organized the signing of the anti-conscription pledge over the next few weeks. Its profile was high at this point, and it even gained the kudos of being proclaimed a 'dangerous association' in some areas. During the crisis it expanded even more dramatically than Sinn Féin itself – according to its 1918 Convention report it grew from 100 branches in 1917 to 'considerably over 600' a year later. (At that Convention, though, there were nothing like 600 delegates – maybe only a quarter of that number; and the RIC counted only 112 branches, with an estimated total membership of 3,691 in September, although those figures were certainly too low.)[143]

As with Sinn Féin, that figure fell sharply in 1919 before rising once more through 1920–21. Total membership was never certain – no systematic roll was ever drawn up. Branch membership was more fluid even than for Volunteer companies, ranging from half a dozen to thirty or so. At a conservative average of ten, there were at least 6,000 active Cumann na mBan women in 1920. But in the end the organization failed to maintain the momentum of its growth, or its position as the near-equal of the (sometimes assertively) male Irish Volunteers.[144] A sign of problems to come was that in 1918 'the spread of Sinn Féin Clubs and the series of by-elections in which members of Cumann na mBan take a prominent part' created 'an impression that our Branches were Women's Sinn Féin Clubs'.[145] This was an impression (shared, incidentally, by the Inspector General of the RIC) that the organization wanted to prove false.

Cumann na mBan emphatically saw itself as a military organization – its badge was formed by its initials, C na mB, resting on the barrel of a rifle. But it equally definitely specified that its military role was auxiliary. Brighid O'Mullane, the organizer for a vast area starting from Sligo, Leitrim and Roscommon, who found that girls' parents were one of the biggest obstacles to recruitment, thought that they were reluctant 'to accept the idea of a body of gun-women'. Yet, for her, the members of Cumann na mBan were 'the pioneers in establishing what was undoubtedly a women's auxiliary of an army' – not quite so shocking perhaps.[146] Whereas women had mainly been held back from the front line by male attitudes in 1916, after that they seem to have deliberately opted out. 'There has always been work in connection with an army that is best done by women,' argued *Leabhar na mBan*, 'such as First Aid and the running of temporary hospitals. But modern warfare has shown the advantage of releasing as many men as possible for the actual firing line by getting women to look after such departments as cooking, catering, stretcher-bearing, and signalling: and in many cases dispatch carrying can be more safely done by women.'[147]

Though the last of these suggestions would prove prophetic, at this point – and right into 1920 – Cumann na mBan was thinking in terms of conventional warfare. Still, it never tried to secure weapons for itself – even on the small scale achieved by the Volunteers before 1920. Rifle practice was dropped from the list of 'suggested military activity' in the Cumann na mBan constitution as early as 1917, and though 'cleaning and unloading of rifles' was added in 1919, it would be replaced by 'home nursing' the following year. This made sense, up to a point: as Cumann na mBan did not intend to take part in armed combat, 'there was little point in training their members in skills that would be of no use to them.'[148] But it widened the symbolic distance between the men's and women's movements and, in a context where deadly weapons were increasingly prized, cannot have bolstered the latter's prestige.

The nature of the relationship – and of Cumann na mBan's social profile – can be sensed in an instruction issued by the Cork Volunteer commander Tomás Mac Curtain some time in 1918, probably during the conscription crisis. 'Write both Cumann na mBan sections at once for three ladies from each side (that is five in all) [sic] to cater for the men in this building [the Volunteer hall]. They will want to start in time to put the place in order, secure tables, etc. Only the six [sic] girls selected will be allowed in the building. They may hire a woman or two to do the rough work but that will be a matter for themselves.'[149] The two organizations were undoubtedly very close. Brighid O'Mullane set up Cumann na mBan branches in her area by getting 'the names of reliable girls' from local Volunteer commanders.[150] (Often they were the commander's sisters or cousins.) But there was never any doubt which was the leader. In 1920 a Cumann na mBan organizer in Leitrim was frankly asked by one Volunteer commander, 'do you expect me to trust these girls with the secrets of the IRA?'[151]

Though its structure survived 1916 unscathed, it was at the same time both more centralized and 'ess solidly articulated than that of the Volunteers. The Dublin Executive overshadowed the local branches. In 1918 the first attempt was made to fit Cumann na mBan branches with IV companies, but the adoption of military ranks was resisted for some time (mothers did not like their girls to join the 'Irish WAAC', it seems), and branches were run by presidents and secretaries, not by captains. In February 1919 the 1st Cork Brigade of the Volunteers wrote to the Cumann na mBan District Council asking it to consider 'attaching a Branch of Cumann na mBan to each Company of Volunteers', ideally covering the same district.[152] But not until 1920 would a fully military structure be adopted, and then only in the most active areas. (Ten-woman branches, or sometimes squads of five, were assigned to each Volunteer company. They were commanded by captains, but still had secretaries and treasurers rather than adjutants or quartermasters. The organizational parallel went up to battalion level – the Cumann na mBan District Council – but no further; there was no Cumann na mBan tier equivalent to IRA brigade councils.)

Cumann na mBan fell far short of matching the Volunteers on a unit-by-unit basis. While the IV Carlow Brigade had six battalions, totalling forty-six companies, for instance, Carlow Cumann na mBan had a single district council with twenty branches; south Leitrim had twenty-six Volunteer companies and sixteen Cumann na mBan branches. Overall, even after post-Truce expansion, Cumann na mBan mustered only eighty-five district councils (of variable strength), alongside the Volunteer total of nearly 300 battalions. So the organization's instructions to its branch leaders remained somewhat theoretical: 'the captain must keep in close touch with the Volunteer battalion or company officer, get his help in organising signalling and other classes, see that he knows how to get in touch quickly with mobilisers, and put herself under his orders in all military operations.'[153] But organizational structure would not be the key link between the women's and men's forces. It is clear that women worked with the Volunteers primarily on the basis of personal contacts. Trust was vital, and the women trusted by Volunteers were their friends and relatives.

There were signs that some in the organization were pushing for greater equality. At the 1918 Convention there were demands for definition of the relationship between Cumann na mBan and Volunteer officers, though the motive for this seems to have been to fend off Volunteer interference in Cumann na mBan activities. It has been suggested that 'the younger women' who joined as the conflict intensified 'proved determined advocates of total militarization', that is to say turning Cumann na mBan into a fighting force. But it is not clear how many did so. The call eventually issued at the 1921 Convention to run the organization on strictly military lines would be defeated.[154] None of this is to suggest, of course, that the women's view of their contribution to the struggle – as being the equal of the men's – was not fundamentally correct. Had the kind of formal military combat still prioritized by the Cumann na mBan leadership actually taken place, things might have been different, but it was rendered more or less irrelevant in guerrilla war. In the sort of war that emerged, women often played a vital role, even if not the one originally envisaged.

'A CERTAIN IDEAL OF FREEDOM'

By the late autumn of 1918, in the view of the Inspector General of the RIC, 'practically the entire Nationalist youth of both sexes' had 'become obsessed with the idea of an Irish Republic'.[155] But just what they understood by this idea was less clear: British military intelligence suggested that it was 'a kind of pious opinion which must be expressed at every meeting, but which nobody from de Valera down ever hopes to see realised'. It seems beyond doubt that, as it had long been, 'the republic' was 'a slogan or a battle cry, rather than ... a concrete objective'.[156] But if there was, as has been perceptively suggested, a key shift from the 'men of words' who had led the 1916 rebellion to the 'men of action'[157] who organized the revolutionary movement at the end of the war, the implication might be that the 'republic' they built was concrete rather than abstract, practical rather than symbolic.

Ideology does not figure prominently in most accounts of the radicalization and mobilization of the national movement. Ernie O'Malley held 'a certain ideal of freedom', but this was quite abstract, and in an odd sense negative. (The opposite of the 'slavery' that so many nationalist ballads equated (identified) with 'English' rule.) As he admitted later, he had 'not one idea in my head as to policy. I know nothing of the application of freedom as I know nothing of the application of tyranny.'[158] This left an extensive empty space for differing conceptions of the republic. The extraordinary public consumption of rebel memorabilia after 1916 has led some to see this new iconography as probably more influential than revolutionary ideas. If so, these symbols seem to have had varying substance. Irish republicanism certainly lacked the consistency of French or American political ideas; it has been said to hang together 'in a logically anomalous but psychologically satisfying way' – another manifestation perhaps of 'elective affinity'. The American conception of the 'masterless' citizen, it has been suggested, never took root in Ireland.[159]

When Sinn Féin adopted republicanism in 1917, it looked like a radical commitment, but for many Sinn Feiners it may have been less a revolutionary line than 'a pragmatic device for winning international support'. America, France and other republics were viewed as potential allies, as was the newly republican Russia. De Valera certainly contended that it was only 'as an Irish Republic that we have a chance of getting international recognition'.[160] The somewhat awkward compromise adopted by Sinn Féin in 1917, that after achieving republican status the people could choose another form of government by referendum, showed how far the party still was from the doctrinaire commitment of the IRB – certainly while Griffith remained prominent in it. The formula was drafted by de Valera and Brugha, according to the labour leader William O'Brien (who knew Brugha well). When O'Brien asked Brugha if this meant that Griffith had 'accepted the Republic', Brugha replied, 'He had to or walk the plank.'[161]

Irish historical experience does seem to have engineered a kind of exceptionalism in the ideological sphere. The polarization of the middle class in nineteenth-century Europe – notably in France, 'where village teacher and parish priest faced each other across a deep ideological divide' – was absent in Ireland.[162] Nationality trumped all political ideas, whether of left or right. Irish nationality was embraced almost as a religious conviction, its truth self-evident. National sentiment was pervasive – a viscerally absorbed story of oppression and expropriation, based on an assumption of the 'righteousness and exclusivity' of a historically distinct people.[163] Children were socialized into this worldview through family and school. Though the Volunteers and Sinn Féin often built history teaching into their programme after 1916 – the Belfast Volunteer leader Roger McCorley said that in the early days there was a 'political commissioner' attached to every company, whose job was to give a talk on Irish history after every parade – most members thought this superfluous.[164] They knew it already. As an American diplomat remarked (and as so many of the participants' memoirs make plain), 'hardly an intelligent Irishman is to be found, in any walk of modern Irish life, who is not steeped in the history of his country.'[165]

Nationalism was a simple but, for believers, all-embracing creed. It has been well said of the Cork Volunteer leader Liam Lynch that he 'made himself a leader out of the force of his own convictions'.[166] He was 'possessed by a sense of mission and by revolutionary ardour', and if nobody surpassed him in the intensity of his faith, many were like him. Explaining Lynch's embrace of the national cause, Florrie O'Donoghue threaded territorial affinity ('the Galtee countryside wove a spell that never lost its magic to the day of his death') together with the master narrative of expropriation ('three hundred years of Irish history is reflected in miniature in what happened in this locality').[167] And he instinctively reached for organic metaphors rather than ideology in explaining the process of mobilization: 'powerful spiritual forces stirred the heart of the nation.'

But though national consciousness, or nationality, seemed simple and self-evident, nationalism was a different, more problematic issue. Nationalism has proved hard to define, but it is undoubtedly a political programme, assuming that nations are natural entities that must become sovereign polities to ensure their survival. But the famous question, 'What is a nation?', has produced many answers. The language issue in Ireland – the Gaelic League's effort to reverse the gradual extinction of what had recently come to be called (in English) 'the Irish language' – pointed up key differences between Ireland and Europe. Continental cultural nationalism regarded language as the vital defining feature of nationhood. The national language determined the national consciousness. The fact that in Ireland the majority of people – both Catholic and Protestant, nationalist and unionist – spoke English, the 'language of the oppressor', was problematic both in theory and in political practice. For nationalists, following Daniel O'Connell, using English was simply a matter of practicality, but for many unionists the non-use of 'Irish' was a political point: they came to see the Gaelic language as the emblem of a hostile political movement.

Though the death of the old language might be mourned by unionists as well as nationalists, its revival was a divisive project. As the language became a symbol of national revival, it signalled a redefinition of Irishness. The politicization of language reached an extreme in the thinking of Terence MacSwiney, who explicitly identified language, together with the sea, as one of Ireland's two 'frontiers'. He argued that an 'Irishman' who spoke English was now 'asked to adopt the language for Ireland's sake as a nation and for his own sake as a citizen'. MacSwiney did not mince words in spelling out the exclusionary implication of this: 'if he prefers English civilisation he should go back [!] to England.'[168]

The new separatist leaders did not see it as necessary to analyse the 'self' that was to exercise self-determination, or to waste many words in defining the republic that would give it political form. Sinn Féin's 1917 formula almost reduced the title to a token. There was clearly more to it than this, but exactly how much? What future did republicans really envisage? Though there was some enthusiasm for the creation of a 'Gaelic state' – Darrell Figgis wrote a book on the topic in 1917 – the contours of such a state remained vague. Gaelicists believed that devolution of power to localities could recover the primitive democracy of clan society, a system more like the Russian than the English version. Some indeed squarely rejected western representative democracy as a sham, embracing the kind of local corporativism that had sprung up in the Russian soviets in 1917, and would briefly flower in the German councils movement just after the end of the war. Proto-communism and proto-fascism commingled in Aodh de Blacam's *What Sinn Féin Stands For*, the nearest approach to a coherent republican political-theoretical tract. 'That parliamentary government ... is played out, seems to be agreed by all advanced political thinkers.' The answer would be, in the first instance, 'something of a state-socialistic policy'. He predicted that 'revolutionary conditions' would produce the same government 'by centralised and iron-handed authority' in Ireland as in Lenin's Russia. 'So backward and disorganised a country as Ireland requires an iron Bismarckian phase.' But eventually it would be followed by the decentralization that fitted 'Irish instinct'.[169]

The schoolteacher Seán Moylan no doubt knew what he meant when he spoke of 'men of a more intensely Irish character and outlook', but since he assumed his readers did also, he did not explain it. Irishness was obviously not a negative quality, but much of the Irish-Ireland movement had framed it in terms of de-Anglicization that set English-ness as the negation of Irishness and vice versa. Urbanization, for instance, was, if not anti-Irish, at least unIrish – Aodh de Blacam argued that all Irish social thought saw Gaelic society as essentially rural. Irish nationalists often expressed a visceral hatred of 'England' rather than Britain. The slippage between the words Britain and England was 'one of those little traps . . . into which many of our people unconsciously fall', Art O'Brien thought. 'Our fight is against England,' as he insisted to Collins.[170] But disentangling them was not easy. When Thomas Ashe graphically told Florrie O'Donoghue, 'I never see that flag but I want to piss on it,' he was of course talking of the Union, not the English, flag.[171] He may well never have seen a St George's Cross in his life.

Separatist republicanism was primarily constructed in moral rather than ideological terms. 'Manliness' was the most vital quality of true Irishmen; degeneracy was the distinguishing mark of their enemies. Seán Moylan suggested that it was the 'demand for a recognition of their manhood and for their rights as men' that had been 'the real source of revolt in Ireland'.[172] (Admittedly, he was arguing deliberately against the idea of economic motivation.) This echoed Joe Plunkett's assertion in early 1914 that with the launching of the Volunteer movement the Irish people had 'reassumed [its] manhood'.[173] Englishness was marked by immorality, 'obscenity and Birmingham-filth'. Anti-conscription propaganda extended prewar condemnation of the British army as the most immoral in the world, riven with 'loathsome diseases brought on by per-sonal immorality'. In 1918 nationalists raised energetic alarms about the likely return of servicemen suffering from 'the vilest diseases known' – more specifically, syphilis, 'this foulest and most shameful of diseases'.[174]

Republicans always asserted, and probably believed, that republican-ism was non-sectarian – heir to the United Irish aspiration to replace denominational labels with 'the common name of Irishman'. But the Enlightenment atmosphere that had nurtured that secularist movement had long since been submerged in a tide of religious revival – both Cath-olic and Protestant. Ireland was not like the west European Catholic countries where 'anti-Catholicism or anti-clericalism were almost inev-itable concomitants of radical or revolutionary ideology'.[175] By 1916 the handful of advanced nationalists from a Protestant background can have been in no doubt that republicanism was unambiguously, and almost assertively, Catholic in ethos. One authority has called the republicanism of 1916 'expressly Catholic', another has observed that the meaning of the Irish national community 'was derived from its Catholicism'.[176]

This was in one sense simply a reflection of the fact that the overwhelming majority of Irish people outside Ulster were Catholic. When Volunteer companies paraded after mass they were doing what was convenient. Likewise the church provided the obvious place (at least until the town halls fell under Sinn Féin control in 1920) to take the anti-conscription oath, or subscribe to the Republican Loan (see p. 90 below). But the connection went further. The instinctual Catholicism of republican organizations could be seen, for instance, in the fact that the nationwide meetings for Lá na mBan ended with the women reciting the rosary in Irish.[177] Seamus Robinson set his memoir in the frame of his Catholic philosophy, starting from the declaration 'as sure as life there is a God.' He wanted to prove that all his actions from the Soloheadbeg ambush through to the civil war in 1922–3 'were carried out ... not only in good faith but as an incumbent duty' – a religious duty that was, he held, denied only by the 'Jansenistic-Gallicanism' of the majority of the Irish Hierarchy. For Todd Andrews, the 'profound Catholic faith' of the Volunteers meant that any nationalist beliefs had to be essentially religious, since 'it would have been quite impossible for us to imagine ourselves breaking the First Commandment.'[178] Atheists, especially militant ones like Frank Busteed of Blarney, were extremely rare among republicans. Busteed, whose father was a Protestant, was brought up as a Catholic, but felt that his Protestant name impeded his progress in the Volunteers. He seems to have thought that his atheism did not produce such discrimination. Even anti-clericalism was less prominent than it had been among nineteenth-century Fenians. The IRB man P. S. O'Hegarty, urging Terence MacSwiney that 'nothing but strong determined actions will break' the clergy of their political habits, remarked that 'it is only when a man leaves Ireland that he starts to see straight on some things, this among them.' 'We have to put them in their places if we are going to do anything.'[179] O'Hegarty, originally from Cork, worked for the Post Office in London. His childhood friend MacSwiney, who did not leave Ireland (except to be interned in Frongoch camp in Wales in 1916), simply equated anti-clericalism with atheism.

'THERE ARE DEAD MEN VOTING HERE TODAY'

The general election at the end of the war was a showdown not only between Sinn Féin and the Irish party, but also between moderate and radical republicans within Sinn Féin. Darrell Figgis thought that the showdown should have been won by the moderates: the 'Griffith school' reaping the 'harvest of their victories' over conspiratorial physical-force republicanism in 1917. Indeed the very strategy of fighting elections was a Griffithite victory. The fact that Sinn Féin candidates were abstentionists, promising never to attend Westminster, made it more palatable to republicans, but only a little. In the event, though, as Figgis lamented, the physical-force men of the IRB and Volunteers displaced the moderates from the party platform.[180] Figgis himself was a notable casualty of the process, perhaps the most outstanding Sinn Féin figure to miss out on selection. Prodigiously talented, a brilliant writer with an immaculate record of imprisonment (he was swept up in the German Plot arrests, and was in gaol during the election), he suffered from 'unbounded egotism'. Robert Brennan said 'he made enemies more easily than any man I knew.' Whether for this reason or because he was identified as representing 'old' Sinn Féin, Figgis would never find a suitable role in the struggle thus redefined.

Sinn Féin followed the old parliamentary party's system of controlling its candidate selection from the centre. Harry Boland became 'chief broker in the allocation of seats', winning, for instance, a dispute with Austin Stack (SF's titular election director) over whether to put up Eamon de Valera against Joe Devlin on his home ground in Belfast (Falls Division). He co-drafted the 'Manifesto to the Irish People' with O'Flanagan, Tom Kelly and Robert Brennan. The manifesto insisted that Sinn Féin was 'not a political party', but 'the natural successor of that great body of the Irish nation, that never . . . surrendered the right of Ireland to absolute independence'.[181]

Initially, Sinn Féin faced the possibility that the labour movement would challenge this claim by fighting the election in its own right. In August 1918 the Irish Trades Union Council changed its title to Irish Labour party and Trades Union Congress, and its president William O'Brien declared that 'we are a political party, independent, erect, free ... We must secure Labour representation, independent, able, strong, efficient and constructive on all our public elective bodies.' The Labour National Executive in September unanimously resolved 'in favour of entering the field at the coming General Election with a number of Labour candidates fighting as an independent political party'. But the leadership was in fact far from unanimous on this crucial issue. While Tom Johnson was in favour of a pact with Sinn Féin, at least for the first postwar election, Louie Bennett denounced the lack of any revolutionary principle in the Sinn Féin programme. Jim Larkin went further: 'the Irish Republic the Sinn Feiners are after is but the counterpart of France and America where year after year the capitalist sweats dividends out of his helpless workers.' But though Larkin might rail against Sinn Féin – 'the Griffith gang' – and its view of socialists as 'antiChrists', and ask why the Irish labour leaders were allowing it to monopolize the national resistance to conscription, his stentorian tones were muted by distance since he had gone to the USA in 1914. Peadar O'Donnell (who was intellectually qualified to take up James Connolly's mantle) regretted that when Connolly died in 1916 radicalism died with him. He 'left no successor'; the Labour leader who best understood Connolly, Cathal O'Shannon, was 'on the payroll of the Transport Workers' Union, and was very much under the influence of Bill O'Brien'.[182]

Boland himself, still – more or less – a working tailor (like William O'Brien), may have been inclined 'towards elements of socialism'. But he was happy to assure Cathal Brugha – whose unreconstructed Fenian view was that it was 'a pity that Labour people have not the intelligence and patriotism to let their class claim wait until we have cleared out the enemy' – that his overriding commitment was to the Republic.[183] Though Boland's complicated manoeuvres over the selection of candidates in Dublin led some republicans to fear that 'we were selling the pass to Labour,' in the end the pressures were all the other way. A special Labour conference in November eventually accepted Johnson's argument that the movement should change its posture, because the nature of the election itself had changed since the Armistice: no longer the 'War election' they had envisaged, it had become the 'Peace election'. There would be 'a Grand Inquest of the Nations', and Labour should withdraw to allow national unity on the self-determination issue to be demonstrated. This was agreed by 96 to 23 – an outcome with farreaching consequences for the labour movement, and one which satisfied even Brugha, who exulted, 'Could not be better!' Labour's decision to stand aside was probably the most emphatic evidence of Sinn Féin's transition into a national movement. It was becoming, as has been said, 'increasingly difficult for any political group to maintain independence in the circumstances of Irish life'.[184]

The election was a historic moment. The dramatic enlargement of the franchise in the 1918 Representation of the People Act – which trebled the Irish electorate – and the lapse of time since the last general election in 1910, meant that three-quarters of voters had never previously cast a vote. Women (over thirty) were enfranchised for the first time, and a last-minute provision in November confirmed that women could stand for election – paving the way for Countess Markievicz to become the first woman elected to Westminster. (Sinn Féin put up only two women candidates, in fact, and the other – Winnie Carney – stood for the Victoria Division of Belfast where, with 'neither personation agents, committee rooms, canvassers or vehicles' to support her, she could muster only 395 votes.)[185] These structural changes were not decisive in themselves – in Longford, for instance, they merely cemented Sinn Féin's already established dominance – and probably did not secure Sinn Féin's victory, though they helped to increase its margin. The result was one of the greatest electoral landslides of the century in western Europe.[186]

Volunteer election activity was well established by this time – the Dublin Brigade had mustered 100 men to send to south Armagh 'to prevent the blatant [loyalist] intimidation that was going on'. Joe O'Connor noted that election duty was popular with officers – it enhanced the men's 'sense of discipline', and gave officers practice in handling them in public. This was normally risky, but 'the British could not very well interfere with our endeavours to keep order' at election meetings.[187] This time Volunteer activity was systematically planned. In mid-November GHQ issued orders that brigades should appoint a director of elections for every constituency to take charge of all Volunteer activity. It instructed that '*for election purposes only*' all battalions 'and odd companies' should 'respond to the orders' of this officer. Volunteers were to guard 'Republican Candidates' Committee Rooms' and provide protection for candidates at election meetings. They were to provide 'peace patrols' – GHQ reminded them that the organization was 'a national one, and the freedom that is desired for ourselves must not be denied to others'. They would guard polling booths to prevent intimidation and molestation of voters, escort the ballot boxes to the place they were deposited between polling day and the count, and guard these depositories. (All these functions would usurp the role of the police.)[188] In Dublin they threw themselves enthusiastically into more directly political activity like canvassing. In College Green Division 'Volunteers ... spent whole nights addressing envelopes, sending off literature, as well as preventing ... ex-soldiers creating any disturbances.'[189] Elsewhere 'Volunteers carried out a thorough canvass of the area and on polling day acted as personation agents and also organised transport to bring voters to polling booths.'[190] Cumann na mBan 'made and distributed a large amount of flags and emblems', catered for the Volunteers on election duty, and 'personated extensively'. Those who, like O'Connor, were less happy about Volunteers taking on electioneering work were relieved when 'as the day of the polling approached we were able to draw off the Volunteers into more soldierly duties' such as maintaining order.

Despite a mini-run of by-election victories in the preceding months, the old parliamentary party was faced with annihilation. Even so, the election was a strangely quiet affair compared with the ferocious contests of the past. There were exceptions: in the Redmondite stronghold of Waterford, for instance, Volunteer election parties were fired on by ex-servicemen armed with rifles, 'a couple of our lads who had revolvers replied to the fire and dispersed the attackers'; but they had to use sticks or hurleys 'on many occasions'.[191] And Kevin O'Shiel (who contested both South Antrim and North Fermanagh) had his most violent election experience in Falls Division at the hands not of loyalists but of the old party's enforcers – 'I shall never forget that wild, yelling, maddened Hibernian mob that pelted us for two hours with sticks, stones, rivets, rotten eggs, dead cats and rats.'[192]

When the polls were declared on 28 December, Sinn Féin swept the old party away. The near-totality of its obliteration was of course due to the British electoral system, and was belied, to some minds, by the modest proportion of the overall Irish poll Sinn Féin secured – not quite 48 per cent. But its share of the vote outside the six north-eastern counties – where Sinn Féin fielded candidates in hopeless contests – was probably a truer reflection of Sinn Féin's strength: 68 per cent. Sinn Féin now had sixty-nine members of parliament (all but twenty-six of whom were in gaol). Sinn Féin and the Volunteers together seem to have overwhelmed the opposition both physically and psychologically. (Boland's opponent in South Roscommon philosophically accepted defeat as 'the passing away of a great movement, to be succeeded by another'.)

Sinn Féin's victory was secured in part by the intensive campaigning of the Volunteers, seasoned with a fair amount of personation – Cumann na mBan women celebrating the extended franchise with special enthusiasm. 'We dressed in different clothes and voted in the name of absentee voters.'[193] Some activists liked to boast in later years that they had voted dozens of times.[194] Republican crowds intimidated some polling officials to overlook under-age voting. Intimidation was nothing novel in Irish elections, however, or particular to Sinn Féin. In the old party stronghold of Waterford during the March 1918 by-election, 'no man could walk out singly carrying a Sinn Féin emblem without being almost beaten to death.'[195] The high proportion of uncontested seats in the general election has often been seen as evidence of intimidation, but actually fewer seats were uncontested in 1918 than had been normal in the first decade of the century – twenty-five as against forty-one in 1910. And the influence of intimidation and personation should not be over-stated: much of it was done out of bravado rather than a belief that it was necessary.[196] It was a function of Sinn Féin's organizational strength, and may indeed be seen as a reflection of a wider pressure for unanimity – or intolerance of dissent – characteristic of 'rural Ireland'.[197] The election as a whole was, in comparative perspective, fair enough: the voters made a clear choice of party. But whether they really knew what the party stood for is another issue.

Ever since, there has been some doubt about the precise platform Sinn Féin fought the election on. This was an issue that grew dramatically in importance three years later when many republicans based their rejection of the Anglo-Irish Treaty on the popular mandate for independence they claimed the election result represented. All later recollections were inevitably but perhaps fatally coloured by the eventual murderous split between pro-Treaty and anti-Treaty republicans. But it seems undeniable that through 1918 Sinn Féin's policy, even after the 1917 Convention, had remained 'studiously vague'.[198] At the hustings some candidates declared that a vote for Sinn Féin was a vote for the Republic, while others later claimed they had never used the word. The Volunteers in Cork certainly complained about their inability to hear the word at election meetings.[199] It seems likely that more people talked about freedom or independence than invoked the Republic as such. Figgis thought that most of the speeches in the election built on the theme of Woodrow Wilson's speeches of 4 July and 28 September 1918 – in other words, national self-determination. Some indications were quite gnomic. One candidate declared that 'Sinn Féin stood by the policy of Parnell,' another that it would 'carry out the programme of that flag that was hoisted upon that occasion'.[200]

According to its manifesto, which Sinn Féin campaigner Kevin O'Shiel thought 'wordy', Sinn Féin gave Ireland 'the opportunity of vindicating her honour and pursuing with renewed confidence the path of national salvation by rallying to the flag of the Irish Republic'. It aimed at 'securing the establishment of that Republic', by 'withdrawing the Irish representation from the British Parliament' and 'making use of any and every means available to render impotent the power of England to hold Ireland in subjection'. It 'stands by' the 1916 proclamation in 'reasserting the inalienable right of the Irish Nation to sovereign independence'.[201] O'Shiel thought that 'the Republic was there certainly, but, as P. S. O'Hegarty writes . . . "in fact what was sold to the electorate . . . was not Sinn Féin, not the Republic, but Easter Week".'[202] Even those who, like Boland himself, invoked their own action in 1916 spoke of 'fighting for Ireland' – rebutting the charge that they had treacherously fought for Germany – rather than for the Republic. Kevin O'Higgins and indeed Michael Collins himself made no mention of the Republic as such in their election addresses. Collins held out 'the supreme, absolute and final control of all this country' as the objective.[203] But there is no doubt that their opponents denounced them as republicans. The old party's key argument had always been that the Sinn Féin programme was 'impossible to realise' precisely for that reason – Britain would concede Home Rule but never a republic. In the end, SF Vice-President Michael O'Flanagan recognized that while 'the people have voted for Sinn Féin, what we have to do now is explain to them what Sinn Féin is'.[204]

'THE IRISH PEOPLE CAN PRODUCE THEIR REPUBLIC AT WHATEVER MOMENT THEY LIKE'

Sinn Féin's post-election strategy had been mapped out long in advance by Arthur Griffith. Abstention from Westminster was the most un-ambiguous plank in the Sinn Féin platform, and though Lord French predictably suggested that the new MPs would be unable to resist the lure of £400 a year, there was never any question of abandoning it. (Markievicz did apparently sneak into the Palace of Westminster to see her name on the brass plate by her coat-hook, a forgivable lapse for the first woman MP perhaps.) Less certain was the way that Griffith's concept of a constituent assembly or 'National Council' would be brought into being, and what this would mean in legal terms. Even before the election results were announced, on 19 December, the Sinn Féin Executive decided to 'convoke the Dáil Éireann' – the national assembly – as the October 1918 Ard-fheis had resolved, and a committee under Seán T. O'Kelly set about preparing for this. Several questions were aired at this stage: were there enough representatives (even if they were all at liberty) to constitute a credible assembly? (The number having, of course, been set by the logic of the UK system.) If not, could others be co-opted? Should the assembly declare a republic?

The fact that the decision to declare an independent republic seems to have been unproblematic reflected the untheoretical nature of repub-licanism itself. The issue was simply not considered. It would, in theory, have been possible to take the view that the creation of the new state was the task of the constituent assembly – that was certainly Figgis's and most probably Griffith's view – and should not be pre-empted. The initial (private) meeting of all available Sinn Féin members – called 'Deputies of the Dáil' in English, in Irish 'Teachtaí Dála', but usually re-Anglicized as 'TDs' – on 7 January 1919 seemed to follow this line. The group pledged merely to 'work for the establishment of an inde-pendent Irish Republic'. But it was soon clear that the work would be brief, and that the Republic was already effectively in being. It seems to have been assumed that there had to be some kind of notional state underpinning the assembly, and as the Dáil's first Speaker Michael Hayes put it, 'what other name could it have been given?' Interestingly, though, the constitution prepared for the first meeting actually made no mention of a state – it was not the constitution of Ireland, but the constitution of the Dáil.

This was to be a single-chamber parliament with an internal cabinet type of executive. The British constitutional model was reflected here, as in all the Dáil's rules of procedure, and in its general working assumptions. For instance, although this was effectively a one-party assembly, the practice of 'whipping' was started immediately (with Piaras Béaslaí as chief whip) to assemble the 'Republican Representatives' for the first private meeting on 7 January. That meeting was 'modelled on established parliamentary procedure, with carefully organised Orders of the Day', including motions to appoint select committees to draft a constitution and standing orders, along with the declaration of independence.[205] This burst of casual Anglicization did not pass entirely unchallenged. One contributor to the radical journal *New Ireland* charged the Dáil with being 'simply Westminster put into Irish'. But nobody in the assembly seems to have been unduly concerned.

The proceedings of the first public session of Dáil Éireann on the afternoon of 21 January, carefully stage-managed by Béaslaí, a veteran of many amateur theatricals, were described as 'dull, but ... electric' – an interesting paradox. They were conducted soberly, in Irish (aside from Count Plunkett's warning to the small audience not to cheer), and – sending another unconscious message – opened with a prayer read by Fr Michael O'Flanagan, the Vice-President of Sinn Féin. This must have seemed natural enough, though it confirmed, in unionist eyes, that the Republic was a Catholic project. It was the historic significance of the event itself that was most clearly felt – the 'enormity' of the occasion, as one reporter put it.[206] The precise form of the constitution and the three declaratory statements adopted by the assembly may have seemed less important. Kevin O'Shiel remarked that none of the six articles of the 'extremely brief' constitution contained 'any reference to, much less a definition of, the Irish Republic or what area it covers'. But it did set up the executive apparatus of a new state, vesting 'all legislative powers' in Dáil Éireann and 'all executive powers ... in the members, for the time being, of the Ministry' (Aireacht). The 'President' of the ministry – not, it should be noted, of the Republic – was to be elected by the Dáil. ('It was manifest', Béaslaí insisted, 'that Dail Eireann could not arrogate to itself the right of electing a "President of the Irish Republic".')[207]

If, as *New Ireland* had claimed, 'the Irish people can produce their Republic at whatever moment they like', the three headline statements adopted by the Dáil at its first meeting did something, but not much, to flesh out the nature of the state it represented. The Declaration of Independence ratified the establishment of the Irish Republic ('proclaimed in Dublin on Easter Monday 1916 by the Irish Republican Army acting on behalf of the Irish people'), asserting that 'the Irish people is resolved . . . to promote the common weal, to re-establish justice . . . with equal right and equal opportunity for every citizen.' The Message to the Free Nations of the World called on 'every free nation to support the Irish Republic by recognising Ireland's national status' based on the natural 'radical' distinction of its race, language, customs and traditions from those of 'the English'. Ireland was 'the last outpost of Europe towards the West', whose independence was 'demanded by the Freedom of the Seas'.[208] The Democratic Programme – 'hastily prepared', Béaslaí suggested, though it had actually been carefully prepared by Tom Johnson and hastily edited by Seán T. O'Kelly – gestured in Pearsean style towards a wider social responsibility. (Indeed it contained 'more of the social doctrine of the Proclamation of the Republic than the electorate could be considered to have sanctioned'.)[209] The fact that it was not in Griffith's style was not insignificant.

With most of the moderate leadership in prison, Dáil Éireann became (as the imprisoned Figgis lamented) 'less a house of consideration than a regiment of battle' in which a military kind of discipline would rule: 'most would look to a few men who knew what that duty should be.' First among those few on this day was Cathal Brugha, elected 'President of the Ministry *pro tem*'; whose brusque assertion after the Declaration of Independence was adopted – 'Deputies, you understand from this that we are now done with England' – pushed the Sinn Féin spirit to its limits. For Figgis, Brugha had 'a Republic as clear before his eyes as the sun in heaven'. Roger Chauviré saw the same Sinn Féin trope he recognized elsewhere operating here. When one Sinn Feiner explained to him that the Dáil, as the only government acknowledged by the Irish people, 'was the *de facto* Government', Chauviré naturally corrected him: '*de jure* if you like, but not *de facto*; the *de facto* Government is the one that sends its opponents to prison.' The reply was simply 'English rule . . . being illegal, *does not exist in fact*.'[210]

'A COUNTRY'S CONSULS ARE ITS MOST VALUABLE CIVIL SERVANTS'

The international situation looked to be exceptionally propitious for the new-born Republic, as the world's statesmen assembled in Paris to settle the new global order on the basis of the Wilsonian principle of national self-determination. Everyone who had studied the national movements of the nineteenth century knew how Cavour, by sending a contingent to fight in the Crimean War, had secured a place for Piedmont at the 1856 Paris Peace Conference, and paved the way for the unification of Italy. Indeed the reasoning of Redmond's party had been exactly that by playing its part in the war Ireland would earn its freedom at the end. Unfortunately, the separatists had opposed this line, and to the extent that they had taken part in the war, it was on the wrong side. The connection with Germany was not in itself fatal to any favourable response to the appeal to the 'free nations', but the situation was less promising than Sinn Féin believed. (Quite apart from the legacy of 1916, Griffith had queered the pitch with France by his intemperate wartime propaganda portraying Germany as a 'free state' fighting against 'imperial states' that had 'blotted out the local self-governing communities'.)

The Declaration of Independence may have been the inevitable result of Brugha's dominance; but Figgis thought it was a strategic error in international terms. The Peace Conference would now be asked not to investigate and adjudicate a national claim, but to recognize an already existing republic, approving an act hostile to a great power. This may well have made a favourable outcome even less likely, but one was scarcely on the cards in any case. The Dáil's three appointed delegates to the Peace Conference, Plunkett, Griffith and de Valera, never even managed to get visas to travel to Paris. Though for a while optimists could believe that the Irish-American lobby would be strong enough to overcome British resistance, this was highly improbable. The hard-headed Hanna Sheehy Skeffington, who had secured a meeting with Woodrow Wilson in 1918 to present a Cumann na mBan petition urging Ireland's claim to self-determination, was optimistic about the President himself. 'From my experience, from what he said and left unsaid, I am convinced that while he might have preferred the Irish question to be settled domestically [by the Irish Convention], he will now see the force of having it settled internationally for the sake of the peace of the world.'[211]

Seán T. O'Kelly, who managed to get to Paris as a representative of the Dublin Corporation and then declared himself to be the 'Representative of the Provisional Government of the Irish Republic', may have damaged the Republic's position by the 'pompous' letter he sent to Woodrow Wilson. While O'Kelly might conceivably have secured a meeting with Wilson as representative of the Corporation (which had sent the President an invitation – albeit unanswered – to visit the city on the way to Paris), in his new guise he had no chance. But in any case Wilson was already in retreat from his commitment to general self-determination. When the Irish-American delegation met him shortly after a US Senate resolution on 6 June that the Irish delegates should be heard by the conference, he explained that the Big Four had agreed that no delegations would be accepted without their unanimous consent. Beyond polite expressions of sympathy, representatives of other states would not take any action without the direct intervention of a great power. Clemenceau did go as far as considering a commission of inquiry into the Irish case, but this fell far short of the republican call for recognition of the already expressed will of the Irish people. Though efforts continued to secure recognition in Europe after the Peace Conference was wound up in July, they led to nothing, as did the attempt to secure membership of the new League of Nations.

These hopes have been dismissed as illusory, perhaps rightly, but the dashing of them was felt as a definite setback. 'So ended in failure all the careful plans that had been made during two years. So fell the brave structure of hopes . . .'[212] Though some Gaelic revivalists wanted to close Ireland off from the corrupting world, mainstream Sinn Féin, certainly as articulated by Griffith, was internationally minded. One of Griffith's favourite pastimes in the early years of the century had been to plan out networks of Irish representatives abroad. He had urged people to study not only the Hungarian model, but also the way that Norway, partly by securing its own consular service to support its expanding overseas trade, had freed itself from Sweden. 'A country's consuls are its most valuable civil servants.' A consular service would enlarge Irish commerce as well as enlarging foreign understanding of

Ireland, teaching the world that it was distinct from Britain. (It was Europeans, as he had lamented in 1905, who addressed communications to him 'at Dublin, Angleterre'.)[213] The size of the Irish diaspora offered a unique prospect of global impact. But in any case, to counter unionist arguments about the advantages of attachment to the British Empire, Griffith had long held that small countries like Ireland – especially Belgium, Denmark and Switzerland – were fully viable in the modern world. Indeed, 'the day of the little nations has returned', and greatness would be measured not by a people's size but by its spirit.

Now Griffith was free to appoint consuls, and indeed envoys or quasi-ambassadors – at least within the constraints of the Dáil's finances. (One part-time consul, Leopold Kerney, remembered Griffith advancing him the first quarter of his annual salary 'in a back parlour of a shop in Parliament Street'. Along with Kerney's credentials as trade representative of the Elected Government of the Irish Republic to France, Griffith 'produced from one of his pockets £50 . . . in £1 notes, the dirty appearance of which struck me very much'.)[214] Griffith seems to have used his position as vice-president to act as foreign minister, although Count Plunkett was formally given the portfolio.

Seán T. O'Kelly was followed as envoy to Paris by George Gavan Duffy, and eventually moved on to Rome as envoy to the Papacy. The vital London office was entrusted to Art O'Brien, a man with aspirations to turn his post as envoy into a full ambassadorship. A Londoner by birth, and a former civil engineer, now in early middle age he was manager of the *Music Trade Review*, a leading figure in the Gaelic League and President of the Sinn Féin Council of Great Britain. He constructed a complex network of undercover contacts to spread information, gather intelligence and acquire arms, as well as an open pressure group, the Irish Self-Determination League of Great Britain. In the process he spent a lot of money – keeping up the style he believed was necessary to the dignity of the Republic's representative. Cars waited outside while he took tea or dined at the Savoy. (His secretary, who thought he was 'more concerned with the official dignity attached to his position than with the national cause', would eventually resign in disgust when O'Brien admonished her for offering a cup of tea to one of the many messengers he kept hanging about his office.)[215]

Kerney was proud of his achievements in Paris – such as getting Irish toilet soap on sale in France (and importing French household soap to

Ireland), and establishing a trade in rabbit skins. He 'met with some success' in getting 'jambon de York' relabelled as 'Irish ham', though perhaps his greatest feat – 'not easy', as he said – was to get the French commercial guide to give Ireland a separate entry, distinct from Britain. In general, as Briollay noted, the Irish envoys in Paris were 'at first repulsed because of the fervour of the Anglo-French Alliance', but a growing French 'bitterness begotten of English selfishness' led them to take a new interest in Ireland's claims.[216] Even so, no concrete action followed.

The Republic's apparently most promising bids for external recognition targeted America and Russia. Though Irish opinion inevitably expected more from America, such expectations were rooted in a common delusion about the nature of big-power politics. In reality, the US would never directly dispute Britain's view of the position in Ireland. In 1919, the weak and isolated infant Soviet Union was actually a better bet. There were a number of contacts that year (including a loan of $20,000 from Irish-American funds against the security of some supposed Russian Crown jewels), which eventually crystallized in summer 1920 in a draft treaty. But the Republic's Ambassador-designate, Patrick McCartan – previously the envoy to Irish-America – did not set out for Russia until December 1920, by which time the USSR's position was strengthening and the Bolshevik interest in stirring up anti-imperialist activity weakening. The delay killed the Irish–Soviet treaty. McCartan blamed it on de Valera's hesitation, and the President's belief in the possibility of gaining US recognition of the Republic dominated all his actions for nearly two years following his decision to travel to the USA shortly after being sprung from gaol (as we shall see) early in 1919.

De Valera's twenty-month American mission was the most high-profile effort to set the Republic on an international stage. Many have wondered, then and since, whether the results justified such an extended absence. The mission took out of the republican leadership in Ireland not only the President himself but also Harry Boland, who had crossed the Atlantic as envoy to the Clan na Gael in mid-May. Patrick McCartan had already been sent there by the IRB to lead the effort to secure recognition. Other exiled 1916 veterans in America included Diarmuid Lynch – deported in 1918 for his part in organizing the 'food control' scheme – and Liam Mellows (though Mellows eventually became disenchanted enough with America to go back to the rigours of life as a rebel leader). Boland had barely begun to navigate the shoals of the fractious Irish-American leadership when the unexpected news of de Valera's arrival reached him on 11 June. Suddenly demoted from envoy to 'valet, shepherd and manager' of the socially awkward President, he stayed on – with a month's break in Ireland in May 1920 – until after the 1921 Truce. (When he returned in August 1921, Collins wryly christened him 'the Visitor'.)

Even Boland's skills as a fixer, though, were not enough to smooth relations between the 'stubborn' de Valera and the imperious Irish-American leaders – the hard-bitten Fenian veteran John Devoy, President of the Clan na Gael, and Judge Daniel Cohalan, who effectively controlled the new Friends of Irish Freedom – who themselves were at loggerheads with McCartan. The Irish leaders were fortunate to have one ally on the Clan Executive, the Philadelphia liquor trader Joe McGarrity, who became a crucial supporter and consistent confidant over the following years. 'Great soul', Boland called him: 'love him more and more.'[217] A gifted businessman, and dogged tax avoider, McGarrity shifted from liquor to real estate when prohibition came in in 1920. His lantern jaw and solid build (the writer Padraic Colum described him admiringly as 'a Donegal gallowglass ready to swing a battleaxe with his long arms') unfortunately disguised a less robust constitution, and his 'breakdown' in spring 1920 set limits to his political activity. But he had a 'deep reverence' for de Valera, and 'spent fortunes on the Irish cause', among other things founding the Philadelphia *Irish Press*.[218]

The Friends of Irish Freedom, through its Irish Race Conventions and fund drives, was raising $2,000,000 for its Irish Victory Fund. It financed the three-man delegation that was sent to Paris. But it proved very reluctant either to disgorge its funds in the direction of Dublin or to support the idea of the Dáil Loan when it was launched later in 1919. One of the delegation's members estimated (on the basis of the activity he had seen on his way back from Paris) that the republican government would not cost more than $50,000 a year to run. Cohalan also argued that it would probably be illegal for an unrecognized state to issue bonds. It was not until late 1919 that an accommodation between Cohalan and de Valera allowed the Dáil bonds to be sold from January 1920 onwards. But tensions persisted and the Irish-American effort was never fully unified, even after the two chief protagonists formally composed their differences in a pact 'ratified in the most solemn manner – all present kneeling and receiving the blessing of Bishop Turner of Buffalo'.[219]

On the face of things, de Valera's American mission looked triumphant in mobilizing public support. 'If cheers and parades mean anything we have won,' Boland noted in October 1919; but he added, 'Wish we could translate cheers etc into deeds.'[220] De Valera's presidential status became informally recognized – 'governors, Senators and Mayors pay court to him and do him honor.' His speeches had a big impact on audiences often reaching 30,000. As McCartan put it, 'de Valera as President issued and sold bonds of the Republic of Ireland, and as President of that Republic asked the American people to recognise it.' (Indeed it was this personification of 'the cause', McCartan lamented, that 'left us without the power to challenge him'.)[221] His prestige as 'the Chief', backed by efficient organization, ensured impressive success in fundraising: over a quarter of a million Americans subscribed to the 'external' Dáil Loan in 1920, and over $5,000,000 was eventually raised. Even though much of this money did not reach Ireland in time to help the Republic (half remained 'buried in American banks' through the 1920s), it transformed the counter-state's resources. But the 'deed' the republicans desired above all, formal US recognition, remained elusive. De Valera had probably done little to advance it by denouncing the League of Nations, Woodrow Wilson's most cherished international project, as an 'unholy alliance' in his first statement to the American press.[222]

De Valera lacked one big advantage that the original 'Chief', Charles Stewart Parnell, had possessed, as had Roger Casement: he was not a Protestant. American Protestant sentiment was worryingly vulnerable to the anti-Catholicism of a well-organized unionist mission demanding self-determination for Ulster. De Valera's assertion that 'religion is involved only as a rack on the pegs of which England exhibits Ireland's political differences before the world', and his assurance that the Irish nation was 'as homogeneous as any nation upon the earth; but under England's influence the elements of Irish life are made to appear to repel each other', were likely to convince only those who had already adopted the nationalist view.[223] Though he won his long feud with Cohalan, the bitterness of the feud itself was worrying. So, though it did not leak into the public sphere, was his long bickering with the Dublin leadership – Collins in particular – over such issues as the date from which interest on the Dáil Loan should be payable.[224]

'DON'T ARGUE, BUT SHOOT!'

Moderate Sinn Feiners like Darrell Figgis might complain that the displacement of politicians by soldiers in the Dáil ensured 'the shock of violence where violence might conceivably have been avoided'. But, from the standpoint of fighting men like Seamus Robinson, things looked quite different: there was still far too much avoidance of violence. Calling them 'fighting men' may seem premature, since no serious fighting had yet taken place, but they had already made up their minds to dedicate themselves to soldiering. Robinson 'had taken a solemn resolution on Easter Monday morning . . . that I'd soldier for the rest of my life or until we had our freedom'. The notion of soldiership was absolutely central to the attitudes and actions of the group – formed really by this outlook rather than by any direct links – that would press the Volunteer organization on into guerrilla warfare. (Dan Breen would describe himself as 'a soldier first and foremost'; Sheila Humphreys would say that Ernie O'Malley was 'a soldier, above all'.) Since 1916 Peadar Kearney's song, 'Soldiers are We', adopted by the Volunteers before the Easter rising, had become the unofficial national anthem of the Republic.

Soldiership meant military-mindedness, but this did not necessarily mean militarism. It was a matter not so much of rejecting politics as of embracing the professional dedication necessary to make the use of violence effective and give it some prospect of success. All Volunteers were well aware of how little they knew about military matters at the outset, and most were eager to learn. In the words of Seán O'Sullivan, a Longford company captain, 'The work went on powerful every man make himself a better soldier and even yet I feel the pride knowing I was a sworn soldier of Ireland, and same I could see in both officers and men.'[225] This was not just a matter of mastering military technology and techniques, vital though these were – O'Malley's notebooks were filled with fieldcraft diagrams and instructions on dismantling various weapons – but still more of internalizing military values. This was not easy for an organization that could make only restricted use of traditional military symbolism, such as uniform. The 1916 rebels had sported all the paraphernalia they possessed, but in the kind of guerrilla actions their successors were limited to, uniform would be a liability

73

(useful, indeed, only to decoy the enemy). Its importance at the kind of events where it could feature, like weddings and funerals, can hardly be missed. Still more importantly, as in all citizen armies, Volunteer leaders were quite well aware of the difficulty of inculcating the central military value, discipline, into soldiers who could not experience the total bonding of regular military units. Here the local nature of the army, and the personal familiarity of its members, was a key asset. When it failed to work, the risk of insubordination, and even the breaking away of whole units, was always present.

The boundary between military-mindedness and militarism was a fragile one, though. Seán Moylan felt that the mantra 'You must think militarily' had its downside: 'as an instruction given to men who had come to despise parliamentarianism, it was not wisely conceived.' Its least pernicious product might be the apparently sensible prioritization of Liam Lynch's dictum 'the army should hew the way for politics to follow.' But at its worst it could lead to a perilous Coriolanus-like contempt for the very people whose freedom was the cause, and even to a belief that only the fighting men were entitled to political power. Ernie O'Malley would reflect bitterly during the Truce that popularity was worse than contempt – 'the crowd cheering you today would cut your throat tomorrow, if they had the pluck.' At the height of the civil war Lynch would reportedly dismiss the ordinary people as 'merely sheep to be driven anywhere at will', and O'Malley would brand them as 'slaves' with the 'slave mind', 'slaves' meannesses and lack of moral qualities'.[226]

Attending training lectures was one thing; fighting was another. 'The Volunteers would have to be brought by gradual stages to the sticking point –' as Seamus Robinson put it, before adding, 'I mean the bayonet-sticking point.'[227] Volunteer activity had started to become violent in many places in 1918 – in February the Volunteers in Ennistymon, Co. Clare had attacked two RIC men escorting a family which was involved in a land dispute, and seized their carbines. In March the first shot fired in anger at the police had been fired at an 'officious' constable there, who had been keeping a close watch on arrivals at the railway station. 'The shot lifted him like a wounded rabbit,' according to the man who pulled the trigger of the shotgun, Tosser Neylon. 'Although it did not kill him, it put him out of action for a good while and he gave no trouble after that.'[228] That month the RIC barrack in Eyeries was raided and four rifles taken, Westport RIC barrack was attacked with a bomb, and British soldiers were stoned in Limerick city. In April, Volunteers seized 250 pounds of gelignite at Newtownbarry in Wexford, and in June a policeman was wounded when an RIC patrol was attacked in Tralee, Co. Kerry. Sentries had been disarmed in several places. So far, though, the only policeman to be killed had died in a prank, when he was shot by one of his comrades while pretending to be a rebel raider.

Confrontation receded along with the conscription threat. Public drilling, for instance, intense in early 1918, became less visible. Some activists who had been given short gaol sentences for drilling, and warned that a repeat would incur much stiffer penalties, had backed off. The Executive advised Volunteers generally not to court arrest. In its effort to construct a national army, GHQ was (and would remain) acutely conscious of regional inconsistencies, striving to push the localities into line with its pattern of soldiering. This could stifle as well as stimulate local energy. The few organizers it sent out across the country were a drop in the ocean, often self-taught officers – like Ernest Blythe – only moderately qualified to impose their ideas. Though GHQ would try to use the promise of weapons as a stimulus, it would never be in a position to guarantee supplies to local units. The experience of John Patrick McCormack's Belmont company in Galway was all too common: 'a sum of £18 for the purchase of three rifles was collected . . . and handed over to the battalion officers' in 1919, but 'no rifle was ever delivered to the company.' McCormack himself (who had contributed much of the cash with three friends, hoping to get first call on the guns) would not get a rifle until he joined the Tuam battalion flying column in 1921.[229] GHQ's hesitancy was sometimes quite justified. The mines it supplied to the Wexford Volunteers were never used, and 'some companies buried their weapons when the fighting started.'[230]

GHQ's prime function was perhaps to transmit a vision of national armed struggle that could provide a template for local activity. Its journal An tOglaċ (the Irish Volunteer), edited by Piaras Béaslaí, and circulated quite openly until the Volunteer organization was banned in late 1919, was the most effective vehicle for this. Its first number set out the Irish Volunteer credo: the Volunteers were 'the Army of the Irish Republic, the agents of the National will, an instrument framed by Irishmen to further Ireland's determination to be free'. If there was a hint here that the army might be representative in a political sense, this was carefully adjusted by the insistence that Volunteers were 'not politicians' – 'they were not created for the purpose of parades, demonstrations or political activities'; they did not follow 'any political leader as such – their allegiance is to the Irish Nation'. This slightly awkward formulation reflected the Chief of Staff Richard Mulcahy's fixed belief (which would ultimately play a key part in the shaping of the Irish state) that modern armies must be utterly unpolitical – political 'mutes' in the French army's famous self-description. 'The Volunteer does not talk, but acts.' Yet the Irish Volunteers were inescapably engaged in a political activity – nation-building. The duty of their leaders was to 'conform' Volunteer policy to the 'National will' by 'cooperating on the military side with those bodies and institutions which in other departments of the National life are striving to make our Irish Republic a tangible reality'.[231] That Republic, as *An tOglac* reminded its readers, had been 'established' by the Volunteers themselves in 1916.

Once the Dáil was in existence, *An tOglac* reinforced the equation of nationalism with republicanism. The election had proved that the Volunteer leaders of 1916 'had truly interpreted the heart of Ireland'. Their successors had not only to 'safeguard the Irish Republic' but also to 'interpret the national will, now rendered vocal and authoritative in Dáil Éireann'. (This interesting formulation seemed, perhaps unintentionally, to imply that the Dáil's voice might need to be 'interpreted' by the Volunteers.) Spring 1919 was 'one of the most critical periods in the history of the country'. 'The fate of the Irish nation is trembling in the balance'; everything depended on the army. Now the Republic had 'a properly constituted government, the *de jure* government of Ireland', the task was 'to convert the *de jure* republican government into a *de facto* government'.

The 'military side' was to be co-ordinated with the civil, but what military action was to be taken? During the final spasm of the conscription menace, the language was becoming more openly belligerent. In mid-September 1918, *An tOglac* counselled its readers, 'don't argue, but shoot!' If conscription was imposed, martial law would 'be imposed *on both sides*'. It would be in effect a state of war: 'the military authorities of the Irish Republic will become the persons to whom *all* Irish Republicans, whether combatants or not, must look for light and leading.' So every Volunteer officer must 'contemplate the possibility of finding himself called upon to act as the chief military authority in his district, to undertake the administration of all public affairs during a time of crisis'. Under this military rule, 'ordinary civilian pursuits and conventional political methods will be practically suspended, and schemes of "passive resistance" based on the theory of normal conditions, must prove unworkable.' Everyone of military age (not only men, it appears) who accepted the 'republican ideal' would be required 'to enlist in the Army of Ireland, in a fight of self-defence'.[232]

A month later, *An tÓglác* published one of its most resonant articles, 'Ruthless Warfare', warning that the coming struggle would be 'more and worse than war'. War, as it pointed out, was 'the combat of one armed force against another', but a conscription campaign would be 'an onslaught by an army on a civilian population'. It would be an 'atrocity', and if 'England' decided on it, 'then we must decide that in our resistance we shall acknowledge no limit and no scruple.' Whether this deliberately shocking essay was intended primarily to warn the British government or to prepare the minds of the Volunteers themselves it is impossible to say. But it launched a series of radical statements. After the Declaration of Independence, *An tÓglác* explained that it was 'the will of Ireland' that 'the state of war between this country and England shall be perpetuated until the foreign garrison have evacuated our country.' The responsible government that thus expressed the people's will 'sanctions the employment by the Irish Volunteers of the most drastic measures against the enemies of Ireland'.[233] By this point the full battery of warlike language had been deployed.

Still, these were declarations of intent rather than a specific programme of action. That would take time to put together. The formula developed by *An tÓglác* was to combine rousing exhortatory editorials (written by Béaslaí) with technical columns ('Notes from H.Q.', mainly by J. J. O'Connell) that could be used by local units for training and planning, and these offered clues to the kind of military action envisaged by GHQ. So the very first number, which spelt out the mission of the 'Army of the Irish Republic', also carried a feature pointing out that 'for the first time in the establishment of an Irish Volunteer Army, a serious and systematic effort is being made to incorporate an Engineering arm.' The implication was in part that reliable mines and 'bombs' (as hand grenades were often called) would make more ambitious operations possible. But as later 'Engineering Notes' would make clear, sabotage should also play a part in hampering British action. Envisaging

large-scale railway demolition, *An tOglac* advised that the 'ideal point
to damage' was a single-track section either on a short, sharp curve or
on a bridge, as far as possible from any highway. In the same issue as
'Ruthless Warfare', GHQ offered notes on 'Hedge-fighting for Small
Units', as it did at several points over the following months. Among the
defensive devices suggested was one used by the Turks in Mesopotamia –
trous de loup, pits filled with sharpened stakes, simple and deadly, but
also slightly barbaric. These, sensibly perhaps, seem to have stayed
on paper.

GHQ may have declared war on paper, but in terms of encouraging
actual violence it was cautious. Mulcahy told Michael Brennan, even
late in 1919, that 'the people had to be educated and led gently into
open war.' Seamus Robinson had an interesting take on this. Arguing
that 'nothing would be done by a large body of Volunteers until a lead
was given by a few,' he suggested that 'GHQ would not give permission
before the whole country was ready.' By that time, though, 'common-
sense dictated that . . . they would probably all be in jail.' Robinson
claimed to have developed by 1918 a clear vision of the kind of military
campaign that should be fought. 'It became abundantly clear to me that
we could hope to survive and win only if we were a ghostly army of
sharpshooters operating all over the country combining to deal with
small bodies of the enemy and making Ireland too costly to hold; always
choosing our own ground, and our own targets.' The sophistication of
this admirably concise formula may have owed something to later writing on guerrilla warfare, but Robinson had a simpler and more urgent
justification for taking immediate small-scale action rather than waiting
until the country was 'ready'. 'It was becoming increasingly difficult to
keep proud young men merely drilling and getting jailed or interned for
it.' To this he added a telling political point. While protesting that 'we all
heartily desired the formation of a Republican government,' he worried
that 'once formed, being our moral superiors, a state of stalemate would
be inevitable unless war was begun before the Dáil could take over
responsibility.' What this slightly odd phraseology seems to mean is that
the republican government would be bound for political reasons to prohibit or delay violent action, unless responsibility had already been
taken out of its hands.

From this perspective, the coincidence between the first meeting of
the Dáil and the action of Robinson's Tipperary Volunteers at Solohead-

beg in South Tipperary takes on a different aspect. Robinson found himself in a race against time to strike a demonstrative blow before the Dáil met. Shortly after Christmas 1918 he and Seán Treacy worked out the project. 'After tea the two of us went out to the haggard [hay shed] where he told me of the gelignite that was due to arrive at Soloheadbeg quarry in two or three weeks.' Treacy wanted to know if they should try to seize it. There was 'the possibility of shooting'. Robinson said 'Go ahead,' and when Treacy asked him, 'Will you get permission from GHQ?', Robinson just gave him a quizzical look 'to see if he were serious'. When Treacy asked, 'Who will take responsibility?', Robinson said, 'I will.'[234]

The Soloheadbeg ambush was a small-scale action even in guerrilla terms. Eight men, with a single rifle (a Wild West-style Winchester repeater) and a miscellaneous collection of pistols, waited behind 'the white-thorn bushes that lined the ditch of Cranitch's field' for the cart carrying the explosives, guarded by RIC men.[235] The instructions were that, if there were two police, they should challenge them; if six, open fire without warning. Just organizing an action by inexperienced men was a challenge. (Robinson recalled Dan Breen, the brigade quartermaster, 'declaring with grinding teeth in a very high-pitched excited voice that he'd go out and face them'; 'I made a mental note that that man should never be put in charge of a fight.') But just as worrying for Robinson was the issue of timing. Being 'most anxious not to compromise the Dáil', he 'thought long, deeply and anxiously and I almost panicked when I saw the date of the Dáil meeting drawing near and no sign of the gelignite coming'. Would he have abandoned the plan if the gelignite had arrived after 21 January? It seems unlikely, but in the event it turned up just in time. The escort consisted of only two constables; they were both killed.

Soloheadbeg was an elementary, even primitive operation – just a matter of lying in wait and hitting a weak, isolated target. What distinguished it from the bushwhackings of the agrarian struggle was its strategic purpose: the seizure of explosives indicated the vision, however weakly focused as yet, of a new mode of combat. Later targets would become stronger, and compel the ambushers to develop much more sophisticated techniques if they were to have any chance of success. In a sense, the whole dynamic of the war of independence would lie in this reciprocal process. The reaction of the police and later the army – the Crown forces – would confirm the credibility of the republican challenge. As Michael Collins saw with his trademark clarity in the early summer of 1919, 'as they pass on so to speak from the police patrol to the military lorry, they positively put more and more weapons in our hands.'

These words were written five days after the dramatic rescue of Seán Hogan at Knocklong railway station. If the direction of the republican campaign was uncertain after Soloheadbeg, its momentum was restored by this operation, and confirmed by its aftermath. Plenty of doubts had indeed been voiced in the weeks after 21 January – the killing of policemen provoked criticism not just from unionists and moderate nationalists, but also from many Sinn Feiners. British reactions did not go down well: South Tipperary was made a Special Military Area, with burdensome restrictions on travel, and on commercial activities like fairs and markets. Many ordinary people bridled at this. The Tipperary men were determined to keep the campaign going, but seemed uncertain how to go about it. Robinson tried to respond to the military control measures by issuing a proclamation announcing that any policeman in the county after February 1919 would have forfeited his life, but GHQ refused to agree. (At that stage he 'lost confidence in GHQ's vaunted "ruthless warfare"', and came to regard its caution as 'the better part of cowardice'.)[236] The eventual decisive operation was simply a reaction to the arrest of Seán Hogan, but the speed of its planning, and the ferocity of its execution, catapulted it into the realm of resistance myth and ballad.

J. J. (John Joseph, known to republican publicity as Seán) Hogan, a playboy who relished the glamour of the rebel gunman, was arrested after spending an evening at a local dance and going off with a girl – evading his Volunteer minder, Mick Davern, assigned to escort him precisely because his dashing habits were well known to his chief. When Seán Treacy was told, he was angrier than Davern had ever seen him, but decided immediately to rescue Hogan. Treacy and Robinson intended the rescue operation to be a sensational public statement of Volunteer determination. Planning it was not easy; even Treacy found it hard to get information about when Hogan would be taken from Thurles, where he was being held, and where to – Cork or Dublin. His men loafed about Thurles station looking for any sign of his movement. Then, on 13 May, Hogan was put on a train to Cork. At Knocklong halt the train was rushed by a hastily assembled group of Volunteers, and in a fierce gunfight two of the police escort were killed. Hogan was rescued. The aftermath was almost more significant. Dan Breen, who was wounded in the fight, remembered the attackers being 'vehemently denounced as cold-blooded assassins', and certainly clerical condemnation was unambiguous. The coroner's inquest on the dead policemen, however, created a different impression. While expressing sympathy with the men's relatives, the jury called on the government to 'cease arresting respectable persons, thereby causing bitter exasperation among the people'.[237]

The Tipperary leaders made themselves scarce, heading to Cork and then on to Dublin, where they had a telling encounter with Collins, 'waiting for us on the street with his note book out'. This was their 'first indication . . . that if we . . . were not exactly personna non-grata [sic], at best we were decidedly not warmly welcome in any HQ office'. Collins told them that everything was 'fixed up' and they should be ready to leave in a day or two. The assumption was that they would get away to America. Robinson refused, protesting that 'running away' would look like a confession that the killings had been murder. When Collins asked what they proposed to do, Robinson said, 'Fight it out of course.' At that point, Collins 'suddenly closed his notebook with a snap' and strode off with a faint smile saying, 'That's all right with me.'

For Robinson's group, the war had really begun. But their decision to stay in Dublin rather than going back to Tipperary – which certainly puzzled many there – meant that the local war was still on hold. In the summer of 1919, according to the Cork Brigade adjutant Florrie O'Donoghue, 'the absence of a military policy comprehensible to the average Volunteer' combined with shortages of arms and 'the distraction of political activity' to plunge the movement into crisis. O'Donoghue's commander Liam Lynch was depressed by the 'reluctance on the part of GHQ' to take responsibility for military actions. He thought that arms could never be bought or imported in sufficient quantities, and that only by attacking British military and police forces could a campaign be got going. To O'Donoghue, that campaign started from the pressure put on GHQ, mainly by the southern brigades, to approve such attacks.[238]

Within the national leadership there was resistance to pushing the campaign forward. Considerable caution was shown by both GHQ and the Volunteer Executive – often assumed to be effectively identical bodies, though the overlap was only partial. But, perhaps unsurprisingly, the politicians seem to have been still more cautious. An interesting case in point was the springing of de Valera from Lincoln gaol on 3 February. In conception this operation looks like a classic Collins project, and it seems to have been fully supported by his colleagues. Skilfully planned and executed, it brought into play the special abilities of men who were becoming key – if self-effacing – members of the staff, like Fintan Murphy. Formerly a small businessman, now a full-time (though unpaid) member of the Executive, Murphy was a 1916 veteran whom the British had tried to prosecute for avoiding military service, on the grounds that he lived in England. (He had been successfully defended by George Gavan Duffy.) Now he was literally a 'key man', as he carried one of the four cakes with the gaol keys used in the escape, as well as acquiring a rope ladder and bringing it from London to Collins and Boland in Manchester. Just as importantly, he ran the operation control centre in Worksop, linking a chain of safe houses.

On the night of 3 February Collins and Boland cut through the perimeter wire, while de Valera with Seán Milroy and Seán McGarry let themselves out with the duplicate keys. The operation was not flawless, but the prison staff seem to have been fairly lax – or so the disapproving de Valera thought – and the escapees and organizers got away unscathed. The escape was a brilliant success, but its aftermath was less impressive. Collins wanted to arrange a 'state entrance' into Dublin for de Valera, crossing the Grand Canal at Mount Street Bridge (where an outpost of de Valera's 3rd Battalion had staged an epic defence during Easter Week). The police picked up a Sinn Féin Executive announcement – signed by Harry Boland – that 'the Lord Mayor ... will receive him at the gates of the city, and will escort him to the Mansion House ... it is expected that the homecoming ... will be an occasion of National rejoicing.' Recognizing the tremendous symbolic force of this project, the British authorities moved swiftly to ban this 'first act of acute defiance of His Majesty's Government in Ireland'.[239] The Chief Secretary berated the Lord Mayor for his intention 'to receive, as His Majesty alone should be received ... a man who claims unlawfully to be the President of an Irish Republic'.[240] For Collins this was a moment when it was vital not to be intimidated, but the Sinn Féin Executive turned down his plan. De Valera and Brugha took the lead in this, with vocal support from Darrell Figgis, who had retreated from politics into journalism. De Valera publicly explained that 'the present occasion is scarcely one on which we would be justified in risking the lives of citizens.' ('We who have waited know how to wait.') Collins sharply disagreed. 'We are having our "Clontarf Friday",' he fumed; 'it may not be as bad [as Daniel O'Connell's disastrous abandonment of his Monster Meeting at Clontarf in 1843 under a similar threat] but it is bad and very bad.' (Joe O'Connor made the same point to Arthur Griffith, who 'needless to say ... did not agree', asserting that while O'Connell had actually been afraid of defying the government, 'fortunately we could not accuse De Valera of being afraid.')[241]

'THIS INVISIBLE STATE'

Sinn Féin had had plenty of time to prepare its plans for civil resistance. Fifteen years had passed since Arthur Griffith had completed the laying out of his 'Hungarian policy', and a decade since Bulmer Hobson's *Defensive Warfare* (a booklet that should have had the same effect on its generation as Che Guevara's *Guerrilla Warfare* would have on the revolutionaries of the 1960s) had shown how the ideal of 'self-reliance' could shape strategies for building a counter-state. Indeed, when Sinn Féin was founded in December 1905, Griffith and like-minded people had already been exploring and debating ideas about a new Irish society for half a lifetime. At least some of the many hours occupied by the weekly meetings of Sinn Féin clubs must have been spent in discussing such issues. There was a general sense of what had to be done. The passive-resistance policy had to work both negatively and positively. It would involve refusing to co-operate with the authorities, and also trying to replace them. Undermining the already fragile legitimacy of the UK regime might not be too difficult, but it was crucial to construct an alternative focus of legitimate government. Nobody put this more clearly than Diarmuid O'Hegarty – not a minister in the new Dáil government but its secretary, the head of the embryonic alternative civil service (as well as Director of Communications at Volunteer GHQ). 'Actual constructive work will leave a bigger mark on people than *political* work. It makes them think more, and besides it invests the *Government* with tangibility.'[242] This would prove crucial.

On 10 April 1919 – nearly two years after it had begun – the boycott of the RIC, 'England's Janissaries' as de Valera described them, was officially confirmed by the Dáil. The form of words drafted by O'Hegarty pronounced them 'guilty of treason to their country', and 'unworthy to enjoy any of the privileges or comforts which arise from cordial relations with the public'. Constance Markievicz achieved one of her many periods of imprisonment for publicly urging the ostracism of the police. (At her trial, a police sergeant told the court that he had heard her instructing people to treat them like 'leepers'; it took her a while to work out what he meant.) There were wilder allegations that she had preached 'a general pogrom of the police', though she insisted that the aim of the boycott was only to 'render them harmless, and prevent them getting information, and also make them ashamed of themselves'.[243] But when local Volunteers set about enforcing the policy, the tone certainly changed. South Tipperary's proclamation threatening the RIC with death might have been forbidden, but in their mouths the declaration that the police should be 'treated as traitors deserve' was far more menacing than the Dáil's formulation. When Frank Thornton addressed the assembled battalions of the Longford Brigade later that year he told them that the RIC had 'taken arms against the IRA by orders of England', and that the IRA were to 'meet this force with a vengeance, we were to give no quarter *whatsoever* until we wiped them out'.

Markievicz's main job (nominally at least) was as minister for labour, in the Dáil ministry remodelled by de Valera on 2 April. The group of ministers labelled 'the Cabinet' in frankly British style was the core of the counter-state which set out to purloin the national administration from beneath the noses of the British authorities. De Valera himself became 'Príomh-Aire' (rendered in English as 'president', though possibly better understood as 'premier' or prime minister; de Valera occasionally described himself as 'chief minister'). 'Home affairs' went to Griffith, defence to Brugha, finance to Collins, foreign affairs to Plunkett (who was later promoted to fine arts), and local government to W. T. Cosgrave. Eoin MacNeill was moved from finance to become minister for industries, and there were two non-Cabinet directors, Laurence Ginnell of propaganda, and Robert Barton of agriculture. Two days later de Valera added Ernest Blythe as director of trade and commerce.

The virtual state initially faced what might now be called a credibility deficit. When Blythe's appointment seemed to create 'two ministers for one department', MacNeill happily admitted that he 'had no special fitness' for the post, and most people would have agreed.[244] It quickly became clear that he had no intention of doing anything: he never came to meetings or set up any ministerial staff.[245] Even sympathetic commentators found it difficult to see the republican government as anything more than a propaganda ploy. The *Manchester Guardian*, succumbing to an uncharacteristic fit of Englishness, had archly suggested in January that 'the Ministers of Finance, Home Affairs, and all the other dignitaries will be hard put to it to find an outlet for any executive capacity they may possess.'

In general, the British press initially shared the government's dismissive view of the separatist movement's prospects. As the year went on, though, perceptions began to change. In May, Robert Lynd of the liberal *Daily News* – a rare Belfast Presbyterian nationalist – offered a remarkably perceptive take on the Sinn Féin strategy of resistance: 'They seem to have a paradoxical belief that England cannot injure them without terribly injuring herself.' Lynd reported that Sinn Feiners did not believe they could defeat the armed forces that might be sent against them, 'but they believe that they could defeat the purpose of those who make use of the armed forces.'[246] In November 1919 the radical commentator H. N. Brailsford penned a striking assessment of the phenomenon of the counter-state. To an outsider, he thought, the confidence with which the Irish 'possessed their own mind' was 'first startling and then unspeakably impressive'. Sinn Féin 'in its own amazing way has attained a positive result in spite of the stranglehold of the army of occupation. It has boldly declared that the Irish republic exists, and faith is realising this invisible State.'[247]

How widely the faith was shared would become a key question. Robert Barton later suggested that though 'to the outside observer the demand for complete independence may have appeared to spring from the people, in reality the people were influenced by the leaders.' To him the national demand had an egg-like quality: 'So long as the shell was intact, compromise and disruption were impossible. The army and political leaders were the shell, the people were the fluid contents.'[248] For three years, the shell held. The Dáil Cabinet, alongside Volunteer GHQ, was the most consistent institution of the Republic. It met weekly, in various places – a favourite being Sheila Humphreys's big Ailesbury Road house – without ever being discovered. It did come close once or twice – the Harcourt Street headquarters had to be abandoned after Collins made a rooftop escape from a raid. Collins used the threat of a raid to keep discussions short, trying to limit meetings to one hour – roughly the time a raiding party would take to arrive after information reached them. Discussion was in any case often perfunctory, in part because most ministerial activity was 'semi-fictional', and the struggles over spending that form a large part of real governmental activity were minimal. But things were not entirely harmonious; according to Ernest Blythe, 'there was from the beginning a certain amount of friction or tension' between two leading ministers, Collins and Brugha.[249] Brugha would bristle at opinions expressed by Collins (who was famously intolerant of fools) which he might have accepted from other ministers.

'TO MAKE THE IRISH REPUBLIC A LIVING FACT'

A crucial issue that arose as soon as the Dáil government was established was the relationship between the new government and what was coming to be called 'the army'. Cathal Brugha, the Minister for Defence, pressed for a declaratory oath that would make the implicit subordination of the Volunteers to the Dáil government explicit. After several months a formula was reached: every Volunteer would swear (or affirm), 'I do not and shall not yield a voluntary support to any pretended Government,' and 'I will support and defend the Irish Republic, and the Government of the Irish Republic, which is Dáil Éireann, against all enemies, foreign and domestic . . .'

This was not quite the end of the issue. Florrie O'Donoghue sketched the official view of the process in a chapter of his biography of Liam Lynch, entitled 'The army swears allegiance', but his own unpublished account shows that it was not so simple. O'Donoghue noted that the decision to approve the oath was taken on 20 August 1919, but the oath was administered 'during the autumn of 1920'.[250] This delay is an indication that things were not straightforward. The Volunteers did not go quietly into 'regular' civil–military relations. The revolutionary flux, as one Executive member later noted, threw up 'a set of circumstances and organisations in which the Volunteer Executive was the first in order of time, and practically the creator of that which subsequently became the superior body'. Some members of the Executive unsurprisingly held to the traditional Fenian physical-force line that politicians were not to be trusted, and that the Dáil might at some stage prove less steadfast for the Republic than 'the army'. A similar view was indeed expressed in the Dáil debate on the issue by Alderman Tom Kelly, who invoked the fate of the original Irish Volunteers in the 1780s: when the Volunteer movement declined, the political gains it had secured were lost.

Beyond doubt, Brugha had reasons beyond impeccable liberal-democratic principle for pressing the oath. It would supersede the oath that bound together the IRB, an organization that he (like de Valera) believed should not have survived into the post-1916 national movement. Now the secret society was at best irrelevant, and at worst a threat to the supremacy of the Dáil. The IRB naturally did not share this view, seeing itself as a crucial guarantor of republican principles. *Sub rosa* resistance to the formal subordination of the Volunteers to the Dáil was led by the President of the IRB Supreme Council, Collins. 'Collins and the IRB section contended that as most of the Volunteers had already taken a republican oath it was unnecessary for them to take a second oath,' and that the Dáil was still 'to some extent an unknown quantity' – 'members of it might be unstable in their political views.'[251] The issue was in part a symptom of the growing personal antagonism between Collins and Brugha – which one of Collins's biographers calls a 'feud' – as well as of the awkward relationship between the Dáil and the IRB. Collins was already in effective control of the Volunteer organization; Brugha was and remained marginal to it. As Mulcahy dismissively put it later, 'Brugha did no systematic work in connection with carrying on of the military organization.'[252] When provincial military leaders came up to Dublin, they almost all saw Collins, but seldom if ever met Brugha. Collins was ubiquitous and endlessly energetic, Brugha was at best a semi-active minister; most tellingly perhaps, the British took no interest in him.

The path to acceptance of the oath was paved by an odd compromise reminiscent of the Sinn Féin formula of 1917 (and maybe adumbrating the later dual-power arrangement of the Dáil and the Provisional Government after the Treaty): the Volunteer Executive was to remain in being as an advisory body to the Defence Minister (Executive member Seán MacEntee described it as 'a sort of Cabinet and Directory for the Minister for Defence and the HQ Staff'). This arrangement would persist until the summer or autumn of 1921, when the Executive wound itself up. This odd compromise had no direct impact on the control of the army before 1922, but it would then provide republicans with a lever to set the army against the Treaty. There seem to have been no open divisions between the Minister and the Executive, but the suggestion of conditional allegiance was unmistakable, and its implications were potentially dangerous. And it is by no means clear whether the oath had any effect on the operational autonomy of the army.

It was still true that, 'in terms of strict procedure, the Volunteers never ratified the change in their status,' or made the appropriate alterations to their constitution.[253] The Executive intended to recommend acceptance of the oath to the next Volunteer Convention, but in the circumstances that kind of full-scale assembly could not be risked. In June 1920, however, 'it was unanimously agreed that there was no prospect of holding in the near future the Convention already arranged for' (for which delegates had been appointed at brigade conventions in November 1919). Still, the Executive accepted that 'the development of the National situation called for the immediate formal establishment of the Volunteers as the Army of the Republic,' and its General Secretary called on all delegates to sign a form agreeing to the proposed oath ('to reach me *without fail* by Wednesday 9th June').[254] Local units were eventually ordered to administer the oath, or signify that they refused to do so. In July GHQ issued a general order that the oath be 'forthwith administered to' all Volunteers – allowing that those with a conscientious objection should be allowed to 'affirm' rather than 'swear' allegiance. (GHQ called it an 'Oath of Allegiance to the Irish Republic' rather than to the government.) A special register of those who had taken the oath was to be prepared for each company, and each battalion and brigade staff. 'Members of a Volunteer Company who for any reason are not present at the special company parade shall have the Oath administered to them in the presence of the Company at the next parade at which they are present.' The process was to be completed by the end of August.[255]

It looks as though the majority, perhaps the overwhelming majority, agreed; James Dorr, captain of the Kilmore company in Roscommon, recalled that 'we had no objectors'; O'Donoghue held that 'the decision was practically unanimous.'[256] Some areas seem to have assembled substantial meetings. The Clogagh company sent two representatives 25 miles to a battalion 'convention' at Charagh 'for the purpose of ratifying the Agreement under which the Volunteers came under the control of the Dáil'.[257] Some at least made it a memorable occasion, like Seán MacEoin in Longford. Seán O'Sullivan's battalion, part of MacEoin's command, was assembled in a hollow square to be addressed by Frank Thornton. 'He told us we no longer Volunteers [sic] were Soldiers of the Irish Republican Army and from hence forth every Soldier would have to take oath of alegeance and further that we were going to fight and that very soon, the Irish Republic was proclaimed and England had declared war on us … Make no mistake the IRA were going to fight and going to make the Irish republic a living fact.'[258] But surprisingly few Volunteers seem to have recalled taking the oath. For some it was not a good idea. Todd Andrews 'thought, or rather felt, that no outside organisation should have any say in the activities of the Volunteers … Nor did I like the change of name … to Irish Republican Army. The word "army" seemed to have overtones of professionalism which conflicted with the idealism of the Movement.'[259]

It remains unclear whether the oath was in fact 'administered to every man in the army', as O'Donoghue said, in 1920. Some units took the oath collectively, and some seem not to have taken it at all. What is clear is that the idea that the Volunteers 'became' the Irish Republican Army is too simple. Indeed the emergence of the title is something of a mystery. Though many (like Liam Deasy) remembered discussing in 1919 an order specifically transferring 'the Volunteer organisation – under the title of "I.R.A." – to the control of Dáil Éireann', it seems likely that (as Piaras Béaslaí said) the title 'IRA' never had any official standing. An tOglác sometimes referred to the Volunteers as 'the Army of the Irish Republic', following 1916 usage, but that was, as Béaslaí noted, 'a very different thing'.[260] Presumably, however unofficial, the phrase 'Irish Republican Army' simply came more easily off the tongue. But its exact usage remains obscure. While it was back-projected by some to 1916 – even though Pearse had definitely used the title 'Army of the Irish Republic' – in 1920–21 its use may have been mainly oral and unofficial. Many units were still using the correct official title of the Irish Volunteers, Oglaich na hÉireann, right through to the end of the fighting. It would be tempting to suggest that this merely reflected the inconvenience of ordering new headed stationery, but the old title persisted in typed reports as well.

SINEWS OF POWER

The general consensus that Michael Collins was the most effective member of the Dáil ministry seems likely to endure, even if his military credentials – and indeed his character – may be impugned. His technical qualifications in finance were not particularly remarkable, but his phenomenal energy ensured that he got sensible, useful things done. His central challenge, obviously, was not so much to regulate expenditure or set economic policy – the functions of 'normal' finance ministers – as simply to generate income. The counter-state had no access to taxation; funds would have to come from public contributions. (Even Collins seems not to have considered the possibility of compulsory loans in the form of armed bank robberies, of the kind favoured by later urban-guerrilla revolutionaries.) Tantalizingly, big money had been collected in the USA by the Friends of Irish Freedom – over $1 million by mid-1919.[261] But surprisingly little of this was actually finding its way to Sinn Féin's treasury. The Dáil government set out to secure funding through its own Republican Loan. Within days of Collins's appointment on 2 April, the Dáil authorized the ministry to 'issue Republican Bonds to the value of £250,000 in sums of £1 to £1,000'. On 10 April de Valera enlarged the scheme to the value of 'one million sterling – £500,000 to be offered to the public for immediate subscription ... in bonds of such amounts as to meet the needs of the small subscriber'. Half was to be subscribed at home, half abroad (that is, in the US). The publicly stated aim of the loan would be to give Irish trade and commerce 'free access to the markets of the world', to develop and encourage sea fisheries, reafforestation and industrial effort, and to establish 'a National Civil Service' and National Arbitration Courts as well as a Land Mortgage Bank ('with a view to re-occupancy of untenanted lands'). It would be used 'to end the plague of emigration, by providing land for the landless and work for the workless', and for 'all purposes which tend to make Ireland morally and materially strong and self-supporting'.[262]

This was an ambitious project, even in a country with a tradition of political subscriptions reaching back to O'Connell's famous 'penny rent', and including the Parnell tribute of the 1880s. The parliamentary party had never succeeded in raising much money by subscription. The fact that the 1918 anti-conscription fund had raised £250,000 might be a promising sign, or a warning that Ireland was 'subscribed out'. (It turned out in fact that most of the money had been returned to subscribers; a grand total of £12,237 was passed on to the Dáil government in 1919.) Collins, typically declaring that 'it will be essential to get on with a rush', organized a 'big advertising campaign', involving printing a quarter of a million prospectuses and commissioning a short publicity film (in which he appeared with Griffith and MacNeill cheerily issuing bond certificates outside St Enda's – using as a table, with a nice symbolic sense, one of Pearse's most treasured relics, the block on which he believed Robert Emmet had been beheaded). Volunteers across the country persuaded cinema managers to screen it.[263]

But a series of delays meant that by the time the campaign got under way the obstacles to it had multiplied. The British had, as we shall see, at last decided to suppress the Dáil and all its works, while in the USA Judge Cohalan made much of the difficulty that since the Irish Republic did not exist in law its bonds had no legal status.[264] Even when press advertisements for the loan in Ireland avoided using the name Dáil Éireann (and the title 'Minister for Finance' as well, merely describing Collins as the 'Director' of the national loan), none of the national papers would risk running them. When the *Cork Examiner* and some twenty provincial newspapers ran them, they were promptly suppressed. Correspondence and prospectuses were seized 'in various parts of the country', leaving Collins 'extremely rushed as a result'.[265] This 'interference' went on, and was more threateningly supplemented during the winter by British investigations of the undercover bank accounts used to conceal the Republic's funds. (Collins, a finance minister with the unusual advantage of also running a death squad, would respond lethally by having the principal investigator, Alan Bell, hauled off a Dublin tram and assassinated in March 1920.)

But British action was not the only obstacle to raising the loan. Though half a million prospectuses were sent out in 1919, distribution and bond sales depended on local Sinn Féin organizations, and especially local TDs who became the principal loan agents. Collins urged 'the great need for increased individual effort on the part of all members of An Dáil'.[266] Local leadership proved (as in other spheres) highly variable. The Munster constituencies (with Limerick in the lead) subscribed almost as much as the rest of Ireland put together. Kevin O'Shiel's North

Fermanagh constituency subscribed just over £1,700 – a small amount by southern standards, as he said, but not bad for such a deeply divided area. He even got a few unionist subscribers – 'chaffed by their fellow Unionists', not for disloyalty but for stupidity: 'they'd never see their money again.' (The subscribers would eventually have the last laugh.) Terence MacSwiney in Cork was notably energetic, calling for 5,000 additional prospectuses at the end of September, 'as we are about to begin the house-to-house canvass'. By February 1920 he had raised £4,817 in pound notes and £500 in gold. Collins told him in December 1919 that it was 'very refreshing to have such a satisfactory account from you . . . It shows what work and energy will do.'[267]

But energy was just what was missing in many places. Collins darkly hinted that while he disliked drawing comparisons with other areas, 'some will suggest themselves at once,' and told MacSwiney that, if he could see the returns made by some areas, 'they would simply drive you mad.' In the spring of 1920 Collins wearily complained to Boland in America that 'this enterprise will certainly break my heart if anything will,' and that he had 'never imagined there was so much cowardice, dishonesty, hedging, insincerity and meanness in the world'. He was provoked into furious exhortatory strategies, including a loan 'black-list', which could alienate as much as inspire. Con Collins (no relation) lamented that this 'sort of thing takes the heart out of a man . . . God knows I find it hard to ask for anything since reading it. What are our Teactas [Deputies] doing at all? Half of them at least might have done as well as we did. Is it all talk and suggestions once again?'[268]

In spite of all the difficulties, the public response was remarkable. (It was materially assisted, O'Shiel was convinced, by the active part played by 'the younger clergy'.) Many were surprised 'to see how well the people responded to the call, even those who had supported the Parliamentary Party in the elections'.[269] Though barely £10,000 had been received by the end of October 1919, the sum had risen by nearly £150,000 in April 1920, and rose almost as much again in May and June. By the summer of 1920 the first issue of the loan was oversubscribed by £40,000. Griffith hardly exaggerated when he credited the Finance Minister with 'one of the most extraordinary feats in the country's history'.

As the money came in, Collins could act more like a normal finance minister, setting departmental budgets, hiring and firing government employees and commissioners. The proto-state had run up significant bills even before the loan was launched. The Irish Film Company's promotional film for the loan itself cost £600, for instance. The President and the Secretary, Diarmuid O'Hegarty, were paid £500 a year, ministers £350. TDs were unpaid (sacrificing their Westminster salaries), but had travel and accommodation expenses of £250 a year. Darrell Figgis was appointed secretary of the Commission of Inquiry into the Resources and Industries of Ireland at £350 a year (with hotel expenses and third-class rail travel). Fintan Murphy, one of Collins's assistants in Finance (and also an unpaid member of the Volunteer GHQ), had his annual salary raised to £180 in July 1919.

The Commission of Inquiry into Resources and Industries was a flagship project with strong ideological underpinnings. It reflected Griffith's faith in autarky, the national self-sufficiency preached by one of his heroes, the German economist Friedrich List, as well as the deeply entrenched nationalist belief that Ireland had been systematically impoverished by British policy. (Collins reiterated this in his first statement of the national finances, when he alleged that Ireland had been overtaxed by £290 million up to 1893, and another £100 million since.) Its mission was 'to put the Nation in possession of exact information in regard to the national resources, and the best methods by which they could be brought into service'. The Commission had the advantage of being fairly cheap, and being concerned with future possibilities rather than actual policies; other Sinn Féin policies aiming at reafforestation and rebuilding the fishing industry quickly ran into problems. Envisaged as a broad national body, many of its forty-nine members were not Sinn Feiners. But expertise was in short supply in some areas: perhaps inevitably in light of Ireland's economic structure, very few of the commissioners were industrialists of any kind. Despite its seemingly uncontroversial nature, the Commission's activities came under the British ban on the Dáil, and it soon found it impossible to work openly. While its opening meetings in Dublin late in 1919 were undisturbed by the DMP, when it went out into the provinces it ended up playing hide-and-seek with the police in various towns. Its progress became disappointingly slow. Collins, who expected something to show for his investment, made no secret of his impatience with Figgis, even though the latter's reputation was briefly enhanced by his repeated narrow escapes, which generated some international press interest.

Other elements in what would be labelled the 'constructive work of Dáil Éireann', though in theory more difficult, were pushed ahead with more visible results. One striking initiative was the establishment of a Land Bank, aimed at breaking the financial bonds between Britain and Ireland as well as fostering a programme of land reoccupancy. Robert Barton, a Wicklow landowner who had moved from unionism through constitutional nationalism to Sinn Féin since 1916, and had some experience as chairman of a co-operative bank, headed the National Co-operative Mortgage Bank established with a £200,000 deposit of Dáil funds in September 1919.

PROJECTING THE VIRTUAL STATE

The British would eventually blame their loss of Ireland in large part on the effectiveness of republican publicity. Propaganda had become big political business during the war, and was widely thought to have the power to influence entire populations. Leading 'information' manipulators like the press baron Lord Northcliffe, who had become Britain's first propaganda chief, were credited with having changed the course of the war. A natural propagandist like Arthur Griffith, who had battled skilfully with British censorship throughout the war, looked poised to exploit its power. In the event, the machinery of republican publicity was surprisingly slow to get moving. In spite of the fact that republicans constantly complained of getting a bad press from the mainstream Irish newspapers, no single republican agency to speak to the Irish people was ever set up. The *Irish Independent* and the *Freeman's Journal* were in a sense the last bastion of Home Rule constitutionalism, even if their instinctive distrust of Britain made their coverage look 'disloyal' to British eyes.

When the Dáil first met, Sinn Féin already had a publicity section, run by Robert Brennan, producing the journal *Nationality*, and as we have seen the Volunteer journal *An tOglaċ* was being issued by the GHQ Director of Publicity, Piaras Béaslaí. A Dáil Department of Propaganda was set up immediately, but its Director, Laurence Ginnell, had not got very far by the time he was arrested in May 1919. When his successor Desmond FitzGerald arrived there to replace Ginnell, the department's target audience (as he stressed in his first departmental report to the Dáil) was outside Ireland, and 'our chief means of publicity was by means of pamphlets.' These were prepared by Sinn Féin's Foreign Relations Committee, and distributed by Sinn Féin supporters wherever they could be found. The foreign press got its Irish news stories from correspondents in London, so the reporting tended to follow the British line. FitzGerald found that making effective contact with the foreign press was difficult, not least because 'war experience has made them very chary of anything in the nature of propaganda.'[270]

Oddly enough, both FitzGerald (who had been brought up in England) and the man he recruited as his deputy, Erskine Childers, spoke with markedly English drawls. It is possible that this, together with their cosmopolitan intellectual credentials, enhanced their international plausibility. Childers had made plenty of journalistic contacts in the course of a fairly distinguished career. He was an established author, who had written a study of cavalry tactics and an account of his own unit, a horse artillery battery attached to the socially exclusive Honourable Artillery Company, in the Boer War. His 1903 novel *The Riddle of the Sands*, one of the most brilliant of the emerging genre of spy stories, was a best-seller. It was not least a fascinating study of the technique of sailing small yachts, and Childers had translated that skill into spectacular political action when he ran a thousand rifles into Howth for the Irish Volunteers in July 1914. His politics were complicated: *The Riddle* had pulsated with fear of German power, and when war broke out he did not hesitate to rejoin the British forces, becoming a seaplane pilot, 'a brilliant officer and utterly fearless'.[271]

In May 1919 Childers travelled to Paris, intending to join the Irish delegation to the Peace Conference, and spent the summer struggling to persuade French journalists to take the Irish case seriously. His clashes with arrogant English colleagues – his 'blind fury' at 'these cultured, cold-blooded, self-satisfied people making careers out of the exploitation of humanity' – finally resolved his political ambivalence, and he moved house from London to Dublin in September. FitzGerald started a brief mimeographed news-sheet called the *Weekly Summary of Acts of Aggression by the Enemy* in July, and in early November the two of them launched a more substantial production, the *Irish Bulletin*. This was issued five times a week, and the Propaganda Department maintained this rate with impressive consistency through the next twenty-two months of intensifying conflict. In its first year its content mostly dealt with the crimes of England rather than the achievements of the Republic, recording police actions in a dry quasi-official style designed to bolster credibility. Until the Dáil complained in February 1920 that 'just lists and bare details of incidents' were inadequate, the *Bulletin* did not try to cover events in any depth. But it offered a useful alternative to British official sources, and the tendency of established journalists to buy the government line seems to have been redirected by the steady flow of counter-information. As republican publicity gained a hearing, and steadily enlarged its credibility, it increasingly threw the authorities on to the defensive.

Childers took a distinctive line from the start. He later recalled that as soon as he had joined the department he had been struck by 'the failure of the political side to take definite responsibility for the Army and its work – a fatal failure because the propaganda of the enemy was that the Army was a "murder gang"'. Only by 'insisting that it was waging a legitimate war of defence' could the 'torrent of defamation' be met. Childers was clear that Griffith was responsible for 'this curb on propaganda' – 'how far Collins opposed or conceded to him on this point I do not know' – and that the argument would not be properly made until de Valera returned from America at the end of 1920.[272]

Republican news secured a dramatic coup when, on 10 November 1919, the Archbishop of Dublin contributed £105 to the Dáil Loan. He emphasized his action through a public letter to Cardinal O'Connell in Boston, declaring that 'none of our papers dare publish the fact' that he was subscribing. 'We are living under martial law,' he explained, 'and amongst the numerous devices to which our present Government has had recourse in its foolish attempts to crush the national spirit of our people' was a 'military order' giving newspaper editors and managers 'notice ... of the fate that awaits any newspaper venturing to publish the names of contributors'. Driving disaffection underground, he said, was responsible for the upsurge of 'crime'. 'The "competent military authority" does not seem to realise that there is no possible remedy for this lamentable state of things, so long as the source of all the evil, the present system of military rule, is maintained.' This intervention raised the possibility that the Catholic Church might, directly or indirectly, be moving to recognize the legitimacy of the republican counter-state. Though he described violence as 'crime', Archbishop Walsh clearly blamed it on the British authorities. Archbishop Gilmartin of Tuam went further, declaring that 'in this country at present people are engaged in a struggle for the natural right of self-government' – 'a distinct nationality such as we are, has a natural right within the limits of the moral law to govern itself.' Archbishop Harty of Cashel denounced the government as having 'proved itself an abject failure': it had 'trampled on the will of the people' and 'excelled acts of in repression and coercion'. The only 'remedy for the Irish upheaval' was 'freedom'.[273]

Not until de Valera returned from America did any republican leader launch a deliberate effort to secure formal recognition of the Republic from the Catholic Hierarchy. But if they had, it would have failed. Patriotic prelates like Walsh were probably in a minority, and the Hierarchy's head, Cardinal Logue, Archbishop of Armagh, resisted any such political engagement. This did not make his stance at all acceptable from a British point of view: he declared that the 'military regime rivall[ed] in severity even that of countries under the most pitiless autocratic government'. But he insisted that republican armed action was 'lawlessness, retaliation and crime such as any man guided by God's law must regret and reprobate'. Logue's colleagues were not all so sure. When, in October 1919, he pressed the Hierarchy to issue a firm condemnation of violence, the bishops were divided enough to force him to drop the idea. In January 1920 they eventually issued a statement that followed only part of Logue's line – the government with its 'principle of disregarding national feelings and national rights' was responsible for the 'dreadful confusion and disorder' of the country.

Though this unquestionably helped to delegitimize the UK state in Ireland, it fell far short of formal recognition of the Republic. Still, there was a general assumption that, while the higher clergy tended to hold aloof from politics, a large proportion of the lower clergy supported Sinn Féin, and some even assisted the Volunteers.[274] By contrast clerical condemnation of republican violence tended to be muted. In terms of open speech, this belief is hard to sustain: the number of recorded public interventions on both sides of the issue is very small, but clerical opponents of violence outnumbered its defenders by almost three to one. (While 144 out of some 3,700 Irish priests – less than 4 per cent – were recorded as speaking out against Volunteer military action between 1919 and 1921, a mere fifty explicitly supported it.) There is certainly evidence that some priests held arms and ammunition for their local companies, and that the soul-searching of many Volunteers about the legality of killing policemen and soldiers was eased by the tacit support of priests and curates. But recent research suggests that priests also continued to denounce crime – murder above all, but also other actions that damaged public security – most intensely where Volunteer activity was itself most intense.[275] A resonant clerical warning shot was fired in 1919 by the Professor of Theology at Maynooth, Walter McDonald, in his book *Some Ethical Questions of Peace and War*. McDonald brusquely dismissed nationalist arguments about the continuity of Irish national identity reaching back to pre-Norman times, and insisted that the use of force in pursuit of independence was unethical. Full independence was not a legitimate aim.[276]

As a declared advocate of Home Rule as against separatism McDonald was probably unrepresentative of the clergy in general, but his refusal to accept that republican armed action could be regarded as legitimate warfare was much more widely shared. This refusal was to be most sharply put by Cardinal Logue, when he asked after an attack in August 1920, 'Am I to be told that this is an act of war? That it is lawful to shoot at sight anyone wearing a policeman's uniform and honestly discharging a policemen's duty?' His answer was that it should be called 'by its true name – a cool, deliberate, wilful murder, pure and simple'.[277] The Soloheadbeg killings had been condemned as an 'inhuman act' by a Tipperary priest, who called on his congregation to 'denounce it and the cowardly miscreants who are guilty of it'. A Thurles curate took the same view after the shooting there of an RIC district inspector in June 1919: 'the memory of that awful deed would haunt the guilty man all his life, and would rise up before him on his death bed.'[278] Others warned their flocks that defiance of God's law, and usurping God's unique power of life and death, might bring awful punishment on the community as a whole.

'A CONDITION OF VEILED INSURRECTION'

Cardinal Logue's 'pitiless autocracy' did not yet quite live up to its billing. Some of the 'acts of aggression' paraded in republican news-sheets were not, it has been suggested, 'exactly of the type that would ignite world indignation' (for instance, the police raid on a hairdresser's displaying a Dáil Loan poster in October 1919, in which the poster was 'completely defaced' with penknives).[279] Even in the late autumn the authorities were only slowly putting together anything resembling a coherent policy for throttling the nascent Republic. The first meetings of the Dáil had impaled the Irish administration on the horns of a dilemma. Was an assembly of MPs illegal? Could it be connected with the violence in Tipperary? Such questions paralysed British policy, or at least Ian Macpherson, who had just succeeded Shortt as chief secretary, and who helplessly confessed to the Prime Minister on 8 May 1919, 'We did not and do not know how to act.' Lloyd George was then away in Paris drawing up the new world order. He and his Cabinet colleagues certainly took the same view of the Dáil as did such intelligent English newspapers as the *Manchester Guardian* ('theatricalism') and *The Times* (a 'stage play'). When Macpherson asked for Cabinet guidance on the government's Irish policy, the Deputy Prime Minister, Andrew Bonar Law – a hardline unionist – suggested that it had been 'clearly defined'. When the incredulous – and speechless – Macpherson 'demurred by a gesture', Bonar Law just went on to tell him he could 'do whatever he liked'.[280]

Britain's Irish policy faced pivotal decisions, with no real sense of direction. Shortly before the end of the war, Lord French had put his views in uncompromising terms: 'every day that has passed since I became Viceroy of Ireland has proved more clearly the unfitness of Ireland for any form of Home Rule.' He did not say 'ever' but rather 'now, or in the very near future', but even so, this was a straight negation of the policy enshrined in the 1914 Home Rule Act, which was due to come into effect after the war. When Asquith's government had pushed the Act through under the wartime 'party truce', he had promised that the unionist north-east of Ireland would be given some (as yet unspecified) special treatment. But Ireland was certainly due to receive a national parliament with substantial legislative powers when the war ended. Asquith's successors were not above deferring this commitment by defining the end of the war as the day on which the last peace treaty was signed (which they expected in 1919, though in the event this would not have come until 1923). But they accepted that the commitment could not be deferred indefinitely, and set about reframing the Act to make it workable.

The committee eventually set up in November to find a new formula for the relationship between the prospective Irish parliament and Westminster, and above all for the exclusion of Ulster from the Dublin parliament's authority, would take six months to come up with a draft bill. In the meantime, Macpherson and French were left to find a way of controlling the situation. The two key issues that French pressed were the extension of military powers and the suppression of Sinn Féin and the Dáil as well as the Irish Volunteers. French wanted to put Ireland under martial law as it had been in 1916 – only more effectively. This was never on the cards in 1919. All that could be done was to react to local challenges by creating Special Military Areas under the 1887 Criminal Law and Procedure Act, with tightened controls on movement and assembly. This move was the reaction to the Soloheadbeg attack in South Tipperary, and also to an attempt to rescue Volunteer and trade union leader Robert Byrnes from Limerick prison in April. Limerick was proclaimed a Special Military Area on 9 April, but the public assumed it had been placed under martial law – an irony French cannot have relished. The local reaction to this – the establishment of a 'soviet' – was disconcerting. The Limerick Trades and Labour Council declared a general strike, set up a governing committee that effectively took over the city, imposed its own controls on movement and issued its own currency.[281]

The Limerick Soviet was shortlived (only ten days), and was probably inspired at least as much by memories of the bitter industrial dispute of 1913 as by Russian revolutionary ideas, but inevitably it fed the British government's mounting alarm about the wave of industrial unrest sweeping postwar Europe. Indeed it may well be that industrial conflict looked more immediately threatening than the separatist movement in the spring of 1919. But fears of 'Bolshevik' revolution, fanned by the conservative press, should have been moderated by the unenthusiastic response of the labour leadership in Ireland to the Limerick confrontation.[282]

These local measures of 'pin-pricking coercion' were a poor substitute for a general strategy, but it was not until the autumn of 1919 that French's demand for direct measures against the republican leadership was accepted by the Cabinet. The coalition government was divided on party lines: its Liberals were dismayed by the idea of proscribing a political party and an elected assembly, however disagreeable. Conservatives were less squeamish; but even the high Tory Walter Long opposed proscription when it was proposed in May. He thought the Irish Executive machinery too weak to make a ban effective, so the government's credibility would be damaged. This clear-eyed line of argument did not survive the heightened challenges of the summer of 1919. The assassination of RIC District Inspector Hunt in Thurles on 23 June spurred French to renew the demand that Sinn Féin be 'proclaimed' as 'an organised club for murder of police'. The ban was to be local, but when the Cabinet discussed it, only Shortt upheld the Liberal argument that ministers should try to drive a wedge between moderates and extremists, not drive them together. Critical public reactions to the violence in South Tipperary had suggested that this would be a possibility. 'No one would be more relieved than the Sinn Feiners if the Irish Volunteers were proclaimed,' Shortt suggested. This insight was brushed aside by the Cabinet, along with any doubts about the propriety or advisability of banning a political party. On 4 July Sinn Féin, the Volunteers, Cumann na mBan and the Gaelic League were all declared illegal in Tipperary, laying the ground for the blanket ban of all separatist organizations throughout Ireland in September. This included Dáil Éireann, a body whose members had been elected by the British democratic system. The fierce attempt to suppress the Dáil Loan, with a mass of prosecutions and the suppression of several mainstream newspapers, suggests that the government grasped that its challenger was now moving from 'theatricalism' to real action. Macpherson's explanation of the ban was that the Dáil had been allowed to meet '*in consultation*', but when it 'conspired by executive acts . . . to overthrow the duly constituted authority, then we could act.'

But could they? There might (more or less) be a will, but it was not clear that there was a way. The attempt to suppress the loan was widely denounced as an attack on the press, and was seen even by government supporters as counter-productive. The army complained, not for the first or last time, that 'the situation would be perfectly simple to deal with if the Government only had a policy.' The weakness of the police had if anything increased as the boycott steadily drove them away from the community; as the Galway RIC reported in late 1919 they were 'receiving no support from the people'. A trickle of resignations – giving up a secure job with a good pension was not an easy matter – suggested the possibility of a flood. The military garrison was numerically under-strength, and full of raw recruits thanks to the 'first in, first out' postwar demobilization policy. Senior commanders were particularly concerned about the quality of the officer corps, and worried that the troops 'being taunted by young Irishmen . . . are getting in such a state that they may take the law into their own hands'.[283] Though it increased funding for the RIC and the DMP Special Branch, the Cabinet was still reluctant to give French all he wanted, in particular the extension of powers of internment and deportation under Regulation 14B. In late September the Home Office accepted that there were 'of course strong objections to extending the DRR [Defence of the Realm Regulations] now that the war is over', but thought that nonetheless 'the condition of Ireland is such as to justify the full use of the powers given by the DRA [Defence of the Realm Act]' – notably curfew powers. It even considered making Ireland an area where the operation of Section 1 of the Defence of the Realm Amendment Act 1915 was 'suspended'.[284] Since the 1915 Act prohibited internment of British citizens without trial, this would in effect mean the suspension of habeas corpus – which had not been done in peacetime since 1866.

French would go on chafing against the Cabinet's restrictive view of the powers that could be exercised in peacetime Ireland. 'I have means of gauging the feeling of the country which Mr Shortt does not possess,' he insisted. He had 'lived a good deal in Ireland, and amongst Irish people', and 'frequently visit my home [Drumdoe in Roscommon] in one of the most disturbed districts of the west'.[285] 'I feel that all [Shortt's] training and experience render him peculiarly incapable of arriving at just conclusions when dealing with a people who nourish secret sedition and are in a condition of veiled insurrection.' This could only be 'held at bay by careful military vigilance'. He still believed that, as he told Lloyd George, it was because of Shortt's 'inexperience in such matters that you sent me to Ireland to exercise the full functions of a Governor-General *de jure* and *de facto*.'[286] Eventually, in mid-November, the Cabinet agreed to the replacement of jury trial in Ireland, in serious criminal cases, by a special court of three high court judges. French was told that it would be 'inconvenient' to bring the so-called 'Three Judges Bill' before the Christmas recess, but was given (or so he believed) 'a perfectly free hand as regards "deportation" and possibly the introduction of martial law'.[287]

The Cabinet was acutely aware of the political risks of using special legal powers. In the executive sphere, though, it was more easygoing. French, in cahoots with Walter Long, was allowed to reconstruct the police in a way that would have huge repercussions on the legitimacy of the British state in Ireland. At the end of the year an order was issued, in the name of the Inspector General of the RIC, authorizing recruitment of non-Irish personnel into the constabulary.[288] French had been pushing for this radical step for months, against the Inspector General Sir Joseph Byrne's dogged resistance. For the IG it was a question not only of principle, but also of the kind of recruits that were in practice likely to appear: war veterans who might not be controllable by the RIC's disciplinary code. Back in May, Long had snorted that 'the head of the police has lost his nerve,' and on 4 November French delivered a virtual notice of dismissal, telling the Chief Secretary that 'Byrne is still showing great weakness.' It was 'most prejudicial to the accomplishment of what we have to do that he should remain in his present position'. The last straw for French came when he ordered the arrest and deportation of seventeen 'of the worst suspects' early in December. The police chiefs had repeatedly assured him that 'they knew always where they could lay their hands on these men', but 'when everything should have been in complete readiness, it appeared as a matter of fact that nothing was ready.' 'The Police Officials met, consulted, pondered, then decided to do nothing!'[289]

But it was not easy to remove someone in Byrne's position quietly. Until a new job was negotiated, he was simply ordered to go on leave 'for the benefit of his health'. (He was not keen to quit, and demanded a colonial governorship as the price of his departure.) More importantly, perhaps, his objections to what would become a drastic change in the nature of the old police force were pushed aside. Lloyd George, accepting that Byrne had 'clearly lost his nerve', added a remarkable rider: 'It may, of course, very well be that the task in Ireland is a hopeless one and that Byrne has simply the intelligence to recognise it.' But for the time being, 'until we are through with Home Rule a man of less intelligence and more stolidity would be a more useful instrument to administer the interregnum.'[290] A few days after the New Year, the first British recruits began to arrive: the 'Black and Tans' were born. Their notoriety would in the event give this 'interregnum' a dangerously unstable character.

French hinted darkly that it would be 'necessary to increase considerably the numbers of people to be sent away for the benefit of their health'. He thought that the administration was 'totally inadequate' to enforce its legal powers. The attempt to conciliate Catholic opinion had produced 'a dual control in the inner circle of Government officials', leading to 'great friction and serious leakage of official secrets'. The head of the DMP, Colonel Edgeworth Johnstone, 'in many ways an excellent commander', had been 'overtaxed by the tension of the work', but French hoped that the new Assistant Commissioner, William Redmond, would help to 'infuse new energy and fresh brains into the police command'. He had no doubt that the situation could be saved, bad as it looked. Although 'the campaign of outrage and murder is growing in strength and intensity every day', it actually represented 'the last desperate struggle of Sinn Fein', and if it could be put down, the prewar political atmosphere could be restored. 'The Irish are an impulsive and quick-witted, but not a deep-thinking people,' he once again insisted. They had 'no will of their own' and were simply intimidated and 'mentally paralysed' by Sinn Féin. The 'real feeling of the country was never in favour of a Republic, or indeed any form of complete separation'. Sinn Féin's attempt to create a rival state structure had, he believed, failed. 'After nearly a year's trial no one in the country can discern anything but the same bombastic talk which has brought no change whatever in the life of the people.' Just before Christmas, he concluded that 'in short, the year 1919 has seen the ruin of Sinn Fein as a clean, sane, and ideal organization, and has reduced it to the level of a foul murder club.'[291]

'THE INCULCATION OF THE PRINCIPLES OF GUERRILLA WARFARE'

Many Volunteers could not remember any novel 'military' activity in 1919; if anything the year seemed less exciting than 1918. Most units went on with training and occasional arms raids. Even these were often less than dramatic – in Closetoken, Co. Galway, for instance, it was 'hardly correct to term them raids as the people handed over any arms they had quite willingly'. Others continued with the public displays that had been largely abandoned a year before: in the 5th Battalion of Kerry No. 2 Brigade, 'we were adopting a defiant attitude ... by parading within sight of the RIC and marching to local sports' meetings.'[292] Even in the most active areas, actions were sporadic, and hard to identify as the beginnings of a coherent campaign. In Tipperary, the dramatic shooting of DI Hunt in Thurles was not followed by any significant escalation of operations. One of the most successful of all Volunteer operations, the raid on the guard post at Collinstown aerodrome in March 1919, was not obviously linked to previous or subsequent patterns of activity. The haul of seventy-five rifles (with seventy-two bayonets) and 4,000 rounds of ammunition was simply enormous in relation to the stocks held by Volunteer units, and would never be exceeded in the whole course of the struggle. The Fingal Brigade seems to have done little with this hoard, if it held on to it: it remained 'peaceful' in 1919 and into 1920; Walter Brown's battalion still had no 'proper arms' at the time of the Truce.[293]

As late as September 1919, local IV units still probably had little idea what, if any, overall plan of action was favoured by GHQ. The bolder and more adventurous were testing the limits, experimenting with possibilities. A classic case in point was the action of the North Cork Brigade at Fermoy. On 7 September a party of fifteen men of the East Kent Regiment on their way to Sunday worship at the Wesleyan chapel were rushed and disarmed. The project had been worked out by Lynch and the Fermoy battalion commander George Power in July, and submitted for GHQ approval. When this came, it was on the condition that the attack could be carried out without loss of life.[294] This suggests a persistent anxiety about the public reaction to violence; the condition carries a whiff of refusal to take responsibility. In the event – as GHQ must surely have suspected – it could not be met: despite careful restriction of the lethal weapons carried by the thirty attackers (six had revolvers, the rest 'short thick clubs'), one of the soldiers was killed in the affray. GHQ's caution may look excessive, since at the inquest the local coroner's jury refused to describe the death as murder – on the grounds not only that the attackers had only intended to disarm rather than kill the troops, but also that the attack had been a regular act of war. This indicated at least some public acceptance of, if not enthusiasm for, the escalation of conflict. The furious reaction of the military garrison to this verdict, charging out into the town and wrecking the shops of some of the jurors, was the first serious 'reprisal' of the conflict. But this may well have been the kind of escalation GHQ feared, and its effect on public opinion was probably double-edged. (It seems to have cowed as many townspeople as it antagonized.)

But the Fermoy attack was undeniably a conspicuous military

success. Fermoy itself was a challenging target, a major garrison town (the HQ of the British army's 16th Infantry Brigade) on the edge of Lynch's North Cork Brigade area. The brigade acquired thirteen service rifles, about as many as it had possessed when it was created in January 1919. On the same day, 7 September, the 8th Battalion of Cork No. 1 Brigade attacked a military patrol at the Slippery Rock near Coolavokig, capturing several rifles and bicycles. GHQ's restrictive attitude began to ease over the next few months. In mid-October, Liam Deasy of West Cork went to Dublin for meetings with two sets of national leaders. At Vaughan's Hotel – where he met Michael Collins, Gearoid O'Sullivan, Seán Ó Muirthile, Diarmuid O'Hegarty, Peadar Clancy and Dick McKee on the 14th – he was impressed by the comradely and non-chalant atmosphere. At Lalor's on Upper Ormond Quay next day he had a less informal meeting with Collins, Mulcahy and Brugha. 'In an atmosphere of military efficiency', various reports were analysed. 'It was clear that military efficiency was the target to be aimed at ... and that the inculcation of the principles of guerrilla warfare was to be an essential part of all training.' Most significantly, it seems Deasy was quizzed on his brigade's capacity to 'carry out attacks on enemy barracks'. He left (according to his memoirs) with authorization to mount such attacks in the new year.

Deasy's account suggests a logical planning process and a harmonious working relationship between GHQ and the local units (and also, incidentally, between Brugha, Collins and Mulcahy). The reality was certainly not so harmonious. Mulcahy later wrote rather acidly that among the regrettable effects of the South Tipperary violence was that the British counter-measures 'pushed rather turbulent spirits such as Breen and Treacy into the Dublin area ... where their services were not required and their presence was often awkward'.[295] The acid view was reciprocated, certainly by Seamus Robinson, who along with Breen and Treacy joined the 'Squad', GHQ's full-time unit, when Tipperary became 'too hot for them'.[296] Robinson had griped about GHQ's 'insatiable maw for written reports' and the security risk they represented. (He recalled that when Ernie O'Malley went to Tipperary he brought an office typewriter – with a porter to lug it – to churn out reports, but after some of his dispatches had been captured in a raid he saw the sense in Robinson's declaration that 'we would stand for no more written reports ... being sent to Dublin'.) For him GHQ meant dead bureaucracy: 'Not a single member of the GHQ staff ever came down to the country to see things for himself.'[297]

Robinson's dim view extended beyond Mulcahy to Collins himself – 'a bit of an artful dodger'. In an odd episode, Collins allegedly told the Tipperary men there would be an attack on Lord French on his way from Kingstown to Dublin, and placed the Tipperary men at the last point before the Viceroy's convoy reached Dublin Castle. 'We were told that the convoy was to be attacked all the way from Dunlaoghaire [then Kingstown]; if French escaped these ambushes we two were to see to it that he didn't get past us alive.' Instead of a Viceregal convoy, Robinson and Treacy, nerved up for the fight near the Castle gates, heard 'a number of men ... talking loudly and laughing' coming round the corner from Dame Street – Collins, with Seán McGarry and the Cork Volunteer commander Tomás Mac Curtain, shouting, 'It's all right ... he isn't coming!' In fact, French had never been planning to make this journey. 'Mick was able to give the impression to the Volunteer officers from all over the country that he not only organised the attacks on spies that had begun in Dublin but that he also led them, taking part in them!'

Just before Christmas, this hoax was followed by the real thing, when the Tipperary men took up position behind a hedge and dung-heap on the left of the road out of Phoenix Park, some 60 yards from Ashtown Cross. This time the Viceroy's three-car convoy did indeed come, and 'several shots were fired and hand grenades thrown'. Though the second car was 'smashed up' by grenades, French in the leading car drove through unscathed. According to Dan Breen, the attackers' attempt to block the road with a cart was stopped by a local policeman; in any case, they had been told to ignore the first car.[298] One of the attackers, Martin Savage, was killed, but the only governmental casualty was one of the G Division detectives, who shot himself in the hand while trying to fire back at the attackers.[299] Lloyd George shocked Macpherson by laughing the attack off ('they are bad shots'), but its impact was very real. As the *Daily Telegraph* commented, even if unsuccessful, it was 'elaborately planned and carried out with remarkable daring and determination'.

The Ashtown attack signalled that GHQ's resistance to risking fatalities and public rejection was being adjusted. The attack's logic looks straightforward: killing the Viceroy would conform to time-honoured traditions of targeted assassination – traditions shared with many nineteenth-century revolutionary movements, including the Anarchists. (In fact, no Irish Viceroy had ever been assassinated, though one Chief Secretary had.) In this sense it was not a turning point or a signal of any new strategy. Some other attacks were more prophetic. The first, like the Soloheadbeg and Knocklong incidents, was in Tipperary six months earlier. The assassination of RIC District Inspector Hunt in Thurles in June had demonstrated not only the new aggression towards the police (no senior police officer had ever been shot down like this), but also the growing alienation or intimidation of the public. The attack was carried out in broad daylight in the middle of summer in the central square of the town, and the killers were undisguised. Yet no witnesses would come forward. Compared with Soloheadbeg, criticism of the deadly attack was muted. Indeed, the very next day the Irish bishops issued a statement denouncing British methods as 'the rule of the sword, utterly unsuited to a civilised nation'.

The second kind of attack would have a material effect on the governance of the whole country. In late 1919 a number of units tried to rush their local RIC barracks, and though most of these assaults were unsuccessful, they triggered a radical shift in policing strategy. As early as August, some stations in Clare, Galway and Limerick were shut down. By the beginning of November, the RIC concluded that no barrack could be 'considered immune from attack', and on the 8th the immediate closure of vulnerable stations was ordered, 'to augment the force in the remainder for defensive purposes and to enable patrols to be strengthened'. As the Inspector General gloomily reported, this 'has caused apprehension among law-abiding citizens ... who feel they are left without adequate protection'.[300] Such apprehensions would prove to be well justified.

Assaults on a much more serious scale began in Cork early in January 1920.[301] The Midleton battalion of Cork No. 1 Brigade, led by Mick Leahy, assaulted the RIC barrack at Carrigtwohill, blowing in a wall with explosives and forcing the garrison to surrender. This was the first time a semi-fortified police station had been captured. The idea for the operation – in fact for a somewhat more ambitious one – seems to have come from GHQ. The frustrated Cork city leadership, Tomás Mac Curtain (Lord Mayor of Cork and commander of Cork No. 1 Brigade) and Terence MacSwiney, who had suffered sharp criticism for their failure to 'rise' in 1916, first proposed mass attacks on all the police barracks in late 1919, as did Michael Brennan in east Clare. Though GHQ shied away from this, the Corkmen came back with the idea of a local 'rising', MacSwiney arguing that 'they could last for a fortnight and in six weeks time the same could happen in Galway.' Mulcahy again rejected this 'travelling rising' concept, but suggested instead that Cork 'select three barracks in the brigade area and arrange to attack them all in one night'. The attackers should 'go about their business the following morning as if not a dog had barked in the area'. In the event, one of these three attacks failed, and another was aborted. (Even so, a 33 per cent success rate would prove hard to sustain.) Mulcahy claimed that he had still insisted that 'every possible precaution' be taken 'that those engaged in the attack will suffer no loss of life' and not kill anyone inside the barrack.[302] Once again this was an odd precondition for an armed assault.

For Mulcahy, looking back later, the Carrigtwohill attack, which was closely followed by an attack by sixty men of the Macroom battalion on the barrack at Kilmurry, marked the transition to 'war', or 'the beginning of the nationwide offensive in reply to the suppression of Dáil Éireann'. (In the same vein Lord French told the Chief Secretary that the Cork barracks attacks 'are nothing less than acts of war'.)[303] At the time, even so, GHQ's vision was less clear. Whatever Deasy's experience, until November at least GHQ had been trying to create small squad-like units to carry out 'special operations', rather than launch general guerrilla war. It envisaged a single fighting force for each county, its ranks to be filled by men taken from local units. Since they would still have been part-time soldiers, their operational capability would have been quite restricted. A key advantage of this plan from GHQ's viewpoint was that it would have brought professionalization along with central control – a tighter arrangement than the full-time flying columns that would eventually emerge.

GHQ did not get its way. Cork No. 1 Brigade dutifully polled its battalions about the scheme, and reported at the beginning of November that all but one had agreed to it. Plainly, though, the views of the dissentient battalion (the 1st) were shared by the brigade staff. Mac Curtain warned that the scheme would mean that units from which men were selected for the special unit 'would fizzle out'. It was 'difficult enough to keep the organisation going at the present time', he pointed out, 'and I am now convinced that the proposition would have a bad effect on the men *not* selected; they would get the idea of not being required, and would fall out altogether.'[304] He reiterated his and MacSwiney's belief that 'to keep things going some action must be taken which will give *all* the men a chance of doing something.' All the officers (battalion commanders and brigade staff) at a brigade meeting on 31 October had been 'unanimous in requesting GHQ to reconsider the position'. Cork No. 1 wanted to be able to 'carry out the work for which we were making arrangements at the time you summoned us to Dublin and called it off in favour of the other idea'.

Mac Curtain had particular reasons for worrying about the cohesion of his command. He had commanded the Cork Volunteers in 1916, when they had stayed holed up in their drill hall through Easter Week. While he remained a model of GHQ-style caution, some of his men had begun to break free of his control. Riobard Langford, a Gaelic Leaguer and founding member of the Cork Volunteers, had left for Dublin after Easter Week frustrated with his leaders' inaction. When he returned next year, he fell in with a group of like-minded 'disgruntled militants' led by Seán O'Hegarty, and together they carried out an unauthorized raid on the Cork Grammar School armoury, seizing nearly fifty rifles. For this, Mac Curtain had him court-martialled, though he could not make the charge stick.[305] The brigadier's desire for 'some action ... which will give *all* the men a chance of doing something' suggests that he could envisage his command unravelling. When the militant group started taking potshots at policemen early in 1920, he again threatened disciplinary action. 'We can't have men roaming around armed shooting police on their own,' he insisted after an off-duty constable had been killed on 19 March. A few hours after issuing this warning, he himself would be shot dead in his own house.[306]

PART TWO

Two Governments: 1920

Looking back, it was easy enough to see the winter of 1919–20 as a step-change, from confrontation to war. At the time, things were not so clear. Guerrilla fighting is a protean form of warfare, and has taken many shapes throughout history. As a strategy, it would become familiar as the twentieth century went on: famous texts, by leaders like Mao Zedong and Che Guevara, set out blueprints for the escalation of guerrilla action, and dramatic guerrilla triumphs, like the victory of the Viet Minh over the French army, or Fidel Castro's overthrow of the Cuban government, would astonish the world. In 1920, though, guerrilla warfare was not well understood. Some people might know of the Spanish resistance to Napoleon's empire, and a few might even have read Clausewitz's short chapter on 'people's war' in his great work *On War*. More would certainly have known of the surprising success of the Boer commandos against the British in the South African war – especially in Ireland, thanks to the role of John McBride's Irish Brigade alongside the Boers. But military experts dismissed South African conditions as irrelevant to European warfare. The orthodox view was that victory would always lie with the 'big battalions' – as indeed it eventually had in South Africa. The Great War seemed to confirm that military power was above all about gargantuan forces and resources.

In 1920, the potential of guerrilla fighting was emerging. That year 'Lawrence of Arabia' first published his argument that the Arab revolt against the Turks launched in 1916 had demonstrated a new kind of revolutionary war, in which irregular forces would turn the very strength of regular armies into weaknesses. By reversing conventional military logic, dispersing rather than concentrating their forces, taking their time and getting the people on their side, insurgents could seize and retain the initiative.[1] But few if any Irish Volunteers were likely to have come across Lawrence's inspirational article, published as it was in the British *Army Quarterly*. Even Ernie O'Malley, one of the best-read republican activists, does not seem to have read Lawrence until several years later.

At GHQ there were long-standing advocates of irregular warfare, but they had never managed to explain how it could overcome the army of a major power like Britain. A strategic appreciation that fell into police hands early in 1920 was still contemplating 'taking to the field' in something like open combat. Recognizing that an outright offensive would be suicidal, it argued that if all RIC barracks and post offices across the country were attacked simultaneously, three-quarters of the country would fall into the hands of the Republic. The Volunteers could then conduct an 'offensive-defensive', in which British counter-strokes might be parried; it even contemplated the concentration of 'larger bodies of Volunteers on the garrison towns with a view to at least holding the military' there.[2]

There was still some way to go before a realistic fighting method would be found, and it would be found by instinct rather than theory. Without a credible doctrine, the only way forward was trial and error. GHQ remained cautious: Patrick Riordan was summoned to Dublin early in 1920 to discuss the situation in Kerry; he remembered that Mulcahy 'impressed on us not to tackle too much'.[3] The future direction of the campaign seemed to be pointed by the Carrigtwohill attack, and a series of assaults on barracks, ten in January, nine in February, across several counties – Longford, Wicklow and Monaghan as well as Cork and Tipperary – helped to create a sense of coherent purpose and momentum. But though the RIC Inspector General (somewhat defensively) said that 'all the attacks showed careful preparation and good discipline', the learning process was erratic. The few successful attacks were heavily outnumbered by failures.

One of the successes, the attack at Ballytrain on 14 February, the first significant operation north of the Boyne, showed what it took to overcome even quite small police posts. Although the barrack was isolated, and garrisoned by no more than six police, the operation was meticulously planned by Eoin O'Duffy, who organized the blocking of approach roads and the cutting of all telephone and telegraph lines before the village was occupied by a substantial Volunteer force (all masked according to press reports). Ernie O'Malley, a GHQ organizer, arrived in time to watch the attack, and provide a demonstration of 'the correct method of throwing a hand grenade'. The attackers opened fire around 2 a.m., to cover the laying of a mine under the gable wall. (O'Duffy seems to have hoped that the heavily outnumbered garrison would quickly surrender, but it contained two sergeants, one Protestant and the other Catholic, who were determined not to lose face. 'We had no notion of giving in till we had to.') When the mine exploded, O'Malley saw a policeman who had been at prayer blown through a partition wall without injury. At this point the garrison gave up the fight. Though one of them was seriously wounded, nobody was killed on either side.[4]

If the mine had failed to explode, the attack would almost certainly have failed with it. This was the reason for the abortive attack at Aghern, Co. Cork two days later, for instance, and it would recur all too often despite persistent efforts to professionalize the engineering sections of local battalions. The surprise, perhaps, was the effect that even a handful of successes had on the RIC's comprehensive network of garrisons across the country. After the Ballytrain attack, the RIC abandoned half a dozen other small posts in Monaghan, leaving much of the county unpoliced. The same thing sometimes happened even when an attack failed – as at Allihies in Co. Cork, where the garrison fought on after the barrack wall was blown in by a mine, and the attackers eventually withdrew. The barrack was abandoned, along with most of the other small barracks, so that 'a large part of the Beara Peninsula was cleared of enemy forces and made available as a safe place for tending wounded Volunteers of the Brigade.'[5] In Mayo, the number of police garrisons fell from forty-seven in January 1920 to twenty-three a year later; eighteen out of sixty-one Tipperary barracks were abandoned in the same period. The abandonment of police posts became a sort of index of Volunteer activity. In the north of Ireland, for instance, the situation was quite different – no stations in Co. Londonderry were abandoned.[6]

When some units started burning down the vacated barracks, GHQ came up with the idea of a nationwide conflagration to celebrate Easter Week. Aside from the problem of finding enough petrol, the simultaneous burning of some 300 empty buildings on the Saturday night of Easter weekend did not present any military difficulty. (Only occasionally, as at Mayobridge in Co. Down, the neighbours went in and put the fire out after the Volunteers had left.)[7] But it had a striking public impact, and Volunteers themselves were impressed. One 'was very nervous as I felt sure that details of a plan on such a large scale were nearly certain to reach the ears of the enemy', but when he read of the nationwide destruction in the Sunday paper 'I realised that our organisation was effective and watertight.'[8] Income tax offices in the main cities were also raided at the same time, and all their tax records burned – the Sinn Féin strategy of non-violent resistance being given a push by non-lethal violence. The torrent of arson advertised the retreat of government. By July, over 400 vacated barracks had been destroyed, along with nearly fifty courthouses.

But even this spectacular demonstration did not mean that the Volunteers had yet found a coherent plan of campaign. Many local units had still not taken any action, and GHQ's small band of organizers was still stretched very thin. Ernie O'Malley, for example, was supposed to be sent to Kerry, but the Tipperary men in Dublin seem to have persuaded Mulcahy to divert him to South Tipperary in May 1920. O'Malley was acutely conscious of the weakness of the provincial Volunteer organization, and the rarity of determined leaders like Seamus Robinson and Seán Treacy – 'officers who were really interested in their work and who understood it'. O'Malley liked to see himself as a non-political military technician; 'in our minds Seán and I left the building up to the Irish Republic to others.' But even he had no idea about the strategic direction of the Volunteer campaign. 'Our fight was a beginning not an end we knew, but in what direction would it go?' As the trio toured the brigade area, poring over 'the microscope of our maps' to assess the possibilities, it became clear that short-paced, pudgy Seamus Robinson, despite his appalling lack of any sense of direction at ground level, 'was in advance of us in thinking things out'.[9]

Military experience was rare; though some British army veterans joined the Volunteers, at this stage they often had to overcome a barrier of suspicion before they were trusted with responsible roles. The rest were marked, as O'Malley saw it, by a pervasive unfamiliarity with military culture. 'Officers and men have not the faintest idea or at most only a very faint idea of military work in general,' he reported to GHQ in December 1919. 'They know very little of the organization and systematic training necessary to turn out an efficient soldier.' O'Malley fretted that outside the bigger towns the Volunteers did not 'possess sufficient status'; 'often a man – a non-Volunteer – will point with pride and awe to the local President of the Sinn Féin Club,' but 'would not dream of doing so where the local Volunteer Captain was concerned'. What was needed was 'military propaganda'. In the meantime the minimum requirement was to get men to turn up at all: 'I have instructed officers to court-martial men who have missed more than three consecutive parades.'[10]

Unfortunately the officers themselves were not much more soldierly. Most of them were 'absent without explanation or excuse' from O'Malley's battalion classes. But if they were less than keen on lectures, they could be interested in active training. 'It was something new and it gave them more confidence,' O'Malley later wrote. He thought it was not hard to teach 'the applied use of weapons', but characteristically believed that 'with rifles and machine guns there was a great deal of musketry theory to be taught.' This went less well. Fieldcraft, 'the use of ground in relation to movement and formation', was likewise easy, but 'the applied tactics of weapons in relation to protective formation, ground and movement was harder.' O'Malley found himself battling what he considered a dangerous mindset – the idea that 'guerilla warfare should be waged without any regular army groundwork in technique.' The danger of this was that they would not be able to anticipate their opponents' likely methods. They tended to underestimate, if not despise their enemy – 'there was a great contempt for the English as fighting men.' This had its uses – it made it easier for 'untrained boys' to think of taking on the British army – but it needed to be adapted to deal with the reality.

O'Malley theorized that they lacked not just training, but – 'disarmed since the time of Elizabeth' – any inherited familiarity with firearms. 'Most of them had never had rifles or revolvers in their hands; hardly any had seen hand grenades.' It was difficult to build up confidence for fighting unless men knew and believed in their weapons; the shortage of guns and ammunition made this a slow process. The sheer variety of rifles (O'Malley listed fifteen different types in the South Tipperary area) made regular musketry training complicated, even without the ammunition problem. O'Malley could only guess at the actual numbers of guns in the hands of local companies. 'It was impossible to extract a reliable list of names, arms and stuff from a Brigade QM [quartermaster]. Companies were afraid the battalion wanted to distribute some of their arms to other companies; the battalion was afraid the brigade would transfer stuff to other battalions. The brigade always made the poor mouth to GHQ to extract more arms.'[11]

O'Malley's style did not work with everyone. He was, as he himself wrote, 'on the outside'. (His theory about the disarmed Irishry had an

Anglo-Irish tinge.) In a Roscommon company where he spent a week in the autumn of 1919, parading, drilling and instructing, he was 'generally . . . not liked'. 'He was too much of the "officer" class and did not succeed in getting himself down to the level of the ordinary country Volunteers and appreciate their problems.'[12] Some came to accept that his intolerance of slacking or incompetence was driven by his passionate commitment to making the Volunteers into real soldiers, but other organizers faced similar problems where local officers were reluctant to accept external direction. The inculcation of military standards, especially of discipline, was not simple. Inevitably, a largely self-created and self-sustaining militia such as the Irish Volunteers had discipline issues rather different from those of a regular army. On 26 May 1920, GHQ found it necessary to issue a general order that 'no action of anything like a military nature shall be taken or ordered to be taken by any Volunteer except insofar as this is covered by definite orders or permission actually received from his superior officer.' Quite what problem this characteristically convoluted syntax was grappling with is not clear, but GHQ added another explanation – 'the fact that actions of a certain type take place in one Brigade or Battalion area does not constitute such an order or permission.'[13]

In March, the commandant of the Wexford Brigade, Thomas Sinnott, was court-martialled on two rather different charges of 'grave neglect of duty'. One was that he had failed to discipline one of his battalion commanders who had told his drinking companions in a pub about an upcoming operation. Worse, perhaps, he had not reported this, and it accidentally 'transpired in conversation with the Chief of Staff some weeks later' about the delaying of the operation. The other charge was that he 'failed to have issued properly and without delay Headquarters Order dated 19th January 1920' (on 'Raids and Robberies'). He was reduced to the ranks, and made ineligible to hold commissioned rank for a year.[14] Other officers were court-martialled for such offences as 'attempting to coerce an Officer of the Limerick City Battalion into joining another organisation', and 'instigating raids and robberies without the sanction of GHQ'.

Such irregularities would persist, but by May there was a sense that the Volunteers' military capacity was firming up. The tempo of attacks on barracks increased. On the 10th, O'Malley and Robinson led an assault on Hollyford barrack in Tipperary. They had to climb up on to the roof carrying 'two revolvers each, grenades, bursting charges, supplies of fuse, detonators and hammers to smash the [roof] slates. On our backs a tin of petrol was tied, sods of turf which had been soaked in oil hung around our necks from cords. The oil sopped into our clothes . . .' They poured in petrol and threw blazing peat through the holes they smashed; O'Malley's bursting grenades pelted him with fragments of slate. 'My hands and face were burning hot, my hair caught fire . . . My coat was alight.' The defenders hung on desperately and the attackers were forced, after a four-hour battle, to withdraw. Their equipment was dangerously crude, but with enough determination it could be made to work. On the 25th, Kilmallock barrack in Limerick, which had been attacked unsuccessfully by the Fenians in 1867, was destroyed in an assault led by Seán Forde (the *nom de guerre* of Tomás Ó Maoileoin). By July, sixteen occupied barracks had been destroyed and twenty-nine damaged.

In North Tipperary, though, the attack on Borrisokane RIC barrack reverted to the Hollyford pattern. An imposing force of 200 men was assembled by the brigadier, Frank McGrath, and all the approach roads were sealed off. But attempts to pour oil in through the roof were thwarted, and the use of grenades was inexplicably forbidden by the commander. After two hours of fighting, with the barrack in imminent danger of catching fire, a false alarm of approaching British troops led McGrath to order a retreat. The garrison was forced to abandon the building shortly after the attackers decamped, and one senior officer alleged that McGrath was afraid of reprisals against his own property. Even this failed operation, however, had some positive effects. 'It was our baptism of fire,' said Dan Gleeson of the Toomevara company. 'It glamourised a lot of lads' – 'You know he was at Borrisokane' became a local saying. But as Gleeson ruefully recalled, 'if you were out five miles away, blocking a road, you got no mention.'[15]

'TWO GOVERNMENTS WAGING WAR'

Alongside the escalation of the military campaign came significant political developments. Mid-January 1920 saw the first round of local government elections, in the municipalities (the rural council elections were to take place in June). These were a crucial test of Sinn Féin's capacity to displace its rival parties, and of Dáil Éireann's status as an alternative government. Its Local Government Minister was a veteran Sinn Féin politician, William T. Cosgrave, with long experience on the committees of the Dublin Corporation to add credibility to his brief military flowering as a member of the 4th Battalion of the Dublin Brigade fighting at the South Dublin Union in 1916 (though it was the latter that had ensured his election as MP for Kilkenny in 1917). In the longer perspective, this ministry became 'a real government department', not only trying to keep local government functioning as disruption spread across the country, but embarking on fundamental reforms which would be continued by the independent Irish state.[16] In 1919, though, Cosgrave's department had not hit the headlines (he seems to have spent much of his time working on a scheme for municipal milk distribution), while his colleagues focused on housing issues and Poor Law reform. But now as the elections approached things were hotting up. At the end of October the Dáil approved his proposed pledge to be taken by candidates – 'I recognise the Republic established by the will and vote of the Irish People as the legitimate Government of Ireland.'

Not only Cosgrave himself, but Sinn Féin more generally had 'a strong tradition in local government'. A tenth of the Dáil's members had some local government experience – an unintended consequence of the British local government reform at the end of the nineteenth century, which created the modern borough and county councils. The party held twelve seats on the eighty-strong Dublin Corporation by 1911, representing significant opposition to the dominant nationalist party, which it persistently charged with jobbery, corruption and inefficiency. Griffith regularly subjected both local authorities and the Local Government Board to his lacerating critiques. The 'Corpo' was a fair target, but there was a negative side to the deep immersion of men like Cosgrave in local battles: his political horizons, some thought, had been narrowed.

Local elections, due in 1917, had already been postponed several times. In 1919 the British government decided to adopt proportional representation (to be introduced for Irish parliamentary elections by the new Government of Ireland Bill). Justified on the grounds of 'minority protection', PR was expected to peg back Sinn Féin gains. But by an agreeable irony it was actually an established Sinn Féin policy: Arthur Griffith had been advocating it for over twenty years, and so indeed had parliamentarian nationalists like John J. Horgan. The British had naturally not noticed this. So the slightly odd situation emerged in which (as the *Daily News* observed) 'instead of opposing a change declaredly designed to cripple its power', Sinn Féin 'willingly helped in its development'. The party approached the elections cautiously, all the same, fielding just over 700 candidates for the 1,816 seats at stake – not many more than Labour, or indeed independent candidates. The election lacked the electric atmosphere of December 1918, and Volunteers seem to have been much less prominently involved, despite the temptation of a strong British presence in many towns. But there was a high turnout, and a substantial Sinn Féin victory, producing republican–Labour control of nine out of eleven municipalities and sixty-two out of ninety-nine urban councils. Though the unionist press first suggested that the outstanding feature of the elections was Sinn Féin's 'failure to sweep the country', by the end of January 1920 the *Irish Times* recognized that 'the local administration of the South and West of Ireland is in the hands of a party which publicly repudiates British government'. The resolution of Cork and Limerick corporations to pledge allegiance to the Dáil represented 'deliberate and audacious declarations of war'.

This step was not one to be taken lightly. When the Dáil approved the form of the resolutions of allegiance, it asked Cosgrave to draw up a report 'showing definitely the results of taking a stand against the Local Government Board'. But it was fairly obvious that defying the LGB would mean at the very least the loss of central funding, with no immediately available alternative source. Though all the Sinn Féin-controlled authorities refused to put up people to act as high sheriffs, a fair number – led by Dublin Corporation itself – temporized for three or four months on the issue of pledging allegiance, and some waited on the outcome of the rural elections in June. Dublin confined itself to symbolic actions, such as (inevitably) flying the tricolour over City Hall and dispensing with the mace as the token of authority – though even Cork did not dispense with the title of lord mayor. When Dublin finally plumped for recognizing the authority of the Dáil on 3 May, it made sure to ask the Minister for Foreign Affairs to communicate its resolution to the US Congress.

The Dáil Local Government Department tightened its grip on the process after Cosgrave had been arrested and replaced by Kevin O'Higgins, a man 'diametrically opposed . . . in temperament, intellect and outlook'.[17] Even so, the complexity of the financial issues involved, and the daunting implications of the shift, made it hard to fix a policy. A new committee consisting of two lord mayors, two council accountants and one council secretary had not come up with a definite recommendation by the time of the June elections. At the end of June yet another Dáil commission, of twenty TDs, councillors and local officials – together with a lone woman, Jennie Wyse Power – was set up, but had not met a month later. Eventually it was the British government which forced the issue at the end of July by demanding that all local authorities should declare allegiance to the LGB by formally undertaking to obey its rules and submit all their accounts for audit. This triggered a gradual evaporation of support for the LGB as councils made up their minds to reject the ultimatum.[18]

The second round of elections, the rural council elections in June, underlined Sinn Féin's dominance. On the platform of a properly local policy – expanding public housing, health and education – the party and its allies gained control of twenty-nine of the thirty-three county councils. At the same time, the party was becoming militarized; the Volunteers were more active in the elections than in January, and growing British pressure encouraged the military leaders to exert more influence. In Monaghan, candidates were selected by the brigade commander, who picked young men with little fixed property that might be at risk if the council defied the LGB. A judicious mixture of 'intimidation and organization' ensured that all the rival nationalist candidates in the county withdrew before the election.[19] Likewise in west Clare, an officer of the 2nd Battalion, Mick McMahon – who thought that GHQ had issued 'instructions for the Volunteers to get control of the Local Government bodies' – was selected as a candidate for the county council by 'a joint convention of Sinn Fein and brigade staffs'.[20]

But though the unionist press denounced the use of Volunteers to guard polling stations during the election as intimidation, the electoral process seems to have been reasonably free, and the result was indisputable. The Local Government Department issued new instructions that chairmen, vice-chairmen and county council representatives to the General Council of County Councils 'should be most carefully selected' with 'due regard being paid to National principle, ability and knowledge of local administration'. Most interpreted this as advice to elect Sinn Féin members – many of them Volunteers – even where they were in a minority on the council. The learning experience of Joseph Clancy, the East Clare Brigade's training officer, was typical. With 'no experience whatsoever', he was elected chairman of Tulla Rural District Council. 'All the new members were nominated by the Sinn Féin organisation but, like myself, many of them were "wanted men".' The council could not use the council offices, and 'had to assemble secretly in all kinds of strange places'. Local Volunteer companies provided the protection for these meetings, which concluded 'without being interrupted even once'.[21]

The new councils adopted – often unanimously – resolutions acknowledging 'the authority of Dáil Éireann as the duly elected government of the Irish people' and undertaking 'to give effect to all decrees promulgated by the said Dáil Éireann in so far as same affects this council'. (However, Cosgrave's department waited until 12 August – a bit behind the wave – to issue a letter calling on all bodies to sever their connection with the LGB.)[22] The 'First Republican Council of Leitrim' ostentatiously congratulated 'the forces of the IRA on their many successes during the past year, and the many fortresses and seats of oppression destroyed, and we earnestly hope that they may continue their successes until victory crowns their arms'.[23] Meath Council resolved that 'the Republican flag fly over the County Hall', and later voted to strike a rate of one and a half pence in the pound towards 'the upkeep and maintenance of the Volunteers of this county'. Neighbouring Louth was less enthusiastic, though, worrying about the likely implications of transferring allegiance to the Dáil, and inducing Alderman Philip Monaghan (the Louth Brigade commander) to promise that 'armed force would never be resorted to unless circumstances made it absolutely necessary.'[24] In Monaghan it was thought wise to assemble the Sinn Féin councillors for instruction (by Fr McNamee) before the council met: 'we were to repudiate the British local government and to stop paying the rates to them.'[25]

In May the *Irish Times* lamented that the 'whole south of Ireland has fallen under the government of Sinn Féin'. In trying to alert Britain to the scale of the threat to the Union, it may have exaggerated a little, but not much. At the beginning of March, *An tOglac* delightedly noted that a French newspaper had just described the situation in Ireland as 'two governments waging war on one another'. This was some way short of the international recognition originally hoped for, but it was heartening. The shift of the Propaganda Department's efforts from turning out pamphlets to the regular production of the *Irish Bulletin* was having its effect. Its tempo, five issues a week, was important in ensuring that the official British version of Irish news items was permanently disputed. It was carefully targeted – circulated not just to press correspondents, but also to politicians, churchmen and other leading figures in several countries (including Egypt and India). The print run increased from fifty in 1919 to 600 in late 1920, and eventually to 2,000 (though the last figure may have been massaged by the department).

The *Bulletin* tirelessly depicted the conflict as a foreign invasion of an independent sovereign state. The Republic existed *de jure* and *de facto*; after the second round of local elections the Dáil government had 'the allegiance of 83 per cent of the Irish people'. (The identity of the remaining 17 per cent, and their grounds for refusing allegiance, were left vague.) In repudiation of the British authorities' description of republican attacks as 'outrages', all British official actions were seen as 'aggression'. The *Bulletin* attacked the distortions of British press coverage, notably the failure to report violent police actions ('terrorism' in republican parlance). In presumably deliberate contrast to *An tOglac*, the republican military actions themselves were downplayed or ignored – at least until Erskine Childers took over as editor in 1921. Childers himself characterized the 'war' in 1920 as a clash between 'an organised army' and a 'well-nigh helpless' civil population – a rather different perspective from the Volunteers' self-image.[26] Positive coverage of the Republic's administration had to focus at first on the loan and the various commissions. These were not tremendously dramatic, and the long delays in producing reports did not help. In 1920, though, a project took shape that gave new substance to the image: the supersession of the British legal structure by republican courts and police.

'AN ILLEGAL GOVERNMENT HAS BECOME THE *DE FACTO* GOVERNMENT'

Bit by bit, a truly revolutionary change was taking place: the popular takeover of the justice system. 'People's courts' were part of the folk-memory of the Land War, and the memory of rural 'midnight courts' stretched further back still. Not all the memories were good ones, but there was a real basis for the emergence of an alternative law. As early as December 1917, republicans like Eamon O'Dwyer were urging people to ignore the official courts, and promising that arbitration courts would be set up. When the Dáil finally announced a scheme of national arbitration courts at the beginning of August 1919 it was if anything a belated response to the resurgence of agrarian agitation. The potential significance of this project was unmistakable, but its implementation at national level was plagued by delays. The National Arbitration Courts Committee twice failed to meet, once when its planned meeting place was raided by troops, the second time when no one but the chairman turned up. No publicity was given to the scheme, since no details had been fixed, so hardly any cases came on – in fact only two by October.[27] In west Clare, though, the local TD, Brian O'Higgins, pushed the idea on by calling a conference which set up a district arbitration court. 'A constitution was drawn up with the aid of local lawyers, together with rules of court; judge-arbitrators and registrars were appointed, and a scale of court fees, costs and fines was settled.'[28]

Mayo and Galway followed suit, but 'the great bulk of constituencies preferred to await the national scheme of Courts.' When it finally met at the end of September, the national committee warned that 'the election of justices in a very large number of districts was impossible owing to the ban on public meetings,' and in any case elections would take 'a considerable time'. In the meantime, 'there were unauthorised courts being set up every other day in a haphazard and slipshod manner, with grave possibilities of irregularity.' Litigants were using the 'English courts' because of the delay in setting up 'the machinery so long promised'. It was important that 'some system which could be temporarily set up which would give a sense of confidence in its impartiality and efficiency' should be 'put in motion without delay'. The key point was that 'once the people were brought into touch with such actual courts well and justly managed, a feeling of respect for the Decrees of the Republic and a sense of individual trusteeship for its welfare would be engendered in the people.'[29]

The Dáil received a sensible assessment of the existing 'English courts', analysing their technical defects ('apart from National considerations'). The county courts, for instance, were 'not unpopular', though they were 'unscientific'. The system of double hearing was unique to Ireland. Appeals from magistrates' courts were perpetually rushed, and often 'dealt with in a wholly unscrupulous way by partisan judges contemptuous of peasants and free from fear of appeal'. The system was 'cheap and popular' in spite of all this, and 'often does rough justice outside the law'. Since it developed in eighteenth-century Ireland it was 'to that extent a native product'. (National considerations resurfaced here.) The high court was different – uncorrupt but expensive; its costs were out of proportion to the amounts in dispute, and its 'paraphernalia copied from England' was 'larger than our country requires'.[30]

The logic of creating a national court system was persuasive; but the cost was daunting. The Dáil ministry did not approve the idea until 7 November, and subject to an estimate of its costs. In the meantime, courts were being set up on a local basis, with prominent people (often priests) acting as judges. In March 1920 the annual cost was worked out at £113,000, with rotary courts costing £26,000 a year. Austin Stack, the new Minister for Home Affairs, recommended a less expensive 'small scale experiment', costing only £11,300 – seven justices on £750 a year, four registrars on £300, with thirty-seven county clerks on a nominal £50 honorarium (plus expenses).[31] Not until May did Stack come up with a national arbitration court scheme, issuing a circular instruction authorizing the election of three arbitrators – to be paid £1 per day – by each parish to adjudicate small claims (less than £10). The new element in this was a right of appeal to a district court of five arbitrators elected by the parish courts, with unlimited jurisdiction.

Stack had not been responsible for the courts policy until late November, when he took over from Arthur Griffith as home affairs minister. (Stack, who had just escaped from gaol, was brought into the Cabinet by the absent de Valera; he was confirmed in the post by the Cabinet on 16 January 1920, though not by the Dáil until 29 June.) Griffith may have handed the fledgling ministry over with a sense of relief. It has been suggested that the slow progress up to that point was 'due more to apathy on the part of the Irish people than to a lack of urgency on his part'.[32] But it seems that Griffith, who famously disliked speechmaking, was not much happier with the routine of ministerial office. Stack, though a little more conscientious, was also an erratic administrator. (A year later, after the Truce, Michael Collins would blame the stalling of the courts policy on the fact that 'the machinery was not held together'; 'not enough work' was done 'locally or at headquarters'.)

By June 1920 the police in many areas reported that 'Sinn Féin

Courts' had 'practically put an end to Quarter Sessions and Petty Sessions'. But it is clear that some of these were Volunteer 'courts martial', sometimes used in cases where no republican judiciary had been set up. Many were run by local factions. The pressure of land cases was threatening to overwhelm the system such as it was. The disappearance of the RIC opened up many rural areas to the revival of longstanding disputes, and in spring 1920 the auctions of eleven-month lettings proved acutely frustrating to the tenants. The anti-'ranch' impulse exploded into life again, with disturbing political volatility. One group marching to seize grazing land under the tricolour, when they were told that Sinn Féin was opposed to land seizures, simply tore the orange and white strips off the flag and marched on as Hibernians.[33] Art O'Connor, who succeeded Robert Barton as minister for agriculture in April, said that the land trouble that broke out in Kerry in early 1920 and 'raged with such vehemence . . . showed all the symptoms of finally taking the form of a civil war of a kind which would undoubtedly have spread to the calmer parts of the country, and probably involve the Government itself in general ruin'. When British law enforcement was withdrawn, 'the Dáil itself seemed overwhelmed by the suddenness with which responsibility of Government had been thrust upon it.' O'Connor suggested that the Dáil ministry 'seemed to shrink from its duty' ('as one shrinks from the fulfilment of an unexpected joy', he added), and that during the winter of 1919–20 government 'seemed to stand stock still'. (Kevin O'Shiel later suggested that 'the Dáil Government was as surprised and shocked at its staggering success as was Hitler at Dunkirk.') The people of the west, 'intoxicated with the wine which they drank to the dregs . . . confused license with liberty'.[34]

O'Connor had a reason for painting such an apocalyptic picture: it was he who fronted the recovery to order from 'the mad onrush of the revolution'. The emergency forced the ministry to take direct action. Appointed as the Dáil's special judicial commissioner (rather like one of the *representants en mission* of the French revolutionary Republic), O'Connor arrived at Ballinrobe, Co. Mayo, on 13 May, and set up a provisional arbitration court for the constituency 'to operate until the Dáil had definitely decided on a national scheme'. The lawyer Kevin O'Shiel helped to draft the procedural rules. The first case heard by the first court sitting directly under Dáil authority, at Ballinrobe on 17 May, could – O'Connor claimed – 'be properly described as the cornerstone of our Judiciary'. It adjudicated a dispute in which two landowners – of 60 acres each – were being intimidated and boycotted by a group of smallholders claiming their land. The court set a significant precedent by finding against the claimants, adding the nakedly political advice that they should turn their attention to a nearby 700-acre farm owned by the Congested Districts Board, the British government quango. But it immediately faced a direct challenge when the claimants refused to accept the verdict, and demonstrated outside the courthouse 'waxing eloquent on the futility of the Dáil's authority'.

With the credibility of the new justice system on the line, the local Volunteer battalion commander was called in to arrest four of the claimants' leaders. They were held prisoners on an island in Lough Corrib until they agreed to accept the court's authority. The commandant seems not to have relished this task, but it set a pattern that would underpin the republican courts for the rest of the conflict. A 'Republican Police' service, drawn at first from the Volunteers, soon began to be put together on a regular basis. The extent of Volunteer involvement remained hard to pin down, though reports of people being kidnapped and brought before Dáil courts – presumably by the Volunteers – were widespread in the summer of 1920, and the police counted over 100 cases in July alone.[35]

Just as significantly, arbitration courts (which were perfectly legal in themselves) began to be replaced by courts of original jurisdiction (which were definitely not). The former were consensual, but the latter could, theoretically at least, force defendants and witnesses to attend. Whatever his executive frailties, Stack did at least think big: he saw the arbitration courts as only a first step in the creation of a comprehensive legal system, and reported that at the end of January his department had considered forming courts 'to whose jurisdiction litigants might be compelled to submit their cases, instead of to an enemy tribunal'. On 21 May he presented proposals for a system of parish and district courts, and on 8 June asked O'Hegarty to ensure that this issue of criminal jurisdiction was discussed at the next Cabinet on the 10th. (The correspondence implies that Stack was not attending Cabinet meetings.) Ministers remained cautious, telling Stack to hold back plans for the 'dislocation of enemy courts' until the republican courts were fully operational. Six days later he urged the ministry to empower him to push ahead the process of appointing arbitrators, and the Cabinet finally resolved to authorize the establishment of parish and district courts with criminal jurisdiction in areas the Home Affairs Minister thought suitable, together with a supreme court. This decision was confirmed by the Dáil on 29 June – its first meeting for eight months. In all this, though, the republican government 'merely endorsed a trend which had already begun'.[36]

At the same time the Dáil moved to dam up a torrent of spurious or extravagant property claims, often based on assertions that 'claimants or their ancestors were formerly in occupation of the property.' Some of these, it suggested, 'seem to be of a frivolous nature, and [are] put forward in the hope of intimidating the present occupiers'. In April, Sinn Féin announced that 'anyone who from this forth persists in pressing a dispute will do so in the knowledge that he or she is acting in defiance of the wishes of the people's elected representatives and [to] the detriment of the National cause'.[37] Two months later the Dáil urged that 'the present critical time' was 'ill-chosen for the stirring up of strife amongst our fellow-countrymen'. 'All our energies must be directed towards the clearing out – not the occupier of this or that piece of land – but the foreign invader of our Country.' So it decreed that 'pending the international recognition of the Republic, no claims of [this] kind shall be heard or determined by the Courts of the Republic, unless by written licence of the Minister for Home Affairs.'[38]

By this time the new court system had become something of a media sensation. Even the hostile *Irish Times* conceded in June that 'the King's writ runs no longer in many parts of the country'; the Sinn Féin 'tribunals' were 'jostling British law into oblivion, as a fast motor-car jostles foot-passengers off the road'. Next month a prominent landowner, Lord Monteagle, told the paper that he had become a convert to the 'Sinn Féin courts and government', which had shown 'extraordinary fairness' and been 'extremely just'. Similar messages were transmitted by the British press – the *Daily News* reporting that 'Sinn Féin law has a sanction behind it such as no other law in Ireland has had for generations.' The *Manchester Guardian* saw the courts as 'the natural result of the strong common will for national responsibility'. Stephen Gwynn wrote in the *Observer* in July that though they had been 'an improvisation to meet a need', nothing had brought Sinn Féin so much prestige as the courts. 'Nothing goes so far to give reality to the claim that there is an Irish Republic in being.' This was confirmed by Lord Dunraven, a prominent unionist, who told *The Times* (not without, we may suspect, a certain *Schadenfreude*) that 'an illegal government has become the *de facto* government. Its jurisdiction is recognised. It administers justice promptly and equitably and we are in this curious dilemma that the civil administration of the country is carried on under a system the existence of which the *de jure* government does not and cannot acknowledge, and is carried on very well.' Foreign journalists went out west in some numbers, and were given access to the 'underground' tribunals by the Propaganda Department.[39] The Chairman of Mayo County Council could declare at the beginning of August that republican plans had been turned 'from alleged dreams into practical realities'.[40]

'THE RAPID DEVELOPMENT OF THE CIVIL SIDE'

For Arthur Griffith, the resort to coercion was a regrettable development, tainting the utopian image of the arbitration concept. But coercion had really been there from the start. The west Clare parish and district court rules, used as a model for the June 1920 scheme, spoke of mandatory judgments alongside voluntary arbitration, and the use of 'guards' to preserve the peace and impose fines for breaches of licensing laws. In January 1920 a Clare litigant who had refused to transfer his case from the 'enemy' courts to the Sinn Féin court was boycotted, his house placarded, and shots were fired outside it.[41] Coercion was, ultimately, a vital element in the state-building process; the republicans needed to ensure that their proto-state exerted a monopoly of it. *An tOglac*, announcing in May that the Volunteers had been 'entrusted with the duty of enforcing the decrees of the courts established by Dáil Éireann', made the point that 'as long as the state of war continues, the Army of the Irish Republic must remain the chief executive instrument of the Irish Republic.'[42]

Many Volunteers were not much happier than Griffith about enforcing the justice system: Cathal Brugha himself 'had no use whatever for Courts of any description'. When asked to authorize Volunteer assistance during the Ballinrobe stand-off, he told O'Shiel that courts and police were irrelevant to the military effort, and would have to wait until the war was won. 'His simple credo was that the nation was engaged in a deadly war with England, and accordingly that every fibre of energy, every atom of strength, every pound collected should be concentrated exclusively and solely on that war.'[43] Local commanders often agreed, seeing the additional duty as a tiresome distraction and a burden. Fortunately for the Republic, others embraced the new dimension with enthusiasm. Patrick Hargaden in south Leitrim thought that, though police duty 'threw a lot of work on the shoulders of the officers and Volunteers but it was a novelty for them and they entered into [it] with great spirit'. 'Their reward ... was that the confidence of the people in them flourished and they came with their troubles to the Volunteers.'[44] Areas where the Volunteers had few weapons discovered a new sense of purpose – for one battalion in the Fingal Brigade, which had 'no arms of any kind' when it was formed, and would still be without any 'proper arms' by the time of the Truce, policing 'gave them work to do and was a decided change from the monotony of parading and drilling and helped to build an esprit de corps'.[45] The moralistic – a powerful element in the movement – found themselves at last empowered to reorder some outstanding social defects, the demon drink above all. Many Volunteer units conducted regular raids on the poteen makers who multiplied as the RIC abandoned its normal policing activities, fining the distillers and destroying stills or seizing the equipment for display outside churches. They enforced licensing hours, forbade publicans to serve 'the tramp class' and fined them for tolerating drunks on their premises.[46] There must have been a number who, like Commandant P. J. O'Daly in Monaghan, 'loved to preside at midnight courts, to take witnesses out of bed at all hours and to use Volunteers to do it. He loved the sense of power it gave him.'[47]

Like so many revolutionary developments, republican policing emerged out of local initiatives. A Dublin Volunteer unit, for instance, arrested four thieves, tried them and sentenced them to whipping, as early as May 1919. The Dáil referred to 'Republican police' acting in the Millstreet bank-robbery case in November. But it took rather longer to set up a national system, thanks to Brugha's 'resolute opposition' to the creation of a police force recruited from Volunteer ranks – the only possible source at that point. In January 1920 GHQ warned 'that a definite effort may very soon have to be made by Volunteers towards the protection of the general public against the raids and robberies that have become so prevalent recently in many districts'. But exactly how they were to go about this was left uncertain. The Volunteers had neither the resources nor the training to step straight into the gap left by the British system. 'The Volunteer organisation is not in a position to take up the policing of the country,' as GHQ made clear in May 1920. Where 'courts martial' were used, the procedures were – approximately – based on the British system. But, as GHQ acknowledged, the issue of enforcing penalties was 'very difficult'. There was 'only one punishment which we can with convenience to ourselves mete out to such people' – that is, death – but 'unless it can be shown clearly that such persons are a danger to society in your area, you may not carry out the extreme penalty.' The only realistic alternative was deportation. Imprisonment was seen as impracticable at this stage, though it would be used on an increasing scale later. The 'important thing' in most robbery cases was that 'the goods are recovered and restored.'[48]

The Millstreet case provided a shining example. Liam Lynch's arrest of a gang of armed robbers, who had seized over £16,000 from two bank officials near Millstreet, Co. Cork, on 17 November 1919, was motivated by the widespread rumour that the Volunteers were themselves responsible for the robbery. Lynch wanted to vindicate his own organization as well as to combat 'the menace of a criminal element in the community capable of carrying out robbery on this scale'. It was not easy, as the gang had planned their disappearance carefully, and until mid-March 1920 no clues had been found to their identity. Finally Lynch went directly to the Millstreet area, set up a formal investigation and put in a passable performance as a detective superintendent. On 24 April he issued warrants for the arrest of ten men, and eight of them were picked up by the Millstreet Volunteer battalion that night. They were 'held in custody' and tried by 'a special Court' – over which Lynch himself presided – three days later. Several of them had confessed – whether or not under duress we do not know – and nearly £10,000 was recovered. Seven of the eight were found guilty, two of them expelled from the brigade area and five deported from Ireland (for periods of eight, ten or fifteen years).[49]

Reports in the nationalist press indicated a range of republican policing activity, including arrests for house-breaking as well as 'riotous behaviour' and fraud (the guilty party being a bookmaker who had made off from Barrastown Races in Tipperary with £67 12s in unpaid bets). Punishments included flogging as well as restoration of goods or repair of damage, fines, and removal to 'an unknown destination'. In some places 'prisoners were made to work on the bogs and farms until their charges were disposed of' by the republican courts.[50] When the RIC reported finding a group of convicts serving a three-week prison sentence on an island off the west coast, the prisoners refused to leave, declaring that they were loyal citizens of the Irish Republic. (No doubt, as one historian has suggested, allowing themselves to be liberated by the police would have exposed them to the risk of worse punishment – but this in itself showed how the republican justice system was securing credibility, a crucial precondition of legitimacy.)[51] Where islands were not available, though, detention of prisoners was (as O'Malley said) 'a drain on us'. They had to be fed and guarded, even though the guards 'played cards with them, smoked, chatted and swapped stories'. O'Malley once 'found the guard asleep in a deserted house whilst their prisoners were out on sentry duty with shotguns'.[52]

On 19 June 1920 GHQ came up with a formula 'pending the development of a criminal department by the Dáil'. Instead of inflicting punishments, 'the convicted parties will be retained in custody until the following Sunday,' when they would be paraded after mass, and 'their name and address and offence ... publicly announced'. Recognizing 'the rapid development of the Civil side of responsible Republican Government', a Republican Police Force was to be established, initially drawing its personnel from the Volunteers. Three or four men per company should be enrolled in the force, to work under policing officers appointed by the brigade commandant. This makeshift set-up was turned into a regular, distinct organization in November, when GHQ declared that 'the point has now been reached in the development of the civil functioning of the Republic when it is becoming necessary to define more clearly the position and work of the Police Force.'[53] The work had 'hitherto been borne entirely by the IRA', but the police were now to become a separate force. This assertion may have been more rhetorical than real at this stage, since it would have to be reiterated more than once over the next twelve months.

Critics have depicted the republican justice system as irregular and unsystematic, a prey to 'parochial faction-fighting', whose formal elements like procedures had great propaganda value but less practical content. It has been argued that, judged by its own pretensions, 'republican justice was a sham'.[54] A key exhibit in this picture is the case in which two priests, Fathers Michael McKenna and Patrick Gaynor, faced down an ex-RIC man who had taken over a relative's farm on the authority of the local republican court. McKenna (who actually commanded the local Volunteer battalion) arbitrarily dissolved the court, and personally confronted the ex-constable, Michael Connors, striking him 'a hard blow on the face'. Then Gaynor – who was also close to the Volunteers though not actually a member – appointed himself acting police chief, and organized a convention of 'all the authorities under the Irish Republic in West Clare' to annul the previous order. When Connors – who carried a gun – refused to leave the farm, Gaynor issued an unambiguous threat: he would be back in half an hour, 'but not alone next time: you have to decide whether you will walk out alive or be carried out dead'. He mustered three Volunteers to eject Connors from the farm, telling them that 'they were in a position similar to that of organised armed forces in any country and were free, if necessary, to open fire on Connors without any qualm of conscience.' In the end Connors 'did not dare use his revolver against a priest and Volunteers on duty', and gave way.[55] All this demonstrates, it has been suggested, that 'neither priests, policemen nor Volunteers showed great respect for the Dáil courts as constituted, though all shared a robust faith in the efficacy of *force majeure*.'[56]

Yet something prevented the eruption of general gang warfare or vendetta. While republican publicity certainly exaggerated the regularity of the system, it does seem to have rested on some underlying consensus. The Dáil courts were able to rely on 'the goodwill of litigants and communal pressure to make their decisions effective'.[57] The local justices, officially called brehons, may have known nothing of the ancient brehon law that now supposedly superseded statute, but they were sensible people whose judgments reflected common sense (as the originals no doubt also did). Without idealizing it, it may not be too much to suggest that there was a real sense of public ownership of the republican court system.

'A PANIC MEASURE OF RAISING 8,000 SCALLYWAGS'

The erratic emergence of the republican guerrilla campaign had a compensating advantage: it helped to disguise from the authorities the scale of the threat they confronted. Emerging low-level insurgencies are not easy for governments to identify, and the measures needed to choke them off are uncertain. Over the next century this problem would be faced, with mixed success, by many states across the world. (Within a decade, indeed, a new Irish state would itself be grappling with the problem of liberal-democratic constitutions that 'envisage no intermediate situation between profound peace and open civil war'.) At this point, Britain was baffled by the new phenomenon. The police force it had created in Ireland was designed to deal with occasional insurrections, and the rest of the time to monitor small, secret revolutionary groups. By the end of 1919, these functions were obsolete. The accumulated expertise of generations of intelligence-gatherers, 'the eyes and ears of Dublin Castle', was all but irrelevant. There was a substantial British military garrison in Ireland, some 40,000 troops in all – and though the number of 'effectives' fell from 25,000 in 1919 to fewer than 20,000 in early 1920, that was still more than twice the strength of the police. Yet the peacetime law made the use of military force problematic.

Lord French, as we have seen, immediately identified the first attacks on barracks as 'nothing less than acts of war'. The police were already a broken reed, especially in Dublin itself. 'As the situation gets worse, Johnstone and the DMP appear to show greater and greater hesitation.' But though he himself was always clear that the only possible response must be military rule, the GOC, Lieutenant General Frederick Shaw, did not see it the same way. 'You know Shaw's dislike to the proclamation of martial law,' French told the Chief Secretary early in January 1920. At least 'he has voluntarily suggested that the military should take up a great deal of the duty which now falls upon the police – in fact that the military should come first and the police second,' or rather, as French preferred to put it, 'the military take the initiative and the police follow'. But would this be enough? Either 'a large number of men must be arrested and deported, *or else we must have martial law*.'[58] As before, though, neither would happen.

The decision to pull back from the smaller police stations, which looked in retrospect like a serious political mistake, was practically unavoidable. The RIC was somewhat under strength in 1919 – nearly 1,000 below its establishment of 10,166. Even at full strength, it would have been overstretched as soon as its dispersion in over 1,300 local posts came under challenge. Many of these posts could not have been held even if reinforcements had been available. Most were either vulnerable because of their position, or structurally indefensible, whatever efforts were made to fortify them with sandbags and new steel shutters. The small garrisons frequently put up a sturdy and often effective fight, but the prospect of repeated attacks in isolated areas was hard to contemplate without strong mobile reserve forces to support them. Such forces would be created later in the year, but by then the traditional policing structure had been swept away, and in many areas the only viable police activity took the form of fairly strong patrols from central barracks.

At the end of January 1920 the army launched an intensive programme of raids and arrests – which it thought were 'the first arrests by military authority', under Defence of the Realm Regulation (DORR) 55 – using police intelligence information. The results, according to the GOC, included 'the capture of most valuable documents from which the organization of the Irish Volunteer Army has been deduced'. It was recognized to be 'a very powerful organization'. Large numbers of its members were arrested: by mid-April 317 had been arrested and 250 interned. Hundreds were deported under DORR 14B, including twenty-seven brigade and sixteen battalion commandants. The biggest contingent of deportees by far were from Cork (eighty-three), Tipperary (forty-one) and Limerick (twenty-one); twenty went from Dublin, fifteen from Clare, nine from Kerry and one from Longford.[59] This military surge initially seemed to seize the initiative from the republicans. But, as the army later admitted, 'many of the raids and searches carried out during this period were . . . somewhat aimless.' The impact on Volunteer operations of the military offensive was disappointing: apart from a brief drop in late March, the totals of 'Sinn Féin outrages' (as classified by the police) went on climbing as the year progressed.

The core problem was that the programme of arrests made clear 'how completely the RIC service of information was paralysed'. 'The lack of information made success very difficult.' The information supplied to the army was sketchy, 'the police lists were out of date and to them every Sinn Féin club was a battalion.' They had made no attempt to construct what the army would call the 'order of battle' – that is, the unit structure – of the Volunteers, and it was up to military intelligence to identify the military status of individuals listed for arrest.[60] At this point the army realized that it would have to construct its own full-scale intelligence system, something that would take months if not years. But, as the GOC observed, even if the policy of arrests was hampered by defective intelligence, 'no other course is possible'[61] – apart, that is, from restrictions on movement, and curfews: in Dublin, from 23 February, no 'civilian' was allowed outside their home from midnight to 5 a.m.

The speed and completeness with which the RIC was neutralized should not be exaggerated. The situation was obviously difficult: in May 1920 there were still many isolated rural stations with garrisons 'so small that they were practically confined to their own immediate neighbourhood by day, and to their barracks by night'. Supporting them was a headache for the army, which had no spare wireless equipment and no trained wireless personnel, a problem that would persist throughout the conflict.[62] Intimidation of the families of policemen reached a peak in the spring and summer of 1920: some 70 per cent of the 280 recorded threats, sometimes oral but usually written (certainly an underestimate, since successful threats were not likely to be reported), were made between March and October.[63] Yet republicans still mostly held back from direct confrontation, and the police (as some of the tenacious barrack defences in early 1920, notably at Kilmallock, showed) were not as demoralized as many have assumed. Though resignations increased, a slight but noticeable surge in recruitment within Ireland indicated that the force had some hope of holding on even as it became more embattled. But British policy did not come to its rescue. Britain had already undermined the Irish party, its main Irish political ally, by delaying Home Rule. Now it effectively undermined its own 'army of occupation'. It did this in two ways: first by turning the police into something much more like the 'army' of nationalist propaganda than the old RIC had ever in reality been; and second by political steps that multiplied the force's pessimism and removed the restraints on its behaviour.

The dangers of militarizing the Irish police remained clear even after Joseph Byrne's removal. But by the spring of 1920 the process had achieved a momentum that proved irreversible. Oddly enough, this happened in spite of the government's clear determination to rein back the power of the Viceroy himself, the man most directly committed to the expansion of the police by recruitment in Britain. The military surge of January–March proved to be General Shaw's last hurrah. To French's dismay he was replaced in April by a new military commander, General Sir Nevil Macready, accompanied by a new chief secretary, Sir Hamar Greenwood. Greenwood insisted that the traditional primacy of the

Chief Secretary be restored. A group of key civil servants were transferred from Whitehall to Dublin Castle, to beef up what Disraeli had once called 'the weakest executive in the world'. Ironically, this was a response to French's own criticism of the Irish Executive, especially of the Under Secretary, Sir James MacMahon – 'quite estranged from all of us owing to his violently Catholic leanings'. (French had effectively cut MacMahon out of the Castle decision-making process in 1919.)

Sir Warren Fisher, the head of the UK civil service, who arrived to audit the administration in early May, reported witheringly that 'the Castle administration does not administer.' What he called the 'mechanical side', which had never been good, was now 'quite obsolete'; in the still more vital sphere of policy formation 'it simply has no existence.' The real answer to the problem, he hinted, was to combine the civil and military command (a rather unBritish idea that prefigured some later set-ups, such as Malaya after the Second World War). Macready, he thought, was 'admirably equipped to play the dual role of Under Secretary and GOC'. But this notion was too radical to implement. Instead Fisher proposed sending a 'powerful civil servant' to get the administration in order. He picked the outstanding official of his generation, Sir John Anderson, who joined Macready in Dublin on 22 May, bringing with him a hand-picked group of London officials headed by the former excise detective 'Andy' Cope as assistant under secretary. Interestingly, Anderson's predecessor MacMahon was kept in post (apparently to avoid the political effects of sacking a Catholic). The odd arrangement of having two under secretaries might well have made the chaos in the Castle even worse, but MacMahon – already sidelined – evidently accepted his ornamental role.

Macready was a significant choice as commander-in-chief because he had unique experience of internal crisis management. He had commanded the troops during the miners' strike in South Wales in 1910, had been selected as the possible military governor of Belfast at the height of the Ulster crisis in 1914, and had run the strike-afflicted London Metropolitan Police after the war.[64] He was put in place as a 'political general' in the good sense, a soldier with a 'civilian mind' and an alertness to public opinion. But when he arrived in Dublin his first reactions compromised his whole mission. He told Walter Long that within a few hours he was 'honestly flabbergasted at the administrative chaos that seems to reign here'. Unfortunately for those who wanted him to take up joint command of the army and the police (a limited version of Fisher's proposed civil–military union), he decided that the police were past saving. He turned down the double appointment, but then could not get his own preferred candidate to take the job as head of the police. What followed was a damaging divergence between the two arms of the Crown forces that would become more serious over the next year.

Macready also lost influence over the recasting of the police. The first British RIC recruits were already present in some numbers, but distributed across the country in small groups to reinforce individual barrack garrisons. The new chief of police, Major General Hugh Tudor, a friend of the War Secretary, Winston Churchill, supplied the regular RIC with much more military equipment – replacing their traditional carbines with rifles, for instance – but he also planned to set up a separate, special counter-insurgency force. The higher military authorities, including the Chief of the Imperial General Staff, Sir Henry Wilson, were horrified at the idea (which may in fact have come from Churchill himself) of creating a 'gendarmerie' for Ireland recruited from ex-soldiers – a 'panic measure of raising 8,000 scallywags'. 'I can't imagine what sort of officers and NCOs we can get,' Wilson wrote in his diary. 'I can't imagine what sort the men will be, no one will know anybody, no discipline, no esprit de corps, no cohesion, no training . . .'

Wilson somehow got the impression that Macready himself wanted to 'draft these mobs over to Ireland at once & split them up into lots of 25 to 50 men over the country so there would be no hope of forming & disciplining this crowd of unknown men'. ('It is truly a desperate & hopeless expedient,' he fumed, which was 'bound to fail'.)[65] In fact he was quite wrong about Macready, who took exactly the same view as he did. Macready chaired a War Office committee that met at the same time Wilson was raging, and pointed out that police discipline would be 'too weak in the circumstances now prevailing in Ireland' to control the kind of men they were expecting to recruit, who would 'need the strictest discipline'. It proposed to create eight 'garrison battalions', which could be deployed only within the UK, but which would be under full military discipline. Though the Cabinet was uneasy about this proposal on political grounds – 'it would be represented as the beginning of a reconquest of Ireland' – it was never definitively turned down, but it disappeared into a kind of administrative limbo. A month later, Tudor was able to head it off with the argument that 'the formation of ex-soldier battalions would probably militate against recruiting for the RIC.'[66] His contention that it was far better to 'very largely increase the RIC' chimed with Churchill's ideas, and he was eventually able to set up a force according to his own recipe. This would become ADRIC, the Auxiliary Division of the RIC.

Tudor's appointment was as 'police adviser' (presumably to the Irish Executive, though this was never exactly clear). Eventually – when the last Inspector General was finally retired – the inspector generalship was placed in commission and he adopted the title 'chief of police', whose unEnglish ring said much about Tudor's assumptions and policy. The government clearly wanted to rein back French's power, but in Tudor it provided a full-blooded enthusiast for French's long-held belief that the police must be stiffened for the fight against 'Sinn Féin'.

'YOUR COUNTRY SUFFERS FROM CANCER'

British policy contained a fatal contradiction. It was committed to Irish self-government, but it required that the Irish people follow British rules of constitutional behaviour. It rested on the assumption that the great majority of Irish people remained law-abiding moderates, who would accept a Home Rule settlement that fell far short of independence. Militant opposition was dismissed as extremist – the Volunteers were always described as fanatics, gunmen or thugs. Even those who took the 'Volunteer Army' more seriously assumed (like the GOC in March) that the arrest of its leaders would cripple it. Yet little was done to encourage moderate nationalists. Thus the new Home Rule measure, intended to set up two separate Irish parliaments in Dublin and Belfast, was not launched until February 1920, and then pushed slowly through parliament as the year wore on. Key provisions such as the size of the area to be governed by the Northern Parliament had not been decided until the last moment. There was no sense of urgency, because the government held that a 'return to constitutionalism' was a vital precondition for the concession of Home Rule, even in the restricted, partitionist form of the 1920 Government of Ireland Bill.

Britain's fourth attempt at a Home Rule measure was a sad admission of its inability either to find a way through the impasse created by unionist resistance or to give definite shape to the proposed devolution. The fact of partition, giving the six north-eastern counties equal status with the other twenty-six, was a heavier blow to nationalist expectations than anything considered possible before 1916. But the powers to be conceded to the Irish parliaments were also disappointing. Early drafts of the bill restricted them so sharply that even the Cabinet recognized that the new parliaments would be little more than glorified local councils. The 'reserved services', to remain under Westminster control, included not just defence and foreign policy, judiciary and income tax, but also postal services, transport, agriculture and health. There was a striking novelty in the new bill, the provision for a Council of Ireland, a device seemingly designed to encourage the two parliaments to unite. If they co-operated to form such a joint Council, it would be given enlarged powers – notably over the judiciary, post and income tax. But not many people took this prospect very seriously, and with some reason. Ministers had grumbled that conceding such powers would give Ireland something akin to Dominion status – and that 'had never been contemplated'.[67] Yet Dominion status (the favoured model was Canada) was by now, almost certainly, the minimum concession that constitutional nationalists could hope to sell to their voters. In effect, Britain was proposing a measure of conciliation which could be imposed only by coercion.

The authorities in Ireland may have dimly grasped that the task of crushing extremism without antagonizing the moderates on whom the viability of the Home Rule policy rested might be difficult, if not indeed impossible. Certainly Warren Fisher recognized how faulty the measures of the previous year had been. He deplored the blanket ban on Sinn Féin and Dáil Éireann, and the failure to distinguish between Sinn Féin and the violent activists – 'as if retired warriors and dowager ladies who denounce socialism in England were to secure the banning of the Labour Party'. Sinn Féin was a political party 'however much people may dislike it'; if parties were required to have programmes containing 'nothing anathema to people of different political complexions, then I can't imagine any party which ever could be recognised'. Military and police methods were just as faulty as political policy – no better than 'blind hitting out'. Fisher thought only Macready himself was opposed to the use of indiscriminate violence.[68]

This fierce critique delivered by the state's top official was more or less ignored. Hamar Greenwood as chief secretary proved energetic but less politically alert than the new military commander. As a Canadian – like the press magnate Lord Beaverbrook only without the ability – he supplied a useful transatlantic gloss to the government, but beyond that he offered little. His style did not work with the senior civil servants at the Castle, notably Anderson himself, who was all too conscious of his own intellectual superiority. They quietly hoped that his more intelligent (and socially acceptable) wife would influence him. He was described by one of the officials who came over with Anderson as a man of 'one idea at a time'. Some have thought this meant that he was 'incapable of handling more than one idea at a time', though in fact it was a New Liberal nostrum which called for policy to be tightly focused.[69] (Irish Home Rule had once been the Liberals' 'one idea'.) Greenwood did strike some as a crude thinker, but Anderson's assistant, the perceptive Mark Sturgis, who at first thought him a 'play actor', came to see him as 'much more than that', even if he lacked the 'instinctive' grasp of things that his wife had. Greenwood was well aware of the need, in principle, to hold some balance between coercion and conciliation, but in practice he concentrated on the restoration of order. His monument in Ireland would be a law bearing that title.

It was certainly an odd situation where the head of the civil government was a greater believer in the effectiveness of force than the head of the army. Macready was not just against 'indiscriminate violence', he was deeply pessimistic about the viability of any repressive policy. Much as he might try to humour the hawkish Henry Wilson, Chief of the Imperial General Staff – and an aggressively unionist Ulsterman – their views were basically opposed. 'In one sense you are right in saying we must go deeper down, and hit harder, before we get to the root of the matter,' Macready wrote in May 1920. 'But I feel very strongly that your country suffers from cancer, and though you may operate severely upon it, it grows again in worse form later.' For him, the only possible 'cure' was political; 'drastic measures would leave a fresh wound on the already scarred body of this blooming island of yours.' Characteristically, though, he added a hesitant gloss: 'whether it is your business or mine to look ahead, or only to do our blind duty, I am not quite sure.'[70]

Macready's first experience in Dublin was a serious crisis. The hunger strike of republican prisoners in Mountjoy gaol launched on 5 April created an electric public atmosphere. The strike, led by Peadar Clancy, vice-commandant of the Dublin Brigade, demanded that DORA intern-ees should be treated as prisoners of war – an issue skilfully chosen by the propaganda chief Frank Gallagher. They called for 'proper' food, separation from 'criminals', no compulsory work, access to books, a weekly bath and the right to smoke as well as to have five hours' exer-cise in the open air each day. The term 'political prisoner' was to be applied to all those convicted of unlawful assembly, possession of arms, drilling and making seditious speeches.[71] The strikers turned down an offer of 'ameliorative' treatment, and by 9 April ninety men were on hunger strike. Two days later Mountjoy's medical officer warned the Castle that fatalities were imminent. The pressure was intense; and the potential impact of any deaths was certainly not underestimated. Sir Edward Troup, the top Home Office official, had reacted to a threat-ened hunger strike in Wormwood Scrubs prison by warning the Home Secretary that if any prisoner died 'his death will be made an excuse for the attempted murder of Ministers in this country.' (In spite of this, the government had stood firm against concessions there.) On 13 April the Irish party MP T. P. O'Connor brusquely told the House of Commons that Thomas Ashe's death on hunger strike was 'the reason we have seven representatives here today instead of 77'. The Cabinet lectured the authorities in Dublin that 'if these men die one by one, there will be an outcry in this country which will become exceedingly dangerous.' Its predictable conclusion was that 'if we were then forced to make any change the effect ... would be much worse than if a change were made now.'

Thousands (on 12 April the army estimated 5,000, the police 10,000) of keening women surrounded the prison; scuffles with the troops on guard outside became menacing. 'The futility of committing troops to hold back such a crowd ... was soon obvious.' Improvised barricades 'were soon trodden down by the leading ranks of the crowd being pressed forward from behind; even tanks were no obstacle.' The army turned to the desperate expedient of having aircraft buzz the crowds on the 13th – despite a 50 mph gale – one 'flew along a broad street below the eaves of the houses'. Even the use of Lewis machine-gun fire from the air seems to have been considered.[72] That day Dublin was paralysed by a one-day labour strike. French, who had dismissed the demand for prisoner-of-war status as absolutely unacceptable, was driven by the

Cabinet's logic to concede it, only to be confronted with the demand for the release of all the hunger strikers. Next day, sixty-six men were certified as being in 'immediate danger', and, though later experience would suggest that this was unlikely, French and Macready – knowing that the government was rattled – decided to release them on parole. The official who wrote the release order failed to note that half the parolees, as sentenced men rather than internees, were 'in no case entitled to be released on parole', as Bonar Law helplessly explained to parliament.[73] The error delivered a dramatic republican triumph and a correspondingly staggering blow to the morale of the forces of order. The military programme of searches and arrests since January, whose impact had been steadily growing, was thrown into reverse. Military and police 'secret service' agents were 'virtually driven off the streets, owing to those whom they had arrested now being free, and in many cases able to identify' them. Imminent republican defeat 'was turned into unqualified victory'.[74] Its impact on the behaviour of the police would be far-reaching.

'THROTTLING THE RAILWAY SYSTEM'

Republican resistance was supported, at one remove at least, by industrial action. Meeting on 20 May, a group of Dublin quayside workers declared that they would not handle 'certain war material' being brought into Ireland. Shortly afterwards the dockers at Kingstown (Dun Laoghaire) refused to unload a freighter, the *Polberg*. The cargo had to be taken off by troops – and was then left at the docks when the railwaymen there refused to take it on. (It eventually turned out not to be munitions, but tins of bully beef.) This action was not, officially at least, initiated by the Irish labour leadership, which carefully avoided direct engagement in the republican campaign. Though Tom Johnson had played a leading part in the anti-conscription movement, and produced the original draft of the Dáil's Democratic Programme, the ILP/TUC and its affiliated unions did not recognize the Dáil government. To be able to go on negotiating for their members, they could not risk British retaliation. Nora Connolly, who took a dim view of Johnson's and William O'Brien's (and even Cathal O'Shannon's) neutralism, snorted that 'building up the bureaucracy of the ITGWU ... seemed to be all that mattered' to them.[75]

The transport workers' action revealed the limits of organized labour's revolutionary ideas. The Irish Transport and General Workers' Union (ITGWU) certainly supported them, instructing all its members to back the embargo. But the railwaymen's own union, the London-based National Union of Railwaymen, took a different line. When the railwaymen appealed to the NUR for support, citing the embargo imposed on munitions exports to Poland by British workers as part of the 'Hands off Russia' campaign, the NUR Executive – 'up against a very difficult test case of the use of the strike for political purposes', as one journal put it – urged them to go back to work while it negotiated with the government. No strike funds were released. By early June, railwaymen at the North Wall alone had lost over £5,000 in wages, while barely £100 had come into the Munitions of War Fund launched by the ILP/TUC. (One local magistrate noted with exasperation that month, however, that even 'Government Officials have given large sums to the Munitions Strike Fund.')

Although railwaymen offered to work normally on all trains not carrying armed troops, police or munitions – so technically were not on strike – the railway companies responded by dismissing all those who had taken part in the embargo: over a thousand were out of work by August. The result was a large number of immobilized trains, as the action spread across Ireland (apart from Belfast) in June. Troops and police were ordered to stay on trains until they were moved, even though Irish Command was unhappy at being forced 'to have recourse to such undignified methods', on the principle that if they could not move, nor could anyone else. Unfortunately, as Anderson reported on 26 July, there were simply not enough of them to 'bring things to a standstill', and 'at the present rate, we shall be broken sooner than the railway companies.'[76] Next month the Cabinet was told that, although some 1,000 railwaymen had been dismissed, dismissals were now 'being conducted in a half-hearted manner, and there was no doubt that the officials and men were being subjected to intimidation'. The idea of closing lines down one by one was mooted, but found to be too expensive since the government would still have to 'make up the [companies'] receipts under guarantee'.[77] Instead it racked up the pressure on the companies by threatening to withdraw their subsidies, for failing in their obligations as 'common carriers'.[78]

It seemed obvious to republicans as well as unionists that the transport workers had, as the *Irish Times* fumed, 'declared [their] alliance with those endeavouring to institute an Irish Republic'. The Dáil contributed £5,000 to the Munitions of War Fund, and Sinn Féin instructed all its branches to organize collections, which helped to boost the fund eventually to some £120,000. Funds were also raised locally to support dismissed railwaymen – as at Carrick-on-Suir where a committee collected around £2,000.[79] The Volunteers, who clearly saw the military as well as the propaganda value of the embargo, weighed in with direct action. In some places they provided alternative transport for civilian passengers stuck on immobilized trains. A sharp-eyed foreign observer of the situation saw this happen at Dundrum, where he shared the platform with 'three RIC with a sergeant, forty infantrymen in full war equipment under an officer', waiting for a train. When the train arrived, 'the four policemen get into a compartment – the guard gets out of the van.' While a bystander took the guard to the bar for a drink, 'a young man with nothing about him to indicate his importance, save the instant obedience which he commands – he is the commandant of the local volunteers – exerts himself to make order out of chaos, regulates the despatch of the passengers, women first, to the nearby town of Tipperary. Side cars and motors have been procured, and each individual goes off in his turn, as he is told . . .' His counterpart took no interest in all this: 'All the time, in the background, beside the fixed bayonets, the British officer stands against the wall, inactive, ignored, inexistant and seemingly bored.'[80]

The army was keen to strike back at this republican mobility by imposing a counter-embargo on motor fuel, but the Cabinet would not agree. 'Although . . . the IRA were commandeering cars and lorries freely for moving about the country, we were unable to stop them from getting petrol.' The Volunteers went beyond the provision of relief transport. Their encouragement often took the negative form of intimidation, 'pour encourager les autres'. Although the notice allegedly sent to railwaymen in the name of the 'Government of the Irish Republic', forbidding them to 'assist in any way, the transport of armed forces of the English Government', was possibly a forgery – it was signed 'Ministry of War', a British rather than republican title – there is no doubt that a policy of this kind was implemented.[81] The Chairman of the Great Northern Railway reported that 'generally speaking, the staff know that

it is safer to refuse to work government traffic than to do their duty.'
The IV Cavan Brigade (whose area did not contain any major rail lines)
reported that 'on three occasions' drivers who had replaced dismissed
men 'were arrested and tried by courtmartial', and usually given 'a fine
of £10 with the necessary unde ʰaking not to drive the ℬritish Forces
again'. The third man so arrestᵉd, an engine driver named McGuigan,
who 'refused to pay the fine imposed and give the necessary undertaking', was 'held in custody for some days'.[82] Likewise in Cork, in the 'few
instances where some weaklings refused to obey the call of the "Munition Strike" ... they were severely dealt with'. Blacklegs were arrested
and released only when they signed a declaration that they would not
reoffend.[83] Some drivers who – whether for political reasons or simply
to save their jobs – drove troop trains were tarred and feathered.

Macready took a glum view of all this: 'no amount of Martial Law
or any other form of repression will make the men drive the trains, and
if we put them all in prison, I fancy there will be more than the prisons
over here can hold.' All in all, he thought it 'a little difficult to see where
it will eventually end'.[84] In late September Greenwood told the Cabinet
that the situation had hardly improved over the last two months: 'the
Irish Government is very seriously embarrassed by the denial of the use
of the railways, and its position is humiliating and discreditable.'[85] Publicly, the government maintained that the railwaymen were 'bitterly
opposed' to the action, 'but such are the methods of intimidation
employed by the Republicans that they have no option.' Privately, it
stepped up the policy of 'throttling the railway system'. Mark Sturgis
was put in charge of a small committee set up by the Minister of Transport, Eric Geddes, to control this. They even experimented with putting
up bogus military stores to widen the stoppage still further, but soon
abandoned this reckless stratagem. Otherwise, there does not seem to
have been much substance to the 'Geddes–Greenwood Plot' to starve
Ireland into submission, reported in dramatic terms by the mainstream
nationalist press.[86]

On 9 November a meeting between the railwaymen's leaders and a
group of TDs looked, to Sturgis, like a sign that the workers' resistance
was crumbling. 'We're on top and I'm sure they know it.' In fact, the
rate of stoppages was still increasing sharply, peaking in the week ending 20 November. But at the National Labour Conference at the Dublin

Mansion House that week there was plenty of depressing realism on display. Though a Derry representative insisted that 'in the North they would carry the foodstuffs in their bare feet on their backs through the country rather than give in,' the representative of the Broadstone men said there would soon be over 15,000 railwaymen out of work, and supporting them was simply impossible. They 'would never be found wanting in their duty to their beloved country', but 'were not going to be content with false talk about fighting on when they knew in their heart and soul that they could not'. Others warned of the wider effects of a total paralysis of the rail system, suggesting that over 100,000 could be put out of work. 'Mock heroics' could not keep them alive. Tom Johnson issued the grimmest warning, that fighting on could risk 'throwing back the social life of Ireland by a hundred years'.

But he also made the moral case for the strike in passionate terms that transcended 'mock heroics'. Refusing to do work of 'an abominable kind' was part of a wider social struggle – asserting 'that as workmen they had a right to be conscious co-operators in the end that was being sought . . . not merely cogs in the machine, but human beings'. Cathal O'Shannon argued that it was a model of popular resistance, a 'new weapon' against which 'all the tanks, the machine guns, the "Black and Tans" and all their bombs, cannot in the end win out'. For others, the issue was a purely moral one: the men 'were not waging this fight because they had a chance of success, but because they were right'.[87]

The conference voted almost unanimously to keep up the embargo. But pressures to abandon it were mounting, notably in the mainstream nationalist press. On 15 December the ILP/TUC Executive issued a statement that 'the British authority which assumes governmental power in Ireland' had deliberately undermined the plans drawn up to maintain food supplies and transport in the event of a total shutdown of the rail system. 'They have seized the papers and records of our Food Committee, have arrested and imprisoned without charge the members of these committees, and have placed a barrier against the organisation of the motor transport service for the distribution of fuel supplies.' Two days later a party of armed troops was carried for the first time on the Great Southern and Western Railway. On 21 December the railwaymen met at the Mansion House and voted unanimously for an unconditional return to normal working.[88]

'IT WOULD BE DIFFICULT TO SHAKE THEIR BELIEF IN THE REALITY OF A REPUBLIC'

The summer of 1920 was a crunch moment for the government. The positive appeal of the republican courts, coupled with systematic intimidation of jurors and witnesses by the Volunteers, brought the British court system 'virtually to a standstill', as Sir John Anderson told the Cabinet on 25 July. In Monaghan, for instance, both magistrates and witnesses failed to turn up for petty sessions, and the summer assizes were adjourned when one plaintiff abandoned his case, explaining that 'his life would not be worth very much' if he persisted.[89] (Direct threats were usually unnecessary: the general apprehension was enough.) Litigants were turned away by republican pickets; prospective jurors received notices that obeying the summons to attend Crown courts would 'be considered an act of treason against the Irish Republic'. By August, over 300 magistrates had resigned, either out of patriotism or out of fear.[90] The failure of the Summer Assizes represented, for Britain, a massive blow to the state's legitimacy. Combined with the outcome of the county council elections, it could only be read as proof of the failure of British policy up to this point.

'Everybody is yielding to Sinn Féin whether they approve of it or not,' a Mayo resident magistrate reported. 'They say they can do nothing else, and that the Government cannot or will not protect them, and the police can barely protect themselves.' Republican police 'patrol the town wearing the badge inscribed "Irish Republican Army" on their sleeves. They have been regulating the supply of flour ... questioning people as to their movements, and regulating the control of licensed premises.' In Galway 'Sinn Féin activities have brought about almost a revolution in local affairs.' In Leitrim 'even loyal people are asking for republican permits and attending Republican courts.' And though a Clare resident magistrate reported 'considerable annoyance at the rate levied by Sinn Féin (6d in the £) from householders for the payment of their police', in Roscommon the republican courts seemed to have 'impressed the people to such an extent with the power of Dáil Éireann that it would be difficult to shake their belief in the reality of a Republic'.[91]

An almost random incident rammed home this reversal of power.

On 26 June the commander of the 17th Infantry Brigade in Fermoy, Brigadier General Cuthbert Lucas, was kidnapped by the Cork No. 2 Brigade. He was on a fishing trip with two of his staff colonels, when the fishing lodge was stormed by a Volunteer group led by the brigade's top officers – Liam Lynch, Seán Moylan and George Power. The motive may have been, as Moylan later wrote, to cut the British officer class down to size – 'pull them down and see what made them tick'; or, as Lynch seems to have thought, to trade them for republican prisoners. Either way, the effect was dramatic, especially in London, where Churchill ordered a large-scale 'drive' to find Lucas, overriding Macready's protest that this might endanger the general.

Macready had wanted to 'arrest six men who were reported to be leading members of the Cork No. 2 Brigade IRA and lock them up until Lucas was forthcoming'. But 'the civil and legal element' had argued that they had no evidence of the personal involvement of the men, and – perhaps more significantly – 'if they went on hunger strike and were allowed to die, we should be reverting to the former policy of interning untried and uncharged men.' Henry Wilson fumed that Churchill and the Cabinet treated the capture of Lucas 'as some sort of joke', and utterly failed to grasp what needed to be done. 'To drive Munster is a childish expedient' – the only way out was 'to declare war on the Sinn Feins'. (Struggling to find eight extra battalions to reinforce Macready, he added that 'if we had 80 instead of 8 the present policy would make the presence of 135 battalions a useless waste of money.' Having 100 to 150 detachments scattered across the country, 'rolling a few soldiers around in 3-ton lorries' while allowing the Sinn Féin courts to operate, he pronounced 'an absolute waste of time'.)[92] Churchill certainly suggested that Lucas had only himself to blame for his 'carelessness', which had put Britain's prestige on the line. When the drive, and all later search efforts, failed, the government's sense of frustrated powerlessness was palpable. This was indeed 'a sensation', as the *New York Times* reported, and shockingly bad publicity.

Lucas himself was well treated, and was distinctly impressed that his captors had the power to allow him regular mail deliveries – as well as plenty of whisky, tennis and regular walks, on one of which he eventually made a dash for it. Seen from the other side, the incident revealed the limits of the republican machinery. Capturing the British officers turned out to be the easy part; simply moving them by car from the fishing lodge allowed them the chance of an escape attempt (planned by Lucas and Colonel Danford speaking, apparently, in Arabic) resulting in a violent fight. Though Lucas was successfully shuttled twice between Limerick and Clare, after a month looking after him and providing constant security became a heavy burden, effectively shutting down the normal operations of the unit responsible for him. As it became clear that the government would not negotiate for his release, the Volunteers faced the choice of killing him – an option they seem never to have entertained – or letting him go. In the end, as Michael Brennan's account shows, they made no effort to stop him escaping.[93]

With its authority collapsing, the British government faced a choice between stepping up repressive measures and making significant political concessions. Anderson came out unambiguously in favour of a 'Dominion Home Rule' offer, suggesting that there could well be no alternative 'not foredoomed to failure'. Indeed the whole new Castle administration, together with the Irish Law Adviser, William Wylie, formed a kind of 'peace party' urging an immediate political settlement. Once again the government preferred to ignore the advice of its top officials. But it now had to face the unwelcome fact that the shelf life of its prime repressive legal device, the Defence of the Realm Act, had expired. It was a war emergency law that was supposed to lapse at the end of hostilities – just as the Home Rule Act was supposed to come into force. The old Crimes Act was being used to create Special Military Areas, which allowed the authorities to control movement and ban public events, but without DORA it would be impossible to go on interning republican prisoners. If there was to be any move to use military courts to stand in for the crippled legal system, it would need new legislation – unless martial law was to be declared, as French had long urged. Ministers toyed with this option once again, but still found its political costs too high. As Macready told Greenwood in mid-July, 'I do not for one instant think that the British public would stand for Martial Law for one week over here.'[94] Instead, the optimistically named Restoration of Order in Ireland Act (ROIA), rushed through parliament in the first week of August, merely retitled the well-known DORA regulations. (So DORR 14B, allowing internment without trial, became ROIR 14B.)

The justification for these emergency powers, instead of DORA's 'public order and the defence of the realm', became the 'restoration or maintenance of order in Ireland'.[95] Like so many of the special coercive laws passed under the Union over the previous century, it confirmed Ireland's separateness from British norms. Along with the headline powers like trial by court martial, the Act suspended normal inquests involving coroners' juries of the kind that had brought in verdicts of murder against the government in the Mac Curtain case. The Military Courts of Inquiry in Lieu of Inquest which replaced them were supposed to consist of two officers with a president 'not under the rank of field offi-cer' (that is, a major or colonel), except when one was not available – 'with due regard to the interests of the public service' – in which case a captain would suffice. This proved quite often to be the case, as did a failure to display the 'ordinary diligence' enjoined on them in taking evidence. As a result the courts of inquiry, which became known as 'courts of acquittal', did little to deflect public suspicion that the Crown forces were at the very least trigger-happy. Over the following months they would consider the deaths of 182 policemen and 463 civilians, 233 of whom they would find to have been killed 'by Forces of the Crown in the execution of their duty'. Of these, seventy-eight had failed to halt when ordered to, and thirty had attempted to escape after arrest. Eventually one court sug-gested that 'in serious cases of arrest [sic] the prisoner should be at once handcuffed or otherwise secured, so . . . obviating the need for shooting,' but this was a rarity.[96] There were four cases of justifiable homicide, and only two people were found to have been killed illegally.

The ROIA has been described as 'a halfway house towards martial law', but the second part of the journey was much more sticky than the first.[97] Political resistance to martial law was deeply entrenched, as we have seen, and this step would never be taken except in a limited and circumscribed way. While the Cabinet jibbed at extending wartime legislation into supposed peacetime, the army would pronounce ROIA procedures 'too slow and cumbrous to be really effective against a whole population in rebellion'[98] (a situation, of course, that the govern-ment preferred to deny). Still, the Act had dramatic effects on the republican campaign, even if the most important of them were unin-tended. By widening the use of military courts, it returned the army to the forefront of the counter-insurgency effort for the first time since April. A new surge was launched, but the army's repertoire of anti-guerrilla methods was still restricted. Henry Wilson's dismissive view of 'drives' said much about the army's limitations. The heightened military pressure resulted not so much in more Volunteers being picked up as in more going 'on the run', and the result, as will be seen, would be a key development in republican military capacity. But on the vital issue of unity of command, the ROIA did not deliver. Outside the army, only Mark Sturgis in Dublin Castle seems to have grasped the importance of this. Early on he argued for a 'dictatorship' or at least a properly constituted war council to direct policy. But it never came. Months later, when Warren Fisher returned to reassess the Irish administration, he too came out for giving supreme power to the military C-in-C, but with no effect. Sturgis was still baffled by the fact that Lloyd George, who had firmly grasped the need for a single command on the western front, could not see 'the absolute necessity for it here'.

As so often in situations of apparent strategic stalemate, the army reached for technological solutions. It looked to speed up its search operations by increasing motor transport, and strengthen patrols by adding armoured cars. But it would never have enough lorries, and many of those it had were already worn out by war service and 'had to be carefully "nursed"'. ('The Disposals Board appeared to have sold all the best vehicles,' the 5th Division believed.)[99] Tanks had already been found to be of little use, and most of the armoured cars were obsolescent. When the new Peerless cars began to arrive in July 1920, they were too heavy (over 7 tons loaded) for any but the best roads – and in anything but fine weather. The best armoured cars, the Rolls-Royces, did not arrive until the beginning of 1921, and then only ten of them for the whole country. The army was forced to rig up its own fighting vehicles by 'up-armouring' its normal tactical lorries.[100]

Was a miracle weapon lurking in the wings? Alongside martial law, the use of aircraft had been one of French's key ideas. It had come to nothing so far, but Macready took it up again in the early autumn, urging that there were 'undoubtedly cases where fire from aeroplanes would materially assist the forces on the ground, with little or no danger to harmless individuals'. This danger, of course, was the key reason why the Cabinet had so far jibbed at the use of aircraft. The C-in-C now suggested that air–ground communications had improved, and that since aircraft could fly much lower in Ireland than they had been able to in France – because there was no risk of anti-aircraft fire – target identification would be easier. He thought that crowds might be fired on, if a warning had been dropped. And echoing French's gleeful notion that air patrolling would 'put the fear of God into these playful young Sinn

Feiners', he opined that 'a few rounds fired from the air would have a great moral effect, even if no casualties were inflicted.'[101]

When Macready's request arrived at the War Office, it was enthusiastically received – 'the Cabinet ought definitely to approve in principle' bomb-dropping and machine-gunning by aircraft in Ireland, a senior member of the general staff thought. But he added, 'I doubt if they will as it is a pretty big proposition.' He was of course right, though this time it was not the politicians but the airmen who scotched the idea. The Chief of Air Staff, Sir Hugh Trenchard, bluntly dismissed 'the policy advocated by the C-in-C' as 'both ineffective and highly dangerous'. Macready's arguments were all wrong, he said: the difference between friendly and hostile people 'would *not* be obvious to a man in an aeroplane', and this 'would lead to endless mistakes'; while as for the idea of dropping warning notices over a crowd, 'I cannot believe that anybody who has had experience of aircraft can believe' it could be done. Worst of all, the 'reckless use of a powerful arm' would lead to 'a great popular outcry against the unfortunate pilots', and 'great bitterness will be engendered.'[102]

Trenchard's alertness to the inaccuracy of air action, and his sensitivity to public opinion in Ireland, certainly diverged from the argument he was pressing in favour of 'air policing' in the Middle East and other parts of the empire at this time.[103] But in both cases they were what the Cabinet wanted to hear – with one exception. Winston Churchill, the Minister responsible for both army and air force, was an enthusiastic supporter of air policing, and indeed may be seen as its primary instigator. He held that aircraft could provide 'great protection to armoured car work on the road and a great deterrent to illegal drilling and rebel gatherings', and put pressure on Trenchard to triple the miserable total of eighteen serviceable machines in Ireland. But amid political and professional resistance a truly effective way of applying this seductive technology remained elusive.[104]

'STAMPING OUT TERRORISM BY SECRET MURDER'

On the morning of his arrival in Dublin on 22 May 1920, Sir John Anderson had a sobering interview with the Inspector General of the RIC, who told him that 'he was in daily fear either of wholesale resignations or of his men running amok.' Either would mean 'the end of the RIC'. The implications were stark. If there were not to be outright military rule, the police must be completely reconstructed. Macready, who judged them 'hopelessly out of date', said that 'as regards the RIC we are sitting on a volcano'. He had no doubt what needed to be done: 'if they were turned into an ordinary unarmed police force,' he told Anderson, 'they would fulfil their functions in time of peace a good deal better than at present.'[105]

The problem was that it was a time neither of peace nor of war – as conventionally understood. On 1 June the newly appointed RIC Divisional Commissioner for Munster submitted a lucid assessment of the state of the country. The people were 'completely terrorised', and 'the situation with the police themselves has been very ticklish.' The police felt 'let down' and 'unsupported', and their complaints were 'hard to find answers to'. He protested that nobody should 'suppose they are frightened – they are not'; but they were hard to hold together. The support that he had been promised would be crucial – if that failed, the situation would be 'beyond retrieving'. At national level the Inspector General reiterated his warning that, as the boycott of the police was still growing, it was 'questionable how much longer the force will stand the strain' without vastly more support.[106]

The kind of support that the police might receive raised some delicate questions. Ministers were clearly looking to provide moral back-up at least. On 22 July Lord Balfour (who had – or believed he had – suppressed the Land War agitation of the 1880s) expressed 'surprise that the military had on all occasions been defeated and that they shot nobody'. Some of his senior colleagues had already, they thought, found a way of overcoming this problem. Earlier that month Henry Wilson was surprised to find the Prime Minister nursing a 'ridiculous belief that Tudor has organised a counter-murder society'; a week later he repeated the same 'amazing theory that Tudor, or someone, was murdering 2 S.F.s to every loyalist the S.F.s murdered'. To Wilson's dismay, Lloyd George 'seemed to be satisfied that a counter-murder Association was the best answer to the S.F.'s murders'.[107] The Munster Divisional Commissioner was evidently already aware of this idea: 'when the support we are promised arrives, we shall know how to employ it in carrying out the policy outlined to me.' The 'main particular' of that policy, he noted with startling candour, was 'the stamping out of terrorism by secret murder'. (Significantly, though, he doubted if this would work: he was 'still of opinion that instant retaliation is the only course'.)[108]

Was a 'counter-murder association' set up? Some such killings had certainly happened, though it is still hard to say how organized they were. A prime example was the assassination of Tomás Mac Curtain, commandant of the Cork No. 1 Brigade and Lord Mayor of Cork, on 19 March 1920. The government claimed that the killers were dissident republicans – a suggestion that may have looked plausible in the light of Mac Curtain's dispute over tactics with the aggressive 'active squad' in his brigade (also known as 'Hegarty's crowd') led by Seán O'Hegarty. Since the local RIC inspector, Oswald Swanzy, was well aware of this split, and saw Mac Curtain as the lesser of the republican evils he faced, killing him was not logical; but there would be plenty of even more illogical police actions in the months to come. The police never troubled to investigate the murder, a fact that is suggestive in itself.[109] Though there was no direct evidence, the coroner's jury brought in a verdict of murder against not only DI Swanzy and 'unknown members of the RIC', but also the Prime Minister, Viceroy, Chief Secretary and Inspector General of the RIC. It may have been somewhat wide of the mark at that point, but the gap would soon close. If Mac Curtain was indeed killed by disguised police (who apparently failed to disguise their 'English accents' – unless these were part of the disguise), the killers were leading the way to the counter-murder policy soon to be approved by General Tudor. A series of night-time assassinations by 'death squads', as they have been called, followed in Cork, Tipperary and Limerick.[110]

The identity of these squads has so far eluded the most careful historical investigation.[111] Republicans certainly believed in their existence as 'associations', and some linked them to Freemasonry, which they saw as a specially diabolical force. Immediately after Mac Curtain's death a *Daily Mail* journalist reported 'a theory gaining ground' that he had fallen 'victim to a new secret Anti Sinn Fein organization modelled and run upon the exact same lines as the famous Ku-Klux-Klan'. The similarity was allegedly 'startling', and 'men best fitted to judge' were predicting 'an ugly triangular duel between the forces of the Crown, Sinn Féin, and private bands of avengers'. Not until July, though, did a grouping calling itself 'the Anti-Sinn Féin organization' carry out an attack (on a schoolteacher in West Cork), and another month elapsed before four Roscommon Volunteer officers received death threats from

'The All Ireland Anti-Sinn Féin Society'. Another two months on, the Mayor of Wexford received a threatening note from the 'Anti-Sinn Féin Society, Wexford Branch'. After that there was a spate of warning notices from either the Anti-Sinn Féin League or the Anti-Sinn Féin Society.[112]

The Cork Volunteers took the Anti-Sinn Féin Society to be, as had been rumoured in April, a vigilante group consisting of prominent local businessmen. Connie Neenan, OC 2nd Battalion, later insisted that 'the Anti-Sinn Féin Society was mostly composed of Protestants who were running businesses in the City'. Whether or not these pillars of the community had really started killing 'Sinn Feiners' by night, the Volunteers set about killing some of them (albeit an odd selection). It seems more likely, though, that the 'Society' was no more than a front for the *sub rosa* action of the new police recruits, some of whom certainly did aim to terrorize those they saw as enemies of the state. Whoever they were, though, their choice of language was significant: it showed that they saw Sinn Féin as the animating spirit of the republican campaign. Of the dynamics of the republican movement they apparently knew, and probably cared, little.

The first British recruits to the RIC went out to stations, after a few weeks' training, in late March. They would rapidly become etched in the popular memory – maybe more deeply than accurately. As stocks of the RIC's bottle-green and black uniform quickly ran out with the sudden expansion, the makeshift use of some khaki military kit led to the new recruits immediately being christened 'Black and Tans'. They were marked out in other ways as well, not only by their speech – their accents surely grated – but also by their stature. The RIC's old 5 foot 9 inch height requirement was dropped by 4 inches, and even if only a small proportion of the new men scraped in at the lower end, they looked different to those accustomed over generations to guardsman-sized police. They were, too, non-Catholics, and – in equally sharp contrast to most of the old RIC – mainly men of the urban working class.

They were enlisted as regular constabulary, but the addition of khaki undoubtedly hinted (even if accidentally) at a quasi-military role. Even after the regular RIC's uniform shortage was cleared up, at the end of 1920, the soubriquet 'Black and Tans' stuck to the British recruits – and maybe to Ulstermen as well. It was extended also to the new temporary force which Tudor began to assemble in August. The RIC Auxiliary

Division, recruited from ex-officers, did not mix police and military uniform, though: it sported purely military battledress and greatcoats, topped off rather oddly with Kilmarnock bonnets (popularly called 'tam-o'-shanters'), in the style of the British army's Scottish regiments. The reason for this particular symbolic choice remains obscure. The harp badge they wore was the only item that identified the 'Auxies' as having any connection at all with the RIC. The second generation of Black and Tans neither looked like police nor behaved like them.

It has usually been assumed that it was the arrival of these new, battle-hardened reinforcements that triggered the upsurge of counter-terror in late 1920. In Leitrim, the RIC 'had become remarkably quiet and were practically doing no duty' up to that time, but then many of them 'became just as aggressive as the Tans or Auxies'.[113] Indeed as the summer crisis of authority deepened, the constabulary had shown signs of wanting to opt out of the repressive campaign altogether. One of them, Timothy Brennan, the member for Leinster on the RIC Representative Body, circulated 2,000 pamphlets urging his comrades to support Dominion Home Rule and refuse to carry arms on duty. He was brought to Dublin Castle to face Anderson's deputy Andy Cope ('assisted' by the Inspector General, according to Mark Sturgis, who was also there). When he refused to repudiate his circular, or even agree to 'take a good responsible position in another country', they remonstrated with him, the Inspector General protesting, 'You will destroy the Force and leave the men with families with nothing to live on.'[114]

Significantly, though, they did no more than remonstrate. Sturgis noted that the seriousness of the problem was 'slightly lessened' by the fact that Leinster was the quietest part of the country, but as he wryly added, 'if it spreads, a bonny job to start Coercion by having to coerce the RIC . . .'[115] The crisis of authority in the country was echoed within the RIC itself, once ruled with an iron hand. The most startling manifestation of this unravelling was the mutiny launched in Listowel, Co. Kerry by Constable Jeremiah Mee and a few of his comrades. After forcing the abandonment of a small post by refusing to garrison it (in protest against the behaviour of the Black and Tan reinforcements there), in mid-June the group went on to refuse to obey orders transferring them to other stations. On his own account, Mee put the issue to his comrades in terms of deciding 'whether we are going to be on the British side or the Irish side, since neutrality will be out of the question'.

(Somewhat inconsistently, but in line with the pessimism by now ingrained in the force, he added that since the RIC would suffer whichever side won, they should make 'a stand against being involved in the conflict' at all.) The garrison agreed to refuse to hand over their barrack to the army as ordered.

This mutiny duly brought a visit from first the County Inspector (CI) and then, on 19 June, no less than the Police Adviser himself, accompanied by two of his new divisional commissioners. Their approach to the mutineers spoke volumes. On Mee's account, at least, instead of berating them – much less threatening them with punishment – the Munster Commissioner, Gerald Smyth, tried to ginger them up by promising them much greater freedom of action against the republicans. Martial law would soon be declared, and the police would be able to shoot suspicious characters on sight; 'the more you shoot, the better I will like you, and I assure you that no policeman will get into trouble for shooting any man.' (For this he was assassinated the following month.) Failing to persuade the men to agree to their transfers, the posse of commanders eventually retired, leaving the mutineers in possession of the barrack.[116] The reaction of the RIC chiefs to defiance was unprecedented, but – presumably not for this reason – the Listowel mutiny failed to spread.[117] Mee himself may have gone too far, in his comrades' eyes, in pushing them towards absolute disengagement. He even tried (without telling most of them) to make contact with the republican leadership in Dublin, to secure some support for the mutiny – without result. He was aware that most would still have regarded this as 'treachery', and it is clear that whatever the pressures on it the force's *esprit de corps* remained stronger than the British authorities feared. RIC men generally wanted to keep their heads down, and do their best to get on with the job of being policemen. A few, though, certainly reacted much more positively to Commissioner Smyth's exhortation.

'THE NIGHT CAN SWEAT WITH TERROR'

The stresses on the force had become barely tolerable by this time. They stemmed partly from the threat of violence, partly from social pressure. Overall police casualty figures were not excessively heavy by military standards – deaths and injuries ran at around 10 per cent. But policemen actually caught up in fighting suffered much higher casualties – 24 per cent were killed and 42 per cent wounded – and even the lower figure was of course quite dramatic for a civil police force, which is what the majority of the RIC perceived it to be.[118] Moreover, before the casualty list began to lengthen in 1920 the boycott had set adrift most of the normal bearings of life for rural policemen. Where the boycott was applied systematically, it actually threatened them with starvation and left them no option but to take supplies by force. Shopkeepers would not serve them, but would watch while policemen took goods and left money on the counter; in pubs they would pull themselves pints and sit and drink them in silence. Whether goods were taken actually or metaphorically at gunpoint, the experience was utterly destructive of the traditional role of the policeman.

The boycott seems to have intensified in the summer, pressed more directly by the Volunteers. Early in June a GHQ general order instructed Volunteers to 'stimulate and support' the boycott, and compile lists of people in their area who associated with the police.[119] Republican enforcement became tougher. When a Cork undertaker allowed his hearse to be used at the funeral of an RIC man in July, the vehicle was set alight on its way back from the cemetery. In Kerry, two sisters had their hair cropped at Portmagee for being too friendly to the police, and an RIC man's sister at Annagh was assaulted in the same way. That month the Roscommon RIC picked up notices from the North Roscommon Brigade's 'Competent Military Authority' announcing that as of 14 July 'all intercourse of any kind' between 'citizens of the Irish Republic' and 'that portion of the Army of Occupation known as the RIC' was 'strictly forbidden'; 'all persons infringing this order will be included in the said boycott.' Shortly after this, a woman accused of supplying the police in Frenchpark, Roscommon, had three pig rings clamped to her buttocks.[120] Such heavy intimidation might be seen as an indication that public opinion was not solid against the police, but at this stage they were too disoriented to take comfort from that. As one county inspector in the west lamented in midsummer 1920, 'they are shunned and boycotted . . . held up and shot at on every opportunity . . . intimidation broods everywhere and the dark hours are dreaded in many places.' The conditions in many areas were imposing 'a strain which very few bodies of men, however highly disciplined, could be expected to bear', the Inspector General warned in August. They were 'boycotted, ostracised, forced to commandeer their food, crowded into cramped quarters without light or air, every man's hand against them, in danger of their lives, and subjected to the appeals of their families to induce them to leave the force'.[121]

The boycott perhaps came closer to a general popular action on the 'defensive warfare' model than any other republican policy. Even so, it was never complete. In some places traders went on supplying the police, while claiming that the supplies had been commandeered. The cost of refusing trade mounted as time passed, and by the summer of 1920 some chambers of commerce were openly resisting the boycott. It may well have been in general decline by the end of the year. It never produced the 'wholesale resignations' feared by the Inspector General, if only because of the lack of alternative employment. But it made policemen 'sullen and arrogant towards the people'.[122] As the psychological assault was followed by a mounting physical threat in 1920, the withdrawal of local police into bigger depots shifted the issue from individual psychology to group ethos. Nothing in the police tradition was designed to cope with the kind of provocation they now faced. (That, indeed, had been the argument of both Byrne and Macready that military rather than police forces were needed.) It is clear that many turned to drink. For those who did not try to opt out, the almost inevitable outcome was retaliation. This was at least indirectly encouraged by the *Weekly Summary*, a news-sheet distributed by Tudor's headquarters from August onwards in an attempt to sustain morale and contradict republican propaganda. To one of its readers, Douglas Duff, it was the most 'fatuous, childish and lying ... Government publication' he ever saw; its ways of trying to 'rouse our blood' would have been 'laughable had they not been so dangerous'.[123] But Duff (who would go on, after serving in the Palestine police, to become a successful writer of action stories) was an unusually thoughtful kind of Black and Tan. And even he – who some think inspired the phrase 'duffing up' – was a firm believer in physical force.

The most notorious 'police reprisals' were to take place in September and October 1920, but even as late as September did not necessarily involve the new British recruits. When the *Manchester Guardian* investigated a serious incident in Tullamore at the end of October, it concluded that the outbreak could 'stand as a type of reprisal by the old RIC'. That 'type' was clearly quite well established by then. No Black and Tans had been involved when police rioted in Tuam on 20 July, or in Galway on 8 September – that riot followed the killing of the lone British recruit posted there.[124] The most notorious outbreak, the 'sack of Balbriggan' on 20 September, when some fifty houses were burned down and two 'suspected Sinn Feiners' killed, certainly involved Black and Tans. But these men did not, as the received version has it, get out of control and break out of their barrack at Gormanstown. They were led by their officers and sergeants – 'Irishmen all'.[125]

One of the minority of Catholic officers in the regular RIC, who was on the staff of the Munster Divisional Commissioner, Cyril Prescott Decie, wrote later that 'those police quickest to avenge the death of a comrade were Irishmen ... Black and Tans, having drink taken, might fire out of lorries indiscriminately, loot public houses, or terrorise a village, but the Irishman would avenge his comrade when absolutely stone cold sober and on the right person.' 'When men were on duty after the murder of a comrade feeling hatred in their hearts for the murderers and dissatisfaction at the conditions under which they were compelled to fight, they started shooting on the slightest provocation, if not indeed from a spirit of bravado, and once it started it was infectious.'[126] Of course some Black and Tans certainly did live up, or down, to what would become the standard picture of them – as one old RIC man put it, 'rough, very rough, f-ing and blinding and drinking and all. They'd have shot their mother, oh desperate altogether.' How far they were encouraged in roughness became a big issue. Even before the end of August, Macready was telling Wilson that he was becoming 'more anxious' every day about 'the action of these "Black and Tans" of Tudor's'. If the military were 'brought face to face with some of the wild acts of retaliation which these men are carrying out', they would have to intervene.

At the beginning of September Sturgis reported a rumour (from Belfast) 'that Police reprisals are due entirely to the known approval of such by General Tudor!!' But he twinned it with a second rumour, that 'Jonathan [John Anderson] is the man responsible for the policy of arming the Ulster Volunteers!!' Since he knew this was quite wrong, he seems – as his double exclamation marks indicate – to have disbelieved the Tudor story too. He saw Tudor almost every day, so could claim some authority here. Immediately after the Balbriggan reprisal, Tudor had 'quite agreed ... to my view that had they confined themselves to the dignified shooting of the two prominent Sinns, notorious bad men, the reprisal would have been not so bad'. The notion of 'dignified shooting' is significant here, as is his comment that in any case 'worse things can happen than the firing up of a sink like Balbriggan.' He also invoked the logic of collective punishment: 'surely the people who say "Stop the murders before all our homes go up in smoke" must increase.' But he could not 'see any middle course between punishing someone and admitting that such a job is our war policy'. This would mean martial law, in effect: such things could be done by soldiers as 'part of a war policy', but he demanded plaintively, 'what in the name of Goodness are *we* doing as a *Civil* Authority in such a business!'[127] Two days later he dismissed the possibility of 'punishing someone', asking 'how the devil can we round up and try 50 policemen when we know that they know that the bulk of their officers up to the top agree in principle with their action' (even if, as he added, 'they prefer shooting to burning'). Maybe the rumour from Belfast was not so wrong.

Another suggestive rumour appeared after the Chief Secretary had visited the RIC Depot in Phoenix Park to hand out medals – as well as a stern injunction against reprisals. As a result, the RIC 'settled to chuck down their guns', only changing their minds when 'their officers explained to them that it was a Show for the benefit of the press.' Sturgis once again dismissed this rumour; but at the same time he heard from Andy Cope, who had just visited Gormanstown and Balbriggan, that 'the RIC are *not* out of hand but are systematically led to reprise by their officers.' This led Sturgis back to a familiar argument – 'it's tragic that these men cannot see that indiscriminate burning is idiotic,' whereas 'a little quiet shooting' would be just as effective; and shooting 'a known bad man who, if he hasn't just shot your comrade, has no doubt shot somebody else' was 'morally much more defensible than this stupid blind work'. A few days later it became clear that the same view was taken by the Prime Minister. Tudor 'says L.G. is all against burning but not gunning, and told him as much himself'.[128]

Against the traditional view that the Black and Tans led the way in retaliation, it can be argued that when British police and Auxiliaries took reprisals, they were merely following the bad example set by their Irish comrades.[129] But they might just as well have been following the example of the British troops. Their comrades-once-removed in the army had been striking out in revenge attacks on the civil population since late 1919 – at Fermoy – and though the C-in-C later claimed that there had been only one unofficial military reprisal during the whole conflict, he was certainly wrong. There were at least four in the first six months of 1920. General Macready's defensive line reflected the extreme unease, even alarm, that the military authorities felt in face of this phenomenon. It would lead him eventually to institute a policy of 'official reprisals' to channel the retaliatory instincts of his troops – because, as he said, a unit that was not infuriated by the killing of any of its members would be so lacking in spirit as to be militarily useless. An example of this approach came in September when, as he told Wilson, 'down at Ennistymon the Royal Scots carried out certain retaliations "by numbers" under order of their CO.' He believed that 'the men were so maddened by the sight of the bodies of the Police who were killed and mutilated by expanding bullets' that 'if the CO had not done what he did, he would probably not have held his men.' 'As the regiment is a good one, I shall merely tell him not to do it again.' But Macready was coming to the conclusion that 'retaliation by numbers' was the only way. And as was becoming clear, reprisals (even, perhaps especially, indiscriminate ones) worked.

The September reprisals evoked the uneasy confession from Macready that 'the whole atmosphere' of the districts where reprisals had occurred had 'changed from one of hostility to one of cringing submission'. People were reported to be touching their caps to military officers in Galway, and, more importantly, to be starting to provide information. Some police officers were openly jubilant – one western county inspector reported that 'the dread of reprisals' had played a major part in 'crippling Sinn Féin prestige and power'. If 'quietly and systematically continued', the process would 'knock the bottom out of the Sinn Féin movement in a short time'.[130] Even the least hawkish ministers, such as the Chancellor, Austen Chamberlain, were impressed by such assertions; Chamberlain told his sister that it was 'a fact that the reprisals have secured the safety of the police in places where previously they were shot down like vermin', and had led the people to give information about ambushes. His Cabinet colleagues even credited them with 'driving a wedge between the moderates and the extremists in the Sinn Féin camp'.[131]

Troops and police lashed out, spontaneously or otherwise, for many reasons; but underlying them all was the paralysis of the judicial system.

By the summer of 1920 it had become effectively impossible to punish those the police believed guilty of murder and 'outrage'. Sometimes they simply could not be found or identified, thanks to the failure of witnesses to speak up; but even if they could, the prospect of securing a court conviction was remote. When those who attacked the Crown forces could not be brought to justice, direct action against them or the communities assumed to shelter them became likely, especially if such violence appeared to make people more co-operative. The likelihood was strengthened by the governing British official belief that (as Mark Sturgis put it) 'the entire population of this God-forsaken island is terrorised by a small band of gun men.' Without the terror of 'Sinn Fein on one end of the stick and Orange on the other', the people would embrace a political settlement. Now, terror would be countered and perhaps neutralized by terror.

The perilously seductive arguments for reprisals were not borne out by their actual effect on republican activity. It would be found, in the end, that in the competition of terror the rebels could easily outbid the authorities. As early as July 1920, Volunteer GHQ raised the question of 'counter-destruction of houses'. Making clear that such a policy was merely being 'considered', it asked some brigades to draw up lists of '20 possible houses that would not injure our own people', if retaliation was agreed to.[132] When the British military finally initiated 'official reprisals' on the first day of 1921 the policy of systematic republican retaliation took off, and ensured that official reprisals weighed at least as heavily on loyalists as on republicans. Thereafter the policy's attraction would inexorably wane.

If there was a representative reprisal, it happened perhaps at Tubbercurry, Co. Sligo, on the last night of September. It was not the first or the most violent: reprisals had struck Thurles, Upperchurch and Limerick in July, Templemore in August, and there had been a destructive series of them in late September – Balbriggan on the 21st, Ennistymon, Lahinch and Miltown Malbay next day, Trim and Listowel on the 27th and 28th. Others would follow, climaxing in the 'burning of Cork' in December. (The list has been said to 'read like a sombre catalogue of small towns throughout the length and breadth of the south and west'.)[133] But Tubbercurry showed what came to be thought of as key characteristics of a reprisal. Following the ambushing of a police inspector at Chaffpool on the Sligo–Tubbercurry road on 30 September, military and police reinforcements arrived (from Sligo) late in the evening – the telegraph wire had been cut, and men had to drive from Tubbercurry to Sligo to get help. They found DI Brady had died of gruesome wounds inflicted (allegedly) by dum-dum bullets. 'His naked body was lying on the kitchen floor [of Tubbercurry RIC barrack], being washed by one of his comrades. The three ghastly wounds made by the shots were in full evidence.' His head constable had 'the calf of his right leg practically blown away', and another badly wounded constable was wandering about in distress. The troops and police stormed off, firing rifles, hurling grenades and shouting 'Come out, Sinn Fein! Where are the murderers?' They burned down three shops on the town square and wrecked several others – eleven according to the veteran Irish correspondent of the *Daily News*, Hugh Martin, who arrived two days afterwards. Finally the officers got the men under control and back in their vehicles, but the police then drove off to the nearby co-operative creamery and burned it down, as well as the creamery at Achonry.[134]

By late September the liberal press in Britain was on the alert, and reports in the *Daily News* and *Manchester Guardian* mean that the Tubbercurry outbreak was particularly well investigated. The papers reported (contrary to the official story) that as soon as they had arrived in the town, the troops and police broke into a pub, drank what they could and destroyed the rest, before torching it. They replied to their commanding officer's orders with defiant verbal abuse, and the CI was reduced to begging his men to spare the town's biggest business. Locals testified that, rather than careering from one creamery to the next, as the CI reported, the troops and police had headed out in two groups in different directions, seemingly going to both creameries at the same time. This had an air of deliberation. The destruction of shops had been common, but the targeting of creameries – on which hundreds of small farmers depended – was a far-reaching development.[135]

Tubbercurry was (unusually) the subject of an official communiqué, admitting that Crown forces had 'broken out of hand' and that 'reprisals continued till early in the morning'. It added that 'a creamery in the neighbourhood was burned,' though without actually admitting that the police had done it. Greenwood, though, with more nerve than honesty, not only refused to admit that the Tubbercurry creamery had been burned down in reprisal, but told the House of Commons he had 'never seen a tittle of evidence' that any creamery had been destroyed by

Crown forces. He accepted that 'there was a reprisal,' but set it in an almost heroic frame: the men 'saw red' when they found Brady lying on the floor: 'They knew him. They loved him. Soldiers and policemen trained under the British flag love their officers. They so love them that they go to their death for them.'[136] The Chief Secretary's invocation of Britishness, whether instinctual or aimed to evoke the patriotism of MPs, pointed up the impossibility of appealing to both British and Irish opinion.

Reprisals were coming to worry many beyond the liberal press. At the end of September, Mark Sturgis would note that other big issues like hunger striking had 'faded into insignificance' beside them. His diary logs the evolution – if that is not too progressive a term – of official thinking around them. With his 'nebulous position' as assistant to the civil servant most closely involved with the police, Andy Cope (he was never formally appointed assistant under secretary, for fear of seeming a rival to the neurotic deputy under secretary), he heard every opinion on the question. The most consistent view, as he noted after Macready had issued a general order forbidding reprisals in August, was that 'reprisals do good of a sort.' Tudor was 'sure of it'. Sturgis then thought that to countenance them was 'death to a disciplined force', but 'if they some-times give a man, caught red handed in some minor outrage, a damn good hiding instead of arresting all the minnows, it's all to the good.' There was also the argument that whatever their effect on the 'enemy', they were unavoidable. In private, Macready himself made the point that 'a regiment that did not try to break out' when they heard a story – even if untrue – that one of their comrades had, say, been thrown into the Liffey and shot at 'was not worth a damn'. He 'had to be careful not to make them sullen and take the heart out of them'. He agreed that 'if a policeman put on a mackintosh and a false beard and "reprised" on his own hook he was damn glad of it.'

Sturgis went on trying to distinguish between acceptable and unacceptable reprisals. On 24 August he noted that 'we are being urged quietly and persistently that Reprisals are the only thing to put down the Gun men,' and he was 'begin[ning] to believe it'. But 'the sort of reprisal that burns half the town of Lisburn because the DI was mur-dered' was 'the wrong sort'. He had just interviewed a 'professional reprisaler', a DI from Thurles, who explained that his district was quiet because they 'have the local blackguards marked – *and they know it* and know that they personally will pay the price if a policeman is shot'. The view that shooting was good, burning bad, turned into a sort of ortho-doxy. Sturgis wavered on the issue of whether reprisals should be open or concealed: at the end of August he judged it 'a tragedy ... that we blame SF for fighting underground when we ourselves have driven them to it and now our undoubtedly useful card "reprisals" is used under-ground by us instead of being *an act of war*'.

It seems beyond question that, while reprisals were officially con-demned, the condemnation was limited to indiscriminate 'bad' reprisals. 'Good' reprisals, targeted assassinations, were encouraged. The Cabinet tacitly accepted this when it failed to come up with any substitute action. Where Sturgis and the Prime Minister diverged was over the pol-icy implications of this. For Sturgis, reprisals were 'not really *possible* without Martial Law to regularise them'. It seemed incontrovertible to him that if they did not stop after Greenwood's speech at the RIC Depot the surviving credit of the civil administration would be 'done', and 'we *must* give place to a military régime.' That, just as clearly, was the last thing that Lloyd George wanted.

Though Sturgis made a kind of moral judgment on reprisals, his pri-mary criticism of bad reprisals was that they were idiotic, stupid. Even he seems not to have suspected how disastrous their impact on Britain's reputation outside Ireland would be. Yet as he wrestled with the issue, the tide of public outrage was welling up. In late September the *New Statesman* drew attention to the difference between spontaneous outbursts by ordinary troops and policemen in an intolerable situation – 'provocation ... difficult to resist, no matter how good their discipline' – and the actions of the Auxiliaries. With them, 'there is clear evidence that methods of terrorism are adopted less from passion than from policy.' The *Observer* editorialized about the 'immense weakening of Britain's moral position', and even the *Daily Mail* protested at the beginning of October that 'half the world is coming to feel that our Government is condoning vendetta and ... lawless reprisals': the 'slur on our nation's good name' was becoming 'insufferable'. On Armistice Day Hugh Martin of the *Daily News*, who had been a particularly ten-acious investigator of police retaliation, penned an agonized lament for his country's reputation. 'Three months ago, the word "reprisals" merely recalled the later stages of the Great War. Today, to the whole of the English-speaking world it means one thing and one thing only – the method by which Great Britain is waging war upon Ireland.'[137]

Reprisals made headlines, and nobody could doubt their republican propaganda value. But pervasive casual brutality may have played a bigger part in constructing the popular image of the 'Tans'. Their body language was consciously aggressive, and they exercised to the full the freedom to intimidate an uncooperative public. 'Those Black and Tans can do what they like, and no check on them,' as Lady Gregory heard a friend say after a particularly ghastly incident near her home at Kiltartan, Co. Galway, in October. Ellen Quinn and her child were shot by the roadside as a police patrol drove by firing at random, and 'the Head Constable [an old RIC regular] was afraid to take a deposition from Mrs Quinn before she died,' even though he was in her house.[138] Sturgis lamented, 'I wish these lorry loads of police could be restrained from this idiotic blazing about as they drive along.' Once again he called it idiotic rather than unacceptable; he merely observed that 'it can do no conceivable good.' The army, though, did see 'promiscuous firing' as something more dangerous: a sign of the failure to impose discipline on the police. Even where it did not produce such deadly results as at Kiltartan, the practice seriously undermined any claim the force had to the status of 'guardians of the law'.

Auxiliaries in particular, who might be called the 'real' Tans (they remained separate from the regular RIC, and were clad in khaki), often appear to have assumed that brutality was capable of converting people to the government cause. Hugh Martin wrote sardonically of their habitual 'whipping, kicking and otherwise instructing [young men] in the elements of British citizenship'.[139] On occasion, brutality could be choreographed around the central symbols of the conflict. In Ballina, Co. Mayo the chemist watched as ADRIC assembled:

> in the main street, in front of the Moy Hotel, a number of the most respectable citizens and men who were whole-heartedly Sinn Feiners . . . and after handcuffing them . . . tied the Tricolour to the last prisoner, trailing it in the mud of the streets and with an itinerant musician marching in front, took them to the Market Cross where the prisoners were beaten and kicked to their knees in an effort to make them kiss a Union Jack placed on the roadway.[140]

Their frequent bursts of drunkenness were in one sense an even more shocking lapse from the standards of the old police than brutality, but it was sustained violence that inevitably generated most resentment and hostility. Beatings were regularly vicious, and mock executions seem to have been alarmingly frequent. Even less serious assaults were conducted as deliberate humiliation, and as one man who had been whipped told Hugh Martin of the *Daily News*, 'the indignity was worse than the pain.'[141] But there were moments of truly gruesome violence. The Loughnane brothers, arrested on their Galway farm in November 1920, were taken away by Auxiliaries, and found ten days later in a pond – one of them 'a mass of unsightly scars and gashes; two of his fingers were lopped off; his right arm was broken at the shoulder, being almost completely severed from the body ... nothing remained [of his face] save the chin and lips'. Harry Loughnane's suffering had a dramatic sequel: his shattered and long-dead corpse was seen to bleed when it was pulled from the water, and 'hundreds dipped their handkerchiefs in the martyrs' blood.' At the brothers' funeral, the Volunteers fired three volleys over their grave.[142]

Women were targeted less often, though dozens of members of republican families or of Cumann na mBan had their hair cut off with scissors or razors – in mirror images of Volunteer assaults on women who were seen with policemen or soldiers.[143] Many more were verbally abused and intimidated, usually deliberately, though of course any night raid was inescapably alarming to the women who experienced it. Kathleen Clarke, a highly prejudiced witness, nonetheless has the ring of truth in her account of a raid in which a 'Black and Tan' (Auxiliary) 'armed with a rifle ... put the muzzle resting on my chest. He was so drunk it seemed as if he was keeping himself standing by holding on to the rifle resting on my chest ... he kept on saying "I'll teach you".'

There must also have been some sexual violence, though it was much less well attested. There were undoubtedly cases of rape, probably more than the few that were formally reported – which may indeed be 'surprisingly few', certainly by the depressing standards of the contemporary world.[144] As one witness told the American Commission on Conditions in Ireland, 'we were so accustomed to hearing of sex excesses in Belgium' that the 'marked contrast' in Ireland was striking. Ellen Wilkinson (representing the Women's International League) told the commissioners that she had 'found no case at all where sexual outrages on women have occurred'. International comparisons will not have meant much to Irish people, naturally, and even a few cases will have spread fear and alarm. The truth remains obscure: as the Cork Gaelic Leaguer Caroline

Townshend said, 'it is very difficult to get facts about such cases.' In November 1920 Lady Gregory heard from her doctor in Galway that 'the family of the girls violated by the Black and Tans wish it to be hushed up,' and 'another case of the same sort in Clare' was also 'to be kept quiet'.[145]

Police brutality converted countless moderate nationalists into separatists. The journals of Lady Gregory vividly demonstrate not just the construction of a popular myth, but also how 'establishment' people came to use the word 'terror' to describe government policy rather than republican activity. Throughout the autumn and winter she recorded seemingly endless instances of Black and Tans dragging young men out and whipping them, forcing men to salute the Union flag, stealing money and livestock, staging mock executions, getting drunk and loosing off their guns. 'Such a thing could hardly happen in savage lands out in Turkey,' as one friend said of the Loughnane killings. By December 1920 Yeats's sister Lily would write, 'As you know I was no Sinn Feiner a year ago, just a mild nationalist, but now –'[146] For her brother, the autumn of 1920, and in particular the murder of Ellen Quinn, seemed to herald a new barbarism. When 'a drunken soldiery / Can leave the mother, murdered at her door, / To crawl in her own blood, and go scot-free; / The night can sweat with terror' – as if we had never 'pieced our thoughts into philosophy'.

'THE FIRST DIRECT ATTACK MADE UPON THE IRISH REPUBLIC'

For a long time, even before Eoin MacNeill published his famous article 'The North Began' in 1913, it had been difficult to fit that 'North' into the trajectory of the Irish revolution. MacNeill had to resort to some counter-intuitive, even sophistical arguments to attempt to contend that, by arming themselves to resist Home Rule, the unionists had 'knocked the bottom out of Unionism' and become, in effect, home rulers. Though the north was claimed – especially by northern nationalists like MacNeill – as an integral part of the Irish nation, the majority of its inhabitants saw things differently. The differences between Protestants and Catholics were more than simply political: in their social complexity they amounted to two distinct cultural systems.[147] Nationalists resolutely ignored this awkward fact, and Sinn Féin had not put together any coherent northern policy, beyond an insistence that unionists had no right to secede from the 'Irish nation'. De Valera's threatening attitude was typical. In 1918 he had likened the Ulster case for self-determination to a 'robber coming into another man's house and claiming a room as his'. The alienation in this view was more than implicit. Unionists 'represented only English interests, and as they were in the minority they had nothing to do but give way to the majority'. This was public rhetoric, intended to provoke nationalist cheers, but as critics like the parliamentary party leader John Dillon repeatedly warned, all the more dangerous for that. Its only effect was to solidify Ulster hostility to republicanism.[148]

Sinn Féin quietly accepted the distinctness of 'Ulster', the only province in which it failed to bring down the old Irish party in the 1918 election. Though it had struggled in one or two party strongholds in the south (notably Waterford), the task in the north was doubly difficult. The strength of the unionist opposition forced it into an electoral pact under which the eight marginal seats were divided equally between Sinn Féin and the Irish party. (Some local republicans, admittedly, saw this as a panic measure that lost some seats that could well have been won.) Occupying the front line in Ireland's most vicious battles over two generations had produced a resilient nationalist organization, backed by notoriously tough – and sectarian – street-level enforcers in the Ancient Order of Hibernians. The Ulster leader Joe Devlin's public denunciation of Sinn Féin was blistering – their 'phantom republic' was a fraud, the abstention policy 'a false pretence'. Sinn Féin would 'go down in the ridicule of the nation'. He mocked the Sinn Féin tricolour's contamination of the old green flag – in which there was 'no white streak – no, nor yellow streak either'. In East Belfast he trounced de Valera by 8,488 votes to 3,245. This triumph helped to disguise the narrowness of the old party's majority in other non-pact constituencies – Sinn Féin lost by only 500 in the Hibernian stronghold of South Derry – but it was striking enough.[149]

The Dáil had no Belfast deputies, and only a handful of leading Sinn Feiners (Eoin MacNeill, Ernest Blythe and Seán MacEntee) came from the north. There were some signs in 1919 that the seriousness of this problem was recognized. A pushy Ulster Protestant, adoptive Canadian and Sinn Féin convert, William Forbes Patterson, was asked by Sinn Féin in June to investigate the northern situation. His verdict on repub-

1. Volunteers in uniform: Dan Breen and Maurice Crowe, 1918. Crowe has a regulation British outfit complete with Sam Browne belt; Breen's rigout is more imaginative.

2. Volunteers in mufti: Seamus Robinson, Seán Treacy, Dan Breen and Michael Brennan together 'on the run' in 1919.

3. The counter-state embodied: Dáil Éireann before Eamon de Valera's departure to the USA. A rare image of Michael Collins beside Cathal Brugha, with Arthur Griffith on de Valera's right.

4. Woman power: an anti-English demonstration in Dublin, 1920.

5. The priest-king and the cardinal: Eamon de Valera and Archbishop Hayes of New York, who contributed $1,000 to the Republican Loan.

6. Comforting the poor: Constance Markievicz with the children of political prisoners.

7. Warriors and civilians: steel-helmeted British troops and curious young people in Dublin.

8. Culture clash: Auxiliary RIC cadets raiding the headquarters of the Gaelic Athletic Association in Dublin.

9. Ambush: a Rolls-Royce armoured car and its crew with police under fire.

10. Martyrdom: Terence MacSwiney's coffin being taken to Cork, escorted by Auxiliary police.

11. Master and commander: Winston Churchill and Nevil Macready go into a Cabinet conference, at Gairloch in Scotland after the Truce.

12. Street fighting: journalists and spectators watch a British raid on a Dublin store.

13. Official reprisals: a store in Dillons Cross, County Cork being wrecked by a tank, early in 1921.

14. The offensive against communications: a Rolls-Royce armoured car negotiates a road pit, June 1921.

licanism there was bleak: it was effectively stillborn. But he believed that unionism was vulnerable to the (slowly) growing labour movement, and Sinn Féin could do worse than support labour. There were signs of cross-communal industrial action – notably the general strike in Belfast early in 1919 – although, as he saw, the British Labour party was unlikely to escape from its 'English outlook'. The prospects for military confrontation were grim, Forbes Patterson thought. If faced with a 'pogrom', republicans could not cope.[150]

Tensions mounted after the January 1920 municipal elections brought the city of London/Derry back under Catholic/nationalist control for the first time since 1690. This was a shocking moment for unionists, psychologically, and very dangerous in political terms, since it undermined their claim to exclusion from Home Rule. The new Mayor, Hugh O'Doherty, removed Lord French's name from the list of Derry city's freemen, and refused to attend any functions involving a declaration of loyalty to the Crown. In April clashes between youths and soldiers sparked 'wild' rioting in the city, and the Catholic clergy intervened to patrol the streets and enrol citizen volunteers to keep the peace.[151] In mid-June the violence became more serious, and nineteen people (fifteen Catholics and four Protestants) were killed in what Eoin MacNeill labelled the 'Derry pogrom' – alleging that the rifles wielded by loyalists had been supplied from London. On 21–23 June, Orangemen (allegedly supported by troops) mounted attacks on St Columb's Diocesan College, and the attempts by Volunteers of the Derry battalion under Michael Sheerin to defend it ended in humiliation as the Volunteers broke and ran, throwing away their weapons. 'The discarding of rifles and ammunition and the hasty disappearance of men', Sheerin later wrote, 'was not edifying.' The garrison cowered in the college with the lights out as outside armoured cars with a searchlight 'drove up to vantage points in the College grounds and proceeded to break every window and outside door'.[152]

At this stage, Volunteer operations – however alarming to unionists – were far from formidable. Sheerin's company of fifty was 'the only unit functioning' in Derry, and even that was 'unenthusiastic', mainly 'held together by threats'. As in Londonderry county, nationalists were simply too conscious of the danger that any activity would rebound on their own community.[153] When Thomas Fitzpatrick's battalion attacked some military vehicles in Low Market in March 1920, they took care not to get permission from the brigade, which was 'averse to activities in Belfast for fear of reprisals on the Catholic population'.[154] The first operation 'carried out against the enemy in Belfast for the purpose of killing' did not take place until January 1921, according to Seamus McKenna. Roger McCorley thought that coherent military activity of any kind started only at Easter 1920 with the burning of the income tax offices: all but one of the offices in Belfast were burned out, and the last was torched a few days later. (Fitzpatrick's battalion apparently was not asked to take part.) But armed engagements were much more problematic. An attempted attack on Cookstown barrack in Tyrone failed, and Patrick Loughran became the first Volunteer to be killed in the six counties. No explosives had been available; and those that were used in an attack on the barrack in Irish Street, Armagh were wasted. (These were packed in a box on a cart and rolled up to the barrack wall; the explosion did more damage to the houses opposite than to the barrack.) McCorley's first serious action was the attack on Crossgar RIC barrack in east Down, carried out inevitably with mostly untrained men with no experience of such actions. Though they were provided with Mills bombs – very sophisticated munitions by the standards of most rural units – using them called for some basic training. The men detailed for the bombing party 'had no idea of the mechanism', and McCorley was given the job of instructing them. He was called away to fix a dismantled rifle after explaining to the group that they must 'keep their hands on the levers after pulling the pins'. He returned to find one of them 'with the pin extracted . . . just about to let the lever fly off. He appeared to be under the impression that nothing would happen if he did not throw the bomb.'

There was near-chaos in the training hall; it was difficult to keep the men under control, and as they moved around they would find themselves detailed to 'two or three different parties'. It took so long to sort the attacking force out that the operation began late, and never got beyond a ragged exchange of fire. 'Before the bombs went off one of the party panicked and ran into the street screaming,' so alerting the police. McCorley decided to withdraw, but could not give the signal – a whistle blast – because 'the officer in command forgot to bring a whistle.' In the end 'the attack more or less broke itself off.' Though about half the garrison had been wounded, the barrack held out; still the action 'served a purpose by showing us our own weaknesses' – and also 'exposed a certain lack of determination to carry an operation through even at a certain cost in casualties'. The leadership were reluctant to take any risks, in his view, and too inclined to prohibit proposed activities 'on the off chance that the Brigade would decide to carry out something in the future'.

The 'fear of reprisals' that paralysed the brigade may well have stimulated McCorley and the other younger Volunteers, thinking that reprisals would radicalize the people. The problem in Belfast was the same as elsewhere in respect of central command at least; 'targets of opportunity were the only ones that could be effectively attacked,' and operations calling for long-term planning would be 'few and far between', and unlikely to 'put [the enemy] off his stride'.[155] But even at a lower intensity than further south, the development of the republican campaign had an explosive impact in the north. The attacks on tax offices triggered the revival in June of Sir Edward Carson's prewar Ulster Volunteer Force. The 'raising of Carson's army from the grave', as Macready put it with a mixture of alarm and contempt, would have immense consequences, as the authorities looked for a way to contain and channel the upsurge of sectarian confrontation.

Tensions were inevitably racked up higher still on the Twelfth of July, and decisive and disastrous events followed a few days later. The assassination of the RIC Munster Divisional Commissioner, Colonel Smyth, in the Cork County Club on 17 July happened a long way away, but had a tangible impact in the north when Smyth's funeral took place in his home town, Banbridge, Co. Down. Catholic property in Banbridge and other towns was attacked, and loyalist press alarms about the advance of Sinn Féin became increasingly strident. A meeting of 'Protestant and Unionist' shipyard workers at Workman Clark's south yard on the 21st denounced the IRA campaign and the Sinn Féin 'penetration' of Ulster. The ILP/TUC were identified as the industrial wing of the republican movement. An immediate purge of socialists and Catholics in the Harland and Wolff shipyards was launched by a force of apprentices and 'rivet boys'; many were 'severely beaten', according to police reports, and some 'thrown into the water and compelled to swim for their lives'. Gunfire across the city added to what the *Irish News* called 'a carnival of terrorism', and within three days eighteen people were known to have been killed. Within the week, 5,000 Catholic workers had been driven out from the yards and from factories such as the

Sirocco engineering works. (There, the workers resolved to refuse 'to work with those men who have been expelled recently until the Sinn Féin assassinations in Ireland cease'.)[156] Mixed residential areas were purged – in both directions, as hundreds of Protestants were also forced from their homes – and the longstanding sectarian geography of the city was more sharply etched.

Over the next two years, more than 450 people would be killed – over two-thirds of them Catholics – and over 8,000 driven from their homes. More than 600 houses and business premises were destroyed. The most prominent Catholic businesses – public houses – were systematically looted and their contents helped to fuel the rampages. This was a working-class war, but with just a single exception no trade union made any public effort to halt or discourage it. This no doubt reflected the fact that most trade unions represented the skilled trades, and the great majority of skilled workers in Belfast were Protestants. But this is not to say that Protestant workers as such formed 'an aristocracy of labour'; the majority were still semi- or unskilled.[157] Communal violence in Ulster was certainly not in any simple sense a conflict between superior and inferior economic classes. Nor was it a crude sectarian conflict. It was intensely political, framed by national symbols – as when the unionist leader Sir James Craig urged people to 'rally' to 'shatter our enemies and their hopes of a republican flag'.[158] The violence, murderous as it was, was also less extreme than in some of the internecine conflicts taking place in other parts of Europe. The most outrageous, 'transgressive' acts, like mutilation and rape, so characteristic of modern ethnic struggles, hardly figured.[159] If this was war, it was limited rather than total.

'IT WAS EASY FOR LINEN TO BURN'

It did not, of course, look this way to its victims. Nationalists were deeply shocked by the explosion of violence and immediately labelled it a 'pogrom' – to show the outside world that the real problem was not the attitude of loyalists but the machinations of the British government and the unionist employers. From this standpoint, the republican response was visceral rather than logical. On 6 August 1920 a 'memorial' was presented to the Dáil by Seán MacEntee, representing nationalist members of Belfast Corporation, urging action to stop the 'war of extermination being waged against us'. MacEntee told the Dáil that it was responsible 'as the only custodian of public order'. The 'bitter persecution and repression' in Belfast was 'a consequence of the establishment of the Republic', and actually represented 'the first open act of rebellion against the Republic' – 'the first direct attack made upon the Irish Republic'. Republicans were not in a position at that moment to take military action, but 'there was the more potent weapon of the blockade.' The Dáil should enforce a commercial boycott, since 'the chief promoters of the Orange intolerance here are the heads of the distributing trades throughout Ireland.' This was a slightly dubious contention, but the real intent of the petitioners was more emotively put – to 'fight Belfast' ('the spear head of British power in Ireland').[160]

The reaction to this fighting call in Dublin was cautious. Ernest Blythe, one of the few northerners in the republican leadership, warned the Dáil that 'an economic blockade of Belfast would be the worst possible step' – it 'would destroy for ever the possibility' of a united Irish nation. Moreover it was highly doubtful that it would have anything like the intended effect – Constance Markievicz thought it could not be made effective, and would be 'playing into the hands of the enemy'. Desmond FitzGerald bluntly said that a blockade would be 'a vote for partition'. Collins even condemned the attempt by MacEntee 'to inflame the passions' of the members of the Dáil, insisting that 'there was no Ulster question'. Arthur Griffith denounced the motion as 'practically a declaration of war on one part of their own territory', and urged instead that it be declared 'illegal for any employer to impose a test on an employee'. Then if the Belfast employers refused to comply within seven days, 'a blockade of Belfast could be declared.' The Dáil, the great majority of whose members, Blythe thought, had at first been quite ready to consent to the boycott, accepted these arguments.[161] But the pressure kept on mounting, and five days later the ministry authorized a boycott of banks and insurance companies whose headquarters were in Belfast. To get maximum local involvement, this was to be implemented by the Local Government Department via the General Council of County Councils. Support was not hard to drum up, since the threat of partition in the Government of Ireland Bill had already triggered spontaneous boycotts in Galway and Mayo early in the year. (On 4 February, Ballinrobe District Council had called on traders to close accounts with north-east Ulster firms that failed to 'declare themselves anti-partitionist'.)

By September, boycott resolutions had been passed by local authorities all over the country, and enforcement by Volunteers in some places was enthusiastic. Local enthusiasm directed the boycott not only at Belfast but at a range of northern towns – such as Lisburn, Dromore and Newtownards – where there had been anti-Catholic violence. It also quickly went beyond the limits of bank and insurance companies; the Volunteers proscribed 'goods manufactured in or distributed from Belfast'.[162] Orders from Belfast suppliers were cancelled, and Volunteers heaved a carload of such stuff into the River Erne at Ballyshannon. It seems clear that the campaign focused a lot of instinctive hostility towards the industrial north, but lack of organization lefts its exact logic vague. Even before the director of the Central Committee for the Belfast Boycott, Leo Henderson, was arrested in October, there was little co-ordination of the actions of the eighty or so local committees, and no blacklist of firms was drawn up until the following year.

Some localities applied the boycott more enthusiastically than others. Eoin O'Duffy, for instance, backed it strongly from the start, so that it was enforced more effectively in Monaghan than anywhere else. His forces picketed Protestant stores, imposed fines on blacklisted businesses, harassed Catholics who patronized them, set alight delivery vans from Belfast and sabotaged the Great Northern Railway (most of whose workers were Protestants). Intimidating railway workers on this line meshed with the enforcement of the munitions embargo.[163]

The boycott of 'Belfast goods' was intended to emphasize the industrial city's dependence on its Irish hinterland. In political terms, though 'it was easy for linen to burn', the bonfires had the opposite effect, heightening the unionist sense of alienation and accelerating the process of partition. In mixed areas like Monaghan, the fault line in the tacit coexistence between the two communities was sharpened. The two commercial groups, the (unionist) Traders' Association and the (nationalist) Traders' Committee, diverged gently but unmistakably. The former passed a resolution condemning the victimization of Catholics, but insisted that it could not give any undertaking to limit its members' business activities in any way that would compromise their commercial freedom. The latter found itself reluctantly 'compelled to take all measures within its power to prevent the sale of Belfast goods in the town'. The result was 'a temporary rupture of the good feeling hitherto existing between Protestants and Catholics in the district', and the rupture would not be as temporary as the local paper optimistically suggested.[164] By the end of the year, indeed, sectarianism had reached a level at which the police warned that violence was 'likely to occur on the slightest provocation'. In Meath, just as ominously, the refusal of the Dundalk Property Owners' Association to condemn events in Belfast, on the grounds that 'there was no intolerance in Dundalk', provoked the burning down of three Protestant stores, in which three people died.[165]

For the northern Volunteers, and the nationalist community as well, the most critical single event of the summer was the killing of RIC District Inspector Oswald Swanzy on 22 August. Swanzy, named by the coroner's jury as one of those responsible for the murder of Tomás Mac Curtain, had been transferred to Lisburn, Co. Down – where Collins had little difficulty in finding him. Collins's determination to avenge Mac Curtain was almost ostentatious: he sent up a leading member of Cork No. 1 Brigade, Seán Culhane, to carry out the killing, and presented him with Mac Curtain's own revolver for the purpose. Culhane initially took a party of no fewer than four men of his brigade, but, after the first assassination attempt had failed, sent them home and did the job with just one, Dick Murphy, assisted by two local scouts. Swanzy was shot down as he left Lisburn Cathedral after matins. The relationship between the Cork and Belfast contributions to the attack would remain contentious. Some of the Belfast men contended that 'the Cork men were guests,' and one of the supposed scouts, Roger McCorley, claimed that they actually took part in the shooting.[166]

Militarily, the Volunteers saw this attack as a striking success. Revenge was sweet, and Collins (emphasizing his ownership of the operation) brought the two Corkmen back to Dublin, where he and Richard Mulcahy, the Chief of Staff, were 'profuse in their congratulations'. But as Culhane left Belfast he could see the fires in Lisburn as his train passed.[167] Whatever fears the Belfast commanders had of reprisals were amply fulfilled in the onslaught on the Catholic population, nearly all of whom were driven out of the town, with over 300 of their homes left in ruins. The famous UVF gun-runner Fred Crawford was reminded when he visited 'of a French town after it had been bombarded by the Germans'; he was told that there were 'only four or five RC families left in Lisburn'. He picked up a small pair of nail scissors lying in the street, which had survived the destruction, 'as a souvenir of the event'.

Any brief sense of triumph on the Belfast Volunteers' part was followed by the realization that the mass violence had 'shown them up' as 'inactive, small in number and hopelessly isolated'. They had been unable to do more than respond episodically to the 'ebb and flow of sectarian violence'.[168] Even that passive role was resisted by the Belfast command, which tried to sideline it as 'a purely sectarian affair'. Roger McCorley recorded, with characteristic venom, that 'Brigade Head-quarters even went as far as to courtmartial one officer for taking part in the defence of his own particular area against the attacks of the Orange mob.' His defence, that to stand by and allow someone else to defend his home would be undignified and unbecoming a Volunteer offi-cer, pointed up the absurdity of the official policy. Under pressure the brigade relented to the extent of authorizing Volunteers to fight British troops if they were directly attacking the civil population. In reality, it was unthinkable that Volunteers would not take part in the battles with the 'disciplined and undisciplined Orange factions', as Seamus McKenna of 1st Battalion put it – 'if the Catholic population were to survive at all'.[169] The real problem was not whether but how to play any effective part.

The summer violence in the north-east, harrowing as it was, was rec-ognizably part of a longstanding tradition of sectarian conflict. In political terms there was some justification for the Belfast Brigade's pious wish to ignore the whole bout of 'fratricidal strife'. The Lisburn assassination was different, and its impact had a baleful influence on the nature of the emerging Northern Ireland polity. Though Macready reflected that 'it rather shakes one's faith in the "discipline" of the Ulster people when one sees the destruction in Lismore [sic], and no attempt made to stop it,' his objections to 'arming the Protestants' were finally overcome.[170] Greenwood – ever the political simpleton – had wanted to 'enrol loyal men in the North as Special Constables', but both Macready and Ander-son rejected this as virtually an official recognition of civil war. Not that anyone doubted that a kind of civil war was indeed in progress – but as the local police and military commanders protested, 'to arm one side and not the other in civil war of this sort is madness.'[171] Mark Sturgis found it a 'comfort' that 'they have not yet sold Belfast to the Ulster Volunteers.'

After Swanzy's death, though, the idea gained a heavyweight supporter – Winston Churchill. Just as crucially, a separate under secretary, Ernest Clark, was placed in Belfast in September to lay the groundwork for a six-county administration. Clark immediately accepted the need for a local security force, and set about energetically constructing one.[172]

A special constabulary would be enrolled; the only remaining question was whether it would be an all-Ireland force. Even those who supported this principle accepted that, since in practice the force would recruit only in the north-east, it would only serve to emphasize the virtual partition of the country. By now, though, this seemed inevitable. Finally, on 22 October, the Ulster Special Constabulary (USC) was inaugurated – two months before the Government of Ireland Act created the polity it would serve. Its three-tier structure – Class 'A' of paid full-timers, the part-time Class 'B' and the elderly reservists of Class 'C' – was planned to provide no fewer than 32,000 men in total, three times the strength of the old RIC.

The USC was a potent force in making virtual partition a reality. Its title enshrined the separate Ulster identity that had been mobilized for unionism and supercharged in the political drama of 1912. Macready's alarmed opposition to 'raising Carson's army from the grave' rightly identified its political significance. He was wrong, though, to imply that the old UVF had died. It certainly became quiescent after 1914 – though the idea that it was transformed wholesale into the British army's Ulster Division and killed en masse at the battle of the Somme is a myth. In 1920 its veterans were plentiful. One of the most senior of them, Brigadier Hacket Pain, who had been chief of the UVF staff, became the RIC divisional commissioner for Ulster. The Irish Office in London, hard as it may be to believe, had no idea 'what position (if any) he held in Carson's Army'.[173] After the war, there seemed to be some reluctance to reconstitute the UVF formally; one or two leaders tried to raise unionist militias under different titles (like Basil Brooke's Fermanagh Vigilance, or the Ulster Imperial Guards formed in the Belfast shipyards). But the UVF reappeared in July 1920, and a fair proportion of its members joined the USC. The new force, however, particularly the 'B' Class, recruited strongly among younger men who had missed out on the great Ulster crisis. As one Londonderry USC commander put it, 'the younger and wilder they are the better.'[174]

THE ARMY OF THE REPUBLIC

The oath of allegiance to the Dáil, even if only partially adopted, was a key symbolic instrument in cementing the claim of the Volunteers to be the Irish national army. Though the title IRA was only patchily – and never apparently officially – adopted, the military side of the republican movement was increasingly described as 'the Army'. The question of how far, in reality, it could develop the machinery of a regular military force was one that preoccupied many at GHQ, above all Mulcahy himself. It was well enough understood that a regular system of top-down command was for various reasons either impracticable or undesirable in the circumstances of guerrilla warfare. Just how far GHQ could control local units has remained uncertain. Some localities were clearly very independent-minded, but others – such as Longford – preferred to follow GHQ's lead. Significant action began there only when GHQ sanctioned attacks on RIC barracks at the start of 1920, and according to Longford's outstanding military leader Seán MacEoin, the first attack was planned in conjunction with GHQ. 'There is evidence that GHQ was directing much of the activities of the Longford IRA throughout 1920,' and GHQ was 'involved in the escalation of the war in Longford' towards the close of the year. The key point here is probably not so much what GHQ itself did as that the Longford Brigade 'was willing to submit itself to GHQ direction'.[175]

Others were less willing. All local units certainly deferred to GHQ in principle, but since the intensification of the shooting war the early practice of seeking authorization for any action had lapsed in the most active areas. In some, feelings of (barely) concealed animosity towards GHQ emerged, starting from the sense that it was hampering the initiative of local units, and bolstered by a sense that it was withholding supplies of arms – something Collins certainly tried to do to encourage local action. GHQ marked out the general structure of the army, and fretted endlessly about the need for uniform standards of command. Though it could sometimes replace unsatisfactory local officers with its own appointees, this was not a simple or systematic process. It had two primary means of influencing the action of local forces: it could send them organizers, and it could send (or deny) them arms. Neither was ever done on the scale that Mulcahy would have thought remotely adequate. Until 1921 organizers were thin on the ground, and even then their arrival could easily create tensions with the local men, and 'proved counter-productive in many cases'.

Complaints and charges of unequal or unfair distribution of arms tend to be impressionistic: hard statistics are few and far between. A rare snapshot of central arms distribution has survived in the GHQ arms ledger kept by Fintan Murphy, meticulously logging all transactions for May–June 1920. This shows that GHQ had £355 worth of stock on hand on 19 April, and over the next five weeks spent £493 on arms and £88 on ammunition: these included twenty-one Lee-Enfield rifles (at a cost of £112) and 2,469 rounds of .303 ammunition (£27 7s 6d). Over that period it sold on £508 worth of arms and £113 worth of ammunition to local units. Eighteen brigades bought arms: in all, thirteen Lee-Enfields went to Cavan (two), west Clare (three), Dublin (three), Offaly (one), North Tipperary (two) and north Roscommon (two). Twenty-two brigades bought ammunition. The biggest consignments by far went, unexpectedly perhaps, to Mayo. In mid-April south Mayo spent almost £80 on twelve Webley revolvers (at £6 each), 300 rounds of .303, thirty rounds of .45 ammunition, and five dozen sticks of gelignite. Next month it bought one .32 and sixteen .45 revolvers at a total cost of £98. Cork No. 1 Brigade, by contrast, received a single Parabellum and two .45 revolvers (all at £6 apiece); Cork No. 2 got fifty rounds of .45 ammunition and ten bundles of gelignite.[176] Though it is isolated, this fragmentary record suggests a fairly comprehensive arms-distribution system.

The greatest military change for the army was what may be called the transition from essentially brief local actions by part-time forces to mobile operations by full-time units. The shift was impelled by the stalemate that emerged in mid-1920. Barrack attacks became increasingly difficult if not impossible for local units as the police concentrated in more substantial stations. But the Volunteer army remained a part-time organization whose members naturally wanted to hang on to their jobs and homes. The fact that it could operate only at night imposed strict limits on its operational repertoire. Its enemy's fixed points were becoming too strong to attack, but it was unable to engage his moving forces consistently. Gradually a way out of the impasse emerged, but, as Michael Brennan was at pains to emphasize later, this was not a deliberate policy conceived at command level. His account makes clear its elementary logic. In east Clare there were only three or four 'wanted men', who kept themselves going as best they could.

> As the year wore on the pursuit became tougher and we were inclined to drift together, partly for company, but mainly because the 'safe areas' were now fewer and we usually met in them. The local Volunteers always

posted men at night to warn of raids, and it was as easy to warn four as one and much easier than to get a message to four widely separated men ... We very quickly discovered that moving around in a group gave greater security and without any actual orders being issued other men 'on the run' drifted to us and our numbers grew.[177]

This was the genesis of the 'flying columns' that began to appear, impelled by the same logic, in various south-western areas as the tempo of the British counter-offensive heightened in the early autumn. Exactly adapted to the circumstances, their organic development governed their capacity. 'The problems of food and billeting prohibited a very large group, and it was necessary to keep the regular column men down to about twenty.' Whether these columns, officially labelled active service units (ASUs), were originally conceived at GHQ level remains a matter of disagreement. According to Artie Barlow, the concept was discussed as early as June 1920, and was another of Collins's bright ideas. Mulcahy was 'not too keen', but Collins insisted, 'We'll have to get these bloody fellows [on the run] doing something.' As Ernie O'Malley noted, at that time they were too often 'a bloody nuisance', lounging around, sleeping late, eating local units' food without contributing any work for them. A number of battalion 'columns' seem to have been set up over the summer, but on too small a scale to have much effect.

Eventually, on 4 October, GHQ issued a general order suggesting that 'the most effective way of utilising' the 'large number' of officers and men on the run in various parts of the country 'would seem to be by organising them as Flying Columns'. The reason offered, in what looks like Mulcahy's cast of thought, was that 'instead of being compelled to a haphazard and aimless course of action, they would become available as standing troops of a well trained and thoroughly reliable stamp'; their actions could be 'far more systematic and effective'. The attraction of 'standing troops' had clearly overcome any initial reservations Mulcahy might have had. 'Permanent troops of this kind', the order went on, 'would afford an exceedingly valuable auxiliary arm to the remainder of the Republican Army,' which was still largely a 'part-time militia'.

The flying columns, 'having to serve actively all the time, would have to be kept fully equipped and supplied with all necessaries'. As 'the work required of them would be very exacting', they were to 'consist only of first-rate troops'. They were to be organized like the cyclist half-companies of the 1914 Volunteers – with a lieutenant and two section commanders, each heading two squads of four men under a squad commander, together with an adjutant and a quartermaster – a maximum total of twenty-six (sic) combatants. ('A larger number than this had better be formed into two Flying Columns.') They should be 'thoroughly familiar with cyclist tactics' – studied via British manuals – but since the superior enemy forces would often deny them the use of roads, they should also be 'minutely trained as Infantry'. GHQ envisaged most members of the columns being officers, some of these being battalion commanders temporarily attached for training (perhaps a tribute to the impression made by the 'elite' ADRIC ex-officers).

The columns would undertake two 'quite distinct types' of action – 'auxiliary' and 'independent'. In the first case, brigade commandants would be able to assign the column as a 'very valuable' extra force to any battalion for the kind of local operations already taking place. The second 'would supply a striking arm not hitherto in our possession', able to undertake 'enterprises requiring to be taken on at instant notice and liable to be endangered by delay. Flying-column commanders would have 'a wide discretion as to enterprises they may undertake'.[178] An attached Operations Memorandum ordered that columns should 'adopt guerrilla tactics generally', and suggested specific actions ranging from field service training, through 'harassing small and quieter military and police stations', interrupting and 'pillaging' enemy stores and interrupting communications, to 'covering towns threatened by reprisal parties'.[179] This last proposal, with its hazardous hint of regular defensive fighting, was the nearest the GHQ order came to identifying what would become the most celebrated item in the flying columns' operational repertoire, the ambush.

The flying-column ambush would become the iconic act of the republican guerrilla campaign – even though not many successful ambushes were ever mounted. Though the number of columns snowballed, many, if not most, of them would not even attempt one. By the time of the GHQ order, a fair number of columns had already appeared, and thereafter there was a rush to form them. But then and later they never conformed to any fixed pattern, in size or style. They could range in size from about ten to over a hundred in the most active areas.[180] The biggest and most aggressive brigades – where, obviously, the most men had gone on the run – established one or more core columns, which moved through their areas picking up local forces to assist with operations. The appeal of the columns for GHQ was obvious. For organizers who had struggled for years to foster a military attitude among the Volunteers, they offered a shortcut to professionalization. In the more intense atmosphere of the ASU, training could be more or less continuous, as in a regular army. This is vividly illustrated in one account of the preparation of the 3rd Tipperary Brigade's second flying column, where the influence of Ernie O'Malley on the two-week training camp was evident. 'Our drill and training was gruelling ... Often after a strenuous day of fatiguing work, during the night we were suddenly called for a "Stand To". This meant that every man was to be fully equipped and standing to attention within 3 minutes' – a drill all too familiar to regular soldiers. 'A night route march often followed.' The aim was to 'submit each member to the acid-test of his durability and stamina and readiness to endure the hardships and dangers that were yet to follow'.[181] This was a question not just of 'hardening' men to outdoor life, but also of trying to instil a self-belief that would sustain them in combat.

The attractions of going 'on the column' were considerable – otherwise they would not have existed, however keen GHQ might have been. Revolution on the hoof offered the young an escape route from the constriction of rural life – 'they went "on the run" not only from the police but from their childhood.' The columns offered safety and status as well. There was some security in numbers – up to a point – and even columns which failed to get into action seem to have had more prestige than local units. This added glamour seems to have meant that there was not much difficulty in finding 'column men'. Roger Rabbitte of the Kilterna company in Galway attended a battalion meeting late in 1920 at which 'we were ordered to make a list of all the men in our companies who would be ready and willing to go on full-time active service if and when called upon.' In the event, when the column was formed early in 1921, Rabbitte was instructed not to join but to stay and keep his company going as a unit – especially for routine work like dispatches. He concentrated on organizing dances and raffles, handing the proceeds over to the battalion quartermaster for the upkeep of the column.[182]

On the other hand, columns were far from invulnerable, and always depended on local auxiliaries for survival. Some men never found life on the run very agreeable. In areas where the people were unsupportive, the life was hard and stressful. Like 'real' soldiers, column men learnt that most of their time was spent in waiting for action. On the whole, they seem to have thrived none the less. Men who were not already hardy became so. A Carrick-on-Suir doctor, Patrick Murphy, who looked after two South Tipperary columns, thought that 'generally speaking, the men were always in the pink of condition', though their feet were often in need of treatment. The worst affliction was 'that dreadful visitation known as the Republican itch' – scabies, caused by diet. The West Clare Brigade's history recorded that 'the invariable prelude to retiring for the night was, in the vulgar parlance, "an hour's scratching".'[183] It was treated by washing and rubbing in copious quantities of sulphur ointment: at one point Dr Murphy treated all forty men of Dinny Lacey's column by having them bathe in a lake before applying the ointment (to his discomfiture, the big tins marked with his hospital's name were found by the British).[184] The daily life of most columns was some way removed from the GHQ ideal; most did little more than survive. Survival meant evading British forces by moving constantly between safe areas, 'guided and guarded by local Volunteers'; these moves have been dismissed as 'rambles', but though they may have had a certain aimlessness, the bottom line was that survival was more than a negative achievement. In publicity terms it was priceless. However much the columns varied in reality, in the pages of the *Irish Bulletin* they were all equal. As long as the columns existed, they represented a massive challenge to the British state – out of all proportion to their actual military capacity.

Even if only a small minority of columns ever managed a successful ambush, the transition to 'active service' was a game-changing move for the Army of the Republic. High-profile operations such as an ambush at Rineen in west Clare on 20 September, in which a district inspector of the RIC was killed, and the police retaliated by burning down twenty-six buildings and killing four people in the nearby towns of Ennistymon, Lahinch and Milltown Malbay, got international coverage. The British army reluctantly began to recognize that it was confronting a kind of war that regular soldiers deeply disliked. Even in places where they faced little open opposition, units noted the distinctive topographical features of their area for the conduct of guerrilla warfare: the 14th Brigade at the Curragh, for instance, could see that 'enclosed and winding roads, the peculiar type of Irish bridge, bog roads' afforded 'special facilities to guerrilla forces for laying ambushes and blocking passage of military vehicles'.[185]

THE INTELLIGENCE WAR

The Volunteers' transition into a viable guerrilla force rested in part in the development of specialist technical departments like engineering and signalling. In these services it had some success, though less than might have been hoped – certainly less than GHQ hoped. The Dublin Brigade developed a 5th Battalion devoted to engineering and signals, one of the highest concentrations of expertise anywhere in the country. Its members, however, seem to have hankered after playing a more direct part in the fighting, and though they were strictly forbidden to do so by the Director of Engineering, Rory O'Connor, it is easy to see why they wanted to. In their specialist work they struggled to make a tangible contribution. For instance, Liam Archer, a senior member of the battalion, recorded that when they got hold of a British aircraft wireless transmitter late in 1920, they set up a listening station with a full-time trained operator. 'But I do not recollect that we secured any tangible results.' Experiments with explosives were interesting, and the battalion played a part by running training courses for provincial specialist units, and producing manuals. But, as Mulcahy would later argue, the overall contribution was disappointing.

The most effective special service created by the Volunteers was intelligence. The basic spur in this was defensive; previous attempts at rebellion had usually been stymied by penetration by state intelligence agencies. The IRB's oathbound secret structure had been developed precisely to guard against this. The more open, and more potent, post-1916 military organization was also more vulnerable – or felt itself to be. In fact, as we know, beyond making a fair effort at counting heads in the Sinn Féin clubs and Volunteer companies, British intelligence agencies had a fragile grasp of the republican movement's inner structure. Even in the matter of simply identifying dangerous individuals they had been a big disappointment to Lord French. But some of them, notably the detective division of the DMP, did possess knowledge, derived from long hours of tailing suspects, that was potentially a threat. The Volunteers needed to find ways not only to counter this threat, but to acquire information themselves on a scale that would enable them to plan and carry out operations.

The 1916 Volunteers seem to have had virtually no intelligence system, but their successors soon saw that the kind of conflict they were likely to get into would be defined by a contest for information. According to Florrie O'Donoghue, 'the need for an organised intelligence service became obvious' early in 1919. Even small actions 'required the gathering of some information in advance', and this was 'the basis of all intelligence activity'. He himself became one of the IRA's most successful intelligence officers, not least because he had a clear conception of the level of organization needed. He saw the need for two 'branches', the first military and the second incorporating 'a wide variety of men and women, individually selected', who could acquire information about the enemy. Developing the military intelligence was a matter of finding officers who shared his dedication and his belief in the centrality of intelligence. He himself was fortunate to recruit (and marry) a particularly effective example of the civilian branch.

The development of the republican intelligence system as a whole – for all its legendary status, and real importance – has not been fully charted. The story of local intelligence activity has appeared only in fragmentary form. Most attention has always focused on the 'intelligence war' in Dublin, directed by Michael Collins personally. The most substantial recent account of this devotes only a few lines to the 'national IRA intelligence system' of which the GHQ Intelligence Department supposedly formed the 'apex'.[186] But it is clear that the GHQ intelligence organization could not in fact 'contribute a great deal directly to the operational conduct of the war outside Dublin'.[187] Operational intelligence had to be the responsibility of the local units which needed it, and the quality of their intelligence work was closely related to their military efficiency as a whole.

The low military priority at first given to intelligence is indicated by the fact that GHQ entrusted it to Edmund [Eamonn] Duggan, a sensible if not very imaginative solicitor. It began to move into the limelight after Collins replaced Duggan as director of intelligence – or director of information as he was usually called at this time – in mid-1919. According to Piaras Béaslaí he had actually 'been Director of Intelligence in fact, though not in name, for several months past'.[188] Collins's takeover of

GHQ intelligence was a natural outgrowth of his phenomenal net-working skills. It had been the 1918 German Plot that brought him into intelligence work, though the warning of the impending arrests actually came from someone Collins did not know at that time. Ned (Eamon) Broy, the clerk of the DMP Special Branch (G Division), was passing messages to Duggan, but they were never acted on quickly enough. As soon as Collins met up with Broy, he adopted him as his personal contact. The relationship became the cornerstone of what has been called his 'intelligence franchise', as Collins 'worked his way into the intelligence business', using his privileged information to ease Duggan out.[189] The organization he built, and especially its methods, bore his personal stamp, though it was not entirely his personal creation. Duggan had already taken on the Dublin Brigade's Intelligence Officer, Liam Tobin, as his deputy, and Collins's decision to retain him as his chief intelligence officer was apparently taken mainly in deference to the Dublin brigadier, Dick McKee.

The intelligence staff 'was built up slowly, as suitable men were not easily found', as Piaras Béaslaí explained. Fortunately the core organizing group were strikingly capable and energetic. Collins himself, who seemed to be good at everything, had a marked gift for intelligence work, thanks to a mix of tireless activity and prodigious memory. Tobin turned out to be no mere deputy: he, not Collins, 'was the real Intelligence man in Dublin', one insider said, adding that 'Collins would be the first to admit that.'[190] Tom Cullen and Frank Thornton completed a central quartet who – quite apart from the question of ability – worked together far more harmoniously than their opponents. They set up the first intelligence HQ, with characteristic nerve, over Fowler's premises in Crow Street – 'right bang up against Dublin Castle'. Collins conducted much of his administrative work in offices, but famously preferred public bars in Parnell Square (Vaughan's Hotel at first, and later Devlin's opposite the Rotunda) for face-to-face meetings in the evening. These might have seemed rather exposed, but Thornton suggested that 'a headquarters of this kind in the heart of the city was valuable ... for, being a public house, no notice was taken of people continually going in and out.' Devlin's, remarkably, was never searched, even on the night that Parnell Square was systematically raided. Troops once entered the bar and searched the customers while Collins and his group were in the dining room, but went no further in.

Beyond trying to foster a countrywide organizational structure,

GHQ's capacity to increase general operational intelligence was limited. But it was uniquely placed to penetrate the official structure in the capital. According to Thornton, they had 'one individual who was working with us from the very commencement in records, who secured for us photographs and the names and addresses and history of practically all the typists and all the clerical workers in the most important departments of the enemy'. Armed with this priceless information their agents were soon able to find 'quite a number' who agreed to work for them.[191] The most useful, perhaps, were women like Lily Mernin who worked on British military and police documents. The key step, the creation of a small dedicated counter-intelligence unit, was launched by the Dublin Brigade under McKee, who had already assigned men to tail the DMP detectives and record their movements, and it was McKee's energy that ensured that the unit worked. Mick McDonnell, another Frongoch-camp veteran, 'advocated the execution of those who were responsible' for identifying the 1916 rebels, and eventually persuaded McKee and (presumably) GHQ to agree to this. McKee called some selected men to a meeting 'and asked us if we had any objection to shooting enemy agents'. Most seem to have done, but a handful – like Jim Slattery – said they were 'prepared to obey orders'.[192]

The first action of this 'special duty' squad – which became known as the Squad – was the shooting of a detective sergeant they called 'the Dog', Patrick Smyth, on 30 July 1919. It nearly failed, through inexperience and inappropriate weapons – .38 revolvers, quickly replaced by .45s. After that a steady sequence of shootings brought G Division to the point of paralysis by the end of the year. In January 1920 the Assistant Commissioner in charge of the Division, William Redmond, was killed. This was a psychologically stunning blow, coming only a few weeks after he had been brought to Dublin from Belfast to rebuild the detective service. The aura of omniscience and omnipotence that began to surround the GHQ intelligence outfit was powerfully enhanced. The shock effect echoed throughout the police service and beyond. The struggle went on for a few more months, but the old 'eyes and ears of the Castle' were effectively closed. Just how formidable 'the G' had really been is open to doubt; though Broy painted a picture of an elaborate network of undercover operatives, the organization was certainly more dangerous in the imagination of its targets than in reality. The DMP detectives might be hated and even feared, but the 'almost flawless

system of espionage' conjured up in Dorothy Macardle's great republican history was a nationalist myth.[193] The police had a unique store of
personal knowledge, but no organization of spies or undercover agents,
and no proper record system. Their operating procedures – they 'spent
a lot of time at railway stations to see who got on or off trains' – meant
that 'far from being an invisible hand', they were quite well known to
their targets.[194] When one of them was killed, a significant chunk of their
database effectively went with him.

In neutering the British capacity to get at the republican organization, the most successful action was the assassination of Alan Bell on 26
March. A former resident magistrate, who had once pursued the funds
of the Irish Land League, and was now (among other things) President
of the Irish Banks Court, Bell was burrowing into the network of concealed bank deposits housing the Republican Loan funds. His investigation
was far too effective for Collins's liking. Remarkably, though two
attempts seem to have been made already to kill him, Bell went on taking the tram to work. When a stranger asked him, 'Are you Mr Bell?', he
confirmed that he was. The questioner was Mick McDonnell, who
immediately announced, 'Come on, Mr Bell, your time has come,' and
together with Liam Tobin dragged him off the tram into the street,
where they shot him in the head and chest. The tram passengers were
told by other Squad members to 'sit there quietly and everything will be
all right'; they did so, and no passer-by seemed to pay any attention to
the 'respectable young men' who walked away from the corpse.[195] This
daylight public assassination was both dramatic and effective: it appears
to have brought the pursuit of republican finances to a permanent halt.

The destruction of the police intelligence service in Dublin was a real
success, but it did not provide a template for the development of an
intelligence service suitable for the army as a whole. Usable operational
intelligence information could not usually be acquired through insiders,
but needed a very wide spread of informants. Building up such a broad
network proved to be a slower process. In fact, in GHQ's view, this task
was never properly engaged with. Its highly critical review of local units
in March 1921 would find a 'very faulty grasp generally' of the key
value of intelligence. This verdict is oddly similar to that of a British
intelligence chief, who pointed out that with the 'manifest advantages'
republican intelligence possessed, 'it is surprising that it has not been
better.' He may well have been right about the basic reasons for this as

well. Although frequent mail raids generated some high-grade material for a time, once the British stopped using the mail this source dried up. 'The constant capture of complete offices belonging to leading rebels', as against the 'immunity to capture of those belonging to the Crown Forces', gave the British a definite advantage. The republicans did not produce formal methods 'to crystallise the Intelligence gained' (in none of the many offices raided, for instance, had 'any card index system been found').[196]

'ANOTHER MARTYR'

At 5.40 a.m. on 25 October 1920, Terence MacSwiney died in Brixton prison on his seventy-fourth day of hunger strike. He had been arrested in a raid on Cork City Hall on 12 August – a few days after the passage of ROIA – and began a hunger strike even before he was tried. The raid was triggered by information that 'persons holding important positions of command in Cork Brigade unit of the Republican Army had received "official" summons to attend a meeting in City Hall . . . A meeting of Commandants of Cork Brigade was being held either simultaneously or under cover of an arbitration court.'[197] MacSwiney was in fact presiding at the Brigade Council meeting; he had succeeded Tomás Mac Curtain as Cork No. 1's brigadier as well as lord mayor. Fortunately for Cork 1, the British did not know who any of the leaders were. They netted nearly all the brigade staff, including Seán O'Hegarty, with Liam Lynch (who had come for an IRB meeting later that day) as a bonus. This might, as O'Donoghue said, have been a 'staggering blow'.[198] But in an almost incredible intelligence failure, they released the lot apart from MacSwiney four days later. And, surprisingly anxious to demonstrate that 'no interference with a Sinn Féin arbitration court was contemplated by the authorities', they charged him only with possession of a police cipher (which, ironically, he had not possessed: O'Donoghue, one of the few who got away, had had it).

MacSwiney's trial proceeded on the assumption that he was a republican official, and he replied in the same coin: 'You have got to realise, and will have to realise it before very long, that the Irish Republic is really existing. I want to remind you of the fact that the gravest offence that can be committed by any individual is an offence against the head of the state. The offence is only relatively less great when committed against the head of a city.'[199] Only at the time of his death did the British finally realize that he was a senior Volunteer officer.

Immediately after his arrest, MacSwiney stopped taking food, and by the time he was sentenced (to two years' imprisonment) he was in the fifth day of what would become the most epic hunger strike of the revolutionary period. He told the court that he would 'be free, alive or dead, within a month'. In the event, he survived seventy-three days. His 'almost miraculous' survival as his hunger strike lasted into its second month gave the British authorities plenty of opportunity to reflect on the significance of his protest. Although some ministers thought that MacSwiney had done nothing worse than 'things ... done by some of the leaders of the Ulster party', the Cabinet this time dug its heels in, holding that 'to give in to hunger striking meant paralysis of the law'. Releasing him would, Lloyd George insisted, 'completely disintegrate and dishearten the police and military in Ireland'.[200] Many thought that MacSwiney must be secretly receiving some nourishment.

Eleven prisoners in Cork gaol were on hunger strike at the same time as MacSwiney. It is clear that the government was less preoccupied with the likely consequences of their deaths than of MacSwiney's, but it is not clear whether that was because of his status or because he was being held on less serious charges.[201] Still, there was no concession. The humiliation of the Mountjoy releases was still fresh in official memory. Collins thought that 'the British Cabinet mean to finish this hunger strike weapon of ours, and do not intend releasing you.' He ordered MacSwiney to 'give up the strike as you will be ten times a greater asset to the movement alive than dead'.[202] (He and Griffith would lead the way in bringing the hunger-strike policy to a halt after MacSwiney's death.) At the Home Office, on the other hand, Edward Troup was writing, 'I believe the Sinn Féin organisers think that the Lord Mayor will be worth more to them dead than alive.' Like most British perspectives, this belittled MacSwiney himself, but it was a sharp view of the government's dilemma.

MacSwiney was the first republican leader to die on hunger strike since Thomas Ashe, and his death had the same kind of impact. His hunger strike had become a global media event, and the authorities could not prevent his funeral from being turned into another great republican manifestation. When his emaciated corpse was taken from

Brixton to the Catholic cathedral in Southwark, it was laid out in his Volunteer uniform, and the bier was draped in the tricolour. After the service on 28 October, the funeral procession set out for Holyhead, with a huge crowd following it across London. The *Daily News* editor Robert Lynd suggested that 'London learned more Irish history yesterday than it had ever learned before' (he added realistically that perhaps it 'only half-learned it'). 'What London saw yesterday is an image of all Ireland.' At Holyhead MacSwiney's body was rerouted to Cork instead of Dublin, on Henry Wilson's insistence, to prevent much greater demonstrations in the Irish capital. But even in its absence a requiem mass was performed by Cardinal Walsh in the pro-cathedral, and the streets were thronged with people. In Cork, at the lying in state, 'the people . . . have filed past the open coffin in unending procession all day.' The Dáil declared the day of his funeral, 31 October, a day of national mourning. In an open letter the Bishop of Cork set MacSwiney's 'heroic sacrifice' alongside the deaths of legendary nationalist martyrs Lord Edward Fitzgerald, Robert Emmet and Pearse: he 'takes his place among the martyrs in the sacred cause of the freedom of Ireland'.[203] At the very least, Lady Gregory hoped – noting that *Punch* had just published a cartoon of the 'Irish Volunteer Army' featuring the kind of simian stereotypes for which it had been notorious in the past – the Lord Mayor 'had not given his life in vain if only to contradict that'. His portrait was in all the national papers – 'all the American ones' as well.[204]

MacSwiney's ordeal had effects that rippled out beyond the ordinary media. It came to preoccupy Gregory's friend Yeats, and precipitated his decision to publish, at last, his poem 'Easter 1916', which appeared in the *New Statesman* on 23 October (four years after it had been written). For all its studied ambivalence, its validation of the 1916 leaders was a potent indication of the way moderate nationalists were becoming increasingly 'republican'. It brought his 'great weight of cultural influence to bear on the unrest and discontent', as Gregory had earlier urged him to. But whereas Gregory directly likened the Volunteers to the Italian fighters she had read about in G. M. Trevelyan's *Garibaldi's Defence of the Roman Republic*, Yeats held back from celebrating the rebels – rather he lamented the collapse of standards on both sides. With rules gone, 'we . . . are but weasels fighting in a hole,' he wrote in 'Thoughts on the Present State of the World'. The Lord Mayor of Cork was perhaps an exception. Yeats now decided to mount MacSwiney's play *The*

Revolutionist at the Abbey Theatre in Dublin. It was 'not a good play' –
MacSwiney had, he judged, 'lived among harsh political types' for too
long – but it 'certainly increases ones [sic] respect for the Lord Mayor.
He had intellect & lived & died for it.' Its 'last pages would greatly
move the audience who will see the Mayor in the plays [sic] hero', and
the play was indeed a big success.[205]

A second notable death followed shortly after MacSwiney's. In Dublin on 20 September a group of twenty-five Volunteers had jumped a
military ration party collecting bread at a bakery in Church Street. After
they had called on the troops to surrender their guns, a brief blaze of fire
broke out before the attackers ran off. Three of the escorting soldiers
were killed, and one of the attackers – Kevin Barry, a second-year medical student – was found under the military lorry with a loaded
Parabellum. (It had jammed, demonstrating why many preferred to use
less fancy revolvers.) Barry's capture itself hinted at some of the Dublin
Brigade's operational problems. He had joined the attacking party at
the last minute, having just heard of the plan the previous day. The
attack went wrong – possibly because, as the military account had it,
the Volunteers started shooting prematurely, or, as the Volunteers'
account had it, the attackers called on the troops to surrender their
arms, but failed to cover one of the soldiers, who opened fire.

Barry was one of the few republican fighters to have been captured
while 'levying war', and was tried by court martial under ROIA. He
refused to recognize the court, offer any evidence or cross-examine the
witnesses, and was sentenced to death by hanging on 20 October. The
sentence was confirmed by the C-in-C on the 27th, two days after Mac-
Swiney's death. At this point the publicity machines of both sides swung
into action. Collins and McKee ordered Barry to swear an affidavit
detailing his ill-treatment under interrogation, and Griffith announced
that his execution would be 'an outrage upon the law and customs of
nations'. He should be treated as a prisoner of war. Griffith's description
of Barry as 'a boy of 18' was not relevant to his argument, but turned
out to be the biggest issue of the whole case. The British authorities
made the same point. As Macready told Wilson, 'of the 3 men who were
killed by him and his friends two were 19 and one 20' – and as these
were 'army ages', they were probably younger. But their identities had
no resonance in Ireland, while Barry inspired one of the most resonant

of all republican ballads. Archbishop Walsh and the Lord Mayor of Dublin led a campaign to secure a reprieve.

It was hardly surprising that Barry was roughly treated by the unit he had attacked, and he certainly suffered a sprained arm. He was widely said to have been tortured, though there is no direct evidence for this. The issue may have been less significant in the end than the fact that the authorities went through with his execution, bringing an English hangman over for the purpose. 'In order to avoid any bungling we ought to engage a professional from England if possible.' (John Ellis was engaged for a fee of £15, with an assistant at £5; the Irish Office in London helpfully suggested that 'if rope and other apparatus are required, Dublin Castle should telegraph' – though 'probably they have a set.' Also, police protection might be necessary on their way back from the prison.)[206] Barry's execution was a highly charged symbolic moment. He was to be hanged 'like a dog', not shot 'like a soldier', in the words of his ballad. This was a notable shift from the procedure used in 1916, but the alternative never seems to have been entertained.

Macready insisted that if 'Berry' were reprieved 'it will irritate the troops to a very great extent, because here is a clean cut case of murder without any doubt . . . and if the man is not hung, how on earth can we prevent troops making reprisals?' The government accepted that any flinching at this point would be a fatal blow to the credibility of the 'restoration of order' campaign. As Sturgis reflected, 'I can't see any reason to let him off if we are ever going to execute anybody.' He sat in on 'a really impressive interview' on 31 October as Lord French reviewed the case – 'His Ex said at the beginning that a life was at stake and the proceedings were thorough and anything but perfunctory.' The Irish Lord Chancellor, Sir James Campbell, unlike the Archbishop and the Lord Mayor counted Barry's youth as a mitigating factor – though Sturgis contemptuously judged that Campbell's opinion was the product not so much of legal reasoning as of cold feet, or as he put it, 'the frozen toe'. French overruled his advice. Whether this was a case of the law taking its necessary course, or a deliberate act of political propaganda, its effect was the same.[207] It was left to an anonymous balladeer to ensure that Kevin Barry would become 'another martyr for old Ireland' and a deathless symbol of struggle for 'the cause of liberty' (though he is, rather oddly, included as one of the so-called 'forgotten ten').*

* Republican prisoners executed in Mountjoy gaol.

'A CAMPAIGN THAT DID NOT SEEM TO BE LEADING ANYWHERE'

Dublin District Command believed that there was a significant shift in the balance of power in late October 1920. Terence MacSwiney's death 'had a far-reaching effect in reviving confidence' in the government's firmness of purpose, and 'a further deterioration' of IRA morale was noticeable. Significantly, 'for the first time ammunition was found abandoned by rebels,' and several substantial 'rebel arsenals' were captured.[208] On Armistice Day a lorryload of Auxiliaries pulled up in College Green at 11 a.m., 'tumbled out and stood to attention for the two minutes'. The crowd – 'many Trinity College students among them, no doubt', as Sturgis reflected, 'but still the Dublin crowd' – sang God Save the King and cheered the Auxiliaries as they drove off; 'I can't think that anything of this sort would have happened a month ago.'[209] On 14 November a military raid on the Republican Stores in Talbot Street was believed to have surprised a high-level Volunteer meeting. Seán Treacy, who ran out into the street and opened fire to distract the troops, was killed.

In some rural areas, there seems to have been a sense of frustration towards the end of 1920. In the 3rd Tipperary Brigade, which lost its three leading lights when Robinson, Treacy and Breen went to Dublin, a group emerged 'who wanted a new plan of campaign, who thought that ambushes and lying in wait might create a certain type of man that we did not want'. They seem to have wanted a more open kind of war. Eamon O'Dwyer (who had originally persuaded Seamus Robinson to move from Glasgow to Tipperary) represented them on a trip to Dublin to try to get more weapons. He met Brugha, the Minister for Defence, and told him 'that it was very difficult for us to continue without a reasonable supply of arms; that we had quite a considerable amount of funds, probably £1,000'. Brugha 'seemed to think that there was no difficulty in the matter'; he was 'full of fight and the only question was to get the arms and go in and get the enemy, attack . . . them every way'. But when he was asked to make arrangements, he 'told me that it was not in his hands, that I should see Michael Collins'. Collins, however, 'was quite indignant that I should be looking for something which . . . I knew was not there' – 'there were no arms to be got.' When any became available they would get their share, but they 'must carry on some way without arms'. When O'Dwyer suggested that 'a good many of the crowd were not prepared to carry on a campaign that did not seem to be leading anywhere, only producing certain types we did not want,' Collins made light of the issue. O'Dwyer 'alluded to some of those things that had happened, such as robberies for personal gain, but he said the IRA ought to be strong enough to deal sternly with those fellows'. Collins ribbed him – 'we seemed to be a very purse-proud crowd in Tipperary with this £1,000 we had to spend' – and 'on this jocose note we parted.' O'Dwyer went on to talk to Griffith – acting as president in de Valera's absence – who 'did not like the situation that had developed and he feared for our ability to stick it out'. But as to what to do, the acting President was unclear. About the 'departure from national idealism of some of our people' he was 'non-committal'. Asked whether he thought they should turn from ambushes to 'strike big blows in other ways', he 'referred me to the army authorities'. O'Dwyer had come full circle: 'I had got nothing for my journey.'[210]

Mulcahy always urged local units that they could significantly increase their striking power by producing their own weapons. The manufacture of firearms was out of the question, but ammunition such as shotgun cartridges was relatively simple to make. Mines, too, which could play a key part in ambushes and attacks on barracks, were theoretically quite simple. Constructing reliable ones, though, proved to be a huge problem in most places. Rifle ammunition called for quite sophisticated machinery. The most useful weapon that could be home-made was the hand grenade. The Dublin Brigade showed what could be done, in the arsenal it set up in the basement of a Parnell Street bicycle shop. A group of engineers under the direction of Matt Furlong built a foundry, and cast iron cases (called shells) three days a week, and brass bodies for the firing mechanisms (called necks) one day. Casting brass created a large volume of white smoke, and 'the filling of Parnell Street with a white cloud became so regularly a weekly occurrence that no one ever took any notice [or] attempted to send for [the] Fire Brigade.'[211] In fact DMP detectives paid two visits, but took so long to look round the shop upstairs that the men in the basement were able to cover up their lethal products. The shells were finished on a lathe (which had been commandeered by the British from a Dublin jeweller but returned at his request), and safety levers cut from sheet iron by hand. The finished grenade shells were 'no larger than a large duck egg', and with firing neck attached would fit in a normal hand. Finally they were taken to a workshop in Dominick Street to be packed with gelignite and primed. By mid-1920 the output reached a hundred grenades a week, distributed among Dublin companies at the cost of manufacture, nine shillings each.

Operationally, these were formidable weapons. They were set with a four-second fuse, much shorter than the seven-second Mills bomb – so that they could not be thrown back, as the Mills could at close quarters. This was cut again to three seconds in response to the fitting of wire cages to ADRIC tenders as protection against grenade attack. Many grenades burst on the cages, leading to a popular misconception that the grenades had hooks to catch on the wires. In fact, the IRA engineers made strenuous efforts to produce an impact grenade, but without success. There would also be more upsetting failures.

In the autumn of 1920 the intrepid Parnell Street engineering section tried to raise the stakes by building a version of the Stokes trench mortar. The prototype was successfully trialled with blank shells in October, but when live ammunition was tried, they could not get it to hit the ground nose first. Patrick McHugh believed that the problem was that the shell needed greater weighting at the front, but Matt Furlong decided to adjust the shell and try again. McHugh tried to dissuade him, but Furlong, 'who was a very strong willed man . . . would not give in . . . He accused me of being windy and ordered me away from himself and [the] gun.' As he was walking away he heard a muffled explosion – 'the gun had disappeared and Matt was lying on the ground . . . the whole left side of his body was a frightful sight.' Furlong's first question was 'Is the gun alright?' Peadar Clancy, the new GHQ Director of Munitions, who was watching the trial, called an ambulance and took him to the Mater Hospital in Dublin, where he died. That was the end of the mortar-production programme.

McHugh lamented that this was 'a severe blow to Dublin Brigade and IRA generally'. They 'could have easily shelled British positions . . . by mounting [the] gun on a small lorry' (something the IRA would eventually get around to in its attack on Downing Street in 1991), and 'it does not require much imagination to realise the effect such attacks would have had.' But though McHugh wanted to go on, Clancy 'seemed to have lost faith in our ability to produce a trench mortar'. Worse was to follow. Clancy himself, who had not been long in the job of munitions director, would be killed, not long after Furlong's death, on Bloody Sunday. The workshop at 198 Parnell Street succeeded in doubling its production of grenades after the mortar disaster, but was eventually discovered in an Auxiliary search operation on 10 December. Though the engineers escaped, and mingled with 'the usual Dublin crowd ... watching our beloved premises being dismantled', this was a definite blow: 'our one and only working munition factory' was gone.[212] No successor to Clancy was appointed until late January 1921, and it took even longer to set up a replacement factory.

'THE VERY AIR IS MADE SWEETER'

The questions that can be posed about the efficiency of the Volunteer intelligence service generally can also be directed to the section directly under Collins's control, and particularly to the most emblematic action in the Dublin 'intelligence war', the assassinations of 21 November 1920 – 'Bloody Sunday'. Was this, as the legend has it, a singularly professional and decisive intelligence operation? It was unquestionably a dramatic one. Around 9 a.m., eight addresses – all, apart from the Gresham Hotel, in south Dublin streets like Morehampton Road, Upper Mount Street, Baggot Street and Earlsfort Terrace – were 'visited' by armed Volunteers. Twelve British officers were killed in their lodgings – nine of them still in their pyjamas – and several wounded; two Auxiliaries who found themselves at the scene of the attack in Upper Mount Street and tried to run back to the ADRIC depot at Beggars Bush barracks for help were also killed in the street.

The drama went into a second act in the afternoon, when Croke Park Gaelic football stadium was raided by Crown forces, apparently on the assumption that some of the attackers would be there for a big Dublin–Tipperary game. The operation, using a substantial body of troops with armoured cars, ADRIC and regular police, aimed 'to surround the whole enclosure and search the people as they were passed out'. Just before the game started, and more crucially before the military cordon had been set up, the Auxiliaries drove up to the entrance. The plan of ordering the spectators to leave the stadium immediately broke down. Claiming that gunshots had come from the grandstand, the Auxiliaries fired into the crowd – for three minutes, until 'the attackers' fire was silenced', according to the official account. Gunfire erupted all around. A military machine gun (possibly in an armoured car) posted by the entrance fired off fifty rounds, according to the military court of inquiry; and at least 220 shots were fired by the Auxiliaries. Twelve people died and eleven were seriously injured, either shot or crushed in the panicking crowd.[213] The army blamed the Auxiliaries, and the Auxiliaries blamed the regular police. The whole operation looked to many people like a reprisal.

A final act was to follow. In the early evening, three men who had been arrested the night before and were being held in the Dublin Castle guardroom were killed; one was the Dublin Brigade commandant Dick McKee, another was his former vice-commandant, Peadar Clancy. These high-profile Volunteer officers joined the list of those 'shot while attempting to escape' – which they may indeed have done, though as in other cases it was never clear why they had to be killed. Republicans have always believed that their interrogators tortured and mutilated them, though there is no evidence for this. (Edward MacLysaght, a friend of the third man killed that evening, Conor Clune, saw all the corpses when he collected Clune's body from the military hospital, and insisted that 'they were not disfigured.')[214] But they were indisputably dead – and apart from the unlucky Clune, who had no military role, the deaths were a serious blow to the republican command.

Why were the morning attacks launched? It is worth raising this question, in light not just of their deadliness but of their still deadlier sequel. The Castle shootings were a personal disaster for Michael Collins. Did he believe that the British secret intelligence group had really been on the point of blowing his own organization apart? There was some evidence to suggest this; in October Liam Tobin and Tom Cullen had been pulled in for questioning, and Frank Thornton held for ten days. Did this mean that 'it was only a matter of time before they and he [Collins] were finished'?[215] Or was the operation essentially a gesture, designed primarily for its psychological impact – demonstrating the power and ruthlessness of Collins's outfit? It has been suggested that its primary significance was as 'a calculated political act'.[216] Collins himself justified it, rather oddly, as 'the destruction of the undesirables who continued to make miserable the lives of ordinary decent citizens'.[217] If, as Thornton and others always maintained, all the targets were secret service agents, their actions would surely not have affected anyone outside the IRA.

A careful recent study sets the operation in a context where the balance of power on the Dublin streets seemed to be teetering.[218] Conditions in the capital were hard to compare directly with those in the provinces, but the level of threat through most of 1920 was lower. Though the city's military command identified a dozen 'Bad Areas' in May 1920 (areas like Upper Sackville Street, Parnell and Capel Streets, North King Street, Aungier Street and Portobello Bridge), it was not until October that it felt it necessary to issue a warning that all troops should expect to encounter 'resistance' in moving about.[219] The attack in North King Street on 20 September was the most serious so far.

The Dublin Brigade's response to the arrival of the Auxiliaries had been ineffective; McKee had still not set up ASUs for the brigade itself, so that in effect the Squad was the only full-time striking force operating in the capital. Harry Colley believed that the brigade's morale was being undermined by the fact that 'the Auxiliaries were now so much in evidence everywhere and we seemed to have withdrawn completely from the fight.' There was a feeling that 'some action would have to be taken to counteract this influence.'[220] Mulcahy said, 'the pressure on us was very great; we were being made to feel that they were very close on the heels of some of us.' He suffered a serious, potentially disastrous loss when a case full of his papers was seized in a mid-November raid.[221] Collins himself was definitely upset by the execution of Kevin Barry on 1 November. So were ordinary Volunteers like Todd Andrews, who recalled the 'deep emotion' with which his company debated how to make 'some gesture of retaliation'.

According to Thornton, a joint meeting of the Dáil ministry and GHQ (the only one before the Truce) was convened to approve the operation. Who decided to call it, and why, is not known – nor which ministers were there, apart from Brugha and Collins. They were evidently presented with a target list, with Thornton's assurance that 'each and every man on my list was an accredited secret service agent of the British government.' Brugha seems not to have challenged the concept of the operation, but tinkered with the hit list on the grounds that there was not enough evidence in some cases. But evidence of what? It is not clear exactly how the threat the agents presented was described or assessed. The term 'Cairo Gang' was later used to suggest that they were an organized group – but while some took this to mean that they had formed in Cairo, a centre of British wartime intelligence, others said that they frequented the Cairo Café, a well-known place on Grafton

Street, one of Dublin's busiest (which would seem odd for secret agents). Ironically, a much more concrete threat was posed by the information captured in Mulcahy's collection of documents – 'some amazing good stuff' as Mark Sturgis exulted – in which some 200 Volunteers were identified (and classified as 'very good shots, good shots, etc.'). The British started to raid for 'these beauties' on the night of 19 November.[222]

In later statements we find dramatic assertions such as that 'the life of every IRA man in Dublin was at stake.'[223] Assuming that the intelligence group was believed to pose an immediate threat, and the attack on them was likely to be a one-off operation that would be impossible to repeat, it was obviously vital that all the men targeted were actually members of this group, and that as many of the group as possible should be hit. The list of men attacked on 21 November would seem to fall some way short of such an operation, but the original list was evidently much more extensive. Even attacking eight addresses simultaneously was a big operation that called for well over sixty gunmen (in squads of at least eight, led by a Squad member and a GHQ intelligence officer), together with scouts a total of more than a hundred men. Seán Russell, given the task of co-ordinating the operation, had to bring in many untried men. Todd Andrews – like a number of men who had backed off from service in the Squad – worried about the morality of the operation ('killing a man in cold blood was alien to our ideas of how war should be conducted'), as well as its likely risks, now looming larger thanks to the 'terror' inspired by the Auxiliaries ('I had increasing fears that we might be surprised by the Tans').

Simon Donnelly warned McKee of the difficulty of getting enough volunteers. (He recalled later that one of the officers of his battalion, 'when detailed for the job, asked permission to be relieved of his part in it as he had some scruples about this type of operation'.)[224] McKee's reply was simply 'if we don't get them, they will get us.' Russell's plan sought to reduce the risk of the attackers being recognized by having them operate outside their own battalion areas, though this brought problems of unfamiliarity. To minimize the risk of uncertain gunfights, targets were to be attacked while still asleep at 9 in the morning (Sundays were notoriously lazy days). To calm the nerves of the attackers, quite elaborate plans were made for their escape.

No copy of the original target list has survived; presumably the list Thornton presented to the joint meeting was etched into his memory, but he did not reproduce it in his later account. It was undoubtedly longer than the eventual casualty list, but we do not know how much. Some targeted men were certainly missed – two escaped even from the scene of the heaviest slaughter, at 28 Upper Pembroke Street – and other men were killed in error. There are many vividly detailed accounts, but, like most recollections of intense violence, they do not dovetail exactly. Clearly not all went to plan in the Pembroke Street attack, though the attackers were helped by the maid, a contact of the Squad man Charlie Dalton. Dalton recalled the attack as 'the longest five minutes of my life – or were they the shortest? I cannot tell, but they were tense and dreadful.' The caretaker was shaking out the doormats when the eight attackers – supported by fourteen scouts – walked up the steps at 9, so the front door was fortuitously open. In the hall they split into two groups of four to go up the two thickly carpeted staircases, and on the landing Dalton's group split again into two to enter two bedrooms simultaneously. They identified the men they wanted, who each had a revolver at his hand, but both were shot before they could use them. Dalton was supposed to search for papers, but his unit commander, Captain Paddy Flanagan, brusquely dismissed him with 'Get the hell out of this!'[225]

Todd Andrews could not decide 'whether I was glad or sorry' that his target, 'a man who was regarded as a key man in the British network', who 'went under the *nom de guerre* of Captain Nobel' and lived in Ranelagh with 'his wife, or some woman', was not at home when his group arrived. They found only 'a half naked woman who sat up in bed looking terror-stricken' – as well she might – and causing the chaste Andrews 'shame and embarrassment' despite his excitement. He was surprised when two armed men, 'from Collins's squad', turned up to search for papers, and so apparently was his company commander, F. X. Coughlan. When they started 'behaving like Black and Tans ... overturned furniture, pushing the occupants of the house around, and either through carelessness or malice set fire to a room in which there were children', Coughlan was furious, and insisted that his unit put the fire out. This took them half an hour of forming a bucket chain from the only tap in the house, in the basement, to the burning room on the first floor.[226]

Many believed that only one mistake was made – Captain McCormack, shot in the Gresham, 'an innocent veterinary officer' in the words of one historian. Even this low error rate was disputed by an author who analysed the victims' service records. McCormack was not on the Army List, but his career pattern 'indicated' Secret Intelligence Service; this appeared to be confirmed by a remark in Mark Sturgis's diary that 'two secret service men were assassinated in the Gresham Hotel.' The fact that McCormack had recently arrived from Cairo was suspicious in itself, and there was 'the possibility that he was in Ireland to assess the threatened use of germ warfare by the IRA' (a threat revealed in Mulcahy's lost documents). 'The professionalism of Michael Collins's organization and the quality of his information' meant, it has been suggested, that 'there was a specific reason for the presence of each man on his list.'[227]

But Sturgis had no special knowledge of the 'secret service', and of course the list was not drawn up by Collins himself. As he admitted in a remarkable note to Mulcahy in 1922 – when McCormack's mother protested against the suggestion that her son was a British spy, and offered a quite plausible explanation for his visit to Dublin – 'we had no evidence that he was a Secret Service Agent.' Moreover, 'several of the 21st November cases were just regular officers. Some of the names were put on [the list] by the Dublin Brigade.'[228]

Lieutenant Colonel Woodcock, wounded in the Pembroke Street attack, has been identified as 'probably the officer in charge of the intelligence group', because his military record 'speaks for itself'. It certainly spoke of exemplary military service, though not obviously of the 'swashbuckling bravery common to men of the intelligence service'.[229] (Woodcock had a DSO but not, for example, a Military Cross.) He was actually commanding a battalion of the Lancashire Fusiliers, and living in Dublin with his wife (like a number of the victims). She gave a remarkable press interview the day after the attacks, later written up as an article and then a book.[230] In it she made no attempt to deny that 'hush hush men' were known to be living in the lodgings, but insisted that her husband was not one of them. Was this an elaborate hoax by the secret service?

The British authorities never denied that some of the men killed on Sunday morning were indeed undercover intelligence agents. But while their claim that many of them were merely 'court-martial officers', and that half were not serving officers at all, may be partly true, they naturally did not offer any direct evidence. The republican case was that their targets represented an immediate and deadly threat to them. (In view of this, and the risks the attackers faced, the fact that they made even a few mistakes may seem surprising.) The precise balance may never be established beyond doubt, though the most careful recent analysis has concluded that, as far as concerns the twelve members of the Crown forces killed, 'if there was a Cairo Gang' (in the sense of a group trained in Egypt) 'these men were not in it.'[231]

There is a slightly different issue to consider as well: how effective was the operation? Frank Thornton grandly claimed that 'the British Secret Service was wiped out on 21 November 1920' – understandably enough, since he had drawn up the original hit list. But even if we add the qualification 'in Ireland', the claim is obviously overblown. The fact that at least one attack, on the Standard Hotel in Harcourt Street, was aborted, shows that a number of the intended targets were missed. Some have suggested that this attack was abandoned because the targets were absent, others that the commanding officer got cold feet. Dan Bryan of C Company, 4th Battalion, who would later become head of the Irish intelligence service, joined one of the attacking units at the last moment. It was 'regarded as a big job', with men from two companies involved, and his company commander after 'some conference with the other officers' in the street decided 'it was . . . too big.'[232] This seems to suggest that several targets were missed here.

Oscar Traynor, McKee's successor as commander of the Dublin Brigade, suggested that the military intelligence system in Dublin was completely paralysed. If we add 'temporarily', this may be plausible. The shock effect of the morning attacks was tremendous – on the city as a whole as well as on the intelligence service. But in the longer term Collins 'knew the operation had fallen far short of his vaulting ambitions'. As far as the 'intelligence war' went, it was not decisive. The British intelligence machine was still in its infancy, and this was a beginning rather than an end. The loss of even ten agents was not like the earlier crushing of G Division. More survived than were killed, the institutional memory survived, and security lessons were learnt. Indeed, the British military command in Dublin did not interpret the attacks as targeting the intelligence system at all, hypothesizing (even with the benefit of two years' historical perspective) that 'the object of this outrage was probably to smash the machinery of Dublin District Headquarters.'[233] The addresses 'visited' were all houses where Dublin District staff 'lived out', and they still believed that 'the murderers became confused and took lives that were not intended.'

And in any case, as the army dismissively put it, 'Secret Service was on the whole a failure in Ireland.' It simply did not represent the threat that Mulcahy implied when he later talked of 'a scheme that was, in a considered and deliberate way, planned as an espionage system for the definite purpose of destroying the Directing Corps of the Volunteer activity', and said that killing the agents 'completely saved the situation' by allowing Dublin to remain the seat of republican political and military power.[234] But, seen as an element in the wider republican resistance, the Bloody Sunday attacks were far more effective. Their public impact was huge. Big crowds lined the Liffey banks and bridges when the bodies of the dead officers were taken to North Wall on their way to London; 'reverent and quiet', according to one British reporter, who did not see 'any man who did not take off his hat and stay uncovered until the gun-carriages had passed' (though he also heard that elsewhere 'a great many hats and caps were forcibly removed by Auxiliaries and thrown into the Liffey').[235] In London the victims were given a state funeral, with a procession down Whitehall to Westminster Abbey. This no doubt generated an impulse to revenge in some; but it also strengthened the views of the small but thoughtful 'peace party' which accepted that some compromise settlement must be found, the sooner the better. The day after the attacks, Griffith received a message – apparently from Lloyd George – urging him 'for God's sake to keep his head, and not to break off the slender link that had been established. Tragic as the events in Dublin were, they were of no importance. These men were soldiers and took a soldier's risk.'[236]

Collins found 'the very air is made sweeter' by Bloody Sunday morning, though in the end the day's outcomes were less agreeable. The afternoon killings formed a grim kind of balance to the morning's. Collins never ceased to lament the loss of McKee in particular, and neither he nor Mulcahy would afterwards have the same close relationship with Oscar Traynor and the Dublin Brigade. For the British, 21 November was a step-change. While the police were blazing away at Croke Park, a meeting of the Irish Executive launched a new military programme – large-scale searches, roadblocks, curfews and internment on suspicion. Military personnel would no longer be allowed to live outside barracks in 'no man's land'. Five hundred arrests were made by the army inside a week (including Arthur Griffith, arrested in defiance of political instructions). This stepping-up of the counter-insurgency campaign certainly intensified the physical pressure on the republicans: raiding made the maintenance of administrative offices much more hazardous. But raising the stakes also carried a psychological cost: the more the British took the gloves off, the greater the expectation that they would land a knockout blow.

Fortunately for the Volunteers, the intelligence service on which the British campaign rested was still less efficient than theirs. Though Collins may have played a complicated game in Dublin, the Volunteer intelligence organization was essentially a single system. The British state, like so many others, undermined its own intelligence capacity by creating multiple agencies with different agendas and operating principles. When the army took the lead role in early 1920 it judged police intelligence useless, and had to start from scratch. Although it made fair progress, the intelligence effort 'unravelled overnight' after the release of the hunger strikers in April. The new intelligence chief appointed in May, Ormonde Winter, was an artilleryman like Tudor, and a friend of his. These facts, rather than for any skill or experience in either intelligence or police work, seem to have been the reason he got the job. He certainly cut a distinctive figure, striking the layman as the perfect image of a spymaster. But cloak-and-dagger operations, however attractive to him and to many historians, could not be his main concern. He was well aware that building up an effective intelligence system was a slow business – 'not a task that can be accomplished in a day, a week, or a month' – but that time was not on his side. He had to make the best of the system that existed, and that meant using what survived of the old police structure. 'The psychology of the police sergeant must be taken into consideration.' This meant that the parallel systems of police and military intelligence, which Macready believed it was Winter's purpose to bring together, remained separate – indeed increasingly so as time went on. Winter himself attributed this to two things: 'one was a large increase in the activity of the rebel organisation, and the other the fact that the Army itself became a target for attack'. Why these things should have had this effect is not clear.

But Winter exemplified the besetting failing of all British intelligence work – internal competition. In the summer Charles Tegart, a brilliant Indian CID officer, was co-opted – apparently on Lloyd George's

personal initiative – as Winter's chief assistant. A Trinity College gradu-
ate, who would go on to become a leading troubleshooter in imperial
counter-insurgency campaigns, Tegart had become famous in Whitehall
for his success in countering terrorism in Bengal. In reality, he was probably far better qualified than Winter to direct the intelligence effort now
needed. He did not last three months. His view that Ireland required the
same building-up of an organization for 'five years plodding and patient
investigation' that had succeeded in Bengal was anathema to Winter,
and more fatally to Lloyd George as well.

'THEY SHOT THE WHOLE LOT OF THEM OFF?'

Bloody Sunday's significance was ambiguous – and the same was true of
the iconic fight of the West Cork flying column near Kilmichael a week
later. This small battle, the climax of the autumn campaign, was the first
to be seen by the British (at least privately) as 'a military operation', and
it certainly altered the psychological environment. In the most active
republican areas of the south-west, the arrival of the Auxiliaries had a
similar effect to that in Dublin. Volunteers were conscious of failing to
counter the reputation of the new force as 'super-fighters and all but
invincible', and the impact of the intensified programme of raiding and
patrolling.[237] The two cadets killed in Mount Street on Bloody Sunday
were in fact the first members of the division to die. The first deliberate
stroke against the Auxiliaries was planned in West Cork by a man who
had a personal as well as organizational point to prove. Tom Barry – no
relation of Kevin – was a veteran of the Mesopotamia campaign. As an
artilleryman in the Tigris Corps that failed to relieve the siege of Kut in
early 1916, he had developed a healthy disrespect for the quality of the
British (or at any rate the Indian) army's officer corps. (He later breezily
asserted that Kut 'would have been relieved by one battalion of aggressively led troops'.)[238] Like other war veterans in the Volunteers, his
military experience was respected, but nobody was unaware that it was
gained on the wrong side. In late 1920 he was in provisional charge of
the Cork No. 3 Brigade flying column, and in November took it into
combat on his own responsibility. His target was the ADRIC company
stationed in Macroom Castle.

Barry, following the standard republican publicity line, held that the Auxiliaries were 'openly established as a terrorist body' aiming to break Irish resistance to British rule by armed force. (In his last book, he repeatedly referred to them simply as 'the terrorists'.) Even their special uniforms, he suggested, were 'calculated to cow their opponents'. He painted a picture of their 'special technique' in garish colours. 'Fast lorries of them would come roaring into a village, the occupants would jump out, firing shots and ordering all the inhabitants out of doors. No exceptions were allowed. Men and women, old and young, the sick and decrepit were lined up against the walls with their hands up, questioned and searched.' They would invariably beat up at least half a dozen people with their revolver butts. 'For hours they would hold the little community prisoners, and on more than one occasion . . . they stripped all the men naked in the presence of the assembled people of both sexes, and beat them mercilessly with belts and rifles.' The fact that so far 'not a single shot had been fired at them . . . by the IRA in any part of Ireland' had a 'very serious effect on the morale of the whole people' as well as the Volunteers. Barry's conclusion was that 'there could be no further delay in challenging them.'[239]

Barry, like many others, stressed the indiscipline of the Auxiliaries. But Macready, who had warned about this issue from the start, pointed out that ADRIC companies varied a lot in this respect. Some, under effective commanders, were well controlled, and C Company at Macroom under Lieutenant Colonel Crake seems to have been one of these. Though they had killed one man, James Lehane, in disputed circumstances, they spent most of their time fruitlessly patrolling. Did they operate as Barry described? Undoubtedly they saw their mission as to impress if not intimidate the people, and they found the people 'hostile and unfathomable'. The result was a high degree of casual brutality in their day-to-day encounters. But, even short of information, the effect of their intensified patrolling activity in an area which had been effectively abandoned by the security forces for six months was marked, turning an area described by the County Inspector at the time of their arrival as 'practically in a state of war' into 'about the quietest part of the county' just before the Kilmichael attack.[240]

Their most serious error – fatal for them – was their failure to vary their patrol routes. As winter came on, patrolling in open trucks became a 'most unpleasant' activity, and the cold men, whose coats could not keep out the rain, were less inclined to 'deviate from known roads'. No. 2 Section always took the same road towards Dunmanway and on to Bandon. This enabled Barry, with a force made up of men from the training camp he was running at Clogher, to select the ambush site near Kilmichael with some confidence. Or at least he did according to his own later account. In the first written report of the fight, included in a collection of captured IRA documents assembled by the British army in mid-1921, the 'OC Flying Column, 3rd Cork Brigade' described it a little differently.

> The column paraded at 3.15 am on Sunday morning [28 November]. It comprised 32 men armed with rifles, bayonets, five revolvers, and 100 rounds of ammunition per man. We marched for four hours and reached a position on the Macroom–Dunmanway road in the townland of Shanacashel. We camped in that position until 4.15 pm and then decided that as enemy searches were completed it would be safe to return to our camp.

On this account, it would seem that the column moved not to mount an ambush but to evade a British search operation. In contrast to Barry's later version, the fight that followed was not planned, but happened by chance: about five minutes after the column started the return journey, 'we sighted two enemy lorries moving along the Macroom–Dunmanway road at a distance of about 1,900 yards.' The column was in an exposed position – the terrain being 'of a hilly and rocky nature', suitable for fighting but not for 'retiring without being seen'. So 'I decided to attack the lorries . . . I divided the Column into three sections, viz – one to attack the first lorry. This section was in a position to have ample cover and at the same time to bring a frontal and a flank fire to bear.' The second section was 120 yards further up the road: 'its duty was to let the first lorry pass to No. 1 section and attack the second lorry.' The third section 'was occupying sniping positions along the other side of the road and also guarding both flanks'. 'The action was carried out successfully, 16 of the enemy who were belonging to the Auxiliary Police from Macroom Castle being killed, one wounded and has escaped and is now missing.' The column had captured fourteen rifles, five bayonets, seventeen revolvers, 719 rounds of .303 and 136 of .45 ammunition, with equipment – and the two lorries, which were burned out. It had lost one man killed in the fight, and two who died of their wounds. In a postscript, the column commander attributed these losses 'to the fact that those three men (who were part of No. 2 section) were too anxious to get into close quarters with the enemy. They were our best men and did not know danger in this or any previous actions.' They had 'discarded their cover'; 'it was not until the finish of the action that P. Deasy was killed by a revolver bullet from one of the enemy whom we had thought dead.'[241]

Tom Barry later published more than one account of the ambush (in the *Irish Press* in 1932, in his celebrated *Guerilla Days in Ireland* in 1949, and finally in his angry rebuttal of Liam Deasy's memoirs, *The Reality of the Anglo-Irish War*, in 1974), and several members of the column also wrote accounts. These vary on several points of detail, such as the number of riflemen in Barry's column, the number of scouts attached to it, and the number of sections in the ambush position (two in some, four in Barry's 1949 account). But they agree on others, notably that the column lost three men in action and, more importantly, that the ambush was deliberate: the column moved into the ambush position after breakfast on Sunday and stayed there all day until the Auxiliary patrol appeared around dusk. Barry's most detailed analysis of the distribution of his force made the military logic of the operation clear.[242] The position was chosen because a sharp bend in the road would force the patrol to slow down (the column had no mines with which to spring the ambush), and the sections were posted to deal with at least two vehicles. It is also undisputed that the decision to mount the operation was taken personally by Barry, without consulting the brigade commandant. This, coupled with the fact that the ambush took place outside the brigade area, has been suggested as a reason why it might initially have seemed a good idea to report it as an encounter fight.

It has also been suggested that, to justify the annihilation of the police patrol, Barry later rewrote the story, alleging that some of the Auxiliaries had opened fire after their surrender had been accepted. As he told it in *Guerilla Days in Ireland*, after killing the nine occupants of the first lorry in ferocious hand-to-hand combat (with no survivors or prisoners), he and the three riflemen of his Command Post section ran back to attack the other group in the rear. 'We had gone about fifty yards when we heard the Auxiliaries shout "We surrender." We kept running along the grass edge of the road . . . and actually saw some Auxiliaries throw away their rifles.' When some of No. 2 Section stood up, the police drew pistols and fired at them – whereupon Barry ordered fire to be kept up until they had all been killed. In Barry's account, the three fatal casualties his column suffered resulted from men standing up after this false surrender. He reacted angrily to the publication of Paddy O'Brien's account of the ambush (in Liam Deasy's memoir *Towards Ireland Free*), which he felt depicted him as 'a bloody-minded commander who exterminated the Auxiliaries without reason'. Yet the earlier bald accounts, which ascribed the casualty level simply to the intensity of the hand-to-hand fighting – 'they like the IRA had fought to a finish' – had not seemed to carry this implication.

There is a hint of this false surrender in the original account, and the six accounts of Kilmichael in the Bureau of Military History's collection of witness statements certainly suggest that some of the Auxiliaries surrendered and were then killed. The wounds of some of the dead, the medical evidence suggested, indicated that their arms were raised when they were shot. It seems entirely possible that several of them surrendered individually, while others were still firing. But some of the column men interviewed by Fr John Chisholm on Liam Deasy's behalf said that no surrenders were accepted.[243] 'They shot the whole lot of them off?' Chisholm asked Ned Young, who replied 'They did.' In the chaos and stress of any fight, even a small one like this, participants always remember different things. In his rebuttal of O'Brien's 'fantastic story', Barry snorted that 'O'Brien has Lordan wounded when he was not even scratched'; yet others had the same memory as O'Brien. The recollection of some that there was never any intention to take prisoners seems perfectly plausible, since the column could scarcely have coped with them, but that would of course not have been admissible in public since the Volunteers claimed to observe the laws of war. (The killing of prisoners has been lamentably common in regular war, though never admitted.) Though all sources are consistent in their account of the column's casualties, the witness statements suggest that the men who died were shot earlier in the action, and not as Barry described.

Barry's whole story has been dismissed as a fabrication, though it remains unclear why he would want to invent it. He never saw any need to justify the extermination of the police in the first tender, and in one later study which he endorsed he is recorded as telling his men before the fight, 'See to it that these terrorists die and are broken!'[244] Others have equally vigorously defended it – among other things, by declaring that the 1921 report was a British forgery. This cannot be proved or disproved, since the original copy has not survived. The British army believed it to be genuine – to use a fake report as part of an analysis of the operating methods of their opponents would have made no sense – though it may well have come to them from the police. Some of its details, such as the provision of 100 rounds per man, do sound more like a regular military than Volunteer level. But we may wonder how forgers could have known some of the other details, such as the division of sections, and the death of Pat Deasy. Yet again, it is not clear that merely failing to mention the false surrender – as several of the Bureau of Military History witnesses did – should be taken as implying that it did not happen. As always, there can be inconsistencies even among genuine testimonies, and these events are unlikely ever to be precisely reconstructed. The most systematic attempt so far made to weigh all the evidence and interpretations of the fighting runs to over thirty pages, and finds no clear way out of the tangle.[245]

Barry was a man who had a point to prove; as an ex-soldier he was going to hit a glass ceiling in the Volunteer command structure unless he could – as he did – demonstrate a wholly exceptional decisiveness and ruthlessness in taking the fight to the British. On his own account, he set up the operation in a way that seems to have been designed to maximize the risk run by the attackers. The attacking force was posted very close to the road, and Barry made a point of stressing that there was no line of retreat – 'there was no plan for retirement until the column marched away victoriously.' (The first report likewise dismissed the possibility of retreat, but presented this as a topographical fact rather than a deliberate decision.) His decision to lead the attack from the front – stepping out into the road himself to slow down the leading tender – broke more than one elementary rule of military command, limiting his ability to direct the fighting and making it impossible for him to communicate with his reserve force. One military analyst has called this 'foolish and careless', and condemned the idea of deliberately making retreat impossible as 'downright foolhardy' and 'recklessly irresponsible'.[246]

'A MORE DEFINITELY MILITARY CHARACTER'

In late September 1920 the RIC Office issued a circular responding to the 'many reports of alleged acts of reprisal by police and soldiers' that had appeared in the press. While protesting that these press accounts were 'generally thoroughly misleading' – often misrepresenting acts of justifiable self-defence as reprisals – it admitted that 'there are cases in which unjustifiable action has undoubtedly been taken.' The order 'repeated and emphasised' that 'reprisals will ruin the discipline of the Force and cannot be countenanced by those in authority'. But the circular's wording was hortatory rather than mandatory. 'The great provocation under which men suffer who see their comrades and friends foully murdered is fully recognised, but the police are urged to maintain, in spite of this provocation, that self-control that has characterised the Force in the past. By so doing they will earn the respect and admiration of the majority of their fellow countrymen.' The destruction of buildings and institutions would 'impoverish the country and increase want and disorder', so negating the fundamental police duty to 'restore and maintain order'. In line with all the pronouncements of the police authorities, this order ended by reasserting that 'the effective use of weapons when threatened or attacked' was legitimate self-defence, and that the duty of the police was to 'hunt down murderers by every means in their power'. In this they would be 'fully supported and protected in the discharge of their duties by every means available'.[247] When the order was translated by the *Weekly Summary* for the benefit of ordinary constables, the insistence that 'reprisals . . . are bad for the discipline of the force' and 'bad for Ireland' was balanced with the assertion that 'reprisals do not happen wholly by accident. They are the result of the brutal, cowardly murder of police officers.' To stop reprisals, 'stop murdering policemen.'[248]

For the British authorities, the fundamental contradiction in their understanding of the Irish problem was becoming more awkward. It may well be that a majority of the policy community still believed that the Republic was a product of terror rather than consent. The RIC naturally led the way in this. 'Much of the moral and material support lent to Sinn Féin is due to fear,' it argued in November, 'and with the growth of the realisation that the Government is beginning to get a grip of the situation there are indications of a return to sanity and revulsion against Sinn Féin on the part of the more responsible persons.' In some places – such as Galway – 'matters are well in hand and the murder gang is on the run.' Indeed, in Limerick 'we are now able to have a dance organised by "Black and Tans" as they are called. These have been most successful and show a good spirit returning.'[249] Just as naturally, Liberals and moderate nationalists stressed the malign effects of reprisals. Edwin Montagu, the Secretary of State for India, told his Cabinet colleagues at the same time, 'I feel a growing conviction that even if the murder gang in Ireland can be destroyed by this process – which I doubt – the younger generation is being educated in murderous thought.'[250]

There was no reprisal after Kilmichael, but on 1 December Montagu's colleagues finally bowed to what now seemed inevitable: because 'the recent outrage near Cork ... partook of a more definitely military character than its predecessors,' martial law would be declared. 'Greenwood inferred that he had always been in favour of it,' the Chief of the Imperial General Staff, Henry Wilson, contemptuously noted, 'and so did Winston, their only doubt being whether we had enough troops! What amazing liars.' Wilson himself thought that with martial-law powers, fewer troops would in fact be needed, but his vision of martial law was not quite the same as that of the politicians ('frocks' in his argot). Mark Sturgis, with his usual clear-sightedness, noted in his diary that the soldiers expected 'to have full control of everything in two two's'; their watchword was 'No more damn civilians'. The Prime Minister's idea, by contrast, was 'to have Martial Law in the distant provinces, a cloud on the horizon, leaving the seat of Government, Dublin, free for them as wants to negotiate'. But this, he could see, was 'tricky work' – not least because the army simply 'have not grasped' the idea.[251]

Leaving Dublin free of martial law certainly made no sense to the soldiers. Even as the proclamation of martial law in his name was being finally drafted, Lord French was spluttering that it would be 'folly' to exclude the capital from the proclaimed area. For ten days General Sir Hugh Jeudwine, deputing as C-in-C while Macready was on leave in the south of France, had fought tooth and nail to persuade Greenwood that martial law would work only if it embraced the whole country. Twice he thought he had convinced the Chief Secretary, only to find him once again 'affecting surprise' at the very idea.[252] The eventual proclamation of martial law on 11 December was restricted to four south-western counties (Cork, Kerry, Limerick and Tipperary). When four further counties (Clare, Waterford, Kilkenny and Wexford) were added in the first week of 1921, this was merely to make the Martial Law Area (MLA) fit the area of General Strickland's 6th Division. Though French once again insisted on the 'vital importance' of including the major ports, especially Dublin, the capital remained outside. Moreover, the army had early warning that even within the MLA its power would be limited: crucially, the police would not come under military control. Macready angrily warned that 'Strickland will have to watch the police very carefully' – his RIC Divisional Commissioner, Brigadier Prescott Decie, would 'certainly . . . think that martial law means that he can kill anybody he sees walking along the road whose appearance may be distasteful to him'.[253] This bitter black humour showed how bad relations between the army and police were becoming. In fact, the Cabinet worried enough about this to count it a reason for considering negotiations with Sinn Féin.

The first fruit of martial law was a reprisal on a scale beyond anything yet seen, putting the whole coercive policy under a baleful spotlight. On 11 December 1920 an ADRIC patrol was ambushed in Cork, barely 200 yards from Victoria barracks: that evening a group of the newly arrived K Company went into the city centre and set fire to a large section of the main shopping street, as well as the City Hall and Carnegie Library several blocks away across the river. No fewer than three inquiries followed in quick succession. The second, by General Strickland himself, confirmed the view of the first that the responsibility lay with the local Auxiliary police, but added a criticism of the 'higher authority who ordered a unit in so raw a state' to such a dangerous area. The government had promised to publish the 'Strickland report', but this open criticism of Tudor changed its mind. The suppression of the report became a serious publicity own-goal. Tudor for his part held his own inquiry, which shifted the blame away from the police.[254] On 14 December he issued a circular order deprecating reprisals by burning – at which, the veteran General Sir Hubert Gough (a leader of the 1914 Curragh mutiny) wrote, 'we may well stand aghast.' 'It is not an order, it is merely an "appeal".'[255]

Stung by the *Daily Telegraph*'s suggestion that 'the chiefs of the terrorist organisation' were quite capable of staging the arson attack to stop 'any talk of peace' by moderate Sinn Feiners, the Irish Labour party protested that 'the Government which stoops to such methods is not only a bully but a sneak.' When the government refused a judicial inquiry, the ILP/TUC held its own, assembling more than seventy eye-witness accounts for its report, *Who Burnt Cork City?*[256] As it happened, the British Labour party's Commission to Ireland was taking evidence in the south-east at the time of the burnings, and the report it presented in London on 29 December was deeply subversive of the official line. The commissioners soberly observed that 'in every part of Ireland that we visited we were impressed by the atmosphere of terrorism which prevailed.' But this was not, as the government maintained, the result of republican violence. British reprisals, 'a cruel and inhuman policy', were 'a confession of bankruptcy of statesmanship and the desperate expedient of men lost to all sense of humanity'. Echoing the Volunteers' own language, they argued that the republican army could not be beaten because 'it lives and fights dispersed; it is everywhere all the time and nowhere at any given moment.' Only negotiation could end the conflict.[257]

Under the pressure of these events the machinery of government was audibly creaking. Three days after 'the burning of Cork city', Auxiliary Cadet Harte shot a young man and an old priest by the road near Dunmanway in southern Cork. Lloyd George furiously called for Harte to be tried by drumhead court and hanged on the spot, but Macready insisted on a proper trial, at which Harte was found insane. Reflecting that the killer in one of the worst excesses of the 1916 rebellion, the shooting of Francis Sheehy Skeffington, had also been found insane, Sturgis raged that if Harte was mad those who let him 'loose on the world . . . armed to the teeth should take his place in the dock'.[258] In the Commons, Joe Devlin bitterly denounced government policy: 'you have fanned the flames of hatred . . . you have gone on from bad to worse.' The Archbishop of Tuam warned Churchill that even in 'peaceful' districts like Galway, 'the auxiliary Police are exercising terror & torture unchecked, & still the spirit of Sinn Fein is as strong as ever.'[259]

PART THREE

War and Peace – Trials of the Counter-state: 1921

With the declaration of martial law, Britain's Irish policy was balanced on a fine edge, teetering between repression and concession. Martial law represented the legal extreme of repressive policy – the last throw of the political dice. Conciliation, pushed into the wings since the summer surge, gingerly returned to centre stage when the Government of Ireland Act at last reached the statute book on 23 December 1920. For the ten months of its halting passage through parliament, the 'partition act' had evoked very little nationalist enthusiasm, but in spite of that it had stoked Ulster unionist fears of betrayal – with deadly consequences. Now Britain faced a real political reckoning. The elections to the two Irish parliaments would be a showdown in which the offer of limited devolution would be tested against the republican claim to independence, and the effectiveness of the Restoration of Order in Ireland Act and martial law measured against the strength of republican armed resistance.

Martial law was restricted to the south-west to keep Dublin open for those, in Sturgis's jokey phrase, 'as wants to negotiate'. A few on both sides seem to have wanted to. They found a new intermediary in Patrick Joseph Clune, Archbishop of Perth, a man with some experience of the war – he had been visiting his native Clare at the time of the Rineen ambush and the reprisals that followed it, and his nephew had died in Dublin Castle along with McKee and Clancy on Bloody Sunday. Shortly after the Kilmichael ambush he was enlisted by Joe Devlin as a go-between, and spent most of December moving between Dublin and London, talking to Griffith in prison, and twice to the Prime Minister, who certified him as 'thoroughly loyal'.[1] He seems to have drafted agreed truce terms that included immunity for Collins and Mulcahy.

Lloyd George was clearly interested in the idea of a truce, but he was equally adamant that the Volunteers must surrender their arms to get one. The permanently optimistic Chief Secretary, Greenwood, told him that Clune's intervention should be read as a sign that the republican 'cause and organisation is breaking up'; they needed to keep up the pressure. Griffith, who had been arrested on 27 November – some have suggested to make it easier for negotiators to talk to him, though this had never been a problem – was clearly ready to look on the bright side, thinking that Lloyd George 'wants peace but is afraid of his Militarists'. Collins, who had succeeded him as acting president (though Griffith may, odd as it appears, first have offered the post to both Brugha and Stack), seems to have been more sceptical, seeing the move as an attempt to wrongfoot them. Certainly Clune was never able to shift Lloyd George on the arms-surrender issue. Neither side was yet really under enough pressure from events or its own public opinion to compromise its objectives. More 'Peace Balloons', as Mark Sturgis called them, would float up and burst in the coming days, and the fact that others went on appearing suggested that 'there *must* be a very real anxiety to settle.' But the episode threw a shadow of distrust, as he discovered months later – Sinn Feiners remained convinced that Clune 'went to London with terms in his pocket and was led on and then turned down'; they had been 'tricked and sold'.

Negotiation was still not the British government's preferred path. Instead it chose, in effect, to fix a date by which military repression should have pacified Ireland enough to make it possible to hold 'free' elections to the new parliaments – elections whose result would not be dictated by republican intimidation. Unfortunately for itself, the army was persuaded to set that date. On 29 December the Prime Minister raised the question of a temporary truce (a month or two) with Macready, Anderson, Tudor and the divisional commanders. All seem to have been taken aback. Although Henry Wilson fumed that Macready was 'not nearly strong enough against . . . so fatuous and fatal a policy', they stood firm. To fend off the proposal, Macready promised that the 'terror could be broken' if martial law was extended across the whole country. Strickland rather recklessly went further, promising that in any case there would be 'definite and decisive results in four months' time'. The elections were accordingly set for May 1921.

'IF IT IS WAR WE MUST HAVE A VIRTUAL DICTATOR'

To achieve 'definite and decisive results', the British army could now deploy fifty-one battalions of infantry (twenty of them in Strickland's division and twelve in Dublin District) – a substantial force, though hardly overwhelming even if the units had been at full strength. In fact most would struggle to muster half their nominal strength – 400 men; most of the troops were raw recruits, young men whose 'fine drawn' physique, as Macready complained, was stretched to the limit by incessant guard duty, little sleep and patrolling under constant threat of ambush. These pressures made normal training impossible. Persistent shortages of key equipment, especially lorries and armoured vehicles, were aggravated by obsolescence and unreliability.[2] But more serious than these problems was the army's painfully slow adaptation to the military environment created by the republican campaign. Contemptuous of their opponents, many officers still did not take their challenge seriously. Intelligence, the service on which any realistic prospect of locating or confronting the Volunteers depended, remained marginal, consigned to junior officers who would often be posted away just as they were developing the local knowledge and contacts needed. Like most regular armies, the British wanted to believe that success would be achieved by technology and large-scale operations.

But the soldiers' key weapon, they hoped, was martial law. They expected many things from it. Maybe the least definite (and most seductive) was its 'moral effect'. It was indeed a menacing concept, reawakening memories in Ireland of the 1916 regime of General Maxwell – even though, ironically, Maxwell had not been permitted to exercise what he saw as martial-law powers. Many people were apprehensive. According to General Strickland's divisional staff, it was 'a noticeable fact that during the first few weeks of Martial Law, more dumps of arms and ammunition were discovered than at any other time' – a direct result of a quickened flow of information from the public. But this flow seems to have dried up again later. Once the shock effect of proclamation had worn off, what real powers did it give?

General Jeudwine, arguing with Hamar Greenwood for 'full' martial law, made a list of its advantages. Military courts would impose 'heavy sentences for carrying or being in possession of arms' and for 'harbouring known rebels'. The 'internment of *suspects*' (Jeudwine's emphasis) would be possible 'at discretion of Military Governor'. He could also impose restrictions on movement and identity checks, and exert 'control of the press' (one of the army's most cherished objectives). But at the top of his list were 'promptitude in action and administration' and 'unity of command'. When his fellow divisional commander Gerald Boyd worried that martial law might be a last resort – 'our last reserve' – committed prematurely, and that if it failed it would make the situation worse, Jeudwine confidently assured him that any drawbacks would be outweighed by 'one great advantage', unity of command.[3]

It was not only soldiers who lambasted the dysfunctional structure of the British administration. 'Lack of unity of Command is most hampering,' Sturgis had noted in mid-August 1920, after confusion in the arrangements to take Terence MacSwiney to England. 'Soon we *must* have a central Dictator, civil or military, to be obeyed by everyone.' A few days later he repeated that 'if it is war we must have a virtual Dictator.' 'As it is we are a great, sprawling, jealous hydra-headed monster spending much of its time using one of its heads to abuse one or other of the others by minute, letter, telegram and good hard word of mouth.' But of course it was not 'war' in the government's view, and Sturgis remained in a minority. When Ernest Clark was made under secretary in Belfast to start setting up a Northern Ireland administration, Sturgis saw this as another retrograde step – 'too many heads already'. A long letter to Lady Greenwood (not, significantly, to her husband) urging the need for unity of command, perhaps through some sort of war council, got a reaction only from Macready, who predictably 'would prefer a Military Dictatorship to a "War Council"'.[4] He sent a copy to Warren Fisher, who had criticized the disorganization of the Irish Executive, but nothing changed.

On the face of it, martial law should have resolved the issue; as Sturgis noted, the army expected 'to have full control of everything in two two's'. But the government had no such idea. Paradoxically, martial law not only would fail to deliver military control over the police and administration, but would actually reduce the unity of the army itself. 6th Division became more of an 'independent force', with the central control and co-ordination of intelligence 'more difficult than before'. When Fisher returned to Ireland in February 1921 he was amazed to find the situation even worse than on his first visit nine months before – not only was 'the use of force not singly directed', but there were undoubted signs of 'an untimely lack of sympathy and uncomprehension' between the military, police and civil 'elements'.

The most serious failure to secure unity came in the vital sphere of the law itself. When the Cabinet discussed martial law it was clear how little the principle of it was understood; martial law had never been used in Britain in modern times, and its use in South Africa had been highly contentious. It had been formally declared in Ireland during the 1916 rebellion, but in practical terms this had meant very little. No martial law tribunals had been held; the rebels had been tried by courts martial under the Defence of the Realm Act. The distinction was lost on most people, though: Ireland was believed to have been under martial law, and the government was left in no doubt that in political terms it carried a heavy cost. Hence Lloyd George's determination to restrict its operation in 1921. Even so, the army assumed that where it *was* applied, the civil courts would be superseded by military courts, and that the normal appeal processes would be suspended.

In the event, things proved more complicated. Appeals were launched on behalf of the first men to be sentenced to death by military tribunals in the Martial Law Area, Joseph Murphy and John Allen, in January and February 1921. Allen's case seemingly produced a decisive military success, when the high court ruled (on the basis of Macready's affidavit that a state of war existed in the MLA) that it could not, '*durante bello*, control the military authorities or question any sentence imposed in the exercise of martial law'. That seemed to be that; but just a day after the Allen judgment two local military governors (the commanders of 16th and 17th Brigades) were served with writs in actions for damages caused by 'official reprisals'. In March the King's Bench issued writs of habeas corpus for the seven men sentenced to death after being captured at Clonmult.[5] The case of *Garde* v. *Strickland* in early April advanced the argument that the Restoration of Order in Ireland Act had actually circumscribed the Crown's powers and made it impossible to declare martial law except by statute. Despite the obvious dangers of this argument, Anderson thought that since the appeal was lodged in Dublin, it would have to proceed as long as Dublin was not under martial law itself. Macready protested that the functioning of civil courts under martial law was 'an anomaly', and in mid-April he was driven to issue a proclamation suspending the jurisdiction of 'all Courts of Justice' in the MLA.

The reality of martial law fell short of the soldier's dream – or the politician's nightmare – of instant, untrammelled repressive action. Macready's staff grumbled that 'an arrangement by which the Military Authority is publicly made responsible for the government of a country, but in reality is not responsible at all' was 'illogical'. They could have been forgiven for choosing a stronger adjective. In political terms, the

Military Governor's acts were 'still those of the Civil Authorities, who behind the scenes claim not only to dictate what his policy is to be, but the exact manner in which he is to carry it out'.[6] In military terms, the army's repertoire remained constricted. The history of one new measure, 'official reprisals', illustrates this. The justification for it was more negative than positive. The War Office had been as worried as the C-in-C about the involvement of soldiers in 'unofficial' reprisals, which the army liked to attribute to the police. In September 1920 the Director of Military Operations suggested that 'the only solution to this problem' was 'to institute a system of *official* reprisals'. He proposed that if a 'definite scheme' was set out, it would make it easier to 'get the troops to restrain their unofficial efforts'. As a bonus he added the argument, familiar by then, that 'the deterrent effect on the Sinn Fein cannot be inconsiderable'. Macready had immediately backed this idea by pointing out that, however worrying from a disciplinary standpoint, wherever reprisals had taken place the 'whole atmosphere of the surrounding district' had changed: hostility had given way to 'cringing submission'. And not only were the people tipping their caps, they were starting to give information. Macready had pressed for the destruction 'as a military operation' of houses from which shots had been fired, or whose occupants 'must have been well aware' of a nearby ambush.

This was not likely to appeal to either the Prime Minister or the War Secretary, with their known preference for 'gunning' rather than burning. Churchill only put it up to the Cabinet with obvious reluctance, and his colleagues unsurprisingly decided (on 10 November) that the moment was 'inopportune' for a decision. The idea was notably missing from the plans for action under martial law set out by General Jeudwine in his discussions with Greenwood, but it suddenly resurfaced on 29 December, when six houses in Midleton, near Cork, were destroyed after an ambush. Technically known as 'punishments', these actions were to be authorized by brigadiers who were satisfied 'that the people concerned were, owing to their proximity to the outrage or their known political tendencies, implicated'. The punishments were 'to be carried out as a Military Operation'.[7] After their inhabitants had been given an hour to remove their possessions (except furniture), the targeted homes were blown up. In the case of terrace houses, to avoid fires, the furniture was hauled out into the street and burned there. Sometimes, though, even the army was so short of explosives that it could destroy the buildings only by fire.

More than thirty official reprisals were carried out every month across the MLA over the next five months. They alienated many more people in Ireland than their direct victims. Like most collective punishments they also made British liberal opinion very uneasy. And of course these dismal little dramas were bad publicity. The proof of implication in IRA activity was often alarmingly vague (where it was recorded at all), and even if the tenants were disloyal, the financial loss of destruction was very often carried by landlords who were the government's allies. Indeed the first official reprisal cost the Earl of Midleton, a prominent Conservative and former Cabinet minister, £1,500. He duly made his annoyance clear to the helpless Hamar Greenwood.[8] But the most damaging effect of official reprisals, in political terms, seems to have taken the military authorities by surprise. They had not considered how easy it would be for the Volunteers to carry out their own counter-reprisals, burning 'big houses' after the British troops had destroyed the cottages and terraces. After the practice began to spread outside the MLA – the RIC Divisional Commissioner in Galway launched a programme of official reprisals in March–April without any authorization – political disapproval hardened.

The deterrent effect of martial-law measures as a whole was harshly assessed, two months after the first proclamation, by Sir Warren Fisher. The 'gunmen', he said, had set out to make martial law look silly by concentrating 'most of their best organisers and most of their best trained fighters' in the Martial Law Area. This shows that Fisher's confidence in his own judgment was not equalled by his knowledge of the real situation; but the feeling that they had been made to 'look silly' certainly afflicted the army. The soldiers knew where the responsibility lay – the independence of the police, the geographical limits of martial law and the persistence of the civil courts – but still they were troubled by martial law's failure to live up to its fearsome billing.

'THE NATIONAL ARMY OF DEFENCE': REPUBLICAN ARMY AND STATE

For all the defects in the martial-law regime, the British counter-insurgency effort at the turn of the year was the heaviest and most sustained pressure yet exerted on the republican structure. Could it withstand it? Early in the new year, Volunteer GHQ produced a fairly sober assessment of the shape of the republican military campaign. Its opening claim, that, 'having carefully weighed all the circumstances, the Irish Republican Army Command elected to adopt the method of guerilla warfare,' was slightly disingenuous: it hardly had any choice. But in saying that it 'realizes the indecisive nature of such warfare and does not seek immediate results', it said something important. Strategically, 'such warfare if conducted with skill always preserves the initiative.' Whereas 'the Regular Army by its very nature presents objectives everywhere, the guerillas never form an objective at any time or place' (a phrase that suggests the writer may indeed have read T. E. Lawrence). 'Guerilla strokes may be laughed at as "flea bites", but those of the Regular Army are blows in the air.' This had an air of sophisticated theory.

GHQ insisted that the republican army could 'fairly lay claim' to a number of achievements in 1920. It had 'destroyed the unique efficiency of the RIC, and thus struck an irreparable blow at the English Administration in Ireland'. Its campaign had cost 'England' a million pounds a week, 'gravely inconvenienced the English Army by the special type of operations imposed on it', and incidentally 'hampered the power of England to interfere' in the rest of the world. It had 'militarized the young men of the country', and 'formulated a system of guerilla warfare capable of being continued practically indefinitely and with ever-increasing effect'. Finally, it had inflicted serious blows on 'English prestige, both in the ethical sphere and by exhibiting how far England is from being invulnerable'.[9]

These level-headed assessments showed a clear-eyed grasp of the strengths and limits of the Volunteers' military capacity. They were almost certainly written because a critique of the military campaign was emerging within the republican leadership. The sort of worries expressed by Eamon O'Dwyer about the moral implications of the ambush system were amplified at the end of the year when Eamon de Valera at last returned from the USA. For various reasons (Collins thought they included delusions of grandeur), the President suggested that the style of operations looked too much like bushwhacking and too little like a war of national liberation. He clearly believed that guerrilla warfare was not generating the kind of image that republican propaganda required. For the first time, there was a whiff of dispute, or at least debate, about strategy at the highest level.

Politically, as Liam Mellows pointedly told the Dáil on 25 January 1921, the elaboration of republican institutions had not altered the basic relationship between the army and the counter-state. 'Were it not for the Volunteer movement, they could not talk of Ireland abroad, and if it were not for the Volunteers they could give up any idea of the Republic.' Although the IRA had taken an oath of allegiance to the Dáil, the Dáil had still not assumed public responsibility for the army. This was a situation that probably suited Mulcahy, the Chief of Staff, who was unquestionably dedicated to the principle that the army was subordinate to the government, but not at all happy that ministers should interfere in actual military decisions. The first serious discussion of military methods in the Dáil, a month after de Valera's return, indicated that the President was starting to push for greater political control over military policy. The debate showed that while some TDs were unhappy with the direction of the campaign, most disliked de Valera's suggestion that the Volunteers might reduce the threat of reprisals by 'delaying' some of their actions. They thought that easing back would indicate weakness. Mulcahy avoided commenting on policy, merely insisting that communication between parliament and army should take place only through the Minister for Defence. In a situation where many TDs were also army officers, the possibilities of irregular contacts and pressures were obviously worrying to him. For Mulcahy, the absolute separation of army and legislature was a hallmark of the democratic state, but there was little chance of securing it in these circumstances.[10]

De Valera was determined to link the military campaign to the governmental mandate of the Dáil. He insisted that the 1918 election had placed 'the Republic of 1916', which had previously been 'provisional and liable to question', on 'a foundation of certitude'. Those who questioned its moral validity 'now must challenge the foundations of Democracy and the constitutional rights of peoples everywhere'. Because it would be 'vain and contemptible' to wish for independence without being willing to 'make the efforts necessary to achieve it', the government of the Republic had gone beyond principles to action. It had 'undertaken the responsibility of marshalling the resources of the nation and directing its strength'. Crucially, 'from the Irish Volunteers we fashioned the IRA to be the military arm of the government.'[11] This notion of deliberate 'fashioning' became vital. De Valera's pamphlet *The Irish Republican Army* set out to calm any fears about the army's potential political role. He insisted that it was 'A REGULAR STATE FORCE under the civil control of the elected representatives of the people, with an organisation and a discipline imposed by those representatives, under officers who hold their commissions under warrant from these representatives'. This suggested a degree of control which the Dáil had never tried (or indeed wished) to exert. In spite of this, he declared that 'the Government is therefore RESPONSIBLE FOR THE ACTIONS OF THIS ARMY.' His point was to insist that 'these actions are not the acts of irresponsible individuals or groups,' and that the IRA was 'THE NATIONAL ARMY OF DEFENCE' and not 'as the enemy would have you believe, a praetorian guard'.[12]

The strict constitutional relationship between army and state does not seem to have been a concern; the casual intimacy and overlap between ministers and military staff felt as useful as it was inevitable. In retrospect, though, Ernie O'Malley identified the porous border between military and political leaderships as a problem. 'Why didn't the Staff pay attention to pure staff work, leaving the political field to others? The Chief of Staff was a member of Dáil Éireann, the Director of Intelligence was a Minister of Finance, the Director of Organization was a Secretary to the Dáil, the Director of Engineering was the Secretary of the Local Government Board [sic].'

De Valera's effort to shape military policy contrasted sharply with Griffith's sense of powerlessness. Griffith had no aptitude for controlling either military or civil policy; he remained at heart an agitator rather than an administrator. De Valera was very different; on his return he called for a briefing on the state of affairs from every department, and tried to ginger up departments that had lost their way, or their nerve, under the impact of the British autumn surge. He had no dislike of long committee discussions; his preference was to reach agreement by letting Cabinet meetings go on until dissent was silenced by persuasion or exhaustion. According to Ernest Blythe he now tried Collins's limited patience by frequently regaling ministerial meetings with anecdotes of his American experiences. When he described one of his stays at the Waldorf Astoria in the suite once occupied by the Prince of Wales, the Finance Minister chided him for extravagance. Another time, when he started to tell a story he had told twice before, Collins brusquely pulled him up short.[13]

De Valera now made a determined effort to have Collins take his place as the Republic's representative in America. On 18 January 1921 he sent Collins 'formal confirmation of the unanimous approval of the Ministry' of his proposal that 'the Minister of Finance be asked to proceed to the United States as a Special Envoy on behalf of the Republic'.[14] Among the arguments he deployed was Collins's 'fame, or notoriety if you prefer it' (an interesting psychological sideswipe). He instructed him 'not to be too modest to exploit' this to impose order on the American finances, open American agencies for republican enterprises, encourage the American boycott of British goods, improve communications, undertake relief work, promote propaganda, bring back into the official fold 'many of the excellent people in the Clan who have been misled', and 'execute commissions for the Minister for Defence'. He added a further argument that the Republic should not 'have here, so to speak, all our eggs in one basket'; in America Collins would be out of Britain's reach, and that 'whatever coup the English may attempt, the line of succession is safe, and the future provided for.'

The question whether this could outweigh Collins's value in Ireland itself has led to some speculation about the President's motives. Did he see Collins as a political rival? Or did he, as has been suggested, want 'to eject another rotten egg from his "basket"'?[15] The motives of Harry Boland – de Valera's presumptive successor as 'special envoy' – were clearer. 'It would be a very good stroke for Gould [a codename for Collins] to come,' he thought, even though he could see that the mission would be bound to expose him to publicity that might be awkward: 'it will be very hard for him to be in this country and to remain quiet.' Quite apart from his personal friendship with Collins, Boland had a particular reason for wanting the movement's leading 'genius for organisation' with him in the USA. After a series of mistakes – including buying 600,000 rounds of Colt .45 ammunition in the wrong format – he had secured the most spectacular of all republican arms deals. Early in January he ordered a hundred of the state-of-the-art Thompson sub-machine guns (first produced in 1919) at $225 each. GHQ immediately saw the enormous potential of these weapons and Collins told Boland that Seán MacMahon, the Quartermaster General, said 'they should be got at any price.' At the end of March Boland accordingly ordered another 653 of them – a huge batch which even after negotiating a 20 per cent discount still came in at the awesome total of $133,000.[16] He understandably 'hesitated for long' before committing to the purchase, and his action would come back to haunt him later when Cathal Brugha heard of it. But still the biggest difficulty remained – storing the guns secretly and shipping them to Ireland. Given his complaint that he had previously had to use men of unknown capacity to transport ammunition, and that it was really GHQ's responsibility to send out reliable men for such work, it is not surprising that he was eager to get the Republic's outstanding executive officer on the case.

Collins, however, had other ideas. He stalled for some weeks on the (fairly plausible) excuse of being unable to find safe passage, and eventually the project of sending him to America was quietly put on hold. Boland succeeded to the post of envoy, but the task of getting the Thompson guns to Ireland remained formidable. Thirty of them reached Cork late in April, and another fifty were landed in Dublin just before the Truce. But in June there was a disaster: after he had successfully spirited a vast batch of 495 into the bunkers of an American ship (chartered by the Irish White Cross to take coal to Dublin) at Hoboken, they were discovered shortly before it sailed.

'THE MACHINERY OF THE REPUBLIC'

At the start of the year the republican effort to control local government was faltering. 'County Council and other public bodies functioning under the Dáil Local Government Department were having a bad time . . . Raids had been made by Crown Forces on Offices and premises of individual [rate] collectors and public money confiscated.'[17] Up to this point the British had done remarkably little – certainly with remarkably little success – to inhibit the Republic's implementation of its local government policies. These focused on slashing expenditure, which 'the young puritans and Tammany-bashers of Sinn Féin' saw as inflated by nepotism and corruption. (Since 1898 the Irish local authorities had operated in a climate of British largesse.)[18] Sinn Féin's solution was to close workhouses and amalgamate hospitals. The first of these policies was sensible and generally popular, but the second ran into local resistance. Progress was erratic; only Roscommon had put through a comprehensive scheme by the time of the Truce.

Cosgrave's Local Government Department has been seen as one of the most effective instruments in turning the Dáil administration from 'another Irish exercise in "let's pretend"' into 'an everyday reality out-side Dublin and some of the bigger towns', where the old regime clung on.[19] Cosgrave and O'Higgins 'found themselves, in effect, running a local government system under the noses of the Castle and the Custom House'. They had to grapple not only with the British system, but also with local ratepayers and vested interests – entrenched councillors and officials. In the new year, this battle reached a critical point. Just before Christmas O'Higgins had written to all rate collectors reminding them that the Dáil had decreed the complete break of public bodies from the LGB in September after the 'enemy Government declared its intention to set the so-called "grants" against damage to persons or property'. To remain in office after that was 'a tacit acceptance of the new situation and all the duties it involved'. The threat of dismissal of rate collectors was a bluff – 'considering that the English LGB has itself been dismissed by the Public Bodies of Ireland, this bluffing should not impress any-one.' Unfortunately it did. Some rate collectors had met in Dublin and advised their colleagues 'to cease work of collection until the Councils come to terms with the English LGB'. This, O'Higgins declared, was 'an utterly impossible position for officials of Public Bodies to adopt'. They must either carry out instructions from their councils or resign.[20]

O'Higgins reported the problem to the Dáil ministry with more than a hint of alarm, declaring that 'A crisis has arisen in Local Government affairs.' The Dublin rate collectors had resigned in a body without hand-ing in the council funds they had collected. They had since 'been visited, placed under open arrest, and compelled to sign bearer cheques for the full amount of rate money in their possession' (totalling some £10,000). But 'this merely solves half the problem,' since 'many ratepayers will refuse to pay the new collectors who will have to be appointed' by the Dublin Corporation. Outside the capital, the issue of treasurership was becoming critical – 'the position in the North Riding of Tipperary was so bad yesterday that I wired the Chairman agreeing to a tentative reso-lution passed by the Council reappointing the Bank as Treasurer.' But O'Higgins confessed, 'I do not see a way out of the present difficulties.' County councils were 'clamouring to be allowed to reappoint the bank as official treasurer', promising that 'this will not be a step towards re-opening communication with the English LGB.' But O'Higgins doubted whether 'under existing conditions in the country it is possible to so stimulate and mobilise public opinion as to ensure that the rates will be got in to any extent that will appreciably alter the situation'. All the consequences of the financial shortfall were 'being laid at our door'.

The basic issue was that 'to attempt with a small staff and working in secret to exercise the control and supervision of local administration hitherto exercised by a huge staff of officials at the Custom House is a difficult undertaking.' 'Frankly,' he admitted, 'the problems of this Department are becoming too great for me.'[21] But his ministerial colleagues were not entirely sympathetic. The Local Government Department's report was scathingly criticized as showing 'no appreciation of the point of view of the Ministry as a whole'. It took no account of the fact that the Dáil government had agreed to grant a loan of £100,000. 'The whole thing ought to be rewritten with some spirit and vigour' – 'Its melancholy defensive is very disheartening.'[22]

Cosgrave's department eventually responded with a fighting manifesto aimed at the recalcitrant collectors. (Though its drafting was again criticized, as 'not nearly as telling as it could be made', the proposed circular was 'of tremendous importance' and its terms would be 'quoted both at home and in foreign countries'; 'really the Department should have a document like this almost perfect before it is sent for final sanction.') Declaring that 'the rates struck and the monies levied by the local governing authorities are for the express purpose of providing essential services for the community,' it warned that 'to divert these is to make war on the sick and the helpless poor, the mother, the infant, and the aged.' Those who acted 'as agents and instruments of the enemy in this attempt' were 'guilty of the highest crime against the State'.

'SKATING ON VERY THIN ICE'

The musculature of the Republic was still primarily provided by the army; but the progress of the military campaign was a cause for concern. Mulcahy was once again advising local commanders – in line with the realism of GHQ's overall strategy – not to attempt too much, just to keep going. 'A little action wisely and well done must be our motto at present,' he wrote to the Mid-Clare Brigade in February 1921. Such sober limits were imposed by necessity as much as by choice in many places, and they implied a reassessment of the flying columns' ability to transform the war. Far too many columns had been set up in the heady enthusiasm of the autumn, and too few of them were really effective.

Mid-Clare was typical in this. It was 'a desperate wish ... to do something big, as big as what had been done in other counties', that pushed it to assemble a large column in late 1920. One of the more aggressive column men, an ex-serviceman who had led the ambush at Rineen, 'regarded the Barretts [two brothers, Joe and Frank] ... as men who wanted to be officers without having to do any fighting', and had threatened to start his own column if they did not fight.[23] Joe Barrett assembled an impressive-looking brigade column, 'practically the flower of Mid-Clare', including most of the brigade's battalion officers. Fewer than half of its fifty-five men were armed with rifles, though its shotguns were made more deadly by a simple technique of pouring molten candle wax into the shot (a technique that seems to have been confined to Clare).[24] The captain of the Ennistymon company, Tosser Neylon, suggested that though the column was 'the cream of the brigade', many of its members had never met or worked together when it was sent into action at Monreal in late December. Joe Barrett had, Neylon thought, been 'too much influenced by the pressure ... [and] was a bit forced in his decision'.

The target at Monreal was a British joint military and police patrol, expected to be in one or two lorries, but which turned up in three. The column had no mine, and though it had some captured grenades, no attempt was made to use them. The first lorry was able to drive through the ambush position under heavy fire, and the third stopped short of it, so Barrett's column was quickly threatened on both flanks. His choice of ambush position meant that the column had to retreat across ground with little cover. Four of its men were wounded in the process, and, perhaps worse, one of its rifles was lost.[25] After two more attempted ambushes with no greater success, the column was eventually split up into three smaller units. The intelligence problem evident at Monreal afflicted the Mid-Clare Brigade as a whole. Over a seven-month period up to June 1921 it succeeded in only fourteen out of over 140 attempts to make contact with the enemy. Its commanders alleged that the British forces had stopped coming out of their posts, but Mulcahy evidently disagreed. He sternly lectured the brigadier, Frank Barrett, that his April operational diary indicated 'the absence of practically any military intelligence or technique'. The Volunteers had been watching constantly for the enemy 'in a district in which there is almost daily activity on the part of the latter, yet contact with the Enemy is only established on three days in the month'. And he warned that 'if there should be found in the heart of Clare anything like stagnation or inefficiency' it would be 'a disastrous thing'.[26]

A new organizational structure laid down in March disbanded several brigade columns and set out a pattern for new, smaller ASUs. 'The men for the ASU will be drawn from each Battalion, and will consist mostly of officers, possibly experienced ones. Men from the ranks will not be drawn upon save – (a) When their area is too hot to hold them; (b) When they possess technical knowledge, e.g. motor-driver, machine gunner; (c) When they have had considerable fighting experience; (d) When they are likely to assume commissioned rank.'[27] Brigades would be 'responsible for supplying the necessary arms, ammunition and equipment and military books', battalions would provide the men with 'necessaries'. The strength of an ASU would be twenty-one, including a unit commander and two squad commanders. The men should be numbered, and 'generally known by their numbers'. Each of the squads was to be capable of independent action. The new instructions stressed the need for battalions to provide billets, and for the units to develop night-defence schemes. On the move, 'men will always move in Patrol Formation.' (This would 'need to be insisted on'.) Marching from one place to another, or going into action or retiring, units must be 'properly protected against surprise'. And because intelligence organization was important, local battalions 'might' provide a daily intelligence report to the OC unit. A communications system 'would need to be perfected'.[28]

Next month an even more substantial guide to 'the Function of A.S. Units' came from the Director of Training. This said that ASUs had a dual purpose – to act not only as 'a standing force of Shock Troops' but also as 'training units'. The latter, in fact, was 'their most important function': the hope, evidently, was that they would accelerate the diffusion of GHQ's ideas of regularization into the provincial units. 'Even on active service, only a very small proportion of a soldier's time is spent in actual fighting: as much as possible of the rest must be devoted to training.' The ASUs should be 'Officers Training Corps on active service'. Every officer in an ASU's area should spend a period of service with it, and when all officers had passed through, the NCOs should follow them, and finally 'the best men of the rank and file'. That way, 'we can count on a uniform standard of command.'[29]

The size of ASUs was fixed accordingly – 'as large as can conveniently be trained and supervised by an Officer under A.S. conditions'. They should be strong enough to 'take care of themselves under all ordinary circumstances', but were never meant to be 'suitable for operations on a mass scale'. (So the suggestion of conventional warfare in the term 'shock troops' was clearly unintentional.) Their characteristics were 'hardiness and mobility', and their motto should be 'Everywhere all the time, but nowhere at a given moment' – another Lawrence-like mantra. The Director of Training handed out yet another sermon on the vital need for formal discipline – the erosion of differences of rank found in one ASU by a GHQ inspector, where 'Battalion Commandants and simple privates were cheek by jowl', was 'altogether wrong'.

But in early 1921 there was still only a loose fit between these formulae and the reality of flying-column activity, even in the most active areas. An attempted ambush near Dripsey by the 6th Battalion column of Cork No. 1 Brigade on 28 January, for instance, carried mixed lessons. The intended target was an Auxiliary supply convoy, usually twenty-five to thirty men strong in seven tenders, which travelled weekly on the same road between Macroom and Cork. As Frank Busteed, the column commander, reported:

> At 7.30am we got into position and remained there until 4.30pm, but during that time no lorry turned up – at that time we got word from the Priest in Coachford that the military were aware of our position but as he is against the cause and ambushes we did not pay much heed to him, but at the same time we considered that there was no use remaining any longer and as we were making arrangements to retreat I discovered a party of military advancing along the road from Dripsey.

The column took up a fighting position, but when a scout reported that 'the military were on our left and trying to surround us', Busteed decided, 'as the fields were very large', to retreat. In the retreat three men were wounded, and 'as far as I can ascertain there are 7 others missing.' (He was uncertain because they were not men from the attacking party of the column itself, but 'scouts and flank guards'. At the end of the report he listed the names of six of the missing men.) According to the battalion commandant, Jackie O'Leary, the column lost 'about three rifles and some shotguns, also some bombs' (the surprising imprecision here being due to the fact that 'some' of these items had been hidden during the retreat, and might be recovered).[30]

Part of the column's problem was one of simple planning and discipline. Busteed later admitted that the operation was 'a bit of a debacle'. One of the column men, Denis Dwyer, recalled that they were almost surrounded because their scouts, exhausted after being on duty for twenty-four hours without food or rest, had gone into nearby houses for refreshments. Once in retreat, other problems appeared. The column's line of retreat 'lay up high ground through a plough-field, which was under enemy fire'. They had to use a narrow lane, in full view of the enemy, and then climb the gate at the end of the lane, which had been 'locked and barred by the owner, who was hostile to the IRA'. The last man over slipped and trapped his leg, and was saved from capture only by the battalion quartermaster, 'who came back at great personal risk, and released me'. Dwyer had 'experienced some very tough and trying situations in France in 1916 and 1917, but this, while it lasted, surpassed any of them'.[31]

O'Leary made clear, however, that the key problem was one of intelligence. Because the military had 'attacked from the front, rear and left flank and also scoured the roads all round', it was 'evident that they got information'. They got it, in fact, from Mrs Mary Lindsay, a stubborn loyalist going to collect her motor permit (an action frowned on by the republican authorities). Stopping in Coachford on her way to Ballincollig RIC station, she met John Sweeney, a grocer's assistant who had been ordered out of his house by Busteed's men, and who warned her of the danger on the road to Ballincollig. Instead of turning back, as most sensible Protestants would have done, Mrs Lindsay went straight to the RIC, who alerted the army. While a force of seventy men of the Manchester Regiment rushed to the ambush site, she herself went back home, telling the Coachford parish priest of the ambush on the way. Three weeks later she and her chauffeur were seized by Volunteers, and held hostage against the lives of the captured column men. Cork No. 1 Brigade wrote officially to General Strickland – a personal acquaintance of Mrs Lindsay's, as it happened – that her life would be spared if the prisoners were treated as prisoners of war. They got no reply.[32] On 28 February, five of the six men named in O'Leary's report were hanged, and on 9 March the hostages were shot.

The mixed messages of the Dripsey ambush persisted. The 3rd Cork Brigade column's attack on Drimoleague RIC barrack, for instance, saw the first successful detonation of a mine under the barrack wall, but in spite of that the structure stayed intact and the barrack was not captured. On the same day, an attack on a train carrying troops at Drishanebeg (Millstreet) netted a haul of fifteen rifles and 700 rounds of ammunition. This showed effective co-operation between local companies and the battalion active service section, though the brigadier's decision to give all the guns to that section angered the company commanders. 'I only admire them for their fighting spirit, but we must make the best use of the arms,' he reported.[33] Unfortunately a more ambitious attempt against a troop train at Upton station on 15 February went awry when the troops turned out to be in greater numbers than expected, and were distributed through the train instead of occupying separate coaches. Three Volunteers were killed and several others seriously wounded (including the brigade commander); six ordinary passengers died in the gunfight and another ten were wounded. This setback – which Liam Deasy judged 'the most serious reverse suffered in the Brigade' – was due simply to inadequate information.[34] Five days later the twenty men of the 1st Cork Brigade's 4th Battalion column were surprised in a supposed safe house at Clonmult: after a desperate struggle twelve were killed and eight captured, the Volunteers' biggest loss in a single action.

This was a shocking blow – 'a very grave disaster', as Seán Moylan said – which underlined the perilous situation created by inadequate intelligence. (Although the British account did not mention prior information, suggesting that the rebels had revealed their presence by opening fire as troops approached, the IRA blamed the disaster on an informer.) The same fate might have overwhelmed the 1st Cork Brigade column itself, which after taking up an ambush position at Coolavokig, near Ballyvourney, went back to it three more times after the expected patrol failed to turn up. The news may have reached the local ADRIC Company (J), which sallied out on 25 February in almost full strength – seventy cadets with seven regular RIC men – though it then drove right into the ambush site rather than deploying to surround or outflank it. Even so, the ambushers were surprised – 'there was a great deal of scampering and confusion.' (The brigade commandant, Seán O'Hegarty, saw this as evidence that the Auxiliaries did not have information – or they 'would have come in greater strength and in open order'; he blamed his scouts for failing to signal the enemy's approach.)

This strong column – fifty-six riflemen and ten shotgun men, with two Lewis guns – ended up retiring in some disorder, thanks to one of the Lewis gunners running off, forcing his co-gunner to abandon his ammunition and get his gun away. 'Some of our men in the eastern portion [of the position] evacuated their posts without orders, and so gave the impression to some of the men in the western portion, who were not in action, that something like a retreat was on foot. Some of them, too, became demoralized.' When orders were sent to the western section to move up to encircle the police cars to the east, 'it was found that the section commander had evacuated his post practically at the first shot and demoralized 9 men, all of whom had retreated.' By the time '[Lewis] Gun No. 2 and sufficient force had been swung round it was found that all our eastern positions had been evacuated and 2 pans [of ammunition] left in the position of Gun No. 1'. The remaining column men concentrated their fire on a house where several of the police had taken shelter, but shortly after 10 a.m. reinforcements from Macroom approached. 'It was found necessary to break off the action, and a general movement north was carried out, without any enemy pressure.'[35] GHQ's verdict was damning: 'Bad scouting, bad inter-communication between units, bad control of units, lack of initiative and sense of responsibility on part of subordinate commanders'. The column commander should not have been engaged in 'eleventh-hour reconnaissance'. But for the 'bold and steady action of small groups, which did not operate as one whole, but in isolation', it 'might easily have been a disaster'. Operating like this was 'skating on very thin ice indeed'.[36]

Things looked up next month. At Clonbannin in Kerry on 7 March the commander of the British army's Kerry Brigade, Colonel Hanway R. Cumming, was ambushed and killed as he drove from Killarney to Buttevant in a touring car escorted by an armoured car and troops in three Crossley tenders. Seventy men (fifty from 4th, 6th and 7th Battalion ASUs of Cork No. 2 Brigade and twenty from Kerry No. 2) under the vice-OC of Cork No. 2 (Seán Moylan) had taken up an ambush position for two days before deciding to move ('as the fact of our party being in ambush was known to all the countryside'). 'It was a beautiful calm morning, and we had an unusually strong force,' Moylan later wrote.

'We also had one of the Hotchkiss guns captured at Mallow and half a dozen road mines.' The ambush positions were set by Paddy O'Brien, the Kerry No. 2 commandant, while Moylan supervised the laying of the mines. They had changed their intended target from an ADRIC pay detail to General Strickland, the MLA commander, who they had heard was on an inspection tour in Kerry. 'At 10.30 hours three Crossley lorries went west and took no notice of our positions,' according to Moylan's official report. Why the ambushers left them alone is not certain: Moylan later asserted that he and O'Brien had 'made it quite clear that General Strickland and his party were the objects of our attack and we intended to ignore every other opportunity ... no matter how tempting'.[37] This seems doubtful (good targets were too rare to be ignored), and O'Brien remembered it differently: they had indeed intended to attack, but Moylan's detonator failed and – by a bizarre coincidence – O'Brien's own rifle round proved to be a dud. 'In that minute of anticlimax the three lorries passed through the position, a soldier in one of them playing an accordion, the others singing, blissfully unaware of the mishaps that saved them from disaster.'[38]

Around 2 p.m., after another 'weary wait', compounded by anxiety that 'if our prediction was wrong any shred of reputation we had was lost,' Cumming's convoy was reported approaching from the west.

> We attacked but our mines failed to explode owing, probably, to the knocking about on the journey from Kerry. Our men opened fire on the leading lorry, and stopped it by killing the driver. The second lorry pulled up, and the touring car and armoured car almost dashed into it ... The rear lorry came on until stopped by our rifle fire. There must have been a big roll of casualties in this car, as a very effective fire was poured into it from the north and west. After a 2 hours' fight, in which the enemy machine guns searched the whole countryside, and which finally developed into a series of skirmishes over a large area, we retreated in good order after inflicting heavy casualties and without suffering any on our side.[39]

In fact the British had four killed and three wounded.

The 6th Division called Clonbannin 'one of the worst reverses suffered by the Army', and Cumming's death was a sensation almost as great as Moylan would have achieved if he had got his intended target. His body was taken to Dublin and a big funeral parade escorted it from

Arbour Hill barracks to the North Wall for its journey back to Britain. But the attack was not an unqualified success for his killers. Though the men had all 'fought well', and the signallers had played a vital role, Moylan reported that one section leader 'showed a regrettable lack of initiative'. 'It is difficult to keep in touch with all sections during an extended fight,' so 'we need to train more section leaders.' The multiple mine failures were just as significant. He later explained that he had targeted the armoured car for the middle of his three mines. 'As it passed over the mine I pressed the switch on the battery. I got a shock that almost knocked me over. It had short circuited.' The Cork brigades' semi-official historian, Florrie O'Donoghue, offered a slightly different explanation: the first mine failure (which Moylan omitted from both his report and his memoir) was found to have been due to using 'high tension wires ... with a low tension battery'; as a result, during the afternoon ambush 'no attempt was made ... to use the mines.' But the bottom line, as O'Donoghue said, was that 'the Cork Brigades were all handicapped by lack of expert knowledge of road mines.' Though units had been instructed to establish engineering sections many months before, the 'slow process of trial and error' was not delivering results.

The brigade command itself was not entirely harmonious, either. While Moylan and O'Brien were waiting for Strickland to arrive, 'a messenger arrived from the Brigade OC in search of me. A meeting of the Brigade Council had been called while we were in Kerry and due to the secrecy of our movements the Brigade Despatch Riders had been unable to get in touch with me.' The messenger told some of Moylan's men that 'the Brigade OC was in a towering rage with me.' The Brigade Council members had been waiting for him at brigade HQ for several days, and Lynch 'had had no report from me for more than a week'. Moylan remarked that Lynch's 'pre-occupation ... with written reports was too much for men who had been constantly hunted and harried for several months', and they 'suggested with, I'm afraid, an insubordinatory lack of respect for the Brigade OC that if he was so fond of reading and had no other business in hands [sic] he might concern himself with the reading of the newspapers of the past few months'.[40]

Outside Munster, there was a welcome ray of hope for GHQ that the burden of fighting might be spreading, with the North Longford Brigade ASU's brilliantly successful ambush of an eighteen-strong ADRIC patrol in two tenders at Clonfin on 2 February. Its commander, Seán MacEoin, was becoming celebrated as 'the Blacksmith of Ballinalee'. His role in the successful fight in his home town in November 1920, when a large British force was driven back by a flanking attack, has been disputed. The manoeuvre, some said, had been devised by an ex-British army sergeant who died in the battle and never got the credit for it.[41] But MacEoin's skilful choice of ground and posting of his fifty men at Clonfin was beyond doubt.[42] Moreover, his mine worked effectively for once, destroying the first of the two tenders, and the result – killing four Auxiliaries and capturing ten, along with all eighteen rifles – could plausibly be seen as a triumph. (A Lewis gun was also taken, though it seems to have been disabled.) MacEoin apparently had to intervene to stop his men killing the prisoners, and was fulsomely praised by the surviving Auxiliaries for his chivalry.

In late March, West Cork's most successful engagement suggested a step-change in the whole campaign – 'the nearest approach to actual warfare, as contrasted with ambushes, that has yet occurred', in Macready's judgment. A major British search operation in the area around Crossbarry (based on information from a prisoner taken at Upton) found the 3rd Cork Brigade flying column on 19 March. It was lying up after an abortive ambush attempt at Shippool on the Bandon–Kinsale road, and once again was taken by surprise. It suffered a serious blow when the brigadier, Charlie Hurley, who had been badly wounded at Upton, was killed. But it was an unusually strong unit – it had been reinforced to a total of 104 men – and Tom Barry directed a skilful fighting retreat. His decision to throw his whole force at the nearest of the approaching British units can be seen as brave or reckless – especially since he seems to have thought his opponents much stronger than they actually were.[43] But, with the luck that successful commanders need, he picked the weakest point in the loose British attempted encirclement, and encountered a British officer who broke the basic rules about maintaining flanking guards. After a sequence of firefights and cross-country movements, Barry got his column away, a remarkable enough achievement even if the casualties inflicted were lower than he claimed. (The British army lost eight men killed, with two men and two officers wounded; they laid some of the blame for the setback on the poor physical condition of the young soldiers themselves.)[44]

BATTLING FOR DUBLIN

Dublin lacked an ASU until December 1920, thanks perhaps to Dick McKee's relaxed approach. But the city presented a very different military environment from the rural areas which had generated the column idea. Urban anonymity and a mesh of backstreets provided a substitute for the protection of open countryside, but the idea of a full-time unit subsisting on local hospitality was inconceivable. Though ambushes were carried out, they had to be very quick operations. (The high risk of collateral damage to civilians also made them very unpopular.) Fighters could not think of staying in position for a day or more to wait for the enemy, and no ambush site was more than a few minutes away from major British military or police bases. Even the limited protection that could, as will be seen, be secured by cutting rural roads could not be provided in the city. Moreover the complexity of the street network, though it offered some security of movement to attackers, also meant that their targets were unlikely to be confined to a single road, as they so often were in rural areas.

It has been suggested that apart from the headline operations – assassinations – mostly carried out by the Squad, most Dublin units found little to do in the way of meaningful military action. This was not because of munitions shortages. Ammunition supplies seem to have been less critical than in rural areas (men bought their own at 4d a round). Simon Donnelly of 3rd Battalion stoutly maintained that 'the Dublin Brigade and ASU had hundreds of brilliant operations to their credit all during the reign of terror,' but he admitted that some of their key targets – notably the so-called 'Igoe Gang', a group of police intelligence officers who patrolled the streets on the lookout for wanted men – were never hit. His battalion OC Joe O'Connor (the battalion claimed forty-six 'attacks' in 1921) noted a little lamely that even though 'the whole Dublin Brigade were watching them', and they always operated on foot, 'they seemed to be fortunate in evading all our attempts to trap them.'[45] Donnelly attributed the fact that the IRA 'never got a favourable opportunity of attacking this murder gang' to the strict rules of engagement imposed in 1921. 'The IRA made many efforts to engage this gang in a position favourable to themselves,' but 'to have attacked when and where seen would have entailed considerable casualties on the civilian population.' Because of the number of units operating in the city, 'very careful planning and supervision became an urgent matter to guard against any two units of the IRA clashing in their anxiety to engage the enemy.' Eventually all operations had to be approved by either GHQ or Dublin Brigade, and 'instructions were issued that street attacks and ambushes would have to be more carefully planned and the points selected to be such as would cause the least casualties or inconvenience to the civil community.'[46] This was a potentially crippling restriction.

The difficulty of making contact, and the likelihood that most contacts would be accidental, was recognized in the emergence of a more flexible form of action – the patrol. Dublin units were urged to patrol their areas constantly, but though plenty of patrol reports were submitted to GHQ (particularly copious for April) it is hard to judge how effective they were. According to Joe O'Connor, patrols had an advance party of two unarmed men, with the main group and their officer following, then a rearguard of two armed men, with another two unarmed men behind them. 'When the leading man saw enemy forces he gave a pre-arranged signal to the man behind, also unarmed. He passed the signal back to the armed party ... That prevented their being taken unawares. They had to keep constantly moving.' This suggests that they were not really disputing control of the streets so much as laying down a symbolic marker. O'Connor 'admired the courage of the unarmed men in doing their particular task as they were very often the first to be shot down by the quickly advancing enemy sometimes before the actual fight opened'. Company patrols had 'very emphatic' orders to 'avoid prolonged action', since there was always an enemy post within a few minutes' drive of any action. Patrols were also forbidden to go to help other patrols, 'this to avoid big formations'.[47]

The brigade ASU under Paddy Flanagan (also of 3rd Battalion) necessarily remained a part-time unit. Its target strength of 100 men was probably never reached. In effect it remained four units, one drawn from each of the city battalions. With a more fluid operational procedure than the rural model, the ASU linked up with either local company men or the Squad for particular jobs, most of which were planned rather informally, through personal contacts as much as formal brigade-level planning. Though it was tasked with confronting the ADRIC, there was not much sign of any systematic approach to this. Influenced, naturally enough, by the environment and the precedent of the Squad, the ASU aspired to headline-grabbing targets such as the British police and military chiefs, Tudor and Macready. Several attempts were made, but never came close to success. Dublin units seem to have had less reliable operational intelligence than their country cousins – urban anonymity may have cut both ways – and spent 'most of their time . . . wandering around their battalion area looking for an opportunity'.[48]

The brigade operations diary begins on 10 January 1921, when seven men of the ASU mounted an attack on an 'enemy motor car' at Charlemont Bridge. As normal in Dublin, the men were armed with handguns (in this case revolvers, more reliable than automatics) rather than rifles. They claimed to have wounded one of the car's occupants. Heavier attacks on enemy lorries followed in Bachelors Walk (13 January), Harolds Cross on the 18th, Parliament Street on the 19th and Ushers Quay on the 26th, when the attackers used five grenades and killed five of the enemy. On the 23rd C Company of 4th Battalion burned 650 shell boxes at a depot by the Grand Canal. The total of thirteen operations, the majority in the last ten days of the month, suggest a rising tempo of attacks. Their outcomes were sometimes modest, however, as when an enemy car was 'temporarily disabled' in a grenade and revolver attack by E Company of the 3rd Battalion in Mespil Road on the 30th. There was one serious setback: when the ASU attempted an ambush at Drumcondra on the 21st, the nine-man party was surprised by the enemy and had six men captured, one of whom died from a serious stomach wound.[49] This disaster seems to have been due to a surprising decision by the unit's leader to move to Drumcondra Bridge after his first attempt at an ambush at the Royal Canal Bridge had failed. This meant that his men walked nearly half a mile up the main road in full view. Was this carelessness or overconfidence in their invisibility? According to the ASU commander, 'Lt. . . . instead of dismissing his men proceeded to the Tolka Bridge to prepare a new ambush. He had only reached the bridge when a tender of Auxiliaries came along towards the city. Two of the men captured opened fire with grenades without orders.' They then retreated down Richmond Street, 'but soon found themselves inside an enveloping movement'. Several 'cars of B. and T.' arrived from different directions, together with two armoured cars.[50] The British alleged that the captured men's revolvers were loaded with dum-dum bullets, and four of the five surviving prisoners were executed.

Several things had gone wrong here, notably that the unit's movement was seen and reported, and that there seems to have been no prepared escape route. As outside Dublin, things would improve, with a heightening tempo of operations – twenty-five in February and fifty in March – even if success remained patchy. On the evening of 7 February, for instance, 2nd Battalion tried to mount an ambush on an ambitious scale near Amiens Street station. Crown forces were to be drawn in by a telephone message to Dublin Castle reporting Volunteer activity in Seville Place. Parties of twenty men from C Company and thirty-five from B Company occupied posts round the railway bridge between Seville Lane and Coburg Place, while forty men armed with shotguns and grenades 'commanded the bridge facing Portland Row', with another ten covering the rear of 100 Seville Lane (an escape route that the fake warning call had drawn to the Castle's attention). Another forty men of F Company were placed in Portland Row. Together with other outpost groups, this elaborate plan involved a total of 165 men – a big investment in what turned out to be a hit-and-miss plan. 'After a period of half an hour's waiting, there appeared to be no sign of the enemy approaching the vicinity of our positions, with the exception of two armoured cars (fitted with searchlights) and three Crossley tenders containing a force of RIC, who drove swiftly down Amiens Street, past the mouth of Seville Place at 7.50 pm, and proceeded in the direction of Fairview.' The armoured cars pulled up at 8 p.m. and played their searchlights on the railway line 'as if endeavouring to locate the position of our men'. At 8.15 'it was deemed advisable to begin to retire'.[51]

The battalion report dwelt admiringly on the orderly retirement of the various sections, and the British intelligence officers who analysed it grudgingly acknowledged that the Volunteers had not been 'afraid of assembling 165 men, armed with such visible weapons as shot guns, in a busy part of the city'. Their dispositions were 'carefully thought out'; but 'as always when they have been in position for any length of time, they soon became nervous of discovery and departed without firing a shot.' Some of Dublin's wider operational problems can be glimpsed in a GHQ memo in late March, noting that bombing lorries had been only 'partially successful', especially at Broadstone, 'a death trap at present for our fellows'. The Director of Organization raised the rather elementary question, 'do all the bombing squads take into consideration the speed at which lorries move?', and suggested that in any case 'Peter the Painters [Mauser automatic pistols] and revolvers of heavy calibre' would be more effective, or at least more reliable, than bombs.[52]

WOMEN'S WORK

It is not easy to recover anything like the full measure of women's contribution to the republican campaign: it remains more or less a footnote in most accounts. In the 'Fighting Stories' series produced by the *Kerryman* in the 1940s – and still current – 'the role of the local Cumann na mBan branches', as one historian says, 'was relegated to a couple of pages at the end – presenting a definite appearance of an afterthought'. Even when women were accorded a special essay, as in *Dublin's Fighting Story*, most of it focused on 1916, with a short paragraph on the war of independence.[53] After all, the *Kerryman* billed the story as 'told by the Men Who Made It'. Although nearly 150 women supplied witness statements to the Bureau of Military History, a significant number, they still formed well under a tenth of the total. Women's applications for military pensions repeatedly fell victim to the attitude expressed by Ernest Blythe when, as minister for finance in 1927, he flatly denied that Cumann na mBan was a military organization.[54] But it can be argued that the armed conflict 'revolutionised the role of women in the republican movement'. Women had become 'the idealised republican citizens' through their support for the military campaign, and 'in the process they had transformed themselves'.[55]

In the most active areas, the Cumann na mBan organization was recast after 1919 to mesh more closely with the Volunteers. The Director of Organization told local units in March 1921 that the CnmB Executive proposed 'to place at the disposal of the O/C in each fighting area four or five well qualified girls who would superintend the arrangements for tending the wounded. They would be directly under your orders and could be moved around particularly in any operational areas.'[56] It seems that in some places the Volunteers actually directed the recasting – the brigade intelligence officer in south Leitrim 'organised a branch of the Cumann na mBan' with about fifteen 'girls', who 'worked for us much in the same way as the Fianna boys'. ('They were getting to be extremely useful when the Truce came along,' he added.)[57] Though in Leitrim their activities remained auxiliary, their range was clearly extended – the organization later judged that five-sixths of its functions were 'concerned with military matters – first aid, dispatches, carrying arms, transferring arms, intelligence, etc', entailing 'running into serious risks'.[58] The first of these, like activities such as fundraising, and the catering and mending frequently cited by Volunteers, was a traditional female task, but the rest were not. Ironically, it was gender stereotypes themselves that enhanced women's usefulness in these guerrilla activities. Only fifty or so women were arrested during the 1918–21 war. 'By reason of our sex we could get through very often with dispatches where men would not have a hope. The enemy did not always have lady searchers with them,' and even when they did, 'only in very limited numbers'. The British gradually became conscious of this problem, and sometimes (so Bridie Doherty believed) cheated – once she was 'put into a room in my house where I was undressed almost naked by two female searchers. I am positive that one of the searchers was a man dressed up as a woman.'[59] The intelligence work done by women such as Piaras Béaslaí's cousin Lily Mernin in Dublin, Josephine Brown O'Donoghue in Cork city, Siobhan Lankford and her successor (after Lankford aroused suspicion and lost her job) Annie Barrett in Mallow Post Office made a vital contribution.

Though many stories of women's aptitude for underground work have survived, many more have been lost. When Auxiliaries raided one of Collins's offices, at 5 Mespil Road, and waited for Collins to turn up, a woman doctor, Alice Barry, was able to spirit material out. Under the pretext of visiting a patient, who was one of Collins's secretaries, she picked up a set of files, 'stuck them inside my jumper and put on my coat. The Auxies were in the hall and let me pass without question.' Dr Barry judged them 'an innocent, unsuspecting crowd to allow anyone in or out of the house in those circumstances without searching them' – adding sharply that 'the Free State soldiers would not have been so remiss at a later stage.'[60] (It must be added, though, that the Auxiliaries seem often to have been just as easygoing with men – Oscar Traynor's driver recalled the ease with which he got a carload of gelignite and bomb-making equipment past them by throwing a few cabbages over it.)[61]

At the height of the guerrilla struggle, women were probably closer to full equality than ever before. There may still have remained a common assumption that women could not enter into the full sacrificial role available to men; they were 'in no real danger of execution if arrested'.[62] And unfortunately, perhaps, from the feminist viewpoint, it was traditional attitudes to femininity that remained most effective in propaganda terms. These invoked a more passive role, in which women were helpless victims rather than active participants. Republican publicity repeatedly stressed the traumatic effect on women of police or military brutality – during house searches especially. A series of articles by Erskine Childers for the New York-based *Irish World*, for instance, carried headline titles like 'Wrongs and Indignities Our Irish Sisters Endure at Hands of Brutal English Soldiers', or 'Defenseless Irish Women Robbed of Money and Jewelry in Their Own Houses'.[63]

Women were, naturally, praised for sacrificing their menfolk – another deeply traditional female role. Here, though, a less traditional political development took place as some of the bereaved women went beyond merely preserving the memory of their dead husbands and brothers to become active custodians of their ideological position – and indeed perhaps to reshape that position. Mary MacSwiney, for instance, would go on to deliver 'seemingly authoritatively' her brother's 'putative views about events that happened after his death'.[64] In early 1921 she was wowing audiences in the USA on a lecture tour – including many who, she thought, had 'never before heard a word on the Irish Question', but who had been impressed by the saga of her brother's hunger strike.

'TINKERING WITH THE HONOUR OF THE NATION'

In March GHQ set out to assess 'the war as a whole'. It divided the country into four – the 'War Zone' (the area under martial law in the south-west), the secondary country areas, the Dublin area and 'Ulster'. Surprisingly, perhaps, it classed the south-west, formidable as its forces were in comparison to those in the rest of the country outside Dublin, as 'a secondary theatre'. This was because its 'geographical circumstances' made it 'impossible to ever secure a decision within it'. GHQ argued that if 'feeding the battle in the War Zone resulted in a real deprivation of other areas, then it would mean that the Enemy had secured the initiative and was making us conform to his strategy' (though just what that was GHQ sensibly did not say). An 'exact balance' must be achieved. The factor GHQ identified as vital was that, unlike any previous struggle for independence, 'the National Military Command is securely established in Dublin.' In all previous efforts, the English hold on the capital had 'turned the scale'.[65]

Its grand strategy therefore hinged entirely on Dublin. 'The grip of our forces on Dublin must be maintained and strengthened at all costs,' while 'strong flanking units' in the rural hinterland should 'bring the Capital into closer touch with the Country'. Ulster, which had now become the 'vital bridgehead' for the English with their 'loss' of Dublin, must be 'attacked steadily and persistently'. But the message was unequivocal – 'it cannot be too clearly stated that no number or any magnitude of victories in any distant provincial areas have any value if Dublin is lost in a military sense.'[66] The terminology used here – like 'flanks', 'bridgeheads' and 'winning' and 'losing' a city – lay at an odd tangent to the IRA's developing doctrine of guerrilla warfare, the war 'without fronts'. It was indeed potentially quite misleading if it was read in a technical rather than metaphorical sense, and it would perhaps have a bearing on GHQ's eventual view of the possibilities of continued resistance.

It is not easy to evaluate the IRA's performance at the height of the war. The repeated failure of operations did not necessarily indicate weakness. Attempted ambushes, even if abandoned, arguably showed that the Volunteers were in business, that public support was keeping their movements safe, and perhaps that the Crown forces were keeping out of the way.[67] This may have been particularly true in urban areas like Cork and Dublin, where guerrilla action was difficult, police and military were present in strength and could more easily vary their patrol routes. Even so, most Volunteers probably did not see things like that. They hankered after dramatic action. There was a hope, even in 'quiet areas' – of which there were too many, as GHQ well knew – of emulating the most aggressive Volunteer units. But the odds against doing this were lengthening rather than shortening in 1921. Despite GHQ's persistent efforts, the War Zone was never significantly enlarged. Areas which had not developed a fighting capacity early found it difficult to get going, not least because in 1921 enemy activity grew increasingly effective.

For Ernie O'Malley, Kilkenny was a prime example of the uneven development of the republican campaign. 'County Kilkenny was slack.' It was difficult to meet officers, and communications had been neglected: 'dispatches took a long time to travel.' Observing a brigade council summoned to elect a brigade staff, O'Malley judged it 'poor material ... no direction from above and no drive'. Their answers to questions 'showed that none of them had tried to solve the problem of their commands ... Quietly, somewhat dully, they sat around the table in awe.' Unlike the opinionated, energetic Corkmen whose 'intelligence flared up' in meetings, they 'would talk when the meeting was over', but 'whilst they voted a staff there was mute acceptance'. Unimpressed by the new brigadier's lack of 'any show of energy or resolution', he concluded that 'in an area that had not seen fighting the elective system was not satisfactory.'[68] But the situation there was not helped by O'Malley's own capture, complete with a notebook naming all the officers of one of the brigade's more active battalions, several of whom were rounded up.

After his column had been surprised at Uskerry when the enemy came from an unexpected direction, the brigadier noted that 'our men were all raw as they never were in anything before.' The commander of the Kilkenny Brigade flying column told the Adjutant General, Gearoid O'Sullivan, 'we did not know for a long time that a Brigade existed in Kilkenny'; 'we never got any assistance from the Brigade.' According to the commandant of the 7th Battalion 'there was no such thing as Brigade orders ... We had no contact with Brigade Headquarters and, in fact, [in April 1921] ... I do not think we even knew who our Brigade Commander was.'[69] After congratulating the brigade on the 'dash and coolness' of the men involved in an April operation, Mulcahy dismissed its call for more weapons by mildly pointing out that 'Kilkenny is much better armed than some areas who do a considerable amount of work.' Later the brigadier, George O'Dwyer, was charged by some with responsibility for the failure of an ambush on 18 June, and with general cronyism – 'men are shoved on by him for Commissions to which they have no qualifications or right.' 'Dry rot and canker is setting in rapidly.'[70] The brigade reported that although dugouts had been made in most company areas, many had to be abandoned 'owing to location by civilians'.

In some areas, the situation was critical. 'I assure you', the South Roscommon brigadier told Mulcahy on 26 March, 'it takes a great amount of zeal to keep many of the (so-called) companies here in existence at all.' There had been 'wholesale desertions' in places. GHQ became seriously alarmed about this, and held that 'the death penalty should be inflicted for the graver class of crimes if the situation calls for it.' Unless sharp disciplinary measures were taken, there was 'a good prospect of large numbers running away in the Western areas'. It was 'absolutely essential to stop this rot'.[71]

In late March, just after he had escaped from prison, Simon Donnelly, vice-OC of 3rd Battalion, Dublin Brigade (with which he had served under de Valera in 1916), was given the task of inspecting no fewer than eleven brigade areas for GHQ. They included all three Clare brigades and mid-Limerick as well as Meath, Athlone, Mullingar, Offaly, Leix and Kildare. 'I was ordered to carry out inspection of Battalion and Brigade staffs and discuss the general situation, give lectures and reprimand officers and staffs who were not producing results.' He was told to 'brush aside' such excuses as shortage of arms. Ginger O'Connell 'called me [to] one side and in a personal chat, asked me to stress the importance of increased activity and the continuous blocking of roads, etc.'.[72] But the most crucial issue was still the quality of officers. Mulcahy urged that inspectors like Donnelly 'should be given a formula as to the way in which they will proceed to remove Officer after Officer, until they get the best men available'.[73] He told Liam Lynch next month that he was 'sending a memorandum suggesting how to allot marks to officers and companies generally in order to assess "military worth" of various companies in a battalion area'. This would have been an instructive document, but it does not seem to have survived.[74]

Donnelly's mission followed a highly critical assessment of 'Serious Deficiencies in Country Units' drawn up by GHQ earlier that month. Local units were widely convicted of 'failure to recognise responsibility for coordination', or 'to recognise the relative importance of internal Brigade Organisation'. Company councils were too casual – without agendas or minutes; orders were 'verbal and inexact', and statistical information was not readily available. Special services were still neglected – specialist officers failed to work up their subjects. Most strikingly perhaps, intelligence work was castigated; even at this late stage, as we have seen, GHQ denounced the army's grasp of the subject as 'very faulty', and insisted that men who 'clamoured for arms' would do better to work on this branch, which they 'can perfect unarmed'.[75] Mulcahy's criticism of some units was blistering: he excoriated the 'whole story of incompetency and slovenliness' revealed in Offaly No. 2 Brigade's reports, for instance, telling the brigadier that 'work of this kind is simply tinkering with the honour of the Nation and playing with the lives of the men who are acting under you.'[76]

Even as late as May 1921 the flying-column men's healthcare was still poor. Bad hygiene – simple 'lack of cleanliness' – was the reason that scabies, nits and foot infections were 'very prevalent'. GHQ urged that all column men should carry field dressings, and that columns should set up field dressing stations 'in a safe place where a member of Cumann na mBan should take charge'. All company captains needed to instruct their men to take care of their feet, and change their socks regularly. Men with scabies should be isolated, and not allowed to go back to the column until passed fit by a doctor. After-treatment was too often neglected. Each province needed to compile a list of surgeons 'who will volunteer to operate in the country'; this evidently had still not been done by June.[77]

The 'continuous blocking of roads' mentioned to Donnelly by O'Connell was becoming the most prominent 'unarmed' strategic action. GHQ eventually called it the 'offensive against communications', though it began as a defensive strategy, to restrict the movement of Crown forces and protect ASUs. The targets in this were roads and bridges, which began to be systematically blocked or broken from January 1921 onwards. The British army first noticed this in Kildare and Meath, and it soon spread. Seamus Robinson claimed to have had the original idea: noticing that Crossley tenders often broke their axles in potholes, he suggested to GHQ that the holes might usefully be enlarged. GHQ came back with a ruling from the Local Government Department that there was to be no 'destruction of the people's property', but Robinson's argument that it would have real military uses eventually prevailed. His own brigade orders specified that gaps be left between pits to allow small local vehicles to pass.[78]

At the end of February 1921 GHQ added a more aggressive dimension to the offensive with an instruction that 'enemy transport shall henceforth be subjected everywhere to a vigorous and persistent offensive.' It was to be 'attacked wherever found, and searched out where necessary', to make it 'impossible for it to move unescorted in town or country'. The target here was not so much motor transport as the supporting transport hauled by animals: GHQ stressed that 'in this connection mules are far more valuable than horses.' It sombrely added the advice that 'in cases where animals are attacked with the Revolver it is essential that where possible a .45 calibre revolver is used.'[79]

Other units evidently followed Robinson's idea of digging pits that would halt military vehicles without preventing movement by ordinary people, but some ingenuity was needed for this. (Ernie O'Malley sketched several possible designs in his pocket books, eventually preferring 'a new style of Road Pit 7 × 8 × 3 in series of 3'.) More and more energy was applied to the contest, as the British responded by rounding people up to refill the trenches. Dublin District wryly noted that 'troops were instructed to invite the local natives to repair the cuts' (the damage to bridges, though, was often 'irreparable except by experts'). Volunteer units soon found that 'the majority of the men in the local companies were engaged nightly on these activities'.[80] Eoin O'Duffy, the Monaghan brigadier, still a civil engineer by profession, earned useful bonuses by supervising the repairs to damage caused by his own men overnight.

Some British military units started to carry bridging equipment with larger patrols, and to sweep the surrounding hills for snipers. GHQ's Engineering Department explained how to counter this with 'covered road pits (improperly called trenches)'. Pits were to be 'dug diagonally across the whole (or portion of the) road according to local circumstances to a depth of about 2ft, by 3ft wide'. The excavated material should not be left in view. 'Across the top should be placed strong laths, say 1½ inches square, at intervals of not more than 1 foot. On top of these should be stretched canvas, or cardboard, or very light timber,' with a 2-inch topping of road stones.[81] Other British units 'evolved a nasty habit of leaving grenade traps behind' in road repairs; after that, 'partly repaired trenches were . . . left untouched and new ones opened.'[82] Ever a fount of useful stratagems, Mulcahy suggested that local units sometimes 'select for cutting a point in a road not so much because of its being a suitable point for cutting, but because it is a point which you can command from some very suitable position at a distance of, say, 500, 600 or 700 yards from it'. Then put 'half a dozen or ten of your picked shots' there.[83]

Road cutting could certainly be a key tactical device, and it became possible to calculate its impact on British movements. When Mulcahy criticized a northern unit for being surprised by a British 'drive', he asserted that 'in the most active areas such as Munster this work has been systematised and will delay the enemy not less than 35 minutes.'[84] Even so, not all units were convinced. Whereas in east Clare the brigadier emphasized in April the 'utter impossibility of campaigning under present circumstances in level country unless the roads are made impassable', his Leitrim counterpart took the opposite view: 'I do not believe it is much use cutting the roads.'[85] Tipperary No. 2 grumbled that the only result of intensive road trenching had been the strengthening of enemy patrols 'and the sending of an armoured car ahead to reconnoitre'.

Another response to the cutting of roads was for British troops to make more use of bicycles on patrol. GHQ offered helpful advice on how to deal with the cyclist patrols of eight to fourteen men that had been observed in April. Ambushing these would require at least three men to every two-man file of the patrol; twenty-two men would be needed to ambush a patrol twelve strong. It suggested that if the patrol was ambushed in the open, its lack of cover should make 'our cover less important'. Maybe the rearguard alone might be attacked. 'Where men are picked shots and have thorough knowledge of one another's positions and are calm masters of the situation, risks may be taken with one another's fire which in other circumstances might not.' 'Technical games', such as having attacking parties on opposite sides of the road, could be played. In any case, 'the operation of small bodies of picked shots at long or short range against enemy cyclist patrols should provide very interesting and instructive work.'[86]

The IRA's own mobility might well have been improved. Collins, who had heard that 'in Cork No. 3 the enemy has already commandeered 50 bikes in a district', suggested in mid-April that across the MLA 'on a particular night, as soon as possible, all civilian bikes should be commandeered by us.'[87] He was by no means the first to see that 'a plentiful supply of bikes would increase the efficiency of our Army,' but little had been done about it. Although units such as the 2nd Battalion of Cork No. 1 had in fact seized large numbers – 'hundreds' – of bicycles due for delivery to the British army in late 1919, this seems to have been a random event.[88] Collins was (unusually) unspecific about the efficiency he envisaged, and he was probably not thinking of forming cyclist units as such. This was something the pre-1916 Volunteers had favoured, though they were preparing for a more open kind of warfare than their successors in 1921. Then, bikes were used all the time by many couriers (and of course, famously, by Collins himself). They were commonly used by scouts – Cumann na mBan women on bikes had scouted for Tom Barry near Kilmichael, and the British army recognized the effectiveness of IRA cycle scouts in Dublin ambushes like those on

Terenure Road and at Rathmines Church in early 1921, and on Great Brunswick Street in March. In fact, the British seem to have paid more systematic attention to their utility than the Volunteers did. When a British cycle patrol was ambushed in Kilkenny, and the troops abandoned their fifteen bikes, the Volunteers 'were afraid to keep [them] as they were easily identifiable, so [they] decided to break them up' (though they did not all agree about this).[89] Units that followed Collins's suggestion and seized all the bicycles they could find 'for use by our own forces' seem to have had no clear ideas about such use.[90] It is possible that rural column men might have been hampered as well as aided by them. In favourable terrain, though, they might well have had the military efficacy Collins seems to have had in mind. No unit appears to have complained that shortage of bikes was a problem for them, however.

'NO IRISHMAN HAS A RIGHT TO A POSITION OF NEUTRALITY'

Republican military operations undoubtedly ran against the grain of local feeling in many places. This reality jars with the dominant nationalist story of the independence struggle, a story that has been widely echoed by later writers. By 1920, it has been maintained, 'the Irish were a people in arms, committed to the IRA.'[91] But that commitment was not universal. Certainly when active units moved outside their comfort zones they could be dismayed by the attitudes they encountered. After billeting itself on some distinctly hostile farmers early in the new year, Cork No. 2 column plaintively asked, 'what is to be done with such people?'[92] When the East Clare Brigade column moved into south Galway in the early spring to attempt an ambush, it 'met nothing but lies, inaccuracies, disappointments, and incompetencies of the worst type'. ('To make it more sickening,' the brigadier added, 'heavy rain fell the whole time'.) After sending home most of the local Volunteers he decided to make an example of one 'notoriously bad district' – 'we rounded up all the passers-by and imprisoned them in the lodge' (of Dolystone House), reasoning that 'such a display would have a good effect locally'. He urged 'a wholesale wiping-out policy for people associating with the enemy'.[93] In one west Donegal village 'all persons found abroad were subjected to a search and questioning.' As the people were 'on good terms with the RIC, no quiet measures were taken, but everyone was roughly handled.'[94] When Tom Barry's West Cork column went into Skibbereen to confront the police, it was 'compelled to hold up over 100 civilians, most being anti-Sinn Féin'. But, Barry noted with grim satisfaction, 'they were all loudly singing "the Soldiers Song" when we left three hours later.'[95]

Many things, from political disagreement to the fear of reprisals, could combine to set people against the republican forces. In 1921 the Volunteers' need for funds was bearing more heavily on local communities. The Waterford Brigade was occupied in May and June 1921 collecting a 'levy imposed by order of the brigade on farmers and business people'. Over £300 was collected in the 4th Battalion area. 'As a rule the people paid up' – whether cheerfully or not – but some farmers refused outright. When this happened, local commanders sometimes 'took cattle in lieu of payment and used the cattle to feed the men'.[96] When the 4th Battalion of Cork No. 1 struck a levy 'according to what the local company believed a man could pay', it had to deal with organized resistance, whose leader was tried by a republican court and fined for 'having attempted to prevent people from contributing to the levy and spreading false reports about the IRA'. (The recalcitrants had alleged that the funds were being siphoned off by rogue Volunteers.) When he refused to pay, they seized some of his livestock – a punishment that seems to have produced a 'good collection' in the end.[97] Some units imposed a tax on 'young men who are not in the Volunteers'. The OC of the 5th Battalion of Cork 1 noted that 'Whitechurch is one of the richest districts in the county and it only paid £49 to the Brigade.' (He estimated that, on the rates subscribed elsewhere, it should have coughed up about £1,000.) When he took command, 'the Volunteer movement was ridiculed by farmers' sons in this area.' It was 'good enough for the labouring class but beneath them'. Though the Volunteers levied 'a tax according to means', they 'would not pay neither would they fight'. One dismissively said 'he would not be made a cock-shot of.' The only way the battalion could collect the 'tax' was to make a blacklist and instruct the owners of threshing machines to turn these men away until they paid up. At the end of October, some had still not done so.

The 'offensive against communications' also brought ordinary people into the fight more directly. By and large they seem to have put up with the disruption. The mid-Clare brigadier noted that although road cutting definitely affected the life of the community, 'as far as I can ascertain they see the matter in the proper light and accept the consequences in a grand spirit.' But people did not resist British demands that they repair the damaged roads. In May, Liam Lynch complained to Mulcahy that the enemy's commandeering of labour for this purpose was threatening to 'nullify the advantages gained by the cutting of roads', and suggested that 'the civil population should be asked to make a united stand against doing this work for the enemy.' Lynch thought that if only Volunteers were so instructed they would be arrested en masse, but a call by the Dáil to the people at large would be 'unanimously obeyed'. Then the enemy might be deprived of all heavy transport. Just as important, as the Adjutant General commented, was the pressing need to 'get away from the "thin Green Line" which holds the enemy at present. Every citizen of the Republic should help.'[98] GHQ issued a clarion call for public support, *An tOglac* declaring that 'no Irishman has a right to a position of neutrality. It must be all or nothing. Money, time, goods, houses, lives must be placed freely at the service of the Republican State.'[99]

Reading between the lines, we may suspect that there was more public 'neutrality' than the republican leadership found entirely comfortable. Such neutrality might take many forms, of course, ranging from lack of support through covert to open opposition. The motives for it might be equally varied. A dislike of revolutionary taxation, such as the Volunteer levies, did not in itself represent political dissent, and most of the non-cooperation that Volunteers found objectionable or inconvenient probably also stemmed from the simple wish to be left undisturbed. But political differences undoubtedly existed. Even Sinn Feiners were not united in support of the military campaign, many disliking the use of violence on either principled or pragmatic grounds, and many apprehensive about the implications of the army's increasing domination of the separatist movement. The kind of pessimism about the physical-force campaign that suffused Eimar O'Duffy's 1920 novel *The Wasted Island* must have been shared by many. The same must have gone for the voters who gave Sinn Féin control of local government in 1920: to vote for the republican counter-state was not necessarily to vote for the military campaign. Old party people may have deserted wholesale to Sinn Fein after 1918, but a minority must have maintained their critical view. Occasionally they did so publicly. Two of them had defied the republican call for a national day of protest when Terence MacSwiney's remains were returned to Ireland in November 1920. William Kennedy refused to close his chemist's shop, and T. J. O'Dempsey started a legal action for intimidation. Both had been active Redmondites (O'Dempsey a close associate of Tom Kettle) and both were shot dead.[100]

Dissent could carry a high price, and dissident voices have, mostly, been silent in the histories written since 1921. Not only triumphalist nationalist histories but also republican elegies like Dorothy Macardle's *Irish Republic* depicted the Irish nation as united behind the IRA in the struggle against Britain. Few people wished to dispute this in later years; dissidents had no interest in drawing attention to their former opposition. Protestants, especially, widely presumed to be passive if not active supporters of the Union, kept quiet – then and subsequently. Speaking out during the war 'could be terribly dangerous', and the habit of self-censorship persisted.[101] Many recent writers – including specialists on the subject of guerrilla or 'people's' war – have followed the nationalist line. Their argument about the level of anti-republican dissent is essentially negative. Without the support of 'most of the population', the IRA could not have survived as long as it did.[102] So public opposition must have been marginal. But careful analysis of the operational records shows, as we shall see, that however small the minority was it posed increasing problems for the republican forces in 1921. Non-cooperation could be troublesome, but giving information to the authorities represented a potentially lethal threat.

'DRASTIC ACTION WAS TAKEN'

In 1921, as many Volunteer units became alarmed at the apparent seepage of information to the Crown forces, a neurosis about 'spies and informers' spread across the organization. In some places, whole units were 'largely occupied' in 'observation of enemy spies'. South Roscommon asserted in January that 'we must first wipe out spies and informers before any action of importance is successful'. In March, Cork No. 2 suggested that 'we rigidly put in force' an order that none of the civil population were to speak to the police or military. 'We cannot afford to wait to find spies,' it said. South Roscommon was still looking in April – even dressing in 'Enemy uniforms' to visit suspects and question them about Volunteer movements. Once they were found, wiping them out might mean killing, expelling or merely fining them. In one case, that of 'an extra well-to-do farmer' who had 'wired the enemy that rebels had trenched the roads in his vicinity', Cork No. 2 requested GHQ permission to fine him £50. The brigadier also proposed to have the charge read out at the principal mass in the local Catholic church (the farmer was a Protestant): 'I mean to have him in the vicinity with the charges pinned on him.' Mulcahy breezily told him, 'if you think you could get £100, do so.'[103]

Pits in roads were hardly high-grade information, and the point here was one of principle. Where more vital information was concerned, action was more coercive. Cork No. 1's intelligence officer noted that 'civilian spies were considered by us to be the most dangerous of all. They were well acquainted with the IRA men in the different localities in which they operated (being natives of the district in certain cases),' and might 'create havoc in our organisation'. 'Drastic action [was] taken to put a stop to their activities.'[104] The two men who gave information to the disguised Volunteers in South Roscommon were summarily 'executed'.[105] The killing of Mary Lindsay was an unusually (and unwelcomely) high-profile case; more often the fate of the alleged informers was obscure, as indeed was their precise offence. The concepts of spying and informing were flexible. In Lindsay's case we know enough to be sure that she was not an informer in the normal sense – she betrayed no trust in giving information. Nor was she a spy in the normal sense (if there is such a thing); she was not using any kind of cover or false identity – indeed she was an openly proclaimed loyalist. Other victims of the spate of killings in early 1921 may also have been ambiguous. In January and February the Cork No. 3 Brigade, for instance, killed at least ten suspected spies. Pinning notices – such as 'Convicted Spy. Informers Beware. IRA' – to their corpses underlined the linkage of the concepts. The implication of conviction after due process was, inevitably, often misleading. GHQ certainly worried about the escalating rate of executions, and instructed local commanders to 'convict' only on definite evidence. The 'language of due process' was clearly vital to the members of IRA military courts, but short of confession – which might be extracted by extreme duress – their proceedings were less exact. A brigade court martial in Limerick, for instance, was set up with considerable formality – a president, two members, a clerk, plus prosecution and defence counsel – but its report showed that the latter two joined the discussion which produced a guilty verdict and a death sentence.[106] One general rule – that women spies should not be killed but exiled – seems to have been followed in all but the Lindsay case. Just how many women acted as spies, though, can only be guessed at.

In Kells 'a man named F. Dooner believed to be an informer was fired at, wounded in the head and stomach but did not die.' On 24 March the Dublin ASU shot an unidentified 'enemy spy' in Thomas Street, expending a dozen rounds of .45 ammunition in the process – wounding him badly but not killing him.[107] A typical case, which Mulcahy inquired about, was 'a man of the tramp class, aged 30', who was reported in the press on 28 March to have been found shot, 'with a card attached to him "Spies beware IRA"'. Kerry No. 2 Brigade explained that 'Barraduff Company had an ex-soldier of whom they were suspicious. They handed him over to the Flying Column. The Commandant questioned him, he admitted that he was receiving 8/- a week from a Capt. O'Sullivan Killarney, to track down "wanted men". He also gave the names of four men in Killarney who are on the same job. He was executed on 24th inst.' 'The names of the four men . . . proved to be bogus.'[108]

The 6th Battalion of Cork No. 1 Brigade arrested 'a British soldier in uniform without badges', who said he was a deserter. He was held for two days while inquiries were made. 'We were very suspicious of him for . . . many of the alleged deserters were British spies,' and 'it was eventually decided to execute him.' According to Denis Dwyer, one of the execution party, the fact that he 'died very bravely without the slightest flinching . . . convinced us that he was a British Intelligence Officer'.[109] One commander, in Offaly, neglected to clear an execution with GHQ, but claimed he had done so with his local priest. He arrested John Lawlor, who had failed to 'clear out' of the district as ordered by a Volunteer court martial, after 'going into houses for a glass of milk' and being 'seen in company with the military and police on two occasions'. 'I told him that I was going to shoot him as he was spying and looking for information [on] men on the run. Seeing that I had found him out in his manuvers [sic] he asked for forgiveness . . . I told him to prepare for confession and I went for a Priest . . . After he had his confession told, the Priest called me to one side and asked me did I hold a court martial on him and I told him I did. He said that was right and I was doing my duty.'[110] The report was headed 'execution of enemy secret service agent'.

When the 1st Battalion of the South Roscommon Brigade arrested 'a strange man passing the house . . . in civilian attire and riding a bicycle' who 'seemed to be taking a great interest in the house in which we were', they found him to be carrying a Webley revolver. He was apparently a Black and Tan in mufti. Their immediate response was to get him to agree to see a Catholic priest, although he 'professed no religion'. As soon as the priest had baptized him 'we bound him and drowned him by throwing him into the river Suck at Dunammon.' Though this was evidently a combatant, since he 'admitted that he was on intelligence work', he could be treated as a spy. (The Volunteer officer who drowned him went on to become a sergeant in the Irish police force after independence, the Garda Síochána.)[111]

Evidently stung by some of GHQ's comments, the intelligence officer of 1st Southern Division eventually took it to task 'with regard to this matter of spies'. GHQ had 'somehow got the idea that in the Cork Brigades, and especially in Cork No. 1, men are being shot as spies more or less on suspicion'. The reality was that 'the greatest care is taken in every instance to have the case fully proved and beyond all doubt.' Most of the men shot had in fact admitted their guilt before being executed. So upset were the Corkmen by Dublin's attitude that they were now 'seriously considering whether instead of shooting any more of them we will no—' (what they threatened to do remains unknown, since the rest of the sentence was cut out of the document at some stage).[112]

The punishment of informers in Cork created a new problem for the Volunteers. Their houses were burned, 'as it was decided that all convicted spys should be executed and "burnt out" as well'. Their lands and stock were 'confiscated to the government of the country'. But sometimes it was clear that other motives were at work. 'The people . . . want to divide his farm up among themselves.' As Tom Barry made clear in the case of T. J. Kingston of Burgatia House, Rosscarbery, and several other cases, 'we are not allowing the sales of those farms.' The brigade quartermaster had become responsible for working them, and was holding the profits in trust: 'He is at present awaiting instructions as to where to send the money.'[113]

It is impossible at this remove to assess the assertion (or admission) that spies represented a major threat to the IRA's survival. It is hardly easier to assess how effective, overall, the IRA's detection and punishment of informers was. Its procedures had, as we have seen, definite weaknesses. The East Limerick Brigade was never able to trace the source of the 'very pointed information' which had led the British army to discover an elaborate arms dump at Thomastown on 8 May.[114] This was not unusual; many informants survived. Though things may possibly have been different in areas with diligent intelligence officers (such as Cork No. 1), the most careful historical analysis strongly suggests that a large proportion of those killed as spies did not give information to the authorities. They had fallen foul of the republicans for other reasons. (Only one out of twenty-two names on the West Cork Brigade's list of 'Enemy agents and other suspects' in July 1921 reappeared on the list compiled six months later, suggesting some erratic evaluation. The diary of a British intelligence officer in Cork, listing all his informants, indicates that none of the people the IRA accused of giving information in the district had in fact done so.)[115] The second of four charges against Patrick O'Gorman, a farmer executed by the 2nd Battalion of the East Limerick Brigade in March, was 'that he was living up to the date of his arrest with a woman to whom he was not married'.[116]

But the sheer scale of the internal security campaign, which one historian has called 'a civil war within and between communities', is beyond doubt. And a myth of IRA omniscience and ruthlessness, which drew on folk memories of earlier secret societies, was certainly created, and grew in the subsequent telling. Whereas in Frank O'Connor's short story 'Jumbo's Wife' the informer was discovered only when his wife took one of his money orders to the local Volunteer captain, a twenty-first-century novelist would use the organization's capacity to pursue a traitor across the Atlantic as a key plot device.[117] Such beliefs may have played some part in protecting republican fighters in the field, but they were probably balanced at the time by an understanding of the organization's limits. The security of the Volunteers was maintained by consent as well as by fear.

REPUBLICAN LAW

After the heady days of 1920, the Republic's justice system was also stumbling a little. Indeed in some marginal areas, such as Donegal, the republican courts had been abandoned because Volunteer commanders refused to provide men for police service.[118] Austin Stack, the Minister for Home Affairs, had to acknowledge the 'partial' success of the enemy's 'ruthless campaign' against the courts. While 'the Justices and Registrars who are at large seem to be bestirring themselves in many places,' the key individuals at constituency level were underperforming. 'I regret to have to report that I have received no response from 14 members of the Dáil (all at liberty) to two communications soliciting assistance in reorganising the Courts. Other members have merely acknowledged and promised Reports.' He reiterated his 'appeal to members to give me all the help in their power'.[119] The Sligo Brigade reported in June 1921 that resident magistrates were being brought in from 'the North' to try to revive the British courts, and asked GHQ if it would be justified in shooting them. Mulcahy temporized: this would be 'a portion of the ground that would be covered by the Offensive against Enemy Civil Administration'. This was evidently a new concept, since its 'main lines' had not yet been agreed on. (Brugha also agreed that it would be 'better to hold it over until we have fully considered the whole matter'.)[120]

There was also an attempt to regularize the republican police. In May, Mulcahy told Simon Donnelly that he had promised 'to send an Army officer to the Department of Home Affairs to bring into being a Civil Police Force', and gave Donnelly this task. On 1 June he ordered that there was to be 'a police force to the number of ten in each company area'. The force would be 'detached from the Army', though it would 'have at all times the Army to fall back upon'. Any member of the IRA who joined the force should be relieved 'of all work connected with the Army'. Those who went from the army to the police 'must be good intelligent men'; if necessary the remainder of the force would be 'drafted from outside the IRA'.[121] At the time Donnelly became chief of police, there were only six full-time – paid – police officers in Dublin, 'assisted by, for want of a better name, the spare time Company and Battalion Police'. His first task was to make sure that each of the seventy-two brigade areas had at least one full-time officer. These were drawn 'mainly' from the Volunteers, but some 'civilians' also had to be recruited. Volunteer ambivalence about police work clearly persisted; as late as November 1921 the Adjutant General found it necessary to insist that 'close co-operation with the Police in a spirit of true citizenship is demanded of all Volunteers.' He urged them to 'appreciate the fact that in the Police is developing another most important branch of the machinery of the Republic'.[122]

The general policing situation was, Donnelly thought, not easy – illegal fishing, poteen making, emigration, cattle-driving and school truancy had all 'got somewhat out of hand'. Looking for alternative forms of punishment to the generally impracticable imprisonment, he asked for authorization to flog 'incorrigible criminals'. But his proposal was turned down, 'as it was considered a barbarous form of punishment'. The republican police in a major port like Dublin had an additional burden, enforcement of the Dáil ministry's restriction on emigration. As early as July 1919 the Department for Home Affairs had prohibited emigration without a permit for men of military age. Volunteers could go only if they had the signed consent of their brigade commandant. When the Dáil confirmed this policy in August, an amendment proposing delay until 'a scheme for providing employment in Ireland for intending emigrants' had been set up was defeated, though only by the unusually narrow margin of 23 votes to 16.[123] Whether any scheme could have coped with the situation is doubtful. In 1919, with wartime restrictions still in place, only 3,000 had emigrated, but in 1920 that total rose tenfold. De Valera warned that the 'effect' of large numbers arriving in the USA was 'very bad', and the 'danger' emigration represented became a more pressing issue for local Volunteer units in 1921. In March, Cork No. 1 Brigade pressed for authority to shoot emigrants, and in May GHQ aimed to persuade the 'younger clergy' to launch an 'anti-emigration crusade'. Unfortunately, as it noted, the areas where emigration was 'rampant' were 'districts where it is very hard to organise anything'. (These presumably included impoverished western counties like Donegal; it was not clear whether the Republic wanted to stop the traditional seasonal labour migration from there to Scotland.) If the younger clergy failed, there was of course a rougher alternative. GHQ wanted 'suitable action' taken against families sending men of military age out of the country, and thought that if 'exemplary punitive measures' were taken against deserters, but not advertised as such, 'the effect will be better, as it will be assumed they were shot for emigrating.' It brutally observed that 'the type of man who runs away now will be very amenable to such reasoning.'[124]

After Donnelly had taken command, 'a number of young men trying to leave the country were apprehended by us as they were about to go aboard ship at the North Wall. We took all their personal belongings (except money), also their tickets and papers, and they had to return home.' Local police were instructed to keep an eye on them. 'Our people' in America also made life 'difficult' for emigrants who arrived without a Dáil permit – 'work being hard to get and so on'. Donnelly tried to get all shipping agents to sign an undertaking that they would not sell tickets to anyone without an official emigration permit – 'the vast majority signed'. The fact that a minority did not is hardly surprising. When Thomas Cook's agency 'was hesitant', Donnelly sent some of his men over to 'interview the Manager'. They were given a time when the manager would be available. Donnelly was 'anxious to force the matter' – it was just before the Truce – but when the republican police went back they were 'arrested by Crown Forces in mufti'. Donnelly urged Stack that such 'defiance of the authority of the Republic', and 'treachery' in informing the enemy, merited condign punishment.[125] He wanted to shoot the manager or one of his staff, or at least destroy their premises. Stack told him to ask Brugha to authorize this, but the arrival of the Truce seems to have suspended the matter.

Donnelly claimed that the republican police successfully maintained a wide range of laws previously enforced by the RIC – notably the regulation of licensed trading hours and the prohibition of illicit distilling, protecting freshwater fish during the close season and even enforcing school attendance. In 1921 they were faced with 'a perfect epidemic' of crimes like obtaining money under false pretences and issuing dud cheques.[126] He thought that the 'greatest handicap' they faced was the fact that they were 'operating in their own areas', among friends and relations. In an unintended tribute to the procedures of the RIC (which had led to that force being branded an army of occupation), he noted that 'human nature being what it is, there was always the danger or weakness that the police officers, without realising it, would not display that absolute impartial spirit necessary.' Donnelly suggested that this was fortunately 'offset' by the co-operation of the people, though he did not say just how.[127] In July he had to issue an order in response to 'numerous complaints as to people receiving notices of a threatening nature, purporting to come from republican sources'. It must be clearly understood, he instructed, 'that threats must not be made by any of our Police officers'. They had no power to inflict punishment without authority from HQ, and must 'not adopt a threatening or intimidating attitude in the execution of their duty'.[128] But people were, not surprisingly, easily intimidated – especially in rural areas. A republican court official in Wicklow recalled that 'when serving summonses, civil bills etc., in the remote country districts, the people appeared to be afraid. They would offer you money, butter, eggs or fowl.' He thought 'it was fear of the name, IRA'.[129] In the weird quasi-war atmosphere of much of the country, republican police could hardly have risen far above the conflict. But at least some seem to have tried.

CHURCH AND COUNTER-STATE

At the turn of the year the Republic's legitimacy was dealt a blow by the Bishop of Cork. Though he had generally followed the Hierarchy's conservative line, and had been notably slow to subscribe to the Dáil Loan, Bishop Cohalan had praised the republican court system and in August 1920 went as far as to say that 'the capacity for government exhibited by Sinn Féin has won the recognition and admiration of friend and foe.'[130] If this looked like a tacit recognition of the Republic, that would change dramatically at the end of the year. After the reprisals in Cork on the night of 11 December he delivered a sermon denouncing the republican contention that 'the murder of policemen' was justified because it had liberated part of the country. 'No', said the Bishop, the killing of RIC men was 'murder' and the burning of barracks was 'simply the destruction of Irish property'. He declared that reprisals and counter-reprisals, starting from the killing of Mayor Mac Curtain, had become 'a Devil's competition'. Ambushers who left 'the lives and property of . . . innocent people unprotected and undefended to the fury of reprisals at the hands of the servants of the government' could not be justified. He went on to excommunicate all murderers.[131]

When the Lord Mayor of Cork and Cork City TD J. J. Walsh protested to the Hierarchy against the 'false supposition' that there was 'no such thing as an Irish Government and Irish Army' and 'no right to strike back at the criminals who are attacking us', Cohalan responded by explicitly denying the legitimacy of the Republic. On 19 December he issued a pastoral letter challenging 'the false teachings of persons who should know better, that Ireland is at the moment a sovereign independent state, and that consequently Irishmen have authority to kill

England's forces and to burn English property in Ireland'. In February 1921 he homed in directly on the republican government's claim to sovereignty. 'If Ireland is a sovereign state she has the right to use physical force,' he wrote, 'but if Ireland is not a sovereign state the physical force policy is unlawful.' Where, he asked, was the 'competent authority' which could declare war? 'The question is: was the proclamation of an Irish Republic by the Sinn Féin members of parliament after the last general election sufficient to constitute Ireland a republic according to our Church teaching? I answer that it was not.' However much people might wish for independence, 'we cannot hold that the proclamation of Dáil Éireann constituted Ireland validly a sovereign state.'[132]

Bishop Cohalan's previous history with the Volunteers was ambiguous. In 1916, as assistant bishop, he had put heavy pressure on Mac Curtain and MacSwiney, telling them that to send their men to fight without adequate munitions would be criminal. Some held him responsible for Cork's resulting inaction, and still more for the humiliating deal he helped to broker, under which the Cork Volunteers surrendered their weapons to the British army at the end of Easter Week. Cohalan indicated that they would be returned later, but in fact the army had not agreed to this and, unsurprisingly, held on to the guns. The effect of his 1920 anathema was mixed. Cork City's other TD Liam de Roiste had to deal with the fact that Cohalan's 12 December sermon appeared to justify English rule, 'and condemn *every* action on the part of the Irish people to defend themselves or assert their independence'. But he argued that a careful reading of it showed that 'His Lordship really does not express this view.' Unfortunately, 'the censure is very ill-timed owing to the excited feelings of the people.' De Roiste was right about Cohalan's 'real' view, in the sense that he was an Irish nationalist at the very least. The Bishop went as far as to say, 'When you come with an army able to fight the enemy and defend the weak and unprotected, I will act as Chaplain.' But this was to impose a very stern test, which many conventional armies of established states would have failed.

Cohalan's action was dismissed by some. A Co. Louth priest averred in March 1921 that thanks to his 'precipitancy and flippancy' Cohalan was 'now without a particle of influence over his own people'. His excommunication decree had 'missed fire'.[133] In general, Volunteers seem to have regarded all clerical denunciations of violence as political interventions, and some abandoned religious practice.[134] But in Cork some Volunteers were troubled by the decree. When the nationalist *Cork Examiner* endorsed it, they smashed its presses. Florrie O'Donoghue sought the view of the Capuchin father Dominic O'Connor (who had been a chaplain with the forces at Salonika in the Great War). O'Connor confirmed that those taking part in ambushes or killings were exempt as long as they were acting 'with the authority of the state – the republic of Ireland'.[135] He went further, indeed, airily assuring him that 'just as there is no necessity telling a priest that you went to Mass on Sunday, so there is no necessity to tell him one has taken part in an ambush.' But since he had adopted – presumably unofficially – the role of 'brigade chaplain' to Cork No. 1, he was a rather untypical priest. The Volunteer leaders who snorted that Cohalan 'was never taken seriously by us' (Connie Neenan), and that 'nobody minds him now' (Liam Lynch), probably well knew that their men were not immune to 'the nightmare horror' of the decree.[136]

Fortunately for the Republic, Bishop Cohalan was not representative of the Church leadership as a whole. Even the deeply conservative Cardinal Logue had been moved by Bloody Sunday to come off the fence and say that 'if a balance were struck between the deeds of the morning and those of the evening, I believe it should be given against the forces of the Crown.'[137] But any prospect of direct recognition of the Republic by the Church remained a distant one. Although de Valera's absence in the USA meant 'he had lost many opportunities to develop ... a good working relationship with the hierarchy', others clearly aimed to make the Republic a more explicitly confessional state. O'Hegarty reported to him in February 1921 that he had received a letter from Cosgrave proposing a 'Theological Senate'. It suggested that 'there should be a sort of "upper house" to the Dáil consisting of a Theological Board' which would decide whether any of the Dáil's enactments were 'contrary to Faith and Morals'. There was also 'a suggestion that a guarantee be given to the Holy Father that the Dáil will not make laws contrary to the teachings of the Church, in return for which the Holy Father will be asked to recognise the Dáil as a body entitled to legislate for Ireland'. O'Hegarty's opinion of the idea was scathing. Noting that Cosgrave's letter had been 'mislaid for a few days', he added that 'it would seem to have been mislaid for nine hundred years.' In his view the Board would not work, 'and might lead to grave trouble'. Most importantly, perhaps, 'for the Dáil to admit that there existed a necessity for such a check on their legislation would, I think, be a fatal error.' Whether or not de Valera agreed, he laconically instructed O'Hegarty to 'tell Liam MacC that I read his theological proposal, and there is no necessity at the moment to consider it further'.[138]

It was the threat of a papal intervention condemning the republican military campaign that did most to bring the Church and the counter-state into line. Even moderate prelates were roused to quite extreme expression. Bishop O'Doherty, in his capacity as secretary of the Hierarchy's Standing Committee, wrote 'English violence and oppression our people can endure; English slanders they despise. But ... it would be utterly heartbreaking to them if Rome were to step into this quarrel on the side of the enemies of their race and faith.' Bishop Mulhern of Dromore issued a not very veiled threat: 'it has often been said that if the Irish people become alienated from the faith and their priests, it will be the fault of the priests.' The bishops clearly feared British influence in Rome, though in the event the Pope's letter proved to be a study in the evenhanded condemnation of violence. 'We do not see how the bitter strife can profit either of the parties' when 'on both sides a war resulting in the death of unarmed people, even of women and children, is carried on'. From the British viewpoint, such balance amounted to a publicity disaster. 'HMG are placed in exactly the same category as the authors of arson and cold-blooded murder,' as the Foreign Office complained. The letter put the government 'and the murder gang on a footing of equality', and the Pope could even be seen as 'coming down publicly on the side of the forces of disorder'.

DECENTRALIZATION AND DIVISIONALIZATION

On 11 March the Dáil tackled the question of how the republican government could be carried on if, as de Valera put it, 'their numbers went very low'. (There were actually twenty-five present at this session, only eight fewer than had constituted the Dáil's first meeting that had issued the Declaration of Independence.) This indirect tribute to the pressure exerted by British military measures produced some interesting reactions. Mulcahy's proposal that TDs should have a substitute (nominated by them and confirmed by their local Comhairle Ceanntair – Sinn Féin district executive) was turned down. De Valera proposed that, if so many deputies were imprisoned that the Dáil could not function, governmental power should pass to the army. This – not something that Mulcahy can have relished – also failed to gain approval. Instead the Dáil resolved that if its numbers fell to five, these survivors should constitute a 'provisional government'.

Another line of approach was to reduce the government's exposure to British repressive action in Dublin by decentralizing the administration. It was noted later that year (by Aodh de Blacam) that the Dáil had 'initiated a system by which its various works would stand by themselves if the central authority were smitten out of existence', though just what this involved was not clear. The Dáil apparently did not consider turning the provinces, 'which would have seemed the most logical basis of decentralisation', into governmental units.[139] What we do know is that the army was, at this time, taking steps to decentralize its own command structure. Mulcahy might not relish having the army replace the government, but he obviously shared the anxiety about being 'smitten out of existence'.

There were worries about resilience in the provinces as well. Liam Lynch pointed out that military co-operation across local boundaries remained lamentable. Often one brigade might be 'hard-pressed by the enemy, while neighbouring Brigades are listening to the guns and do nothing, often perhaps allowing enemy reinforcements to pass through unmolested'. He believed that 'at the present moment the Enemy is out to try and squash our Brigade'; it had 'too many gun-men on active service while some of our adjacent Brigades are inactive'. It would be an advantage to be able to 'cross over the border now and then'.[140] Given the persistence of territorial jealousy, the answer seemed to be to create a divisional command. 'All the officers at the conference were in favour of it except Cork No. 1, but since then the military situation has changed there considerably.' Lynch characteristically asked Mulcahy not to insist that he should take up this command: it would mean 'being responsible for the war zone and I consider myself far from being able to fill such a position'. One of the 'old dogs' in the area should do it and let him stay 'with the brave fighting men here'. But the Chief of Staff was clearly less impressed by the alternative candidates, and Lynch was appointed the IRA's first divisional commander a few weeks later. On 26 April nine brigades – three from Cork, three from Kerry, two from Waterford and one from Limerick – convened at Kippagh, near Millstreet, to constitute themselves the 1st Southern Division.[141] (Lynch had advised that Clare should be left out – 'except one of the Brigades' – but that a GHQ representative would be a better judge of the situation.)

This was a dramatic step. Over the next three months another six to eight divisional commands were set up, half of them in the north. The idea did not come out of the blue; the notion of establishing divisions had been discussed as early as 1918, and in mid-1920 a number of southern brigades had been identified as capable of benefiting from a joint organization, though it was clear that any extensive co-operation would be difficult to implement in practice.[142] Psychologically, the idea cut both ways: it was attractive as a sign that the Volunteers were steadily growing more like a real army, but less so insofar as it threatened to disturb the tight military groups which had proved their capacity to survive in sometimes difficult environments.

The primary justification was to rectify the kind of problem Lynch had identified, or as Mulcahy put it in his somewhat ponderous autodidactic military language, 'the necessity for harmonising the nature and direction of operative activity in adjoining Brigade areas which are so placed as to influence the Military Situation in one another'.[143] A secondary but also vital function was to push on professionalization via the 'Divisional School of Administration and Training'. The underlying aim was systemic resilience. Mulcahy later acknowledged that a series of successful British raids meant that 'we never knew when the blow would come and ... GHQ might be wiped out.' 'We therefore set out from the beginning of 1921 to divisionalize the country ... we had about 15 divisional areas where we knew there was military capacity among the people there ... so that if Headquarters here was wiped out there would be sufficient authority and prestige attached to local groups to ... get on if they were driven to get on without us.'[144]

At the time, he headlined more positive arguments. 'Diminishing the number of units coming directly in contact with GHQ' would enable 'more attention to be given to the main problems of each individual area', and also facilitate 'much closer cooperation between the several Divisional areas'. As he instructed one western brigadier, 'the immediate primary object in the setting up of Divisional Commands' was 'the harmonising of operations in contiguous areas, whose operations react on one another'. It was 'essential that the Divisional Commander have the power to transfer arms and men from time to time' when he judged it necessary. So he could 'dispose of [sic] any arms in your Area'.[145] Paradoxically, given that a new tier of command was being created, it was argued that 'the machinery of administration will be greatly simplified, and there should be a very pronounced increase in speed and efficiency of working.'[146] This would be because the brigades could be in closer contact with divisional HQs than they had been with GHQ. Decentralization would reduce GHQ's contact points and free it to concentrate on strategic planning.

Mulcahy held that 'each Division must come more and more to regard itself as a definite Unit capable of carrying on a formidable campaign unaided ... an army in miniature.'[147] Divisions are of course the basic strategic elements of regular armies, but in a territorial guerrilla force like the IRA the same terms could just as well be applied to brigades or battalions, if not indeed even smaller units. Its local resilience meant that, unlike in regular armies, its units had no real need to co-operate. Greater acceptance of higher authority might well go some way to bringing them together, but nothing like the integration implied by the divisional concept could ever really be achieved as long as units remained essentially local. Another argument rolled out as the programme expanded was that divisionalization would bring 'quiet areas' under closer control and stimulation. GHQ was acutely conscious of the contrast between the War Zone and the main part of the country, which it blamed primarily on inadequate leadership rather than objective conditions. It had stepped up its own efforts to gee up the laggards over the last year, but the results were meagre.

One argument that stayed in the background, but clearly carried weight, was that GHQ was simply overloaded. Diarmuid O'Hegarty, the Director of Organization, spelt this out: in the previous summer, as he wrote on 10 March, 'we were dealing with about 45 units more or less and had about 4 organisers.' Now 'we are dealing with 100 units direct and we have to supervise the work of 32 Organisers.' Considering that 'this includes dealing with monthly reports from all units, alterations and ratifications of officers of all ranks, general discipline, records and numerous other matters in the case of 100 units, as well as the receipt of and attention to fortnightly reports, queries etc, from 32 Organisers and their payment, it will be readily observed that the increase in this Department's work is very large'. Two of the voluntary members of his staff had left, and the third had 'lost much of his utility' because the curfew regulations stopped him working regularly. He himself found his duties as secretary to the ministry more 'various and irksome' since de Valera's return to the country. He could no longer get any help in his civil work from his Assistant Secretary, who was fully employed on Volunteer work. He had also recently been deprived by 'an unfortunate accident' of his Volunteer office. As a result of all this, he had decided to employ a lady clerk (an 'exceptional girl' with 'considerable experience of similar work') at £3 10s a week. (This brought the weekly expenditure on staff to £12 10s, but as he pointed out 'it is obvious that a Department which expended between £600 and £1000 per month cannot be effective without a whole time staff'; up to this point, the salary cost of its officers at HQ had been nil.)[148] This bureaucrat's grumble was in part a preface to giving up his double civil–military life in April 1921. But it indicated the knife-edge on which the administration worked.

Some divisional areas decided themselves naturally, while others seemed more artificial. Most of the country was far less developed in terms of military organization than the south-west. While only two divisions were needed for the War Zone, five were created in the north where the infrastructure was much more rudimentary. In some cases, existing brigades were simply redesignated divisions, presumably in the hope that the promotion would inject new energy. (Hitler would do the same thing with his forces in the final months of the Second World War.) Probably only the south was really ready to be reorganized in this way, and the structure may have been extended across the country to give an impression of greater regularity and uniformity than actually existed. This image-creation loomed large in Mulcahy's mission and vision: it was one of the key reasons for relentlessly pushing proper military procedures (reporting, form-filling) in face of persistent uncooperativeness or outright resistance. There was a dramatic acceleration in the frequency of written reports around this time, often on new proformas (for instance, for intelligence reports and information on the enemy order of battle). New divisional commanders were required to send reports listing 'criticisms of reports you have received, notes on how you propose to remedy problems and defects, and any suggestions for developing your area'.[149] This reflected Mulcahy's belief in the importance of uniformity, which still left some unconvinced. Not many officers rose to the level of perfection Mulcahy found in, say, Eoin O'Duffy as commander of 2nd Northern Division. The Chief of Staff was 'struck by the excellence and comprehensiveness of your general agenda', adding that 'your "unerring instinct" is much appreciated by me and everyone else.' When he drew Oscar Traynor's attention to one of O'Duffy's reports – 'Isn't that a magnificent report?' – the Dublin brigadier brusquely replied, 'what strikes me about that man is that he must have plenty of time on his hands.'[150]

But even the exemplary O'Duffy had reservations about the divisionalization process. Trying to set up the 2nd Northern Division in April 1921, he reported scathingly on the state of Tyrone: 'working here practically in the dark without any orders from GHQ', he found 'the standard of efficiency at a very low ebb: very little knowledge of close order drill, no knowledge whatever of extended order. No special services . . . & absolute ignorance of the care & use of arms'. He calculated that an astounding number of rifles (maybe sixty) had simply been lost and most of the rest, revolvers as well, were 'in a filthy condition from rust'. 'Thousands of rounds' of .303 ammunition had also been lost, and thousands 'have got useless from damp'. (He blamed this on the fact that units had not had to risk their lives to get their guns.) Discipline was feeble – 'what would be considered reasonable orders in other counties' would be regarded here as 'Prussianism'. The worst battalion in Tyrone (Gortin) was dedicated to poteen making, and O'Duffy 'scrapped all the officers and made new appointments'. The battalion would recover, he said, though it would 'be much smaller'.[151]

O'Duffy also worried that taking over Tyrone might damage his position in his own county, Monaghan – 'After years of building it up alone & unaided I would not like to lose my grip on it.' In the south, opposition was more strident, often on the grounds that divisions were artificial and impracticable, a paper exercise of the sort you would expect from the Dublin desk soldiers. Did the divisional areas make real military sense? GHQ put quite a lot of effort into drawing up strategic appreciations clarifying the strengths and weaknesses of various divisions. These are the most substantial surviving evidence of republican military thinking, and their survival is indeed remarkable. Mulcahy noted the 'danger that if any of this material falls into enemy hands' (which, as his own experience showed, was quite possible) 'it discloses our mind fairly completely to them.' But he thought that less dangerous than 'not setting down our ideas'.[152] Only by setting them down could they 'hope to have a uniform outline or a uniform understanding of the main lines along which we should work and develop'. To Mulcahy these were self-evidently desirable.

What he did was essentially to codify as doctrine the methods which active areas like Cork had developed more or less instinctively. So their general policy was 'to hem them [enemy forces] into a few big stations and repossess the countryside outside'. This applied above all to Cork city itself: it was 'most important for us to have the firmest grip possible on Cork, both to use its resources ourselves and to dispute the Enemy's use of its facilities'. Mulcahy insisted that 'our War is distinct from all other Guerrilla Wars' in being 'the Guerrilla War of a civilised modern people'. Urban areas were vital; it was 'not enough to maintain ourselves indefinitely in remote areas'. 'The more effort we put into Cork City and the more strain we put on enemy in and around it the greater relief we afford to outlying areas.' If the enemy was 'resolutely tackled in suburban areas' – 'largely peopled by his adherents or people over-used to his exhibited strength' – this would (as they had discovered in Dublin) have a significant impact on his prestige. 'Such operations manifest the "imperturbable offensive spirit" because they tackle the Enemy where it would suit him to have his hands free.' But hemming the enemy in must not involve risky operations; 'small jobs' and sniping could be enough. 'It is not very important what post is attacked, nor when, nor how often – the great thing is to have every attack that is made successful.' Again, obvious as it might seem, this was a key insight.

Seán Moylan, who took over Cork No. 2 Brigade when Lynch became divisional commander, left an account of the 26 April meeting at which the 1st Southern Division was set up. It was the first time that he met Tom Barry or Seán O'Hegarty. He could see the benefits of inter-brigade co-ordination, and in this sense the creation of divisions was 'a natural growth fostered by conditions'. But like some others he was less impressed by the GHQ input, delivered by Ernie O'Malley as GHQ representative. 'Those who wrote such communications at GHQ seemed to have as bedside book and Bible General Lettow Vorbeck's story of the war in East Africa. From this and "Infantry Training, 1914" I assume came the inexplicable military periods and inapplicable military proposals ... which roused the ire of men of long fighting experience and terse speech.' Seán O'Hegarty, a 'master of invective, tore the communication and its authors to ribbons'.[153] According to Moylan several others, not just Tom Barry, joined in the assault – though Barry's condemnation echoed loudest down the years – divisionalization did not contribute 'a man, a gun, a round of ammunition, a shilling or a plan of action'.[154] Mulcahy's wider state-building ideas bounced off these 'fighting men' like peas off a wall.

Ernie O'Malley, who chaired the meeting, recalled O'Hegarty's 'biting gnarled tongue that flayed', demanding arms not memoranda. 'Why was the pressure on the South not relieved? Why didn't some other part of the country begin to fight? And why doesn't HQ organize or train the Midlands, the West or the East? And why doesn't Dicky Mulcahy or Micky Collins come down to inspect brigades in Tipperary, Cork and Kerry? Then they could see how things were.' O'Hegarty's 'acrid spleen' was unusual, but he only 'voiced our general discontent'. The mood of the meeting brightened when it turned to a project of running in a really big arms shipment – 20,000 rifles with 200 rounds of ammunition each, and 600 machine guns, 150 tons in all – to West Cork. This, O'Malley estimated, would give the two southern divisions some thousand rifles between them. 'Our faces shone ... Here were we, who thought in terms of seventy or eighty rifles to a brigade and an odd machine-gun, talking of thousands of rifles and millions of rounds of ammunition.'[155] Landing points were discussed and evaluated in detail, and plans made for transporting the bulk of the arms on through to 'the Midlands and the North'. The great gun-running did not, however, materialize.

'IN HOSTILE TERRITORY'

The northern divisions were sometimes referred to as 'Ulster' divisions – a slip which indicates how far the sense of separation had already gone. (The other provinces were never linked to the divisional structure.) Their limited military capacity inevitably reflected the very different political demography of the north. The potential citizenry of the Republic were, in practice, never more than a minority. The Volunteers in Crossmaglen were not unusual in keeping a low profile. 'No person seemed to have any idea what it was possible to do or make any effort to do anything.' It was not, Thomas Luckie of the Crossmaglen company thought, a matter of 'trying and things not working out' – 'as far

as I know no effort was made even to make plans to carry out operations.'[156] Even in the more active areas, like the Newry Brigade, the first
serious attack – on the RIC barrack at Camlough – did not come until
December 1920. Only after that was there enough British pressure to
generate a flying column 'of sorts'.[157]

GHQ's grand strategic analysis identified Ulster – or, as Mulcahy
preferred, 'the six Carsonia Counties' – as the 'vital English bridgehead',
which must be 'attacked steadily and persistently'. Whatever that meant,
it was easier said than done. And while it may have been encouraging
for 2nd Northern to hear that 'although the fact of a large unfriendly
population' (or, in the case of 4th Northern, 'operating in hostile territory')
'has serious disadvantages, it also has counterbalancing advantages',
the northern commanders were not told just what these were. Mulcahy's strategic memoranda often talked about 'flanks' as if there were
big regular military forces on the ground. 1st Northern Division was
told that it 'menaced the western flank of Carsonia along its entire
length', and that an advance from Donegal to Omagh would 'outflank
the disaffected territories in the Foyle valley'. But since it had neither the
capacity nor presumably the wish to invade and capture these territories, the relevance of such information remained obscure. 2nd Northern
was told that a 'proper military grip' on its area would 'result in breaking up Carsonia internally'. The centre of its area was a 'continuous
mountain mass', and it should aim to 'establish a solid base in the mountains and develop outwards from it'. Operations should focus on cutting
communications, to bring 'economic pressure on the hostile population,
and prove to them that adherence to the Enemy is not a paying game'. If
the strategic position of 4th Northern Division was 'turned to the fullest
possible account . . . Belfast can be brought to the brink of ruin'.[158]

That division should form the 'spear point of the offensive for which
the driving power would be supplied from the South'. The republican
leadership in Dublin naturally tried to push northern activity into a
single national framework. From a northern perspective it might look
exploitative; GHQ has been criticized for 'using northern Volunteers
for its own southern priorities'.[159] But of course its fundamental ideas
made this inevitable, and it would not have seen its priorities as anything but national. To treat the north differently would have been, in a
sense, partitionist. But if there was indeed a 'cynical undercurrent' in
Dublin operational policy, it perhaps appeared in the decision to send a

northern force to Cavan in May 1921. 3rd Northern Division (mainly the Belfast Brigade) was ordered to create and equip a column, to assemble on Lappinduff Mountain, meeting up with a Cavan column under the command of the GHQ organizer Seamus McGoran. The thirteen Belfast men travelled to Cavan by rail in small groups, while their arms were brought up by Cumann na mBan women. Unfortunately, Cavan did not prepare to receive them as ordered, and munitions promised by GHQ did not appear. After two days preparing its own base, the column was surprised by a big search operation. 'Enemy forces numbered about 350, with ten lorries and one lorry of hostages picked up on way. These passed houses in different directions but strange to say none of the inhabitants came to inform us of such enemy movements . . .' The column men were either 'without instructions as to their fighting dispositions or ignored it [sic]'.[160] After a two-hour fight in which one of the column was killed and one wounded, ten men surrendered.[161] The Belfast men's commander had 'cleared off' during the fight, according to his lieutenant, Seamus McKenna. Even though he could see 'the hopelessness and utter futility' of their position, McKenna would always regret the surrender: hearing the enemy cheer 'as they jumped to their feet from where they had been concealed and danced with joy' was 'the most bitter moment of my life'.[162]

This deadly fiasco has been seen as 'little short of blatant exploitation' of the Belfast men by Dublin, trying to stimulate activity in a quiet area. Mulcahy, though, would no doubt have defended the idea as a way of giving field experience to urban Volunteers. But the bottom line was that it revealed the 'very appalling want of elementary training' among all concerned. This situation endured. As late as mid-June 1921 the commander of 1st Northern Division reported that 'organisation is so poor that it will be some time before operations can be attempted in the divisional area.'[163]

THE REPUBLIC'S FIRST GENERAL ELECTION

As the date for the Irish elections loomed, the British government could see that the military promise of 'definite and decisive results' by April 1921 had been over-optimistic. There were few illusions in London about the likely outcome of an election at this point: whatever the Irish people really thought, no candidate would stand against Sinn Féin in the existing circumstances. (If there were a few exceptions, they were not very encouraging: the Dr Ash who visited the Castle to ask for financial support led Sturgis to reflect that if he had any supporters, 'their patriotism does not reach to their pockets.') The Cabinet debated whether to postpone the elections, or to call a truce while they were held, in the hope that this would allow some moderates to stand. By 21 April it had decided against postponement, mainly because of the need to get the northern legislature up and running.

The truce issue was more complicated. In a two-day discussion, Churchill, now Colonial Secretary, urged the 'great public importance' of getting 'a respite in Ireland'. He worried that 'we are getting an odious reputation' and 'poisoning our relations with the United States'. The improved military situation meant that a truce would not be seen as a sign of weakness, and if it was maintained it would produce a 'tremendous advantage' – the IRA would 'have great difficulty in getting men to go back'. Balfour, the Lord President, was more hawkish. He accepted that 'naturally we should wish to end this uphill, sordid, unchivalrous, loathsome conflict – we are sick of it,' but argued that halting military action would 'add no freedom of election', while at the same time it would be seen as giving 'your imprimatur as if the elections were "fair"'. Both the military and police warned that a truce would hand a big advantage, particularly in intelligence, to the IRA. Ministers were clearly surprised that the C-in-C Macready – a home ruler with 'a good civilian mind' – should be against a truce. John Anderson also thought that the government's growing military advantage should be kept up, and this led Austen Chamberlain to change his mind during the discussion. He still worried, though, that a 'wartime' election would be bound to reinforce Sinn Féin's hard line on the Republic.[164] In the end, the Cabinet suddenly realized that the election period had already begun: as nominations were taking place next day, it was already too late for a truce to affect it.

The republican government had by now decided to use the electoral machinery of the Government of Ireland Act, despite the risk of appearing to recognize the British right to legislate for Ireland – and still more dangerously, perhaps, of recognizing partition. Though all republican discussions put the twenty-six-county 'Southern Ireland' entity conjured up by the new Act in mocking quotation marks, mockery might turn out not to be enough. As Collins had written to de Valera in January, 'up to recently I was strongly of opinion that it was never intended to set up the Northern Parliament, but I have changed this view.' Much as many republicans might have preferred to ignore the north, this was not an option. On 13 January de Valera told the party General Secretary, Paidin O'Keeffe, that preparations must be made for the northern election, but worried that the Sinn Féin electoral machinery had fallen apart – now it would have to 'be reassembled under conditions of extreme difficulty'.[165] Though SF's Standing Committee had (uncharacteristically) voted £1,000 towards 'organising Ulster' in August 1920, the violent disturbances had scotched whatever efforts were made. Now the ministry decided to provide Sinn Féin with £4,000 to help reorganization in the north – to the annoyance of O'Keeffe, who fumed that the '80,000 Catholic families in the North should be easily able to raise £20,000 for the election'. If they would not, they should be left to their fate.

De Valera weighed the issue of boycotting the Northern Parliament. It was not a simple one; if Sinn Féin did not win at least ten seats in it, it would look, he told Collins, as if 'these counties were practically a homogeneous political entity, which justified partition'. And standing for both parliaments carried a financial cost. Even though the Senate created by the Act was studiously ignored, fielding 140 candidates would entail putting up £21,000 in deposits (£150 a head), and since none would take their seats the money would be lost. But failing to contest the north would drive nationalists to vote for the old party, and this, as he warned the Cabinet, 'might later have a dangerous reactionary effect, by contagion, on the South'. And the election had massive propaganda potential – 'the will of the people [could] once more be demonstrated.'

The party manifesto, as drafted by de Valera, largely steered clear of substantive policy options. It headlined 'the legitimacy of the Republic', Ireland's right to self-determination, the guarantee of minority protection, and devolved administration. It relied on a set of simple oppositions: 'for Ireland against England; for freedom against slavery, for right and justice against force and wrong'. Voting Sinn Féin would be voting against the external enemy and also 'the traitorous or pusillanimous within'. But as an organization Sinn Féin, long sidelined by the army's priorities, was now a shadow of its former self. Austin Stack, who became the party's director of elections, faced an uphill task to restore its infrastructure.

It was not only in the north that the party machinery had atrophied since 1918. In Sligo, for instance, the Sinn Féin clubs were in no state to dispute the Volunteers' primary role in selecting candidates, who all turned out to be senior officers, initially led by the Sligo brigadier Liam (Billy) Pilkington and including several battalion commandants. The leading Mayo Sinn Feiner Joseph MacBride's attempt to get Michael McHugh adopted as a candidate was squashed by the west Mayo ASU's choice of its former commander Tom Derrig. As soon as it was announced that this was 'an IRA selection, there was no more about it'.[166] The south Mayo flying-column commander, Tom Maguire, was selected as a parliamentary candidate while lying wounded on a hillside after an ambush; 'I knew nothing about it at the time.'[167] The five candidates put up in West Cork included Seán Moylan, Seán Hales and Daniel Corkery, commandant of the Macroom battalion. Though the Volunteers did not always get their way – when Seán O'Hegarty demanded that the Cork City TDs, J. J. Walsh and Liam de Roiste, be replaced by Volunteer officers, he was overruled by de Valera – they increasingly tried to influence public appointments as well. Cork No. 1's 8th Battalion, for instance, got the Macroom board of guardians to overturn the election of a woman doctor as dispensary medical officer (apparently because they felt uncomfortable undressing in front of a woman). Military service was becoming a qualification for public office: Paddy Cannon was nominated as accountant general to the Central Home in Mayo on the basis of his participation in four major IRA actions.[168] All this demonstrated a shift in the internal balance of the republican movement towards the military side.

As the police had predicted, no candidates were put up against Sinn Féin in any but four of the 128 seats in the 'Southern Parliament'. (Hence it has been said, with perhaps a little exaggeration, that the second Dáil was 'not elected at all'.)[169] The four Dublin University seats were inevitably conceded to unionists. The Irish party had disappeared from the political picture, and Labour continued to stand aside – it decided to contest elections in the six counties but not the twenty-six. It explained its withdrawal from the southern elections as a repudiation of the Government of Ireland Act, which had 'no valid sanction, being in contravention to the declared will of the Irish people'. Labour's rejection of partition sat rather oddly with its decision to fight in the north, and its repudiation of the legitimacy of the Act sat oddly with Sinn Féin's effective acceptance of its machinery. But Labour was in a fix – its constituency 'had been drawn to the militancy either of Sinn Féin or of Unionism', and a decision to stand would have been 'disastrous', even under PR.[170] Instead it urged workers to 'demonstrate their loyalty to Ireland and to freedom' by supporting only candidates who stood for 'the ownership and government of Ireland by the people of Ireland'. As in 1918, and in contrast to 1920, Labour adopted a role as auxiliary in a national liberation front.

Though Labour polled weakly in the north – winning only two seats – Sinn Féin itself managed to secure just six (tying with the old nationalist party) against thirty-six unionists. No Sinn Féin candidates were 'Ulstermen'. This marginal presence was in sharp contrast to the resounding endorsement of the Republic in the south. British electoral reform had endowed the second Dáil with significantly more members than the first, and its 125 deputies were less like Sinn Feiners than before. Nearly a third were Volunteer officers – up from a bare fifth of the first Dáil – including six members of GHQ, three divisional commanders, two divisional staff members and seven brigadiers. (Even more – 42 per cent – were Volunteers.) Of the seventy-seven TDs who were currently at liberty, fifty-two were on the run, and as Diarmuid O'Hegarty noted, 'the task of bringing together ninety [sic] members including several well-known ladies' for meetings would be 'a big one'. Various ways of coping with this were mooted: Collins thought that no more than half of them should meet at any one time, de Valera proposed creating a series of twenty-strong committees, and the Cabinet opted for a grand committee of thirty-one.

De Valera took control of the process of winding up the first Dáil ministry and inaugurating the second, holding that as president he stood above the national assembly. Ministers would 'resign their portfolios through the President', who would summon the new Dáil. Whether this was strictly constitutional was an issue that did not bother people at this stage (though it would have ramifications later). Though de Valera had been routinely called the President of the Irish Republic while in the USA, and had come to think of himself as such, he was actually President of the Dáil, in English terms prime minister ('Príomh-Aire' in the 'original' Irish version). The constitution had not yet provided either for a head of state or for a dissolution of parliament. Nor had the issue of pay been worked out. TDs – unlike Westminster or indeed Belfast

MPs – were unpaid, but quite a few of the second Dáil held paid posts either in the administration or in the army. Collins thought that paid administrators should give up their jobs to be TDs, though he did not make the same demand of Volunteer GHQ or divisional commanders.

In fact, it was not always easy to get these officers to accept salaries. Ernie O'Malley had the distinction of being the first paid field commander in the Volunteers, at £5 a week. Although he must have shared the aspiration towards professionalization that underlay the proposal to pay divisional staffs, he refused the salary, no doubt influenced by Seamus Robinson's view that 'it looks as if they want to have men in charge of divisions they can call [G]HQ men.'[171] He received a stiff note from the Director of Organization, Eoin O'Duffy – 'As regards you not accepting a salary, you at least shall be paid direct from here. You are our Officer and represent GHQ in No. 2 Division.' All divisional officers devoting 'their whole time to responsible Army work' must accept an allowance as decided by GHQ. (O'Malley had of course been a paid GHQ organizer for several years.) He was bluntly instructed to 'forward a covering address'.[172] Mulcahy saw this (as Eamon Price told O'Malley) as a disciplinary issue, but even after being charged with 'indiscipline' O'Malley remained defiant. He himself said that he eventually accepted the money on behalf of his unit. But the Department of Defence accounts show that 'owing to some disagreements between the senior officers of [2nd Southern] Division', the first payment of £20 – four weeks' pay in advance – was returned. Since 'it was felt that it was only a question of verbally explaining certain outstanding questions', the money was not passed back into the accounts. The dispute clearly continued over the following months. 'A number of letters passed between the Director of Organisation and Commandant O'Malley' about this and the general question of payment of divisional staffs, 'but agreement had not been reached before the Treaty was signed.' The cash seems to have remained in limbo.[173]

THE MILITARY BALANCE

Even though the Crown forces had not come up with 'decisive results' in time for the May elections, they believed they were now getting the upper hand. Admittedly, Macready maintained his professional pessimism. ('Whatever we do, we are sure to be wrong,' he had glumly said when the question of postponing the election was being discussed.) But in the most active commands, the Martial Law Area – which Macready never visited – and Dublin District, the military leaders were distinctly optimistic. 'By the beginning of April,' 6th Division said, 'the initiative had passed definitely to the troops.' The following weeks were a period 'of almost unbroken success', Irish Command later claimed. 'Assisted by the fine summer weather, encouraged by the promise of further reinforcements and increased powers in July, everybody threw themselves with still greater energy into the struggle ... Large Mobile Columns and small Officers patrols scoured the country ... No place, however remote, could be regarded as a safe retreat for the "wanted men".' In Dublin a series of successful raids in late April netted four machine guns, thirty rifles, some 150 revolvers and over 20,000 rounds of ammunition in the space of a few weeks – a huge blow. At the end of the month no fewer than forty Dublin Volunteers were captured in a raid on Blackhall Place.[174] In 6th Division area, 'the rebels had suffered severely, and were in no mood to join issue with the troops', while the military forces were 'spoiling for a fight'.[175]

Sadly, this cheerful picture contained one annoying blemish – it was still 'very difficult to "get at" the extremists, except by hunting them down'. However keen the troops might be, 6th Division recognized that 'the one problem confronting the military authorities was how to run the various rebel bands to earth.' This might be portrayed as just a single problem, but it was really crucial. General Strickland might predict that 'One good encounter, where heavy casualties are inflicted on them, might bring their activities to a speedy end.' But without accurate information such an encounter remained impossible to engineer. Pressure exerted on the community through collective punishments (including the closure of such co-operative creameries as had survived police reprisals) touched people's pockets, 'but in most cases they took no action to stop outrages, and merely gave vent to their woes.'[176]

Police indiscipline was becoming ever more worrying. At the end of February, the commander of the RIC Auxiliary Division, Brigadier Frank Crozier, resigned when his attempt to discipline the men he held responsible for wanton damage during a raid in Trim was overruled by Tudor. This was a publicity setback, since Crozier proved highly vocal in giving his version to the press (though he waited nearly ten years before publishing his account in book form). There was another in April, when a party of Auxiliaries raiding a hotel in Castleconnell killed a police sergeant who was drinking at the bar and one of themselves in a burst of firing in the courtyard outside. They were accused by one guest of rampaging around 'like demented Red Indians', and leaving dum-dum cartridges at the scene, and since the guest was the brother of the eminent Liberal peer Lord Parmoor the issue was brought (complete with dum-dum bullet exhibit) to the floor of the House of Lords. The army fumed that the Auxiliaries 'had the wind up, blood up, and did what they used to do in the trenches in France'. They might not, in the circumstances, be criminally responsible, but 'they are not fit to be policemen.'[177]

Time was almost up for the reprisals policy. At the beginning of June the Cabinet heard Macready's admission 'that we were getting into a difficult position' – 'if the military burned a cottage, then the Sinn Feiners burned two, then the military four, and so on'. In Cork, for instance, when four houses were destroyed in Blackpool by troops as a reprisal for an ambush in which three policemen had been killed, the IRA burned down the houses of four prominent unionists next day, as well as that 'den of imperialism' the Douglas Golf Pavilion.[178] The 6th Division claimed in mid-May that 'there has been no recurrence of counter-reprisals by the rebels,' thanks to 'our determination to increase the ratio of destruction indefinitely'.[179] But this seems to have been dangerous bravado. Cork No. 2 Brigade was pressing for a wider targeting of 'Active Enemies of Ireland': such families 'should be ordered out of the country and their lands confiscated' (though they would be 'allowed to dispose of their stock'). Mulcahy was concerned that unionists and Orangemen should be classified thus only if they were 'actively anti-Irish in their outlook and actions', but this limitation was alarmingly vague.[180] In June the IRA was formally instructed to answer British reprisals with counter-reprisals, 'stopping only when the district has been entirely cleared of active enemies of Ireland'.[181]

When the Cabinet's Irish Committee had asked Macready why he could not simply stop reprisals, he said that he would then have to 'get something else' – he would have to enforce the order against carrying arms 'by punishment of death'. He had not done this so far because it seemed 'difficult' with martial law only partially in force. But soon afterwards, on 3 June, official reprisals were indeed abandoned. One brigadier in the MLA reassured his units that this Cabinet decision had 'not been arrived at because of the vapourings of some insignificant member of the House of Commons' – it was largely due to the King's influence, 'so we can all be perfectly happy about it.' Instead there would be drumhead courts martial for possession of arms – the Fermoy commander instructed his officers to 'regard the Drumhead Court Martial as one of the most important weapons in your armoury', to be treated as being 'as important as a tactical operation'.[182] Pressure in Cork No. 2 Brigade area was mounting; in March a search operation in the Boggeragh Mountains narrowly missed capturing the brigade HQ at Nadd, and the brigade commandant, Seán Moylan, was arrested on 16 May (carrying among other documents a cheque for £115, which was gleefully cashed by the HQ of the Kerry Infantry Brigade.)

Through May and June 1921 the war of independence hung in the balance. Republican military activity peaked, in numerical terms, and the Crown forces – whose casualty rate had dropped to below thirty a month in March and April – suffered record losses. From the beginning of the year to July, 94 soldiers and 223 policemen were killed, nearly double the totals (47 and 127) for the last six months of 1920. In the last twelve weeks of the conflict, the toll of military and police deaths (48 and 114) amounted to a quarter of all their fatalities since January 1919. On 6 June the Chief Secretary reluctantly acknowledged that there was 'a very marked increase in rebel military activity throughout the country'. Even though the bulk of that activity took the form of 'small jobs', sniping, assassinations and road cutting rather than quasi-regular flying-column actions, it was (as Mulcahy had urged) none the less effective in psychological terms.

Early in June the Dublin Volunteers attacked a military motor transport depot known as the 'Shell Factory', destroying forty vehicles (including five of the new Peerless armoured cars) and other stores to the value of £88,000. Nobody was killed, so this operation was not a headline-grabber, but it was a real success, and pointed a new direction in which a great deal of expensive damage could easily be inflicted. So far, and perhaps surprisingly, sabotage had been neglected. A couple of weeks earlier, a different operation had showcased the IRA's repertoire of skills. In an attempt to rescue Seán MacEoin from Mountjoy gaol, members of the Squad seized a Peerless armoured car and drove it into the prison yard. Emmet Dalton and Joe Kehoe in British uniform, posing as court-martial officers from Dublin District HQ, presented a warrant to remove MacEoin for interview. When the prison governor insisted on confirming this with Dublin Castle they tied and gagged him, but any chance they had of getting to MacEoin ended when firing apparently broke out in the prison yard. Still, they managed to get away – the army, which had no record of any firing, said they had not been recognized as hostile.

Even the crusty Dublin District staff, usually dismissive of rebel capabilities, recognized this raid as a 'brilliant achievement'. The armoured car had been escorting a lorry delivering meat to the Dublin Abattoir, and its crew (half trained like most of those drafted to man the new Peerless cars) had fallen into a routine, failed to maintain normal precautions and panicked when attacked. They 'tamely surrendered their arms and their car'. The driver even helped the raiders to restart the machine and advised them on its gearbox – for which he was court-martialled.[183] But their attackers were undeniably daring: when the phone in the abattoir office rang, one of them had even taken an order for meat from the Curragh and asked them to ring back in twenty minutes, before hanging up and cutting the line. After driving the armoured car away, they were forced to abandon it on the Malahide road (either because it had overheated or because its fuel line had failed). They carried off its two Hotchkiss machine guns, though they left behind not only two spare barrels and 1,500 rounds of .303 ammunition for the guns, but also three of their own pistols. If they had succeeded in springing MacEoin this would have been one of the most remarkable successes of the war – it was 'frightfully disappointing that he should have been missed', as Mulcahy ruefully reflected, since 'everything went so well . . . it was only a matter of another 8 or 10 seconds.' Even so it created a striking impression.

In between these successes, Dublin staged an attack more in tune with de Valera's idea of warfare. Arguing the need to 'deliver a smashing blow', the President had persuaded the GHQ staff to look at the possibility of attacking either Beggars Bush barracks (close to the site of de Valera's garrison in 1916) or the Custom House. Asked to investigate, the Dublin brigadier reported that the first target was unfeasible.[184] Accordingly, on 25 May some 120 men of the Dublin Brigade entered the Custom House, spread petrol throughout the vast building and set it alight. This really was a big operation, and the destruction of a mass of local government, Inland Revenue, Stamp Office and Stationery Office records could be portrayed as a lethal blow to British rule. *An tOglac* proclaimed it as signalling 'the final collapse of English civil administration in this country', even though the Land Office records were actually as useful to ordinary people as to the government. It was a spectacular action in the grandest part of official Dublin: the image of the great building in flames across the river was unforgettable. But it came at a high price. Though the operation went on for three-quarters of an hour without attracting attention, a passing group of Auxiliaries were fired on by scouts outside the building, and a general affray broke out. Six men were killed and over eighty captured. If this was a victory, it was a Pyrrhic one; after follow-up arrests had brought the total to over a hundred, the 2nd Battalion effectively ceased to exist.

British intelligence raided one of Collins's offices on 26 May and found a letter written that morning regretting 'that we lost all those gallant fellows yesterday at the Custom House'. Charlie Dalton and his surviving colleagues 'spent a very gloomy night thinking of the serious losses we had sustained', and the following weeks were 'very trying for us'.[185] In an attempt to 'conceal our crippled state from the enemy', the survivors stepped up the tempo of their activities. The arrival of two Thompson sub-machine guns opened up new possibilities for demonstrating republican strength, but when Dalton was selected to make the first use of one in an ambush of a train at Drumcondra on 16 June, he was given no instruction on how to fire the weapon.[186] In fact, he had never had one in his hands until the time came to open fire, and 'it took me a minute to locate the various gadgets,' by which time the target had passed by. He did not get another opportunity to use one in action.

The intensification of republican military activity was more ambiguous than it might look, however. Flying columns made a sharply declining contribution to it – indeed it has been suggested that most of them found their position 'untenable' in spring 1921, as British activity increased and night hours diminished.[187] Many had as much difficulty in making contact as their opponents did. The Galway Brigade's 2nd Battalion column 'prepared six ambush positions which we occupied and remained in position all day, but no enemy forces came . . . on [the] routes which we expected the enemy would travel'.[188] A GHQ strategic assessment had identified Longford as 'a very valuable focus of action in the North-Midlands', and on the basis of the success of Seán MacEoin's north Longford ASU, GHQ planned to 'make the Longford Units the nucleus for working up the entire region'. It had already sent Seán Connolly to organize Leitrim, and now wanted to encourage neighbouring units to send men to get experience with the column. Just at that moment, however, MacEoin had been arrested (at Mullingar, returning from a meeting with Brugha in Dublin). Connolly was ordered back from Leitrim, but before he could leave he was ambushed and killed at Selton Hill. Some infighting over the succession to MacEoin seriously damaged the cohesion of the north Longford force.[189]

At the same time Leitrim went from bad to worse. Ordered to investigate how Connolly's unit had been 'given away', the brigade intelligence officer identified a culprit – on rather circumstantial evidence. He 'did not contact [him] before he was shot', since 'that would have shown me up.' After apparently receiving compensation for his death, his family 'deserted their farm'. GHQ sent an inspecting officer, Captain Paddy Morrissey, to reorganize the brigade. He took a dim view of it, telling the 3rd Battalion that 'the South Leitrim Brigade was the worst brigade in Ireland and that the 3rd Battalion was the worst battalion in the brigade.' The brigadier resigned along with his whole staff. (One of them, the vice-OC, returned to the ranks as a scout, emphasizing that this was 'none too safe a duty ... you did not know what you would run into in front and you did not know what you were going to get from behind either'.)[190]

On 3 May the south Mayo column under the brigade commander, Tom Maguire, ambushed a police patrol passing through the village of Tourmakeady. The ambush was successful enough for Mulcahy to exult that it demonstrated that 'we have the intelligence and courage and the military skill to bring the present struggle to a very definite victory.' But the British reaction, a pursuit in which Maguire was badly wounded and his adjutant killed, sounded a warning; his column escaped thanks to the chance arrival of the west Mayo column. Mulcahy advised him to avoid over-ambitious operations, until his men could 'gain confidence in themselves and get the best possible use out of their weapons' through harassing operations. But dispatch work and many other activities became more difficult, one Mayo Volunteer recalled, 'as the roads were swarming with Crown forces, particularly after the fight at Tourmakeady'.[191]

Columns often had similar narrow shaves – one escaped from an attempted ambush on the Piltown–Fiddown road in Kilkenny thanks only to the 'coolness and experience' of an ex-soldier in its ranks, who understood cover and lines of retreat.[192] When Ernie O'Malley met up with Dinny Lacey's Waterford column that month, he reflected that, though Lacey had brought it 'many times through South Tipperary . . . it had seen very little fighting . . . due partly to bad luck, the uncertainty of enemy movement, and our faulty intelligence system'. Local scouts were still unreliable, O'Malley thought: 'they were never alert save when an objective danger was pressing.'[193] GHQ pronounced Waterford No. 2's action at Knockyoolahan on 6 June 'another lost unsuccessful ambush through putting inexperienced men scouting'.[194]

At Rathcoole on 16 June Cork No. 2 Brigade was at last able to combine exploitation of the restrictions imposed by road cutting and belated development of explosives expertise. A big ambush party – over a hundred men from five battalions, with a Hotchkiss gun – laid seven mines in the road, three of which were detonated to trap an ADRIC ration party in four Crossley tenders. These mines were used in a more sophisticated way, and worked better ('fairly well', at least, said George Power) than before, but they were still short on impact. Though the first and last trucks were immobilized, all but two of the police survived the explosions, and were able to hold off the attackers until shortage of ammunition forced them to withdraw after an hour.[195]

O'Malley found that many of the thirty-two battalions in his division remained resistant to development. 'In many companies . . . only a few of the men had seen grenades or rifles, and . . . training schemes had never been enforced or orders carried out.' Some companies failed to block roads even when directly ordered to do so, negligence that exposed 'our small columns . . . to sudden raids or round-ups', as did frequent failure to forward 'information captured or sent through our intelligence'. To sit down and 'attempt to direct' his 7,000 men like a conventional divisional commander 'might have been possible if battalions had any uniformity in armament, ability, experience or desire for action', or if he could get information quickly enough to keep in touch with local situations. But these conditions did not exist. Kilkenny remained notably recalcitrant: 'the brigade staff had seldom sent our orders to battalions; they had never been on inspection.'[196]

The self-critical O'Malley worried that the 2nd Southern Division, the second strongest IRA unit, 'was not fighting enough, and was not helping to draw off troops from the First Southern'. It might have been easier for him to build divisional spirit, he thought, if he had emerged through the local unit structure as Lynch had – having a 'brigade of my own to back me'. But GHQ's efforts to gee up inactive areas were not much more successful, and even Lynch's had trouble with ineffective units, particularly in Kerry and Waterford. The Kerry No. 2 brigadier, John Joe Rice, recalled spending 'all my time tramping from one company to another, fixing disputes and squabbles'.[197] Mulcahy judged Kerry No. 1 'very disappointing', complaining in June that 'probably not three reports of operations have reached me' since brigades had been ordered (in November 1920) to submit a monthly diary of operations and enemy activity.[198]

This was the trigger for one of the most explosive showdowns between GHQ and a local unit. GHQ judged the Kerry brigadier, Paddy Cahill, incompetent, and no fewer than three GHQ inspections in a short space of time produced a comprehensively crushing verdict. There was very little activity and almost no co-operation between battalions; worse, indeed, there was 'an amount of ill-will and in some cases actual clashing of interests'. Although companies mostly met regularly they did little. There was 'no systematic training', especially in musketry – 'hardly ten per cent of the men being able to use a rifle'. One organizer, though he needed more time to make a 'final judgement' on the quality of the officers, suggested that 'the removal of nearly 50 per cent would lead to improvement.' Practically no attention was paid to special services, notably engineering. Though there was 'a fair amount of arms', they were 'badly distributed with regard to suitability of ammunition'. Intelligence and communications were weak. All this was the fault of the brigade, which took no interest in these issues. The brigade HQ itself was wrongly placed, in the Dingle Peninsula, 'strategically at the wrong end of the Brigade', but did 'absolutely no training, its energies being devoted to eating, sleeping and general amusement'. The brigade's only saving grace was that with one exception (Tralee) the battalion commanders were 'fairly good'.[199]

Cahill himself was suspended, but many of his officers cold-shouldered the replacement appointed by GHQ, Andy Cooney, who had previously been the organizer for Kerry No. 2. 'All of us known as "Cahill's men"', the brigade quartermaster wrote, 'absolutely refused to serve under the new man.' One inspector recognized that Cahill's influence was 'enormous', and 'whatever his faults there is a general conviction that no man could have done better.' Liam Lynch apparently agreed and thought that, since no local officer would take on the job, 'it would have been best to leave him.' The problem was that even a better quality of brigade staff might not have helped, since Cahill preferred 'to act by himself without consultation with any staff'. The senior staff were 'never continually in touch with him', and the quartermaster 'could not give me a list of arms in the brigade'. Cahill believed that 'his removal was the result of a conspiracy on the part of GHQ', misled by reports from the previous organizer. As for that officer, his successor caustically remarked that 'even apart from his relations with Cahill, Byrne was a complete failure here, and I can find absolutely no trace of his having done anything by way of organisation.'[200] 'Cahill's men' remained recalcitrant, and eventually GHQ was more or less forced to allow them to form a separate battalion, operating outside the briga-dier's command.

If anyone had read GHQ's memo on 'Serious Deficiencies', they had evidently not felt obliged to respond to it. But though Kerry No. 1 drew a lot of GHQ's fire, it was hardly out of line with many other brigades. Technical services had not kept pace with the development of the campaign. The shortage of key munitions like grenades, landmines and buckshot cartridges remained a crippling problem across the country, and though local workshops kept turning them out production fell far short of GHQ's aim of self-sufficiency. GHQ complained that manufacture of these munitions was 'virtually at a standstill' in June, while far too much attention was being devoted to what it called 'side-shows': 'incendiary bullets, armour-piercing bullets, and bomb-throwers are being experimented with'. None had got past the experimental stage.[201] In fact the Dublin Brigade factory that replaced the Parnell Street work-shop was highly productive – three months after the loss of the old factory it was turning out a thousand grenades a week. In mid-1921 Peadar Clancy's successor as director of munitions, Sean Russell, was organizing production of .303 ammunition. Mulcahy presumably knew this, though according to Patrick McHugh he did not visit the main factory in Luke Street until December 1921.[202]

Mayo was hardly alone in complaining that it had 'absolutely no stuff', but Mulcahy began to bristle at units 'making the poor mouth'. He told the Sligo Brigade to stop complaining about its lack of arms and get organized, asserting that 'with organisation and system, we shall win this War, if we are left with nothing but picks and shovels to wage it'. Grim humour might not be enough, however.[203] Ammunition shortages could not be talked away; they hamstrung even the most active units. Frank Thornton reflected after the Truce that, if the fight had gone on, the shortages would have meant that 'we would have found ourselves very hard set to continue it with any degree of intensity.'

One reason for the increase in British casualties was simply that there was more military action: more searches, more encounters. A dramatic expansion of military strength in June added to Macready's forces no fewer than seventeen infantry battalions, together with a 'mounted rifle' brigade (formed from divisional artillerymen) – an increase of a third in the space of a month. This new surge represented Henry Wilson's last attempt to crush the republican campaign before the nerve of the 'frocks' cracked. It certainly created, maybe for the first time, a real possibility of sustained intense activity in Dublin and the Martial Law Area. It would also make the extension of martial law viable – though, as we have seen, Wilson himself believed that 'real' martial law would not need extra troops to make it effective. 'Round-ups' became more frequent, and commanders were urged to ensure that there was 'no "driving" except with a very definite object'. ('Concentrate on intelligence,' General Strickland insisted, 'and *watch* them.')

The resulting pressure was not yet fully comprehensive. Offensive operations certainly caused a lot of inconvenience. In South Tipperary 'we were subjected to two of those ordeals . . . All young men were ordered out of bed and marched off before the advancing hordes. All were assembled in Hollyford village for inspection and interrogation. Some were assaulted, others threatened, but all were released . . . those of us on the run eluded them each time.'[204] Still, IRA GHQ maintained that drives could be countered. Since the troops could not carry more than three days' rations – more than that must be 'sent up' if it could not be commandeered – 'the importance of trenching and retrenching roads behind British drives, and removing, destroying or hiding food supplies in "drive" area is *obvious*.'[205]

More threateningly for the Volunteers, the British army also began to develop its own 'flying columns', whose aim was 'to get troops and police in touch with the people in a friendly way, so as to enlist the waverers on our side'. They were also intended to search for the dugouts that 'the rebels are getting very fond of making in isolated hilly places'. Their operating logic was simple enough – the fact that 'directly our people appear the gunmen clear out' meant that 'they cut a poor figure'. 'That cannot fail to lower their morale.'[206] Still, this remained an indirect effect of force. Actually locating republican units needed more flexible formations which could mimic guerrilla methods, but in some places – notably in Cork – such methods were at last being tried out.

Perhaps more worrying than any military issues, though, were signs that Volunteer discipline was hanging by a thread in some places. O'Malley reported to Mulcahy in early July that there had been numerous cases of looting in Tipperary No. 2, and that the 'evil influence' was spreading to the neighbouring 3rd Brigade. He thought that nothing short of capital punishment could arrest the spread, but seems to have been unsure whether he could impose it. He was reassured that 'Divisional Commandants have power to inflict any punishment they think fit for military crimes.' O'Duffy suggested that 'if this looting gets started it will be hard to stop it, but if a few are shot now for it, it will be all right.'[207]

THE PROPAGANDA BATTLE

British leaders always felt that, even when counter-insurgency action was successful, its positive effect was negated by superior republican propaganda. They took the propaganda battle seriously, and saw themselves losing it. Some of this they blamed on political restrictions: even the moderate nationalist press could take an anti-government line with impunity. When the Castle belatedly moved in late 1920 to prosecute the *Freeman's Journal* (a far from republican paper) for 'spreading a false report' – a classic wartime charge – the government quickly backed down in face of protests. Macready wrote contemptuously of this 'abject surrender', and went on trying to get both the *Freeman* and the *Irish Independent* suppressed as 'nothing less than daily propaganda of rebellion'. But he also lamented the failure of Britain's own publicity agencies to project a positive image of British policy. The head of the Castle Publicity Bureau, Basil Clarke, had sophisticated theories of news presentation, but though these have been portrayed by some as pernicious, they were not really effective.[208] His bureau never rivalled the *Irish Bulletin*'s influence on British reporting of Irish events.[209]

But the famous republican publicity machine had its share of malfunctions as well, even at this advanced stage in the campaign. At the end of March 1921 the Department of Propaganda suffered a serious setback when a mass of its papers and material was seized in a raid. De Valera was, according to Diarmuid O'Hegarty, very concerned that 'the enemy should not be allowed to feel that he has disorganised us by this capture.' And in fact the captured typewriters and duplicators were used to produce forged issues of the *Irish Bulletin* in April and May. Though the first forgeries were 'obviously bogus', later efforts were more convincing. While the domestic audience could, the department hoped, be 'forewarned' against these, they 'do cause some confusion amongst foreign readers' – who were of course always its main target audience. 'The fraud is one that is exceedingly difficult to counter.'[210] Still, the circulation of the official *Bulletin* was steadily increased. In March it went daily to 200 'English newspapers and public men', and weekly to 300 'other persons including many Continental and Colonial newspapers and journalists'. By May, over 650 copies were circulated.

On 9 May Erskine Childers was arrested, like FitzGerald and Gallagher before him. Unlike them, though, he was quickly released. (Collins was frankly baffled by this, telling Art O'Brien, 'I cannot say I properly understand what the reason of the release was. Their ways are very extraordinary.')[211] In line with the Dáil ministry's acceptance of civil responsibility for the army, Childers modified what has been called the 'reticence' of the *Irish Bulletin* in reporting military operations. Its tone had been 'consistently defensive', in 'sharp contrast with the belligerent *An tOglac*'. But its attitude was still rather different, even after Childers took over as editor. The emergence of the army was portrayed in much less proactive terms than the Volunteers themselves now used. In June the *Bulletin* noted that 'eighteen months ago the Irish Volunteers were a territorial reserve rather than an army in the field. But when a price was placed on the heads of its more active members, these men went into permanent active service, determined to defend their liberty with their lives.' This view of the army as a kind of local self-preservation society was only partly counteracted by the more regular publication in 1921 of IRA GHQ orders implying a regular, centralized national organization.[212]

But a big part of the 'reticence' about publishing details of military operations was due to the sheer difficulty of getting accurate information about them. This seems to have persisted to the end, and was surely a reason for the *Bulletin*'s odd remark in late 1920 that it did not issue statements (beyond 'correcting mistakes') because 'sufficient publicity' was given to military actions by Dublin Castle, British MPs and 'the English Press'. The Propaganda Department had never had great success in persuading republican administrators or TDs to supply accurate (or often any) information either. FitzGerald found it necessary to remind the Dáil in August 1921 that 'information was no good unless detailed and accurate': it 'should stand investigation afterwards'. And however 'belligerent' it may have been in comparison to the *Bulletin*, even the army's own journal had the same problem. Just like his British counterparts, Piaras Béaslaí's temper was repeatedly strained by the reluctance of local units to supply timely information. 'I am greatly hampered in my work by the failure to get vital information,' he complained in early July. A couple of instances show the sort of problems that persisted. When Cork No. 1 Brigade abducted and shot Mrs Lindsay without securing authorization from GHQ, it refused to submit a report of the incident. Her disappearance was a serious propaganda setback, and Béaslaí wanted to construct an acceptable official story. But, though he made 'repeated efforts' to get information from Cork No. 1, he never got it. Just a few days before the Truce he was fed a story that she had been released but was ill in hospital. Fearing that he might 'already have made a serious mistake in handling this matter', he pressed Brugha 'as a personal favour' to get a written statement confirming her fate – and indeed 'what her offence was'. 'It is urgent that I know for certain.'[213]

After labouring to justify, through an editorial in *An tOglac*, another increasingly unpopular policy, street ambushes in Dublin, he found 'casually in the course of conversation' with the Assistant Chief of Staff that an order had been issued to suspend these attacks owing to the danger they posed to non-combatants. 'I do not know who issued the order,' he protested to Mulcahy, 'but I think it is pretty bad that information so vitally important to me in my work was not at once officially conveyed to me.' Even information that was not so time-critical often proved impossible to extract. Early in 1921 – none too soon it may be thought – GHQ had the idea of compiling a 'Roll of Honour' of all the Volunteers who had died in the fight. Brigades had been asked to supply returns of all those 'killed in action or murdered by the enemy'.[214] Béaslaí could see that these would 'give us some chance of comparing our casualties with those of the enemy' ('I fancy the result would be encouraging'), but though he claimed that the President was 'very keen about this matter', no returns seemed to have been received. 'I do not think OCs generally realise the importance of it.'[215] The boot could sometimes be on the other foot, though; in a July article entitled 'Two against Two Hundred', *An tOglac* attributed the action it described to the wrong brigade, provoking a complaint from the east Clare brigadier. ('Now look what you have done,' the Adjutant General chided the editor.)

'IN DEALING WITH THE IRISH YOU MUST SHOW THAT YOU MEAN TO GO ON'

The failure to achieve unity of command, and the persistent divisions between military and police, now threatened to wreck British policy. King George V spoke for many in his dislike of police methods and of the police chief himself – telling Wilson that he wanted to 'abolish all Black and Tans', and that Wilson's predecessor as Chief of the Imperial General Staff, Sir William Robertson, had a low opinion of Tudor. But several ministers – including, crucially, the Prime Minister – took the opposite view. Even as the Cabinet agreed to the programme of reinforcements, Lloyd George insisted that the 'Irish job' was 'a policeman's job'. The military should support the police, not the other way round – if 'it becomes a military job only it will fail'. He backed up Churchill's assertion that 'on balance Tudor and his men were ... getting to the root of the matter quicker than the military.'[216]

Macready (perhaps intentionally) colluded in this by firing off alarming warnings about the resilience of the army itself. In late May 1921, just as the surge was being launched, he presented the government with a deflating assessment of the prospects. Even when strong reinforcements arrived they would need a long time to adapt to Irish conditions. The scope for offensive action was limited. The troops themselves were being stretched to the limit. Officers would soon be unfit to serve without a 'very considerable period' of leave; soldiers, mostly young and 'fine drawn', were under punishing physical and mental strain, worse than conventional warfare. (As Churchill's successor as war secretary, Sir Laming Worthington-Evans, explained, 'there is no back area into which they can be withdrawn.') Unless 'the present state of affairs' was 'brought to a conclusion' by October, virtually the whole force would have to be relieved. Since Macready was 'quite aware' that there would be no troops to replace them, this was a grim ultimatum. Again, in mid-June, as the surge was well under way, he treated the Cabinet's Irish Committee to an even gloomier view. He told them he was 'losing his self-respect' – 'it put him in an absurd position,' for instance, that though he was commander-in-chief of the British forces he was 'unable to buy English goods in Dublin'. He felt he was losing the confidence of his men, and asked 'the Government to bear in mind the personal feeling of the tools they were using' – otherwise 'those tools would break in their hands.'

The King had also queried Macready's suitability, and though Wilson defended him – by blaming the army's underachievement on the 'frocks' who would not permit 'unity of control' – the monarch did have a point. Macready never gave the impression of bursting with energy and ideas for developing the counter-insurgency campaign. His pervasive negativity – verging on fatalism – and repeated assertions that the only possible solution must be political and not military had tried Wilson's own patience. His preference for large-scale operations blinded him to the real challenges of guerrilla warfare. In his May report he had noted the use in some places of 'little expeditions of a couple of subaltern officers and from 12 to 20 men' without apparently realizing that this was the most promising tactical adaptation yet tried by the army.

Worthington-Evans interpreted Macready's assessment in almost apocalyptic terms: unless 'full advantage is taken of the opportunities of the good weather of the summer months', there was 'a grave risk of failure'. In essence they had three months to 'break the back of the rebellion'.[217] After two years or more of 'virtual stalemate', this was asking a lot. In military terms, it may not have looked entirely encouraging that almost a year after the Chief of the Imperial General Staff had pronounced driving 'a childish expedient', the key method identified for taking advantage of the summer weather was that 'drives and other similar intensive operations should be inaugurated.' It is interesting, though, that when news of this was leaked to Collins, the plan sounded more substantial. After the dissolution of the Southern Parliament, martial law 'of the most rigorous' nature would be proclaimed (and Collins was told that the proclamations had already been printed), and civil courts would be put out of commission. Three times the present military strength would 'operate on a scheme of investment of areas, search and internment. All means of transport from push bicycles up will be commandeered and allowed only on permit.'[218]

With a commander-in-chief so committed to 'a generous and definite offer to Ireland', it seems hard to argue that the eventual decision to negotiate a truce represented 'the dominance of political over purely military considerations'.[219] Purely military considerations had never played a part in the British response to the Republic, and indeed it would (as Clausewitz would say) have been absurd if they had. More to the point, it is hard to argue that there was actually a decision to negotiate. Rather, the British government had inadvertently closed off its options when it set the timetable for the implementation of the Government of Ireland Act. If the Southern Parliament was not inaugurated by 12 July, 'Southern Ireland' would revert to Crown Colony status and be ruled, in effect, by martial law. Though a few ministers may actually have relished this prospect, for the majority it was unattractive if not unthinkable. It is hard to believe that they had paid any attention to these remote contingencies when the bill was being drawn up – nobody seems, for instance, to have noticed the significance of the 12 July deadline. The Cabinet's discussions in early June of how martial law would operate cannot have rendered the prospect more inviting.

On 21 June Lord Birkenhead, the Lord Chancellor, one of the few ministers who seem to have faced the prospect of Crown Colony government with equanimity, made a remarkable speech. His recognition that what was going on in Ireland was 'a small war' was unprecedented. He went further, adding that the previous three months had shown 'the failure of our military methods to keep pace with and to overcome the military methods which have been taken by our opponents'. But he asserted that Britain would redouble its efforts to win. Next day, the King opened the Northern Parliament with a carefully phrased kite appealing to 'all Irishmen to pause, to stretch out the hand of forbearance and conciliation'. (A more 'gushing' original draft for the speech by General Jan Smuts had been chilled by the still-hawkish Balfour.) Birkenhead noted the 'apparently harsh disparity' between the two speeches, and thought it 'unfortunate they should come on the same day'. But Lloyd George thought the contrast 'helpful' – 'in dealing with the Irish you must shew that you mean to go on.'[220] That afternoon, a military raiding party unknowingly arrested Eamon de Valera in Blackrock, in possession of a clutch of documents including IRA operation reports. He had given a false name (Crown forces had general orders not to arrest him), but when he arrived at Portobello barracks he announced that he was the 'President of the Irish Republic'. In 'the sort of absurd farce that does happen in this country', as Sturgis put it, Andy Cope had at that moment been 'seeing [Bishop Michael] Fogarty and two other Bishops' to persuade them 'to see the said gentleman today and urge peace!'[221] The 'said gentleman' was hastily released, though not before the military authorities had tried to launch a prosecution for high treason.

Cope had been on this mission, in fact, ever since he arrived in Dublin in spring 1920. Mark Sturgis's diary provides a vivid record of a series of peacemaking moves beginning in July 1920 and recurring at regular intervals after that. The most promising, Archbishop Clune's shuttle at the end of 1920, had, as we have seen, foundered on Lloyd George's demand that Volunteers surrender their weapons. It may also have been undermined by the Wexford TD Roger Sweetman's proposal on 30 November of a conference of public bodies to formulate truce proposals. (Sweetman had become strongly opposed to the killing of Irish policemen, and would quit the Dáil in January.) On 6 December the Sinn Féin Vice-President, Fr Michael O'Flanagan, apparently unaware of Clune's mission, sent Lloyd George a telegram saying that 'Ireland is willing' (to make peace) and asking 'what first step do you propose?' Lloyd George supposedly told Clune, 'this is the white feather and we are going to make these fellows surrender.' But there was rigidity on the other side as well. Griffith insisted 'there would be no surrender no matter what frightfulness was used,' and not only held out against the demand for a surrender of arms, but also held out for the 'republican demand': 'we had a mandate for it from the people and only the people could revoke it.'[222] Collins, who met Clune twice, said he was 'profoundly distrustful' of the whole initiative, which seemed to him 'an effort to put us in the wrong' – both with 'the world' and 'particularly with our own people'. When Collins briefed the newly returned de Valera on the negotiations, though, his comment that Sweetman's and O'Flanagan's 'rushing in torpedoed the efforts' implied perhaps that he had taken them quite seriously.[223] And O'Flanagan himself later said that his intervention had had the 'deliberate intention of spoiling the great negotiations', which he thought were under British control.[224]

In mid-March 1921, de Valera noted that 'feelers are being thrown out in all directions just now.'[225] A senior Cabinet minister, Lord Derby, went over (ostensibly in an unofficial capacity) to meet de Valera and Cardinal Logue in April, but there still seemed little room for manoeuvre – 'an Irish republic they would never achieve so long as England had a man left to fight,' in Logue's view. De Valera was already signalling that any negotiations would depend on the British government taking the republican counter-state seriously. He archly objected to the 'hole and corner methods' being used, which like the 'unofficial intermediaries to the nth degree removed' were not the way to approach questions 'affecting the fate of our nation'.

The departure of Lord French in April was another indication of a shift in the political atmosphere. Though he had long since lost his influence on policymaking, he was undeniably a public symbol of military coercion. He did not go willingly – for one thing, since his house in Fermanagh had been destroyed by the IRA in a counter-reprisal, the Viceregal Lodge was his only home. His replacement, Viscount Fitz-Alan, was a firm enough unionist, but like his fellow unionist Lord Midleton believed that coercion had gone too far. The fact that he was a Catholic – the first Catholic ever to hold the lord lieutenancy – was clearly intended to make a public statement, and the fact that his appointment closely followed the retirement of Bonar Law added to speculation that the hardliners were losing ground.

Some of the shock and mystification caused by the Custom House attack stemmed from its timing – at the exact moment when the peace-niks in the Castle were hourly expecting a dramatic breakthrough. On 19 May Sturgis had fused his two greatest interests, peacemongering and horse-racing, in a 'Peace Stakes' – with no fewer than three separate channels of communication, including his own, in amicable contention. Andy Cope was 'running good and strong right out in front by himself', followed by James MacMahon, the joint Under Secretary, whose extensive contacts with the Catholic leadership had enabled him to come through after being 'nowhere early on', and who now 'lies second making things easy for Andy', while the Quin–Sturgis combination 'are going comfortably about third on the rails'.[226] ('Quin' was his close friend 'Dicky' Wyndham-Quin – the future Lord Dunraven – who was the Viceroy's Military Secretary.) But though 'we are assured' that the republicans wanted peace, they went on 'risking' it by intensified military activity. 'Their mentality has me beat,' Sturgis noted three days later when 'these brutes took a poor devil they had wounded out of the Mater Hospital and shot him dead on the porch.' How could this sort of thing go on 'in spite of negotiations'? When the Custom House went up in flames he could only wonder 'how can this make settlement anything but more difficult' – and in any case burning 'the finest building in one's own capital seems sheer lunacy'.[227]

In early June, Cope and MacMahon were busy enlisting Cardinal Logue's aid to arrange a meeting between de Valera and the Prime Minister elect of Northern Ireland, James Craig – resting on the vital assumption that, as Logue 'said definitely, not even the Extremists wanted a Republic'. In mid-June Collins remarked to de Valera that 'this particular peace move business has been on for some time. They have tried so many lines of approach that it is obvious they are banking somewhat on it.' When he received, through a back-channel, news of the planned British summer surge, he thought it 'quite possible that this is part of the peace move'.[228] Indeed it seems clear that (as the veteran parliamentarian Tim Healy told his brother at this time) Cope was 'continually meet[ing] the Sinn leaders, including Michael Collins'.[229] The prospect of peace talks had been discreetly waved in the President's direction for a couple of weeks, but de Valera had not responded – Sturgis attributed this reticence in part to the fact that the republicans were 'to a certain extent all to pieces'.

'TO LIE DOWN AND BE KICKED BY MURDERERS'

As soon as the King had opened the new Northern Parliament in Belfast, the British government finally felt ready to deal with the rest of the country. On 24 June Lloyd George sent invitations to de Valera – 'as the chosen leader of the great majority in Southern Ireland' – and the new Northern Ireland Premier, Craig, to come to London 'to explore to the utmost the possibility of a settlement'. Over the next few days several republican leaders, including Arthur Griffith and Robert Barton, were released from prison. Surprisingly, to him at least, the unionist Lord Midleton received a telegram from de Valera inviting him 'to come to Dublin with three other representatives of the "Loyal South" to discuss the answer to be given to the Government'. At first Midleton (who had never met or even seen de Valera) assumed this was a hoax, but showed the telegram to Lloyd George. The Prime Minister was plainly relieved – 'they had had no reply whatever to their gesture of amity' – and urged him to go. Midleton went to the Mansion House on 3 July, not having been given a time for the meeting, and was told that the Lord Mayor's secretary would see him. 'A tall spare man with spectacles met us, and in a very friendly way arranged the hour, shaking hands with us warmly at parting and thanking us for coming over.'[230]

De Valera was, as he told Lloyd George a few days later, consulting what he called his 'political minority' before responding to the Prime Minister's invitation.[231] He had invited Craig as well as Midleton and three other prominent southern unionists, but Craig turned him down. On 1 July the Dáil ministry met, and decided to put forward the truce terms they had outlined in December. Lloyd George originally assumed that negotiations would go ahead in London without any formal truce in Ireland. The 24 June letter (drafted in Cabinet, the Foreign Secretary Lord Curzon typically protesting against the 'tragic futility' of collective drafting) avoided any mention of a truce. Churchill proposed simply that 'we should choke off our people and they theirs.' It took 'two long days' debate' at the Mansion House before Midleton went back to tell the Prime Minister that unless he agreed to 'stopping all fighting', it was useless to continue the discussions. The 'rebels' had required that, if there was no truce, 'the troops should be confined to barracks and not show . . . in the streets of Dublin, as they could not prevent their supporters from taking advantage of them. In fact, the position would be impossible.' Lloyd George as usual jibbed, but eventually, 'without recalling the Cabinet, sat down and wrote me a letter conceding the point'.

On 5 July General Jan Smuts also arrived in Dublin as an 'unofficial intermediary' and met de Valera and Griffith, with Eamonn Duggan and Robert Barton. They told him they 'had made up their mind to refuse' the invitation because 'Ulster' would not be involved. The South African elder statesman advised them that they had 'no force but a certain measure of public opinion', which they would lose if they refused this olive branch. Griffith seemed to agree with him, but de Valera 'spoke like a visionary', Smuts noted, 'spoke continually of generations of oppression and seemed to live in a world of dreams, visions and shadows'. They agreed, though, that 'if they were granted a republic, they were prepared to be bound down by limitations.' Smuts deprecated this idea – his experience with the 'limited Republic' of Transvaal suggested it would produce continual disputes culminating in breakdown. 'We fought a three years' war over the limitations and my country was reduced to ashes.' Smuts clearly hoped that this apocalyptic warning would persuade them to accept Dominion status, but he found them determined that the British government 'should make a great gesture' to show it did not distrust the Irish people. 'The conflict is only hardening the spirit of our people.' Any settlement 'must be an everlasting peace'.

When Smuts reported this to the Cabinet next day, the final phrase was warmly greeted by Churchill: 'I would go a long way to humour them.' Lloyd George's private secretary Tom Jones thought that the 'most irreconcilable' minister was Balfour, as he had been all through the recent discussions. Churchill had 'frankly acknowledged the failure of the policy of force', and most of the other ministers were in favour of conciliation. When consulted, Macready now favoured 'an open and formal truce', but Tudor still preferred a 'tacit arrangement', and the Cabinet seems to have agreed with him that any truce 'should be of the "gentlemanly understanding" type'.[232] Yet two days after the generals had gone back to Dublin, a formal truce was agreed. It was Macready, not Tudor, whom Midleton asked along to the Mansion House discussions.

Midleton returned to the Mansion House on 8 July with Lloyd George's agreement to a truce, to find Dawson Street 'blocked almost from end to end'. As a way was made for him through the crowd, the people 'dropped on their knees with one accord in hundreds, supplicating Heaven for peace'. When Macready (whom Midleton had visited at Kilmainham, the Irish Command GHQ, earlier in the day, and found 'protected by every conceivable military device') 'boldly came through the crowd in his motor' he was actually cheered. Once the C-in-C had joined the discussions, they rapidly crystallized into practical truce terms, although he was the only soldier present. The Irish negotiators (de Valera, Brugha, Barton and Duggan) came from the 'state' rather than the 'army' side. Mulcahy, the Chief of Staff, told by Brugha that it was 'not necessary' for him to be there, waited for the outcome at Alice Stopford Green's house around the corner.

Midleton seems to have been content with oral agreement: no Truce document was signed by both sides. Macready thought he had agreed to five terms – the cessation of raids and searches, the restriction of military activity to supporting the police in 'normal civil duties', the removal of curfew restrictions, the suspension of reinforcements from England, and the replacement of the RIC by the DMP in policing Dublin itself – while the republicans had agreed to avoid 'provocative displays', to 'prohibit the use of arms', and to 'cease military manoeuvres of all kinds'.[233] The *Irish Bulletin* published a slightly different version, listing six terms on the British side, including no incoming troops or munitions and no military movements – with the exception of 'maintenance drafts'; 'no pursuit of Irish officers or men or war material or military stores'; 'no secret agents noting descriptions or movements, and no interference with the movements of Irish persons, military or civil'; and 'no pursuit or observance of lines of communication or connection'. The 'Irish Army' had agreed four conditions: no attacks on Crown forces and civilians; no provocative displays of forces, armed or unarmed; no interference with government or private property; and 'to discountenance and prevent any action likely to cause disturbance of the peace which might necessitate military interference'.

These two sets of terms reflected the concerns of each side as much as actual formal agreements. The failure to produce a single version was a fruitful source of dispute, and the atmosphere remained stormy. After a trip to Cork in mid-July, Collins reported to de Valera that 'the spirit animating the enemy' there was 'arrogant and provocative'. He believed that 'they are trying to regard the position not as a truce but as a surrender on our part.' His car was stopped on the road to Clonakilty by troops, 'although they have no power whatever to undertake such action'. In Cork city 'Captain Blest and some companion paraded the streets for half an hour or so evidently hoping to see me. I had it conveyed to them that if they were on the streets when I went out they would be regarded as breaking the truce. I don't know whether this intimation had any relation to the fact that they were not on the streets when I did go out a few minutes afterword.'

But both sides had a strong interest in preventing breakdown. At the high political level, the Truce was a dramatic step-change for the republican counter-state. Lord Midleton hardly exaggerated when he said that 'the proceedings of that week ... in reality decided the fate of Ireland.' The negotiations effectively set what Smuts called 'the Republican Government' face to face with the United Kingdom authorities on a basis of equality. (Even so, Smuts dismissed them as 'all small men, rather like sporadic leaders thrown up in a labour strike' – a comparison they would have found particularly disagreeable.) Since the British Cabinet was well aware of the possible implications of this, it did not happen without a good deal of awkward manoeuvring, and ultimately Lloyd George had been driven to ignore his colleagues' reservations. But they did not protest.

It was different with the front-line Crown forces, for whom the Truce came as a severe shock. Strickland complained that 'the flaunting of Sinn Féin flags everywhere is trying the temper of the Police rather highly.' This was deliberate provocation – 'they are no doubt trying to make them break out' – and it would work. 'It will be beyond human endurance for some people to lie down and be kicked by murderers.' He was plainly baffled by the reversal of power. 'It appears that everything must be done on *our* side to avoid provocation, and *nothing* on theirs – and yet we are, or were, in the winning position.'[234] His regimental officers used less cautious language – one lieutenant in the Essex Regiment fumed that 'the British politicians arranged an armistice just when we could have quelled the rebellion.' His men were defiant: a draft leaving Cork for an overseas posting sang 'We are the boys of the Essex' (a riposte to the rebel song 'The Boys of Kilmichael') on the way to the quay, and one 'swarmed up the rigging of the ship, pulled out a green, white and gold [sic] flag from a pocket, blew his nose on it, put it back in his pocket and came down to loud cheers'.

The obvious bafflement and dismay of the Crown forces cannot have been lost on the people. Republicans were ecstatic; Charlie Dalton, seeing 'our tricolour flag waving from every window, felt like a kid ... unbelieving, blissful!' A series of institutions which had been more or less bending under growing coercive pressure – the ministry, the republican courts, elements of the IRA itself – were able to regroup, rebuild and reinforce. At this level, the eventual political negotiations were in a sense marginal – it was understood by everyone (and enthusiastically predicted by some) that they might break down at any moment. But as long as they lasted, the administration of the country during this odd interregnum was creating 'facts on the ground'.

The ambiguity of the Truce terms meant that some key issues could be a potent source of friction. GHQ's own interpretation, for the benefit of its liaison officers, was that 'neither military nor police forces are to be increased' – which Macready would have accepted. But he would have repudiated the contention that 'there are to be no movements of bodies of British troops or police from place to place except under exceptional circumstances and after consultation with [the] Republican Liaison Officer,' and still more the suggestion that 'police or military carrying arms is to be regarded as a provocative display.' The only exception GHQ admitted was that police on night duty in towns with more than 5,000 inhabitants 'have the right to carry arms for their own protection in the discharge of ordinary civil police duties'. GHQ also demanded that the Martial Law Area should now be 'in no worse position than the rest of Ireland', so that there would be no further banning of fairs or closures of creameries.[235] After a period of contention on the streets, troops and police were mostly pulled back into barracks to avoid confrontation, which seemed like a further defeat to many.

TALKING TO THE ENEMY

The question of liaison between the British and Irish forces during the Truce was as delicate as it was urgent. The British suggestion that RIC County Inspectors should act as liaison officers was dismissed by Collins on the slightly obscure ground that 'it would be impossible to get the necessary men', and that the County Inspectors 'would be much more harmful than regular officers, from the point of view of being in constant touch'. But of course there was a political point here – the recognition of the 'Irish army'. In some places this was conceded with great reluctance, if at all. The 6th Division dismissed IRA liaison officers as 'of little value except as figureheads, to whom episodes were reported as a matter of form, prior to being finally forgotten'. Many British commanders predictably took a dim view of them personally. 'They had no great authority in their own areas, and their personal qualifications were not, as a rule, such as to appeal to the officers with whom they were supposed to have dealings.' (Not only had the first republican liaison officer for the 6th Division area 'organised the Kilmichael ambush', his successor was 'a man who admitted he had assisted in the attempt to murder General Strickland on 24 September 1920'.)

Some saw Tom Barry's appointment as liaison officer as a provocation in itself. He found he could not get the commander of the 17th Brigade, Colonel Commandant Higginson, even to meet him if he insisted on wearing Volunteer uniform. When Barry finally went to Victoria barracks 'in mufti', Higginson opened proceedings by firing the question 'Are you representing Mr De Valera here?' (a not unreasonable question, since de Valera had negotiated the Truce, and none of the army leadership had been involved). Barry indignantly said he was not, 'and wished it to be clearly recognised that I was an officer of the Irish Republican Army'; Higginson inevitably replied that he 'did not recognise' the IRA.[236] This was a shaky start, and things hardly got much better. Barry reported that his British counterpart had told him 'that he had no orders preventing his troops from carrying arms while on duty', and that it was his intention to keep on patrolling. Barry 'pointed out to him that this was a provocative action and a breach of the truce', but concluded that in the 6th Division area 'our protests are futile'. Representation should be made to the British GHQ where they were likely to 'be received with more respect'.[237]

In October Barry resigned – it remains unclear whether his grievance was at all justified, or merely (as Mulcahy put it) an instance of Barry's vanity and his 'petulant and childish' character. Others were less abrasive. The chief liaison officer, Eamonn Duggan, was a lawyer without any blood on his hands. Fintan Murphy, the businesslike GHQ fixer who was sent to Athlone to act as liaison officer for the midlands, had been a backroom worker. Things might have been different there if Collins had had his way – he urged that Seán MacEoin would be 'indispensable' in this post (adding that quite 'apart from the desire to see him out, this is really true'). Murphy's extensive records suggest that the republican authorities worried quite a lot about Truce infringements. But they were inevitably confronted with contradictory statements which they rarely had the capacity to investigate thoroughly. At Loughlynn in Roscommon, for example, it was alleged that 300 Volunteers had carried an empty coffin draped with a tricolour through the streets, passing by the home of a man they had recently shot, and shouting at his son and daughter, 'get inside, you spies.' The unit reported that only twenty men were involved, the coffin had been used for a catafalque during a high mass for the IRA dead, and the flags had been removed before it was taken away in a cart after the service.[238]

Some liaison problems stemmed, inevitably, from the imprecise terms of the Truce itself. One example was the Belfast Boycott. Was it covered by the Truce or not? The Minister for Labour initially instructed 'all the Committees not to take any drastic action in connection with the Boycott' during the Truce – but added, 'I take it they are allowed to note who is breaking the Boycott during the Truce with a view to subsequent action.' At the end of July committees were formally instructed that the boycott did not come under the terms of the Truce, but 'drastic action in connection with it must not be taken' while the Truce lasted. If committees found, for instance, that traders had received Belfast goods, they 'will inform them that they are aware of the fact, but no attempt will be made to raid the shops or railways for the destruction of these goods'.[239] Clearly, 'destruction of property is a distinct breach of the Truce', but 'in other respects the boycott is to continue.' Some people thought, or hoped, that it had been suspended, however. A Granard grocer, complaining to Murphy that 'a consignment of goods from a Belfast firm were [sic] today carried off in the name of the Belfast Boycott', demanded that if the boycott was continuing 'it should be made quite plain in the Press, and not leave people under the impression it has ceased.'[240]

'THERE SHOULD BE NO QUESTION OF VACATION OR HALF-TIME WORK'

'In view of the perhaps very long and hard struggle in front of us, it is absolutely necessary to throw responsibility upon younger men' – even at the cost of 'some present loss'. Mulcahy wrote this to a brigadier he was sacking, but it reflected his concern to use the Truce to reconstruct the Volunteers and provide some space for activities that had never been fully developed. Training camps sprang up everywhere – not least because, as O'Malley said, 'We had to give the officers sufficient work to keep them busy and do our best to prevent them from entering towns and cities where they would become known to enemy intelligence agents.'[241]

O'Malley's own training camp provided fieldcraft and ambush practice as well as parade-ground drill. Cumann na mBan turned out enthusiastically to provide catering – 'If you're good, we'll wash for you also.' 3rd Southern's November camp was hailed as a triumph: 'The men simply eat up the work.' The training 'opened up an entirely new field of work to all officers and showed up the proper working of the

Company in concrete form.' It would seem that this was fairly elementary military training, which was still necessary for most officers and men – another camp report noted that 'on starting it was evident that they were totally ignorant of drill or discipline in any shape or form.' The Dublin Brigade acquired a large property in Glenasmole which gradually expanded to become 'more of a General Headquarters training camp, as men were brought [in] from various parts of the country', mainly for instruction in using the Thompson gun by the brigade's two American ex-officers. But, as before, this consisted only of learning to strip the guns, rather than fire them. (Ammunition may have been short, and in any case the famous thumping 'rattle' of the Thompson was hard to disguise.)[242]

Under the Truce terms road trenching was suspended. On 27 July, GHQ ordered units to ensure roads were made fit for traffic; but to 'bear in mind that those repairs are to be carried out with a view to possible resumption of hostilities'. Munitions supply, on the other hand, was to be increased 'to the fullest possible extent'. 'There should be no question of Vacation or Half-time work on the part of anybody engaged in this department.' If hostilities were renewed it would be 'vital . . . to have a liberal supply of War Material of all procurable kinds'. Since munitions shortages had been, and remained, the biggest single handicap to the Volunteer campaign, this clearly represented an attempt to change the status quo, and so was a breach of the Truce – albeit not in GHQ's view, it appears. Such issues would preoccupy the committee set up in London to monitor the Truce, and would more than once irrupt into the Anglo-Irish negotiations at the highest level.

Truce conditions also allowed a return to drilling, which itself could raise issues which had been neglected during the fighting. The local Volunteers in Ring, Co. Waterford, had 'learned all their drill in Irish', but when the brigadier visited them in September he insisted on the drill commands being given in English. Though this was presumably the brigade's standard practice, it 'caused considerable dissatisfaction among the men, and made a bad impression on the people of Ring'. Another military-language issue remained unresolved. All the Volunteer titles of rank were English, and as (Commandant General) Béaslaí reflected in December, 'it is a pity that we did not devise exclusively Irish titles which could be easily used by the men whether they knew Irish or not,' and which might 'soon become as familiar to everyone as "Sinn Féin" or

"Coiste Gnotha [the governing body of the Gaelic League]"'. Was it too late to do anything about it, he wondered? Adjutant General Gearoid O'Sullivan noted that 'for the moment titles and ranks etc are in abeyance' (presumably while the 'New Army' was constructed), but sent a copy of the proposed scheme. 'If you could draw up similar ones in Irish,' he suggested to Béaslaí, 'the *Irish ones only* should be circulated.' This would be 'good from the point of view of language and association', but also – interestingly – 'would do a great deal towards removing the militaristic and introducing the Volunteer touch into the work'.[243] But, despite his sense of its importance, Béaslaí still took three months to come up with the Irish rank titles; by that time it was indeed too late. The Volunteers were on the brink of dissolution, and even the anti-Treaty IRA went on using English titles. Generations later, the Provisional IRA would still be run by an army council and a chief of staff.

The sense that the Truce would be brief was widespread. It is worth recalling that, as Midleton recorded, the original truce talks had assumed that 'the negotiations would not last more than a fortnight or three weeks'. In fact it took six weeks even to agree the basis for substantive talks in London. After two months the Adjutant General announced that GHQ was 'of the opinion that the truce period is coming to an end'. Ernie O'Malley remembered Eoin O'Duffy proposing to break the Truce, when the London negotiations approached deadlock, by attacking British posts without giving the required seventy-two hours' warning. Though some officers were in favour – assuming that the British would do the same – the divisional staff 'repudiated the suggestion coming as it did from a member of GHQ'. If there was to be a fight it should begin honourably. But exactly how remained unclear. It has indeed been said that the army's preparations for a resumption of hostilities were 'largely a sham', and no evidence exists of any plan being drawn up, or even 'any considered national military strategy'.[244]

O'Malley recalled a group of senior officers going to a meeting with Collins, Mulcahy, O'Duffy and Emmet Dalton in Dublin. (O'Malley was struck by how many commanders were absent – among them Liam Lynch of 1st Southern, Tom Maguire, Billy Pilkington, Michael Kilroy of the 2nd, 3rd and 4th Western, and Frank Aiken of the 4th Northern Division.) They discussed food supplies, and submitted oral reports of their arms stocks, training and potential for active service. 'Some seemed pessimistic, they had little ammunition and felt they could not maintain themselves for long in case of a resumption of hostilities.' O'Malley himself disputed this – 'It is not a question of arms or ammunition. I have never yet met a keen, good officer or Volunteer who did not, by hook or by crook, obtain arms and stuff.' They were asked for their opinions on the 'advisability of fighting in uniform'. (There was a detailed discussion of the new uniform cap – with 'a soft rim of the Kepi type' to distinguish it from the British rim.) Most were apparently in favour of carrying distinctive badges.

The officers had a lecture from Mulcahy on the revised seniority of the higher ranks of the army – the Chief of Staff was to be a general, the Deputy and Assistant Chiefs lieutenant generals. Divisional commanders who had so far been ranked equal to the members of the GHQ staff – commandants general – would henceforth outrank them. (As we have seen, none received Irish titles.) They met de Valera and Brugha next day, who questioned them about the morale of the people, and their likely support in renewed hostilities. Issues of civil administration – collection of taxes, repair of roads, local and district courts, enforcement of the Belfast Boycott and Dáil decrees – were talked about. All these discussions seemed fairly inconclusive.

Arms shortages clearly influenced thinking about restarting the war. GHQ compiled figures showing that the army had on average forty-three rounds per rifle (the average for the three southern divisions was actually slightly lower at forty, while that for the eastern divisions was noticeably higher at fifty-nine), thirty-four per automatic, fourteen per revolver, and a mere six cartridges per shotgun. It is hard to assess whether arms stocks improved or worsened under the Truce. Though the supply of weapons bought or purloined from the British themselves more or less dried up, the Quartermaster General reported to Brugha in December that arms imports since July had substantially exceeded those of the previous eleven months. They included fifty-one machine guns and 331 rifles (as against five and ninety-six between August 1920 and July 1921). Even though rifle ammunition importation fell slightly (from 21,000 to 18,000 rounds), these figures were hardly, as some have suggested, 'insignificant' in relation to existing stocks. As far as GHQ knew, the IRA had only 3,295 rifles in all. The four western divisions possessed no more than 417 between them. Though this was almost certainly an underestimate, the accession of rifles was substantial and that of light machine guns was dramatic: by December there were sixty-one (forty-nine of them Thompson guns) with an average of 500 rounds of ammunition apiece. GHQ arms expenditure also rocketed (to £6,000 a month).[245]

What perhaps made the arms holdings seem more inadequate was the dramatic numerical expansion of the IRA after the Truce. 'The Irish Republican Army was in danger of becoming popular,' as O'Malley wryly reflected; 'recruits came in large numbers. Soon men appeared in uniform who had never shown much anxiety to run special risks when courage was needed.' The army's effective strength in July is admittedly hard to fix exactly. GHQ counted almost 34,000, though some would see this total as misleadingly high.[246] But paper strength leapt up to some 50,000 in October and 75,000 in December. By the following spring it would be well over 100,000 – comparable to the paper strength of the Volunteers before the 1914 split.

This rush of manpower was not altogether welcome, as O'Malley's comment suggests. Ever since the 1914 split, mere numerical scale had been discounted in favour of the strength that came from commitment. The style of fighting adopted after 1919 reinforced, if anything, this priority. The demand for dedication makes it all the odder that the Volunteers had been giving only a limited role to the boy-scout organization Fianna Éireann. This fiercely separatist and militarist group, founded by Bulmer Hobson and Countess Markievicz, had a longer history than the Volunteers themselves, and was a byword for republican purity. Under Hobson's direction they had helped in the landing of rifles at Howth in 1914, and individual Fianna leaders – notably Seán Heuston – had played leading roles in 1916. But the Fianna had never been integrated with the Volunteers. In fact, after 1916 the two organizations moved further apart, as the Fianna asserted their independence from Volunteer control. But though it boasted a general staff, the Fianna organization was loose. In Limerick in 1919, 'the sluaghs [companies] were practically working on their own without any central control'; then 'after a time, the sluagh system seemed to have broken down and all the members were meeting as one unit.'[247] The Fianna apparently discussed raiding for arms like the Volunteers, but turned the idea down. Though they remained, as they had always been, committed physical-force republicans, those who (like Frank Busteed) wanted to fight simply joined the Volunteers as soon as they were old enough.

After the Truce a move to bring the Fianna under the control of the

Defence Department revealed how undeveloped the organization remained. According to the Fianna's Adjutant General, in the seven months since January, 103 Fianna *sluaghs* had sent in reports, forty of them since the Truce. Many were 'newly established, and we became aware of their existence for the first time'. They totalled 2,738 'boys', but the real total must have been bigger, as there were 'many districts which have not communicated with us, in which the Fianna exists in a more or less disorganised state'. The reasons why the situation was so unsatisfactory were obscure. The Volunteers had been ordered by the IV Director of Organization to work with the Fianna, but outside Dublin, Cork and Belfast had not done so. 'The attitude adopted by the IV towards the Fianna', the Adjutant General said, 'is rather incomprehensible,' and it would have to change if recruits were to be drawn from the Fianna. 'We have found that in most cases the I.V. have not made the slightest attempt to avail themselves of the advantages of boys over men' – especially in scouting work. The general Volunteer view was that 'the Fianna are only youngsters and should be treated like children.' But there might have been a less creditable motive. There was a suspicion that in some cases 'the I.V. actually thought that the Fianna would force them to get into the fighting and this would make it uncomfortable for them.'[248]

'WAS IT ANY WONDER THAT THE FIRE OF THE ARMY DIED DOWN?'

The prolonged Truce was later condemned by Mulcahy as 'very bad in every way' – 'excesses of one kind or another arose out of the relaxation of strain, and ... a certain amount of demoralisation took place.'[249] Down south, the flinty Seán Moylan agreed that the 'period of relaxation' brought its own problems – 'the discipline which physical danger imposes had disappeared and ... men had to face the more subtle danger of a fleeting flattery and adulation. For a few weeks there was a certain joyous abandon ... the natural reaction from the strain and tension of the previous years, but with the real fighting men this phase passed quickly.' Still, Moylan also thought there was 'a demoralisation' in the republican movement. 'Round every organisation, no matter how closely compact, there is a nebulous edge composed of men who are in it but not of it.' The Truce allowed such people to pose as 'war hardened soldiers'. 'In public houses, at dance halls, on the road in "commandeered" motor cars, they pushed the ordinary decent civilian aside and earned for the IRA a reputation for bullying, insobriety and dishonesty that sapped public confidence.'[250]

Some of the worst offenders were quite high-ranking officers – thanks to 'the original elective method of appointment'. And the problem 'could not be controlled', Moylan lamented, because the best fighting men had gone back to their farms or any jobs they could find. 'They were the nation's army ... yet the nation made not the least effort to provide for them.' 'Was it any wonder that the fire of the Army died down, that the organisation's strength, in spite of its valiant efforts, waned?' The Truce atmosphere was a peculiar one. Senior officers trod a fine line between embracing the spirit of the Truce and fraternizing with the enemy. The commander of the Athlone Brigade, the Adjutant General was told, had accepted a dinner invitation from the Auxiliaries, 'lost his head altogether with drink' and 'considerably lowered the prestige of our officers in that district'. 'I am given the impression that drinking among our men has come to the point of scandal.'[251]

When a man was killed by north Roscommon Volunteers, who said they were commandeering him to cut roads, the Adjutant General did not believe them. 'These men went to McGowan's house with the intention of murdering him,' he told Collins. 'The three Volunteers who were present should be executed.' But he thought this was not an isolated case: it showed 'an atmosphere of drunkness [sic], indiscipline and blackguardism. Somebody should be sent at once to investigate the state of the organisation in that area.' Shortly afterwards, further problems were reported by the brigade chief of police; cases of 'breaking into houses at night, taking money under false pretences, ill-treatment, threatening at revolver point' were 'blackening the Republican cause'. 'To be candid, some of the people told me that they would sooner have the Black and Tans over them than the present party, who seem to think that they can do as they like to everybody.'[252] Gearoid O'Sullivan concluded next month that the commanders of both Roscommon brigades 'must be removed', adding wearily that 'when the CS [Chief of Staff] returns from the country, I have decided to retire to a Monastry [sic].'[253]

On 21 October 1921 the ministry discussed 'some very serious complaints about excessive drinking' from areas as 'wide apart as Meath,

Kerry, North Roscommon, Tipperary, Wexford and Dublin', and called on Brugha to issue a general order. Mulcahy was instructed to tell all commanders 'to use strict disciplinary methods to have this thing stamped out' (though Brugha noted that the order must be carefully worded so as not to provide the enemy with propaganda material). On 4 November officers 'found guilty after a warning of frequenting Public Houses for the purpose of drinking, or of continued indulgence in drink', were threatened first with reduction to the ranks, and on a second conviction with dismissal from the army.[254] Many commanders shared the experience of Frank Aiken, who had to dismiss two of his officers for drunkenness.[255]

In Kerry No. 1 area, indiscipline might be a thing of the past, but 1st Southern Division said 'the difficulty now is in converting undisciplined men into soldierly units in short time', thanks to 'complete lack of organisation in most Battalion areas'. Worse, Lynch reported that 'gross irregularities' were still occurring, especially in north Kerry; they 'must be put down at once to save the honour of the Army'. But more thoroughgoing changes were not going to happen 'in a few months when so many years were idly lost'.[256] In late October, in what Mulcahy called 'a serious breach of the Truce', the police barrack at Passage East was burned down after it had been evacuated. 'At the moment the alternative to a state of Truce is a state of War,' he warned. 'Serious disciplinary action must be taken in the case of any Volunteer whose action or attitude might involve a return to War illconsideredly [sic] or in a manner prejudicial to the National honour and dignity.'[257]

In some places, the most dramatic of all forms of indiscipline – open mutiny – broke out. Some units tried to break away from the control of officers they disliked, others held that their legitimate grievances were ignored. When three battalions refused to recognize the authority of the Mid-Limerick Brigade in October, claiming that brigade officers were city men who did not understand country conditions, Ernie O'Malley summoned the aid of Eoin O'Duffy from GHQ to enable him to disarm the offenders. (The Assistant Chief of Staff tartly commented that, without the control of the city men, 'these battalions would become mobs.') When the Cratloe company in east Clare mutinied, 'orders were issued for the arrest of everybody concerned, but on the night of the sweep fifteen escaped'; some of them fired on the raiding parties. Michael Brennan, who had also faced mutinies in west Clare and south Galway, sent in 'several hundred' men to search 'every house, field and fence in Cratloe', and all but three were taken and charged with mutiny and attempted murder. 'When this mutiny is finished,' Brennan grimly noted, 'I think we won't have many more mutinies in this Division.' As he reflected, 'if mutineers are dealt with properly and firmly they have a wonderful regard for discipline afterwards.'[258]

Mulcahy found his office 'inundated with complaints' from the public. Some were justified, but he thought many were mischievous – the work of the 'type of polished Irishman' blamed by 1st Southern for deliberately 'misrepresenting' the local Volunteers. (One complainant was 'a staunch friend of the enemy during the critical stages'.) The brigadier of Kerry No. 2 drily urged Lynch to 'try to get the war on as soon as possible', otherwise 'we will have to get another staff to keep contradicting the lying reports which are being sent to GHQ through what channels God only knows. If we are to be persecuted by these civilians we will have to chuck all military work.'[259] Lynch grumbled to Mulcahy that thanks to 'different complications' it was four times harder to run the division since the Truce than it had been during the war. 'I assure you that ye at GHQ have not full knowledge of what discredit the Army is brought to in some areas, discredit of far more serious type than in Cork 3. I assure you we are leaving nothing undone in this matter that the Army may be looked up to by the civil population.'[260]

'COLLECTIONS PURE AND SIMPLE'

One persistent cause of friction with the civil population was the long-established practice of paying for the Volunteer campaign by public levies. These were unlikely, in the circumstances, to be entirely voluntary, though the level of pressure varied from area to area. During the Truce such methods came under sharper public scrutiny and criticism. The republican authorities grew anxious. 'Will you please have it hammered into the heads of all O/Cs', GHQ wrote, 'that Truce time collections must be collections pure and simple, and neither loans nor extortions.'[261] De Valera thought, as he told Collins, that all collections, 'even though they are nominally in the nature of *voluntary contributions* are regarded in fact as levies, and when made by the army units can be open to abuse'. The ministry decided on 19 October that 'these collections, as well as the levies, should be forbidden as from the present date.' Collins, though, was opposed to 'any stop of collections', though not because of Irish public opinion. 'The enemy admitted that we had a right to [them] and I don't think we should abandon this right. It would be making things altogether too convenient for them.'[262] But he did not get his way, and on 25 October Mulcahy circulated a 'Special Memorandum' signed by Cathal Brugha, instructing that 'levies in whatever form must be stopped absolutely' (with the characteristic gloss, 'Weekly Memorandum No. 15 Para. 3 refers'). 'Collections must be carried out in such a way that they will not savour of the levy and that no undercurrent of pressure can be complained of; and they must be carried out by known Volunteers. Our National reputation for honour and discipline is involved in this matter.'[263]

The ministerial order provoked something of a crisis in the south. The Waterford Brigade's publicity officer placed a notice in the press 'to clear the doubt which appears to exist in the minds of some persons as to the Levy in this area', declaring that the Waterford Brigade was 'authorised by Divisional Headquarters to raise funds by means of a Levy'. Duly appointed collectors, carrying written authority, would 'call and collect the sums requested'. Those paying up could 'rest assured that the money will be devoted to placing the Waterford Brigade in a state of efficiency, and ready to do their part in safeguarding the national interests of the people'. His divisional commander, Liam Lynch, immediately ordered the Waterford brigadier to 'suspend this Officer on the charge of a gross breach of Discipline'. But he told Mulcahy that 'some Brigades have already received requests to return collections' after the ministerial order was published. 'You may take it as definite', he warned, 'that all Commanding Officers in the South who adapted [sic] this war measure will not nor could not hold their commission if Ministry ruling is not explained to refer only from Truce date.' If this was not made clear, the government 'will have shown proof not to have stood by our actions'. The problem was that since the Truce 'expenditure is about six times more than during hostilities'. The Volunteers could not depend on subscriptions. But whereas 'during war it was only in a few instances per Battn that levies had to be insisted on as people paid up freely', now 'the situation is certainly different in area[s] where some of population have not developed a war mind.' There was 'a peace at any price group of shoneens who put a few pounds before the Nation's honour and Freedom'.[264]

Mulcahy confirmed that the order referred only to the post-Truce situation, and that GHQ 'realises that it was absolutely necessary to impose such levies in certain places during the fighting period'. (Noting that the instruction had been 'agreed in London', he added the interesting observation 'the fact is that we *are* dealing with some non-war areas which are not very cotrolable [sic]'). He assured Lynch that 'any request for the return of monies collected should not be entertained.' But Lynch – who seemed almost to be looking for signs of betrayal – demanded to know 'whether Ministry sanction or repudiate action of Brigade Commandants in enforcing Levies in the past'. [265] Mulcahy duly referred the problem to Brugha, with a request that he be 'empowered to inform [Lynch] that the Ministry appreciates the circumstances in which some of the O/C's in the South had to organise levies and that they approve of the actions of the Officers'. Brugha's response threatened to take the problem to a new level. The ministry 'could not approve as having been regular what we never sanctioned'; but if local units submitted full accounts of their receipts from levies and their expenditures, they would be credited with 'having contributed to the national exchequer', and the sums raised would be factored into future taxation.[266] When Collins got wind of this he protested that the idea of incorporating levies into the national funds was 'a proposition which I could not advise any Government to accede to', and was 'wholly impracticable' as far as the local commanders were concerned. The matter raised a 'tremendous question' of government liability, since the amount 'levied or collected by semi-levy (it would be very hard to differentiate) probably runs into very many thousands'. It should have been a simple matter to issue 'the necessary endorsement to the O/C 1st Southern' without raising this 'new complication'.[267]

The cost of running the army was now a serious issue. Brugha, wondering whether it could be covered from government funds if levies and Volunteer subscriptions were suspended, asked for an estimate. Mulcahy put it at £200,000 a year – at least. This was 'a very skimpy estimate', which covered merely 'training and administration', and took 'no account of the cost of arms or munitions production. He stressed to Brugha that there was 'a very considerable difference' between 'the cost of running the Army in Truce time and the cost of running it during War'. Some local officers he had spoken to 'considered the comparative cost to be as four is to one'.[268] He had agreed, for instance, that the salary bill for 1st Southern Division staff was to rise from £36 to £100 a week.[269]

NEW GOVERNMENT, NEW ARMY

Late in August 1921 de Valera remodelled the Dáil Cabinet, drastically pruning its core membership to six, with seven subordinate non-Cabinet ministries. Among the latter, J. J. O'Kelly's National Language Department was relabelled Education, while Count Plunkett was pushed out of Foreign Affairs into a new ministry of Fine Arts, which de Valera thought 'gave the appearance of stability and progressiveness to their affairs'.[270] The Propaganda Department became the (non-Cabinet) Ministry of Publicity, with Desmond FitzGerald edging out Erskine Childers to return as minister. Childers concentrated on preparing a series of pamphlets, *The Constructive Work of Dáil Éireann*, which marshalled some fairly impressive evidence of the Republic's administrative achievements. The core ministerial group – Griffith, Collins, Brugha, Stack and Cosgrave – was joined by a new portfolio, Economic Affairs, which was given to Robert Barton. Barton, cousin and friend of Childers and former Agriculture Minister, had been out of the picture between his arrest in January 1920 and his release in July 1921. His inclusion may have been intended to strengthen the republican solidarity of the Cabinet, although it – along with the remodelling of the inner Cabinet – has also been seen by some as shifting the balance away from the fundamentalist republican wing.

The Propaganda Department's change of name pointed to some problems of adjustment to the postwar situation. The department's work had always been aimed primarily at overseas opinion, and it had never developed machinery to address an Irish audience. After the Truce its main publicity vehicle the *Irish Bulletin* suffered, it has been suggested, from 'a lack of appropriate topics to publicise'. Reviewing past brutalities of the British did not have the same capacity to rouse public sympathy as it had during the war. Government publicity may even have suffered from a public sense that the republicans, no longer underground fighters, were now the incumbents.

In the country at large, a growing tendency for the Volunteers 'to domineer over civilians and despise "politicians"' has struck some as a symptom of their post-Truce demoralization. Certainly the army's political dominance, evident in the May election, was cemented after the Truce. The seepage of military leadership into local government had already become pronounced, but this, in a sense, simply mirrored the overlap at national level. Michael Brennan as chairman of Clare County Council, like Michael Collins as minister for finance, or Diarmuid O'Hegarty as Cabinet secretary, echoed the common ancestry of Sinn Féin and the Volunteers. Not everyone seems to have endorsed this position: in October 1921 Mulcahy heard of a case 'in which a Company Adjutant who acted as a district Court Registrar was instructed to resign his court position and that he should not be associated with the civil administration'. He felt it necessary to point out that 'this attitude is incorrect. There is no prohibition preventing a Volunteer occupying any position on the Civil side of our Administration.'[271]

But his efforts to stop the IRA 'interfering in public appointments' still ran up against hard realities. The mid-Limerick brigadier Liam Forde explained that he had put in Dr Brennan, a longstanding member of the Limerick Volunteers, as chief medical officer of Croom hospital in accordance with 'the practice general in all countries of exercising their influence on behalf of the candidate who served in the war'. (Mulcahy underlined this sentence and put an exclamation mark beside it, but seems to have left it at that.) Forde accepted that his 'interference may be considered irregular', but pointed out that Croom was strategically located between the three Limerick brigades, and 'as it will be a point of considerable importance on the termination of the Truce' it needed to be run by 'one whose service on resumption of hostilities would be entirely at the disposal of our army' and could be relied on to 'give secret and unremitting attention to the wounded of the three brigades'.[272]

The erosion of Sinn Féin's party machinery under the impact of two years of war emphasized the resilience of the army's, and this helped military attitudes to harden into something approaching militarism in some places. In Sligo 'major divisions' between the Volunteers and the county council soon became apparent. The non-Volunteer council chairman was denounced as 'wholly unsuitable for the position he occupies', and the question whether one clerk should be retained or let go seems to have produced a division prefiguring the civil war split. (The clerk's supporters would all go anti-Treaty.) There were battles over Poor Law union reform, and the IRA took action against a councillor, Patrick Connolly, who had objected to the idea of adjourning the council as a mark of respect for the commandant of Ballymote battalion (who had drowned the day after the Truce), Tubbercurry Rural District Council being instructed to 'rescind' Connolly's appointment to the council and replace him by 'a better qualified councillor'. The Local Government Department was sufficiently worried by developments in Sligo to send an inspector, who commented wryly that 'Sligo Brigade appears to have declared martial law for Sligo.'[273] This may have been extreme, but it was not entirely unrepresentative.

The ending of active hostilities had a particularly damaging effect on the republican high command. For reasons that are still obscure, Cathal Brugha decided to assert his ministerial authority during the Truce. Mulcahy's biographer thinks he 'resented the fact that Collins and Mulcahy were . . . associated in the public mind with the IRA', and may have 'decided that it was time to break their hold on the army'.[274] Brugha went as far as charging Collins and Harry Boland, the envoy to America, with misuse of funds in buying arms. GHQ's reaction may be judged from the Adjutant General's note asking Fintan Murphy to check the details – 'you need not break your heart about this, as I know you won't.'[275] Mulcahy's later irritated comment that Brugha 'took advantage of the freedom of the Truce' to meet people, listen to their complaints and 'take an active and an interfering part in dealing with arms questions, and indeed with Defence matters generally' seems coloured by the final violent split in 1922. But even in the late summer of 1921 the animosity between them was all too clear. On 30 July Brugha issued a stinging rebuke to Collins over the handling of the case of a man banished from Ireland on erroneous information, charging the Department of Information with 'an amateurishness that I thought we had long ago outgrown'. A more calculated insult could hardly have been devised, and after what seems a very long period of reflection – over a month – Mulcahy opted to respond in kind, declaring that 'the tone of your letter of 30th July is most unfortunate and must have a very destructive influence on the harmony and discipline of the Staff.' He indicated that unless something could be done to 'eliminate the tendency to revert to this tone when differences arise', he could not be responsible for maintaining that 'harmony and discipline'.[276]

This threat of resignation drew from Brugha some of the most remarkable written words that can ever have passed between a minister and a service chief. Wondering 'what good purpose' could have been served by 'writing thus 5 weeks after the event', Brugha suggested that 'it seems a further development of that presumption on your part that prompted you to ignore for some months past the duly appointed deputy chief of staff.' 'Before you are very much older, my friend, I shall show you that I have as little intention of taking dictation from you as to how I should reprove inefficiency or negligence on the part of yourself or the D/I [Collins], as I have of allowing you to appoint a deputy chief of staff of your own choosing.' Brugha went on to add to his criticism of Collins's amateurism a stark denial of Mulcahy's credentials as chief of staff: it was 'scarcely necessary to remind me' of 'your inability to maintain harmony and discipline among the Staff', since 'your shortcomings in that respect . . . have been quite apparent for a considerable time'. Six days later he told Mulcahy that, unless he produced a full dossier on the Robbie case (a businessman who had been ordered out of the country on insufficient information) within twenty-four hours, he would be suspended. Next day he duly told him that his services would no longer be required 'until further notice'.[277]

This was an impossible situation. Forwarding the correspondence to de Valera, Mulcahy fumed that 'it arises purely in a nagging spirit. It must be clear to you that its tendency must be devitalising and degrading.'[278] He frankly – and rather shockingly – declared, 'I cannot usefully discuss any matter with the Minister for Defence,' or 'accede to his request to preside at or be present at any meeting of the Staff'. Unless the position 'be estimated and adjusted without delay', it would 'lead to the destruction in a very short time of the vigour and discipline of the Staff'. Again, such language can hardly ever have passed from a service chief to a head of government. Yet, ironically, Mulcahy was a firm believer in the subordination of the military to the civil authority. Possibly he really thought that Brugha was exceeding his constitutional role; but one gets the sense that these roles were still being 'played' among a group of equals. It is hard to see how he expected de Valera to 'estimate and adjust' the crisis except by removing either him or – presumably – Brugha. The President did neither, however, though he may have calmed Brugha down: Mulcahy was reinstated, but the situation went on.

Robert Barton, who was 'filled with admiration' for de Valera's 'self-control and patience' in trying to 'prevent an open rupture', later noted that he tried several times 'to discover from Collins the root cause of his antipathy to Brugha. I failed.' But he found that 'he bore resentment to de Valera for the impartial attitude he adopted regarding this quarrel.' Fintan Murphy, a useful fixer in the background at GHQ, recalled 'acrimonious' meetings at which it was clear that the majority would side with Collins as they were 'all IRB'. 'Towards the end of the Tan War Brugha was very stiff.' Brugha was, Barton thought, 'a difficult man to work with. A man of iron will and scrupulous honesty he often argued fiercely over details that were of little moment and in a manner that was at times offensive though unintentionally so.'[279] Murphy noted that 'CB was quite the opposite type to Mick C for Mick C would jolly up a situation by saying "Come let us have a ball of malt."' The bottom line for him, though, was simply that 'whatever job he had' Collins 'was running the show'; he 'wanted to hold power and he was not going to surrender his power to the M/D [Minister for Defence].'[280] Sean Dowling, who was with Brugha in Dublin at the outbreak of the civil war, thought he 'hated Collins like poison – it was pathological'. Like many others, Dowling saw it as simple envy of Collins's capabilities. By that time, whatever its origins, it had become a paranoid obsession.[281]

Collins was unlikely to confide in Barton; he was only a little less guarded with his old friend Harry Boland – who had also felt the sting of Brugha's 'unintentional offensiveness' over the issue of payment for the Thompson guns. ('Surely a man of your intelligence must realise', Brugha patronizingly lectured him, 'that our plan of activities here is based upon our having a certain amount of money at our disposal.') When Boland, using the partial code which the pair slipped into erratically, told Collins in mid-May that he understood 'the question at issue between you and Porter', Collins hinted at the depth of the enmity. 'Indeed there is a question between the two men whose names you mention,' and but for his own 'forbearance', 'the thing would be simply a scandal.' Boland, he added, though heavily bruised by American faction fighting, had 'received no treatment at the hands of any of his enemies like one of these has received' (he was referring to himself, not 'Porter'/ Brugha, evidently). He would tell Boland of Brugha's 'real motive' 'Some day . . . when, if ever, we have an hour together.'[282] That hour does not seem to have come before the friends found themselves on opposite sides of a civil war.

In this poisonous atmosphere the Republic embarked on a radical rebranding exercise, the creation of a 'New Army'. This project was designed to remove the remaining ambiguity surrounding the relation-ship between the army and the civil government. As a basis for this, at some point the Volunteer Executive met for the last time to liquidate itself and terminate the independent status of the IV organization. On 15 September 1921 the Dáil Cabinet agreed to the reconstitution of the army, but it was not until mid-November that Cathal Brugha formally notified GHQ of the decision 'to issue fresh commissions to Officers, and to offer re-enlistment to all [other] ranks'. The rationale for this was the need, in view of 'the possibility of further fighting', to 'put the Army in an unequivocal position as the legal defence force of the Nation under the control of the Civil Government'.[283]

This step seems to have taken many by surprise. When the Defence Ministry memorandum was circulated, the commander of 5th Northern Division noted that it was 'the only intimation I have had' of the New Army idea, and announced that he would have to 'communicate with the chief of staff on the matter' before reaching a decision on whether to accept a fresh commission. Seán MacEoin sent an almost identical message four days later.[284] The OC 4th Northern, Frank Aiken, tartly remarked that 'the circular was the first we ever received from the Min-ister for Defence'.[285] Mulcahy himself, before he accepted the offer of a fresh commission as chief of staff, tried to get his powers over appoint-ments to GHQ defined as he wanted. Such appointments should not, he suggested, 'be made against his judgment and without his concurrence'. Unsurprisingly, Brugha replied that while the Chief of Staff's advice would be 'considered', both he and the whole staff would be 'appointed by the Cabinet on the recommendations of the Minister for Defence'.

This was not an abstract issue: as Brugha had pointed out, Mulcahy had been ignoring the man Brugha had nominated as deputy chief of staff, Austin Stack. 'Since I received your letters,' Brugha wrote on 8 October, 'I have asked him did he attend meetings of the Staff lately, and to my surprise he told me that he did not, as he had not been summoned to any meeting.' Brugha also queried Ginger O'Connell's appointment as assistant chief of staff. 'I don't remember seeing the title A/C/S appear-ing until now,' and he clearly thought it was the same post as 'Deputy Chief of Staff – whichever you like to call it'. Had he been kept in the dark, or had he just not been paying attention? In fact Eoin O'Duffy had become deputy. Mulcahy now proposed that the GHQ staff simply be reappointed, but, as he had threatened, Brugha insisted on placing

Stack as deputy (O'Duffy was to be director of organization). The issue was really what role the Minister should play in staff appointments – in essence, whether the post of deputy chief of staff was a military or a political appointment. Mulcahy once again threatened resignation 'if the Ministry decide to make an appointment to such an important Staff position against my judgment'. He also held that Brugha's proposal to reverse the existing seniority system, so that GHQ directors would be outranked by divisional commanders, would create serious difficulties. A meeting between GHQ and the Cabinet on 25 November to resolve these issues actually made the situation worse. O'Duffy had written to Brugha the day before to protest that he was 'reluctantly compelled to interpret the reduction in rank as a personal slight and a grave dishonour which I submit I do not deserve'. At the meeting he became 'a little bit shrill' in repeating this complaint, and his 'slight touch of hysteria' (according to Mulcahy) provoked an alarming scene. De Valera – who had previously tried to uphold O'Duffy's position – 'rose excitedly in his chair, pushed the small table in front of him, and declared in a half-scream, half-shout "ye may mutiny if ye like, but Ireland will give me another army," and dismissed the whole lot of us from his sight'.[286]

De Valera's impatience with the unseemly squabble may be understandable at one level, but he seems to have refused to face the issues put by Mulcahy and rule on them as he was plainly required to do. Mulcahy's demands were not entirely reasonable, but they would have been irrelevant in a less contentious situation. The real issue was psychological; as Ginger O'Connell innocently blurted out at the Cabinet meeting, up to this point GHQ had been 'a band of brothers'. As one historian has observed, he 'could not have put the case both for and against the *status quo* more succinctly'. It is hard not to see in this spat a pre-echo of the eventual split, and de Valera's resort to the word 'mutiny' was ominous. At this point, though, he was not taking sides so much as simply trying to keep Brugha in the frame.

The New Army project seems in the end to have petered out: the Ministry's decision on 25 November to call it the 'Re-Commissioned Army' has been seen as, in effect, an acceptance of the status quo.[287] A few days after the 25 November confrontation, Mulcahy explained to divisional commanders that while 'it might be inferred from this document [the Ministry memorandum] that a New Army is being formed, this is not really so'. The idea was merely 'to offer fresh commissions to certain Officers'. He added that 'the whole situation has been examined at a joint Meeting of the Cabinet and GHQ Staff and an understanding arrived at.' But he did not tell them what the understanding was.[288]

NEGOTIATORS: PURISTS AND PRAGMATISTS?

The New Army plan erupted at a delicate, maybe critical moment in the Anglo-Irish negotiations. It took its place in a series of disputes which gradually fractured the solidarity of the republican leadership. Tension within the supreme command was bad, but not necessarily fatal in itself. Transferred to the political negotiations with Britain its impact was of a different order. The spat over staff ranks and appointments coincided with the process of selecting the Republic's delegation to London and setting out its negotiating stance. Simply getting to the point of agreeing a basis for formal negotiations consumed the best part of three months after the Truce. A seemingly interminable and inconclusive correspondence between Lloyd George and de Valera through July and August left the two sides almost as far apart as at the start. The gulf was bridged only after Andy Cope had persuaded the British Cabinet on 7 September that as long as Britain insisted on allegiance to the Crown as a precondition for talks there would be no negotiations. At the end of the month de Valera finally agreed to negotiate on the basis of Lloyd George's formula – to work out 'how the association of Ireland with the community of nations known as the British Empire may best be reconciled with Irish national aspirations'. This long process had made clear that this 'reconciling' would be extremely complicated, if it could be done at all. The British aim was clearly to adjust Irish 'national aspirations' away from the independence claimed by the Republic, but how far was less clear.

De Valera's decision not to lead the delegation still strikes many as inexplicable. It has been justified by several arguments, which were anthologized by Dorothy Macardle, ranging from the contention that 'during this crisis' the President's place was at home, and that 'the appropriate person to head a delegation to England was the Minister for Foreign Affairs,' to the suggestion (ironic, perhaps) that if a settlement were reached which 'met with opposition from a section of the

Republicans' de Valera would have more influence in recommending it 'if he were outside the Delegation which had effected it'. (Yet since he expected the delegation to be in continuous conversation with the Cabinet, it is not clear that the distinction would have been obvious.) None of these explanations is more than inferential. Winston Churchill got the impression that de Valera had refused to go because 'as a "President" he was senior to Lloyd George.'[289] The selection of delegates has provoked almost as much speculation. Brugha and Stack simply refused to go. Brugha 'refused to leave the army', according to Macardle, but Collins – who could not use that justification – failed to persuade his colleagues that he would be more effective as a distant threat than as a negotiator. It may well be that he was not so much against going as against going without de Valera.[290] His claim that he was no more than a simple soldier was obviously absurd, but the decision to send him still looks bizarre. He had been the most wanted man in the British Empire, and his legendary hair's breadth escapes had created the myth that the authorities had no photograph of him. Now he was to be set in a global spotlight. He could never reoccupy his former role if the war was restarted. Can this have been Brugha's intention?

The division in the Cabinet over the delegation followed the lines that were becoming worryingly familiar. With Collins and Griffith, supported by Cosgrave, pressing de Valera to go to London, and Brugha, Stack and Barton supporting his refusal, the President in effect had the casting vote. The division was transmitted into the delegation, with a new strain of animosity added by the inclusion of Erskine Childers as secretary. This was not helpful: Griffith's bitter dislike of Childers was already clear and it would have very serious effects in the longer term. During the negotiations, as Childers told Nora Connolly, Griffith's 'absolute contempt' for him kept him from playing any meaningful part.[291] Was there any intention of balancing 'more' or 'less' republican commitment within the delegation, or was the key issue that of negotiating capacity? When Mary MacSwiney asked de Valera to put her on the delegation, he apparently replied, 'You would not do, Máire, you are too extreme.'[292] De Valera later told Joe McGarrity 'that Griffith would accept the Crown under pressure I had no doubt'; more surprisingly, 'from my own weighing up of' Collins, 'I felt certain that he too was contemplating accepting the Crown.' His argument that this 'would simply make them both a better bait for Lloyd George – leading him on and on, further in our direction', was a puzzling one.[293]

De Valera's own republican commitment has often been questioned – then and since. Though his messages to America in 1921 necessarily remained unequivocally separatist ('Sinn Féin will conduct no peace negotiations that do not provide for the recognition of the Irish Republic and complete political separation of Ireland from England'), at home his language was less strident. Ernest Blythe had several conversations with him after his return from the USA, and maintained that they had agreed on the inevitability of a compromise settlement. At one point, de Valera perceptively argued that they should try to negotiate while the Lloyd George coalition government was still in office, since they would get better terms from its ministers than from any likely successors.[294] De Valera mentioned the Republic only twice during the extended correspondence with Lloyd George. Opening the second Dáil on 16 August, he seemed to revert to the old Sinn Féin mantra in saying that the people had voted for freedom rather than a particular type of government. 'I do not take it that [the electorate's] answer was for a form of Republican Government as such, because we are not Republican doctrinaires.' But he said 'it was obvious' that 'Irish independence could not be realised in any other way so suitably as through a Republic' – at least 'at the present time'. As the London talks went on, though, he tended to speak of 'our principles' without specifying them exactly. Thus, at Ennis on 1 December, at the crisis of the negotiations, he reassured 'anybody who thinks that we can be driven beyond a point to which we are entitled to go by our principles' that 'we are going to stand upon the rock of truth and principle.'

By contrast, on 16 August Brugha had immediately reminded the Dáil that it had taken an oath of allegiance to the Irish Republic, and added ('not in a threatening sense, but as a manifest fact') that 'the fighting men ... are prepared to stand by that Oath no matter what the consequences might be.'[295] The post-1919 formula was incorporated in the oath of allegiance taken by the TDs four days later to 'the Irish Republic and the Government of the Irish Republic, which is Dáil Éireann'. At a public meeting of the Dáil on the 26th (after a series of private or 'secret' sessions) de Valera's title was apparently changed from president of Dáil Éireann to 'President of the Irish Republic'.[296]

There is some uncertainty about this, though. Seán MacEoin, who proposed this motion, recorded that he was instructed to do so by the previous President of the Republic, but for some reason he did not give his name.[297] Diarmuid O'Hegarty, who certainly should have known, later insisted that the term was never used in the Dáil until the motion to re-elect de Valera after the Treaty vote, and was incorrect even then. The correct title remained 'President of the Ministry or Príomh-Aire [prime minister]' as in the original constitution of Dáil Éireann, revised in August 1921.[298] If O'Hegarty was right, the only individual called President of the Irish Republic at this stage, ironically, was the President of the Supreme Council of the IRB, who had always been given this honorary title.

That President, Michael Collins, went on record as saying, indeed 'emphasising' more than once, that 'the declaration of a Republic by the leaders of the [1916] rising was far in advance of national thought.'[299] That remained substantially true five years later. As Robert Barton glumly reflected, 'great numbers of the people were never Republican.' He believed, as we have seen, that although the demand for independence might have seemed spontaneous, the people were drawn into it by their separatist leaders, and (in a striking echo of de Valera's eggs-in-a basket metaphor) likened the strength of the national demand to the strength of an egg. 'So long as the shell was intact, compromise and disruption were impossible. The army and political leaders were the shell, the people were the fluid contents.'[300]

When the Dáil confirmed the choice of delegates, Mary MacSwiney (just back from eight months in the USA lecturing for the American Association for the Recognition of the Irish Republic) insisted that they were going to England for one purpose only – to secure British recognition of the Republic. Ernest Blythe recalled that 'she wound up pointing her finger directly at me and saying: "If anyone here has a contrary opinion, let him speak now or be forever silent."' This rare attempt to pin down the objectives of the negotiations was sidelined by what has been called the 'casual misogyny' that Blythe shared with many of his colleagues: 'I only laughed at her.'[301] But her suspicions had been growing for some time. While she was in America she had worried about the republican commitment of both de Valera and Collins. Harry Boland had reassured her that both were sound, and that 'there can be no compromise between Ireland and England.' But as they sailed back to

Ireland together in August she had been disturbed by Boland's own conversation – 'the nonsense you talked on shipboard about "Dual Monarchy" etc. etc.' – and warned him that should he go to London 'please leave your Dual Monarchy nonsense behind you. Our oaths are to the Republic, *nothing less*.'[302]

Boland – who would become one of the most prominent casualties on the anti-Treaty side – certainly toyed with various formulations at this stage. This may have been a product of his enforced diplomatic duties (as he told Mary MacSwiney, his experience in the USA had made him cynical, and 'vague and unsatisfactory in my speech and actions') rather than of ideological flexibility. But when he was sent to Scotland in mid-September to deliver one of de Valera's letters to Lloyd George at Gairloch, he was plainly impressed by the vehemence of the Prime Minister's insistence on the impossibility of sovereign independence. That month he remarked more than once that he would be returning to the USA to 'prepare the people for something less than a Republic', 'the fact that we would not be getting a Republic'.

De Valera showed that separatism was not such an unequivocal concept as many republicans believed when, after the preliminary London talks, he began to set out the idea of 'external association'. This was really a recognition that without entrenched security guarantees the British would never agree a settlement. De Valera had long since been prepared to offer such guarantees: in February 1920 he had angered Irish-American hardliners by saying that permanent Irish neutrality might be enshrined in an instrument akin to the 1903 US–Cuba treaty. The problem was how to entrench the guarantee in a form acceptable to both sides. Republicans like Stack and Brugha saw any guarantee as a breach of sovereignty. De Valera struggled to clarify his conviction (most carefully elaborated in a letter to Joe McGarrity after the Treaty had been signed) that external association 'would leave us with the Republic unless the people wished to change it', and 'would commit us to nothing more than consultation with the representatives of Great Britain, Canada, Australia, South Africa, New Zealand, etc., on matters of common concern'.[303] Though it would also 'rid us ... of all British forces in occupation of our territory and coasts', this would happen not immediately but 'after a short period' – a more gnomic formulation.

External association has been recognized as a 'novel and imaginative' attempt to rethink the standard notion of sovereignty to find a way out of the impasse. But it struck most hardline republicans as at best baf-fling, at worst a betrayal. It proved too imaginative not only for Irish republicans, but for the British as well. De Valera's argument that such an arrangement would be no different from any treaty agreed by, say, the French government – and hence a confirmation rather than a denial of sovereignty – showed just why the British would never accept it. For the British, the security guarantee could be entrenched only by a formal recognition of the supremacy of the Crown. In the end, the negotiators did not push the idea very hard. If de Valera had managed to convince his Cabinet colleagues that he was committed to it, they might have tried harder, but it seems clear that neither Griffith nor Collins thought that it represented his 'last word'.[304] And de Valera was quite specific on the point that he could not provide a written draft – the delegates must draft the treaty.[305]

When the delegation arrived in London they carried a letter of accreditation, carefully worded to empower them as 'Envoys Plenipoten-tiary from the Elected Government of the REPUBLIC OF IRELAND to negotiate and conclude . . . a Treaty or Treaties of Settlement, Associ-ation and Accommodation between Ireland and the community of nations known as the British Commonwealth'. (It was signed by de Valera 'as President' – of what, was not said.)[306] Whether the British might have fallen for this indirect recognition of the Republic's exist-ence, or if not whether the talks would have been stymied at the start, are interesting questions. In the event, the delegation's credentials were never asked for and, perhaps more oddly, Griffith made no attempt to present them.

The delegation's powers would eventually become an acutely contro-versial issue. Nobody seemed to be sure, then or later, if they were 'plenipotentiaries' in the normal sense – with full powers to agree a settlement. (So that, as the Viceroy Lord FitzAlan told Lloyd George, they should 'not take advantage of de Valera's absence to delay and refer back to him'.) Since, if Macardle was right, de Valera was already pre-paring for the possibility of dispute over the eventual agreement, it is hard to fathom why the situation was left ambiguous. The instructions issued to the delegation along with their credentials on 7 October 1921 made clear that 'the Plenipotentiaries have full powers as defined in their credentials', but they were to refer 'the draft text of any treaty about to be signed' to the Cabinet, and await a reply before signing.[307]

Any ambiguity here was more apparent than real, since the Cabinet could not reduce the plenary powers conferred by the Dáil. The Cabinet's instructions were 'really nothing more than suggested guidelines'. If de Valera really believed that the two strongest members of the delegation would 'accept the Crown', he must have been, as he told McGarrity, 'convinced that as matters came to a close we would be able to hold them from this side from crossing the line'. This was surely a very high-risk strategy.

'OUR CIVIL FUNCTIONS'

In the midst of the London negotiations de Valera told Collins it was 'very important that you stipulate that our civil functions – police, courts, etc. – go on'. Their work could proceed '*unostentatiously* as I explained to MacCready [sic] initially', but 'cannot be given up, otherwise the truce if continued long enough would mean that we had gone out of business'. The republican justice system had indeed been brought to a near-standstill in the last six months of the guerrilla conflict. Austin Stack admitted that 'owing to enemy action' the courts 'for a time fell into abeyance in many places'. Under the Truce, though, they revived. Stack, as he told the Dáil on 18 August, interpreted the clause prohibiting 'interference with the movements of Irish persons, military or civil' as permitting republican justices, registrars and clerks to conduct their circuits. Courts were to be held 'as publicly as possible, without making the holding of them provocative'.[308] By mid-August, they were 'going again in almost every part of the country'. (In Longford, Dublin city, Cork city and parts of Cork, Clare and Limerick they had 'never for a day ceased work', he claimed.)[309]

But the key figures in keeping the courts going, the TDs and district registrars, still seem to have been doing little. After the Truce, Stack renewed his exhortation to TDs – 'Kindly take off your coat and give whatever help you can in this work, which is of the very highest importance.'[310] He urged registrars to seize the 'great opportunity at present afforded for thoroughly reorganising the Courts in your area'. The local judicial machinery needed 'to be capable of withstanding the most violent attempts that may be made by the enemy to render it ineffective'. Rather mysteriously, he told them that 'should hostilities be resumed, the Courts, for reasons which it is yet premature to disclose, will be called upon to play a mighty part in the struggle.' 'This is the golden hour. Therefore be prepared.' Stack's warning that any justice who was 'not prepared to perform his duty at all costs should resign and make room for a better man' indirectly acknowledged that many had been intimidated by British action. Parish courts, he added, should be 'an easy matter to keep going', and there could be 'no excuse for any Parish which in the future is found wanting'. As long as they had regular fixed sittings – once a fortnight – 'the people will in a short time submit all their disputes to them.' The enemy would try to disrupt them, but 'it should be very easy to outwit the forces of the enemy in holding these.' District courts might be more difficult to convene, but if they were split into five sub-districts, each with its own district justice, the 'work could be done with greater dispatch and less risk of detection'.[311]

Stack instructed the district registrars that 'it is not at present desirable to invite too much publicity'. There should be 'no relaxation of our efforts to empty the enemy courts, but the work should go on quietly and unostentatiously'. The dates of court sittings should not be publicized, and press reports of proceedings 'must be avoided'. Decrees and court orders should be executed 'with as little display as possible'. Early the following month, after the police had dispersed a republican court in Donegal, Stack stipulated that 'should the enemy interfere, the justices should take a strong stand on the matter and point out that such interference is a glaring breach of the terms of the truce.' But he was careful to add a further instruction that 'everything possible should be done to mislead the enemy as to the time and venue of the courts.' Courts confronted with 'enemy interference' should adjourn under protest and report the matter to the Home Affairs Department – 'so that the complaints can be dealt with through the liaison officers'. In case 'interference' was too vague a term, another week later he insisted that 'on no account should the Justices adjourn a Court until force has actually been used to disperse it.'[312]

The courts still touched British nerves. In mid-October Lloyd George brandished in Cabinet a newspaper report of a republican court in Dublin, which had opened with the formula 'I now declare this Court open in the name of the Irish Republic.' Invoking the Vereeniging Conference, the peace talks that had ended the South African war, he fumed that even though there had been a Boer republic before the war, it would have been out of the question for such a court to operate during the negotiations. 'It is to do a thing which was not done before. This is not the status quo. I shall have to tell them that we shall have to scatter these courts.'[313] This was bluster, partly designed to placate colleagues like Birkenhead who said that 'otherwise it would be absolutely impossible to carry on.' But the Irish delegation agreed to a joint declaration that 'no courts shall be held in Ireland otherwise than as before the Truce' – hardly an unambiguous formula, though Collins saw it as a setback. He fretted that it was 'a dam [sic] shame' – 'if the unostenticity part of it had been maintained we would not have been let down like we have been' by this 'cheap bravado'. The military authorities certainly interpreted it as confirming that 'as all Sinn Féin courts were illegal before the truce they are all illegal now.' A local commander who got the impression that courts could be held as long as they were in 'out of the way places', and proposed to tell the republican liaison officer this, was firmly corrected – 'Your proposed course of action would really be an incitement to the rebel liaison official to break the truce.'[314]

'THE CELTS NEVER WERE REPUBLICANS'

How did the opposing delegations match up? Once de Valera had opted out, the Irish team might appear politically inexperienced. On the British side, the Prime Minister led a group of undoubted political heavyweights: the Leader of the House of Commons, Austen Chamberlain, Lord Chancellor Birkenhead and Winston Churchill. Even so there was a potentially fatal omission: Bonar Law, the moving spirit in pushing the Conservatives to the brink of civil war during the 1912 Home Rule crisis – and the man who would head the Tory revolt against the Treaty that eventually brought Lloyd George down – was on the sidelines.

Given their complexity, much time would inevitably be consumed in the issues of delimiting Irish fiscal autonomy and arranging the fiscal balance between Ireland and Britain. But such issues were in principle resolvable. Two others – Ireland's unity and allegiance to the Crown – were not. The issue of unity, for all its nationalist emotional charge, was somewhat illusory (and would be all but ignored in the eventual debates on the Treaty). Because Britain had accepted that there could be no 'coercion of Ulster', partition was already a reality. The majority of British ministers disliked it, but it was effectively irreversible except by bilateral agreement between Dublin and Belfast. Of course the old nationalist belief that Ulster resistance was fomented by Britain and would collapse without British support persisted, and was fervently espoused by republicans. (De Valera would rehearse it to Griffith at a late stage in the negotiations.) When Griffith accepted the compromise developed by the British in late October – exclusion of 'Ulster' from the Irish Dominion, a 'new delimitation' of the boundary on the condition that no new powers were given to 'Ulster' – he certainly believed that this support had now disappeared. ('They are I think willing to go any distance short of using force against Ulster.') In the case of Lloyd George himself, Griffith was right, but his promise on 12 November not to 'repudiate' the Prime Minister 'while he was fighting the "Ulster" crowd' meant that at the crisis of the negotiations the delegation's options were cut. It could not break on the issue of Ulster intransigence, on which British public opinion was likely to be supportive, rather than the issue of allegiance to the Crown, on which it was not.

The most crucial issue was always that of Ireland's sovereign status. Republicans had generally understood their claim, whether for 'independence', 'separation' or simply 'freedom', to mean absolute legal sovereignty. Most rejected any concession on this issue as 'going into the Empire' – a phrase vividly expressing the belief that the Irish Republic was already an independent state. De Valera's position was different: his concept of 'association' would inevitably modify the claimed sovereign powers of the Republic, though exactly how was not entirely clear. In the tussle over this issue, which repeatedly brought the talks to the brink of collapse, the British had a crucial advantage: they knew exactly what they wanted to secure. The 'oath of allegiance' in some form – even though the form might be, and was, significantly modified – represented the symbolic salve to unionist suspicion of Irish separatism.

Addressing the 'conflict of ideas' that shaped the Treaty negotiations, Frank Pakenham's classic study perceptively invoked Carlyle: 'of man's whole terrestrial possessions and attainments, unspeakably the noblest are his Symbols.' Under these 'divine or divine-seeming' things, 'what we can call his Realised Ideals', 'he marches and fights with victorious assurance in this life-battle'. As Pakenham noted, the British saw the existing Imperial symbolism as vital to the Commonwealth, even though (or maybe especially because) it was now rapidly evolving away from British control. Even the arch-unionist Bonar Law (Canadian by birth) had publicly accepted that the Dominions would take 'control of their whole destinies', and that if one decided to go it alone 'we would not try to force them' back.[315] The problem for Anglo-Irish relations was that, whereas for the British what Lloyd George called 'the potency of the invisible bond' was ambiguous and 'not easy to interpret', outsiders – most Irish nationalists certainly included – took the symbolism literally.[316] The story of the negotiations is in essence the story of the movement of two nationalist leaders, Griffith and Collins, away from this literalism to a belief that acceptance of symbolic British suzerainty would no longer compromise effective Irish independence.

For Griffith the move was effectively made already. He was an advocate of dual monarchy on the Austro-Hungarian model, though this did not make him a 'monarchist' in the usual sense of the term. He was (like de Valera) a republican in the sense of being a separatist rather than a 'doctrinaire' supporter of republican forms of government. But for him separation was a practical rather than a symbolic project. This had been what Sinn Féin was all about. In this sense he 'accepted the Crown', as de Valera would allege. Griffith was more interested in effective governing power than in abstract sovereign status – hence the story of how, as he walked down Whitehall with Austin Stack in July, he gestured towards the Home Office building and asked 'Would you like to take that to Dublin with you, Austin?' (Stack by contrast reacted in symbolic terms, protesting, 'look at the dead who have given their lives for the Republic.')[317]

Collins does not seem to have given any systematic thought to the precise nature of freedom, sovereignty or forms of government before he went to London. The negotiations were a kind of crash course in constitutional politics for him, and as usual he was a prodigiously quick learner. 'No man was to be so much influenced by the actual course that the negotiations ran,' Pakenham judged. The result was probably, for de Valera, an unintended outcome of his determination to send Collins to London. Collins found he shared Griffith's 'conception of an Ireland free from British occupation, British penetration and British laws'; they had 'the same concern for practical construction'.[318] This was in sharp contrast to Childers – the Englishman – who never ceased to believe that if Britain was left with any constitutional power over Ireland it would use it. Collins did some reading on the recent evolution of the British Commonwealth and concluded – more perceptively – that it was inexorably turning into a league of free states.[319]

Collins seems to have made a genuine effort to push the external-association concept. At the sixth and seventh sessions in late October, the issue of Irish neutrality was discussed at length. Pithily noting that 'all your argument depends on your security,' Collins said 'we propose a condition which I contend is a better guarantee of security' than naval bases. He drew up in what Lloyd George called a 'formidable document' (and Churchill hailed as a document of 'marked ability') – an example of Collins's rapidly acquired grasp of high-level administrative procedures – detailing a policy of guaranteed neutrality. He went on to argue, perceptively, that the evolution of the British Empire into a freer community of states made some flexibility possible. But at this point in history the British were never going to be convinced by mere neutrality, however guaranteed. As Churchill insisted, 'Ireland's control of her neutrality might be ineffective,' and in any case even 'a completely honest neutrality by Ireland in the last war would have been worse for us' (than its rebellious disposition, presumably).[320] It did not help that the conference atmosphere at this point was poisoned by altercations over breaches of the Truce. The sixth session opened with a complaint by Lloyd George that the republicans were using the Truce 'to accumulate destructive stores for the purpose of manufacturing bombs and arming your forces', and ended with a fierce spat over a bomb factory found in Cardiff – the Prime Minister querulously asking why 'Sinn Féin' did such things, which just lost them (British) public sympathy.

Republican political symbols proved, paradoxically perhaps, ultimately less rigid than the British. A sign of this appeared right at the start of the negotiation process. When de Valera, escorted by Art O'Brien, had first met Lloyd George in July he handed over a document headed – like most official ministry documents over the last couple of years – 'Saorstát Éireann'. In 1919, the 1916 title 'Poblacht na hÉireann' had been superseded, for reasons that were not clear to everyone. Pakenham speculated that Saorstát was 'broader', Poblacht 'more abstract', but it was not a matter of meaning so much as one of linguistic purity. Pearse's word *poblacht* was a neologism, which looked like a loan-word, derived from Latin rather than Gaelic, though it could be seen as evoking the power of the people. *Saorstát* was a new compound of two Gaelic words – 'free state' (the latter itself a fairly recent coinage). Lloyd George, looking as if his curiosity had been aroused, 'began by asking modestly for a literal translation, saying that "Saorstat" did not strike his ear as Irish'. When told, he asked 'what is the Irish word for Republic'? De Valera and O'Brien were apparently unable to provide a satisfactory answer, allowing the Prime Minister – who had been making a great show of Celtic affinity with his Irish visitors (he 'received the Irish Chieftain cordially as a brother Celt', according to Tom Jones) – to ask 'must we not admit that the Celts never were republicans and have no native word for such an idea?'[321]

Frank Pakenham maintained that Lloyd George would not have been guilty of the 'indescribable folly' of deliberately embarrassing his visitor by such a question. He thought the story, which he found in Winston Churchill's book *The Aftermath*, was unreliable because Churchill had not been at the meeting. Actually it came from Jones himself, who was certainly there – though he did not set it down until eight years after the event. Pakenham took the same view of the story (also relayed by Churchill) that the Prime Minister 'discomfited' his visitors by talking with Tom Jones in Welsh while the Irishmen debated the linguistic question in English. Though Jones recorded this with evident relish, it does indeed seem dubious, since it supposedly happened while de Valera and O'Brien were struggling to find a more 'Irish' word than *saorstát* for republic. Jones did not indicate how long the debate lasted, but there were not very many possibilities; one perhaps was *comh-fhlaitheachd*, the term for 'commonwealth' given in Dineen's Irish dictionary, though never adopted by Sinn Féin. If they failed, or refused, to come up with the word *poblacht*, this would seem to have been taking linguistic purism absurdly far.[322]

But, whatever actually happened then, it is quite clear that Lloyd George fixed on the label 'free state' as one he could do business with. Did it carry any different meaning from 'republic'? De Valera seemed to confirm their equivalence by signing the plenipotentiaries' credentials under the letterhead 'Saorstát Éireann/Respublica Hibernica'.[323] Lloyd George appeared content to treat it as equivalent to 'dominion'. The battle over conceding or accepting 'Dominion status' would consume a lot of energy on both sides, and the way forward involved abandoning the term 'dominion' itself (whose undertones definitely sounded very different to British and Irish ears).

The labelling seemed a classic fudge, offering a path for the common desire for a solution to navigate past irreconcilable symbols. This was, as Collins put it in mid-October, 'the first time practically all parties wish a settlement.' Whether the wish was equally strong on all sides was the question. Some of the British negotiators remained acutely conscious that they were sailing very close to the wind – Lloyd George famously said, 'the life of the Government is put in issue by our proposals,' and Chamberlain urged his Irish counterparts, 'do not press it too far I beg. You are not aware of the risks we are taking with our whole political future.' His warning of course applied just as forcefully to Griffith and Collins themselves. Within two years of signing the Treaty, Chamberlain's distinguished political career would indeed be shipwrecked along with Lloyd George's. But, long before that, Collins would be killed in the internecine fight over the Treaty terms.

PART FOUR

The Republic Fractured: 1922–1923

'THE TREATY AS IT IS DRAFTED IS NOT ACCEPTABLE TO US'

By the end of November 1921 the London negotiations had produced a roughly agreed draft Treaty. On 3 December the Dáil Cabinet met in the Dublin Mansion House, with the two delegates who were not members of it, Duggan and Gavan Duffy, and the delegation's secretary, Erskine Childers, to discuss it. It was not an easy discussion, or an amicable one, and it showed how divisive the central points at issue were. As it stood the Treaty would create a twenty-six-county Irish Free State with 'Dominion status'. From a republican point of view, what was striking about it from the outset was not the powers this state would possess but those it would lack. It would not possess full fiscal autonomy; it would have no independent foreign policy; and its defences would be substantially in British hands. Some were ready to break over these issues: Robert Barton believed that fiscal independence was vital, and also achievable. Erskine Childers argued that Articles 6 and 7, which effectively committed Ireland to join all Britain's wars by giving Britain the right to defend the Irish coasts (including the occupation of several ports), would deprive the 'free state' of national status.

The majority seemed able to live with these terms. At least, the discussion was inconclusive (next day in London the delegates could not agree on what if anything had been decided). Two other issues threatened sharper division: partition and the 'oath of allegiance' to the British Crown. For de Valera himself, neither issue seemed absolutely fundamental – he said he could understand giving up independence for national unity, but objected that Griffith had 'got neither this nor that'. Partition could be regarded as a temporary setback; nobody at that stage (including the British ministers) imagined it could be permanent. The 'boundary commission' guaranteed in Article 12 of the Treaty was expected by nationalists to draw a border that would make Northern

Ireland unviable. The issue of allegiance was harder to sidestep. Collins suavely dismissed the oath as the 'sugar-coating to enable the English people to swallow the pill' of conceding real Irish autonomy. According to one account of the meeting, he pointed out that it would not come into force for a year, and proposed waiting to 'see how it would work' – a pre-echo perhaps of his later gradualist approach.[1] De Valera again said that 'if . . . we get all else we want, what harm would it be if we had an oath like this'? Here (as Austin Stack recalled) he 'spoke words paraphrasing the form in the draft treaty' – 'true faith and allegiance to the constitution of the Irish state and to the Treaty of Association', and 'to recognise the King of Great Britain as Head of the Association'.[2] Stack himself at first agreed with de Valera, and tried unsuccessfully to persuade Brugha to agree to such an oath; only later did he decide 'that Cathal was right'. Brugha, of course, refused to entertain any idea of an oath of allegiance to the Crown.

The discussion hinged on Griffith's insistence that the draft Treaty represented the most that could be got from Britain in the existing circumstances. The terms were disagreeable, but they were not dishonourable – and there was no alternative. Barton and Gavan Duffy took the view that they were not Britain's last word. Brugha latched on to the fact that key negotiations had been conducted in small sub-conferences – with only Griffith and Collins on the Irish side. Once again he shocked some of his colleagues with the directness of his accusation: the British had 'selected their men'. Griffith immediately forced a vote requiring Brugha to withdraw the remark. But of course there was some truth in it. The British had preferred to work with Griffith and Collins; but that did not mean that they had (as Brugha's words had, for some, implied) suborned them. Collins simply retorted that he should pick his own – 'get another five to go over' – if he wanted. Barton seemed to take this up, disputing Griffith's assertion that the British were at the limit of their concessions, and again urging de Valera to go to London in his place. De Valera may have reconsidered his position for a moment; he later told Joe McGarrity that he decided once more to stay, 'to get those republicans who desire isolation to consent' to external association, if the British accepted it. At this point Griffith tacked a little. Having first said that he would sign the Treaty (if he thought the only alternative was war) and then submit it to the Dáil, he now said he would not sign it until it had been submitted to the Dáil – and 'if necessary the people'. Brugha, who

15. Motorized force: an Auxiliary patrol in Tipperary. The first and fourth of its Crossley tenders are rigged up with anti-grenade cages.

16. The communications war continued: during the civil war, road-blocking remained one of the primary methods used by the republican IRA, here seen posing with a felled tree.

17. Holding fast to the Republic: most of the fifty-seven members of the Dáil who voted against the Treaty (and one, Robert Barton, who did not) posing with tricolour flag (held by Frank Casey, not a TD), numbered for identification by Free State intelligence.

18. Intelligence notes on the status of the fifty-eight, c. 1923.

1. P. Rutledge. T.D.
2. E. De Valera T.D.
3. A. Stack T.D.(Prisoner) (now prisoner)
4. S.T.O'Kelly T.D.
5. J.Mc.Donagh T.D. (dead)
6. L. Mellows (dead)
7. S. O'Kelly (Sgelig)
8. T. Maguire T.D.
9. Devins T.D. (dead)
10. S. Robinson (Tipp)
11. J. Doherty T.D.
12.
13. Madam Markieviez T.D.
14. Mrs. O'Callaghan T.D.
15. S. Doyle T.D. (Wexford)
16. Cathal Brugha (dead)
17. Mrs. Pearse.
18. Mrs. Clarke.
19. Mary Mc.Swiney T.D.
20. Harry Boland (dead)
21. Ada. English (B'sloe)
22. Dr. Ferran (Mayo) dead.
23. Dr. J. Crowley (Mayo)
24. S. Moylan (Cork)(U.S.A)
25. Prof.Stockley. (Cork)
26. M.P. Colivet (Limerick)
27. Aylward (Kilkenny (chucked in)
28. D. Corkerry (prisoner)
29. F. Fahy. (Gaelic League)
30. Fitzgerald. (Cobh)
31. Phil Shanahan.
32. P. Cahill. Kerry (prisoner)
33. Count P.J. O'Byrne (Roscrea)
34. Frank Casey (Republican Police)
35. R.C. Barton (prisoner)
36. Brian O'Higgins (prisoner)
37. Tom O'Donoghue (Kerry prisoner)
38. John O'Mahony (prisoner Fleming's Hotel)
39. Sean McEntee (Prisoner)
40. G.N. Cout. Plunkett
41. D. Buckley. (Maynooth).

42. J. Ryan (Wexford) prisoner
43. D.O'Callaghan (Cork) U.S.A.
44. Eamon Dee (Waterford).
45. Art O'Connor (prisoner)
46. Con Collins (Limerick)
47. Sean Etchingham (Wexford) (dead)
48. Dr. Brian Cusack (prisoner)
49. Sean McSwiney (Cork)
50. Erskine Childers (dead)
51. C. Murphy.Dublin (prisoner)
52. James Lennon (Carlow)
53. Sean Nolan (Cork)
54. Eamon Roche (Limerick)
55. D. Kent. (Cobh)
56. F. Carty.
57.
58. P.J. Moloney.

19. The handover: National Army troops (and dog) marching into Portobello barracks in Dublin, 1922.

20. The last attempt to keep the army together: Seán MacEoin, Seán Moylan, Eoin O'Duffy, Liam Lynch, Gearoid O'Sullivan and Liam Mellows at the Dublin Mansion House, 8 May 1922. MacEoin's preference for wearing uniform was still unusual among senior military officers.

21. Arguing for the Treaty: Michael Collins outside the GPO in 1922.

22. The edge of civil war: anti-Treaty IRA troops patrolling in Grafton Street, Dublin, 1922.

23. English guns: National troops with an 18-pounder in the attack on the O'Connell Street 'Block', July 1922.

24. Stater generals: Tom Ennis and Richard Mulcahy at Portobello barracks in early August 1922.

25. Stater soldiers: National Army troops in the battle for Limerick city, July 1922.

26. The fall of the Block: the last republican stronghold in Dublin, the Gresham Hotel, ablaze after bombardment by Free State artillery, July 1922.

27. Playing soldiers: despite the intensity of the civil war, the military contamination of Irish society was eventually confined to the perhaps harmless sphere of children's games.

28. Men of the west: a republican IRA column in Sligo, 1922.

29. Kevin O'Higgins, Home Affairs Minister and Assistant Chief of the General Staff, uses a military truck as a platform to call for law and order.

had protested 'you will split the country from top to bottom', seemed to be mollified by this change (presumably in the belief that with this procedure there would be no division of opinion). Griffith, for his part, presumably expected the people to share his view of the Treaty.

But by this stage there was, in reality, very little chance of agreement over any possible Treaty terms. It seems unlikely that de Valera could have persuaded republicans to accept external association, even if the British had been prepared to concede it. When he drew his proposal up under the title 'Document No. 2' it was all too clear that it incorporated the Ulster provisions of the draft Treaty, so accepting partition – for the time being at least – pretty much as Griffith had. Neutrality, a key Sinn Féin idea, had been abandoned early in the negotiations, and the Irish draft proposals dropped it in favour of the 'free state' concept.[3] Document No. 2 followed suit in making no mention of neutrality.

The delegation returned to London with no agreed idea of the Cabinet's position on the key issues. Barton and Gavan Duffy were still holding out for British recognition of Irish independence in principle as a prelude to accepting Dominion status. On 4 December the British negotiators furiously walked out of the talks when Gavan Duffy said that 'our difficulty is to come into the Empire.' This actually echoed Lloyd George's own words when he had rejected the Irish delegates' attempt to modify the first treaty draft in late November. 'If they are not coming into the Empire, then we will make them.' His anger was palpable.[4] The Irish delegation made another effort to get the British to accept de Valera's formula for the oath of allegiance – 'to the constitution of the Irish Free State' (which would imply rather than explicitly specify the Crown) – but failed. Lloyd George's threat of 'war within three days' if the delegation did not sign on the evening of 5 December created a drama that has been replayed many times in print and on screen. Under the pressure of the moment – pressure that seemingly made them ready to be convinced by Lloyd George's theatrical gesture of waving two letters and asking which he should send to Craig that night – Griffith forgot about his undertaking to consult the Dáil before signing. This was no great surprise, perhaps. More surprisingly, even the delegates who, unlike him, believed that it was still possible to get better terms – Robert Barton above all – also failed to telephone their Cabinet colleagues in Dublin. When Barton spoke later of the 'solemnity and the power of conviction' that Lloyd George 'alone of all men I ever met can impart by word and gesture – the vehicles by which the mind of one man oppresses and impresses the mind of another', he was clearly still shaken by it. (He may conceivably have sensed Lloyd George's withering personal estimate of him as 'that pip-squeak of a man'.)

The first direct division resulting from the Treaty came of course in the Dáil Cabinet – with Cosgrave, apparently to de Valera's surprise, clinching the majority in favour – and then spilled into the Dáil and beyond. Just how far beyond is hard to tell. Daniel Corkery (who would vote against the Treaty) thought that 'there was at first a general air of rejoicing amongst the public and the IRA.' Béaslaí suggested that initially there was 'no great public curiosity' about the Treaty's precise terms. For three years 'the people had been trained to place unlimited confidence in the Dáil Ministry,' and he suggested that the 'vague national aspirations' of ordinary people 'had not crystallised into reasoned doctrines'. Even active republicans had generally not constructed 'reasoned doctrines'; but 'the wording of the Treaty came like a shock of cold water to many sincere Separatists.'[5] Todd Andrews's first reaction to reading the oath of allegiance was incredulity: 'something must be wrong with the newspaper report,' since 'Collins could not have agreed to this.' Then, as he 'read the clauses allowing the British to retain the ports, paying pensions to the hated RIC, leaving the defence of our coasts to the Imperial power, substituting the title of Governor-General for Lord Lieutenant', he became literally ill 'through rage and disappointment'.[6]

De Valera's decision to issue a public letter stating his position on 9 December – 'I feel it is my duty to inform you immediately that I cannot recommend the acceptance of this treaty' – accelerated the process of taking sides. The usually influential Diarmuid O'Hegarty had tried and failed to dissuade him. Even if one does not follow Piaras Béaslaí as far as to brand de Valera's action 'insane irresponsibility', he was surely right to say that de Valera's reference to his attitude being 'supported by the Ministers for Home Affairs and Defence' was the 'bare announcement of a "split" ... calculated to open the doors to centrifugal tendencies, to personal loyalties and personal animosities'. The following day, a week before the Dáil debate began, the most important military unit spoke out against the Treaty. The brigadiers of the 1st Southern Division met in Cork on 10 December and resolved that 'the Treaty as it is drafted is not acceptable to us ... and we urge its rejection by the Government.'

This was a serious threat, which the IRA leadership in Dublin moved to neutralize. De Valera had already instructed the army that it 'was the instrument of the Civil Gov[ernment] and must obey the decision of the Dáil'. He 'would not discuss Army Opinion'.[7] (This suggests he may have thought at first that it might not go his way.) Béaslaí echoed this directly in an *An tÓglaċ* editorial on 16 December: 'The Army is the servant of the Nation and will obey the national will expressed by the chosen representatives of the people and expressed through the proper military channels.' Whatever that national decision was, it would be accepted 'in the true spirit of disciplined soldiers'. It was fairly clear what decision was expected. In Dublin on 13 December Liam de Roiste was surprised to find that 'practically all the military chiefs here, and certainly all those directing the operations of the last few years, except the Minister of [sic] Defence, are in favour of ratification of the Treaty.'[8]

The Dáil debate, starting with private sessions on 17 and 20 December, soon took a line that would decide the issue for many. At the first meeting, Seán MacEoin 'reported that he had five thousand Volunteers and ammunition enough to last only seven minutes of hard fighting'. He went as far as to say, 'if England goes to war again she will wipe all out'; and when the people realized that the Volunteers could not defend them, it would be all over. Eoin O'Duffy, weighing the IRA's improved discipline against its still inadequate equipment, concluded that it could not drive out the enemy. MacEoin, Béaslaí, Seán Hales and others drew attention to the dangerously changed intelligence situation. At the second meeting, 'All the officers of GHQ who were members of the Dáil, and several who held commands in the country,' Béaslaí wrote, 'agreed that a return to the war conditions, which prevailed before the Truce, was out of the question.' 'Most of the commandants throughout the country made a report of their fighting strength,' Batt O'Connor told his sister. Nearly all were discouraging. (O'Connor said he could 'go on and fill up this whole page [with] reports from the fighting men[;] they all realised the resources of the country could not stand another year of war'.)[9]

Next day Mulcahy issued one of his beloved memoranda, insisting that the army must stay out of politics. 'The Army is merely an instrument of policy in the State,' he began: 'as such it has no title to express opinion on public affairs.' It should, ideally, have no opinion. But 'contingencies arise in which it is expedient for the State to consult with Army heads.' This was clearly one of them, and there were 'certain questions the army was entitled and indeed duty bound to answer' (the questions were, it is also clear, his own). The first was 'do the Treaty provisions constitute a military menace by reason of the restrictions imposed?' Mulcahy's answer was brusque – 'they do not.' It may be said, he suggested, 'that by the provisions of the Treaty English armed occupation of Ireland comes to an end'. The second question was perhaps more crucial, and certainly more complicated – could the Republic achieve a better settlement by fighting on? Mulcahy sternly lectured his subordinates that 'when the State consults the Army Chiefs, the matter is very simple.' The chiefs 'have only to give their considered opinion as to whether the further objects can in fact be achieved'. If they could not, they 'must advise the State that such is the case, so that the State acts with its eyes wide open'.

Mulcahy's answer here was again definite: even recognizing 'the greater preparedness of the Army as compared to five months ago', they could not. He hinted that this increased military efficiency might be 'counterbalanced by a different attitude of the civil population' (though this was 'an imponderable quantity in any case'). But the real issue was purely military: 'it is evident that the improved power of the Army falls short of that required for a military decision.' Anticipating his much quoted speech in the Dáil debate the following day, he insisted that 'the English could not be driven into the sea, nor even expelled from their fortified centres.' In short, acceptance of the Treaty was 'a quicker way to complete independence' than was rejection of it. To this highly political analysis he added a psychological one which must have been designed to counter the invocation of the republican dead already in full swing on the side of those opposed to the Treaty: 'Any good Irishman, if assured that by dying he would secure for Ireland the benefits included in the Treaty would have died without hesitation.'[10]

'IN ONE YEAR OR TEN IRELAND WILL REGAIN THAT FREEDOM WHICH IS HER DESTINY'

In the first Dáil public sessions, in the council chamber of University College, Dublin, on 19–22 December, the shape of the debate emerged. As people began to grasp the scale of the impending split, many attributed it to deeply opposed attitudes. Frank O'Connor would speak of 'two worlds, two philosophies, running in very doubtful harness' long before the Treaty. He instanced the mismatch between Michael Collins and Terence MacSwiney: 'hard sense and warm humanity' versus 'a fervid nobility' (to the point of priggishness).[11] MacSwiney was gone, of course, but nobody – least of all his sister – could doubt what side he would have taken. For those against the Treaty, the split set principle against compromise; for supporters ('Treatyites' as they were immediately labelled) it pitted reality against fantasy. One Treatyite would identify a 'Scientific Spirit' – accepting doubt – struggling against the 'Romantic Spirit' – cleaving to 'certitude'. (The latter 'start off with a castle in the air, and end up minus two damn fine public buildings'.)[12]

Many neutrals have diagnosed a conflict of idealism against realism, and some participants certainly adopted such roles. Seán MacEoin was an explicit realist: 'To me, symbols, recognitions, shadows, have very little meaning.' What counted for him was that the Treaty would give him 'my own army'. Piaras Béaslaí insisted that 'the bullets and bayonets of the British government' could not be 'conjured away by the repeating of some magic phrases'. He set out what now became the official GHQ interpretation of IRA strategy: 'The reason why we found it necessary to send out our young men half-armed, half-equipped to attack the enemy was not because we hoped to drive him from our country by force of arms – we were not such fools.' The 'true motive' of the war had been 'simply to break down that prestige which the enemy derived from his unquestioned superior force'. Most of those who supported (or accepted) the Treaty took the line that the Volunteers had effectively reached their military limit by 1921. Mulcahy, in ramming this point home, went as far as to say that far from winning 'We have suffered a defeat.'

Some 'anti-Treatyites' may have been 'such fools' as to believe that the IRA could physically drive out the British; others no doubt believed that it remained capable of pushing the process of psychological attrition further. But, for most of them, principle did seem to outweigh pragmatism. Mulcahy's suggestion that 'any good' Volunteer would have accepted the gains secured through the Treaty was rejected. Dan Breen, hearing that Seán MacEoin had said that the Treaty gave him and his comrades what they had fought for, angrily declared, 'I would never have handled a gun or fired a shot . . . to obtain this Treaty.' As so many did, he invoked dead comrades to ram home his point; writing on 'the second anniversary of Martin Savage's death', he asked, 'do you suppose that he sacrificed his life in attempting to kill one British Governor-General in order to make room for another British Governor-General?'[13] The fact that to him a governor general evidently was no different from a viceroy showed how little bearing constitutional provisions had on the republican imagination.

But in the middle, positions were more complicated, or less coherent. Frank Aiken recalled going to a *ceilidhe* in Clones to meet Eoin O'Duffy, 'hoping in a vague way that he might have some explanations to give'. In the presence of Joe McKelvey, Seán MacEoin and several other high-ranking officers, O'Duffy 'assured us with great vehemence that the signing of the Treaty was only a trick'. He would never take the oath, and nobody would have to take it. GHQ had only approved the Treaty 'in order to get arms to continue the fight'. In the same breath, though, O'Duffy fired off a more divisive salvo: 'there are people who are now calling Mick Collins a traitor who were "under the bed" when there was fighting to be done.' This, as Aiken noted, was 'the first time I remember hearing the "under the bed" phrase: alas, it wasn't the last!' Aiken's own reaction to the Treaty was 'instinctively' different. To him, it was 'wrong, and if it were allowed to come into operation it would be an obstacle instead of an aid to independence'. This was because of 'the type of men who would work it' – a warning that Aiken would sound again over the following weeks.[14]

As a northerner, Aiken was bound to see the Treaty – above all its acceptance of partition – as unsatisfactory. But unlike many anti-Treatyites he recognized that the long delay of the Truce had weakened the republican position ('if it had been possible to have had the crisis about two months after the truce, Britain would have got a very different answer to the "Treaty" or "War" proposition'). He also refused to brand the signatories as traitors – this was not just 'untrue' but, perhaps more importantly, 'unwise'. He even argued that public acceptance of the Treaty was 'due, in a large measure, to some people of the Republican side failing to rise above the bitter "you have let us down" attitude'.[15]

On 12 December Liam Lynch wrote to his brother that fighting for the Republic meant not voluntarily accepting being part of the British Empire. But he seemed to think that the Treaty might be worked – 'if we must temporarily accept the treaty there is scarcely another lap to freedom and we will certainly knock her off next time.'[16] But in the new year, his position hardened and the military reaction became increasingly outspoken. Lynch indicated the battle front to Mulcahy on 4 January 1922, writing that his officers and men 'realise that the Government, GHQ Staff and the Army in the rest of Ireland outside the Southern Divisions and the Dublin Brigade have outrageously let them down'. When the Free State came into existence, discipline would 'I have grave fears . . . be hard to maintain'; this would be GHQ's responsibility. Two days later he issued a barely veiled ultimatum to the Chief of Staff. 'It is with deep regret that I have to acquaint you that while at all times I shall do my utmost to carry out your orders, maintain general discipline and above all insist on Truce being maintained, I cannot carry out any order against IRA principles . . . when such principles stand the danger of being given away by our unthankful Government.'

Not all opponents of the Treaty took their stand purely on abstract principle. Liam Mellows contended that 'the Republic does exist.' It was not just an aspiration or an ideal but 'a living and tangible thing'. (Lynch told his brother somewhat gnomically, 'we can scarcely realise what a fine country Ireland will be when freedom comes.') And Griffith's practical arguments may well have meant little even to some supporters of the Treaty. The most persuasive idea was probably Collins's 'stepping stone argument', which deftly preserved the ideal ultimate 'freedom to which all nations aspire', while offering the immediate attraction of seeing the back of the British army. As Seán Hales of Cork put it in the Dáil, 'it is to be a jumping off point' – 'in one year or in ten years, Ireland will regain that freedom which is her destiny and no man can bar it.' Collins seems to have gone further in private, telling Hales (the most important Treaty supporter in Cork apart from Collins himself), 'the British broke the Treaty of Limerick [which ended the Jacobite war in 1691], and we'll break this Treaty too when it suits us, when we have our own army.'[17]

Alongside the kind of otherness that has led some to paint republicanism as 'quasi-millenarian', even suggesting that 'the cult of the Republic stands in for the kingdom of Christ,' we can see disagreements that do not look to have stemmed from a clash of principles. Most republicans read the Treaty in a way that was neither idealist nor realist; they saw the abandonment of republican symbolism as straightforward subjugation to imperial power. In their view the Treaty absolutely

negated national self-determination, and every argument made by separatists for it. It threw Ireland back to the status of a British colony.[18] De
Valera's angry charge that by accepting the Treaty the Irish people
would 'voluntarily abandon their independence and the republican
form of government which enshrined it' not only maintained the republican assertion that Ireland had actually achieved independence in 1919,
it equated the idea of the republic with the idea of national freedom.

This was what many republicans needed to hear, but it was a crude
characterization, certainly by de Valera's standards, and he himself had
already taken a more nuanced line. His argument for external association, which would clearly have modified the absolute legal sovereignty
of the Irish state, was that it would preserve the substance of independence. So the real argument was not about absolute independence against
subjection, but about determining the minimal criteria for 'substantial'
independence. In this argument, elements of the Treaty such as the British naval bases probably weighed as heavily with republicans as the
oath of allegiance itself. The reading of their significance ultimately
rested on conflicting expectations of British behaviour. Would Britain
exercise the power that was implicit in the Treaty relationship, or had
that historical phase passed? The Treatyites perhaps sensed – before the
British themselves did – that in future the crude assertion of old-
fashioned 'hard' power would be in decline. Collins himself, speaking
on 19 December 1921 ('the worst day I ever spent in my life', as he told
his fiancée Kitty Kiernan), identified the underlying shift of power relations that the settlement represented as its key point. 'They have made a
greater concession than we. They have given up their age-long attempt
to dominate us.' This perception was as vital as his famous assertion
that the Treaty gave freedom – not the 'ultimate freedom' but the 'freedom to achieve that end'.

We probably get as close as we can to grasping the contingent process by which individuals made up their minds in Liam Archer's account
of his meeting with Rory O'Connor just after the Treaty was signed.
O'Connor told Archer, a fellow 1916 veteran – and fellow corporation
employee – 'Oh, we must work it for all it's worth,' but added, 'if I could
get enough to support me I would oppose it wholeheartedly.' Many
took the same line, waiting to see how others reacted. The two eventually went opposite ways; as he 'saw the situation deteriorate', Archer
'realised' that O'Connor was aiming to create a situation where the

British would 'return in force for the purpose of establishing "Law and Order" and we would be plunged into complete submission or complete anarchy'. He made up his mind to take the Treaty side.[19]

Those who argued for the Treaty were on the back foot on the point of principle, but they countered by setting what Griffith called in his fierce concluding speech the 'living Irish nation' against abstract ideals that would consign the nation to 'the dead past or the prophetic future'. Béaslaí also pleaded for 'the lives and happiness of the people' against 'sophistries and legal quibbles', but he went further, claiming faith and dreams for his own side. He turned the moral tables by accusing the rejectionists of lacking 'faith in the nation', and shrewdly suggested that their idealism would resist any concrete form. 'Many of us ... bred in this hateful atmosphere of foreign occupation ... eternally struggling against it, have never visualised freedom ... They have not dreamed of the great work of national reconstruction.' Mulcahy used his military expertise to insist on the limits of what could be achieved by fighting, but also found a resonant metaphor in holding that the Treaty formed the only available 'solid spot of ground on which the Irish people can put its political feet'.

THE TRUCE CHRISTMAS

Shot through though it was with anguished soul-searching, the intellectual quality of the Treaty debate has never been much admired. The number of deputies who were swayed by the long-drawn-out sequence of often repetitive assertions and denials can only be guessed at. For many, a stronger influence than the formal debate seems to have been the gelling of opinion during the Christmas recess. Public support for the agreement became more assertive; Harry Boland was one of many who 'had to contend with a chorus of approval' for the Treaty from his constituents.[20] Collins's opponents later accused him of political motives in proposing the adjournment: Macardle suggested that 'had the vote been taken on December 22nd the Treaty would probably have been rejected.' But with over fifty deputies indicating their wish to speak in the debate, it is hard to see what alternative there was, unless the Dáil was to sit through Christmas. This is indeed what Mary MacSwiney urged. It seems, though, that she did not fear the influence of public opinion as much as that of the IRB. But a massive pro-Treaty movement quickly took shape, perhaps appearing even bigger than it was. 'Small miscellaneous groups which assembled to pass resolutions in favour of the Treaty were reported by the Press as important representative gatherings. Public bodies which showed a majority for acceptance were reported as favouring it "unanimously". Letters supporting it were published at full length . . .'[21] Todd Andrews found his college lecturers organizing weekly soirees 'where the evenings were spent denigrating de Valera'.

Public opinion, in 1922, effectively meant press opinion: ordinary people's views emerged only indirectly. The Irish press was not entirely one-sided, but positive endorsement of the Treaty seemed to emerge much quicker than criticism. In Sligo, while the Redmondite *Sligo Champion* hailed the Treaty on 10 December in a long editorial under the title 'Peace' – 'thus ends the long period of misrule and oppression . . . which began . . . in 1172' – the republican *Connachtman* withheld judgment, waiting a week before 'reaffirm[ing] our allegiance' to 'the Republic founded by Pearse at Eastertide 1916'.[22] By that time the national *Freeman's Journal* was suggesting that people in the midlands and west were 'astonished to find a minority in Dublin opposed to harvesting the fruits of the struggle', and referring to the Treaty as 'the Treaty of Independence'.[23] The pro-Treaty press was assiduous in finding supporters of the settlement. On the other side, while many IRA leaders who would come out against the Treaty were chairmen of local councils, they did not try to use them as a public platform.

The Church weighed in with some enthusiasm. As early as August 1921 the Bishop of Killaloe had urged on Collins that 'the people feel that there is in the British proposals something very substantial to negotiate & work upon,' and warned that 'a war of devastation without the good will of the people behind it would be a ruinous disaster.'[24] Immediately after the Treaty had been signed, the Bishop of Cork ordered a series of thanksgiving masses in his diocese. When the Hierarchy met on 13 December, the overwhelming majority approved the Treaty, though the minority ensured that its public statement was neutral. Cardinal Logue held that there was not 'a man alive who ever expected that such favourable terms could be squeezed out of the British government in our time'.[25] Bishop Michael Fogarty was sure that 'the great bulk of the nation want acceptance,' and briskly dismissed the republicans' argument about 'surrendering their birthright' – 'they know their own minds. They have no idea of surrendering any right.'[26] Some clergy seem to have been reluctant to take sides. One parish priest, who wrote to Tom Maguire at Christmas urging him at least to abstain if he could not support the Treaty, admitted that he had been forced to write by his Archbishop. (A second priest, though, wrote to Maguire more aggressively on the issue.)[27] In Sligo, local priests kept fairly quiet until the Lenten pastorals of late February 1922, when the Bishop of Killala urged 'all classes and sections of the people' to give 'the most generous assistance and cordial co-operation' to the Provisional Government, which had by then been in existence for several weeks. The Bishop of Elphin talked of the 'nation's resurrection' (after its 'crucifixion' over the last six years), and urged – uncontroversially enough – that a 'period of national unity and peaceful activity is now essential'.[28]

Republicans detected a great conspiracy to 'stampede the people into a panic-stricken terror of rejection, a blind clamour for surrender', but there were simpler reasons why ordinary people might accept the Treaty. Memories of the grim events of December 1920 were sharp enough to point up the attractions of a normal Christmas. In Seán Moylan's home town the previous Christmas, for instance, an old man had been shot by a stray bullet through the window of his bedroom; now (as Moylan's grandson notes) 'the atmosphere was lighter, less fearful and more hopeful'.[29]

The republican view of public opinion was and remained generally dismissive. Some tried to ignore it, but most merely discounted it. Boland made a point of stressing the weight of the public pressure on him to vote for the Treaty, before declaring that he would not bow to it.[30] The most explicit justification of this position was de Valera's celebrated assertion that 'the people had no right to do wrong'. But the shift in opinion restricted the political options available to him. He told McGarrity in late December that he had 'been tempted several times to take drastic action, as I would be entitled to legally', without specifying what it might have been (perhaps arresting the signatories on their return from London, which some Volunteer leaders urged). Significantly, though, he said that 'the army is divided and the people wouldn't stand for it.' (Todd Andrews admitted that for the IRA to have arrested Collins at that point would have been 'like Tibetan monks arresting the Dalai Lama'.)[31]

By the end of the recess, verbal violence was becoming more personal. Just before the Dáil reconvened on 3 January 1922, the *Freeman's Journal* denounced de Valera as lacking the 'instinct of an Irishman in his blood' and Childers as a renegade Englishman. On the 6th, de Valera used the word 'crookedness' when he and Griffith clashed over de Valera's demand for a Dáil vote on his presidency. The full depth of the split was finally displayed on 7 January when Brugha, riled by Griffith's reference to Collins as 'the man who won the war' (a famous soubriquet of Lloyd George's), went as far as to suggest that Collins's military reputation was no more than a figment of the journalistic imagination. In a speech pulsating with icy fury he denounced this mere 'subordinate in the Department of Defence' as a self-publicist who had deliberately sought notoriety and had been built up by the press as a heroic 'romantic figure . . . such as this person certainly is not'. He dismissed Griffith with equal contempt, saying that if he had not signed up to the clause in the October 1917 Sinn Féin constitution stating that the party aimed 'to secure international recognition of Ireland as an independent Irish Republic', Griffith 'would not be now in public life any more than he was in 1916'.

When the final vote was taken that day, and the Treaty was approved by 64 to 57, Todd Andrews (who had persuaded the University College porters to let him watch the debate from a doorway of the council chamber) 'saw the mixture of triumph, grief and worry with which deputies received the result'. Worry may well have been the majority position, and with good reason. Opinions were unstable: the narrow pro-Treaty majority was actually reduced in the following vote on the presidency, which de Valera lost by a margin of only two. After that his supporters walked out of the Dáil, and the clash of ideas intensified. Republicans naturally cranked up their ideological labelling. Erskine Childers began to issue a twice-weekly news-sheet, the *Republic of Ireland*, subtitled *An Phoblacht na hÉireann*. (The lead title was not, interestingly, 'the Irish Republic': now Pearse's translation into Irish was back-translated.) Early in February de Valera launched a new party, Cumann na Poblachta. Behind its uncompromising republican title, its programme was aimed at finding some means of 'safeguarding the position of the Republic' while ensuring that the country remained 'governed peacefully'. Other leaders were more forthright. Frank Carty in Sligo told an anti-Treaty meeting at the end of February that 'we were elected as Republicans and not as Free Staters or Home Rulers.' The oath he had sworn was 'sacred and binding', and 'the spirit of the Republic is unconquerable.'[32]

The consensual tone of Cumann na Poblachta's programme was dramatically altered in March. As de Valera toured Munster, the mounting strain was beginning to tell: he seems, as during Easter Week, to have suffered a kind of nervous breakdown.[33] At Carrick-on-Suir on 14 March he was reported as warning that 'if the Treaty was not rejected, perhaps it was over the bodies of the young men he saw around him that day that the fight for Irish freedom may be fought.' At Thurles on the 17th he said that to complete the work of the last four years, 'to get Irish freedom', the Volunteers would now have to complete it 'over the dead bodies of their own countrymen'. At Killarney on the 18th he insisted that the Republic must exist, because some of the acts that had been performed in its name would have been immoral otherwise. 'Men and women were shot for helping the enemy, and there would be no justification for the shooting of these if the Republic did not exist.' He repeated still more emphatically that to achieve freedom the Volunteers would have to 'wade through Irish blood, the blood of the soldiers of the Irish Government, and, perhaps, the blood of some of the members of the Government'.[34] This could be seen either as incitement to violence or as an awful warning against it. His insistence that 'the people had no right to do wrong' was less ambiguous. It meant that the Republic could not be disestablished even by an overwhelming popular vote.

HUMAN STRUCTURES OF THE SPLIT

Personal attitudes, loyalties or – as Erhard Rumpf's pioneering social analysis put it – 'temperament' have been the commonest explanations of the choices people made. Rumpf thought it 'hard to believe that the bitter hostilities of 1922–3 sprang simply from the almost academic differences between the Treaty and Document No. 2'. But if the division over the Treaty was indeed largely 'a matter of temperament', then, as he said, analysis could proceed no further.[35] In fact, the differences between the Treaty and the imagined Republic were more than merely academic, but because the status of the Republic, and the nature of national 'freedom', had never been officially defined, the imagination of individuals had been given free rein. So personal outlook or 'temperament' clearly did play a part in their vision. Did it fit, or outweigh, objective qualities like their social status, age, gender, education and occupation?

The second Dáil was cruelly characterized by the veteran separatist P. S. O'Hegarty as 'a collection of mediocrities in the grip of a machine', leaving all its thinking to a handful of leaders.[36] A one-party assembly, the second Dáil was unrepresentative even of Sinn Féin itself, since it was dominated by the militant Volunteer side of the republican movement. Socially it was even less representative, with commercial, agricultural and industrial backgrounds swamped by professional and clerical ones. The slender Dáil majority in favour of the Treaty was certainly narrower than that in the country at large. Teachers – the biggest identifiable occupational group in the Dáil – divided eight–seven in favour of the Treaty. Among 1916 veteran TDs, twenty-three supported the Treaty, twenty-four opposed it. Local government people divided exactly fifty–fifty. The forty-seven IRB men, a hefty segment of the assembly that might have determined the result, also split surprisingly evenly, twenty-seven to twenty. Also surprisingly, for those who saw revolutionary ardour as an attribute of youth, the average age of Treaty supporters (just under thirty-eight) was lower than that of the irreconcilables (nearly forty-two).

Nine out of thirteen GHQ staff were in favour, eleven out of nineteen divisional staffs against, as were a substantial majority (70–80 per cent) of brigades. Florrie O'Donoghue made the point that the seven commanders who would sign the order to call the Army Convention in March 1922 – the decisive breach with the Provisional Government – 'represented' 71,250 officers and men, over 63 per cent of total IRA strength. But this was equally a geographical division – GHQ in Dublin was acutely conscious of the national weaknesses of the IRA, while the opposite view was taken by the most active divisions in the south-west; the less active north-east had most to lose from the Treaty.

Rumpf's work, first published in German in 1959, was a rare attempt at a systematic analysis of the split. Rumpf wanted to demonstrate that rejection of the Treaty could not be 'explained simply in terms of the attitude of a few IRA commandants' – a commendable aim, certainly, but surprisingly hard to achieve. A recent study of the civil war remarks that 'no scholar has convincingly argued that the conflict emerged out of objective social and political conditions.'[37] Few indeed have even tried. Rumpf saw the split as coinciding with a wider line of social division which he called 'the west–east gradient'. The small farmers of the west 'owed the preservation of their traditional Gaelic outlook to a remote situation and economic backwardness'.[38] Rumpf made a larger claim, that the intensity of the 'national struggle' of 1919–21 created a pattern for the anti-Treaty struggle: 'anti-British and subsequent anti-Treaty activity went together,' in fact, indicating that 'the animosities developed during the earlier campaign produced a deep-rooted spirit of intransigence' in the most active areas. The statistics he used to plot the intensity of armed action were fairly crude, however, and he did not resolve the problem that some of the most intransigent anti-Treaty areas had not been in the forefront of the 'national struggle'. Kerry and Mayo, with their erratic military performance, had almost troubled Mulcahy more than they had the British. Their resistance to the Treaty stemmed, perhaps, more from pre-political hostility to government than from political principle.

Were women especially likely to stay loyal to the Republic? Certainly all six of the women TDs voted against the Treaty, and it struck many people that the majority of active nationalist women took the anti-Treaty side. Jennie Wyse Power saw her former colleagues as 'running wild', and thought Mary MacSwiney's influence Rasputin-like. She was stung by their immediate recourse to personal attacks – they were 'very free in their criticisms' – a tendency noticed by many others.[39] To Batt O'Connor, 'the women are "holy terrors", mud-slinging and name-calling'. P. S. O'Hegarty's complaint that 'women jumped to conclusions without any consideration whatever, save their emotions' may look like crude stereotyping. But the most vocal women did seem disinclined to debate the practical merits of the Treaty. The first woman to speak in the Dáil debate, Kathleen O'Callaghan, declared that to her the issue was simply one of 'principle, a matter of conscience, and a matter of right and wrong'. And women did use particularly emotional language: one Cumann na mBan member recalled the movement 'speaking with one clear and emphatic voice rejecting the Treaty of surrender and all that its evil and unnatural clauses stood for, when the people of Ireland staggered under the foul threat of utter extermination'.[40] It seems likely that such intense emotionalism exerted some pressure on men. One English journalist plausibly portrayed the Dáil Cabinet in August 'quailing . . .

before the accusing forefinger of Miss MacSwiney'.[41] Her two-and-three-quarter-hour 'tirade' during the Treaty debate echoed with words like 'dishonour', 'surrender' and 'betrayal'.

Cumann na mBan was the first separatist group to mobilize against the Treaty: they were the only organization demonstrating outside University College on Earlsfort Terrace in December. Wyse Power complained that the Dublin branches had been posting anti-Treaty bills around the streets even before the organization had officially taken up any position on the issue. They went on to circulate all branches to urge them to do all they could to 'secure the adherence of every Sinn Féin Cumann and Comhairle Ceanntair for the Irish Republic' at the upcoming Sinn Féin Ard-fheis. Cumann na mBan's own Special Convention, called for 28 January but postponed until 5 February so that Markievicz could attend, was actually convened in the name of the Republic. In mid-January the Executive publicly 'reaffirmed' its allegiance to the Irish Republic and declared that it could not 'support the Articles of Treaty signed in London'.[42] It seems likely that most of the rank-and-file membership of Cumann na mBan were in favour of the Treaty. Markievicz and MacSwiney, however, were determined to place the organization in the republican vanguard.[43] At the Special Convention (the delaying of which seems to have caused the absence of many pro-Treaty delegates – perhaps deliberately) the organization's leadership was purged.[44] Markievicz was elected president, and after a motion to support the Treaty had been rejected by 419 votes to 63, pro-Treaty members were, as Macardle delicately puts it, 'requested to resign'.[45]

Women's prominence in the anti-Treaty resistance became, if anything, more marked as that resistance became more uncompromising and, ultimately, violent. Ernie O'Malley noted the contrast between the 'Tan war', when 'the girls had always helped but had never sufficient status', and the onset of hostilities in 1922. 'Now they were our comrades': 'loyal, willing and incorruptible'; 'indefatigable, they put the men to shame by their individual zeal and initiative.' (Here, though, in the word 'individual' lurked a critique of the whole anti-Treaty movement: collectively, initiative and indefatigability were in short supply.) Even so, their role remained essentially what it had been in the Tan war: carrying dispatches, supplying food and clothing, and (as at Clonmel, for instance) 'assisting in every possible way' – short of actually fighting.[46]

'OUR CIVIL SERVICES HAVE SIMPLY PLAYED AT GOVERNING A REPUBLIC'

Had the 'band of brothers' at GHQ already, as some republicans believed, admitted defeat long before the Treaty was signed? The suggestion sometimes made that no military plans were prepared for a renewal of hostilities, if the negotiations broke down, might be taken to support this. In fact, GHQ did contemplate a second phase of the war. One staff memorandum, on 'Divisional Offensives', echoed the original reasoning for the creation of divisions. 'Upon the resumption of hostilities it is best to have the Division the operative unit'; each 'should be self-centred and capable of carrying out a vigorous offensive by itself'. They should 'seize and retain the initiative'. Decentralization of command would be 'the keynote of future successful operations'. The GHQ perspective was clear – 'if the divisions fail in their part, too much work will fall on GHQ.' 'If each division acts dependable [sic] then GHQ will be able to deploy them in mutual support.'[47] At local level, there were plans to carry on as before – 'to mine roads at suitable ambush positions and to prepare bridges on all roads for demolition by explosive charges' so that 'our columns could take the initiative at short notice'.[48]

A second memo, produced in late November by the Director of Training, Emmet Dalton, assessed the operational prospects on termination of the Truce, but it focused primarily on likely British action. The brother of the Squad's Charlie Dalton, and a former officer in the Dublin Fusiliers (who had been beside Tom Kettle when he was killed in France, and presumably mentioned this often, since he was apparently nicknamed 'Ginchy'), Dalton was the only member of the staff with direct experience of front-line fighting in the war. He seems to have been the author of another paper discussing the likely struggle for public support if war was renewed. Suggesting that the destruction of the British administrative departments in the Custom House had 'never received the attention it deserved', it argued for much more concerted action against the enemy civil administration. But this argument turned into a lacerating critique of the republican civil administration itself, which needed a 'complete overhaul'. If there was to be 'a sort of national call to arms' in the next round, 'the Nation cannot be fairly asked to rally to institutions that have not stood the very moderate tests to which they have been subjected.' The government 'must give the Nation a lead', but had not done so. 'No single Government Department has been the slightest assistance to the Army and some of them have been a serious drag.' If they could not function 'standing on their own legs', they should abdicate. 'The Army can no longer afford to dissipate its energy in bolstering up any Civil Department without getting a return in kind.'[49]

Dalton considered that the only department 'pulling its weight' was Publicity. (This in itself formed a striking contrast with Liam Lynch's view that 'the press has ruined the country', and that 'it is the action of Fitzgerald [sic] and his type that has brought us to our present position'.)[50] The task of the Local Government Department, by contrast, had 'never been tackled', even though it was 'simple enough'. It had only to 'order its permanent officials to have no dealings with the Enemy departments – and dismiss them if they disobey'. Instead of which it had been swayed by 'stupid' humanitarian considerations of not throwing men out of work. Home Affairs was if anything worse: the judiciary had 'yielded to the first onset of the Enemy when he tried to overthrow our Civil Administration'. Yet 'these officials might without any personal risk have stood up to the usurping Government, and if not technically effective might at least have had some propagandist value.' The arbitration system could have been maintained over 'considerable stretches of the country', and 'the way in which these activities lapsed is thoroughly discreditable.' The conclusion was stark: 'The plain fact is that our Civil Services have simply played at governing a republic.' They had merely developed all the vices of functionaries. 'The calm way our Officials regard their interests as vested for good and all would be laughable if it were not criminal.' In future, ineffective officials must be sacked – after all, inadequate army officers were 'dismissed every week'.[51]

This withering indictment offers a rather different perspective on GHQ's 'defeatism', if such it was. Most of the arguments then and since have turned on the IRA's military capacity to withstand and counter a new British offensive. The republican administration's effectiveness had generally been taken at its own evaluation; but – even with due allowance for the difficulties it operated under – it might clearly be open to question.

THE BROTHERHOOD

For most of the previous seventy years or so, it would have been assumed by separatists – and probably nationalists in general – that the IRB would play a central part in deciding whether any political settlement met republican demands. Since 1916 its position had, as we have seen, become less central; and if de Valera and Brugha had had their way, it would have been marginalized if not cast aside entirely. But it had not. The organization still existed, and the ghost of the old IRB principle that its Supreme Council was the provisional government of the Republic still walked. Since 1916 the Council had contained many pivotal figures in the republican leadership, among them Collins himself (who was president in 1921), Richard Mulcahy, Diarmuid O'Hegarty, Austin Stack and Gearoid O'Sullivan, as well as provincial leaders like Liam Lynch. (O'Sullivan, IRB Centre for Leinster as well as Adjutant General of the IRA, typified the knit.) In late 1921 Seán Ó Muirthile was its secretary and Eoin O'Duffy its treasurer. Collins's position was exceptional, not only because of his key role in the republican administration. It may be that 'in the back of many people's minds he was the Young Pretender to a semi-imaginary throne.'[52] He seems still to have believed in the brotherhood's centrality. Mulcahy thought he saw it as more significant than Sinn Féin and even the IRA. Others thought he valued it as an instrument of his personal power.[53]

Even before the Anglo-Irish negotiations began, the IRB was manoeuvring around their likely outcome. Frank Henderson was sent by Gearoid O'Sullivan to Wexford at the August bank holiday, to take the IRB Circles 'a message from the Supreme Council'. This was a warning that the negotiations 'might possibly conclude with an offer ... of a compromise which could not be accepted by the Republicans, but which would be so tempting that there would be a great danger of its acceptance being advocated by many influential people'. At this point, evidently, the Supreme Council saw itself as standing out against compromise. Who were the influential people it was worrying about? Interestingly, Henderson was told that he would be on the same train as Cathal Brugha, 'and that I was to avoid him'. This was the first disturbing indication he had of 'a serious estrangement between the chiefs'.[54]

The Supreme Council met on 3 December 1921 to discuss the draft Treaty, at the same time as the Dáil Cabinet – where of course Collins was. Without its president, it debated the form of the oath – arguing for the demotion rather than the removal of the King from it – and partition, which it rejected absolutely. Ó Muirthile met up with Collins as he boarded the ferry back to England that evening and briefed him on the discussion. When the Council met again on 10 December, it seemed to think that the final form of the oath was acceptable, even while it noted the survival of partition. In spite of this, a majority appeared ready to give the Treaty a trial. Liam Lynch's fierce opposition forced the Council to adopt a neutral position, but Ó Muirthile contrived to issue a note (dated 12 December) to TDs who were members of the brotherhood, reporting that the Council had decided that the Treaty should be ratified. Individual deputies were, however, left free to vote as they thought best. Though the note adduced, plausibly enough, the old IRB policy of making use of any instruments likely to lead to independence, the Council's tergiversations fatally damaged the organization's tradition of absolute obedience – as the rider to its decision recognized.

Some IRB men certainly followed the Supreme Council's lead: Seamus McKenna, who was still 'undecided' in March, finally took the advice of 'the man whom we regarded as our Republican father', a member of the Supreme Council. He was 'sure that many other IRB men accepted the ill-fated Treaty on the advice of their officers'. Many, though, did not. The moment Tom Maguire arrived in Dublin on 13 December he was met in the hallway of his hotel by his superior in the IRB and told that the senior officers supported the Treaty. But Maguire, no doubt like many others, had 'never had much to do with' the organization, and had little respect for his superior. He ignored him.[55]

Three days after the ratification vote in the Dáil, the IRB held an unprecedented meeting of provincial Centres with the Supreme Council, which showed that it was as deeply riven as the rest of the country. Most of the Centres, unsurprisingly, were against the Treaty.[56] It is clear that the members of the Supreme Council wanted to head off the looming split: hence the December compromise, which kept the organization nominally united. Mary MacSwiney insisted that without the IRB's influence hardly 5 per cent of the Dáil would have accepted the Treaty. Brugha stridently declared that the IRB had been 'prostituted in order to disestablish the Republic'.[57] Others were more sceptical, dismissing the brotherhood as 'semi-moribund' by the time of the Truce. Certainly, under the pressure of disagreement over the Treaty, the venerable organization steadily disintegrated. O'Donoghue paints a fine picture of the three extraordinary IRB conferences held in Dublin in early 1922 in the hope of keeping the organization together. The leading lights, Collins and Lynch, 'admiring and respecting each other, but each apparently immovable in his convictions, wrestled with the grim threat of disunity'. Even though 'each was aware that it had been our fatal weakness in the past,' and was 'impressed by the appalling fear that it might be our undoing again', they could not reconcile their divergent analyses.

Here, as in the wider debate, the belief that the Treaty delivered the substance of freedom ran up against the belief that 'for the first time in our history the people would have, by their own deliberate act, accepted foreign domination.' Assessments of republican military capacity were likewise poles apart. Where Mulcahy frankly acknowledged 'a defeat', the opponents of the Treaty thought that 'we were not beaten in the field; we were in a better position to continue the struggle than at any time since 1916.'[58] To Collins and Mulcahy, even if this were true, it was simply not the point. Nor was it, in the end, for their opponents: 'above all,' as O'Donoghue said, 'members of this organisation had bound themselves on oath to maintain and defend the Republic.' The organization's ultimate failure can be seen in the fact that by the time of the last of these unprecedented conferences, at 41 Parnell Square on 19 April, the anti-Treaty IRA had already begun military action by occupying the Four Courts, a hulking structure on the River Liffey's north bank which housed the Irish high court as well as a mass of government archives.

THE 'YEAR OF DISAPPEARANCES'

The self-image of the IRA as a military force, and of its members as soldiers, had been crucial to its performance in the fight against Britain, and it is hardly surprising that – as with all nationalist movements – an overwhelmingly positive picture of the struggle for independence passed into public memory. The failure of generally inept British efforts to brand the Volunteers as thugs, criminals and terrorists proved a long-lasting one. Such dark deeds as were done were widely assumed, not just in Ireland, to have been carried out by the thugs and terrorists of the Black and Tans. That there might have been a seamy side to revolutionary violence itself was not something to be dwelt on by subsequent generations. More recently, though, it has begun to be uncovered. The process was, somewhat surprisingly, begun by the Provisional IRA, reacting against suggestions – common in the 1970s – that its operations were morally inferior to the military campaign of the 'old IRA'. The British charge of terrorism was sticking to those who claimed to be the Volunteers' lineal successors. *The Good Old IRA*, a pamphlet published by Sinn Féin in 1985, painted an unfamiliar picture of the war of independence. It provided details of the killing of dozens of ex-soldiers as alleged informers, many killings of unarmed police and soldiers, and cases of civilians – women and children included – killed in crossfire during IRA fights. Sinn Féin accepted – in fact clearly hoped – that these details would be 'shocking revelations to those who have a romantic notion of the past'.[59] Even though the pamphlet specifically targeted 'hypocritical revisionists', its content actually looked remarkably like the so-called historical 'revisionism' that was taking shape at the time.

But this new academic history has gone much further in exploring the darker side of the 'good old IRA'. It has produced even more 'shocking revelations', above all that some of the IRA's victims were killed for sectarian rather than political reasons. The most notorious case, the so-called 'Bandon Valley massacre', occurred in April 1922. On 27 April, James Buttimer of Dunmanway was awoken in the middle of the night, and shot in the face when he came to his door. Two other men living in the town's main street suffered the same fate. As one of them, a chemist by the name of David Gray, was shot, his wife heard the killers say, 'Take that, you Free Stater.' Over the following nights, a total of ten men were killed and another wounded. All of them were Protestants. 'The spectre of mass murder', wrote the historian Peter Hart in his reconstruction of the events, 'had long haunted the unionist political imagination; when it arrived, the reality struck with the force of a nightmare.' Hundreds of Protestants now went into hiding or fled their homes as a wave of panic swept through West Cork.[60]

The title of Hart's chapter on the killings, 'Taking it out on the Protestants', spelt out his view that their motive was not 'military', like the executions of 'spies and informers', but sectarian. The killings were carried out by 'committed republicans', members of the anti-Treaty IRA, probably acting on their own initiative but 'with the connivance or acquiescence of local units', which 'must have known what was happening'. The victims 'were shot because they were Protestants': precisely because they were loyalists, they could not have been informers, since they would have had no information. This was borne out by the remark in the British army's 'Record of the Rebellion in Ireland' that Protestants in the south 'rarely gave much information because, except by chance, they had not got it to give'. Indeed Hart held that in the conflict as a whole, 'the great majority of actual informants were never suspected or punished; [and] most of those shot (or denounced, expelled, or burned out of their homes) never informed.'

Hart's arguments have proved highly contentious, and his work has become the subject of a protracted and sometimes bitter dispute unique in recent Irish history-writing. Under a scrutiny more intense than most history books ever experience, some flaws in Hart's use of evidence emerged. An early critic pointed out that the general remark about southern Protestants in the *Record* had been followed by a proviso, which Hart did not quote: 'An exception to this rule was in the Bandon area where there were many Protestant farmers who gave information . . . it proved almost impossible to protect these brave men, many of whom were murdered . . .' Since the *Record* was compiled before April 1922, it cannot have been talking of the Bandon Valley massacre, but it was claimed to modify Hart's essential argument, and indeed to suggest to some that he was guilty of 'elision' – selective quotation (if not outright suppression of evidence).[61]

Some of Hart's critics have backed up their rejection of his argument by pointing to a resolution of the Protestant Convention that met in Dublin in May 1922, to the effect that 'hostility to Protestants by reason of their religion' in the twenty-six counties where they were a minority 'has been almost, if not wholly, unknown'. But there is a problem in taking this as unforced testimony. If Protestants had been subject to 'hostility', or even to what F. S. L. Lyons in a famous phrase called 'repressive tolerance', they would be more likely to play it down than emphasize it.[62] Other assertions, like Meda Ryan's that most if not all of those killed in April 1922 had informed on the IRA, or other republican assertions that the killings were carried out by a maverick IRA group, or by British intelligence agents (trying to provoke a sectarian war which would justify a British return), depend on unrecorded evidence – folk memory. Ryan bases her assessment on a document supposedly abandoned by K Company of the ADRIC when it left Dunmanway workhouse in 1922. Unfortunately this list of wanted IRA men and 'helpful citizens', despite being recognized as 'sensational' and carefully studied by several Cork IRA men, has not been preserved. In its absence, the most striking thing about interpretations like Ryan's is their assumption that those listed as 'helpful citizens' actually gave information to the police – precisely the point that Hart offered concrete evidence to dispute. (She calls it an 'informers' dossier'.) Her suggestion that the document 'confirmed the existence of a British Loyalist vigilante type organisation' called the Loyalist Action Group would seem to go well beyond even the evidence reportedly contained in the lost document.[63]

One initially uncontroversial element in Hart's account was his suggestion that the spate of killings was triggered by the death of Michael O'Neill, acting commandant of the Bandon battalion in a raid on a Protestant house in Ballygroman on the night of 26 April 1922, which ended in a miniature inferno when O'Neill's comrades returned to destroy the house and its occupants the next day. Recently, though, it has been pointed out that three British intelligence officers had been captured by the IRA about twelve hours before the Dunmanway shootings. (They were held by the Macroom battalion in the old RIC barracks, and shot on orders from Cork No. 1 Brigade.)[64] In all, seven British soldiers, two of them senior intelligence officers, were being held by the IRA during the 'massacre' before being executed, and the fact that Hart seemed to see no significance in this has been described as 'remarkable'. Indeed one of his critics asserts that this 'ahistorical' neglect of information has undermined not only Hart's work, but the entire Irish historical profession.[65] Hart has also been accused of 'marginalising' the role of the famously atheist Frank Busteed, whose participation in the killings would, for some, 'indicate a non-sectarian explanation' for them.

How far Hart's general contention that most of those killed as spies and informers had not given information will hold up remains open to question. His statistics, compiled from press reports, may well be adjusted by further research. It has been argued, as we have seen, that the intelligence system in Cork No. 1 Brigade was one of the best in the country, and had the capacity to identify informers with some accuracy. This argument may be extended to West Cork. We should note, though, that while John Borgonovo's research has been taken by some to 'directly contradict' Hart's argument, its conclusions are not entirely dissimilar. Trying to explain 'the high proportion of ex-servicemen shot in the city', Borgonovo suggested that the IRA 'probably found it easiest to assassinate isolated men of low social standing, rather than prominent pillars of the community, close associates, or members of Republican families'.[66]

The precise details of these grim events may forever remain murky, but the interpretation of what they signified is of real public importance. For Hart, the deaths represented 'the culmination of a long process of social definition' – the definition of who was and was not Irish. As another historian has put it, they 'momentarily exposed the embedded belief that Protestants as a community were outsiders and interlopers'; yet another has talked of 'the latent sectarianism of centuries of ballads and of landlordism' welling up in the killing of Protestants.[67] Republicans, on the other hand, have always denied such a view. In formal terms they have held to an essentially territorial definition of Irishness, deriving from the 'United Irish' vision of Wolfe Tone – 'Catholic, Protestant and Dissenter'. Tone's non-sectarian emphasis, of course, itself underlined the power of sectarianism and the threat it represented. The most explosive label in the dispute was not 'sectarian', however, but 'ethnic'. Hart's reference to 'campaigns of ethnic cleansing' sent out real shockwaves. One of his most persistent critics spoke of his 'making the then IRA seem capable of uninhibited ethnic rather than controlled military violence'.[68] ('Uninhibited' was a revealing addition to the debate.) On the other side, it has been suggested that 'Republicanism which has lived off and prospered from a false prospectus of non-sectarianism, has everything to lose if these killings are what they appear.'[69]

Hart was careful later to say 'we must not exaggerate': 'Cork was not Smyrna.' But merely setting 'Munster, Leinster and Connaught' alongside 'Silesia, Galicia and Bosnia' in the wide frame of the 'unmixing of peoples' was highly suggestive, especially as he invoked 'all of the nightmare images of ethnic conflict in the twentieth century' – 'the massacres and anonymous death squads, the burning homes and churches, the mass expulsions and trains filled with refugees, the transformation of lifelong neighbours into enemies, the conspiracy theories and the terminology of hatred'.[70] The fact that Hart linked the Volunteers with earlier, pre-political agrarian secret societies has allowed critics to charge him with espousing 'a wider narrative ... that presents the violence of Irish history as stemming from ancient sectarian hatreds', ignoring 'structural factors' such as the impact of British policy. This wider narrative was supposedly ideological – motivated by hostility to the violent activism of the Provisional IRA – and so was a kind of 'public history', different from neutral academic scholarship. It could be viewed as political propaganda, even if of a very subtle kind. The legitimacy that the IRA of the 1970s drew for its armed struggle from its Volunteer ancestry could be undermined if the original Volunteers' campaign were delegitimized.[71]

The issue of sectarian killing certainly touches a nerve in the public consciousness. While some have angrily repudiated Hart's image of the IRA, for others it has launched a painful re-examination of collective memory. Joseph O'Neill's *Blood-Dark Track*, a remarkable journey into the history of one family, skilfully links south Cork with the Turkish coastal city of Mersin.[72] The sense of a gradual (if still partial) lifting of a veil of silence pervades Gerard Murphy's *The Year of Disappearances*, a large-scale investigation of 'political killings' in Cork in 1921–2, presented as a personal journey of discovery into his community's history. Murphy, one of the many schoolboys who had 'marched dressed in Volunteer uniforms for the 50th anniversary of the 1916 Rising', found that the 'new perspective on the IRA' his inquiries revealed 'did not fit with the image of brave flying columns fighting impossible odds that we had celebrated in 1966'. 'It gradually began to dawn on me that the truth of the time had never been told.'[73] The truth, he says, is that dozens of men 'disappeared' in Cork in the year after the Truce, and were buried in 'killing fields' like the Rea, a few miles north-east of Cork city, and Carroll's Bogs just south of it (now the Cork Municipal Dump). Before being killed, many were held in a vaulted tomb in a cemetery at Knockraha, known as 'Sing Sing'.

The commandant of the 2nd Battalion of Cork No. 1 Brigade, Mick Murphy, told Ernie O'Malley, 'Every spy who was shot in Cork was buried so that nothing was known about them. They just disappeared.' Since only a quarter of the spies executed during the Anglo-Irish war disappeared, Gerard Murphy argues that this recollection 'is far more likely to apply to the period when the IRA was the sole authority in Cork during the spring and summer of 1922'.[74] The number can only be guessed at, and Murphy's guesses – 'up to 35' in total – have been dismissed by some as pure speculation. His suggestion that a primary role in the illegal killings (notably the killing of several boys) was played by

Florrie O'Donoghue and his wife Josephine, and that O'Donoghue used his skills as a historian to construct a cover-up, has shocked many to whom O'Donoghue represented the very model of the 'old IRA'. Murphy's rejection of the IRA's actions does not explicitly imply a rejection of its *casus belli*, but it can look that way – indeed it can be seen to raise 'big questions about the plausibility of the whole Republican interpretation of history'.

Technically, Murphy's approach invites some criticism, as it relies too often on drawing conclusions from coincidences and omissions. Hypotheses are turned into assumptions and then 'presented as factual statements'.[75] His methods, mixing archival research (some of it highly original) with the patient teasing out of local memories, do not convince those who argue not just that the IRA did not do such things, but also that such memories simply could not have been suppressed by whole communities for so long. Murphy's suggestion that 'the secrecy and censorship in place in Cork from February to the end of August 1922 makes a space in which it is possible for all kinds of people to have disappeared' is certainly tendentious. But his suggestion that for southern Protestants 'suppression was the price of survival' rings truer than the argument of those who hold that the failure of Protestant public bodies to protest against the killings proves that they did not happen.

The evidence for the situation of Protestants is mostly indirect rather than direct, but it can hardly be doubted that Protestants felt under threat and that there was often some reason for this. A few republicans were quite open in their view of what Kathleen Keyes McDonnell frankly identified as 'an alien community', the Protestant 'settlers'. 'More than three centuries after the foundation of Bandon, the descendants of the settlers fled before Irish wrath or fell to rebel bullets.'[76] The first action of Tom Barry and the West Cork brigadier Tom Hales when they rushed back to Cork from Dublin after the Dunmanway killings was to place guards on Protestant houses. The South Tipperary brigadier Seamus Robinson had to act to protect Mrs de Vere Hunt, a firm supporter of the Volunteers and reliable provider of hospitality. A 'stately and cultured lady', she was, as Robinson carefully put it, 'a non-catholic', and so 'suspected by the locals to be anti-national'. Robinson was asked to authorize a local Volunteer action to 'remove' the Hunts to get their land for 'division'. He was able to hand out a lecture on how the Volunteers 'should try to win these people rather than alienate them', but this was clearly news to 'the locals'. Likewise a republican police officer in Tipperary, a former flying-column man, recorded that 'many Protestant people' asked him for protection. They were naturally assured that 'they were going to get the protection of the Irish Republican Army and the Irish Republican Police'; but it must be considered significant that they needed it.[77]

HIBERNIA IRREDENTA

In the nationalists' view, sectarian violence was something that happened in the north, and they were its victims. That was largely undeniable, and the northern experience of the Truce was peculiar. It was, as the Belfast Volunteer commander Roger McCorley observed, an 'extraordinary' period. All through it, there was a 'state of affairs in which we had official relations with the RIC and British military and open warfare between ourselves and the Special Constabulary'. According to the Truce terms, 'we were supposed to have our arms in dumps or under strick [sic] supervision in training camps but it was perfectly obvious that this . . . was not being observed by us in Belfast'; the British seemed 'satisfied that it could not be observed while armed attacks were being made on us'.[78] The 'B Specials' became ever more active: 'things they never attempted to do before the Truce', Thomas Fitzpatrick said, 'they did during the Truce.' Seamus Woods, OC 3rd Northern Division and Belfast liaison officer, was instructed not to liaise with the police as they were under the control of the Northern Parliament. 'For some time previous to Xmas and up to the end of December the Catholic population of the city were subjected to continuous and murderous onslaughts from armed Orange gangs,' with 'both the police and the military' acting in conjunction with them. The provocative activity of the Specials and 'those of the old RIC who were connected with the "Murder Gang" during the war' was 'becoming daily more unbearable', and Woods thought liaison was a dead letter. 'Our position in this city is becoming one of fighting for existence with no hope of succeeding.'[79]

Northern nationalist opinion welcomed the Treaty, particularly in the border areas. In Lurgan, nationalist streets were 'decorated . . . with flags and bunting to celebrate the event'.[80] Seán MacEntee was asked to resign his seat by the South Monaghan Comhairle Ceanntair after voting against it. The Catholic Church in the north was firmly against de Valera.[81] The northern IRA also seems to have taken a broadly positive attitude to the Treaty. This was not because it shared Frank Aiken's nuanced assessment of the issues – in fact the men of his division did not. But it seems to have assumed that the partition part of it could never happen. In Belfast, many were simply indifferent to it – as was McCorley himself when Joe McKelvey telephoned from Dublin to tell him that the Treaty had been passed, and ask whether he should come out against it. McCorley said their position would be unchanged either way.[82] With weary resignation he noted that the Volunteers' 'normal wartime footing' returned in early 1922. In fact the Northern Ireland government instructed its security forces just a few days after the Treaty that any restrictions on the 'enforcement of the law' were forthwith cancelled, and that all liaison arrangements with 'the Sinn Féin authorities' would cease as of 1 January.[83]

A medical student at Queen's University in Belfast, Michael MacConaill, a member of 3rd Northern Division's 2nd Brigade, gave a vivid picture of what this meant. Working after hours at the Mater Hospital, he found that 'the mortality rates from gunshot wounds were unduly high' – thanks to delays in getting victims to hospital because of the difficulty ambulances had in entering or leaving conflict zones. 'Scenes which recalled those of the Place de la Guillotine in Paris took place almost daily at the gates of [the] Mater Hospital,' which was in a loyalist area. 'The women of the district used to gather with their knitting and await the arrival of the ambulances'; assuming that all the people brought in 'were Nationalists, in plain words, Catholics', they 'would cheer their arrival, jeer at the patients and often try to tear the clothes from them'. MacConaill felt that 'since a state akin to that of continuous trench warfare existed in Belfast for several years my duties exposed me to the same risks as that of a RAMC man on the Western Front.' He was deliberately fired on twice, and developed a technique for crossing dangerous roads, drawing fire by 'throwing a coat across a side street and then following quickly'.[84] At least this meant that (as McCorley noted) 'we had no difficulty in Belfast concerning wounded IRA men as the hospitals . . . were full of gun-shot wound cases.'

At the other end of the political scale, the three governments (four if the Dáil–Provisional Government be counted double) cobbled together an agreement labelled the 'Craig–Collins pact'. The British initiative in bringing Craig and Collins together stemmed from Churchill's view of Collins as someone he could do business with – in effect, someone who accepted the British government's perspective on the northern issue. Collins did have some interest in an accommodation. It is not clear if he had ever shared the belief that the boycott would overawe unionists, but it now looked sensible to cash in what few chips the republicans possessed, abandoning the boycott if the Northern government undertook to end the discrimination and persecution that had provoked it.

Collins started out with the standard nationalist view that Ulster resistance was entirely created by British interference. He minimized its extent – writing to Art O'Brien that there was 'really only one small question in Ulster and it has its pivot in the Belfast shipyards . . . the spot from which the strength of intolerance comes'. Reacting to MacEntee's call for the boycott he had gone as far as to snort that 'there was no Ulster Question.'[85] When he went to speak to a 'monster meeting' in Armagh in September 1921 he followed the old line that Protestant intolerance was 'the product solely and entirely of British policy', and invited Protestants 'as Irishmen to come into the Irish nation . . . to come in and take their share in the government of their own country'. He could say little else, of course, and it is not clear whether he actually believed there was any chance of this. He did, at the same time, reassure his nationalist audience that whatever happened he would not 'desert' them. When as head of the Provisional Government in January 1922 he had to come up with an actual policy, he decided that 'non-recognition of the Northern Parliament was essential'. Craig's government 'could stop all the outrages in the North if they set their hands to do so'.

When Collins met Craig at the Colonial Office on 21 January, there did appear to be the basis for a working relationship. Not only did Craig agree that the expelled shipyard workers should be reinstated in return for the abandonment of the boycott, he even proposed a kind of all-Ireland convention to determine the relationship between north and south. The two also agreed to replace the Boundary Commission by a direct bilateral agreement. Collins could maintain that 'we have eliminated the English interference' and north and south would 'settle outstanding differences between themselves'. Within a few weeks, though, it was clear that the outstanding differences remained as wide as ever. The all-Ireland conference was immediately dropped, and Craig was forced to reassure the Ulster Unionist Council on 27 January that he would not agree to any boundary change that left 'our Ulster area any less than it is'.

The volatility of the northern situation had been explosively demonstrated just before the Craig–Collins meeting, when the commander of the 5th Northern Division, Dan Hogan, and several of his officers were arrested by police in Tyrone while travelling with the Monaghan Gaelic football team. Early in February the IRA seized forty-two leading local loyalists as hostages, and took them across the border to Clones. On 11 February, in an armed clash at Clones station, a Volunteer officer and four Ulster Specials were killed. The scale of the crisis can be seen from Craig's inquiry whether there would be 'any legal obstacle to our sending a flying column of 5,000 constabulary to recover the kidnapped Loyalists'. Churchill, clearly startled, came up with a political objection – such action might cause the fall of the Provisional Government 'thus creating chaos and leaving the extremists in control'. To limit the damage, he tetchily warned Griffith that 'if your people are going to pop into Ulster and take off hostages every time the Northern Government enforces the law in a way you dislike . . . we will have a fortified frontier,' which would have to be garrisoned by 'Imperial troops'. Churchill set up a triangular Border Commission, with the menacing explanation that it was the alternative to the 'drastic steps' he would otherwise be expected to take 'for securing the area of Northern Ireland'. But this, one more example of London's unrealistic hopes of co-operation, was predictably ineffective, and was abandoned after a couple of months. Still, the border at least remained an open one, for the next half-century.

The Belfast Boycott was wound up, and Collins was probably happy enough with this. Though there were still some believers in its effectiveness, there was also a growing lobby that maintained it was counter-productive. Months earlier Erskine Childers himself, together with the writers George Russell (prominent in the agricultural co-operative movement), Alice Stopford Green and others, had urged that 'continuance of the boycott is not in the interests of Ireland as a whole.' It 'injured the innocent as well as the guilty', and the most guilty – the shipyards – were 'not seriously hampered' by it. People were being driven out of business, and unemployment was hitting Catholics harder than Protestants. Others put it even more strongly: 'in this movement our friends have unwittingly helped the Pogromists'; 'Surely the Boycott weapon was not forged to punish the victims of the Pogrom!'[86]

At some point in January, Collins set up an Ulster Council Command – whose name might be seen as another unconscious genuflection to the unionist doctrine of Ulster's separateness – to co-ordinate the military policy of the northern IRA. Historians have divided sharply over whether this meant that Collins had a serious military strategy for the north, or was simply trying to hold on to the support of northern units on the Treaty issue. At the September meeting in Armagh, Eoin O'Duffy had fulminated characteristically that 'if necessary they would have to use the lead on them' (the unionists), and Collins presumably agreed. But he probably did not share the simple belief – which Frank Aiken, the head of the new Council, admitted that he and others still possessed – 'in the power of the gun alone to cure all evils'. The Council's first function seems to have been to choke off any spontaneous outbursts that might fuel a new round of tit-for-tat violence. As the failure of the first Craig–Collins pact became clear, the Council authorized a series of barrack raids in three border counties.

The calling of the Army Convention (see p. 392 below) threw the northern IRA's position on the struggle over the Treaty back into the balance. Roger McCorley believed that the army should follow the Dáil, and disapproved of the Convention. But he became suspicious of GHQ's motives when it first backed and then banned it, and decided to attend. He disliked the way a 'certain element' took control of the proceedings, making no effort to look for any agreement with GHQ. But since GHQ had done little, in his view, to supply the northern units with arms, he decided to support the Executive. Only when he visited Beggars Bush and had an interview with O'Duffy, who promised him that GHQ would do more to support him, did he change his position. When a majority of his brigade council decided to follow GHQ, the minority almost all fell into line – there was no split.[87]

The sense of latent civil war in the north was intensifying. After the Clones incident, there was a storm of gunfire in the Kent Street area of Belfast that even the hardened *Belfast Telegraph* found 'awe inspiring'. On 11 March Collins protested to Churchill that three police officers, including DI Nixon, who were 'up to their knees in the crimes of 1920–21', were 'the men who keep the "peace" in Belfast today'. Within a fortnight, Nixon had once again proved the point. On 24 March the killing of a Catholic family, the McMahons, by gunmen who broke into their home on the Antrim Road in Belfast – branded 'the most terrible assassination that has yet stained the name of Belfast' by the *Belfast Telegraph* – sent shockwaves that reached beyond the city, as far as London.[88] This act of terrorism, which seemed more alarming because the victims were a well-known middle-class family, jolted the unionist community's sense of moral superiority, and seemed to presage all-out war. Churchill called another north–south meeting in London on 30 March. A second Craig–Collins pact was drawn up (oddly enough, Arthur Griffith signed it alongside Collins and O'Higgins 'on behalf of the Provisional Government'). Verbally impressive enough – eleven articles filling two dense pages – the agreement could scarcely live up to its dramatic Churchillian first article: 'peace is today declared.' Forward-looking provisions such as that 'special police in mixed districts' should be 'composed half of Catholics and half of Protestants', and that a committee ('of equal numbers Catholic and Protestant') should investigate complaints of intimidation and violence, never got beyond the verbal stage.[89] There is little sign that the traditional nationalist dismissal of the credibility or legitimacy of loyalism was changing. The Treatyites held on to the belief expressed by Mulcahy on the North-Eastern Advisory Committee that carrying out all the terms of the Treaty 'will ultimately unify the country and destroy the Northern Parliament'. That committee had been set up in February to monitor northern opinion, but predictably perhaps it heard only from nationalists.[90]

In just over two months, from 10 February to 21 April, 127 Catholics were killed and some 300 injured in Belfast.[91] The Northern government's security measures themselves seemed, to nationalists, to deepen their insecurity. After the passage of the Special Powers Act in April, in effect reviving the Restoration of Order in Ireland Act, Collins told Churchill, 'if these offensive not protective measures are taken against our people ... I cannot be responsible for the awful consequences which must ensue.' The meeting of the North-Eastern Advisory Committee on 11 April, called by Collins to discuss the Craig–Collins pacts, presented a bleak picture. However reluctantly, the sectarianism of the northern conflict was reflected in the 'Catholic ethos' of this meeting.[92] Alongside the Dublin leadership (Collins, Cosgrave, O'Higgins, Griffith, Mulcahy and O'Duffy) and the northern IRA commanders (Seamus Woods and Frank Crummey) were three northern bishops and ten priests. Woods frankly declared that though 'the IRA have the support of the whole people, of every Catholic in Belfast ... you could not fight.' Outside the Falls area (where 'there could be a fight'), people were simply 'striving for existence'. 'Sooner or later we [the IRA] will have to clear out of Belfast.' The veteran republican Fr John Hassan of west Belfast said, 'it is generally admitted that the Catholics in Belfast are on their last legs. They are not even holding on. They are going to Dublin and elsewhere. And the only reason why they are not all leaving is because we can't get away.'[93] The general recognition that, during the 'temporary period' before the Boundary Commission, the only hope for the northern nationalists lay in the Craig-Collins pact foreshadowed the gradual abandonment of the policy of non-recognition of Northern Ireland.[94]

Collins himself was already engaged in preparing a major military action in the north. The rationale of what has usually been labelled the 'joint IRA offensive' – a curious locution reflecting both the IRA's division over the Treaty and its lack of experience of concerted action – is still rather obscure. Some spoke of the planned action as a 'Rising', suggesting that significant hopes were invested in it. It was to be 'a big effort ... to bring about, if possible, the downfall of the six-county Government by military means' – 'on a given date all the Units in the Six County area were to go into action,' with supporting actions along the border.[95] On 22 February Collins approved the creation of the Belfast City Guard, a paid unit of sixty men – fifteen from each of the four city battalions. (Some saw this as a form of outdoor relief for unemployed Volunteers.) Southern commanders such as Seán Lehane of Cork No. 1 Brigade were sent to ginger up some northern formations. Lehane took over the 1st and 2nd Northern Divisions, assisted by Charlie Daly, who had already been removed from command of 2nd Northern Division for attending the Army Convention. The IRB seems to have played its last part here in bringing pro- and anti-Treaty leaders together in a common effort.[96]

Significant arms supplies were promised, on the assumption it seems that weapons handed over to the Provisional Government by the British could be sent to northern units. When it was realized that their serial numbers would reveal their origin, the plan faltered. Removing the identification was a possibility, but a crude and risky one – the motive for removal was likely to be all too obvious. So an arrangement – almost as reckless – was made with Lynch to swap British-supplied guns for those of the 1st Southern Division. 'General Collins insisted that we were to get arms from Cork No. 1 Brigade, and that he would return rifles instead to Cork from those rifles handed over by the British.'[97] This may have produced a few hundred rifles. Thomas Fitzpatrick's brigade got a hundred, brought in to Cushendall on a lorry which broke down, ironically, a mile or so outside Larne – the site of the UVF's celebrated gun-running in 1914. The brigade adjutant succeeded in getting the local British commander to have it repaired, telling him it was a load of petrol. But before that the brigade had barely twenty usable rifles.[98]

All these developments were too little too late. There was no quick fix for the structural weaknesses of the northern IRA, and most units remained seriously short of arms. If any plans for the joint offensive were drawn up, they have not survived. Its start date seems to have been set for early May, but was then postponed for two weeks or more: the vagueness about such a key part of the co-ordinated action played into its confused execution. Severe damage was inflicted on the Volunteer organization, particularly on 3rd Northern Division, when a big cache of papers, which incredibly enough had been kept at the Belfast Liaison Office, was seized in a police raid.[99] The rescheduled offensive was to be preceded by an attempt to seize two armoured cars and 250 rifles from Musgrave Street barracks in Belfast on 17 May. This was nearly a dramatic triumph: with the assistance of an insider, the armoury was actually captured, but the alarm was raised while Woods and his men were bundling up the guns. He decided to retreat, and the attackers all got away, by the skin of their teeth. 'We had hardly reached safety', Woods reported, 'when the area was flooded with Lancias and armoured cars filled with Specials. They swept the streets with machine gun fire and for three quarters of an hour the area was a regular battlefield.' Even so his men 'succeeded in driving them off' with 'rifles and PPs [Peter the Painters]'.[100]

The *Belfast Telegraph* disapprovingly commented that 'all the brains, all the audacity, all the enterprise and all the resources' appeared to be 'on the side of the rebels'.[101] But the appearance was illusory, certainly as far as resources and organization went. The offensive was put off again until 22 May, but communication failures meant that the order did not reach all units. 2nd Northern said it was impossible to cancel since orders had already been issued; there was 'some confusion in some of the areas' about the second date. The Antrim Brigade received orders to launch the operation on the 19th, and committed all its four battalions to attack police barracks. It commandeered a large number of cars and 'for about 48 hours we had complete freedom of movement practically throughout the whole [brigade] area.' But the premature start meant that 'all the enemy forces which would otherwise have been engaged in different centres were concentrated in our area,' and the IRA units were forced to retreat in columns to the hills.[102] Elsewhere a debacle reminiscent of Easter Week followed, though on a much smaller scale, with individual units carrying out uncoordinated sniping and arson attacks. The Tyrone IRA, despite receiving a consignment of rifles with 'a large quantity of ammunition', was still waiting to act when several of its leaders were arrested in a 'sudden large-scale swoop' by British forces on 22 May.[103] The idea of an offensive sputtered on in some border counties, notably Donegal, into the late autumn, but the possibility of united action was effectively ended long before that by the outbreak of the civil war. With a mixed bag of units and a weakly defined objective, the doomed northern offensive starkly revealed the limits of the Republic's capacity to vindicate its claim to the north.

'POWER WIELDED BY MEN WHO HAVE NO LEGAL AUTHORITY'

The Treaty created a complicated authority structure. Some believed that the Treaty vote effectively disestablished the Republic, though most appear to have accepted the republican contention that the Dáil had no authority to do this. Legally, the Treaty had been approved, but not yet ratified: only a new parliament could do this. Until a general election was held the Republic stayed in being, and a system of dual authority emerged. Collins foreshadowed this when he proposed on 3 January 1922 that the Treaty be passed and 'the Provisional Government come into being, subject to Dail Eireann'. (Béaslaí sardonically suggested that the dual set-up would allow 'the opposition' to 'redeem the country ... and take all the kudos', while the Provisional Government could take 'all the shame and disgrace'.) The issue triggered the final fracture of the Dáil. When de Valera resigned as president of Dáil Éireann on 9 January, the proposal to re-elect him as 'President of the Republic' was, as we have seen, lost by only two votes. The pro-Treaty side actually denied that such a post existed – although the title had been in common use since at least August 1921 – holding that such a president could be elected only by the people, not by the Dáil. When Collins proposed Griffith as president of Dáil Éireann, de Valera insisted that his oath of office would bind him not to subvert the Republic. Griffith undertook to maintain the Republic until the people decided the issue, but de Valera said that his commitment to carry out the Treaty would put him in an impossible position, simultaneously maintaining and subverting the Republic. Before the vote was taken, the ex-President and the anti-Treaty deputies walked out.

The ambiguity of authority went beyond the Dáil. Within days of the signature of the Treaty, it was all too clear to the British that there was a 'remarkable misunderstanding' about the powers to be exercised by the Provisional Government. Griffith and Collins clearly thought that it would be able to spend money 'on other things than those for which the British parliament had given authority'.[104] They had also 'not faced the fact that the treaty does nothing to create any organ in Ireland capable of giving a legal sanction to the Irish constitution when framed'.[105] These misunderstandings as the British saw them were in line with the interpretation Griffith and Collins were offering the Dáil: the Treaty would allow bigger powers in practice than a strict reading of it might suggest. The crucial question was whether Britain would be able to compel the Provisional Government to follow the procedures required by British law. On the legal issue, it failed. Without legislation the British government could not give the Provisional Government financial powers, but no new legislation could be brought in before the end of the parliamentary recess in February 1922. The only legal route around the problem was to use the Crown Colony clauses of the Government of Ireland Act, but Griffith and Collins would not tolerate this. So the British were forced to accept an 'admittedly irregular' arrangement in which a 'makeshift' provisional government was said in law to be an *ad hoc* executive committee advising the Viceroy. This fiction would fill the gap until the Irish Free State (Agreement) Act could be passed.

On 14 January Griffith – in his capacity as chairman of the plenipotentiaries – convened the House of Commons of Southern Ireland to approve the Treaty and elect a provisional government to implement it. This second and final meeting of the Southern Parliament brought the four Trinity College members (the only ones who had turned up at the abortive first meeting in May 1921) and sixty pro-Treaty TDs together. Though the assembly had been established by the Government of

Ireland Act, and met in accordance with the requirements of the Treaty, it might possibly have been regarded as the Dáil. In the event, Collins as chairman of the Provisional Government, and Griffith as president of the Dáil, set up two parallel governments. Mulcahy, who became minister for defence in the Dáil Cabinet, had (like Griffith) no position in the Provisional Government, which had no defence minister. Immediately after the Treaty vote, under pressure from de Valera, he had been induced to assure the Dáil that 'the Army will remain the Army of the Irish Republic.' For six weeks or so, this useful fiction held up; in mid-February, though, Mulcahy started to attend Provisional Government meetings, so the government could be in 'closer touch with the Defence Department'.[106] Collins retained his old Finance portfolio in the Dáil government, and Cosgrave, O'Higgins and Duggan occupied the same posts in both executives. This meant that the Provisional Government could be seen as deriving its authority, whether formally or informally, from the Dáil – not from Britain via the Treaty.[107]

Did this dual authority make sense, and did it matter if it did not? It certainly produced some convoluted official channels. For instance, Mulcahy as minister for defence in the Dáil government 'arranged with the Provisional Government to occupy for them all vacated military and police posts for the purpose of their maintenance and safeguarding'. Any expenses incurred would be 'charged to the Provisional Government'.[108] To have two governments of the same territory involved an element of unreality which might undermine either or both. Winston Churchill, who was responsible for pushing the Irish Free State (Agreement) Bill through an increasingly fractious House of Commons in London, angered by the violent incidents in the north, was increasingly alarmed about the situation. Pointing out that the Provisional Government was operating without any official British sanction, he saw it as 'fatal to peace, social order, and good government to have power wielded by men who have no legal authority'. A provisional government 'unsanctified by law' yet recognized by the British government was 'an anomaly unprecedented in the history of the British Empire'.[109] This irregularity may be seen as the first definite indication that Griffith and Collins were right in their understanding of the way the future power relationship between Britain and Ireland would evolve.

The Provisional Government took policing more seriously than the republican administration had; it had no alternative. It had to vindicate the authority of the law simply to survive, and to keep the British off its back. The situation at the turn of the year was dire, and something had to be done. But what? It was politically impossible to adopt the old RIC, in the way that so much of the British administrative apparatus was taken over. The force was doomed by its history, and the republicans' own remorseless denunciation of it as an army of occupation, even though some of those who had battled against it over the last couple of years – Collins in particular – had come to respect its effectiveness as a state instrument. The republican police had never lived up to their publicity image: Collins later excoriated 'the wretched Irish Republican Police System' and its 'awful personnel', condemning its 'lack of construction and . . . lack of control'. Even if its performance had been better, the Treaty split fatally damaged its organization. The Chief of Police, Simon Donnelly, opposed the Treaty and took off with most of his administrative records (and his funds).

In effect, only one police force remained viable. The Dublin Metropolitan Police had mostly been allowed by the IRA to exercise its 'non-political' functions during the war. (It had, for instance, arrested Countess Markievicz for driving without a tail-light.) Even though, as an unarmed force, it represented the tradition of 'English policing' more accurately than did the RIC, it provided a better model for the new state. The decision to create an unarmed national police force, first named the National Guard, was probably the most crucial one taken by the Provisional Government, and contributed more to its ultimate survival than anything else. It was not a simple one. Ernest Blythe remembered some ministers contending that the police 'would be hunted out of their stations within a few days if they had not guns to defend themselves'. This was all too plausible; the counter-argument was that arming them 'would only be to subject them to attack', and if they were not driven out they would be pinned down in their stations. Then 'the position would be worse than if we did not attempt to send out police at all.' The government finally came to the conclusion that 'the only thing that would get real sympathy for the Guards was to have them . . . defenceless against armed attack.' Fortunately, the wisdom of this was quite quickly demonstrated: the public attitude to the new police was 'very different from their attitude towards the RIC'.[110]

The new force emerged by a rather irregular process. Some time after the Truce, Collins had set up an *ad hoc* police unit under Liam Tobin, which did not even have an official name (in 1922 it was simply known as Oriel House, the Westland Row building it operated from). Its responsibilities were at best loosely defined, and included criminal investigation as well as public security and intelligence functions. Since it was drawn primarily from Collins's old Squad, its policing credentials were slender. It was armed, and its dubious discipline and rough-and-ready methods did not endear it to either contemporaries or later historians. What it clearly demonstrated was that in order to crush opposition the new state was quite prepared to go down the same path as the British had. It was not placed under unequivocal civil control until a month after the attack on the Four Courts. Eventually, in August, it was given a name – the Criminal Investigation Department – but it remained a stop-gap unit that could be tolerated only in emergency conditions.

The establishment of a national police force was ordered on 22 January, under the title 'Civic Guard', with the 1916 veteran Michael Staines as its commissioner. Both Staines and Mulcahy (representing the Dáil government) set up committees to suggest structures for the new force. They seem to have more or less agreed on a 4,500-strong unarmed police (about half the strength of the old thirty-two-county RIC). Like both the DMP and the RIC it would be entirely controlled by the government – no hint of the decentralization and local control which was so characteristic of British (and indeed American) police organization. It would take over the RIC barracks when they were evacuated in the spring, and would follow the RIC pattern of service outside policemen's native counties. But, as soon as recruitment began, the force fell victim to the same chaos as afflicted the emerging National Army. For some reason the Provisional Government was, as has been observed, 'a hopeless quartermaster'.[111] The first recruits were unsatisfactorily housed in the Royal Dublin Society at Ballsbridge, and given basic training which included musketry on the old RIC model. Then in April, with the force 1,500 strong, they were moved out to even worse accommodation at the Curragh, where conditions were so bad that the force mutinied on 15 May. For the next month the Civic Guard was under the control of a mutinous committee, and when the Commissioner, who behaved with 'singular ineptitude', turned up on 9 June he was shut out. Two officers he sent to negotiate were chased unceremoniously away and had to take refuge with the Kildare parish priest.

Only after this drama did the mutineers receive their pay arrears, though not before Rory O'Connor sent over a republican group from the Four Courts to pick up the Civic Guard's rifles. At least the men themselves did not go over to the other side. Collins visited the mutineers several times, trying to reassure them of their public value, and promising an inquiry into their grievances. Eventually, the civilians got a better grip on the force, and on the whole policing issue. In mid-July a committee of inquiry headed by Kevin O'Shiel began a considered assessment of the formidable problem of law enforcement in a country with deeply embedded traditions of resistance to the law. It decided that the new police force was altogether too much like the old RIC, with 'a militaristic instead of a peace outlook' that could not 'assure the public that militaristic and coercive policing was at an end'.[112] What was needed was 'a police body that shall be the servants of the people, and have the confidence of the people'. Its 'principal body' should be unarmed, but there should be 'a semi-military body trained to the use of arms' as an HQ reserve, as well as a detective force shared with the DMP. Central control might be modified to the extent that local councils could reasonably 'hold the local police body directly responsible for certain local duties', as long as they did not interfere with 'police duties proper'. Addressing the causes of the mutiny, O'Shiel found that the men had objected to the prominence of ex-RIC men among their instructors. He thought that the new force should be commanded at the top by ex-Volunteers, leavened with one or two highly experienced officers from abroad – preferably 'American, French or German'. RIC officers would be needed to advise the leaders, but such appointments should be seen to be temporary. The most crucial issue for the immediate future, though, was who should be commissioner. O'Shiel proposed that this should not be a role for a politician, offering a decorous way of persuading Staines to give it up. This meant that, with no pool of experienced police officers to draw on, the solution would probably have to be found in the army.

'MANY MORE OF US WILL DIE'

One of the most poignant expressions of 'realism' in the Treaty debate was Seán MacEoin's remark that in fighting for the Republic 'I did not succeed but I did my best.' Other leaders with equally impeccable

military credentials were not prepared to accept this. Nor, just as seriously, would they accept the right of the Dáil to decide the issue. On 6
January 1922, just before the final vote, Seamus Robinson called for a
Volunteer Convention. If the Treaty was 'forced on us without our consent as an Army of Volunteers', 'certain terrible action' would follow.
On the same day, as we have seen, Liam Lynch warned the Chief of Staff
that he could 'not carry out any order against IRA principles' which
were in 'danger of being given away by our unthankful Government'.[113]
After the vote, for Todd Andrews as for many rank-and-file Volunteers,
'nearly all the members of the Dáil overnight became . . . "politicians".'

Ironically the subordination of the Volunteers to the Dáil, including
the winding-up of the Volunteer Executive, had been pressed by Cathal
Brugha, the leading opponent of the Treaty. The anti-Treaty group now
needed to undo his achievement, reasserting both the inherent independence of the army and its essentially political nature. Both these
ideas flew in the face of the professionalization that Mulcahy had been
striving to foster. But they clearly echoed the beliefs of many Volunteers.
Over the following weeks the new Defence Minister trod an awkward
path as he tried to insist on the unconstitutional nature of an army convention without pushing its advocates into open defiance. There was no
doubting the point made by Liam Mellows on 4 January: not only had
men given their lives for the Republic, plenty were 'still prepared to give
their lives'. (Mellows had already predicted to Seán Moylan, 'Many
more of us will die before an Irish Republic is recognised.')[114] Immediately after the 7 January vote the senior officers opposed to the
Treaty – four members of GHQ staff, six divisional commanders and
the two Dublin brigadiers – held 'a series of consultations'. They reached
the more or less agreed view that 'the Army should revert to its status as
a Volunteer force under the control of an elected Executive.' The Executive would be elected by a convention; the fact that no convention had
been held since 1917, and that the Executive had ceased to meet, had
not 'abrogated the constitutional right' of the organization to hold
conventions.

Florrie O'Donoghue thought that 'the best hope of keeping the Army
united and faithful to its allegiance lay in the preservation of its democratic and voluntary character.' The sponsors went to great efforts to
clarify the purpose and mechanics of the convention. On 11 January

they formally requested the Defence Minister, Mulcahy, to call 'a Convention of the Army . . . not later than Sunday, 5th February', to debate three resolutions. The army should 'reaffirm its allegiance to the Irish Republic'; it should be 'maintained as the Army of the Irish Republic under an Executive appointed by the Convention'; and 'be under the supreme control of such Executive'. The Executive would draft a constitution to be considered by a later convention. Delegates to the Convention would consist of all divisional commandants *ex officio*, and others selected from brigade conventions. Mulcahy pointed out on 13 January that the 'supreme control of the Army' was vested in the Dáil, which was 'the elected Government of the Irish Republic'; the proposal to change this was beyond the powers 'vested in the Dáil Executive by the Dáil'. He proposed a conference to discuss the issue, and this met five days later. After the arguments for and against a convention had been aired, Mulcahy surprisingly agreed to hold one within two months, and promised that the army would still be the Army of the Irish Republic. Only Frank Aiken, who wanted to wait until the Free State constitution was published, stood out against the idea.

What would have happened if the Convention had met on this basis? O'Donoghue implies that the fact that each side 'would have had representation roughly proportionate to its numerical strength in the Army' offered 'a reasonable probability of preserving Army unity'. This is not easy to follow, especially in light of his account of Liam Lynch's position. Lynch 'could see the difficulty that any democratic Government would have in accepting the position that the only military force in the country was not in any way under its control; but he was at all times unwavering in the conviction that the Army should not in any circumstances abandon its allegiance to the Republic', or 'be committed to support of the Treaty'.[115] Did he somehow think that these points were not irreconcilable?

In the event, Mulcahy was forced by Griffith and his Cabinet to reverse his position on the Convention. But he still moved hesitantly and reluctantly. In early March Liam Lynch made several trips to Dublin to discuss the issue, and 'although a note of acerbity and partisanship was beginning to appear in public statements, these conferences were not so affected.' Lynch and Mulcahy remained on comradely terms. On 15 March the Cabinet forced the issue, proscribing the Convention on the ground that 'any effort to set up another body [than the Dáil] in control [of the Army] would be tantamount to an attempt to establish a Military Dictatorship.' Mulcahy, out on a limb, still went on looking for a way through the impasse, travelling to a council of the 1st Southern Division at Mallow on the 20th, and securing an agreement to hold yet another meeting – of all brigadiers and divisional commanders – to elect an eight-strong council that would frame proposals 'for associating the IRA with the Government elected by the Irish people'. (Using the concept of 'association' was an interesting parallel with de Valera's alternative to the Treaty.) But this was conditional on the demand that the Civic Guard be wound up, which was inevitably rejected by the Cabinet. When the Republican Military Council of some fifty senior officers responded by formally summoning the banned Army Convention, Mulcahy issued a less than severe rebuke. While the summoning of the Convention 'breaks definitely, to some extent', the 'solidarity and organisation of the Army', it did not, he suggested, break its 'wonderful brotherhood'.[116] At the same time, his instruction to O'Duffy that 'any officer or man attending the Convention will thereby sever his connection with the IRA' surely did – O'Donoghue saw it as 'a disaster, worse than any defeat in the field'.

The echo of that brotherhood did persist even after the 'sectional Convention' eventually met on 26 March. The 200-plus (O'Donoghue says 211, others 223) delegates, representing some 60 (O'Donoghue claims 80) per cent of the army, elected a sixteen-strong IRA Executive (to be elected annually) to exercise 'supreme control' over the army in the name of the Republic, and draw up a constitution for the army. It immediately repudiated the authority of the Minister for Defence and Dáil Éireann itself, pointing out that although the Volunteers had 'agreed to' come under the control of the Dáil, they were never 'formally called together to agree'.[117] A fortnight later the Convention met again to ratify the new army constitution, and the Executive created a new GHQ staff headed by Liam Lynch. (The exact positions occupied by the others – including Rory O'Connor, Liam Mellows, Joe McKelvey – do not seem to have been recorded.) The constitution declared the army's object to be 'to guard the honour and maintain the independence of the Irish Republic', and to 'place its services at the disposal of an established Republican Government'.

THE TAKEOVER

While the army debated, the pace of events was creating its own dynamic. Whether or not Mulcahy was maintaining the army as the Army of the Irish Republic – some republicans were disputing this – he was evidently creating 'a distinct pro-Treaty force', which Liam Mellows charged was 'being superimposed on the Army of the Republic'. As soon as the British began to hand over military installations the question of who would occupy them became urgent. This evacuation – the most visible and symbolic fulfilment of a key pro-Treaty argument – began remarkably soon after the Dáil vote. A big convoy of baggage left Cork on 16 January 1922, and four days later the first infantry unit to leave – the 1st Battalion of the Duke of Wellington's Regiment – sailed from Dublin port. Their embarkation on the SS *Rathmore* aroused 'very little public interest', with no spectators apart from 'a few railwaymen, press photographers and cinema operators'.[118] The first army barrack, at Clogheen in Tipperary, was handed over on 25 January, followed by the legendary Beggars Bush barracks in Dublin, the HQ of the Auxiliary Division, on the last day of the month.

At this point the formal procedures for transferring installations had still not been agreed. But the process was amicable, especially after the British realized that the Provisional Government's authority was under challenge. Emmet Dalton, in charge of negotiations on the Irish side, noted in late February that the British C-in-C wanted to retain Naas barracks until the Curragh had been evacuated. He put the case for immediate transfer 'strongly', so that they could 'send Officers to be trained correctly and in the right environment', to be able to take over the 'cantankerous areas'. 'They appreciated this of course,' Dalton reported to Ginger O'Connell, 'and I am sure they will endeavour in every way to help us.'[119] One simple fact was that the new Free State could not afford to maintain the number of installations that the British army had: closures were inevitable, but local interests made them a politically sensitive issue, and the choice could not be made immediately.

The question of which forces were to take over the British posts became crucial. Discipline and control were hanging by a thread in many areas. Con Moloney, the adjutant of Ernie O'Malley's 2nd Southern

Division, was faced with a spate of robberies in mid-Limerick in January. The brigade adjutant, urging O'Malley to call a special brigade council, said that 'the crisis in the Brigade is getting worse every day.' Cattle were being seized for non-payment of IRA levies (which had already been prohibited). As O'Malley sardonically noted in February, 'the bold troops of the "fighting sixth" seem to have a dash of Black & Tan instilled into them.' One local doctor whose car had been commandeered pressed the invidious comparison further, protesting that 'bad as the Black and Tans were they never interfered with the cars of doctors.'[120]

Beggars Bush was the base for the new force raised by the Provisional Government, which would eventually become the National Army. For the time being, the pro-Treaty command lacked even the clear title possessed by the anti-Treaty 'IRA Executive', and was often known merely as 'Beggars Bush'. The barracks were occupied by the Dublin ASU (the old Squad) and picked Dublin Brigade Volunteers, who marched past Collins on the steps of City Hall on their way. This forty-six-strong group, commanded by Paddy O'Daly, were labelled the Dublin Guards, and would expand to brigade strength by July. Although anti-Treaty republicans took immediate alarm at this development, it was – like so much else in the state-building process – hesitant and confused. This was despite being implemented, under the aegis of the presiding organizers of the old GHQ, Mulcahy and Collins, by the experienced team of O'Duffy, O'Connell and others. The key role was played by O'Duffy, who replaced Mulcahy as chief of staff on 10 January. His biographer calls this a 'shrewd' appointment, as O'Duffy 'was admired by the regional IRA leaders, who perceived him as a fighting man'. But not all did, unfortunately. One who did not was the mid-Limerick brigadier, Liam Forde, who denounced O'Duffy as a traitor on 18 February. 'We declare that we no longer recognise the authority of the present head of the army, and renew our allegiance to the existing Irish Republic.'

This triggered a crisis as the British vacated their posts in Limerick. The RIC left their five barracks on 23 February: a demob-happy crowd of Auxiliaries at Limerick station had the station-master 'frantic with fear' until they were calmed down by a 'large party of the old RIC'. Some IRA men, returning from a training camp, were met with gleeful shouts of 'here are the Sinners!' and 'here are some of the invisible army!' By this time a Beggars Bush force under Michael Brennan was already moving in from east Clare. As soon as he realized this, O'Malley brought up all the men he could gather to dispute the occupation of the city. Limerick's strategic significance was obvious to both Brennan and O'Malley, though it may not have been fully grasped by their superiors. A full-scale armed clash was imminent, and Brennan, who was already referring to the 'Executive' forces as 'mutineers', was conscious of his vulnerability. 'I understand we are to get an ultimatum today,' he wrote to GHQ on 8 March, 'giving us 24 hours to clear out.' Although he had 570 men, only 300 of them were armed, and some of his men had 'too many associations with the Mutineers to be properly reliable'. They had 'only fifty rounds of ammunition per rifle which is not nearly enough for what we are up against here'. He wanted 'a couple of thousand Mills bombs at once as well as 500 rifles', and 'at least one more armoured car, two if possible'. Then he wanted 'a big supply of Thompson ammunition and a few more Thompsons. Any chance of Lewis guns and a few gunners?' He judged all the barracks 'weak' (in spite of three years of British fortification), and thought it 'a foregone conclusion that the mutineers will be able to lock us in'. 'However you manage it,' he urged Ginger O'Connell, 'send 100 of McKeown's men here at once – tomorrow if you can possibly do so'; thanks to MacEoin's reputation they had 'a name which would be very useful to us'. The garrison should be reduced to 500 reliable men, with at least 150 rounds of ammunition each – and he also wanted a tank and armed launches to use on the river.[121] GHQ had no tanks to send (whatever might have been their military utility), but Brennan did receive the first Rolls-Royce armoured car to be handed over to the Free State by the British.

The crisis never came to the crunch. It is no doubt true that, as has been said, 'old friends made reluctant fighters'. But the men on the spot, Brennan – 'puffed out in his uniform like a peacock', as Oscar Traynor snorted – and O'Malley, were clearly up for a fight. O'Malley urged Rory O'Connor to press Seamus Robinson to act more decisively, arguing prophetically that if the republicans failed at Limerick they would quickly be turfed out of all significant posts and lose whatever military advantage they started with. On the other side, Arthur Griffith took the same view of Limerick's significance as an issue in vindicating the authority of government. When the issue was under discussion, he addressed his fellow ministers for nearly half an hour, the only formal speech he ever delivered in Cabinet. The government must live up to its responsibility to defend the people: 'these men challenge our authority and right.' With a verbal pungency more akin to his old journalism than his recent statesmanship, he fumed that 'if we let this situation through our fingers we will be looked on as the greatest pack of poltroons that ever held the fate of Ireland in their hands.' But Collins seems to have been 'lukewarm', and Mulcahy argued that the government's forces were 'not yet ready' either psychologically or militarily to act. Failure would be even more disastrous than inaction. Mulcahy believed, as he would for some time to come, that Lynch would be a force for reconciliation and indeed Lynch saw the situation as 'a disgrace to both sides', and was ready to join Oscar Traynor in a mission to broker a compromise.[122]

Although Traynor celebrated the 'amicable settlement' which led 'about 700 armed troops on each side who were about to engage in mortal combat eventually [to] leave Limerick as comrades', the Limerick clash showed that civil war had already, in effect, begun, and there was nothing to stop it spreading. (Even Traynor, who had 'an awful job' persuading Tom Barry to walk away, found he could do so only by telling him 'that there would be fighting at some time'.)[123] It was only disguised by the leaderships' desperate efforts to hold the issue back from its logical conclusion. A notch down from the top, some were dismayed by the fudge. GHQ was unhappy; on 12 March a group met at the Gresham Hotel to protest against the decision of 'the Staff . . . in connection with the Limerick Mutiny'. They demanded that GHQ meetings be 'properly constituted' and that if any members of the staff voted to 'refer any matter of importance to the Dáil Cabinet', such a course would be adopted.[124] Ginger O'Connell protested directly against the Limerick compromise, and later bitterly reflected that 'all the territory we light-heartedly gave up to the mutineers had later to be hard fought for.'[125] O'Duffy seems to have been more complaisant, and O'Connell certainly blamed him for the failure to create an effective national force in time to get a grip on the situation. 'Worse waste of what was once promising material would be hard to find,' he reflected: 'all because the High Command was totally unfitted for its task'.

Thus far, the republicans' course of action was obvious enough, and effectively unanimous. None dissented from Rory O'Connor's statement in a press interview that 'our view is that [the government] has abolished itself – not exactly abolished but it has done something it has no moral right to do . . . The Dáil, in deciding that the Irish Republic

shall go into the British Empire, has committed an act of national dishonour that we won't stand.'[126] But if the logical implication was that
the republicans must set up their own government, there was less agreement about that, or about whether the next step should be some kind of
open military action against the Provisional Government. The only action
that followed the Executive meeting on 9 April was an attack on the pro-
Treaty press, through the destruction of the presses of the *Freeman's
Journal* and the occupation of some big buildings in Dublin. The biggest
and most symbolic was the vast bulk of the Four Courts. Despite its formidable appearance, the Liffeyside building had effectively buried the
men of Ned Daly's battalion who had occupied it in 1916. One of them
indeed had been driven mad by the grim experience.[127] Sixteeners among
the 130-odd republican troops who shuffled into it on 13 April do not
seem to have had a sense of *déjà vu*, at least to begin with. This was a
gesture rather than a military initiative. In a purely military sense, seizing
buildings was as suicidal in 1922 as it had been in 1916. It made sense
politically only on assumption that either the Treatyites would come to
their senses or – more likely – the British would take military action that
would bring public opinion back behind the republicans.

Michael Collins's comment on the day the Four Courts were occupied, that 'no government in the world could exist' which did not
control its army, set the IRA Executive action in a larger frame.[128] When
a journalist suggested that the occupations represented a 'coup d'état'
or a 'military dictatorship', Rory O'Connor seems to have assented,
though he later denied it. (His easygoing response, 'you can take it that
way if you like,' does have a ring of truth, but it is worth noting that the
phrase 'military dictatorship' had already been put into circulation by
the government itself.) In any case the anti-Treatyites were drifting in
that direction. Their political posture was at best half-baked. In terms of
generating a coherent policy, 'the Executive never fused into an effective
unit,' as O'Donoghue lamented. 'It never had a common mind.'[129]

'A REPUBLIC IN DISGUISE'

The timetable for the general election required by the Irish Free State
Act might perhaps have been taken lightly, since it was set by British
rather than Irish legislation, but Griffith wanted the election held as

soon as possible, by June at the latest. Republicans demanded revision of the 1921 electoral roll, which Griffith refused, but went along with the idea of new elections. In the Dáil on 17 May, Cathal Brugha complained he was 'sick of politics', pleading for all to unite in a 'crusade' to protect their people in the north-east. But de Valera conceded that 'the interests of the country demand that there be stable government' and undertook to 'give . . . assistance in any way' ('so long as we are not committed further than I have stated') to make that possible. He had rejected Collins's idea of a plebiscite to be held on a Sunday outside the country's churches – a 'stone age plebiscite' – but agreed to an electoral arrangement between the two sides of Sinn Féin. Announced on 20 May, the 'electoral pact' would divide the seats in proportion to the 64–57 division in the Dáil vote on the Treaty. The contours of the split would be artificially preserved.

This was pure election-rigging, and Griffith was as dismayed by it as he had been by the Limerick deal. Ernest Blythe remembered that when he was asked to agree to it in Cabinet he seemed to be under 'tremendous emotional stress'. 'He worked nervously with his neck-tie in silence. He took off his glasses and wiped them . . . his hand was shaking so that he could hardly hold them.' For what seemed like three minutes of dead silence round the Cabinet table, he repeatedly adjusted his tie, put on and took off his glasses, and slowly polished them. Only after this agonizing struggle within himself did he say simply 'I agree.' He said nothing more; and from then on, when he referred to Collins, he called him not 'Mick' or 'Collins', but 'Mr Collins', the most distant form of address.[130]

The nervous strain of the situation now threatened Griffith's health. He became convinced that Collins would never nerve himself to take on the government's opponents directly, and would let the situation slide beyond the point of possible recovery. As Blythe said, it was somewhat easier for him to demand a showdown: he was not faced with the prospect of having to use a weapon against former comrades in arms. But the psychological burden of the split was immense for him: no Treatyite liked being accused of betraying Ireland, but for Griffith it was almost unbearable. His hatred of Erskine Childers, whom he now talked of as a British agent, became obsessive.

Many believed that the new Irish Free State constitution would be a vital factor in the election. Collins's assertion that it would be possible to have an essentially republican constitution under the Treaty terms played a significant part in the IRA's spring negotiations. Frank Aiken had urged that no drastic action be taken until the constitution could be studied. Liam Lynch told his brother on 6 March, 'if we can force the Treaty party to draw up a Republican constitution we are A1 again.' This he considered 'quite possible'. Drafting the new constitution was thus much more than a legal exercise. If it indeed proved possible to combine in it both republican and British symbolic elements, it might succeed where external association had failed. This was a task arguably as important as any on the Provisional Government's agenda.

The drafting committee was headed by Collins himself, with Darrell Figgis, returning to (near) centre stage after a long detour, as deputy chairman. Figgis, who had published several essays on the idea of the Gaelic state, was Griffith's choice, and had to do most of the day-to-day committee work. Collins obviously hoped at the start that the new cordiality of Anglo-Irish relations after the often frosty Treaty negotiations would allow some corners to be rubbed off. At first, the situation looked promising. The British government made an effort to accommodate the Provisional Government's wish to 'contend', as Churchill put it, 'that their constitution derived its authority from the Treaty and not from a British act of Parliament'.[131] It was ready to include the constitution as a mere schedule to its bill ratifying the Treaty – in effect smuggling it through. But for this to happen the constitution would have had to be ready by the end of February, and this was impossible. And, as Collins found, there were sharp limits to British flexibility. Even in February, before the threat of civil conflict became acute, his suggestion that the Viceregal Lodge might make an admirable cancer hospital failed to evoke a response in kind. Jokes could be 'so dangerous', Austen Chamberlain chillingly replied. 'The question was of the greatest importance to His Majesty's Government who could not consent to the humiliation of the representative of the Crown.' This set the tone for future British reactions to the Free State constitutional proposals, which became more rigid as the anti-Treaty republican threat to the Provisional Government intensified. The electoral pact was as alarming to the British as to Griffith, but while Griffith had to choke back his rage, Churchill was able to exploit it to insist on incorporation of the symbols of Crown and empire. 'Had the proposed election been a bona fide one,' Churchill noted in May, 'they could have put pressure on us to stretch the

Constitution to suit them'; but 'as no election of value is contemplated we are in a position to be much more searching in our examination of the Constitution.'[132]

Collins told the committee to concentrate on future 'practicalities' rather than past 'legalities', and to aim for a document that would be both concise and, importantly, easy to adapt as Ireland's status evolved. It should contain 'no unnecessary sentiment which might be laughed at'. He was even against the mixing of Irish and English terms (well established by now in republican usage), which he thought had 'a grotesque effect'. He himself quickly drafted a very short constitution – with just ten basic articles – representing, he believed, 'the essence of a Gaelic polity . . . without the trappings'.[133] Unfortunately this difference between 'essence' and 'trappings' bedevilled the entire constitution-drafting process. The committee split three ways, and produced three drafts, all dramatically bigger than his, and with more identifiable ideological freighting. Drafts A (seventy-eight articles) and B (eighty-one) were broadly similar except as regards the structure of the Executive, Senate and Supreme Court. Draft A, for instance, proposed a system of cabinet government on the British model, and gave the Senate more power than B did. The third draft, by Alfred O'Rahilly and James Murnaghan, was a more explicit reflection of Catholic ideas of social justice.

Collins remained oddly optimistic, perhaps through a combination of his intense desire to reconcile the constitution with republicanism and 'breathing the rarefied air of constitutional theory'.[134] He reviewed the drafts on 8 March, and the Cabinet decided that Draft B, which included the idea of an appointed upper house (the Senate) designed to enhance minority protection, and brought in the concept of an executive containing non-elected 'extern' ministers, should form the basis of the proposal carried to London. It approved a declaratory preface asserting Irish sovereignty, though the delegation removed this before presenting the draft to the British on 27 May. Even without the preamble it was immediately identified by Lloyd George as a 'complete evasion of the Treaty and a setting up of a republic with a thin veneer'. The Prime Minister fulminated that the 'republic in disguise' made the monarchy look ridiculous, ignored the oath of allegiance and rejected the idea of a Commonwealth foreign policy. The British might conceivably have accepted that this was what the political situation required, but they were unable to make the kind of imaginative leap needed. The British signatories undoubtedly feared the political extinction predicted by Chamberlain if they went too far. Lloyd George had, the day before, made clear that 'the one thing on which the British government could fight was allegiance to the king.' The government's law officers now delivered a lecture on the centrality of the Crown as the bond of the empire, a role reflected in its position not only as the supreme executive – acting on the advice of Dominion ministers – but also as the final legal authority. (The Irish draft constitution also left out the possibility of appeal to the Privy Council.)

The week-long negotiations that followed were almost as bruising as those over the Treaty. On several issues the attempt to fudge the explicit acknowledgment of British symbols was defeated. The draft avoided using the title 'governor general' for the Crown representative, and also withheld the Crown's power to dissolve parliament, which could only dissolve itself. The British insisted on both the title and the power of dissolution (though the eventual clause was obscure enough that 'no one understood' it).[135] After a long meeting on 30 May between the Provisional Government's law officer, Hugh Kennedy, and the Lord Chief Justice had got nowhere, Kennedy drew up a statement of the Irish position. He argued that the Treaty recognized that the Irish people were to establish a constitution which would be 'their own creation', and that traditional British forms were at best meaningless in Ireland and at worst imbued with negative value. Lloyd George simply refused to recognize this interpretation, repeatedly insisting that the Crown must occupy the same position in Ireland as in the other Dominions. The gulf was never clearer than in a private meeting between Collins, Griffith and Lloyd George on 1 June. Collins, whose humour had soured, berated the British as 'Shylocks' – an apposite tag in the circumstances, even if it did not fit diplomatic conventions. The normally unflappable Tom Jones found him 'pugnacious', 'belligerent' and 'militant'; Lloyd George called him a 'wild animal'. The Prime Minister claimed that as a Celt himself he was eager to see a Celtic nation play an international role, but repeated that the Crown must be accepted as a mystic term that stood for the power of the people. Griffith's objection that in Ireland it conveyed just the opposite meaning cut no ice. The Prime Minister's obtuseness may have been wilful – he was not habitually an obtuse man. His driving of a hard bargain was certainly in part deliberate. His dismissive remarks about Collins after the meeting, however, suggest that he had not troubled to work up much knowledge of the situation in Ireland, and that his understanding of the country remained 'very limited'.[136]

'NOT ONLY THE END OF THE IRISH REPUBLIC, BUT THE END OF REPUBLICANISM IN IRELAND'

The importance of the June election is clear, but just what it represented is less so. It was the Free State's first general election; but in the republican view it was not a 'free' one – not because of the electoral pact, which republicans had signed up to, but because people were in effect coerced by the threat of renewed war into voting against their real beliefs. The threat was certainly an influence, but it had been present to everyone since July 1921, and the Treaty debates had largely hinged on the capacity of the Republic to withstand another, more intense war. Republicans also protested that the Free State constitution was not published until the very last moment before the election – in fact on the morning the polls opened on 16 June. This deprived the electorate of some vital evidence, and it is revealing that Collins earlier admitted (to the British) that 'if they did not have an election till after the Constitution was drafted, the Treaty would be beaten in Ireland.'[137] It can of course be argued that the whole Treaty issue had effectively been put in cold storage by the pact, but republicans also charged that the pact was broken. Collins allegedly repudiated it on the eve of the election. In Cork on 14 June he appealed to his audience to 'vote for the candidates you think best of,' those 'the electors of Cork think will carry on best in the future the work they want carried on'. Admittedly he did not directly urge them to vote for the pact candidates, but his uncharacteristically indefinite phraseology did not immediately strike the press as signalling a break with de Valera. His speech next day in his home town, Clonakilty, was even more ambiguous, asking people to support the pact 'in the spirit in which it was made', before telling them 'their duty was to vote for the people they thought would carry out that policy.'

Republicans might have tried to prevent the election by force, but when this was proposed at the IRA Executive on 9 April, Florrie

O'Donoghue, Seán O'Hegarty and Tom Hales resigned, and the idea was dropped. Some came to regret this. The British-designed PR system used in the 1921 election was carried over, and produced a decisive majority of deputies accepting the Treaty. The long-delayed reappearance of Labour as an independent political party broke Sinn Féin's electoral monopoly, and by the day of the poll a Farmers' grouping and a clutch of Independents had raised the number of non-pact candidates to fifty-one. Only thirty-four Sinn Feiners (half of them pro-, half anti-Treaty) were able to run unopposed. In the end, pact candidates won around 60 per cent of the votes cast. Pro-Treaty Sinn Feiners comfortably outpolled anti-Treaty republicans by 239,000 first-preference votes to 130,000 (fifty-eight seats to thirty-six); but the republicans were also outpolled by Labour with 132,000 (though this tally produced only seventeen seats). Altogether Labour, Farmers and Independent deputies brought the pro-Treaty majority to 92 out of 128, with over 78 per cent of the votes cast. Geographically, there was a striking east–west and urban–rural split: republicans won a bare majority in Connacht, and came close in rural Munster, but lost decisively in Leinster and the Ulster border counties, as well as in Dublin and Cork cities. Dorothy Macardle pronounced the result 'not only the end of the Irish Republic, but the end of Republicanism in Ireland'.[138]

On 18 June, before the results of the election were announced, the third Army Convention debated further reunification proposals. Seán MacBride had returned from a mission to Germany to find that a split had developed within the Executive – 'and it became more and more apparent . . . that this split was on an absolutely fundamental decision of policy.' Lynch, Seán Moylan and Liam Deasy were 'ready to work the Treaty' and allow the IRA to be 'controlled by the Free State Army'. The mood was sombre – Lynch's speech was 'very depressing', and 'everybody was depressed and solemn.' In middle of the debate Tom Barry proposed a motion to resume the war against the British (actually to deliver an ultimatum to withdraw all their forces in seventy-two hours). Though Lynch and Brugha were against it, and both O'Connor and Mellows thought the motion 'a huge mistake' at that point, it was narrowly carried. Then (as MacBride, one of the tellers, recorded) the vote was challenged on the ground that 'there was a Brigade there which wasn't represented at the last Convention.'[139] Eventually the motion was defeated by 118 to 103. The minority split from the Executive, and made

Joe McKelvey their chief of staff. There were now two anti-Treaty IRAs, and as O'Donoghue put it, 'the state of the Army was chaotic.'[140]

'OUR BOAST OF CIVILISATION IN THESE ISLANDS IS STULTIFIED'

British inflexibility, rooted in an entrenched suspicion of Irish separatism, denied the Provisional Government the political advantage of being able to demonstrate that Collins's interpretation of the Treaty was valid. The British were convinced of Griffith's commitment to the Treaty, but it did not take much to persuade them that Collins remained a covert republican. The British government had already ensured the ruin of its most committed allies, the Redmondite nationalists, through a similar lack of political imagination. Luckily for Britain, the Treatyites did not meet the same fate as the Redmondites. But the British could take little credit for securing the outcome they needed. Not only did they insist on a rigid implementation of the Treaty, they became increasingly strident in their insistence that the Provisional Government take direct action to crush republican defiance. Ignoring the potentially fatal risk of confirming the republican charge that the Provisional Government was a British puppet regime, they hustled it on to an open military confrontation.

In June Churchill bombarded Griffith with 'specimens of letters which were pouring into this office' deploring the state of affairs in Ireland: 'Rich and poor turned out of their homes on two hours notice ... leaving behind them the inheritance of generations and generations ... The cattle are killed, the lonely white peacocks hunted to death – some of the scenes are like those of the French Revolution.' Churchill boomed portentously, 'Until somehow or other we find a means of putting an end to this state of affairs, our boast of civilisation in these Islands is stultified.'[141] British pressure reached a peak after Sir Henry Wilson was assassinated by anti-Treaty IRA men in London on 22 June. This sent a shockwave through Westminster and Whitehall, even though Wilson's extremism probably posed more of a threat to British mainstream politics than it did to Irish republicanism. Lloyd George fired off a formal warning to Collins that:

the ambiguous position of the Irish Republican Army can no longer be ignored by the British Government. Still less can Mr Rory O'Connor be permitted to remain with his followers and his arsenal in open rebellion in the heart of Dublin . . . organising and sending out from this centre enterprises of murder not only in the area of your Government but also in the Six Northern Counties and in Great Britain.

If this stayed just about in the realm of request rather than instruction, the following words crossed that fine line: 'His Majesty's Government cannot consent to a continuance of this state of things.'[142]

Belligerent language was almost followed by actual belligerence. Though many provincial military garrisons had been withdrawn, British forces remained in strength in Dublin. When Collins, on a trip to Cork, failed to reply immediately to this ultimatum – in fact the Provisional Government never replied to it – the British Cabinet instructed General Macready to prepare a full-scale assault on the Four Courts using tanks and aircraft as well as field artillery. On 24 June it decided that the attack should go ahead the following day. Macready, unsurprisingly, took a dim view of this project. In his view the assassination had thrown the Cabinet into a panic: he sensed 'suppressed agitation'; 'considerations of personal safety' were contending with 'a desire to do something dramatic'. (Churchill actually took refuge in his attic at Chartwell with a loaded revolver for the night of the 22nd, barricading the door with an iron sheet.) The Cabinet's 'ignorance of the Irish situation blinded them to possible results'. An operation like this could not be carried out without civilian casualties, and would almost certainly backfire fatally.

Though Lloyd George declared that he did not want to publish his letter to Collins, and 'would rather they acted upon their own initiative, rather than with the appearance that they are doing it under compulsion from the British Government', this good sense was spectacularly ditched in the House of Commons on the afternoon of 26 June. Speaking immediately after Henry Wilson's funeral that morning, Churchill, tasked by the Cabinet with making clear that 'the ambiguous position of the IRA must come to an end,' produced a characteristically resonant parliamentary rhodomontade. He declared that 'the prime and continuing cause of all the horrors which have taken place in Belfast is the organisation of . . . two divisions of the Irish Republican Army in Northern territory,' and that 'the greedy and criminal design of breaking down the Northern Government ... has got to die in the hearts of those who nourish it.' He threatened that 'if, through weakness, want of courage' or, he added, 'some other even less creditable reason', the presence in Dublin of 'a band of men styling themselves the Headquarters of the Republican Executive' was 'not brought to an end and a speedy end ... we shall regard the Treaty as having been formally violated ... and we shall resume full liberty of action in any direction ... to any extent that may be necessary'.[143] This was dangerously provocative. Churchill told Collins, 'we had reached the end of our tether,' but that only underlined the failure of understanding.

At least Churchill stopped short of broadcasting the hint that Lloyd George had dropped in his letter to Collins, of direct British military aid: 'assistance has on various occasions been given to dominions of the Empire in cases where their authority was challenged by rebellion.' It would be difficult for the Treatyites to lay the mantle of 'rebels' on their erstwhile comrades. But talks had already begun between Griffith, Emmet Dalton and the British military authorities, about supplying the Provisional Government with the material it needed to eject the republicans from the Four Courts. This massively sensitive issue might have given the government further pause. (Dorothy Macardle would entitle the April–July 1922 section of her epic republican narrative 'English Guns'.) But any worries about its public presentation were eased by the republicans themselves. On 27 June a prominent anti-Treaty IRA commander, Leo Henderson, was arrested while carrying out a raid on a garage in Lower Baggot Street. This was apparently part of the ongoing republican effort to reinforce the supposedly suspended Belfast Boycott – 'the only real activity' of the anti-Treaty forces, Todd Andrews thought. In response, the republicans arrested an even more prominent Treatyite, Ginger O'Connell, and held him in the Four Courts. This 'kidnapping' of a senior National Army officer provided a plausible *casus belli*.

The Provisional Government now warned the Four Courts garrison that unless they left the building immediately, surrendering their arms along with O'Connell, 'necessary military action will be taken at once.' At 3.40 a.m. on 28 June a message (signed by Tom Ennis, OC 2nd Eastern Division) was delivered, requiring them to parade on the Quays by 4 a.m., or 'the building will be taken by me by force.' Collins must have consented to this, though the actual decision seems to have been taken by Griffith. Why did Collins accept that attack was inevitable? He could not have known of the British military preparations (such as they were). The most real fear must have been not that – as later alleged – the republicans were about to stage a coup, but that they would attack British troops and throw the British withdrawal into reverse. The 18 June split made this more than likely.

Overall command of the attack, under the authority of Mulcahy as Dáil defence minister, was given to Emmet Dalton. The precise status of the troops deployed, from Tom Ennis's 2nd Eastern Division and the newly formed Dublin Guard under Paddy O'Daly, was ambiguous. The need to avoid using any British troops was always, as Andy Cope noted, absolutely clear to the Irish government(s). But the Four Courts building was effectively a fortress, and any direct assault on it would require artillery. Macready supplied two 18-pounder field guns to the Provisional Government – in response, he said, to urgent phone calls from O'Duffy, the Chief of Staff (though O'Duffy later denied this). Another two followed later that day, with a handful of British artillery-men to advise on their use. The National Army troops, not just inexperienced but almost all untrained (many of those deployed had not even fired a rifle), now had to learn to fire them in action. Emmet Dalton himself, the only leader with personal experience of modern artillery warfare, was forced to spend three hours serving one of the guns.

Unsurprisingly, the first day of the attack did not go well. The guns had to be aimed by opening the breech and sighting the target through the barrel. Dalton realized that several shells had overshot the Four Courts and landed on the British GHQ at Kilmainham; when he went over to apologize he found himself under the same bombardment. Even the shells that hit their target had little effect on the mighty structure. Churchill was keen for the attackers to use 60-pound howitzers instead, but this offer was not taken up. (Macready was in any case reluctant to give his former enemies such powerful weapons, and Churchill had to tell Cope to lean on him.)[144] Shortage of high-explosive shells – the British had supplied ten per gun – worried Dalton. Macready 'agreed to send him fifty rounds of shrapnel, which was all we had left, simply to make a noise through the night, as he was afraid that if the guns stopped firing his men would get disheartened and clear off'. The next day went no better. 'This is not a battle,' Cope lamented. Garrison and attackers were 'each firing . . . hundreds of rounds with probably remarkably few hits'. Just out of range, 'the people carry on their ordinary business.' By the end of the day, Churchill was talking of air action (a habit the Colonial Office had got into overseas) and even discussing how to disguise British aircraft in Free State colours.

'IT'S GOOD TO FEEL MYSELF A SOLDIER AGAIN'

The attack forced the Four Courts garrison to think about the rationale of their action, and showed that they had no positive idea of how the campaign might proceed. Strong as the building was, its complicated interior made it hard for the 180 men of the garrison to stay in touch with each other. O'Malley rightly judged that they were 'rats in a trap'. They seem to have spent much of their time trying to figure out a means of escape (O'Malley advocated digging a tunnel) and waiting for the arrival of relief forces. Their Rolls-Royce armoured car, wryly christened 'The Mutineer', could do no more than drive back and forth inside the compound, firing on the National troops working their way into the west wing building. Most of the Dublin Brigade were stuck (as O'Malley complained) on the wrong side of O'Connell Street. Todd Andrews had a low opinion of their military leaders – and, with the exception of O'Malley, of the leadership as a whole. After studying them at close quarters for several months, he concluded that 'the man with a record was not necessarily, nor indeed usually, a man with the qualities required to deal with the predicament in which we in the Four Courts found ourselves.'[145] The same went for the republican forces outside, which Andrews later joined. Oscar Traynor was against a repeat of 1916 and in favour of guerrilla warfare, but he went an odd way about it. When Andrews met up with the 4th Battalion in the Hammam Hotel, he found that they were about to barricade it in 1916 style. 'I could not believe that we were going to indulge in such a foolishly futile military exercise. But so it turned out.' They had no doubt that 'militarily we were in a hopeless position,' but simply had no idea what else to do. At least the company of 'a squad, if that is the word, of pretty young Cumann na mBan girls to attend to our commissariat' was agreeable.

Traynor also occupied the luxurious Gresham Hotel, along with the Granville and the rest of the block between Earl Street and Parnell Street. De Valera arrived there to rejoin his old battalion as a rank-and-file Volunteer. The other most senior republican leaders, Stack and Brugha, together with Countess Markievicz, also gathered at 'the block' to confer with Traynor (who was 'in sole and complete charge of military operations', as Andrews pointedly noted). None of them had any specific military or political position. Just before leaving his Suffolk Street office de Valera had issued a press statement characterizing 'the men who are now being attacked by the forces of the Provisional Government' as 'those who refuse to obey the order to yield' to 'England's threat of war'. He declared that 'the Republic' was the 'embodiment' of Ireland's independence. Liam Lynch, over the river at the Clarence Hotel, issued a more direct appeal to his 'fellow citizens ... to rally to the support of the Republic'.[146] Co-signed by fifteen senior republicans (including Mellows, O'Connor, McKelvey, O'Malley, Seamus Robinson and Seán Moylan), this showed that the split-within-the-split was over.

For two days the senior officers in the Four Courts debated the idea of surrender, finally rejecting it as a betrayal of the Republic. O'Malley and Paddy O'Brien, the garrison commander, planned a sortie, but in the mid-morning of 30 June the munitions store (in the Public Record Office wing) was hit by a shell and exploded, stunning the garrison and hurling a stupendous cloud of shredded irreplaceable archival records into the air. Oscar Traynor sent a message arguing that he could not relieve the Courts, and as the senior officer outside he was entitled to order the garrison to surrender. 'If the Republic is to be saved your surrender is a necessity.' His reasoning (influenced, Moss Twomey told Lynch, by Brugha) was that 'the Free State people can reduce any position with artillery and capture the Garrisons and Equipment and thus destroy the morale of our Forces.' But if the Four Courts surrendered, the rest could evacuate their positions 'voluntarily without loss of prestige on the plea that they were occupied only to relieve the pressure on the Four Courts Garrison'.[147] The garrison, exhausted by pointless tunnelling as much as by shellfire, had become equally defeatist: their morale was 'broken by their crowding together in cellars where they could do nothing but listen to the fire ... and hear the explosions'. O'Malley reluctantly accepted that surrender was inevitable, and led out the 130 survivors at 3.30 that afternoon.

'The block' was left as the last republican stronghold. It had a few days' grace as the National troops worked their way up O'Connell Street with great caution, getting within range only on 4 July. Armoured cars drove up, peppering the hotels, whose garrisons broke through the internal walls exactly like Connolly's garrisons in 1916. Artillery shelled the Gresham and the Hammam. By 5 July the buildings were on fire, and de Valera left with Stack and Traynor, assuming that the others would follow. (Markievicz had already left.) When they did not, Traynor ordered the survivors to retreat or surrender, but instead Brugha ran out into Thomas's Lane, at the back of 'the block', where he was mortally wounded. That evening de Valera anxiously wrote to him, 'I had no idea in view of the plan agreed on that you would attempt to hold the Hotels as long as you did ... You were scarcely justified ... in taking the risk you ran.' He added a rare personal note: 'we were all more than vexed with you – But all's well that ends well.' By the time his letter arrived, Brugha was dead. Sadly, perhaps, for the Republic, its most unflinching defender was happier with gun in hand, facing death, than he had been facing political disagreement in the council chamber. Sixty-five Executive and Provisional Government troops also died in the Dublin fighting, as did an unknown number of 'civilians' – possibly well over 250.

De Valera felt that at least 'the opening of the campaign otherwise not to be dreamt of by us gave a definite beginning.' His press statement spoke starkly of 'this war'. But the republicans, though physically better armed than the government's forces, were not psychologically armed for war. O'Malley had not even been able to persuade the Four Courts garrison to occupy the surrounding houses in preparation for the inevitable assault, since they felt that firing on the approaching government forces would create a war situation. He bitterly lamented 'the futile way in which we fought, the air of induced martyrdom in the Courts, and the mysterious occupation of O'Connell Street'.[148] There was no plan of campaign. Traynor believed in guerrilla fighting but found himself sandbagging and loopholing hotels. He had little alternative, perhaps – without work to occupy them, he may well have feared that his men might drift away. But keeping them there made any idea of 'relieving' the Four Courts less rather than more feasible. Traynor hoped that the relief would come from the countryside (just as Pearse had in 1916). For a few days, the possibility of a 'march on Dublin' did exist, but in a sad anticipation of future republican strategy it petered out in a confused muster in Blessington, a village of 'almost one long street below the hills', 15 miles south of the capital.

Gerald Boland, commandant of the 7th Battalion of the 2nd Dublin Brigade, complained that his brigadier, Andy McDonnell, 'took every man he had from Bray to Arklow and left the road [to Dublin] wide open. He brought the whole mob out to Blessington in Furey's Charabancs and not even one loaf of bread'. On 1 July Ernie O'Malley, Seán Lemass and others who had escaped from detention in Jameson's Distillery arrived ('to pester me' as Boland grumpily put it). O'Malley took over, with Lemass as his director of operations and Boland's brother Harry as quartermaster general. His instinct was, once again, to fortify the place – barricades were erected around it, and 'engineers were sent out on the roads . . . to dig up the metalled surface and lay mines to prevent the approach of armoured cars.'[149] He issued orders for the 'destruction of communications, the establishment of our own communications, and the perfecting of an efficient Intelligence system', adding encouragingly (in traditional GHQ style) that 'unarmed men can be as useful as . . . armed men.'[150]

None of this had any effect. When Oscar Traynor arrived at Blessington in the middle of the night on 6 July he found 'everybody asleep' and 'things rather mixed up'. He endorsed Gerald Boland's condemnation of Andy McDonnell's action in 'retreat[ing] from the whole eastern portion of his area, leaving it in the hands of the enemy'. Apparently ignoring O'Malley, he ordered the Blessington position to be abandoned. McDonnell was to 'split his Brigade into columns' and return to his old area. Traynor's idea was 'not to hold towns', but 'to hit and go away'. The force at Blessington, unfortunately, simply melted away, leaving behind trashed houses, robbed banks and 'a terrible spirit of defeat'. Most of the men 'stayed at home and were arrested for they had no leadership either from B[attalion]n or from the B[riga]de'.[151]

No republican leaders emerged with much credit from the Blessington fiasco, or the Dublin fighting. Few seem to have realized it, though. O'Malley agonized over 'surrender[ing] my own command' with 'no excuse that I could see'. 'I felt a sense of disgrace about it . . . nor could I find peace of mind about it.' But his comrades did not feel this way. 'Nobody said what should be said about such a personal failure'; most of them 'were not dissatisfied with the events of the past week'.[152] For them, simply fighting, however incompetently, seemed to be enough. The sense of relief in Paddy O'Brien's words to O'Malley when the Provisional Government's ultimatum was delivered to the Fours Courts garrison – 'It's come at last' – had been unmistakable. Liam Mellows made the point explicitly: 'it's good to feel myself a soldier again after all those futile negotiations.'[153] For Rory O'Connor, O'Malley wrote, 'the fight . . . had been a symbol of resistance. He had built a dream in his mind and the dream was there.' O'Malley thought O'Connor was insulated against the idea of failure – 'he evidently did not sense defeat,' or share O'Malley's idea that it might be more useful to escape from custody afterwards so as to keep up the fight. But in a long reflective letter written in Kilmainham gaol at the end of November 1923, O'Malley also acknowledged that 'fighting was so easy compared with that awful, soul-numbing, uphill fight against one's people's ignorance and prejudice' (a process that might be taken as a definition of political action). 'I had always been looking for fight as it was the best expression of my convictions.'[154]

'WE LET THE REPUBLIC GO BY DEFAULT'

Nobody has ever questioned Liam Lynch's selfless dedication to his cause, but his capacity to direct the republican campaign has come in for plenty of criticism. Not only did he have no policy, he seemed to reject the very notion of having one. He was 'a very good person, but he did not have a revolutionary mind', Peadar O'Donnell said. 'He could not descend from the high ground of the Republic to the level of politics.' Early in September 1922 he asserted unequivocally that there was 'no alternative policy to present one of fighting'. 'At present it is a waste of time to be thinking too much about policy.' If they could just 'strike our hardest for some time . . . this would make the question of policy easier to settle'. This plainly reflected the general dislike of 'politics' that had burgeoned among the republican leadership after the Treaty, as well as Lynch's personal suspicion that the 'Republican Party' had not 'its mind made up to total separation from England' as the army had. But it was problematic in more than one way. To fight without policy was to confirm the public image of militarism so carelessly endorsed by Rory O'Connor, a gift to Free State propaganda. The wishful thought that military action would cut through political complication has been the delusion of many soldiers. Lynch's belief in the efficacy of 'striking our hardest' rested on a misunderstanding of the real basis for republican success in 1920–21, which had not depended on mere striking power. If it were to make any sense, it required that the striking should really be 'hard'. Even by early September, however, it had become all too clear that it was not.

Peadar O'Donnell lamented that 'we were very poorly off politically' in 1922. 'We let the Republic go by default.'[155] A degree of rigidity was perhaps built into republican thinking. O'Malley acknowledged 'a certain hardness in our idealism', which 'made us aloof from ordinary living, as if we were above it'. Men and women of principle were more apt to ignore than to cultivate ordinary people. 'There was insistence on principle, which often stood coldly out where immediate feeling was needed.'[156] Even to discuss policy was to raise the possibility of different priorities. Impelled by conviction rather than analysis, Republican strategic direction was never precisely organized.

The republicans began the war, as has often been pointed out, with some apparent military advantages. Even if the army Executive did not represent 80 per cent of the old IRA, as O'Donoghue implied, it certainly controlled a clear majority – most estimates put it at over two-thirds. So the anti-Treaty forces were distinctly more seasoned than the government's, and – even with only the 7,000 or so rifles they possessed – probably at least as well armed, at the outset. They lacked artillery, but so had the old IRA; they had plenty of experience in conducting the kind of campaign that would render such matériel irrelevant. They had a substantial munitions production capacity in Cork, with Patrick McHugh in charge. (He sent 2,000 grenades to the Four Courts.) McHugh even succeeded in producing the trench mortars that had failed in 1921.

But republican commanders did little to exploit their resources. Most of them were extremely cautious about the kind of operations they might launch. To McHugh, arriving in Cork from Dublin in June, 'it appeared they had no idea that there might be a fight.' Once fighting had started, little changed. Republicans' reluctance to fire on their errant comrades has been widely attested. Not all of them shared it, of course: Walter Mitchell made clear what he thought of the orders his unit received a few weeks into the war to fire over the heads of the Staters: 'They never fired over me.'[157] But the point was that such orders were issued. Oscar Traynor's reasoning went for many others: 'The O/C Dublin', Twomey told Lynch in early July,

> does not consider it wise to resort at the moment to Ambushes in the streets, as it would alienate public sympathy which has much improved in our favour, would antagonise the rank and file of the Free State Forces who he believes are half-hearted and very much susceptible to propaganda influences, and also he favours the continuation of the situation which compels the Free State to make war on us.[158]

All these points made perfectly good sense, but they amounted to a wholly passive defensive policy. It was based on the assumption that time was on the republicans' side: an attractive one, naturally, but one which, if it turned out to be mistaken, would prove fatal.

Initially, the attack on the Four Courts at least had the effect of re-uniting the anti-Treaty forces, and Lynch resumed his authority as chief of staff on 29 June. At the same time, though, he moved out of Dublin and established his HQ at Mallow. This was a perhaps more than tacit recognition of the geopolitics of the struggle, and the effective abandonment of Dublin. Lynch's strategic command was unchallenged, but he did not choose to work out a policy with his peers. Traynor naturally believed Dublin to be vital, and so did O'Malley, who saw clearly enough that 'it is not so much use making the South unbearable for them if they have the Capital.' But he addressed this view to Liam Deasy, not Lynch. Traynor bridled at Lynch's idea of 'keeping [the] route to [the] South open' – with what precise purpose he did not say – and asked whether it was more important than 'the holding of Dublin' itself. But he does not seem to have got an answer. O'Malley himself, instead of returning to 2nd Southern Division, was appointed deputy chief of staff by Lynch. But when Lynch went back to Munster he was left in Dublin, and given command of the whole eastern and northern theatre (the two Dublin brigades, 1st Eastern and all northern divisions) – an area he had no experience of, and which had little or no organizational coherence. This was simply a waste of talent. Twomey maintained that GHQ, or some of it, should be in Dublin, and Lynch may have thought that O'Malley fulfilled this requirement. O'Malley himself repeatedly urged Lynch to establish GHQ in the capital, but Lynch said that while he would 'like to', it was more effective 'here, where we are more in touch with the actual situation and developments' (a telling enough phrase).

The republican high command was shaped in part by accident. Several senior leaders who had surrendered in the Four Courts, notably Joe McKelvey, Liam Mellows and Rory O'Connor, were in prison from that point until their deaths, while O'Malley (with Paddy O'Brien's adjutant Seán Lemass) had escaped. Tom Barry had been arrested trying to enter the building, though he escaped in August. Lynch himself was arrested during the Dublin fighting, along with Liam Deasy, only to be released on Mulcahy's instructions. He was again pulled up in Kilkenny on his way to Cork, and again let go. This coincidence suggested to some that he had given some parole, which the government alleged, and he and Deasy denied. If he had, it would have been out of character. Back in Dublin, on 27 July Oscar Traynor was arrested by a National Army patrol at Baggot Street Bridge. Austin Stack was pitchforked into the job of IRA quartermaster general at the beginning of August after Harry Boland was killed (shot while allegedly resisting arrest in the Grand Hotel, Skerries, though why he was there, in an area of exiguous republican activity, nobody seemed to know). Republican faith aside, Stack's qualifications for this key post were no more evident than they had been for his earlier posting as deputy chief of staff, and, as before, he seems to have put in a patchy performance.[159]

On the map, the republican position looked strong: almost all the main southern centres were in their hands. In 1st Southern Division area, only two posts were held by pro-Treaty forces, and they were immediately taken. Republican forces outnumbered and outgunned the government's. They were certainly adequate for a sudden coup. But when the chance of using this strength to dispute the government's control of Dublin was lost, the balance shifted. Lynch established a defensive line from Limerick to Waterford, but positional defence was ultimately impossible for forces that had few machine guns and no artillery. The republican leadership saw the Limerick compromise (as Con Moloney said) as giving them 'a considerable military advantage as with a comparatively small number of troops held up at Limerick, we have been able to ensure that at least 3,000 of F.S. troops are also held up'. If they had had to fight in Limerick the forces there 'would not only be held there for at least 10 days, but we wouldn't be in a position to re-enforce Wexford–New Ross area. How could we hope to attack

Thurles?' That supposed a large-scale offensive movement towards Dublin, but this never materialized. Instead as National troops concentrated on Limerick, the unsuitability of the republican forces for urban fighting became clear. Hostilities began late on 11 July and remained inconclusive for six days, with key posts in the city centre changing hands more than once. But when O'Duffy arrived on the 27th with reinforcements and an 18-pounder gun, the four key republican positions in the city were swiftly abandoned and left in flames. The battle for Limerick had the air of conventional warfare, but this was belied by the mercifully light casualty rate. Though there were eight days of fairly intense gunfire between the initial National assault on the Ordnance Barracks and the final republican retreat, no more than eight National troops were killed.

The traffic from that point on was almost all one way. Although Liam Deasy's tenacious defence of the Kilmallock front brought the National advance to a standstill, and showed that republican forces could fight positional battles in the countryside, it was undermined by the fall of the main southern towns over the next three weeks. Waterford was taken by National troops under John T. Prout on 23 July – a single field gun again playing an apparently decisive role. Three republican columns assembled by Dinny Lacey in Carrick-on-Suir advanced on Kilkenny through Mullinavant but retreated again when Lacey thought he had lost surprise. In the west, the first coastal landing, of troops embarked at Dublin on 22 July, took Westport on the 24th. Seán MacEoin's deputy, Tony Lawlor, had already advanced through Castlerea, Ballinrobe, Ballyhaunis, Claremorris and Ballaghadereen without meeting resistance, and Castlebar was also captured in late July. At the end of the month, Seán MacEoin told Mulcahy that 'all the reports about fights, and thousands of men, has [sic] faded considerably into thin air.'[160] Tralee was taken by a force under Paddy Daly landing from the sea at Fenit on 31 July. Dublin troops were crucial here, as they were in the decisive landing at Passage West on 11 August which opened the way for the capture of Cork. Lynch's own HQ at Fermoy (where it had arrived after moving from Mallow via Limerick and Clonmel) was abandoned. From then on they reverted to the time-honoured recourse of the weak, guerrilla warfare. This was now called 'forming into columns' in IRA terminology, a revealing usage which indicated that from the deep local structures on which the Volunteer campaign of 1919–21 had rested, only the columns survived.

'Slowly the resistance retrogressed back from some semi-open fighting', as O'Malley put it, 'to disintegrated guerilla war in which smaller and smaller columns and groups took part.' The question became how effectively the columns could operate in the changed environment. As Florrie O'Donoghue succinctly noted, they faced two serious disadvantages they had not faced in the previous fight. 'The majority of the people were no longer with them, and their opponents had an intimate and detailed knowledge of their personnel.'[161] Either would be damaging to the prospects of sustained guerrilla action; both together were really fatal. O'Donoghue might have added a third difficulty – the Church had become openly hostile. Given the republicans' need to commandeer supplies and strike levies to provide funds, the likelihood of any improvement in public support was slender. An appreciation sent to O'Malley on 29 July by the IRA Adjutant General, Con Moloney, showed the scale of the problem. Although 1st Western Division area, for instance, was 'well organised and a tremendous amount of work has been done there', it was 'very hard to do anything effective there as the people generally are hostile and convey intelligence to the enemy'. The 3rd Southern Division area was frankly 'hopeless' – columns had been disbanded because 'the men got dissatisfied and would not destroy roads, nor would they fight Free Staters, nor would they go against the priests etc.'[162]

In guerrilla warfare it is such factors, rather than armaments or supplies, that are the key elements. There is little sign that many, if indeed any, of the local republican leaders recognized this. They were handicapped by their own belief in the Provisional Government's lack of legitimacy, and persuaded themselves that the people would come to share their view of them as usurpers and British stooges. Even allowing for this, though, they did little to assess the situation systematically and take appropriate action. If anything the reverse process occurred, and they reverted to the kind of fragmentation that Mao would later castigate as 'guerrillaism'. Noting that in Dublin 1 'we cannot bring the war home to them very effectively', as 'there are not sufficient funds on hand to even maintain a strong column or a strong ASU', O'Malley added that in Dublin 2 'Petty jealousy, insubordination and organised opposition have prevented columns ... from doing anything active.' The total effective strength of 1st Eastern Division – 250 men ('which may be overestimating') – meant that 'even if it concentrated its available strength round the Curragh district', it 'would not be even able to obstruct the roads there'.

Generally, the arrest of senior officers has 'played havoc with areas in the Command'. There was a complete lack of communication between the three divisions of Western Command. Lynch, fuming about the inactivity of 3rd Western, asked 'Are all rifles in 3rd Western manned? . . . I cannot make out what they are doing.' If they had surplus rifles these should be sent to 2nd Western. 'You must press that all rifles are manned.' Enemy garrisons were no bigger than forty to eighty men, so 'if all our forces on active service are properly organised into columns and well led they should be able to make things very hot for the enemy.'

The one guerrilla advantage retained by the republicans was their ability to exploit difficult terrain – Deasy noted that 'with a very small force we were more than holding our own' in the North Tipperary mountains, but the surrounding area was 'dormant'. Serious reverses like the loss of strategic centres could be mitigated by topography. Even though Free State forces captured Tubbercurry in Sligo, for instance, they never managed to get much further west. Despite repeated sweeps, Frank Carty was able to maintain his power base west of the Ox Mountains. In December his force was said to be in control of the whole area from Ballina to Ballisodare. Such success certainly provided evidence of the resilience of the republicans, and also of the failings of the Free State commanders; but it reflected above all the strategic marginality, if not irrelevance, of the remote uplands.

O'Malley's instructions to his sprawling command (enlarged in late July when Lynch casually threw in '1st Midland Div, that is any Brigades or Units you can have worked up') were ambitious enough. 'Similar . . . methods to those adopted against the British must be enforced' – but they must be 'much more vigorous', he wrote in late July. The IRA focus on obstruction of communications during the civil war has often been cited as evidence of its military weakness, but O'Malley clearly identified it from the outset as 'the work of paramount importance'. 'Half-hearted destruction will not do. Obstructions must be thorough and snipers must make the work of removing obstructions costly.' The point of this was to hamper enemy movements and make it easier for IRA intelligence to track them; 'tactical as well as strategical destruction' should mean that 'a sniper or a small ambush group could inflict casualties and thus make the enemy more wary in advancing.' Enemy posts would become isolated and IRA columns could combine to attack them individually.[163] All this was fine as long as both local units and columns were functioning effectively. But they were not, and the stream of strategic directions looked increasingly like the orders Hitler would issue to imaginary units in his last days in his bunker.

O'Malley's generalship has come in for sharp criticism. 'The rules and regulations he tried to impose, the manoeuvres he learned from his British and French military manuals, were utterly useless ... He had never even been to several of the key areas under his command. The orders he sent were often impractical; they took little or no account of the conditions of the men charged to carry them out.'[164] Certainly O'Malley seems to have lost the close contact with his command that he had maintained in the previous fight. From September until his arrest in November, he lived in some style in the house of Sheila Humphreys – 36 Ailesbury Road, in the 'leisurely, respectable and imperial' Dublin suburb between Donnybrook and Ballsbridge. It was a well-established safe house: Batt O'Connor had built a secret room there during the Anglo-Irish war. (For that very reason, of course, it was known to the National Army commanders as well.) There were servants and a tennis court where he played in the evenings to keep fit. Until the raiding party arrived on 4 November, and he was captured in a dramatic shoot-out, he could hardly have been further away from 'the war'. This was not altogether as agreeable for him as it can be made to sound; he chafed at the inactivity, but seems to have believed it forced on him by his position.

O'Malley at least grasped the need for some larger framework for military action. But when he asked for 'an outline of GHQ Military National policy', Lynch rather testily replied, 'is it necessary to state that our National policy is to maintain the established Republic?', adding, 'as you are already aware, we have no notion of setting up a Government.' Though 'our military policy must be Guerilla tactics,' in the 1st Southern area 'we are convinced of our future success in open country' – this area 'can more effectively wage war by holding certain fronts' (at least, 'for some time').[165] Lynch and his staff seem to have taken a less realistic view of public attitudes than the Volunteer commanders the previous year. His deputy Con Moloney predicted in late September that 'when they settle down to the inconvenience caused by Rail and Road destruction', the country people would 'improve Nationally'. Part of the reason why they did not may lie with the republican forces themselves. When it was decided in late August to issue all IRA units with a free paper under the old title *An tOglac*, third among the four principal objectives (after raising the 'Moral standard of the Army', and making its outlook 'more idealistic than at present') was 'to inculcate virile Republican principles'. The fourth, worryingly, was 'to discourage Intemperance and needless interference with civilian population'.[166]

The fundamental point was that 'generalship' in any conventional sense was not what was needed. What was needed was organizational impetus, of the kind previously supplied by Collins. Collins himself probably did not shine as a 'general' in that sense, and neither did Mulcahy, though even his opponents respected Mulcahy's dedication to duty. But they had always had a clear-eyed view of what could and what needed to be done. They had understood – as the British had not – the nature of the war they were directing. It was at this level that the real failings of Lynch's generalship lay. His strategy was informed by his fundamental assumption that guerrilla warfare could work, as it had against the British, because the Provisional Government was, in effect, itself British. It could be worn down and discouraged by the cost of fighting, and persuaded to give up. But this basic analysis was wrong. The Provisional Government had nowhere to go: it was fighting for survival.

As, of course, was the Republic – except that it did not seem to recognize the urgency of its situation. Even allowing for its strategic misconception, the republican campaign was oddly inert. Lynch's strategy rested on the defence of the 'Munster republic' as a kind of demonstration that the Republic could survive. There was no intention of trying to reconstruct the republican civil administration there, and for many the term was no more than gestural. In Cork itself, for six weeks something like a republican governmental apparatus could be seen. But it was a military government, with Liam Lynch as military governor. Lynch's primary concern was to impose discipline on the Volunteers themselves, and he brought in strong measures to curb irregular requisitioning – which often verged on looting. Nothing was to be commandeered without a form signed by the Cork No. 1 Brigade quartermaster. Motor vehicles across the whole of 1st Southern Division area had to carry permits, to be shown at all checkpoints, partly to control the unauthorized seizure of vehicles.[167] Liquor controls, including the closure of pubs at 10 p.m. and the punishment of publicans who went on serving drunks, were enforced by the republican police, while press censorship was carried out by a publicity department led by Erskine Childers.

Republican control of Cork has been described as 'visible, but shallow'. The IRA succeeded in raising considerable funds – some £100,000 – by annexing the customs revenue of the port. The Inland Revenue office was occupied in mid-July, and the district tax inspector was arrested while trying to leave the country, and ordered to report to IRA headquarters daily. But commerce, already depressed, was further damaged as suppliers refused to send goods to Cork. In an attempt to keep economic life going, shopkeepers who tried to shut up shop were ordered to carry on trading – even without stock. Like most military governments, the Cork republicans found that there were strict limits to their capacity to stimulate the economy.

'IT IS IN THE PUBLIC INTEREST THAT ORDER SHOULD BE RESTORED'

The government's campaign was better conceived – though not much. On the face of things, the best organizational talent in the former republican army was available for it: Collins and Mulcahy themselves above all, but also Béaslaí, O'Hegarty, O'Sullivan and O'Duffy – all practical men, not *têtes exaltées*. The most obviously qualified military men, O'Connell and Dalton, were quickly reinforced by others with direct Great War experience, who had so far been on the fringes of the IRA high command – men such as the Irish-American John T. Prout, a US infantry officer who had served in France before becoming an intelligence officer in the Tipperary Brigade.

On 1 July 1922 Collins announced that the Ministry for Defence was moving into Portobello barracks, and he would take over as C-in-C. Two days later the government authorized recruitment of up to 20,000 temporary troops, on top of the 15,000 regulars. On 7 July it issued a 'Call to Arms' envisaging a six-month enlistment at 10 shillings a week into a reserve. (O'Duffy shortly returned this to the £1 a week originally envisaged.) A War Council was set up on 12 July headed by Collins as C-in-C and Mulcahy as both chief of staff and minister for defence. The creation of five regional commands, under MacEoin (Western), O'Duffy (South-Western), Dalton (Eastern), Prout (South-Eastern) and O'Connell (Curragh), made it possible – at least in principle – to develop a strategic plan of campaign. Dalton took up Mulcahy's long-running effort to create a military culture that echoed the rules of soldierly behaviour set by regular armies elsewhere. The easygoing familiarity of the revolutionary forces would be out of place in the new order – he insisted that seniors be addressed as 'Sir' rather than (as was normal) by name, and that 'horseplay' (where Collins had presumably set a bad example) must stop. In the adjustment of ranks on 15 November, while the traditional Volunteer rank of commandant was preserved, more conventional titles like colonel, major general and lieutenant general appeared.

The regional commands took some time to pull together. O'Duffy denounced the men of the South-Western Command at Limerick as 'a disorganised indisciplined and cowardly crowd. Arms were handed over wholesale to the enemy, sentries were drunk at their posts, and when a whole garrison was put into the clink owing to insubordination etc, the garrison sent to replace them often turned out to be worse.' One group of 300 reinforcements were 'absolutely worthless', 200 of them having never handled a rifle before.[168] No doubt he exaggerated for effect, but the new army was certainly beset by the same problems that had eaten away at the IRA during the Truce, indiscipline and disorganization – even outright mutiny. These weaknesses were now, in part, symptoms of an underlying lack of motivation. (In Limerick, Michael Brennan said, 'I don't see how serious fighting can take place here, our men have nothing against the other lads.') Before O'Duffy took over command of the south-west, the local commanders had defied a GHQ injunction not to agree a truce with the republicans.

Western Command, a large and incoherent area, was instructed that 'the general policy is to prevent enemy troops evacuating barracks in possession of rifles and ammunition and reverting to guerilla warfare.' This was unrealistic, even if the National forces had been much stronger than they were. After the guerrilla phase began, the new National Army faced the classic counter-insurgency problem of how to extend its control outside the urban centres. Small posts would require much bigger numbers than were available, and in any case were undesirable from a military viewpoint. As Mulcahy said, 'We are simply going to break up what we have of an army if we leave it any longer in small posts and do not give it proper military training.' He complained to MacEoin in October that he could not 'sense that there is any solid administration or organisation . . . pressing back the forces of disorder there . . . The people of the area feel that no impression is being made on the situation.'[169] Reorganization was an urgent necessity.

Eventually, the steady transfusion of British weapons guaranteed that, even with erratic organization, the National Army's fighting capacity would increase. By the end of August, it had received nine 18-pounder field guns, 27,000 rifles, 246 Lewis guns, five Vickers guns and 8,496 grenades. In mid-July the army's strength reached some 15,000 men, and in late August the government raised its authorized strength to 35,000. Numbers remained uncertain for some time, though, thanks to the ingrained laxity of reporting. Mulcahy told Collins early in August that while 14,127 regular troops had been enrolled, the total forces reported by units amounted to only 12,270. Seán MacEoin 'admits that there are more than 1000 additional men in his area that he cannot at present indicate the distribution of'.

Collins became, in effect, a kind of *generalissimo*, combining military and political supremacy. Griffith had no desire, or capacity, to dispute the day-to-day conduct of government with him, and while Mulcahy had greater administrative capacity he sensibly deferred to Collins as a strategist and thinker. Collins, relying on his personal ascendancy, did less than he might have done to equip the nascent Free State with what it most needed, a symbolic political objective to match and neutralize the invocation of the Republic as the symbol of independence. When he suggested that the government should issue 'a sort of Official Instruction to me ... appointing me to act by special order of the Government as Commander-in-Chief during the period of hostilities', he also set out the basis of a political programme for the war ('A statement which could be directed to the Army by me as an Order of the Day'). 'It should be pointed out that in the present fighting the men we have lost have died for ... the People's right to live and be governed in the way they themselves choose.' This was 'the same principle we fought the British for'. The army was fighting against 'mere brigandage' or 'opposition to the People's will', and for 'the revival of the Nation'.[170]

Collins was well aware that the negative side of this policy needed to be played down. Speaking of the failed negotiations with the 'reckless and wrecking opposition', he declared, 'we must maintain for [the people] the position of freedom they had secured.' He urged that the 'revival and restoration of order cannot in any way be regarded as a step backwards, nor a repressive, nor a reactionary step'. Yet it certainly could, and would be. Would it be enough to insist that it was 'a clear step forward'? His own political philosophy was still half formed; he has been depicted both as a would-be dictator and as an instinctive democrat.[171] As with the Republic itself, everyone can construct their own Michael Collins. When Horace Plunkett, a man of some experience, met him in the summer of 1922, he judged him 'simple yet cunning'. A recent biographer, who finds him 'thoroughly, even desperately, sincere', but 'a babe in arms' in political terms, suggests that he had never been so unsure of himself as during the split.[172] There were 'bound to be contradictions and paradoxes' in his 'multifaceted personality', while his seeming inertia at the crucial time was due to ill-health. Certainly there was an odd contrast between the prolixity of his style in 1922 and the laconic clarity of his earlier writing.

Collins may have set the government's overall strategy, but its implementation does not seem to have suited his skills. He certainly 'spent little time drawing arrows on maps or reading up on the art of war'. His policy was simple enough – to win as quickly as possible, 'but with the least possible nastiness'.[173] The man who was 'for ever pouring [sic] over maps' was Eoin O'Duffy. 'Full of brains and determination', as one journalist thought, he provided the main supply of energy in prosecuting the campaign. More hawkish than Collins or Mulcahy once the fighting started, he did not flinch from the 'nastiness' that he believed would be inseparable from internecine conflict. O'Duffy's early action in forcing the issue with Frank Aiken, driving him to declare against the Provisional Government, was the kind of thing Collins found exceptionally difficult.[174]

The government's stance was increasingly set by Kevin O'Higgins. He had already signalled his sense of the revolution as a process in which social order balanced on a knife-edge. He has been depicted as a counter-revolutionary, though he was a dedicated Sinn Feiner of the Griffith stamp. He was one of the Treatyites – a minority no doubt – who genuinely saw the Treaty not just as a regrettable necessity but as a remarkable achievement. As a lawyer he may have been particularly alert to the weight and significance of its title. Though its content may have more or less equated to 'Dominion Home Rule', its conveyance in the form of a Treaty was (as in the Anglo-Iraqi Treaty) a concession the British would certainly have preferred not to make. It emphasized the real capacity of the Free State to redefine the relationship in future. O'Higgins might be described as a practical separatist, like Griffith. His understanding of the revolution was limited to the replacement of British rule by Irish self-rule, and for him that rule could be effectively exercised only by responsible, professional people – like himself. The threat, even before the British left, was that the revolution would trigger a breakdown of order, as he had made clear at an early stage, during the struggle to establish the republican courts in 1920. For him the government was, as he put it in January 1923, 'simply a body of men out to vindicate the idea of ordered society and the reign of law'.[175]

Later O'Higgins would famously evoke the confrontation in vividly personal terms – 'eight young men in the City Hall standing amidst the ruins of one administration, with the foundations of another not yet laid, and with wild men screaming through the keyhole'. His derogatory view of the republicans aside, his estimate of the situation was sober enough. 'No police force was functioning through the country, no system of justice was operating, the wheels of administration hung idle, battered out of recognition by the clash of rival jurisdictions.' As a lawyer he perhaps unsurprisingly recognized the working of the legal system as the foundation of civilization in its battle against anarchy.

In this he was of course not alone. There was a sense that guerrilla actions were producing 'a widening deterioration of public morale'. The Catholic Church spoke out at an early stage in words that O'Higgins himself could hardly have improved on. Ten days after the occupation of the Four Courts the Hierarchy called on 'the young men connected with the military revolt' not to 'make shameful war upon their own country'. If they did, they would be 'parricides, not patriots' – 'murderers' if they shot 'their brothers on the opposite side', and 'robbers and brigands' if they commandeered public or private property. Six months later the bishops labelled the republicans as 'a section of the community' who had 'chosen to attack their own country as if she were a foreign power'. What they called a war was 'morally only a system of murder and assassination of the national forces'. They spoke of young minds being 'poisoned by false principles', falling into 'cruelty, robbery, falsehood and crime'. Any 'priests who approve of this Irregular insurrection' were 'false to their sacred office'.[176] The charge of falsity echoed through the pastoral.

(Republicans answered this with their own vision of the moral conflict. 'Ireland can never be free until we win the spiritual battle,' Aodh de Blacam wrote. 'We cannot have spiritual solidarity while the Bishops are against us.' 'The Bishops always smash the national movement at the critical moment for simoniacal reasons, by creating schism in the national spirit.' He thought that 'the clergy themselves realise that the Bishops initiated the civil war,' and was confident that 'a crime like this' – 'the greatest scandal in the history of Christendom', no less – would 'deliver the Hierarchy into our hands'.)[177]

At the risk of being seen as the successors of the discredited Home Rule 'constitutional movement', the Provisional Government laid heavy stress on the republicans' violation of constitutional norms. A recruiting proclamation for the National Guard in May 1922 accused the republican leadership of 'arrogating to itself powers of legislation, contrary to all Constitutional practice', and so 'openly challenging the right of the Irish people to express their will through the medium of the popular franchise'. Republicans had interfered with the rights of free speech and 'threatened to subvert the authority of the Sovereign Irish People duly expressed in accordance with Constitutional practice'.[178] The attempt to identify the concept of constitutionalism, long dismissed by separatists as a byword for compromise, with sovereign authority was bold but risky. Collins, by contrast, tried to take the resonant concept of sovereignty out of the public debate entirely by dismissing it as a 'foreign word'.[179]

The Home Affairs Ministry drew up a formidable list of the threats to public order: 'the peace of the country is at present menaced by the operation of armed bands engaged in robberies of Banks and Post Offices; armed interference with public meetings, suppression of free speech, and of the press. Trains are being held up and goods stolen; business premises are being raided and large quantities of goods removed by force; and large money levies are being made on proprietors of also business premises.' It suggested that 'whatever differences of opinion may exist on other matters, everyone must agree that it is in the public interest that Order should be restored, and life and property respected.'[180]

At an early stage Cosgrave labelled the struggle 'a war upon the economic life of the Irish people'. Griffith asserted that republican action would 'lay Ireland, dishonoured, prostrate again at England's feet'. He lamented that six months after the Treaty vote his great economic programme – 'housing, arterial drainage, afforestation etc' – had not been begun. 'Had the Government got the slightest choice, there would not be today an unemployed man in Ireland and the country would be humming with prosperity. But the Government got no choice.' He bitterly protested that 'although it represented the people it was assailed and attacked and thwarted, by some of those the people had elected.' They 'openly boasted that they would force Ireland back into a state of war with England, although they all knew, none better than the Englishman Childers, that the result of such a conflict would be the physical wreck of the country and the moral destruction of the Irish nation'.[181] The persistent invocation of 'the nation' was the closest the Treatyites got to finding an emotive counterweight to the Republic. 'Do you ever think of the poor Irish nation which is trying to be born?' Béaslaí had demanded in the Dáil debate. Griffith had asked the same question: 'Is there to be no living Irish nation?' The Hierarchy argued that the Provisional Government had been 'set up by the nation'. Factually, this was stretching the point, but rhetorically it was a powerful device.

The government's rhetoric exploited the public consent to the Treaty demonstrated in the general election, allowing it to focus less on the positive aspects of the Treaty than on the negative nature of opposition to the will of the people. Its labelling of its opponents quickly became systematic, though the early temptation to call them 'mutineers', 'murderers' or 'brigands' was resisted in favour of the term 'irregulars'. News reports were required to speak of 'the government' (omitting the doubt-raising qualification 'provisional') and 'the Irish Army', 'national troops' or 'forces', in contrast to 'irregulars', 'bands' or 'bodies of men'. Kevin O'Higgins suggested that it would be 'a generous estimate to say that 20 per cent of the militant opposition to the Government is idealism', and a generous estimate to say that only 20 per cent of it was 'crime'. Most of it, the remaining 60 per cent, was 'sheer futility'.

Harping on the democratic nature of the government allowed it to go further than its British predecessor in calling for direct public assistance. While Cosgrave maintained that republican attacks on communications were a recognition that 'the Irregulars cannot hope to offer successful military resistance to the National Army', he insisted it was 'the duty of the people to act in their own defence and prevent the economic weapon from being used to force them to reject the Treaty'. The government urged the clergy and 'public men' to impress on everyone the importance of 'taking steps to clear the roads wherever they have been obstructed' and repairing bridges. 'The best way to stop the campaign of outrage and destruction is to let it be seen that it is arousing the people to opposition.'[182]

This clearly made sense, so public involvement – in the form of vigilance committees or a citizens' guard – seemed an obvious line to encourage. But things proved more complicated in practice. Collins first backed the idea of a citizen militia for 'preventative' work to supplement the 'corrective' work of the soldiers and police. Local committees would 'promote a feeling of confidence' and help 'the people themselves' to 'become actively interested in the new life of the Nation'. He thought that this would strengthen their 'loyalty to the Government', but began to worry that the local guards might 'develop into a casual Police Force without proper training and without the due responsibility in their work'. The 'wretched Irish Republican Police System and the awful personnel that was attracted to its ranks' showed what could go wrong: its 'lack of construction and . . . lack of control' had led to 'many of the outrageous things which have occurred throughout Ireland'. This pungent morsel of historical revisionism meshed with a larger point about the task of state-building – 'the vital necessity of building up their foundations rather than building quickly'. Organizations that might be 'helpful in the initial stage' might in the longer term 'weaken Governmental control'.[183]

'GIVE THEM NO REST'

The rapid collapse of republican offensive action enabled Mulcahy to assure Collins on 4 August 1922 that the only 'definite military problem' was the Waterford–Cork–Kerry–Limerick area. Everywhere else the problems were minor, and the army should really be operating in support of the police. It was 'essential that the Civic Guard take up their police duties' as soon as possible. Even in the south, the problem was 'not so much the military defeat of the Irregulars . . . as the establishing of our Forces in certain principal points . . . with a view to shaking the domination held over the ordinary people by the Irregulars'. He was confident that 'the establishing of ourselves in a few more of these positions would mean the resurgence of the people from their present cowed condition' and the 'immediate demoralisation of the Irregular rank and file'.[184] A week later Piaras Béaslaí suggested that 'the Censorship can safely be abolished in about a fortnight . . . The crisis is now over.'[185]

Nearly two-thirds of those killed in the civil war died in its first three months (just a seventh would die in the final five months). But, though serious fighting had effectively ended, it takes two sides to end a war, just as it does to start one. Republicans were not ready to accept defeat, and guerrilla action went on. In December a group seized Sligo Town Hall and held it for several hours, making off with twenty-one rifles and 1,300 rounds of ammunition; and on 10 January 1923 a forty-strong republican force comprehensively destroyed Sligo railway station. As in all irregular warfare, the government needed much larger forces to exert effective control. Seán MacEoin, head of Western Command, announced his intention to 'stick it and keep up the pace until the country is pacified'. The plan had been 'to allow no rest. To keep at them the whole time.' This was 'more trying on our troops than on the enemy but the superior discipline of our troops allows us to force the pace'. The enemy's morale had been 'broken', he claimed, and 'if we could get them to surrender their arms on any pretext it would be of great advantage and would shorten the war by two months perhaps by three.'[186]

Keeping up the pace was trying indeed, and there was no sign of any arms surrender. Several Free State commanders were criticized for not pressing their military advantage – as was Prout for not keeping up the pursuit after capturing Kilkenny. In Mayo there were complaints that action against irregulars was so slow and ineffective that 'now they are going about threatening this and other towns and harassing the people in the rural districts by living on them and ill-treating those who refuse to comply with their demands.' Roads were blocked, bridges destroyed, trains attacked, fairs and markets ruined; business was at a standstill. 'Why not use artillery to drive these marauders from their hiding places?' asked Canon d'Alton. Could not General Mckeon [MacEoin] come and follow them up? Instead 'there is nothing but drift.' The local TD complained that failure to deal with roadblocks gave the people a false impression of irregular strength. He urged that 'there is one way to deal with them – General Lawlor's way – follow them, follow them, give them no rest.'[187]

Sporadic and indecisive military actions might be trying to the patience, but were at least mercifully light in human cost. For instance, as many as 400 National troops, with a field gun, were involved in the attack on Collooney in Sligo, where the defenders had two Lewis guns, but not one was killed, and only one republican defender received fatal wounds. Strategically, the classic recourse of retreating from high-value centres to low-value, inaccessible peripheral areas allowed guerrilla units to retain some credibility, and in different political circumstances this level of armed resistance might have been enough to threaten the stability of the new state. But as always the key question was whether the public blamed the government or the insurgents for the disruption of normal life. Now people, including no doubt many who may well have disapproved of the original Volunteer guerrilla campaign, felt freer than before to voice their opposition. People were certainly antagonized by the republican renewal of the 'war on communications', a strategy pursued with unusual consistency – railways above all were attacked much more intensely than during the war against the British. 'Owing to the use of railways by the Free State for the conveyance of troops and war material, the destruction of railways under Free State control is an essential part of our military policy.' Nearly a fifth of republican operations took the form of railway sabotage of some kind, and the objective was clearly not just to deny the railways to government forces, as with the 1920 embargo, but to paralyse the whole system.

Republican inactivity has often been blamed on public hostility, or even apathy. But it is difficult to measure public attitudes amid the fighting. The Free State army's intelligence service usually (in an uncanny echo of its British precursors) insisted that 'the people' would be basically sound but for republican terrorism. Thus in Limerick, even as late as the spring of 1923, though 'the people show no love for the Irregulars, information is slow in coming in' – because of 'fear of the Irregulars having [sic] reprisals afterwards'. National troops were certainly often unimpressed by the level of public co-operation they received. Seán MacEoin complained, for instance, that 'it is very difficult to understand the civilian population of Sligo, as one day they would appear with you and the next against you.'[188] When National troops were ambushed outside Dungarvan in Waterford on 10 December 1922, a crowd of people attending a funeral 'did not tell the officer. They were waiting to see the ambush.'[189] Republican commanders often remained upbeat about the level of public support. Shortly before Christmas Liam Pilkington even felt able to claim that the civilian population was 'generous and sympathetic to us in most of the area', and that 'if our fight is maintained it won't be long until we have the people wholeheartedly with us in our struggle for the life of the REPUBLIC.'[190]

Efforts to reunite the erstwhile comrades of the IRA went on even after the assault on the Four Courts. Frank Aiken, who held his 4th Northern Division in a position of neutrality, wrote to Mulcahy – whose authority he still acknowledged – on 6 July 1922 'to ask you to call a Truce immediately'. This would allow an army convention of 'all sections of the IRA' to meet and elect an army council, and the 'Third Dáil' to frame a new constitution. His reasoning was that:

> although Miceal O Coilean has broken the pact made with E. de Valera, to such an extent that we under GHQ Beggars Bush are only an Army of a political section instead of the Army of the Dáil; although the present position is probably a result of the bad tactics of Rory O'Connor and some of the Executive, if it goes on it will become a war; it will break the republican tradition of the IRA, lessen the morale of all Irishmen and retard or perhaps prevent the gaining of our ideal of an Irish republic.[191]

Next day Aiken 'went south to see Commandant General Lynch, and put to him that he could do more for the Republic by propaganda than by fighting men of the old Army, most of whom thought they were doing their best for the Republic'. He clearly believed that the pro-Treaty section even now would 'never countenance the King in the Constitution'. He advised Lynch that 'although he had the moral right to fight, it was bad tactics, since he could only fight for a few months or years, without any chance of a successful revolution.' Aiken met Lynch in Limerick during the temporary truce, and was still there when it was broken on 11 July. His thoughtful arguments made no impression on Lynch, who took the view that 'the other people had started the fight and it was up to them to take steps to stop it.' 'I failed in my mission and returned to my division.'

Things still seemed to be hanging in the balance. When he got back, he and his staff met Mulcahy to insist that the Provisional Government must 'give the Anti-treaty parties civil and military a constitutional way of carrying on for the republic, such as withdrawing the oath for admission to the parliament'. If they did not, 'we would give them no support moral or material.' Aiken clearly accepted the validity of the parliament itself, and it seems unlikely that even if his conditions had been met he could have persuaded many other republicans to accept them. But they were not. When he next returned to his HQ at Dundalk he found 'orders to attack the Executive forces in my area'. His reaction to this was predictable: he broke off relations with the Beggars Bush GHQ. The orders had come from the Chief of Staff, Eoin O'Duffy, and Aiken pointedly told him 'that if the Minister for Defence attempted to govern, without the consent of the best people, he would be driven to use rotten men and means'. On 17 July his division issued a manifesto. 'Realising that Civil War is suicidal to the Nation, and also that our hands are full at the present juncture protecting our own people against the ravages which are daily being committed against them in the North', they had 'agreed to unite ... to hold intact our forces in face of the common enemy, to resist the second plantation of Ulster by England, and to maintain law and order'.[192] His HQ was promptly seized by men of the 5th Northern Division and he was arrested.

The issue had been forced by O'Duffy, who now saw any negotiations as useless, if not indeed dangerous. In mid-August, he argued to Collins that any peace without a definite 'Military decision' would benefit only 'the Bolsheviks'. The underlying proto-fascism of conservative nationalists came closer to the surface once the traditional enemy had decamped. 'The Labour element and Red Flaggers are at the back of all moves towards "Peace",' O'Duffy warned. The left realized that 'if the Government can break the back of this revolt, any attempts at revolt by labour in the future will be futile.'[193] With Lynch instructing O'Malley later that month that there could be no negotiations except on the basis of recognition of the Republic, such will to compromise as still survived may be said to have finally disappeared.

WILLIAM COSGRAVE ENTERS HIS INHERITANCE

In August 1922 the shape, and the personality, of the Provisional Government changed twice in ten days, when first Arthur Griffith died on the 12th and then Collins was killed in action during a trip to Cork on the 22nd. Griffith's cerebral haemorrhage, at the age of fifty-one, was probably brought on by stress, and a consuming anger against the republican irreconcilables. Collins's death had an aspect of classical tragedy: when his convoy was fired on, there was nothing to stop the car he was travelling in from driving through to safety – nothing except perhaps his desire to demonstrate that he was truly a fighting man, not a pen-pusher. By the time he reached Beal na mBlath, most of the republican ambush party had left, and the rest had dismantled the blockage on the road. Emmet Dalton immediately told the driver to drive on, but Collins halted his convoy and went out on to the roadside with a rifle. He was playing soldiers. The precise source of the shot that hit the back of his head and shattered his skull has been a matter of dispute, but it was his own decision to put himself in its way.

Collins's body was brought back from Cork to Dublin by boat, arriving just before first light. The procession 'when it reached Stephen's Green in the dark grey morning, the coffin on a gun-carriage, a piper in front and a small straggling crowd of two or three hundred people after it', was intensely moving to those who saw it. When the government met that day, Ernest Blythe unsurprisingly 'never . . . saw a more dejected looking group'. The War Council was recast, headed by Mulcahy, who remained defence minister, but also at last became commander-in-chief. Kevin O'Higgins, who had been serving on the military staff, stepped up to a bigger political role as home affairs minister. He proposed that Mulcahy should succeed Collins at the head of the government, though Blythe persuaded his colleagues that to put a second general in that position would send out the wrong signals. Only then was W. T. Cosgrave, who had chaired the Cabinet in Collins's absence, formally confirmed as chairman. O'Higgins then surprised Mulcahy by suggesting that O'Duffy – Mulcahy's 'right arm' – be made chief of police, to kickstart the stalled process of establishing the Civic Guard (soon to be officially named 'Garda Síochána'). Public insecurity, he argued, had reached a critical point – 'foundations are crumbling on the civil side, decrees cannot be executed, debts cannot be collected, credit is therefore at an end, all commercial enterprise is at a standstill.' This was a bigger problem even than the military threat. If the situation was not 'boldly faced', the social crisis could 'shatter all hopes of founding a democratically governed Irish State'.[194]

After Collins's death there was a widespread fear of reprisals by National forces, and with good reason. The Squad veteran Vinnie Byrne, who said that for four or five days 'I'd have shot any bloody Die-hard I came across,' was not alone. Many people assumed that the loss would cripple the Provisional Government. They included de Valera, who assured McGarrity in September that its personnel was 'very weak'; Cosgrave was 'a ninny'. Liam Mellows likewise thought that the Free State 'seems to be a bit groggy these days', and Paidin O'Keeffe predicted that 'the English will be back in a week.' But though many ministers decided to take refuge in Government Buildings for security (echoing the retreat of British officials into the Castle in 1920), the ministry was not seriously shaken. De Valera's judgment was wide of the mark, and Todd Andrews's contemptuous snort that Cosgrave's 'ambition in life was to be accepted as respectable' also missed the point. Cosgrave had a quality of quiet solidity that was most valuable in the crisis of 1922 – his very ordinariness may have been an advantage. (The joke that even his wife did not know what his second initial stood for was double-edged.) Events now pitched him into a unique position: with both Griffith and Collins gone, he took over the headship of both the Dáil ministry and the Provisional Government, moving to resolve the unstable, semi-fictional dual authority that had been preserved since January. As president of Dáil Éireann and chairman of the Provisional Government he was a remarkable – perhaps unique – constitutional hybrid. This hybridity would echo into the institutions of the Irish Free State: after the Republic had finally been formally wound up in December, Cosgrave became a British-style prime minister with the title of president – President of the Executive Council.

The remnant of the second Dáil would have a kind of half-life for years – indeed decades – to come, as the last repository of republican sovereignty. In August Liam Lynch, still looking for ways of pulling the republican movement back together, suggested that 'if the second Dáil, which is the Government of the Republic, or any other elected assembly, carry on such Government, I see no difficulty as to the allegiance of the Army.' Cosgrave explained that 'the functions of the Second Dáil came to an end on June 30th. The meeting which was to have taken place on that date would have been purely formal . . . The Sovereign Assembly of Ireland is now the Parliament elected in June last.'[195] But as that parliament did not assemble until September, the precise source from which Mulcahy and other ministers derived the authority they were exercising could well be questioned. The failure to convoke the parliament led to damaging charges that the government was showing 'as complete a disregard for democracy' as the irregulars. It was acting 'as if it had a clear and unchallenged mandate . . . but it has no mandate at all'.[196]

It is clear that the delay was entirely for military reasons. Mulcahy had warned Collins early in August that it was 'too early to say whether we could establish ourselves' in the south 'in time to have Parliament

meet on [the] 12th. I feel that we shall have to have another postponement ...' But he thought that 'even the political effect of another
postponement would be good.' His reasoning was characteristically military: it would 'prevent the Irregulars in the South feeling that as soon as
we came definitely up against them, we hesitated to face them boldly,
and turned aside from the job, and called Parliament'. He predicted that
if parliament did not meet until 24 August, 'our military position would
be very favourable.'[197] In fact, Collins was killed two days before that
date, and the meeting was put back still further to September.

By the time it met, the legal system had been radically redirected. The
operation of the Dáil courts had been troubling the government for
some time. The court system had been reconstructed after the Truce, and
courts then 'reached the highest point of their effectiveness'; but, if
this was true overall, the local variations were always striking, even
within counties.[198] In Sligo, for instance, the south appears to have
responded adequately to the reorganization while the north failed dis-
mally. There was no attempt to hold a district court until 2 December,
and then it fell through when only one justice managed to turn up. Austin Stack lambasted the 'fiasco', lecturing the justices that 'the courts in
your district are in a most unsatisfactory condition.' Stack's direction of
the courts has been sharply criticized – 'self-important, bullying and
pedantic', he tried to impose 'rigid and unreal demands'.[199] But his
relentless chivvying of local court officials must have had some effect,
and when he quit his post after the Treaty vote, things were unlikely to
improve. Mulcahy complained to Griffith early in February that the
Home Affairs Department was no longer working. 'We are losing terrible [sic] in prestige because the ordinary Petty Sessions are going on,
and going on in court houses, while Republican courts are in the
background.' In a guarded tribute to the former Minister, he noted that
people were complaining that 'whereas they could get a reply almost by
return from Stack, under the present condition they cannot get a reply
even after a number of reminders.' The effect of this disorganization
'cannot but be bad for the Free State'.[200]

The decision to scrap the republican courts does not, though, seem to
be explicable on practical grounds. The system was still working when
the circuit judges were recalled in mid-circuit on 11 July. Two days later
the Supreme Court was abolished, and shortly after that the government
took the remarkable step of formally rescinding the 1920 decree that had

established – or, as the announcement put it, 'purported to establish' – the republican court system. This was the only Dáil decree ever to be formally rescinded, and the fact that it was done not by parliament (which had not then met) but by the Minister makes the step still more remarkable.[201] Here, if anywhere, the need to meet British requirements acted to squeeze the life out of the Irish revolution. The loss of the republican courts seems to have been felt by many: 'I have often heard it regretted since that [they] were not made permanent.'[202]

The new parliament also represented a decisive break from the Republic. If there was any temptation to have it meet as Dáil Éireann – a verbal fudge that might have mollified some lukewarm supporters of the government – it was sternly resisted by Cosgrave. When it eventually assembled on 9 September it was described in firmly British terms as 'the Parliament to which the Provisional Government is to be responsible' under the provisions of the Treaty. Even so Cosgrave, acting as chair pending the election of a new speaker (Ceann Comhairle), casually referred to the assembly as 'the Dáil', as did everyone who spoke. Some deputies indeed spoke of it as the 'third Dáil'. The title 'Provisional Parliament of Southern Ireland' does not seem to have been heard. The political freight carried by formal terminology was emphasized by the veteran deputy Laurence Ginnell, who insisted that he had been elected 'not to attend any such Parliament', but 'as a member of Dáil Eireann', and refused to sign the roll unless he was assured that it was Dáil Éireann. 'Will anyone tell me with authority whether this is Dáil Eireann or a Partition Parliament?' Was it 'the Dáil for the whole of Ireland?' Ginnell's warning that 'the public are watching' did not, however, deter Cosgrave from moving his expulsion, and he was led out of the chamber by the Captain of the Guard (a relief to ministers who saw that he might have been 'very much of a thorn in our flesh' in the next critical months).[203] The chairman made clear that the executive was also changing. When Gavan Duffy asked if 'the present system of dual government would be unified', Cosgrave made clear that the two governments would at last be merged. Even so, the Free State as such could not formally come into being until 6 December, a year after the signing of the Treaty.

Under this second Provisional Government regime, counter-insurgency policy became distinctly tougher. Mulcahy was somewhat 'less sentimental about old comrades' than Collins had been. Cosgrave and O'Higgins were prepared to brand republican fighters as unlawful combatants, in effect criminals. They were unworried by the prospect of using martial law, despite its grim political echoes – and even though Mulcahy had long since judged that the threat across most of the country had been reduced to the level of a police action. Early in September the government discussed the possibility of proclaiming martial law in Cork, but decided to leave any decision to the chairman in parliament. The general confusion over martial-law powers in English law – whether they derived from Crown prerogative or common law – that had vexed the British Cabinet, remained unresolved, and the government eventually opted for statutory emergency powers. On 15 September, Mulcahy outlined the powers required by the army to restore order, and the government law officer was instructed to draw up the necessary provisions.

The result, the Army Emergency Powers Resolution, was introduced on 27 September and adopted next day. It took the form of 'a number of recitals followed by a ratification clause',[204] establishing military courts or committees with powers to impose death penalties on non-army personnel and indefinite detention without trial. Firearms possession was to be controlled by the (National) Army Council. The Council was authorized to create further orders (which would have to be laid before the Dáil), to create offences triable by military courts. Answering Labour criticism of the legislation as a virtual military dictatorship, Cosgrave noted that, although he had always been against the death penalty, he could now see 'no other way ... in which ordered conditions can be restored in this country, or any security obtained for our troops' – or indeed 'to give our troops any confidence in us as a Government'.

Even after nearly four months of fighting, the National Army's military effectiveness was still limited. As in the fight against Britain, the intelligence system remained unexpectedly fragile. Eastern Command, 'with the exception of the 2nd Eastern division, does not show that proper grasp of intelligence work which is absolutely necessary to defeat the present tactics of the Irregulars. We should be in a position to anticipate and frustrate all Enemy activities,' but the reverse was occurring in many places. In the south, the troops gave away information 'and of course the Enemy are often able to frustrate our plans.' In Limerick, the intelligence service might or might not exist – 2nd Southern Division said, 'we do not know ... beyond the absolute lack of any form of communication with this Department.' These were potentially serious problems, but in the end they could be neutralized by the establishment of governmental legitimacy. The most important thing was that the war should be 'made a second-rate news item ... minimising disturbances and emphasising the normalisation of things'.[205]

REPUBLICAN GOVERNMENT

As president of a republic that was effectively disestablished, Eamon de Valera was in a kind of political limbo from the time the IRA Executive set itself up as an independent source of republican authority. Shepherded through the countryside from irregular unit to irregular unit, the awkward symbol of a lost state, he was more alert than his military hosts to the weakness of the republican position. The Dáil meeting of 9 September seemed to push him over the narrow line into outright defeatism, if he had not indeed crossed it already. According to Lynch, when de Valera had left GHQ on 15 August he had been 'most pessimistic and regarded our position as hopeless. He even at that time contemplated taking public action which would ruin us.' Before the Dáil met, Lynch urged that de Valera be told that the military situation had changed, and 'we are so certain of success that we ask that no action be taken by him or Republican Party which would weaken us and may even rob us of victory.' Either de Valera did not receive this reappraisal or he did not believe it. The long and agonized appraisal of the situation he sent to Joe McGarrity the day after the Dáil meeting pithily demonstrated the fundamental impossibility of the situation. Republicans had now to choose 'between a heartbreaking surrender of what they have repeatedly proved was dearer to them than life and the repudiation of what they recognise to be the basis of all order in government and the keystone of democracy – majority rule'. There could be 'no glory and no enthusiasm' in the struggle, and, worse, 'no way out of it'. He was already looking forward to a 'revival of the Sinn Féin idea in a new form' if 'the present physical resistance fails'. He himself was 'almost wishing I were deposed, for the present position places upon me the responsibility for carrying out a programme which was not mine'.[206]

But he was determined to fight for control of the republican funds still resting in the USA. In a postscript he argued that 'they' could not 'make good their title after their performance ... when they would not declare that their Parliament was Dáil Éireann'. The line to take, he wrote shortly afterwards, was that 'the new Dáil is not the legitimate successor to the old Dáil ... The funds are the property of the Second Dáil which has not yet been constitutionally dissolved.' Over the years McGarrity had often done little more than extend a sympathetic ear to his distinguished correspondent, but at this point he made a decisive intervention, urging on 27 September that 'top man' make a 'determined stand'; the second Dáil should be recalled and an all-Ireland civil government 'be boldly declared'. ('You may have a government – that is not known – that is not enough.') 'The bolder the stroke, the more will rally to your banner.'[207]

In fact the policy of establishing a government had already been discussed at some length by IRA leaders. A month earlier, Liam Mellows had urged that 'a Provisional Republican Government should be set up at once.' Writing to O'Malley from Mountjoy gaol on 29 August he argued that 'an object – a target – must be presented for the enemy ... to hit at – otherwise it becomes a fight (apparently) between individuals.'[208] He also argued that 'The Programme of Democratic Control (the social programme) ... should be translated into something definite': this was 'essential if the great body of workers are to be kept on the side of Independence'. Mellows suggested taking the programme that had appeared in the *Workers' Republic* on 22 July – a pretty full-blooded socialist document advocating nationalization of the banks and industry. 'Under the REPUBLIC all Industry will be controlled by the State for the workers' and farmers' benefit ...' For Mellows, if Irish labour could be kept 'for the Republic', it would be 'possibly the biggest factor on our side'.[209] The idea of creating a republican administration was also supported by Maurice Twomey, who asked 'where was the Republic' and who was in charge of it. 'You cannot very well have a Republic without a government.' Other republicans were also reacting to the crystallization of the Free State by focusing on social programmes. P. J. Ruttledge, the only 'politician' on the IRA Executive, had persuaded it to adopt a Land Scheme for confiscating and redistributing 'demesnes and ranches'. But, tellingly perhaps, O'Malley was unable to lay hands on a copy of Ruttledge's scheme.

Lynch still appeared unmoved by such thinking, though. 'Views and Opinions of political people are not to be too seriously considered,' he declared at the end of August. 'Our aim and course are now clearly defined and cut and dried.' Even though 'many influences' would be 'constantly brought to bear to deflect us from them ... these will be brushed aside'.[210] Mellows was evidently one of these: 'his ideals prevent him from seeing the same military outlook as others at times.'[211] But the argument for a republican government was revived yet again when O'Malley's adjutant, Tom Derrig, posed the question 'can we get on without a shield of Civil Authority or civil departments at the very least?' Derrig thought there were three possible courses. The one he preferred was to call the second Dáil, 'dissolve it and form a Government from the Third Dáil which will swear allegiance to the Republic': this would 'strengthen us much more in the eyes of the people and will strengthen our position wonderfully'. Otherwise a number of civil departments (courts and local government, finance, land, food and propaganda) might be set up, or – failing all else – a five-man army council might be set up with one of its members in charge of civil administration. This last, however, was not warranted – was in fact 'discard[ed]' – by 'our military position', and would be utterly impossible unless Lynch's HQ came to 'a more central base'.[212]

O'Malley put Derrig's argument to Lynch on 24 September. 'We consider it imperative that some sort of a Government whether a Provisional or Republican Government or a Military one should be inaugurated at once.' Derrig spoke of the need for 'some form of central control' (probably not very attractive to Lynch) and the role of the government as a 'shield' (perhaps a little more). O'Malley suggested that it was 'essential to fight the illegality of the Provisional Government', and 'time to turn our attention to a constructive policy'. The republicans needed both a legal committee, and a body to tackle 'the food question, Transport, Land and Civil Administration'. He reported that Derrig was organizing a legal committee, and 'working on the Democratic Programme'. Three weeks earlier he had in fact argued that 'the need for a Democratic Republican Constitution is felt', and that it would 'get the workers'. But O'Malley's pressing sense of the need to give some social content to the concept of the republic was not shared by his chief. (Lynch bluntly dismissed the labour manifesto as 'gas' and demanded that workers stop co-operating with the enemy.) He had, as Mellows's biographer Desmond Greaves condescendingly put it, 'been trained as a small-town shop assistant and such matters were foreign to him'.

De Valera took the issue up again with Lynch, telling him on 12 October that in order to provide a rallying point and centre of direction, to preserve the continuity of the Republic and to establish a claim on the republican funds, a government must be restored. Characteristically he also warned McGarrity on the same day that there would be 'grave difficulties', since no body but the Army Executive could 'now get the allegiance of the men who are fighting', and their views on possible peace were 'unlikely to be the same' as his. Lynch had the same idea; though he had decided not to summon the Executive again 'unless a decision is necessary on some vital point of policy', he had told O'Malley that he felt 'sure the decision of the Executive would be to fight to a finish, and accept no more compromises'.

When the Executive discussed the issue over two days on 16–17 October, it might otherwise have been ready to go further than merely calling on 'the former President of Dáil Éireann to form a government which will preserve the continuity of the Republic'. When the second Dáil reconvened in secret on 25 October and reaffirmed that de Valera was its president, the Cabinet he formed had an air of unreality. The ministries headed by Austin Stack (Finance), O'Kelly (Local Government) and Barton (Economic Affairs) simply did not exist, while the Defence Minister, Liam Mellows, was incarcerated in Mountjoy gaol.

'VERY DRASTIC MEASURES'

The death of Collins, and that of his close friend Harry Boland, might be seen as sad accidents. Towards the end of the year, however, there were signs that a vicious spiral might overwhelm the restraints that had so far kept the civil war within bounds – avoiding what Collins had called 'unnecessary destruction and loss of life'. The first executions under the Army Emergency Powers Resolution, of four republican IRA men on 17 November, were followed by the execution on the 24th of Erskine Childers on what many saw as a trumped-up charge. (He had a miniature pistol, a gift from Michael Collins, but his real offence was to be seen as the *éminence grise* of the republican irreconcilables.) Gavan Duffy denounced this execution directly as a political murder. Scrupulous precautions, he insisted, should have been taken against doing an injustice under the new regulations; instead 'unnecessary secrecy' seemed 'to pervade the dealings of the authorities with these strange tribunals'. Three days later an IRA warning was issued to the Speaker of the 'Provisional Parliament of Southern Ireland': 'every member of your body who voted for this resolution by which you pretend to make legal the murder of soldiers, is equally guilty ... unless your army recognises the rules of warfare ... we shall adopt very drastic measures to protect our forces.'

The government reacted to this warning by issuing the so-called 'Orders of Frightfulness' on 30 November. These identified fourteen named categories of people who were to be shot on sight. Barely a week later the leading pro-Treaty TD and former IRA leader Seán Hales was assassinated on Ormond Quay in Dublin. Mulcahy immediately proposed that the imprisoned Four Courts leaders be executed, and the Cabinet agreed. The legality of this action was highly questionable, to say the least. Mulcahy's subsequent announcement of the executions described them as both a 'solemn warning' and a 'reprisal'. It was later said that O'Higgins was dismayed by the addition of the word reprisal, but Ernest Blythe (who accepted that it was a bad choice which drew stern criticism from the Church) was clear that the whole Cabinet had approved the statement. They did not question Mulcahy's selection of names, assuming that it was caculated to strike the heaviest psychological blow possible. The summary executions were not intended to be even pseudo-legal: Blythe bluntly described them as simple counter-terrorism. He argued that if the four men had been brought before drumhead courts martial the effect would have been worse: people would have said that the verdicts were a foregone conclusion in any case, and the government was trying to avoid direct responsibility. The killings had a powerful effect, confirming, ironically, the assertions of hawkish British ministers about the value of strong action in impressing the Irish people with the government's resolve.[213] O'Higgins read parliament a lesson in elementary political theory: all government was ultimately based on force, and 'must meet force with greater force if it is to survive'. *Salus populi suprema est lex*. This was incontrovertible, if remarkably frank: the question of course was what kind of threat to public safety Childers had represented.

Out in the countryside the government forces clearly recognized counter-terrorism as an effective policy. In January 1923 the army's emergency powers were enlarged, to impose the death penalty for a swathe of offences including carrying messages for irregulars, assisting in escapes, using military or police uniforms, and desertion from the National Army. The increase in the level of executions from late December onwards was striking. Whereas the British authorities had executed twenty-four Volunteers up to the Truce, the Free State executed at least seventy-seven (a total enshrined in Dorothy Macardle's republican bible), and probably four more, for political offences. Though the Labour party succeeded in getting the government to talk about the idea of suspending executions to make a settlement possible, it failed to convince it. Meeting with the Labour leadership on 23 February, Mulcahy rejected the argument that executions stiffened republican resolve, and maintained that their effect was to erode irregular morale. The rate of executions actually increased after February.[214] Unknown numbers were shot extra-judicially by police and National troops; the bodies of at least twenty-five republicans were alleged to have been dumped in Dublin streets. In Kerry in particular, a cycle of tit-for-tat killings began in late August 1922 when two republican IRA men were shot after surrendering. It reached a gruesome climax in March 1923 after five National troops searching a supposed republican dugout at Knocknagoshel were blown to pieces by a booby trap. The incident turned out to be a set-up. The local National Army commander ordered his troops to use republican hostages as minesweepers, and can hardly have been surprised when they went on to outdo their opponents by strapping prisoners to a mine of their own.

On 7 March, nine republicans were brought from Ballymullen barracks to Ballyseedy Cross, bound hand and foot and roped together in a circle around a mine buried beneath a log and a pile of stones. When the mine was detonated, eight were killed; one, amazingly, was blown clear and escaped with only slight injuries. The men who rescued him heard a series of further explosions, and believed that grenades were thrown in among the victims.[215] Smaller versions of this massacre were re-enacted within hours near Killarney, where five were killed, and Caherciveen, where four died. Only five of the thirty-two republican IRA men who died in Kerry in March were killed in combat. The massacres were widely believed to be the work of the Dublin Guards, but responsibility was never pinned on any senior officers – or indeed men. According to one National Army officer, the submissions made to the military court of inquiry at Tralee on 7 April which exonerated the troops were, 'to my personal knowledge, totally untrue'.[216]

'THE REPUBLIC CAN NO LONGER BE DEFENDED'

In January 1923 Liam Deasy was arrested, and would no doubt have been executed like so many other irregulars. But he had already decided that it was pointlessly destructive to keep up the fight. Risking the charge that he was acting to save his own skin, he signed a statement accepting 'immediate and unconditional surrender of all arms and men as required by General Mulcahy' and calling on sixteen named republican leaders to give 'a similar undertaking and acceptance'. The statement was drafted by his captors, but it accorded with his own conclusions, as he explained in a personal letter sent to the named leaders. When the government published the appeal on 9 February, it announced a temporary suspension of executions until the republican leaders replied, and offered an amnesty to all irregulars who surrendered with their weapons before the 18th. No reply came.

This was far from the first effort to compose the split within the army. Throughout the fighting, as Ernest Blythe lamented, 'individual Commanders in various areas, instead of pursuing the war with full vigour . . . were inclined to try to make contact with their opposite numbers and enter upon discussions.' This tendency extended, with a few exceptions, 'right through the top ranks of the Army' – including Mulcahy, who at one point left a Cabinet meeting which had decided to prohibit all negotiations, 'got into his car at the door of Government Buildings and drove to a rendezvous with Mr de Valera'. According to Blythe's account, when the Cabinet discovered this, it was unanimous that Mulcahy should hand in his resignation, though 'in view of the state of affairs generally, and . . . the way in which the Government was cut off from the Army, none of us felt that we could make that demand.' But Blythe 'never had full confidence in him afterwards'.[217] No peace talks were ever formally entertained by the government. The civilian Free Staters seem to have made up their minds, probably well before Collins died, that they would accept nothing short of unconditional surrender, expressed in the demand for the surrender of arms.

Throughout the autumn of 1922 there were calls for peace from a series of public and private organizations. Several corporations and councils, harbour commissioners, boards of guardians, the Farmers'

Union, the Gaelic League, the Irish Women's International League and others urged at least a temporary ceasefire. A new organization called Clann na hÉireann was founded in Navan in October, with the support of leading clergy and the Lord Mayor of Dublin, to promote all-Ireland activities as a platform for 'peace with honour'. In November a People's Peace League emerged, backed by the veteran Fenian P. S. O'Hegarty, and proposed that the two sides should meet together at a peace conference. The government's line on such ideas was effectively summed up in Cosgrave's response to a call from a grouping of Wexford Sinn Feiners, Farmers and Transport Workers for an armistice in December. Peace could be established only 'on a sound basis, namely subject to the authority of representative government . . . The time for mercy is being rapidly consumed, and if advantage be not taken of it very shortly, those who are making war on the people will find too late that there is a limit to patience.'[218]

On the face of things, the most plausible peace effort came from the Neutral IRA, a group put together by the Cork Volunteer leaders Florrie O'Donoghue and Seán O'Hegarty at the end of 1922. It claimed a membership of 20,000 'men who had pre-Truce IRA service, and who had not taken an active part on either side in the civil war'. This was a very large number, even if its organization was, as O'Donoghue admitted, necessarily 'loose'. With a majority of republican sympathizers, it was a single-issue group, aimed at ending the war. It 'sprang up spontaneously in every area in response to an appeal for this purpose'. It was able to mount an impressive convention in Dublin on 4 February 1923, with over 150 delegates. They called for the disbandment of both pro- and anti-Treaty forces, and their replacement by a new army recruited from pre-Truce Volunteers (themselves, presumably). The Neutral IRA sent both leaderships an appeal to negotiate a truce in mid-February.[219] The republican view of these activities was pithily expressed by Tom Maguire's contemptuous remark that O'Donoghue 'went from this bishop to that bishop trying to bring the sides together'. Cosgrave was no more receptive. He was recorded as saying, 'if we have to exterminate ten thousand Republicans, the three millions of our people is bigger than this ten thousand.'[220] This was unusually crude language (and grammar), but it essentially reiterated the line that he and O'Higgins had always taken: 'if the country was going to live', the government was not just entitled but obliged to act without flinching.

When the Waterford brigadier Dinny Lacey was killed on 18 February, there were rumours that he had been involved in moves to end the fighting. The IRA Adjutant General wrote angrily to Lacey's divisional commander, 'the propaganda which our own people are furnishing the F.S. "Government" every day is reducing GHQ to a miserable position.' The impression was that 'Officers all over the country are deliberately disobeying orders of GHQ and making individual peace overtures to the enemy.' This encouraged the enemy in 'his "Executions and Surrender" policy'. GHQ – that is, Lynch – insisted that 'a temporary cessation of strife will lead us nowhere,' and added darkly that 'discipline must be maintained at all costs.' 'By remaining firm & united we can secure Independence.'[221]

By this time, most of Lynch's subordinates had reached the conclusion that there was no point in fighting on. All but two of the eighteen commanders who attended a 1st Southern Division Council at Coolea on 26 February gave their opinion that victory was impossible.[222] Lynch himself never accepted this. He had recently declared that the republican forces were 'in a stronger military position than at any period' in their history. The war would 'go on until the independence of our country is recognised by our enemies', and 'victory is within our grasp if we stand unitedly and firmly.' This was not just public morale-boosting. Conversing with Sean Dowling at this point, 'not alone was he planning for mountain cannon to arrive, but he was also formulating the sort of uniform we would wear when we won.'[223] Even the disillusioned de Valera believed, or at least told Joe McGarrity, that 'one big effort from our friends everywhere would finally smash the Free State.' The arguments were extensively rehearsed at a four-day meeting of the Executive between 23 and 26 March, the first to which de Valera was invited – an indirect recognition that the military command had run out of road. In the end, a motion 'that further armed resistance and operations against F.S. Government will not further the cause of independence of the country' was defeated by a single vote. It was still 'impossible to reconcile the divergent views held by members of the Executive'. They decided to adjourn for a fortnight and reconvene on 10 April.

On his way to that meeting, early in the morning of the 10th, Liam Lynch, with a group of officers including Frank Aiken, was caught in a large-scale search operation near the Tipperary–Waterford border by troops of Prout's Waterford Command. Lynch's group climbed along a stream bed towards the grey-brown uplands of the Knockmealdown hills, but when they emerged at the top on to a bare ridge Lynch was hit by a single rifle shot. The others had to leave him, because as Aiken said, 'the papers we carried must be saved and brought through at any cost.'[224] Lynch was picked up by National troops – who first thought he was de Valera, and had to ask him who he was – and died of his wounds in Prout's headquarters town, Clonmel, that evening. Even with Lynch gone, it was not easy to end the military campaign. Aiken, Lynch's successor as IRA chief of staff, took soundings among republican commanders, confirming the pessimism thay had already expressed. But when Austin Stack called a group of them together to sign a statement they all refused to take the responsibility, despite agreeing that it was 'neither politic nor sensible to carry on the war'. Todd Andrews remembered 'seeing the agonising effect Stack's sense of responsibility was producing on him'.[225] A fortnight after Lynch's death, de Valera issued his order to the 'Soldiers of the Republic, Legion of the Rearguard', declaring that 'the Republic can no longer be defended successfully by your arms.' Military victory 'must be allowed to rest for the moment with those who have destroyed the Republic'. Nearly a month after that, on 24 May, Aiken issued the final command to the IRA to dump its arms. There were no negotiations, no truce terms: the Republic simply melted back into the realm of the imagination.

Conclusion

'We have declared for an Irish Republic and will not live under any other law.' Liam Lynch's famous assertion was made even before the formal declaration of independence by Dáil Éireann. For him, and many others, the Republic was an actually existing entity; it had been created by the action of the Irish Volunteers. The first Republic had lasted five days in 1916, the second had lasted nearly two years when the vote on the Treaty was taken. When the crunch came in 1922 many Volunteers plainly believed that they owned it. They had some grounds for this belief. It was obviously the case that 'the Republic had crystallised around the army', and could only exert state-like functions where the army operated successfully. Otherwise it remained a projection of political imagination rather than a functioning political structure.

Paradoxically, though, it was the most enterprising 'republicans' who accepted the Treaty. Those diehards who stood out most vehemently against it had mostly been less committed to the task of turning the Republic from an abstract concept into a functioning machine of representative government. They were and remained hostile to everything that smacked of 'politics'. Those who had worked to make the counter-state a reality were more likely see the point of making the Free State work, to deliver actual self-government rather than imagined 'freedom'. Among the republican leadership, nobody did more to make the Republic a reality than Michael Collins. His energy and what Frank O'Connor called his 'genius of realism' let him conduct his multifaceted executive business almost as if the British authorities were not there. 'He would be made aware of the English garrison as a sort of minor interruption and hit out at it as a busy man hits out at a bluebottle.' 'The word "cannot" was not in his vocabulary,' as the Republic's house solicitor said.[1] Collins grasped, as many of his colleagues did not, that the counter-state was not just a publicity stunt: it had high propaganda value, of course, but ultimately that value would rest on its effectiveness. 'Our propaganda can never be stronger than our actions.'[1]

The Republic's actual performance was crucial to the process of convincing the British that the game was up. In some departments it was impressive, but it could never be more than partial. Ultimately, the Republic was unable to create the means to secure its survival. Republican diehards blamed the failure on lack of will, but it was in the battle of wills of the civil war that they themselves fell short. The will of the Staters to create a functioning structure outweighed the republican will to prevent them. The republicans lost the civil war as soon as they slipped into this negative posture, in effect battling against 'the security of the people, or the security of their lives, and the value of their money', as Cosgrave put it. An assertion like that of Kevin O'Higgins – 'the ceasing of the bailiff to function is the first sign of a crumbling civilisation' – dull as it might sound, represented a passion as vehement as that of any idealist. The Free State's repressive action was more violent than the British had been. From a republican perspective, this should have condemned it to the same fate as the British regime; but it did not.

Fighting wars can, as is all too well known, be a source of national and personal pride. But fighting civil wars usually produces a sense of shame rather than of pride, for victors as well as losers, and Ireland's was not an exception. For many, the response was a deep silence. The lone republican survivor of the Ballyseedy massacre did not speak publicly about it for over forty years. Robert Barton, as the historian R. F. Foster was once 'courteously told', never discussed the civil war at all. The Free State and its successors were hardly more forthcoming; no official history of the revolutionary period was ever produced. Even academic historians shied away from the divisive topic for generations, and the few who addressed the war of independence usually took 1921 as a natural end point. There were good or at least weighty reasons for this. As F. S. L. Lyons wrote in 1971, the civil war was 'an episode which has burned so deep into the heart and mind of Ireland that it is not yet possible for the historian to approach it with the detailed knowledge or the objectivity which it deserves'. Things have changed since then. The knowledge deficit, primarily due to that collective silence, has been greatly reduced. Objectivity may still be more difficult to achieve. The fundamental issues of the Treaty split have not been fully resolved, even if they have been eventually set aside by the mainstream.

The contrast between the heady communion of the 'four glorious years' and the dismal descent into fratricidal violence in 1922 was hard for the 'band of brothers' to grasp. Some – like Michael O'Flanagan – came to think that the split had, in effect, been 'there from the start' in 1917. Surveying the correspondence between Collins and MacSwiney in 1919 led Frank O'Connor to think, as we have seen, that 'within the revolutionary organisation there were already two worlds, two philosophies'. Were the allegiances of the civil war, in essence, predetermined? When the split began, though many people tried to stop it, and many suffered real anguish, very few seem to have had no fundamental conviction about the Treaty. Even Frank Aiken, who hesitated longer than most, clearly could never have actively supported the Free State. The protracted negotiations certainly have an air, in retrospect, of merely delaying the inevitable.

The 'heavily built, Falstaffian' irregular who passed by W. B. Yeats in his Sligo tower, 'cracking jokes of Civil War' as though 'to die by gunshot were the finest play under the sun', perhaps represented that 60 per cent of 'Irregularism' that Kevin O'Higgins attributed to 'sheer futility'. Yeats called him 'affable', and like the lieutenant and his soldiers 'half dressed in National uniform' who also passed by, and with whom the poet chatted about foul weather and storm damage, he brings home that this was a domestic conflict, an intimate, neighbourly war. As in many civil wars, the dynamics of local action were often loosely related, or even unrelated, to the great issues which preoccupied actors at the national level.[2]

O'Higgins's argument, of course, was that in national terms the fight was pointless, and many at the time and since have shared this view. Indeed some have extended the judgment to the 'war of independence' as a whole. As one leading historian has written, 'whether the bloody catalogue of assassination and war from 1919–21 was necessary' to get the Treaty terms 'may fairly be questioned'.[3] C. H. Bretherton of the *Irish Times* pointed out in 1922 that 'the two things at which the Catholic Irish were supposed to baulk were Partition and the King. By the Treaty they accepted both. Had they accepted them in 1914 they could then have had all the self-determination that they are now getting.' Some parliamentarians went further, holding that if partition had been swallowed, even 'more than was got under the Treaty could have been got then'.

The catalogue of blood is grim enough. Some 7,500 people were killed or injured by armed action between 1917 and 1923.[4] In Cork alone over 700 people were killed, 400 of them at the hands of the IRA. Over a third of the dead were civilians. The IRA killed 200 civilians – innocent or not – and seventy of these were Protestants. Many more were driven out by direct or indirect threats of violence. In Peter Hart's words, the 'single greatest measurable social change of the revolutionary era' was the dramatic reduction of the non-Catholic population in the south. The numbers recorded here may be trivial in comparison with the massive dislocation of peoples in Europe, starting with the Greek–Turkish conflict in the early 1920s. Compared with the unrestrained violence so common in civil wars, Ireland's violence was constrained by social mechanisms we do not yet fully understand. This was a mercy, but in other ways the Irish civil war was fully as destructive as most of its kind. There was more to the damage than simple bloodshed. It represented the culmination of a process in which, over three years of guerrilla conflict, violence permeated society. By 1922 many leaders on both sides of the split were concerned about what they saw as a general public demoralization.

While there can be no question that Protestants as a community felt the threat of harm and dislocation with particular acuteness, a sense of apprehension ran much wider as the fighting went on. Normality was unhinged by continual violence, and Ireland became in a sense a war zone. Although observers were often struck by the way ordinary people calmly went about their business while gunfights were erupting near by, the quality of life was degraded by the atmosphere of generalized apprehension. 'The night can sweat with terror,' as Yeats said. We have seen how commonly the armed police loosed off their guns at random, but even the British army, which prided itself on its control of weapons, admitted that in the winter of 1920, in Dublin, 'shots are fired at any time of day or night now and there seems to be little check on ammunition.'[5]

The military inquest files are full of personal tragedies, people caught in the crossfire – not all 'innocent civilians' certainly, but more than enough to spell out the grim hazards of war. None of those killed by Crown forces 'in the execution of duty' was unluckier, perhaps, than

Hannah Carey, a worker at the Imperial Hotel in Killarney, who was shot in the throat on the day of the Truce by a policeman, driving a car with a revolver in his hand. 'When turning at the end of College Street, I mechanically gripped the wheel tighter, making the turn, and it was then my revolver went off, I suppose I must have pressed the trigger . . . we were all rather excited at the time, it was just after two military sergeants had been shot in the street.'[6] A situation in which driving with a loaded pistol had become normal behaviour was, without doubt, a deeply abnormal one. Of the dozens of people shot for 'failing to halt when challenged', many were probably too frightened to realize they were making the wrong choice. One car driver (John Kenure) was shot by troops at 500 yards' range – at which distance he could certainly not have heard the order to halt. Another man who was shot by a military post for failing to halt was at that moment trying to make himself known to another military post near by.

Kevin O'Higgins described the collapsed public structures of Ireland in 1922 as 'battered out of recognition by rival jurisdictions'. At the personal level the clash was disorienting. When District Inspector Gilbert Potter was killed in Tipperary in April 1921, his widow received a weirdly informative letter of explanation from the local IRA commander. 'Your husband was charged with and found guilty of waging war against the Republic. We offered to release your husband if the British Government would release Volunteer [Thomas] Traynor who was similarly charged. Personally I don't believe the offer went past Dublin Castle. Traynor was hanged on Monday, the law had, therefore, to take its course.'[7]

What, in the end, had violence achieved? Terence MacSwiney once quoted Mazzini's warning that a new order of things established by violence 'is always tyrannical even when it is better than the old' – a paradoxical warning from a physical-force man, and one which might well have been heeded by republicans (his sister included) when the IRA set itself up as an independent authority in 1922. In fact, and perhaps against the odds, the emergent Irish state – however tyrannical it seemed to its republican victims – became a remarkably stable democracy. It may even have been too stable. The Staters who battled the Republic to a standstill seemed to have their imaginative horizons shrunk by the experience. Men like Cosgrave, Blythe and O'Higgins became so conservative as to be seen by some as counter-revolutionaries from 1922 on.

The stolid caution they showed, particularly in the fiscal sphere, cast a pall of gloom over the early decades of independence. Blythe's 1924 budget cuts, notably in welfare spending, have even provoked an eminent historian to describe him as 'launch[ing] an attack on the old and blind'.[8]

It may be that if Irish nationalists had been more flexible over partition there would have been no Anglo-Irish war; and if Britain had been more flexible over the Free State's constitution there would have been no civil war. But such flexibility is not usually attractive to politicians, especially when (as in both these cases) they fear being outbid in conviction by more radical groups. At both these moments it was the 'extremists', not those 'in power', who determined policy. In 1914 Ireland, like much of Europe, was spoiling for a fight. In 1921, like Europe, it was war-weary, and this weariness allowed the 'realism' of those who accepted the Treaty to have a purchase on public opinion.

Violence had not initiated partition, but it certainly cemented it. The advance of republicanism after 1916 paralleled the process of establishing a separate northern state, and not by accident. The non-denominational or freethinking origins of republicanism in the 1790s were long since forgotten. The republicans who took control of the nationalist movement as it reacted to Ulster unionist resistance to Home Rule were seen by the majority of Protestants as aiming at Catholic majority rule. In 1916 the future of both republicanism and partition hung in the balance, but the subsequent republican guerrilla campaign produced a violent reassertion of Ulster identity. If any chance remained of reconstructing the unity of Ireland after 1918, it depended on the British government's commitment to implementing the Council of Ireland project in the 1920 Government of Ireland Act, and ensuring that the Boundary Commission envisaged in the 1921 Treaty operated as the negotiators had assumed. As long as the Lloyd George coalition remained in power, both these were possible. But as the Free State sank into civil war, Lloyd George was overthrown with almost shocking speed and finality. During the Treaty split, and through the civil war, the partition issue remained secondary to the issue of 'the oath'; it could be still sidelined because nobody on either side really believed partition could endure. Only when the Boundary Commission set to work in 1924 did reality begin to dawn for most nationalists.

The cementing of partition in the 1920s had consequences for the idea of the Republic. Republican Sinn Féin fell apart after the civil war, and when de Valera led a new party back into parliament its republican credentials were relegated to an appendix (in English) to its Irish title. Even after Fianna Fáil ('the Republican party') gained power and moved in the 1930s to dismantle the symbolic structures of Crown supremacy that had proved so lethally divisive in 1922, de Valera maintained that the Republic could not exist while Ireland was divided. The state he redesigned through his 1937 constitution was essentially republican, but it had to wait until the descendants of the pro-Treaty side returned to power a decade later before it was formally designated a republic. By that time, the real political independence of Ireland had been conclusively demonstrated. Britain responded to the declaration of the Republic in 1949 with the Northern Ireland Act – guaranteeing that Northern Ireland would remain part of the UK as long as a majority of its population wanted this – but not with violence. More crucially, the assertion of Irish neutrality during the Second World War had been maintained in spite of intense British (and American) pressure. The old belief that only direct control of Ireland could guarantee Britain's security had been finally scotched. It had proved, as Collins believed, that Britain no longer had the power or the will to coerce Ireland. The fight for independence had, in that sense, been truly won.

Appendix: Biographical Glossary

Aiken, Frank b. 1898 in Co. Armagh; educated by Christian Brothers and at St Colman's College, Newry; joined Irish Volunteers 1914, Sinn Féin 1917; Chairman of Armagh Comhairle Ceanntair; OC Newry Brigade, Irish Volunteers 1920, OC 4th Northern Division, IRA 1921; tried to stay neutral during Treaty split, eventually took anti-Treaty side 1922; Chief of Staff IRA 1923–5; Sinn Féin TD for Louth 1923, re-elected as Fianna Fáil TD for next fifty years; Minister for Defence 1932–9; Minister for Finance 1945–8; Minister for External Affairs 1951–4 and 1957–69; Tánaiste (deputy prime minister) 1965–9; d. 1983.

Ashe, Thomas b. 1885 in Co. Kerry; Gaelic Leaguer and pipe-band enthusiast; principal of Lusk National School, Co. Dublin; commandant of 5th Battalion, Dublin Brigade, Irish Volunteers 1916; death sentence commuted to life imprisonment; released June 1917; rearrested August 1917; led hunger strike in Mountjoy gaol; died under forcible feeding September 1917.

Barton, Robert b. 1881 at Glendalough, Co. Wicklow; educated at Rugby School and Oxford; joined Dublin Fusiliers 1914; resigned commission 1916; joined Sinn Féin 1917; MP for Wicklow West 1918; TD for Kildare–Wicklow 1921; Dáil Minister for Agriculture, then Economic Affairs; in prison Jan. 1920–July 1921; member of Irish delegation in London 1921; signed but opposed Anglo-Irish Treaty 1921–2; lost seat in 1923, retired from politics; Chairman of Agricultural Commission 1934–54; d. 1975.

Béaslaí, Piaras (Pierce Beasley) b. 1881 in Liverpool; educated at Jesuit school; joined Gaelic League, worked to remove Douglas Hyde as president 1915; vice-OC 3rd Battalion, Dublin Brigade, Irish Volunteers

1916; Director of Publicity, Irish Volunteer Executive 1918; Sinn Féin MP for Kerry East 1918; editor of *An tOglaċ* 1919; TD for Kerry–Limerick 1921, re-elected 1922; official biographer of Michael Collins 1924; d. 1965.

Blythe, Ernest (Earnán de Blaghd) b. 1889 in Co. Antrim; government clerk; junior reporter for *North Down Herald* 1909; Gaelic Leaguer and Volunteer organizer; deported 1915; Sinn Féin MP/TD for North Monaghan 1918; minister in Dáil Cabinet 1919–21; Minister for Finance in Free State government 1922; Vice-President (deputy prime minister) 1927–32; lost parliamentary seat 1933; Senator 1933–6; retired from politics 1936; managing director of the Abbey Theatre 1941–67; repeatedly criticized for hiring actors for their Irish language rather than acting ability; d. 1975.

Boland, Harry b. 1887 in Dublin; apprenticed as cutter in tailoring department of Mary Street store; GAA player and administrator, Chairman of Dublin County Committee 1911; joined 2nd Battalion, Dublin Brigade, Irish Volunteers 1913; in GPO 1916; Sinn Féin MP for Roscommon South 1918; envoy to USA 1919; TD for Mayo South–Roscommon South 1921, re-elected 1922; voted against Treaty 1922; Quartermaster General IRA 1922; killed in Skerries August 1922.

Brugha, Cathal (Charles Burgess) b. 1874 in Dublin; educated Belvedere College; co-founder of candle-making business; Gaelic Leaguer 1899; vice-commandant 4th Battalion, Dublin Brigade, Irish Volunteers in South Dublin Union Easter 1916; seriously wounded and permanently crippled; Sinn Féin MP/TD 1918; presided over first meeting of Dáil Éireann 1919; Minister for Defence in Dáil Cabinet; opposed Treaty 1922; killed during fighting in O'Connell Street in civil war July 1922.

Childers, Robert Erskine b. 1870 in London; grew up in Co. Wicklow; educated Haileybury and Cambridge; Clerk of the House of Commons 1895–1910; fought in Boer War with City Imperial Volunteers; wrote *In the Ranks of the CIV* 1900; *The Riddle of the Sands* 1903; *War and the Arme Blanche* 1910; became a home ruler 1908 and wrote *The Framework of Home Rule* 1911; ran in IV guns at Howth 1914; served in Royal Naval Air Service 1914–19; awarded DSC 1917; Secretary of Irish Convention 1917; Director of Propaganda in Dáil government 1919–21, edited *Irish Bulletin*; Secretary to Irish delegation to London 1921; opposed Treaty 1922; fought on anti-Treaty side in civil war; executed 1922.

Collins, Michael b. 1890 in Co. Cork; Post Office clerk in London; adjutant to Joseph Plunkett in GPO 1916; interned in Frongoch, released December 1916; Irish Volunteer organizer, and Sinn Féin MP 1918; Director of Organization (later Intelligence), Volunteer GHQ; President of the Supreme Council of the IRB 1919; signatory of Anglo-Irish Treaty 1921; Chairman of the Provisional Government and Commander-in-Chief of the National Army, Irish Free State, 1922; killed in ambush, Co. Cork, 22 August 1922.

Cosgrave, William T. b. 1880 in Dublin; Sinn Féin member of Dublin Corporation 1909; captain, 4th Battalion, Dublin Brigade, Irish Volunteers in South Dublin Union 1916; death sentence commuted to life imprisonment; Sinn Féin MP for Kilkenny 1917; released from gaol 1918; Minister for Local Government in Dáil Cabinet 1919; President of the Executive Council (prime minister), Irish Free State, after death of Michael Collins in 1922; leader of Cumann na nGaedheal party 1922–33, and Fine Gael party 1934–44; d. 1965.

De Valera, Eamon b. 1882 in New York; mathematics teacher and Gaelic Leaguer; commandant of 3rd Battalion, Dublin Brigade, Irish Volunteers 1916; death sentence commuted to life imprisonment; released June 1917; MP for East Clare July 1917; President (Príomh-Aire) of Sinn Féin and Irish Volunteers, October 1917; President of Dáil Eireann 1919–21; opposed Treaty and joined IRA 1922; left Sinn Féin party to found Fianna Fáil 1926; President of the Executive Council (prime minister), Irish Free State 1933–7; Taoiseach (prime minister), Eire, under new constitution 1937–48, 1951–4, 1957–9; President of the Irish Republic 1959–73; d. 1975.

Dillon, John b. 1851 in Co. Dublin; nationalist MP 1880–83, 1885–1918 (East Mayo); Parnell's deputy in charge of 'Plan of Campaign' 1886; anti-Parnellite leader 1891–1900; deputy leader of reunited nationalist party (UIL) 1900–1918, and leader 1918 after death of John Redmond; lost East Mayo seat to Eamon de Valera December 1918; d. 1927.

APPENDIX: BIOGRAPHICAL GLOSSARY

Figgis, Darrell b. 1882 in Rathmines, Dublin; family emigrated to India, returned 1892; worked in family tea brokerage in London; joined Irish Volunteers 1913; moved to Achill Island to learn Irish 1913; accompanied Erskine Childers on Howth gun-running 1914; in Reading gaol 1916–17; Hon. Secretary of Sinn Féin 1917; arrested and deported to England 1918; editor of the *Republic*; led Commission of Inquiry into the Resources and Industries of Ireland 1919–21; opposed electoral pact 1922, expelled from Sinn Féin; beard cut off by republicans 1922; TD for Dublin County 1922, re-elected 1923; on Constitution Committee 1922, broadcasting committee 1923; committed suicide 1925.

Ginnell, Laurence b. 1852 in Westmeath; barrister; MP for Westmeath North 1906; organized Ranch War 1906; expelled from Irish nationalist party 1909; independent nationalist MP 1910; ejected from House of Commons for accusing H. H. Asquith of murder 1916; joined Sinn Féin 1917; TD for Westmeath 1918; Director of Propaganda in Dáil government 1919; Dáil representative in Argentina 1920; opposed Treaty 1922; ejected from Free State Dáil 1922; republican envoy to USA 1922; d. 1923.

Griffith, Arthur b. 1871 in Dublin; printer and journalist; founded the *United Irishman* and *Sinn Féin*; Vice-President of Sinn Féin party 1917; Sinn Féin MP 1918; Acting President of Dáil government 1919–20 during de Valera's visit to USA; chief negotiator and signatory of Anglo-Irish Treaty 1921; President of Dáil and Minister in Irish Free State Provisional Government 1922; d. 12 August 1922.

Johnson, Thomas b. 1872 in Liverpool; worked for Irish fish merchant; commercial traveller 1900; Vice-President Irish TUC 1913; President 1915; co-operated with Eoin MacNeill over employers' threats to sack members of Irish Volunteers 1915–16; organized anti-conscription strike 1918; co-drafted Democratic Programme of first Dáil Éireann; Secretary of ILP/TUC 1920–28; TD for Co. Dublin 1922–7 and Leader of Labour party; Senator 1928–36; d. 1963.

Lynch, Liam b. 1893 in Co. Limerick; apprentice in hardware trade in Mitchelstown, Cork, 1910; joined Gaelic League 1910; Irish Volunteers 1913; adjutant, Fermoy battalion 1918; OC North Cork (Cork No. 2) Brigade 1919; OC 1st Southern Division IRA 1921; opposed Treaty 1922; Chief of Staff, IRA 1922; killed in action 1923.

Mac Curtain, Tomás b. 1884 in Co. Cork; Secretary of Blackpool branch of Gaelic League 1902; joined Sinn Féin and IRB 1907; Fianna Éireann organizer 1911; commanded Cork Brigade, Irish Volunteers 1916; imprisoned in Wakefield, Frongoch and Reading 1916–17; Sinn Féin councillor for Cork North-West in 1920 local elections; elected lord mayor of Cork January 1920; assassinated in his home 20 March 1920. Coroner's jury found verdict of murder against the RIC and the Prime Minister, Lloyd George.

MacEntee, Seán b. 1889 in Belfast; educated St Malachy's College and Belfast Municipal College of Technology; electrical engineer and patent agent; with Dundalk Volunteers in 1916, joined GPO garrison; death sentence commuted to life imprisonment; released 1917; Sinn Féin MP/TD 1918; Fianna Fáil TD 1927–69; government Minister 1932–48, 1951–4, 1957–65; Tánaiste (deputy prime minister) 1959–65; d. 1984.

MacEoin, Sean (John McKeon) b. 1893 in Co. Longford; trained as blacksmith in father's forge, took over family firm 1913; joined Irish Volunteers and IRB 1913; OC Longford Brigade 1920; imprisoned for murder 1921; GOC Western Command 1922; GOC Curragh 1927; Chief of Staff 1929; Cumann na nGaedheal TD for Leitrim–Sligo 1929, Longford–Westmeath 1932–7, 1948–65, Athlone–Longford 1937–48; Minister for Justice 1948–51; Minister for Defence 1951, 1954–7; ran for presidency in 1945 and 1959; d. 1973.

MacNeill, Eoin b. 1867 in Co. Antrim; law clerk; co-founder of Gaelic League 1893; editor of *Gaelic Journal*, later *An Claideamh Soluis*; Professor of Early Irish History, University College Dublin 1908; founder and first Chief of Staff, Irish Volunteers 1913; sentenced to penal servitude for life 1916; released 1917; Sinn Féin MP/TD for the National University of Ireland 1918; Minister for Education, Irish Free State 1922; member of Boundary Commission 1924–5; forced to resign ministry and lost parliamentary seat 1927; Chairman of Irish Historical Manuscripts Commission 1927; d. 1945.

MacSwiney, Terence b. 1879 in Cork city; trained as an accountant; philosophy degree at Royal University 1907; co-founded Cork Dramatic Society with Daniel Corkery 1908; plays included *The Revolutionist*, *The Holocaust* and *The Warriors of Coole*; peripatetic teacher, Co. Cork 1911, resigned to become full-time Irish Volunteer organizer,

1915; vice-commandant, Cork Brigade, Irish Volunteers 1916; Sinn Féin MP/TD for West Cork 1918; elected lord mayor of Cork after murder of Tomás Mac Curtain; arrested and sentenced to two years' imprisonment 16 August 1920; died on his seventy-fourth day of hunger strike, 25 October 1920.

Markievicz, Constance (née Gore-Booth) b. 1868 in London; grew up at Lissadell, Co. Sligo; studied at Slade School, London 1893; married Count Casimir Dunin-Markiewicz 1900 (daugher Maeve b. 1901); co-founder of United Arts Club, Dublin 1907; joined Sinn Féin and Inghinidhe na hÉireann 1908; co-founder of Fianna Éireann 1909, and Irish Citizen Army, 1913; in St Stephen's Green garrison Easter 1916; death sentence commuted to life imprisonment; released June 1917; converted to Catholicism; first woman MP (for Dublin) 1918; Minister for Labour in Dáil Cabinet 1919; opposed Treaty 1922; joined Fianna Fáil 1926; TD 1927; d. 1927.

Mellows, Liam b. 1892 in Lancashire; grew up in Co. Wexford; educated Royal Hibernian Military School; clerk in Dublin 1905; joined Fianna Éireann 1909; joined IRB 1912; full-time organizer, Irish Volunteers, Co. Galway 1914–15; deported 1915; returned Easter 1916 to lead Galway Volunteers; escaped to USA after rebellion, worked on *Gaelic American*; agent for de Valera's US tour 1919–20; Director of Purchases, IRA 1921; Sinn Féin TD for Galway 1921; member of Four Courts anti-Treaty garrison in civil war June 1922; executed December 1922.

Mulcahy, Richard b. 1886 in Waterford; educated by Christian Brothers; worked as Post Office engineer 1902; joined Gaelic League and IRB; joined Irish Volunteers 1913; fought with Thomas Ashe at Ashbourne 1916; OC Dublin Brigade 1918, Chief of Staff GHQ 1919; Sinn Féin TD for Dublin North-West 1921, re-elected 1922; Minister for Defence 1922; succeeded Collins as commander-in-chief; Cumann na nGaedheal TD for Dublin North 1923–37; Minister for Defence 1924; Minister for Local Government and Public Health 1927–32; elected to Seanad Éireann 1937; Fine Gael TD for Dublin North-East 1938–43; Leader of Fine Gael party 1944; Minister for Education 1948–51, 1954–7; retired 1960; d. 1971.

O'Brien, William b. 1881 in Co. Cork; joined Irish Socialist Republican party 1898; close associate of Connolly and James Larkin; secretary of lockout committee during 1913 labour dispute; anti-conscription campaigner; deported and interned in Frongoch and Reading 1916; deported to Wormwood Scrubs 1920, released after hunger strike; Labour party TD for Dublin South City 1922–3, for Tipperary 1927 and 1937–8; General Secretary ITGWU; d. 1968.

O'Duffy, Eoin b. 1892 in Co. Monaghan; apprenticed as engineer in Wexford, engineer and architect in Monaghan; joined Gaelic League and GAA 1912; joined Irish Volunteers 1917; imprisoned 1918; OC Monaghan Brigade 1918; OC 2nd Northern Division 1921; Sinn Féin TD for Monaghan 1921, re-elected 1922; Director of Organization, GHQ 1921; Assistant Chief of Staff, GHQ IRA 1921; Chief Liaison Officer in Ulster 1921; Chief of Staff 1922; Commissioner Civil Guard 1922; leader of Army Comrades' Association (Blueshirts) 1933; launched National Corporate party 1935; tried to form Irish Volunteer Legion to fight with Germans against Russia 1941; d. 1944.

O'Higgins, Kevin b. 1892 in Queen's County (Co. Leix); educated at Clongowes, St Mary's Christian Brothers' school in Portlaoise, and St Patrick's College Maynooth; studied law at University College Dublin; joined Irish Volunteers 1915, Sinn Féin MP for Queen's County 1918; Assistant Minister for Local Government 1919; TD for Leix–Offaly 1922, re-elected 1923; Minister for Home Affairs 1922 (renamed Justice 1924); Assistant Adjutant General on army general staff 1922; Minister for External Affairs 1925; assassinated 1927.

O'Kelly (Ó Ceallaigh), Seán T. b. 1882 in Dublin; Gaelic Leaguer, joined Celtic Literary Society; Sinn Féin 1905; Sinn Féin member of Dublin Corporation 1906–26; manager of *An Claideamh Soluis*; General Secretary Gaelic League 1915; in GPO Easter 1916; MP/TD for College Green division of Dublin 1918; Speaker of Dáil Éireann 1919; envoy to international Peace Conference, Paris, 1919; opposed Treaty 1922; joined Fianna Fáil 1926; Minister for Local Government 1933 and Vice-President of Executive Council (deputy prime minister); Minister for Finance 1941; President of Ireland 1945; d. 1966.

O'Malley, Ernie (Earnán) b. 1897 in Co. Mayo, son of a CDB official; medical student at University College Dublin; joined Irish Volunteers and Gaelic League 1917; full-time IV organizer 1918; arrested in Kilkenny 1920, escaped from Kilmainham gaol 1921; OC 2nd Southern Division, IRA 1921; opposed Treaty 1922; Assistant Chief of Staff, IRA, and OC

Northern and Eastern Command 1922; captured 1922; Sinn Féin TD for Dublin North 1923–7; moved to USA, wrote memoir of war of independence and became a full-time writer; returned to Ireland 1936; conducted extensive series of interviews with former IRA men; d. 1957.

Robinson, Seamus b. 1890 in Belfast; left Scottish monastery to join Irish Volunteers 1913; OC 3rd Tipperary Brigade 1917–21; vice-OC 2nd Southern Division 1921; Sinn Féin TD for Waterford–Tipperary East 1921; opposed Treaty 1922; joined Fianna Fáil 1926; member of Seanad Éireann 1928–37; co-founder of Bureau of Military History; d. 1961.

Stack, Austin b. 1880 in Co. Kerry; GAA enthusiast and champion hurler; founder member and commandant, Kerry Irish Volunteers 1913–16; interned 1916–17, led hunger strikes in Lewes prison; released June 1917; Sinn Féin TD for West Kerry 1918; Minister for Justice in Dáil Cabinet 1919; established republican courts; IRA Deputy Chief of Staff 1921; Minister for Home Affairs 1921–2; opposed Treaty 1922; abstentionist Sinn Féin TD 1923; d. 1929.

Notes

ABBREVIATIONS USED IN NOTES

A/A/C/S	Acting Assistant Chief of Staff
A/C/S	Assistant Chief of Staff
A/G	Adjutant General
ASS	Active Service Section
Bde	Brigade
BMH	Bureau of Military History
Bn	Battalion
CnmB	Cumann na mBan
C/S	Chief of Staff (IV)
DAG	Deputy Adjutant General
D/C/S	Deputy Chief of Staff
DE	Dáil Éireann
Div.	Division
D/O	Director of Organization
D/P	Director of Publicity
HLRO	House of Lords Record Office
Inf.	Infantry
IO	Intelligence Officer
IWM	Imperial War Museum
LGP	Lloyd George papers
MAI	Military Archives, Ireland
MCI	Military Court of Inquiry in Lieu of Inquest
M/D	Minister for Defence
MSP	Military Service Pensions Archive, MAI
NA	National Archives, London
NAI	National Archives of Ireland
ND	Northern Division (IRA)
NLI	National Library of Ireland
PRONI	Public Record Office, Northern Ireland
QMG	Quartermaster General

SD   Southern Division (IRA)
S/S   Secretary of State
UCDA   University College Dublin Archive
WD   Western Division (IRA)
WS   Witness Statement

INTRODUCTION: UP THE REPUBLIC!
REPUBLICANISM IN IRELAND

1. Matthew Kelly, 'The Irish People and the Disciplining of Dissent', in Fearghal McGarry and James McConnel (eds.), *The Black Hand of Republicanism: Fenianism in Modern Ireland* (Dublin 2009), p. 37.

2. Florence O'Donoghue, 'Illumination', in John Borgonovo (ed.), *Florence and Josephine O'Donoghue's War of Independence: A Destiny that Shapes our Ends* (Dublin 2006), p. 31.

3. Tom Garvin, *Nationalist Revolutionaries in Ireland 1858–1928* (Oxford 1987), pp. 35, 119.

4. Hayden Talbot, *Michael Collins's Own Story* (London n.d.), q. Brian P. Murphy, *Patrick Pearse and the Lost Republican Ideal* (Dublin 1991), p. 98.

5. Tony Crowley, *Wars of Words: The Politics of Language in Ireland 1537–2004* (Oxford 2005), pp. 137, 150–57.

6. Charles Townshend, *Easter 1916: The Irish Rebellion* (London 2005), p. 35.

7. David Thornley, 'Patrick Pearse – The Evolution of a Republican', in F. X. Martin (ed.), *Leaders and Men of the Easter Rising: Dublin 1916* (London 1967), p. 155.

8. Peter Berresford Ellis, *A History of the Irish Working Class* (London 1972), p. 235. Cf. e.g. Dorothy Macardle, *The Irish Republic 1911–1923* (London 1937), ch. 16; Eoin Neeson, *Birth of a Republic* (Dublin 1998), ch. 6.

9. Joseph Plunkett notebook, NLI MS 4700.

10. Maxwell to Asquith, 13 May, to French, 16 Jun. 1916. Bodleian Library, Asquith MSS 44.

PART I: THE IMAGINED STATE:
1918–19

1. Adrian Gregory and Senia Pašeta (eds.), *Ireland and the Great War: 'A War to Unite Us All'?* (Manchester 2002); John Horne (ed.), *Our War: Ireland and the Great War* (Dublin 2008).

2. Charles Townshend, *Political Violence in Ireland: Government and Resistance since 1848* (Oxford 1983), pp. 67–84.

3. Jim Herlihy, *The Royal Irish Constabulary* (Dublin 1997), p. 75.

4. John D. Brewer, *The Royal Irish Constabulary: An Oral History* (Belfast 1990), pp. 12–13.

5. Irish Command was a subordinate part of the UK Home Command until 1920 when it became an independent command, and its commander a commander-in-chief (GOC-in-C).

6. Memorandum on the Enforcement of Conscription in Ireland, and note by B. Mahon with additions by IG RIC, 26 Mar. 1918. MAI BMH CD 178/1/1.

7. Lawrence W. McBride, *The Greening of Dublin Castle: The Transformation of Bureaucratic and Judicial Personnel in Ireland 1892–1922* (Washington, DC 1991), p. 243.

8. 'Man-Power of Ireland', Memo by the Chief Secretary, 27 Mar. 1918. GT 4052, NA CAB 24/46.

9. John Kendle, *Walter Long, Ireland and the Union 1905–1920* (Montreal 1992), p. 164.

10. War Cabinet, 3 Apr. 1918. NA CAB 23/14.

11. Duke to Lloyd George, 16 Apr. 1918. HLRO LGP F/37/4/51.

12. War Cabinet, 16 Apr. 1918. NA CAB 23/7/392.

13. French to Lloyd George, 5 May 1918. HLRO LGP F/48/6/10.

14. French to Lloyd George, 18 Apr. 1918. MAI BMH CD 178/1/2.

15. W. J. Mc Cormack, *Dublin 1916: The French Connection* (Dublin 2012), pp. 55–65, puckishly labels the process 'baptising the Fenians'.

16. David Fitzpatrick, *Politics and Irish Life: Provincial Experience of War and Revolution 1913–1921* (Dublin 1977), p. 138.

17. David W. Miller, *Church, State and Nation in Ireland 1898–1921* (Dublin 1973), pp. 391–2.

18. Monthly Confidential Intelligence Report, Midland and Connaught District, 30 Apr. 1918. NA CO 904/157.

19. Jérôme aan de Wiel, *The Catholic Church in Ireland 1914–1918* (Dublin 2003), p. 222.

20. Miller, *Church, State and Nation*, pp. 404–5.

21. IG RIC Report, 20 Apr. 1918. NA CAB 24/49/4326.

22. *Tyrone Constitution*, 19 Apr. 1918, q. Michael Laffan, *The Resurrection of Ireland: The Sinn Féin Party, 1916–1923* (Cambridge 1999), p. 137; RIC Report, NA CO 904/105, q. Marie Coleman, *County Longford and the Irish Revolution 1910–1923* (Dublin 2003), p. 83.

23. Monthly Confidential Intelligence Report, Midland and Connaught District, 30 Apr. 1918. NA CO 904/157.

24. C. Desmond Greaves, *Liam Mellows and the Irish Revolution* (London 1971), p. 144.

25. Thomas Johnson papers, MAI CD 258/9.

26. Aodh de Blacam, *What Sinn Féin Stands For: The Irish Republican Movement, its History, Aims and Ideals* (Dublin 1921), p. 93.

27. War Cabinet Memo by W. H. Long, 9 Oct. 1918. GT 5926, NA CAB 24/66.

28. Eunan O'Halpin, *The Decline of the Union: British Government in Ireland 1892–1920* (Dublin 1987), p. 160.

29. Fintan Murphy statement, MAI MSP 34 REF 11815 34A24.

30. BMH WS 1570 (Dominick Molloy).

31. Laffan, *Resurrection of Ireland*, p. 145.

32. Jacqueline Van Voris, *Constance de Markievicz in the Cause of Ireland* (Amherst, Mass. 1967), pp. 246, 251.

33. The phrases are from F. S. L. Lyons, *Ireland since the Famine* (London 1971), p. 386.

34. Joost Augusteijn (ed.), *The Memoirs of John M. Regan: A Catholic Officer in the RIC and RUC, 1909–1948* (Dublin 2007), p. 113.

35. War Cabinet 381A, 3 Apr. 1918. NA CAB 23/14.

36. Liam Deasy, *Towards Ireland Free: The West Cork Brigade in the War of Independence 1917–1921*, ed. John E. Chisholm (Dublin and Cork 1973), p. 8; C. S. Andrews, *Dublin Made Me: An Autobiography* (Dublin 1979), p. 99.

37. On female personifications of the country, see Ewan Morris, *Our Own Devices: National Symbols and Political Conflict in Twentieth-Century Ireland* (Dublin 2005), pp. 22–6.

38. Sylvain Briollay, *Ireland in Rebellion* (Dublin 1922) (originally *L'Irlande Insurgée*, Paris 1921, based on articles written in 1920–21), pp. 18–21.

39. Terence de Vere White, *Kevin O'Higgins* (London 1948), p. 38.

40. Briollay, *Ireland in Rebellion*, pp. 26–9, 35–6.

41. BMH WS 857 (Seamus Finn).

42. W. M. Lewis, 'Frank Aiken and the Fourth Northern Division: A Personal and Provincial Experience of the Irish Revolution, 1916–1923', PhD thesis, Queen's University, Belfast 2011, pp. 64–5.

43. Andrews, *Dublin Made Me*, p. 100.

44. BMH WS 1253 (Joseph Daly).

45. BMH WS 1168 (John O'Keeffe).

46. BMH WS 1314 (Patrick Ryan).

47. Peter Hart, *The IRA and its Enemies: Violence and Community in Cork 1916–1923* (Oxford 1998), p. 248.

48. BMH WS 1349 (Daniel Conway).

49. Military Intelligence report, Midland and Connaught District, Dec. 1917. NA CO 904/157.

50. BMH WS 1770 (Kevin O'Shiel).

51. Fr Michael O'Flanagan, *The Strength of Sinn Fein* (Dublin 1934), q. Murphy, *Patrick Pearse and the Lost Republican Ideal*, p. 104.

52. Barry M. Coldrey, *Faith and Fatherland: The Christian Brothers and the Development of Irish Nationalism 1838–1921* (Dublin 1988), p. 252.

53. Led off in this case by Patrick Lynch's pioneering chapter 'The Social Revolution that Never Was', in T. Desmond Williams (ed.), *The Irish Struggle 1916–1926* (London 1966), pp. 41–54.

54. Fitzpatrick, *Politics and Irish Life*, ch. 7.

55. See e.g. Coleman, *County Longford*, pp. 75–6.

56. Fergus Campbell, *Land and Revolution: Nationalist Politics in the West of Ireland 1891–1921* (Oxford 2005), p. 237.

57. BMH WS 1770 (Kevin O'Shiel).

58. 'The Pig Push' – Dedicated to Diarmuid Lynch, Sinn Féin Food Controller. NLI MS 5637.

59. Campbell, *Land and Revolution*, pp. 106, 240–41.

60. Ibid., pp. 223, 242.

61. Michael Farry, *Sligo 1914–1921* (Trim 1992), pp. 112–13.

62. Cf. Terence Dooley, 'IRA Veterans and Land Division in Independent Ireland', in Fearghal McGarry (ed.), *Republicanism in Modern Ireland* (Dublin 2003), p. 88.

63. J. A. Gaughan (ed.), *The Memoirs of Constable Jeremiah Mee RIC* (Dublin 1975), pp. 51–3.

64. Special Circular re Cattle-driving, 23 Feb. 1918, q. Campbell, *Land and Revolution*, p. 241.

65. BMH WS 1287 (Joseph Noonan).

66. MAI, MSP A/3 (5), Bde Activity Reports, Cork III Bde.

67. BMH WS 1253 (Joseph Daly).

68. *Sligo Champion*, 2 Mar. 1918. Farry, *Sligo 1914–1921*, p. 117. C.S.O. Intelligence Notes, 1918, NA CO 903/19/4.

69. Paul Bew, 'Sinn Fein, Agrarian Radicalism and the War of Independence, 1919–1921', in D. George Boyce (ed.), *The Revolution in Ireland 1879–1923* (London 1988), p. 225.

70. Speech by Edward Dwyer [Eamon O'Dwyer], 6 Dec. 1917. NA CO 904/122.

71. Military Intelligence report, Midland and Connaught District, Mar. 1918. NA CO 904/157.

72. Malcolm Bickle diary, q. Hart, *IRA and its Enemies*, p. 60.

73. BMH WS 450 (Brighid O'Mullane); Sinéad McCoole, *No Ordinary Women: Irish Female Activists in the Revolutionary Years 1900–1923* (Dublin 2003), p. 71.

74. CI West Cork, Monthly Report Apr. 1918. NA CO 904/105.

75. Hart, *IRA and its Enemies*, p. 61.

76. BMH WS 1268 (Patrick J. Hargaden).

77. Liam de Paor, *On the Easter Proclamation and Other Declarations* (Dublin 1997), pp. 48–50.

78. BMH WS 1770 (Kevin O'Shiel).

79. UCDA P104/1309.

80. BMH WS 1166 (Patrick Lyons), WS 1329 (Patrick Walsh); Farry, *Sligo 1914–1921*, p. 95.

81. BMH WS 1114 (John Scannell).

82. BMH WS 1141 (Richard Glavin).

83. BMH WS 909 (Mrs Sidney Czira).

84. Seamus Robinson memoir, NLI MS 21265.

85. BMH WS 939 (Ernest Blythe).

86. BMH WS 959 (Patrick Houlihan).

87. J. J. O'Connell, 'Reorganisation 1917', NLI MS 22117.

88. BMH WS 939 (Ernest Blythe).

89. Desmond Ryan, *Seán Treacy and the Third Tipperary Brigade, IRA* (Tralee 1945).

90. O'Duffy to Cathal Brugha, 24 Nov. 1921. UCDA P7A/5, q. Fearghal McGarry, *Eoin O'Duffy: A Self-Made Hero* (Oxford 2005), p. 26.

91. BMH WS 1672 (Thomas Meagher).

92. BMH WS 819 (Liam Archer).

93. Peter Hart, *Mick: The Real Michael Collins* (London 2005), pp. 139–45.

94. BMH WS 958 (Denis J. O'Sullivan).

95. Hart, *IRA and its Enemies*, pp. 232–4.

96. BMH WS 446 (Frank Hynes).

97. Florence O'Donoghue, 'Guerrilla Warfare in Ireland 1919–1921', *An Cosantóir* XXIII (May 1963), p. 294.

98. Collins to Austin Stack, 28 Nov. 1918. Fitzpatrick, *Politics and Irish Life*, p. 207.

99. Seán Moylan statement, NLI MS 27731.

100. General Richard Mulcahy, 'Conscription and the General Headquarters Staff', *Capuchin Annual* 35 (1968), p. 392.

101. BMH WS 1498 (Michael Murray), WS 1146 (Eugene Kilkenny).

102. BMH WS 1115 (Edward O'Sullivan).

103. BMH WS 487 (Joseph O'Connor).

104. BMH WS 1178 (Andrew Keaveney), WS 1476 (Seán O' Ceallaigh).

105. Cork Bde orders, 2 Oct. 1918. NLI MS 31196.

106. Cabinet Conversation, 16 May 1918. NA CAB 23/17.

107. *Irish Volunteer*, 2 May 1914, q. Matthew Kelly, 'The Irish Volunteers: A Machiavellian Moment?', in D. George Boyce and Alan O'Day (eds.), *The Ulster Crisis 1885–1921* (Basingstoke 2006), p. 75. BMH WS 1634 (Alfred Burgess).

108. BMH WS 1541 (Thomas Meagher), WS 1370 (Joseph Clancy).

109. Deasy, *Towards Ireland Free*, p. 19; BMH WS 1332 (John O'Gorman).

110. Military Council minutes, 17 Jan. 1919. French papers, IWM JDPF 8/2; Guns Committee note, NA HO 20049.

111. BMH WS 1076 (Anthony Malone).

112. BMH WS 1247 (Michael Higgins), WS 1368 (William Hanly).

113. BMH WS 1205 (Patrick Mckenna), WS 1166 (Patrick Lyons), WS 1220 (James Keating).

114. BMH WS 1008 (Thomas Brady); Seán Moylan statement, NLI MS 27731.

115. BMH WS 1393 (Edmond McGrath).

116. HQ Staff order, 11 Jun. 1918. MAI Maurice Crowe MSS, CD 208/1/4.

117. Peter Hart, 'The Social Structure of the Irish Republican Army', in *The IRA at War 1916–1923* (Oxford 2003), pp. 114–16.

118. Ibid., p. 123.

119. Deasy, *Towards Ireland Free*, p. 29; BMH WS 487 (Joseph O'Connor).

120. BMH WS 1076 (Anthony Malone).

121. BMH WS 1434 (Paul Mulcahy); WS 1721 (Seamus [Seumas] Robinson.

122. Florence O'Donoghue, *No Other Law* (Dublin 1954, 1986), p. 20.

123. BMH WS 395 (Thomas Fitzpatrick/Bob McDonnell).

124. BMH WS 1016 (Seamus McKenna).

125. BMH WS 1723 (Joseph Martin).

126. BMH WS 1008 (Thomas Brady), WS 928 (John Shields).

127. BMH WS 529 (James McCullough).

128. Joost Augusteijn, *From Public Defiance to Guerrilla Warfare: The Experience of Ordinary Volunteers in the Irish War of Independence 1916–1921* (Dublin 1996), p. 86.

129. BMH WS 1450 (John C. Ryan).

130. BMH WS 446 (Frank Hynes), WS 1111 (James Daly).

131. BMH WS 1626 (Bernard Brady).

132. O'Malley's notebooks, UCDA P17/B/111, q. Hart, *IRA and its Enemies*, p. 195.

133. O'Donoghue to Capt. J. Crowley, OC 3rd Bn, 16 Aug. 1918. NLI MS 31181.

134. O'Malley papers, MAI CD 53/1.

135. The English version, 'The Irishwomen's Council', though rather flat, was in a sense more national.

136. Margaret Ward, 'The League of Women Delegates and Sinn Féin', *History Ireland*, Autumn 1996, pp. 38–40.

137. Ann Matthews, *Renegades: Irish Republican Women 1900–1922* (Cork 2010), p. 240.

138. Senia Pašeta, *Nationalist Women in Ireland 1900–1918* (Cambridge forthcoming), ch. 10.

139. Sighle Humphreys MSS, UCDA P106/1165.

140. *The Times*, q. in R. C. Escouflaire, *Ireland: An Enemy of the Allies?* (London 1919; translation of *L'Irlande: ennemie … ?*, Paris 1918), p. 215.

141. Shaw Desmond, *The Drama of Sinn Féin* (London 1923), pp. 345–6.

142. BMH WS 587 (Nancy Wyse Power).

143. Cal McCarthy, *Cumann na mBan and the Irish Revolution* (Dublin 2007), pp. 110–11.

144. Margaret Mac Curtain, 'Women, the Vote and Revolution', in Mac Curtain and Donncha Ó Corráin (eds.), *Women in Irish Society* (Dublin 1978), pp. 34–6.

145. Cumann na mBan, *1918 Convention: Report* (Dublin 1918), q. Aideen Sheehan, 'Cumann na mBan: Policies and Activities', in David Fitzpatrick (ed.), *Revolution? Ireland 1917–1923* (Dublin 1990), p. 88.

146. BMH WS 450 (Brighid O'Mullane).

147. 'Military Activities', *Leabhar na mBan* [n.d.]. MAI CD 160/1.

148. McCarthy, *Cumann na mBan*, pp. 117–18.

149. NLI MS 31198.

150. BMH WS 450 (Brighid O'Mullane).

151. Máire Comerford memoir, UCDA P200/65, q. McCarthy, *Cumann na mBan*, p. 120.

152. 1st Cork Bde IV to Sec., Cork District Council, CnmB, 14 Feb. 1919. NLI MS 31181.

153. *Leabhar na mBan* (1919), q. McCarthy, *Cumann na mBan*, p. 118.

154. Margaret Ward, 'Marginality and Militancy: Cumann na mBan 1914–1936', in Austin Morgan and Bob Purdie (eds.), *Ireland: Divided Nation, Divided Class* (London 1980), pp. 103–4.

155. IG RIC Report, Nov. 1918. NA CO 904/107.

156. Military Intelligence report, Southern District, Jan. 1918. NA CO 904/157. Laffan, *Resurrection of Ireland*, p. 245.

157. Joost Augusteijn, 'The Importance of Being Irish: Ideas and the Volunteers in Mayo and Tipperary', in Fitzpatrick (ed.), *Revolution?*, p. 25.

158. O'Malley to Molly Childers, 17 Dec. 1923. Richard English and Cormac O'Malley (eds.), *Prisoners: The Civil War Letters of Ernie O'Malley* (Swords 1991), pp. 123–4.

159. Tom Garvin, *1922: The Birth of Irish Democracy* (Dublin 1996), p. 16.

160. NLI MS 21523, q. David Fitzpatrick, *The Two Irelands 1912–1939* (Oxford 1998), p. 29.

161. BMH WS 1766 (William O'Brien).

162. Garvin, *Nationalist Revolutionaries*, pp. 25, 51.

163. Diarmaid Ferriter, *The Transformation of Ireland 1900–2000* (London 2005), p. 195.

164. BMH WS 389 (Roger McCorley).

165. Consul at Queenstown (Cobh), 30 Sep. 1916. Garvin, *Nationalist Revolutionaries*, p. 112.

166. Hart, *IRA and its Enemies*, p. 205.

167. O'Donoghue, *No Other Law*, pp. 3–4.

168. Terence MacSwiney, 'Frontiers', in *Principles of Freedom* (Dublin 1921) (online edition).

169. De Blacam, *What Sinn Féin Stands For*, pp. 132–6.

170. O'Brien to Collins, 19 Sep. 1920. NLI MS 8427.

171. NLI MS 31367.

172. Seán Moylan statement, NLI MS 27731.

173. *Irish Volunteer*, 7 Feb. 1914.

174. Ben Novick, *Conceiving Revolution: Irish Nationalist Propaganda during the First World War* (Dublin 2001), pp. 155–7.

175. Garvin, *Nationalist Revolutionaries*, p. 125.

176. Richard English, *Irish Freedom: The History of Nationalism in Ireland* (London 2006), p. 274; Jeffrey Prager, *Building Democracy in Ireland: Political Order and Cultural Integration in a Newly Independent Nation* (Cambridge 1986), p. 41.

177. Matthews, *Renegades*, p. 219.

178. Robinson memoir, NLI MS 21265; Andrews, *Dublin Made Me*, p. 99.

179. UCDA P48b, q. Garvin, *Nationalist Revolutionaries*, p. 127.

180. Darrell Figgis, *Recollections of the Irish War* (London 1927), pp. 228–9.

181. David Fitzpatrick, *Harry Boland's Irish Revolution* (Cork 2003), pp. 108–109.

182. Uinseann MacEoin (ed.), *Survivors* (Dublin 1980), p. 23.

183. Fitzpatrick, *Boland's Irish Revolution*, p. 107.

184. Brian Farrell, *The Founding of Dáil Éireann: Parliament and Nation Building* (Dublin 1971), p. 30.

185. Diane Urquhart, *Women in Ulster Politics 1890–1940* (Dublin 2000), p. 114.

186. John Coakley, 'The Election that Made the First Dáil', in Brian Farrell (ed.), *The Creation of the Dáil* (Dublin 1994), p. 31.

187. BMH WS 487 (Joseph O'Connor).

188. GHQ to T. Mac Curtain, 19 Nov. 1918. NLI MS 31191.

189. M. Noyk statement, NLI MS 18975.

190. BMH WS 571 (Michael Newell).

191. BMH WS 1229 (James Mansfield).

192. BMH WS 1770 (Kevin O'Shiel), 804.

193. BMH WS 1193 (Bridget Doherty).

194. Oliver Coogan, *Politics and War in Meath 1913–23* (Dublin 1983), pp. 86–7.

195. NLI MS 18975.

196. Laffan, *Resurrection of Ireland*, p. 164.

197. Patrick Maume, *The Long Gestation: Irish Nationalist Life 1891–1918* (Dublin 1999), p. 213.

198. J. J. Lee, *Ireland 1912–1985: Politics and Society* (Cambridge 1989), p. 41.

199. Laffan, *Resurrection of Ireland*, pp. 163, 244.

200. Q. in Paul Bew, *Ireland: The Politics of Enmity 1789–2006* (Oxford 2007), p. 391.

201. Manifesto to the Irish People, Macardle, *Irish Republic*, App. 1 No. 6.

202. BMH WS 1770 (Kevin O'Shiel).

203. Tim Pat Coogan, *Michael Collins: A Biography* (London 1990), p. 92.

204. Coakley, 'Election', p. 44.

205. Farrell, *Founding of Dáil Éireann*, p. 56.

206. Arthur Mitchell, *Revolutionary Government in Ireland: Dáil Éireann 1919–22* (Dublin 1995), p. 17.

207. Piaras Béaslaí, *Michael Collins and the Making of a New Ireland*, 2 vols (Dublin 1926), vol. I, p. 295.

208. Message to the Free Nations of the World, Macardle, *Irish Republic*, App. 1 No. 10.

209. Lee, *Ireland*, p. 41.

210. Briollay, *Ireland in Rebellion*, pp. 20–21.

211. Hanna Sheehy Skeffington, *Impressions of Sinn Féin in America* (Dublin 1919).

212. Figgis, *Recollections*, p. 251.

213. *United Irishman*, 4 Nov. 1905, q. Gerard Keown, 'The Ideas and Development of Irish Foreign Policy from the Origins of Sinn Féin to 1932', DPhil thesis, Oxford University 1997 (2010), p. 33.

214. BMH WS 825 (Leopold H. Kerney).

215. BMH WS 860 (Elizabeth McGinley).

216. Briollay, *Ireland in Rebellion*, p. 52.

217. Boland diary, 2 Oct., 1 Nov. 1919. Fitzpatrick, *Boland's Irish Revolution*, p. 151.

218. Connie Neenan in MacEoin (ed.), *Survivors*, pp. 250–51.

219. National Council, 18 Jun. 1920. New York, Irish American Historical Society, FOIF papers.

220. Fitzpatrick, *Boland's Irish Revolution*, p. 132.

221. Patrick McCartan, *With de Valera in America* (New York 1932), p. 152.

222. Tim Pat Coogan, *Eamon de Valera: The Man Who Was Ireland* (London and New York 1993), p. 144

223. Eamon de Valera, *The Foundation of the Republic of Ireland in the Vote of the People*, Irish Ireland League pamphlet (Victoria 1920).

224. Coogan, *Eamon de Valera*, pp. 168–9.

225. O'Sullivan memoir (holograph), Seán MacEoin MSS, UCDA P308/1/15.

226. Tom Garvin, 'Unenthusiastic Democrats: The Emergence of Irish Democracy', in R. Hill and M. Marsh (eds.), *Modern Irish Democracy* (Dublin 1993), pp. 14–15.

227. Seamus Robinson, NLI MS 21265.

228. BMH WS 1042 (John J. Neylon).

229. BMH WS 1400 (John Patrick McCormack).

230. Augusteijn, *From Public Defiance to Guerrilla Warfare*, p. 147.

231. *An tOglác*, vol. 1 no. 1 (15 Aug. 1918); no. 12 (n.d. [Mar. 1919]).

232. *An tOglác*, vol. 1 no. 2 (14 Sep. 1918); no. 3 (30 Sep. 1918).

233. *An tOglác*, vol. 1 no. 4 (14 Oct. 1918); no. 10 (?Feb. 1919).

234. Seamus Robinson, NLI MS 21265. In his memoir, *My Fight for Irish Freedom* (Dublin 1924), Dan Breen said that Robinson did not appear in Tipperary until mid-January.

235. Ryan, *Seán Treacy*, p. 63.

236. Seamus Robinson, NLI MS 21265.

237. *Irish Independent*, 21 May 1919.

238. O'Donoghue, *No Other Law*, p. 44.

239. Sinn Féin Executive circular, 22 Mar. 1919, and Chief Sec.'s note. NA CO 904/169.

240. Chief Sec. to Laurence O'Neill, 31 Mar. 1919. NA CO 904/169.

241. BMH WS 487 (Joseph O'Connor).

242. O'Hegarty to G. Gavan Duffy, q. A. Mitchell, '"Exit Britannia" – The Formation of the Irish National State, 1918–21', in Joost Augusteijn (ed.), *The Irish Revolution, 1913–1923* (Basingstoke 2002), p. 74.

243. Markievicz to Hanna Sheehy Skeffington, 26 Jun. 1919. NLI MS 41177/31.

244. Michael Tierney, *Eoin MacNeill* (Oxford 1980), p. 277.

245. BMH WS 939 (Ernest Blythe).

246. *Daily News*, 30 May 1919. Maurice Walsh, *The News from Ireland: Foreign Correspondents and the Irish Revolution* (London 2008), p. 67.

247. H. N. Brailsford, 'Is there a Republic in Ireland?', *Nation*, 22 Nov. 1919.

248. Note by R. Barton, D. Macardle collection, MAI CD 9/6/9.

249. BMH WS 939 (Ernest Blythe).

250. NLI MS 31390.

251. Seán MacEntee to Dorothy Macardle, 10 Jun. 1936. MAI CD 9/6/6.

252. Mulcahy note, Mulcahy MSS, UCDA P7/C/96; Maryann Valiulis, *Portrait of a Revolutionary: General Richard Mulcahy and the Founding of the Irish Free State* (Dublin 1992), p. 43.

253. Kevin B. Nowlan, 'Dáil Éireann and the Army: Unity and Division (1919–1921)', in Williams (ed.), *Irish Struggle*, p. 71.

254. Gen. Sec. GHQ (Seán McGarry) memo, 2 Jun. 1920. NLI MS 31194.

255. IV General Orders New Series No. 11, 23 Jul. 1920. NLI MS 31193.

256. BMH WS 962 (James Dorr); NLI MS 31390.

257. MSP A/3 (1), Bde Activity Reports, 1 Bn, Cork III Bde.

258. S. O'Sullivan memoir, MAI CD 308/1/5.

259. Andrews, *Dublin Made Me*, p. 116.

260. Deasy, *Towards Ireland Free*, p. 82; Béaslaí, *Michael Collins*, vol. 1, p. 377.

261. F. M. Carroll, *Money for Ireland: Finance, Diplomacy and the First Dáil Éireann Loans, 1919–1936* (Westport, Conn. 2002), p. 16.

262. Béaslaí, *Michael Collins*, vol. 1, pp. 344–5. Loan Prospectus, q. Francis J. Costello, *Énduring the Most: The Life and Death of Terence MacSwiney* (Dingle 1995), p. 111.

263. Jack Plunkett, NLI MS 11,981. An eyewitness described Emmet being beheaded (after being hanged) on 'a deal table like a common kitchen table'. Marianne Elliott, *Robert Emmet* (London 2001), p. 97.

264. Carroll, *Money for Ireland*, p. 17.

265. Collins to MacSwiney, 25 Sep. 1919, q. Costello, *Enduring the Most*, p. 112.

NOTES

266. Finance report, Nov. 1919. NAI DE2/7, q. A. McCarthy, 'Michael Collins, Minister for Finance 1919–22', in Gabriel Doherty and Dermot Keogh (eds.), *Michael Collins and the Making of the Irish State* (Cork 1998), p. 55.
267. Collins to MacSwiney, 11 Dec. 1919. Costello, *Enduring the Most*, pp. 112–13.
268. C. Collins to D. O'Hegarty, 15 Mar. 1920. NAI DE2/404.
269. BMH WS 1770 (Kevin O'Shiel), 865, WS 1336 (Patrick Lennon).
270. Report of Propaganda Department, n.d. [May 1920]. NAI DE2/10.
271. Andrew Boyle, *The Riddle of Erskine Childers* (London 1977), p. 221.
272. Childers notebooks, q. ibid., p. 257.
273. *Irish Catholic Directory*, 1921, pp. 499–507, 548–9, q. Dermot Keogh, *The Vatican, the Bishops and Irish Politics 1919–39* (Cambridge 1986), pp. 38–9.
274. T. O Fiaich, 'The Catholic Clergy and the Independence Movement', *Capuchin Annual* 37 (1970), p. 501; Patrick Murray, *Oracles of God: The Catholic Church and Irish Politics 1922–1937* (Dublin 2000), p. 12.
275. Brian Heffernan, 'Catholic Priests and Political Violence in Ireland, 1919–1921', PhD thesis, National University of Ireland, Maynooth 2010.
276. W. McDonald, *Some Ethical Questions of Peace and War, with Special Reference to Ireland* (Dublin 1919; new edn, intr. Tom Garvin, Dublin 1998).
277. *Irish Catholic*, 4 Sep. 1920, q. Heffernan, 'Catholic Priests and Political Violence in Ireland', p. 77.
278. *Irish Catholic*, 5 Jul. 1919, q. Heffernan, 'Catholic Priests and Political Violence in Ireland', p. 68.
279. Mitchell, *Revolutionary Government*, p. 103.
280. War Cabinet, 14 May 1919. WC 567A, NA CAB 23/15.
281. Liam Cahill, *Forgotten Revolution: The Limerick Soviet 1919* (online edition 2003).
282. Tom Crean, 'From Petrograd to Bruree', in Fitzpatrick (ed.), *Revolution?*, p. 152.
283. GS Memo, Oct. 1918, q. Hart, *IRA and its Enemies*, p. 63; Charles Townshend, *The British Campaign in Ireland 1919–1921: The Development of Political and Military Policies* (Oxford 1975), p. 43.
284. NA HO 45/19665.
285. Memorial to War Cabinet by the Lord Lieutenant of Ireland, 8 Oct. 1918. MAI BMH CD 178/1/13.
286. French to Lloyd George, 12 Oct. 1918. French papers, IWM JDF 8/1.
287. Draft memorandum, 17 Dec. 1919. MAI BMH CD 178/1/19.
288. The order has not survived, and it is not clear whether it was first issued on 11 November or 27 December. D. M. Leeson, *The Black and Tans: British Police and Auxiliaries in the Irish War of Independence, 1920–1921* (Oxford 2011), p. 24.
289. Draft memorandum by Lord French, 17 Dec. 1919. MAI BMH CD 178/1/19.
290. Lloyd George to Bonar Law, 30 Dec. 1919. HLRO, Lloyd George papers F/31/1/16.

291. Draft memorandum, 17 Dec. 1919. MAI BMH CD 178/1/19.

292. BMH WS 1137 (Patrick Connaughton), WS 1111 (James Daly).

293. BMH WS 1436 (Walter Brown).

294. George Power memoir, NLI MS 31335.

295. Valiulis, *Mulcahy*, p. 39.

296. Richard Mulcahy, 'Commentary upon Piaras Béaslaí's *Michael Collins*. UCDA P7/D/l/67.

297. Seamus Robinson, NLI MS 21265.

298. Dan Breen, 'Lord French Was Not Destined to Die by an Irish Bullet', *With the IRA in the Fight for Freedom* (Tralee 1955), pp. 45–6.

299. DMP report, 20 Dec. 1919. NA HO 45/10974.

300. IG RIC Monthly Report, 15 Dec. 1919. NA CO 904/110. W. J. Lowe, 'The War against the RIC, 1919–21', *Eire-Ireland* 37 (2002), p. 83.

301. Usually given as 2 or 3 Jan.; BMH Chronology has 4 Jan. 1920.

302. General Richard Mulcahy, 'Chief of Staff 1919', *Capuchin Annual* 36 (1969), pp. 351–2

303. French to Macpherson, 5 Jan. 1920. IWM JDPF 8/2.

304. HQ 1st Cork Bde to D/C/S, GHQ, 1 Nov. 1919. O'Donoghue MSS, NLI MS 31197.

305. Hart, *IRA and its Enemies*, p. 247.

306. Ibid., p. 241.

PART 2: TWO GOVERNMENTS: 1920

1. Charles Townshend (ed.), *The Oxford Illustrated History of Modern War* (Oxford 1997), pp. 160–61.

2. 'The Strategy that the Volunteer Force as at present armed and trained is likely to use in case it takes to the field voluntarily', encl. in IG RIC Report, Feb. 1920. NA CO 904/111.

3. BMH WS 981 (Patrick Riordan).

4. McGarry, *Eoin O'Duffy*, pp. 47–8. Ernie O'Malley, *On Another Man's Wound* (London 1936, Dublin 1979), pp. 116–17.

5. Deasy, *Towards Ireland Free*, p. 94.

6. Leeson, *Black and Tans*, pp. 22–3.

7. BMH WS 853 (Peadar de Barra).

8. BMH WS 1385 (James McMonagle).

9. O'Malley, *On Another Man's Wound*, ch. 11.

10. E. O Mallie to Capt. G. Plunkett, 5 Dec. 1919. O'Malley MSS, UCDA P17 A/1. Charles Townshend, 'The Irish Republican Army and the Development of Guerrilla Warfare, 1916–1921', *English Historical Review*, April 1979, p. 324.

11. O'Malley, *On Another Man's Wound*, p. 149.

12. BMH WS 1008 (Thomas Brady).

13. General Orders, 26 May 1920. NLI MS 31193.
14. Court martial of Irish Volunteers 1920, NLI MS 11406. Also NLI Pos 916, A/0478.
15. Dan Gleeson in MacEoin (ed.), *Survivors*, p. 263.
16. Mary Daly, 'Local Government and the First Dáil', in Farrell (ed.), *Creation of the Dáil*, p. 123.
17. White, *Kevin O'Higgins*, p. 36.
18. Daly, 'Local Government and the First Dáil', p. 126.
19. McGarry, *Eoin O'Duffy*, p. 50.
20. BMH WS 1685 (Michael McMahon).
21. BMH WS 1370 (Joseph Clancy).
22. Macardle, *Irish Republic*, p. 356.
23. Resolution No. 2, in BMH WS 1265 (Paul J. Mulvey).
24. Natasha Grayson, 'The Quality of Nationalism in Counties Cavan, Louth and Meath during the Irish Revolution', PhD thesis, Keele University 2008, pp. 209–10.
25. Q. McGarry, *Eoin O'Duffy*, p. 50.
26. Erskine Childers, *Military Rule in Ireland* (Dublin 1920), p. 3.
27. Ministry of Home Affairs, Interim Report with reference to the Scheme for the Establishment of National Arbitration Courts, 19 Aug.–25 Oct. 1919. NAI DE2/51.
28. BMH WS 1770 (Kevin O'Shiel).
29. National Arbitration Courts Committee, 28 Sep. 1919. NAI DE2/38.
30. 'Proposals for Arbitration', n.d. NAI DE2/38.
31. Report by Stack, 4 Mar. 1920. NAI DE2/38.
32. J. A. Gaughan, *Austin Stack: Portrait of a Separatist* (Dublin 1977), p. 103.
33. Mary Kotsonouris, *Retreat from Revolution: The Dáil Courts, 1920–24* (Dublin 1994), p. 24.
34. Art O'Connor, 'A Brief Survey of the Work done by the Agricultural Department, Dáil Éireann, April 1919–August 1921'. Diarmuid O'Hegarty MSS, UCDA P8/25. BMH WS 1770 (Kevin O'Shiel), 885.
35. Inspector General RIC, Monthly Report, Jul. 1920. NA CO 904/111.
36. Gaughan, *Austin Stack*, pp. 108–9.
37. 'Manifesto!', 'Claims on Property', 26 Apr. 1920. NLI MS 33912 (11).
38. Dáil proclamation, 29 Jun. 1920. MAI CD 264/8/2.
39. Mitchell, *Revolutionary Government*, pp. 141–2.
40. *Irish Times*, 2 Aug. 1920.
41. Fitzpatrick, *Politics and Irish Life*, pp. 174–5.
42. *An tOglác*, 15 May 1920.
43. BMH WS 1770 (Kevin O'Shiel), 905.
44. BMH WS 1268 (Patrick J. Hargaden).
45. BMH WS 1436 (Walter Brown).

46. McGarry, *Eoin O'Duffy*, pp. 52–3.

47. Ibid., p. 51.

48. NLI Pos 916, q. Augusteijn, *From Public Defiance to Guerrilla Warfare*, p. 287.

49. O'Donoghue, *No Other Law*, pp. 63–5.

50. BMH WS 1336 (Patrick Lennon).

51. *Freeman's Journal*, 4, 9 Jun. 1920. Robert Kee, *The Green Flag: A History of Irish Nationalism* (London 1972), p. 679.

52. O'Malley, *On Another Man's Wound*, p. 166.

53. GHQ IV, General Order No. 12, 1 Nov. 1920. Copy in MAI CD 243.

54. Fitzpatrick, *Politics and Irish Life*, pp. 177–80.

55. Gaynor, 'Sinn Féin Days', NLI MS 19826.

56. Fitzpatrick, *Politics and Irish Life*, p. 180.

57. Ibid., pp. 178–80, 182.

58. French to Macpherson, 5 Jan. 1920. IWM JDPF 8/2.

59. Irish Command, 'Record of the Rebellion in Ireland in 1920–21, and the Part Played by the Army in Dealing with it', vol. III: 'Law'. NA WO 141/93.

60. Ibid., vol. II: 'Intelligence'.

61. The Military Situation in Ireland, memo by GOC-in-C, 25 Mar. 1920. CP 1131, NA CAB 24/104.

62. Dublin District Historical Record. NA WO 141/93, vol. IV pt III.

63. Lowe, 'The War against the RIC', p. 99.

64. Charles Townshend, 'One Man Whom You Can Hang If Necessary: The Discreet Charm of Nevil Macready', in J. B. Hattendorf and M. H. Murfett (eds.), *The Limitations of Military Power* (London 1990), pp. 143ff.

65. Wilson's diary, 13 and 12 May 1920, q. Keith Jeffery, *Field Marshal Sir Henry Wilson* (Oxford 2006), p. 263.

66. Police Adviser to S/S for War, 27 Jun. 1920. NA CAB 27/108.

67. Cabinet Committee on the Irish Question, 4 Nov. 1919. NA CAB 24/92, C.P. 56; Cabinet, 19 Dec. 1919. NA CAB 23/18.

68. Fisher to Bonar Law, 15 May 1920. Lloyd George MSS, HLRO F/31/1/33.

69. For this suggestion, Michael Hopkinson, *The Irish War of Independence* (Dublin and Montreal 2002), p. 37.

70. Macready to Wilson, 21 May 1920. IWM HHW 2/2A.

71. Maurice Crowe MSS, MAI CD 208/2/5.

72. Dublin District Historical Record. NA WO 141/93.

73. Bonar Law in House of Commons 15 Apr. 1920, q. Seán McConville, *Irish Political Prisoners, 1848–1922: Theaters of War* (London and New York 2003), p. 721.

74. Dublin District Historical Record, NA WO 141/93; Peter Hart (ed.), *British Intelligence in Ireland, 1920–21: The Final Reports* (Cork 2002), p. 11.

75. Nora Connolly O'Brien in MacEoin (ed.), *Survivors*, p. 209.

76. Cabinet, 26 Jul. 1920. NA CAB 24/109.

77. Cabinet, 11 Aug. 1920. NA CAB 24/110.

78. Charles Townshend, 'The Irish Railway Strike of 1920: Industrial Action and Civil Resistance in the Struggle for Independence', *Irish Historical Studies 21* (1979), pp. 266–72.

79. BMH WS 1197 (Philip Murphy).

80. Briollay, *Ireland in Rebellion*, pp. 67–8.

81. 'I.O.' (C. J. C. Street), *The Administration of Ireland 1920* (London 1921), pp. 249–50.

82. Cavan Brigade history. NLI Pos 915, A/0453.

83. BMH WS 1479 (Seán Healy).

84. Macready to Wilson, 2 Jul. 1920. IWM HHW 2/2A.

85. C.P. 1891, 25 Sep. 1921. NA CAB 24/111.

86. Diary of Sir Mark Sturgis, 11 Oct. 1920, NA PRO 30/95/2; Townshend, 'Irish Railway Strike', pp. 274–5.

87. Report of Mansion House Conference, 16 Nov. 1920. ILP/TUC Report 1921, Appendix, pp. 53, 54, 55, 56, 59, 61.

88. Townshend, 'Irish Railway Strike', pp. 280–81.

89. *Dundalk Democrat*, 10 Jul. 1920, q. McGarry, *Eoin O'Duffy*, p. 50.

90. Mitchell, *Revolutionary Government*, p. 146.

91. Reports from Resident Magistrates, Jun. 1920, circulated to Cabinet by S/S for War. NA CAB 27/108.

92. Macready to Wilson and reply, 28, 29 Jun. 1920. IWM HHW 2/2A.

93. Michael Brennan, *The War in Clare 1911–1921: Personal Memoirs of the Irish War of Independence* (Dublin 1982).

94. Macready to Greenwood, 17 Jul. 1920. Lloyd George MSS, HLRO F/19/2/12.

95. Colm Campbell, *Emergency Law in Ireland 1918–1925* (Oxford 1994), p. 27

96. Military Court of Inquiry on Joseph Taylor, 14 Mar. 1921. NA WO 35/160. For court instructions and findings see Townshend, *British Campaign in Ireland*, pp. 106–7.

97. Hopkinson, *Irish War of Independence*, p. 66.

98. Irish Command, 'Record of the Rebellion', vol. II, p. 10. Townshend, *British Campaign in Ireland*, p. 103.

99. Townshend, *British Campaign in Ireland*, pp. 57–8.

100. William H. Kautt, *Ambushes and Armour: The Irish Rebellion 1919–1921* (Dublin 2010), pp. 66–8.

101. GOC-in-C Ireland to War Office, 20 Sep. 1920. NA WO 141/44.

102. Minute by Deputy Adjutant General, 5 Oct., and Note by Chief of Air Staff, 9 Oct. 1920. NA WO 141/44.

103. Charles Townshend, 'Civilization and "Frightfulness": Air Control in the Middle East between the Wars', in C. Wrigley (ed.), *Warfare, Diplomacy and Politics: Essays in Honour of A. J. P. Taylor* (London 1986), pp. 142–62.

104. S/S for War and Air to Chief of Air Staff, 24 Sep. 1920. Townshend, *British Campaign in Ireland*, pp. 170–71.

105. Macready to Long, 23 Apr., 1 May 1920. HLRO LGP F/34/1.

106. IG RIC Report, Jun. 1920. NA CO 904/11.

107. Wilson's diary, 1, 7 Jul. 1920, q. Jeffery, *Wilson*, p. 265.

108. Munster No. 1 Division Fortnightly Report to AUS, 1 Jun. 1920. NAI P&C Police Reports No. 5.

109. Hart, *IRA and its Enemies*, pp. 240–41.

110. Leeson, *Black and Tans*, pp. 188–9.

111. Notably that of John Borgonovo, *Spies, Informers and the 'Anti-Sinn Féin Society': The Intelligence War in Cork City 1920–1921* (Dublin 2007).

112. Ibid., pp. 7–10.

113. BMH WS 1268 (Patrick J. Hargaden).

114. BMH WS 584 (Timothy Brennan).

115. Sturgis diary, 4 Aug. 1920. NA PRO 30/59/1.

116. Gaughan (ed.), *Memoirs of Constable Jeremiah Mee*, pp. 94–9.

117. Elizabeth Malcolm, *The Irish Policeman, 1822–1922: A Life* (Dublin 2006), p. 166.

118. Leeson, *Black and Tans*, pp. 140–41.

119. GHQ Order, 4 Jun. 1920. UCDA P7/A/45.

120. Weekly Summaries, NA CO 904/149. Lowe, 'The War against the RIC', p. 102.

121. CI Galway West Riding Report, Jul. 210; IG Report, Aug. 1920. NA CO 904/112.

122. Brian Hughes, 'Persecuting the Peelers', in David Fitzpatrick (ed.), *Terror in Ireland 1916–1923* (Dublin 2012), pp. 214–15.

123. Douglas V. Duff, *Sword for Hire* (London 1934), p. 77.

124. Leeson, *Black and Tans*, pp. 195–6.

125. Ibid., p. 196.

126. Augusteijn (ed.), *Memoirs of John Regan*, p. 139.

127. Sturgis diary, 22 Sep. 1920. NA PRO 30/59/1.

128. Ibid., 1, 5 Oct. 1920.

129. Leeson, *Black and Tans*, ch. 7.

130. Memo by GOC-in-C, 28 Sep. 1920. HLRO 103/3/27. CI Report, Mayo, Oct. 1920. NA PRO CO 904/113.

131. Austen to Hilda Chamberlain, 31 Oct. 1920; Cabinet, 1 Oct. 1920. D. George Boyce, *Englishmen and Irish Troubles: British Public Opinion and the Making of Irish Policy 1918–22* (London 1972), p. 55.

132. GHQ to Cork No. 1 Bde, 23 Jul. 1920. NLI MS 311192 (1).

133. Hopkinson, *Irish War of Independence*, p. 80.

134. The accounts by the *Manchester Guardian* and *Daily News* reporters, and by the RIC County Inspector, are analysed in Leeson, *Black and Tans*, pp. 166–70.

135. *Daily News*, 4 Oct.; *Manchester Guardian* 4, 8 Oct. 1920.

136. House of Commons Debates, 20 Oct. 1920.

137. *Daily News*, 11 Nov. 1920.

138. Lennox Robinson (ed.), *Lady Gregory's Journals 1916–1930* (London 1946), p. 143.

139. *Daily News*, 21 Oct. 1920.

140. BMH WS 1569 (George Hewson).

141. Hugh Martin, *Ireland in Insurrection* (London 1921), p. 115.

142. BMH WS 1517 (Pádraig Ó Fathaigh), WS 1652 (Henry O'Mara).

143. Louise Ryan, 'Drunken Tans: Representations of Sex and Violence in the Anglo-Irish War (1919–21)', *Feminist Review* 66 (2000), pp. 79–83.

144. Leeson, *Black and Tans*, pp. 179–80.

145. Robinson (ed.), *Lady Gregory's Journals*, p. 138.

146. R. F. Foster, *The Irish Story: Telling Tales and Making It Up in Ireland* (London 2001), p. 72.

147. See the careful exploration in Donald Harman Akenson, *Small Differences: Irish Catholics and Irish Protestants 1815–1922* (Montreal and Dublin 1988).

148. John Bowman, *De Valera and the Ulster Question 1917–1973* (Oxford 1982), pp. 34–5.

149. Eamon Phoenix, *Northern Nationalism: Nationalist Politics, Partition and the Catholic Minority in Northern Ireland 1890–1940* (Belfast 1994), pp. 54–5.

150. Austen Morgan, *Labour and Partition: The Belfast Working Class, 1905–23* (London 1990), p. 287.

151. Mary Harris, *The Catholic Church and the Foundation of the Northern Irish State* (Cork 1993), pp. 80–81.

152. Lt M. Sheerin, 'Record of Derry City Battalion, Derry Brigade'. NLI Pos 915, A/0464.

153. Augusteijn, *From Public Defiance to Guerrilla Warfare*, pp. 114–15.

154. BMH WS 395 (Thomas Fitzpatrick/Bob McDonnell).

155. BMH WS 389 (Roger McCorley).

156. *Belfast News Letter*, 5 Aug. 1920, q. D. S. Johnson, 'The Belfast Boycott, 1920–1922', in J. M. Goldstrom and L. A. Clarkson (eds.), *Irish Population, Economy and Society* (Oxford 1981), p. 288.

157. A. C. Hepburn, *A Past Apart: Studies in the History of Catholic Belfast, 1850–1950* (Belfast 1996), p. 86.

158. Morris, *Our Own Devices*, p. 117.

159. Tim Wilson, 'Boundaries, Identity and Violence: Ulster and Upper Silesia in a Context of Partition 1918–1922', DPhil thesis, Oxford University 2007, pp. 125–8.

160. Dáil Debates, 6 Aug. 1920.

161. BMH WS 939 (Ernest Blythe).

162. Orders, Sep. 1920, MAI CD 256/3/8.

163. McGarry, *Eoin O'Duffy*, p. 57.

164. *Northern Standard*, 28 Aug. 1920, q. Edward Micheau, 'Sectarian Conflict in Monaghan', in Fitzpatrick (ed.), *Revolution?*, p. 112.

165. CI Report, q. McGarry, *Eoin O'Duffy*, pp. 57–8. Grayson, 'Quality of Nationalism', p. 223.

166. Robert Lynch, *The Northern IRA and the Early Years of Partition, 1920–1922* (Dublin 2006), pp. 32–3.

167. BMH WS 746 (Seán Culhane).

168. Lynch, *Northern IRA*, p. 37.

169. BMH WS 1016 (Seamus McKenna).

170. Macready to Wilson, 28 Aug. 1920. IWM HHW 2/2A.

171. Sturgis diary, 19 Aug., 2 Sep. 1920. NA PRO 30/59/1.

172. Bryan A. Follis, *A State under Siege: The Establishment of Northern Ireland 1920–1925* (Oxford 1995), p. 14.

173. Doolin to Power, 26 Jul. 1920. Irish Office telegrams, NA CO 906/19.

174. Timothy Bowman, 'The Ulster Volunteer Force, 1910–1920: New Perspectives', in Boyce and O'Day (eds.), *Ulster Crisis*, pp. 256–8.

175. Coleman, *County Longford*, p. 164.

176. MAI CD 227/10/1–2.

177. Brennan, *The War in Clare*, pp. 70–71.

178. Director of Organization, Organization Memo No. 1 (1920). Organization of Flying Columns, 4 Oct. 1920. 'The Irish Republican Army. (From Captured Documents Only)'. NA WO 141/40.

179. Operations Memorandum No. 7, 4 Oct. 1920. NA WO 141/40.

180. Augusteijn, *From Public Defiance to Guerrilla Warfare*, p. 132.

181. BMH WS 1701 (Maurice McGrath).

182. BMH WS 1490 (Roger Rabbitte).

183. History of the Anglo-Irish Conflict 1912–1921, West Clare Brigade, p. 191. NLI Pos 915, A/0363.

184. BMH WS 1197 (Philip Murphy).

185. 14 Inf. Bde Orders, 23 Aug. 1920. NLI MS 33913.

186. Michael T. Foy, *Michael Collins's Intelligence War: The Struggle between the British and the IRA 1919–1921* (Stroud 2006), p. 64.

187. Eunan O'Halpin, 'Collins and Intelligence 1919–1923: From Brotherhood to Bureaucracy', in Doherty and Keogh (eds.), *Michael Collins and the Making of the Irish State*, p. 70.

188. Béaslaí, *Michael Collins*, vol. I, pp. 329–30.

189. Hart, *Mick*, pp. 207–8.

190. Tony Woods in MacEoin (ed.), *Survivors*, p. 322.

191. BMH WS 615 (Frank Thornton).

192. BMH WS 445 (James Slattery).

193. Hart (ed.), *British Intelligence*, p. 4.

194. Hart, *Mick*, p. 212.

195. *Irish Times* report of Inquest, 27 Mar. 1920; BMH WS 663 (Joseph Dolan).

196. A Report on the Intelligence Branch of the Chief of Police, Dublin Castle from May 1920 to July 1921. NA WO 35/214.

197. Anderson draft statement, 25 Aug. 1920. NA CO 904/168.

198. O'Donoghue, *No Other Law*, p. 92.

199. *Cork Examiner*, 18 Aug. 1920, q. Costello, *Enduring the Most*, p. 148.

200. Conference of ministers, 23 Aug., and Lloyd George to Bonar Law, 4 Sep. 1920. Sheila Lawlor, *Britain and Ireland 1914–23* (Dublin 1983), p. 68.

201. Michael Biggs, 'Hunger Strikes by Irish Republicans, 1916–1923', Workshop on Techniques of Violence in Civil War (Oslo, August 2004), p. 10 (online edition).

202. Costello, *Enduring the Most*, p. 187.

203. *Cork Examiner*, 29 Oct. 1920. Costello, *Enduring the Most*, p. 231.

204. Robinson (ed.), *Lady Gregory's Journals*, pp. 136–7.

205. R. F. Foster, *W. B. Yeats: A Life*, 2 vols (Oxford 2003), vol. II, p. 181.

206. Assistant Under Secretary, Irish Office, to under secretary, Dublin, 25, 27 Oct. 1920. NA HO 54/24753.

207. M. A. Doherty, 'Kevin Barry and the Anglo-Irish Propaganda War', *Irish Historical Studies* 32 (Nov. 2000), pp. 217–31.

208. Dublin District Historical Record. NA WO 141/93, vol. I pt I.

209. Sturgis diary, 11 Nov. 1920. NA PRO 30/59/2.

210. BMH WS 1474 (Eamon O'Duibhir).

211. BMH WS 664 (Patrick McHugh).

212. Ibid.

213. Report by Chief Secretary's Office, NA CO 904/168. Military Court of Inquiry, NA WO 35/88. Tim Carey and Marcus de Burca, 'Bloody Sunday 1920: New Evidence', *History Ireland* 11 (2003). There is a balanced assessment in Richard Bennett, *The Black and Tans* (London 1959), p. 127.

214. Foy, *Collins's Intelligence War*, pp. 205–6.

215. Coogan, *Michael Collins*, p. 158.

216. O'Halpin, 'Collins and Intelligence', p. 72.

217. Rex Taylor, *Michael Collins* (London 1961), p. 106.

218. Foy, *Collins's Intelligence War*, pp. 173–6.

219. Dublin District Memos, 2 May, 19 Oct. 1920. NA WO 35/90.

220. BMH WS 1687 (Harry Colley).

221. Foy, *Collins's Intelligence War*, pp. 141, 155, gives both South Frederick Street and Longwood Avenue as the location of this raid.

222. Sturgis diary, 16, 20 Nov. 1920. NA PRO 30/59/2.

223. BMH WS 907 (Larry Nugent).

224. BMH WS 481 (Simon Donnelly).

225. Charles Dalton, *With the Dublin Brigade (1917–1921)* (London 1929), pp. 105–6; BMH WS 434 (Charles Dalton).

226. Andrews, *Dublin Made Me*, pp. 150–53.

227. Tom Bowden, 'Bloody Sunday – A Reappraisal', *European Studies Review* 2, 1 (1972), pp. 38–9.

228. Collins to Mulcahy, 7 Apr. 1922. NLI Pos 917. Charles Townshend, 'Bloody Sunday – Michael Collins Speaks', *European Studies Review* 9, 3 (1979), p. 381.

229. Bowden, 'Bloody Sunday', p. 40.

230. Mrs Woodcock, *Experiences of an Officer's Wife in Ireland* (Edinburgh 1921).

231. Jane Leonard, '"English Dogs" or "Poor Devils"? The Dead of Bloody Sunday Morning', in Fitzpatrick (ed.), *Terror in Ireland*, p. 130.

232. Col. Dan Bryan, holograph notes, n.d. [1970]. In author's possession.

233. Dublin District Historical Record, NA WO 141/93, vol. IV pt III.

234. Mulcahy comments, 14 Apr. 1959. UCDA P7c/2.

235. *Manchester Guardian*, 26 Nov. 1920. Walsh, *The News from Ireland*, p. 81.

236. Brian Maye, *Arthur Griffith* (Dublin 1997), p. 149.

237. Tom Barry, *Guerilla Days in Ireland* (Dublin 1949, Tralee 1962), p. 39.

238. Ewan Butler, *Barry's Flying Column: The Story of the IRA's Cork No. 3 Brigade 1919–21* (London 1971), pp. 19–20.

239. Barry, *Guerilla Days*, pp. 38–9.

240. Hart, *IRA and its Enemies*, pp. 27, 29.

241. 'The Irish Republican Army. (From Captured Documents Only)'. NA WO 141/40.

242. Tom Barry, 'Auxiliaries Wiped Out at Kilmichael in their First Clash with the IRA', *With the IRA in the Fight for Freedom*, p. 125.

243. Eve Morrison, 'Kilmichael Revisited: Tom Barry and the "False Surrender"', in Fitzpatrick (ed.), *Terror in Ireland*, pp. 160–64.

244. Butler, *Barry's Flying Column*, p. 64.

245. Seamus Fox, *The Kilmichael Ambush – A Review of Background, Controversies and Effects* (www.dcu.ie/-foxs/irhist, 2005).

246. Kautt, *Ambushes and Armour*, pp. 102–3.

247. RIC Circular Order, 28 Sep. 1920. Richard Abbott, *Police Casualties in Ireland 1919–1922* (Cork 2000), pp. 173–4.

248. *Weekly Summary*, 8 Oct. 1920. Lowe, 'War against the RIC', p. 115.

249. IG Monthly Report, Nov. 1920; CI Limerick Report, Dec. 1920. NA CO 904/113.

250. Memo by S/S India, 10 Nov. 1920. C.P. 2084, NA CAB 24/114.

251. Sturgis diary, 14 Dec. 1920. NA PRO 30/59/3.

252. Jeudwine to Macready, 6 Dec. 1920. Jeudwine MSS, IWM.

253. Macready to Jeudwine, 10/11 Dec. 1920. Townshend, *British Campaign in Ireland*, p. 138.

254. And seems to have convinced Lloyd George at least. Thomas Jones, *Whitehall Diary*, vol. III (Oxford 1971), p. 50.

255. Sir Hubert Gough, 'The Situation in Ireland', *Review of Reviews*, Feb. 1921, p. 35.

256. Irish Labour Party and Trade Union Congress, *Who Burnt Cork City? A Tale of Arson, Loot and Murder: The Evidence of Over Seventy Witnesses* (Dublin 1921).

257. *Report of the Labour Commission to Ireland* (London 1920).

258. Sturgis diary, 19 Dec. 1920. NA PRO 30/59/3.

259. Martin Gilbert, *Winston S. Churchill*, vol. IV: *1917–1922* (London 1977), pp. 468–70.

PART 3: WAR AND PEACE – TRIALS OF THE COUNTER-STATE: 1921

1. Lloyd George to Greenwood, 2 Dec. 1920. HLRO F/19/2/28.

2. Townshend, *British Campaign in Ireland*, pp. 143–5.

3. Ibid., p. 134.

4. Sturgis diary, 17, 19 Aug., 20 Sep. 1920. NA PRO 30/59/2.

5. Townshend, *British Campaign in Ireland*, pp. 146–7.

6. Irish Command, 'Record of the Rebellion', vol. III. NA WO 141/93.

7. GOC-in-C Ireland, Weekly Situation Report, 1 Jan. 1921. NA CAB 627/108.

8. Midleton to Greenwood, 20 Jan. 1921. NA PRO 30/67/44.

9. C/S Memo [n.d.]. NA WO 141/40.

10. Valiulis, *Mulcahy*, pp. 61–2.

11. 'President de Valera states the national position', *International News*, 30 Mar. 1921.

12. President de Valera, *The Irish Republican Army*, n.d. [1921] NLI MS 33913.

13. BMH WS 939 (Ernest Blythe).

14. President to Minister for Finance, 18 Jan. 1921. NA DE2/448.

15. Fitzpatrick, *Boland's Irish Revolution*, p. 218.

16. Ibid., pp. 212–13.

17. BMH WS 679 (John F. Shouldice).

18. Garvin, *1922*, ch. 3.

19. Ibid., p. 70.

20. Dáil Local Government Department to Rate Collectors, 21 Dec. 1920. UCDA P150 1376.

21. Memo by K. O'Higgins, 5 Jan. 1921. UCDA P150 1376.

22. Note to L. Mac Cosgair, 19 Jan. 1921. UCDA P150 1376.

23. BMH WS 1042 (John J. Neylon).

24. Joe Barrett, 'Quick Change of Plan was Necessary to Counter the Enemy at Monreal', *With the IRA in the Fight for Freedom*, p. 137.

25. BMH WS 1042 (John J. Neylon).

26. C/S to OC Mid-Clare Bde, 23 May 1921. UCDA P7/A/19.

27. C/S Memo, Active Service Unit, Mar. 1921. UCDA P7/A/17. (First misdated as 4 Oct. 1920 in NA WO 141/40, then given as 'undated'.)

28. Active Service Unit, notebooks Mar.–Apr. 1921. UCDA P7/A/17.

29. Director of Training Memo, 'Function of A.S. Units', 23 Apr. 1921. UCDA P7/A/17.

30. 1st Cork Bde to A/G, 31 Jan. 1921, encl. OC 6th Bn to OC Cork Bde No. 1, 30 Jan. 1921. NA WO 141/40.

31. BMH WS 713 (Denis Dwyer).

32. O'Donoghue, *No Other Law*, p. 121.

33. OC Cork No. 2 Bde to C/S, 3 Mar. 1921. UCDA P7/A/38. This point was omitted from the version printed in NA WO 141/40 and reprinted in Kautt, *Ambushes and Armour*, p. 129.

34. Deasy, *Towards Ireland Free*, pp. 221–2.

35. Brigade Commandant, Cork No. 1 Bde, Report of Ambush at Coolavokig, 25th February 1921. NA WO 141/40.

36. GHQ Staff Criticism of Engagement at Coolavokig. UCDA P7/A/38.

37. BMH WS 838 (Seán Moylan).

38. O'Donoghue, *No Other Law*, p. 140.

39. A/G vice-OC, Cork No. 2 Bde, 'Clonbannin Attack', in OC Cork No. 2 Bde to C/S, 14 Mar. 1921. NA WO 141/40.

40. BMH WS 838 (Seán Moylan).

41. Walter Mitchell in MacEoin (ed.), *Survivors*, p. 386. For MacEoin's own account, see *With the IRA in the Fight for Freedom*, pp. 101–13. Only three other actions, out of thirty-four in that collection, took place outside Munster.

42. Kautt, *Ambushes and Armour*, p. 168.

43. Ibid., p. 141.

44. Gen. Staff 6 Div., Irish Rebellion in the 6th Divisional Area, pp. 184–5. NA WO 141/93.

45. BMH WS 487 (Joseph O'Connor).

46. BMH WS 481 (Simon Donnelly).

47. BMH WS 487 (Joseph O'Connor).

48. Augusteijn, *From Public Defiance to Guerrilla Warfare*, pp. 139–40.

49. Dublin Brigade Diary of Operations, Jan. 1921. UCDA P7/A/39.

50. OC ASU to OC Dublin Bde, 21 Jan. 1921. NA WO 141/40.

51. Acting Adjutant, Battalion II to OC Dublin, 12 Feb. 1921. NA WO 141/40.

52. Memo by D/O, 22 Mar. 1921. UCDA P7/A/47.

53. R. M. Fox, 'How the Women Helped', *Dublin's Fighting Story* (Tralee 1949), pp. 207–12.

54. Eve Morrison, 'The Bureau of Military History and Female Republican Activism 1913–1923', in Maryann Valiulis (ed.), *Gender and Power in Irish History* (Dublin 2009).

55. Coleman, *County Longford*, p. 190; Margaret Ward, 'Gendering the Irish Revolution', in Augusteijn (ed.), *Irish Revolution*, p. 181.

56. D/O to OC Cork No. 1 Bde, 5 Mar. 1921. NLI MS 31192(2).

57. BMH WS 1263 (Charles Pinkman).

58. MAI MSC/CMB/163.

59. BMH WS 1193 (Bridget Doherty).

60. BMH WS 723 (Alice Barry).

61. BMH WS 1761 (Stephen J. O'Reilly).

62. Jason Knirck, *Women of the Dáil: Gender, Republicanism and the Anglo-Irish Treaty* (Dublin 2006), p. 55.

63. Ibid., p. 54.

64. Ibid., p. 61.

65. GHQ Staff Memo, 'The War as a Whole', 24 Mar. 1921. UCDA P7/A/17.

66. Ibid.

67. See Borgonovo, *Spies, Informers*, pp. 74–5, disputing the view of Hopkinson, *Irish War of Independence*, p. 108.

68. O'Malley, *On Another Man's Wound*, p. 221.

69. BMH WS 980 (Edward J. Aylward).

70. Rev. E. Hartley to GHQ, 15 Oct. 1921. UCDA P7/A/20.

71. OC S Roscommon Bde to C/S, 26 Mar.; GHQ Staff memo, 'The Question of a Disciplinary Code', 30 Mar. 1921. UCDA P7/A/18, 16.

72. BMH WS 481 (Simon Donnelly).

73. C/S to D/O, 20 Apr. 1921. UCDA P7/A/17.

74. C/S to OC 1st SD, 1 May 1921. UCDA P7/A/18.

75. Serious Deficiencies in Country Units, GHQ Dublin, 7 Mar. 1921. UCDA P7/A/17

76. C/S to OC Offaly No. 2 Bde, 21 Apr. 1921. UCDA P7/A/17.

77. GHQ memos, 5, 30 Apr. 1921. UCDA P7/A/18.

78. BMH WS 1721 (Seamus Robinson).

79. C/S Operations Memorandum, 28 Feb. 1921. UCDA P106/1918.

80. BMH WS 1719 (Daniel Corkery).

81. Dept of Engineering, Circular No. 6, 2 Apr. 1921. UCDA P106/1917.

82. History of the Anglo-Irish Conflict 1912–1921, West Clare Brigade, 12 Jun. 1934. NLI Pos 915, A/0363.

83. OC Mid-Clare Bde to C/S, 11 Apr.; C/S to OC Mid-Clare Bde, 16 Apr. 1921. UCDA P7/A/17.

84. C/S to Acting OC 1st ND, 27 May 1921. UCDA P7/A/18.

85. OC E Clare Bde to C/S, 29 Apr.; OC Leitrim Bde to A/G, 18 Apr. 1921. UCDA P7/A/18, 38.

86. General Orders, 28 Apr. 1921. MAI CD 284/1.

87. Collins to Mulcahy, 14 Apr. 1921. UCDA P7/A/17.

88. BMH WS 1676 (Robert C. Ahern).

89. BMH WS 980 (Edward J. Aylward).

90. For example, the Schull battalion, West Cork. BMH WS 1502 (William Crowley).

91. Tom Bowden, 'Ireland: The Decay of Control', in M. Elliott-Bateman, J. Ellis and T. Bowden, *Revolt to Revolution* (Manchester 1974), p. 227.

92. Cork No. 2 Bde ASS to Bde HQ, 22 Jan. 1921. NA CO 904/114.

93. OC E Clare Bde to C/S, 29 Mar. 1921. UCDA P7/A/38.

94. OC W Donegal Bde to [A/G?], Mar. 1921. UCDA P/A/39.

95. Column Report No. 3, w/e 19 Feb. 1921. UCDA P7/A/38.

96. BMH WS 1282 (Michael Cummins).

97. 4 Bn Cork 1 to R. Foley, 7 Mar.; vice-OC to OC Cork 1 Bde, 26 Nov. 1921. UCDA P7/A/27.

98. Note by A/G on Adjutant 1st SD to A/G, 5 May; C/S to M/D, 14 May 1921. UCDA P7/A/18.

99. *An tOglac*, 8 Apr. 1921. BMH WS 615 (Frank Thornton).

100. Bew, *Ireland*, p. 407.

101. Peter Hart, 'The Protestant Experience of Revolution in Southern Ireland', in Richard English and Graham Walker (eds.), *Unionism in Modern Ireland* (London 1996), p. 86.

102. William H. Kautt, *The Anglo-Irish War, 1916–1921: A People's War* (Westport, Conn. 1999), p. 27

103. OC Cork II Bde to C/S, 19 Mar., and reply, 26 Mar. 1921. UCDA P7/A/38.

104. BMH WS 1676 (Robert C. Ahern).

105. S Roscommon Bde reports, Apr. 1921. UCDA P7/A/38.

106. Bde Adj. to OC E Limerick Bde, 22 Mar. 1921. NA WO 141/40.

107. Meath Bde to C/S, 31 Mar.; Dublin Bde Operations Diary, 13 Apr. 1921. UCDA P/7/A/39.

108. C/S to OC Kerry No. 2 Bde, 16 Apr.; Bde Adj. Kerry No. 2 Bde to C/S, 30 Apr. 1921. UCDA P7/A/38.

109. BMH WS 713 (Denis Dwyer).

110. Vice-OC 3rd Bn Offaly Bde to OC Bde, 29 May 1921. UCDA P7/A/18.

111. BMH WS 718 (Thomas Crawley).

112. IO 1st SD to GHQ, 5 May 1921. UCDA P7/A/20.

113. Comdt Tom Barry to C/S, 4 Oct.; C/S to M/D, 7 Oct. 1921. UCDA P7/A/34.

114. Col. J. M. MacCarthy (ed.), *Limerick's Fighting Story* (Tralee n.d.), pp. 134–5.

115. Hart, *IRA and its Enemies*, pp. 304, 307.

116. Bde Adj. to OC E Limerick Bde, 22 Mar. 1921. NA WO 141/40. This document includes a substantial extract from the evidence presented to the court.

117. Frank O'Connor, *Guests of the Nation* (London 1931); Sebastian Barry, *On Canaan's Side* (London 2011).

118. Donal Ó Drisceoil, *Peadar O'Donnell* (Cork 2001), p. 20.

119. Ministerial Report, Home Affairs, ?May 1921. NAI DE2/51.

120. C/S to M/D, and note by M/D, 11 Jun. 1921. UCDA P7/A/20.

121. 'Civil Police Force. Organisation', 1 Jun. 1921. MAI CD 243.

122. Orders by Adjutant General, 10 Nov. 1921. NLI MS 33913.

123. Mitchell, *Revolutionary Government*, p. 240.

124. GHQ memo, May 1921. UCDA P7/A/18.

125. Chief of Police to Minister for Home Affairs, 28 Jun. 1921. NLI MS 11404.

126. Chief of Police to Publicity Department, 15 Nov. 1921. UCDA P80/25.

127. BMH WS 481 (Simon Donnelly).

128. Chief of Police Circular, 9 Jul. 1921. MAI CD 244/1/1.

129. BMH WS 1757 (Patrick L. Rogan).

130. Heffernan, 'Catholic Priests and Political Violence in Ireland', p. 133.

131. Keogh, *Vatican, Bishops and Irish Politics*, p. 60.

132. *Freeman's Journal*, 7 Feb. 1921.

133. NLI MS 22838.

134. Murray, *Oracles of God*, pp. 12–13.

135. O'Connor to O'Donoghue, 15 Dec. 1920. NLI MS 31170.

136. Borgonovo, *Spies, Informers*, pp. 39–40.

137. Keogh, *Vatican, Bishops and Irish Politics*, pp. 56–7.

138. Secretary to President, and reply, 24 Feb., 4 Mar. 1921. NAI DE2/396.

139. De Blacam, *What Sinn Féin Stands For*, p. 134; Mitchell, *Revolutionary Government*, p. 280.

140. OC Cork No. 2 Bde to C/S, 12 Mar. 1921. UCDA P7/A/17.

141. O'Donoghue, *No Other Law*, p. 154.

142. Augusteijn, *From Public Defiance to Guerrilla Warfare*, p. 157.

143. C/S to OC Cork No. 2 Bde, 13 Apr. 1921. UCDA P7/A/17.

144. Valiulis, *Mulcahy*, p. 71.

145. C/S to OC West Donegal Bde, 20 Apr. 1921. UCDA P7/A/17.

146. The Divisional Idea, UCDA P7/A/47

147. UCDA P7/A/21.

148. D/O to C/S, 10 Mar. 1921. UCDA P7/A/17.

149. General Instructions to Divisional Commandants, Apr. 1921. UCDA P7/A/17.

150. C/S to OC 2nd ND, 20 Apr. 1921, UCDA P7/A/17; McGarry, *Eoin O'Duffy*, p. 75.

151. OC 2nd ND to D/O, 22 Apr. 1921. UCDA P7/A/18, 309.

152. C/S to OC 1st SD, 25 Apr. 1921. UCDA P7/A/18, 365.

153. BMH WS 838 (Seán Moylan).

154. Tom Barry, *The Reality of the Anglo-Irish War 1920–21 in West Cork* (Tralee 1974), p. 43.

155. O'Malley, *On Another Man's Wound*, pp. 307–9.

156. BMH WS 672 (Thomas Luckie).

157. Matthew Lewis, 'The Newry Brigade and the War of Independence in Armagh and South Down, 1919–1921', *Irish Sword* XXVII, 108 (2010), pp. 104–5.

158. Memos to 1st, 2nd, 4th ND, Apr. 1921. UCDA P7/A/17.

159. Lynch, *Northern IRA*, pp. 55–8.

160. Cavan Flying Column to OC Belfast Bde, 10 May 1921. UCDA P7/A/17.

161. The incident report in NA WO 35/89 does not detail the strength of the military force, but it would appear to have been considerably less than 350.

162. BMH WS 1016 (Seamus McKenna).

163. OC 1st ND to A/G, 10 Jun. 1921. UCDA P7/A/18.

164. Cabinet, 27 Apr., 11 May 1921; Jones, *Whitehall Diary*, vol. III, pp. 56, 70. Townshend, *British Campaign in Ireland*, pp. 178–9.

165. De Valera to O'Keeffe, 13 Jan., 9 Feb. 1921. Laffan, *Resurrection of Ireland*, pp. 334–5.

166. Ned Maugham interview, O'Malley notebooks. UCDA P17/B/109, p. 55.

167. Tom Maguire in MacEoin (ed.), *Survivors*, p. 288.

168. Mayo County Council Minutes, 17 Oct. 1921, q. Gloria Maguire, 'The Political and Military Causes of the Division in the Irish Republican Movement, January 1921 to August 1923', DPhil thesis, Oxford University 1985, p. 241.

169. Garvin, 'Unenthusiastic Democrats', p. 12.

170. Arthur Mitchell, *Labour in Irish Politics, 1890–1930: The Irish Labour Movement in an Age of Revolution* (Dublin 1974), p. 129.

171. O'Malley, *On Another Man's Wound*, p. 329.

172. D/O to OC 2nd SD, 7 Jul. 1921. UCDA P7/A/22.

173. Director of Training Account, NAI DE3/6/7.

174. Dublin District War Diary, 28 Apr. 1921. NA WO 35/90. Townshend, *British Campaign in Ireland*, p. 176.

175. Irish Rebellion in 6th Div. Area, 'Record of the Rebellion', vol. IV ch. II. NA WO 141/93.

176. Irish Rebellion in 6th Div. Area, pp. 112, 127, 128. IWM P363.

177. Note by DAG Irish Command, 3 May 1921. NA WO 35 157A. Townshend, *British Campaign in Ireland*, pp. 167–8.

178. Borgonovo, *Spies, Informers*, p. 93.

179. 6th Div. Weekly Intelligence Summary, 17 May 1921. 'A Captured Document', MacCarthy (ed.), *Limerick's Fighting Story*, pp. 130–35.

180. C/S to M/D, 14 May 1921. UCDA P7/A/18.

181. Orders by A/G, 22 Jun. 1921. NLI MS 33913.

182. HQ 16 Inf. Bde, Orders 17 Jun. 1921. NLI MS 31223.

183. OC A Company 3rd Tank Bn, memo, 18 May 1921. UCDA P7/A/18. Incident report, NA WO 35/89.

184. HQ Staff Council, 'Burning of Dublin Custom House'. NLI Pos 921.

185. Dalton, *Dublin Brigade*, pp. 165–6.

186. BMH WS 434 (Charles Dalton).

187. Augusteijn, *From Public Defiance to Guerrilla Warfare*, p. 138.

188. BMH WS 1555 (Thomas Reidy).

189. Coleman, *County Longford*, pp. 128–9.

190. BMH WS 1263 (Charles Pinkman), WS 1268 (Patrick J. Hargaden).

191. BMH WS 1122 (Thomas Howley).

192. BMH WS 1672 (Thomas Meagher).

193. O'Malley, *On Another Man's Wound*, pp. 327–8, 329.

194. Reports in NLI MS 33913.

195. OC 1st Bn Cork IV to HQ Cork No. 3 Bde, 17 Jun. 1921. UCDA P7/A/38.

196. O'Malley, *On Another Man's Wound*, pp. 333, 339.

197. O'Malley notebooks, UCDA P17/B/102.

198. General Order No. 14, 28 Nov. 1920. MAI CD 105/2/19.

199. Organizer, Kerry Brigades, to C/S, 23 Jun. 1921. UCDA P7/A/20.

200. Ibid.

201. Memo on Munitions Dept, Jun. 1921. UCDA P7/A/19.

202. BMH WS 664 (Patrick McHugh).

203. Adj. S Mayo Bde to C/S, 28 Apr.; C/S to OC Sligo Bde, 6 Jun. 1921. UCDA P7/A/38, 19.

204. BMH WS 1262 (Phil Fitzgerald).

205. 'A Note on Drives', NLI MS 33913.

206. HQ 16 Inf. Bde Orders, 17 Jun. 1921. Copy in NLI MS 31233.

207. C/S to A/C/S, and note by A/C/S, 12 Jul. 1921. UCDA P7/A/22.

208. See e.g. Brian P. Murphy, *The Origins and Organisation of British Propaganda in Ireland 1920* (Aubane 2006).

209. Boyce, *Englishmen and Irish Troubles*, p. 93.

210. Dept of Propaganda Report, March–May 1921. UCDA P80/14.

211. Collins to O'Brien, 17 May 1921. UCDA P80/14.

212. Keiko Inoue, 'Propaganda of Dáil Éireann', in Augusteijn (ed.), *Irish Revolution*, pp. 92–3.

213. D/P to M/D, 7 Jul. 1921. NLI MS 33913.

214. C/S to A/G, 4 Apr. 1921. UCDA P7/A/17.

215. D/P to C/S, 8 Jul., and to A/G, 20 Jun. 1921. NLI MS 33913.

216. Cabinet, 2 Jun. 1921, Jones, *Whitehall Diary*, vol. III, p. 73; Townshend, *British Campaign in Ireland*, p. 184.

217. Cabinet Memo by S/S for War, 24 May 1921. CP 2964, NA CAB 24/123.

218. Collins to de Valera, 16 Jun. 1921. NAI DE2/244.

219. Hopkinson, *Irish War of Independence*, p. 197.

220. Cabinet, 24 Jun. 1921. Jones, *Whitehall Diary*, vol. III, p. 80.

221. Sturgis diary, 23 Jun. 1921. NA PRO 30/59/4.

222. Griffith to O'Hegarty, 3 Dec. 1920. NAI DE2/234A; Griffith to Collins, 10 Dec. 1920, NAI DE2/251; memo on Clune visit, 13 Dec. 1920, q. Lawlor, *Britain and Ireland*, p. 88.

223. Collins to Griffith, 26 Jan. 1921. NAI DE2/242.

224. *The Plain People*, 30 Apr. 1922, q. Murphy, *Patrick Pearse and the Lost Republican Ideal*, p. 122.

225. De Valera to Collins, 18 Mar. 1921. NAI DE2/244.

226. The letters Sturgis and Wyndham-Quin wrote to the *Irish Times* on 2 and 4 March and 20 April 1921, under the aliases 'M' and 'Paddy-go-Aisy', are printed in Michael Hopkinson (ed.), *The Last Days of Dublin Castle: The Diaries of Mark Sturgis* (Dublin 1999), App. II.

227. Sturgis diary, 19, 22, 25 May 1921. NA PRO 30/59/4.

228. Collins to de Valera, 14, 16 Jun. 1921. NAI DE2/244. These were among a number of documents seized at de Valera's house in Blackrock on 22 June. See NA CO 904/23.

229. Tim to Maurice Healy, 16 Jun. 1921. T. M. Healy, *Letters and Leaders of my Day*, 2 vols (London 1928), vol. II, p. 638.

230. Earl of Midleton, *Records and Reactions* (London and New York 1939), pp. 258–60.

231. De Valera to Lloyd George, 28 Jun. 1921. HLRO LGP F/14/6/4.

232. Cabinet conference, 6 Jul. 1921. Jones, *Whitehall Diary*, vol. III, pp. 84–5.

233. *Arrangements Governing the Cessation of Active Operations in Ireland*, Cmd 1534 (1921).

234. Strickland to Macready, 27 Jul. 1921. Strickland MSS, IWM P363.

235. Instructions to Liaison Officers, 12 Jul. 1921. NLI MS 33913.

236. Barry to O'Sullivan, 15 Jul. 1921. NAI DE2/255.

237. Ibid.

238. MAI CD 227/21/G.

239. Minister for Labour to Chief Liaison Officer, 28 Jul. 1921. MAI CD 227/21/J.

240. MAI CD 227/21/C.

241. Ernie O'Malley, *The Singing Flame* (Dublin 1978), p. 15.

242. BMH WS 340 (Oscar Traynor).

243. Béaslaí to O'Sullivan, 1 Dec., and reply, 2 Dec. 1921. NLI MS 33913.

244. John M. Regan, *The Irish Counter-Revolution 1921–1936* (Dublin 1999), p. 26.

245. QMG to M/D, 19 Dec. 1921; 'Statement of Munitions', n.d. [Dec. 1921]. UCDA P17/E/31, P7/A/28. Table in Valiulis, *Mulcahy*, p. 257. See also Lawlor, *Britain and Ireland*, p. 122.

246. The figure of 33,992 is in a list of divisional strengths in June–July, UCDA P7/A/27.

247. BMH WS 1404 (Thomas Dargan).

248. Fianna Éireann, Report for period ending August 15th 1921. UCDA P7/A/23.

249. Mulcaky, 'Commentary upon Piaras Béaslaí's Michael Collins, UCDA P7/D/I/67, q. Valiulis, *Mulcahy*, p. 87.

250. BMH WS 838 (Seán Moylan).

251. MAI CD 227/21/C.

252. MAI CD 227/21/F.

253. O'Sullivan to Murphy, 10 Aug. 1921. MAI CD 227/21/J.

254. General Orders, 4 Nov. 1921. MAI CD 236/4.

255. Statement [1925]. UCDA P104/1308.

256. OC 1st SD to C/S, 5 Oct. 1921. UCDA P7/A/28.

257. Oglaich na hÉireann, Weekly Memorandum No. 18, 4 Nov. 1921. MAI CD 236/3.

258. A/C/S Report, 4 Nov.; OC 1st WD to GHQ, 10 Nov. 1921. UCDA P7/A/27.

259. OC Kerry 2 Bde to OC 1st SD, 17 Aug. 1921. NLI MS 33913.

260. OC 1st SD to C/S, 7 Oct. 1921. UCDA P7/A/28.

261. GHQ to 1st ND, 21 Sep. 1921. UCDA P7/A/27.

262. De Valera to Collins, 19 Oct., and Collins to de Valera, 21 Oct. 1921. NAI DE2/244.

263. C/S Order, Special Memorandum by M/D, 'Levies and Collections', 25 Oct. 1921. MAI CD 236/1.

264. OC 1st SD to C/S, 25 Oct. 1921. UCDA P7/A/29.

265. OC 1st SD to C/S, 7 Nov., and reply, 11 Nov. 1921. UCDA P7/A/29.

266. C/S to M/D, 14 Nov., and holograph minute by M/D, 17 Nov. 1921. UCDA P7/A/29.

267. Dáil Éireann Dept of Finance, Memo by M. Ó Coilean, 22 Nov. 1921. UCDA P7/A/29.

268. C/S to M/D, 24 Oct. 1921. UCDA P7/A/24.

269. 1st SD Administration Expenses; C/S to M/D, 5 Oct. 1921. UCDA P7/A/37.

270. Mitchell, *Revolutionary Government*, p. 304.

271. C/S Weekly Memo No. 17, 21 Oct. 1921. NLI MS 33913.

272. OC Mid-Limerick Bde to C/S, 7 Oct. 1921. UCDA P7/A/26.

273. Michael Farry, *The Aftermath of Revolution: Sligo 1921–23* (Dublin 2000), p. 27.

274. Valiulis, *Mulcahy*, p. 101.

275. A/G to Murphy, 10 Aug. 1921. MAI CD 227/21/J.

276. C/S to M/D, 2 Sep. 1921. UCDA P7/A/1.

277. M/D to C/S, 6, 12 Sep. 1921. UCDA P7/A/1.

278. C/S to President, 19 Oct. 1921. UCDA P7/A/27.

279. Note by Robert Barton to Dorothy Macardle, MAI CD 9/6/9.

280. Mulcahy notebooks, UCDA P17/b/109.

281. Sean Dowling in MacEoin (ed.), *Survivors*, p. 405.

282. UCDA P150/1125, q. Fitzpatrick, *Boland's Irish Revolution*, p. 218.

283. M/D to C/S, 16 Nov. 1921. UCDA P7/A/2.

284. MacEoin to Brugha, 29 Nov. 1921. UCDA P151/116.

285. Frank Aiken notes, O'Malley MSS, UCDA P17/A/93, q. Valiulis, *Mulcahy*, p. 105.

286. 'Note on the differences between Cathal Brugha and Stack and other members of the Volunteer Executive and Cabinet'. UCDA P7/D/96.

287. Fitzpatrick, *Politics and Irish Life*, p. 342.

288. C/S to Div. Comdts, 30 Nov. 1921. UCDA P151/116.

289. Gilbert, *Churchill*, vol. IV, p. 670.

290. Hart, *Mick*, p. 288.

291. Nora Connolly O'Brien in MacEoin (ed.), *Survivors*, p. 210.

292. Eibhlín Ní Cruadhlaoich in MacEoin (ed.), *Survivors*, p. 352.

293. De Valera to McGarrity, 21 Dec. 1921. Seán Cronin (ed.), *The McGarrity Papers* (Tralee 1972), p. 110.

294. BMH WS 939 (Ernest Blythe).

295. Sceilg [J. J. O'Kelly], *A Trinity of Martyrs* (Dublin 1947), p. 50.

296. F. S. L. Lyons, 'The War of Independence, 1919–21', in W. E. Vaughan (ed.), *Ireland under the Union 1870–1921*, vol. VI of *A New History of Ireland* (Oxford 1996), p. 253; Fitzpatrick, *Boland's Irish Revolution*, p. 228.

297. Gen. Seán MacEoin, 'The Constitutional Basis of the National Struggle', *With the IRA in the Fight for Freedom*, p. 15.

298. Collins pointed out that the Dáil had no power to elect a president of the Republic. In the government accounts, de Valera drew his salary as 'Prime Minister'. O'Hegarty MSS, UCDA P8/9.

299. Hayden Talbot, *Michael Collins's Own Story* (London n.d.), p. 66.

300. Note by Barton, D. Macardle collection, MAI CD 9/6/9.

301. BMH WS 939 (Ernest Blythe).

302. Fitzpatrick, *Boland's Irish Revolution*, pp. 199, 231–2.

303. De Valera to McGarrity, 21 Dec. 1921. Cronin (ed.), *McGarrity Papers*, p. 106.

304. Joseph Curran, *The Birth of the Irish Free State 1921–1923* (Tuscaloosa, Ala. 1980), p. 77.

305. De Valera to Griffith, 14 Oct. 1921. NAI DE2/304.

306. Macardle, *Irish Republic*, pp. 482–3.

307. Ibid., p. 483.

308. Gaughan, *Austin Stack*, p. 121.

309. Ministerial Report, 16 Aug. 1921. Ministry for Home Affairs correspondence, NAI DE2/51.

310. Minister for Home Affairs to P. P. Galligan, 28 Jul. 1921. MAI CD 105/6/1.

311. Memo to District Registrars, 28 Jul. 1921. Galligan papers, MAI CD 105/6/1.

312. Gaughan, *Austin Stack*, pp. 121–2.

313. Cabinet Conference on Ireland, 13 Oct. 1921. Jones, *Whitehall Diary*, vol. III, p. 123.

314. OC 16 Inf. Bde to 6 Div., 1 Nov., and reply 8 Nov. 1921. NA WO 35/182.

315. House of Commons Debates, 30 Dec. 1920; Nicholas Mansergh, *The Unresolved Question: The Anglo-Irish Settlement and its Undoing 1912–72* (New Haven and London 1991), p. 146.

316. Frank Pakenham, *Peace by Ordeal* (London 1935, 1972), ch. IV.

317. Memoir (1923) by Stack, q. Gaughan, *Austin Stack*, p. 156.

318. Pakenham, *Peace by Ordeal*, pp. 100–101.

319. Brendan Sexton, *Ireland and the Crown, 1922–1936* (Dublin 1989), p. 45.

320. Jones, *Whitehall Diary*, vol. III, p. 140.

321. Ibid., p. 89.

322. Winston S. Churchill, *The World Crisis*, vol. IV: *The Aftermath* (London 1923), p. 298; Pakenham, *Peace by Ordeal*, p. 73. Tom Jones himself left no full diary account of the meeting, but later sent Churchill a note for use in his book.

323. UCDA P4/387. Garvin, 'Unenthusiastic Democrats', p. 19.

PART 4: THE REPUBLIC FRACTURED: 1922–1923

1. Colm Ó Murchada's note, q. Regan, *Irish Counter-Revolution*, p. 23.
2. Barton's wording (Colm Ó Murchada, almost certainly wrongly, recorded him as saying 'the Constitution of the Irish Free State'), in Macardle, *Irish Republic*, p. 528.
3. Keown, 'Irish Foreign Policy', p. 156.
4. Jones, *Whitehall Diary*, vol. III, p. 170.
5. Béaslaí, *Michael Collins*, vol. II, pp. 309–10.
6. Andrews, *Dublin Made Me*, p. 203.
7. Childers diary, 8 Dec. 1921, q. Michael Hopkinson, *Green against Green: The Irish Civil War* (Dublin 1988), p. 41.
8. Liam de Roiste's journal, q. Regan, *Irish Counter-Revolution*, p. 46.
9. Batt O'Connor to Marie, 28 Jan. 1922. UCDA P68/4.
10. 'Army and State', 21 Dec. 1921. UCDA P7/A/32.
11. Frank O'Connor, *The Big Fellow: Michael Collins and the Irish Revolution* (London 1965), p. 115.
12. Garvin, 1922, p. 148.
13. Public letter to Comdt McKeon, 19 Dec. 1921. Copy in NLI MS 33914 (4).
14. Frank Aiken memoir, UCDA P104/1308.
15. Ibid.
16. Liam to Tom Lynch, 12 Dec. 1921. NLI MS 36251.
17. Eamon de Barra's recollection of conversation with Seán Hales, 29 Dec. 1921. Coogan, *Michael Collins*, p. 339.
18. Bill Kissane, *The Politics of the Irish Civil War* (Oxford 2003), p. 61.
19. UCDA P53/344. Garvin, 'Unenthusiastic Democrats', p. 22.
20. Fitzpatrick, *Boland's Irish Revolution*, p. 265.
21. Macardle, *Irish Republic*, p. 568.
22. Farry, *Aftermath of Revolution*, pp. 36–7.
23. *Freeman's Journal*, 14 Dec. 1921.
24. Fogarty to Collins, 30 Aug. 1921. Collins MSS, q. Margery Forester, *Michael Collins: The Lost Leader* (London 1971), p. 209.
25. To John Hagan, 10 Dec. 1921, q. Keogh, *Vatican, Bishops and Irish Politics*, p. 80.
26. To John Hagan, 31 Dec. 1921, q. Keogh, *Vatican, Bishops and Irish Politics*, p. 81.
27. Tom Maguire in MacEoin (ed.), *Survivors*, p. 289.
28. Farry, *Aftermath of Revolution*, pp. 53–4.
29. Aideen Carroll, *Seán Moylan: Rebel Leader* (Cork 2010), p. 173.
30. Fitzpatrick, *Boland's Irish Revolution*, p. 265.
31. Andrews, *Dublin Made Me*, p. 205.

32. Farry, *Aftermath of Revolution*, p. 45.

33. Dermot Keogh, *Twentieth-Century Ireland: Nation and State* (Dublin 1994), p. 5.

34. He later denied using any of these phrases. Coogan, *Eamon de Valera*, pp. 312–13.

35. Erhard Rumpf and A. C. Hepburn, *Nationalism and Socialism in Twentieth-Century Ireland* (Liverpool 1977), pp. 32–3.

36. P. S. O'Hegarty, *The Victory of Sinn Féin* (Dublin 1924), p. 77.

37. Kissane, *Politics of the Irish Civil War*, p. 14.

38. Rumpf and Hepburn, *Nationalism and Socialism*, pp. 61–2.

39. Knirck, *Women of the Dáil*, p. 97.

40. UCDA P61/4(50), Brigid Gallogly questionnaire.

41. Garvin, *1922*, pp. 96–7.

42. Lil Conlon, *Cumann na mBan and the Women of Ireland 1913–1925* (Kilkenny 1969), p. 255; McCarthy, *Cumann na mBan*, p. 177.

43. Matthews, *Renegades*, pp. 313–15.

44. Ann Matthews, 'Women and the Civil War', *Irish Sword* XX, 82 (1997), p. 381.

45. Macardle, *Irish Republic*, p. 598. Jennie Wyse Power told her daughter that Markievicz and MacSwiney had earlier tried to persuade her not to resign. Jennie to Nancy Wyse Power, 15 Jan. 1922. UCDA P106/740.

46. MAI CW/OPS/1/A, q. Gemma M. Clark, 'Fire, Boycott, Threat and Harm: Social and Political Violence within the Local Community: A Study of Three Munster Counties during the Irish Civil War, 1922–23', DPhil thesis, Oxford University 2010, p. 115.

47. 'Divisional Offensives', UCDA P7/A/31.

48. BMH WS 1719 (Daniel Corkery).

49. 'The Enemy's Civil Side', n.d. UCDA P7/A/31.

50. OC 1st SD to C/S, 6 Jan. 1922. UCDA P7/A/31.

51. 'The Enemy's Civil Side', loc. cit.

52. Tom Garvin, 'Dev and Mick', in Doherty and Keogh (eds.), *Michael Collins*, p. 151.

53. Mulcahy, 'Commentary upon Piaras Béaslaí's *Michael Collins*', UCDA P7/D/I/67. The IRB is mentioned more than fifteen times in the first volume of Béaslaí's work, only once in the second.

54. BMH WS 821 (Frank Henderson).

55. Tom Maguire in MacEoin (ed.), *Survivors*, p. 290.

56. Seán Ó Murthuile, 'History of the Irish Republican Brotherhood', q. J. O'Beirne-Ranelagh, 'The IRB from the Treaty to 1924', *Irish Historical Studies* 20 (1976), pp. 28–9.

57. Dáil Éireann Debates, 19 May 1922.

58. O'Donoghue, *No Other Law*, p. 232.

59. Sinn Féin Publicity Department, *The Good Old IRA: Tan War Operations* (Dublin 1985), q. Brian Hanley, 'Terror in Twentieth-Century Ireland', in Fitzpatrick (ed.), *Terror in Ireland*, pp. 14–15.

60. Hart, *IRA and its Enemies*, pp. 276–7.

61. Brian P. Murphy, 'The IRA and its Enemies', *The Month*, Sep.–Oct. 1998, pp. 381–3; John M. Regan, 'The "Bandon Valley Massacre" as a Historical Problem', *History* 97 (2012), pp. 73–4.

62. This point is emphatically registered in the richly detailed (albeit often speculative) investigation by Gerard Murphy, *The Year of Disappearances: Political Killings in Cork, 1921–1922* (Dublin 2010), e.g. in ch. 50, pp. 266–76.

63. Meda Ryan, *Tom Barry: IRA Freedom Fighter* (Cork 2005), pp. 209ff.

64. BMH WS 1719 (Daniel Corkery).

65. John M. Regan, 'Dr Jekyll and Mr Hyde: "The Two Histories"', *History Ireland*, Jan./Feb. 2012, p. 13.

66. Borgonovo, *Spies, Informers*, p. 91.

67. Coogan, *Michael Collins*, p. 359.

68. Niall Meehan, 'Troubles in Irish History', in Brian P. Murphy and Niall Meehan, *Troubled History: A 10th Anniversary Critique of Peter Hart's The IRA and its Enemies* (Aubane Historical Society 2008), p. 12.

69. Jeffrey Dudgeon, 'Dunmanway and Peter Hart', *Irish Political Review* 27, 2 (2012), p. 18.

70. Peter Hart, 'The Protestant Experience of Revolution', in *IRA at War*, p. 240.

71. Matthew Reisz, 'Between the Lines of a Tale of Murder and Motive', *Times Higher Education Supplement*, 24 May 2012, pp. 20–21.

72. Joseph O'Neill, *Blood-Dark Track: A Family History* (London 2000).

73. Murphy, *Year of Disappearances*, pp. 243, 9.

74. UCDA P17/B/112, q. ibid., pp. 26, 250.

75. Eugenio Biagini, in *Reviews in History* 1053 (21 Mar. 2011).

76. Kathleen Keyes McDonnell, *There is a Bridge at Bandon: A Personal Account of the Irish War of Independence* (Cork and Dublin 1972), p. 7.

77. BMH WS 1721 (Seamus Robinson), WS 1348 (Michael Davern).

78. BMH WS 389 (Roger McCorley).

79. Liaison Officer Belfast to C/S, 6 Jan. 1922. UCDA P7/A/31.

80. BMH WS 1096 (J. J. Murray).

81. A. C. Hepburn, *Catholic Belfast and Nationalist Ireland in the Era of Joe Devlin 1871–1934* (Oxford 2008), pp. 232–3.

82. Jim McDermott, *Northern Divisions: The Old IRA and the Belfast Pogroms 1920–22* (Belfast 2001), p. 151.

83. Watt to Wickham, 12, 22 Dec. 1921. PRONI HA 32/1/4, q. Lewis, 'Frank Aiken', p. 132.

84. BMH WS 567 (Michael MacConaill).

85. Coogan, *Michael Collins*, p. 337.

86. Belfast Trade Boycott Central Committee papers, NAI DE2/110.

87. BMH WS 389 (Roger McCorley).

88. Tim Wilson. '"The Most Terrible Assassination That Has Yet Stained the Name of Belfast": The McMahon Murders in Context', *Irish Historical Studies* 37 (May 2010), pp. 83ff.

89. Heads of Agreement between the Provisional Government and Government of Northern Ireland, paras 3, 5. Macardle, *Irish Republic*, App. 24.

90. North-Eastern Advisory Committee minutes, NAI D/T S1011.

91. UCDA P24/554.

92. McDermott, *Northern Divisions*, p. 207.

93. North-Eastern Advisory Committee minutes, 11 Apr. 1922. NAI D/T S1011.

94. Phoenix, *Northern Nationalism*, p. 212.

95. BMH WS 389 (Roger McCorley).

96. Robert Lynch, 'Donegal and the Joint-IRA Northern Offensive, May–November 1922', *Irish Historical Studies* 35 (Nov. 2006), pp. 189–90.

97. Seán Lehane to MSP Board, 7 Mar. 1935. NLI MS31340.

98. BMH WS 395 (Thomas Fitzpatrick/Bob McDonnell).

99. McDermott, *Northern Divisions*, pp. 187ff.

100. 3rd ND Report, 19 May 1922. UCDA P70/173.

101. McDermott, *Northern Divisions*, p. 225.

102. BMH WS 395 (Thomas Fitzpatrick/Bob McDonnell).

103. BMH WS 928 (John Shields).

104. Cabinet Committee on Irish Finance, 12 Dec. 1921. NA CAB 21/248. John McColgan, *British Policy and the Irish Administration 1920–22* (London 1983), p. 91.

105. Memo by Lionel Curtis, 10 Dec. 1921. McColgan, *British Policy and the Irish Administration*, p. 92.

106. Valiulis, *Mulcahy*, pp. 122, 125.

107. Mansergh, *The Unresolved Question*, p. 208.

108. Dáil Éireann debates, 1 Mar. 1922.

109. Churchill, *Aftermath*, p. 320.

110. BMH WS 939 (Ernest Blythe).

111. Eunan O'Halpin, *Defending Ireland: The Irish State and its Enemies since 1922* (Oxford 1999), p. 6.

112. Report of Commission of Inquiry into the Civic Guard, 12 Jul. 1922. UCDA P80/7: Report of Kevin O'Shiel and Michael MacAuliffe, 17 Aug. 1922. NAI D/T S9045.

113. OC 1st SD to C/S, 6 Jan. 1922. UCDA P7/A/31.

114. BMH WS 838 (Seán Moylan).

115. O'Donoghue, *No Other Law*, pp. 211, 213.

116. Memo by M/D, 23 Mar. 1922. UCDA P17/A/49.

117. IRA Convention, Memo by the Executive of the IRA, 28 Mar. 1922. UCDA P17/A/5.

118. *Irish Independent*, q. Anthony Kinsella, 'The British Military Evacuation', *Irish Sword* XX, 82 (1997), p. 277.

119. Officer I/C Evacuation to A/C/S, 28 Feb. 1922. NLI MS 22126.

120. Barry to O'Malley, 25 Jan.; O'Malley to Moloney, 18 Feb. 1922. UCDA P9/23, 142, 154.

121. OC 1st WD to A/C/S, 8 Mar. 1922. NLI MS 22127.

122. O'Donoghue, *No Other Law*, pp. 206–7; Hopkinson, *Green against Green*, pp. 63–4.

123. O'Malley notebooks, UCDA P17/B/95.

124. Note of meeting, 12 Mar. 1922. NLI MS 22127.

125. 'Account of events re setting up of National Army', NLI MS 22126.

126. But O'Donoghue, *No Other Law*, p. 219 suggests somewhat opaquely that these words 'did not accurately represent Liam Lynch's position'.

127. Townshend, *Easter 1916*, p. 206.

128. Collins to Daly, 13 Apr. 1922. NAI D/T S2978.

129. O'Donoghue, *No Other Law*, p. 230.

130. BMH WS 939 (Ernest Blythe); Hart, *Mick*, p. 373.

131. Cabinet Conclusions, 23 Jan. 1922. NA CAB 21/252.

132. Memo by W. S. Churchill, 23 May 1922. NA CAB 21/256.

133. Notes by Miceál Ó Coileán, Mar. 1922. NAI D/T S6541.

134. Curran, *Irish Free State*, p. 204.

135. Sexton, *Ireland and the Crown*, pp. 56–68.

136. Curran, *Irish Free State*, p. 211.

137. Hart, *Mick*, p. 362.

138. Macardle, *Irish Republic*, p. 657.

139. Notes by Seán MacBride, Jul. 1922. NAI D/T S1233.

140. O'Donoghue, *No Other Law*, p. 246.

141. Churchill to Griffith, 10 Jun. 1922. NA HO 24183.

142. Lloyd George to Collins, 22 Jun. 1922. UCDA P4/174.

143. Gilbert, *Churchill*, vol. IV, pp. 735–8.

144. Hopkinson, *Green against Green*, p. 120.

145. Andrews, *Dublin Made Me*, p. 226.

146. Macardle, *Irish Republic*, pp. 679–81.

147. Twomey to Lynch, 3 Jul. 1922. UCDA P69/77.

148. O'Malley, *Singing Flame*, p. 138.

149. Ibid., p. 129.

150. GHQ Blessington to Bde and Bn Comdts, 3 Jul. 1922. UCDA P7/B/106. Fitzpatrick, *Boland's Irish Revolution*, p. 310.

151. George Gilmore in O'Malley notebooks, UCDA P17/B/106, q. Hopkinson, *Green against Green*, p. 143.

152. O'Malley, *Singing Flame*, p. 132.

153. Ibid., pp. 95–6.

154. O'Malley to Mollie Childers, 28 Nov.–1 Dec. 1923. English and O'Malley (eds.), *Prisoners*, p. 86.

155. O'Donnell statement, MacEoin (ed.), *Survivors*, p. 23.

156. O'Malley, *Singing Flame*, p. 285.

157. Walter Mitchell in MacEoin (ed.), *Survivors*, p. 388.

158. Twomey to Lynch, 3 Jul. 1922. UCDA P69/77.

159. Gaughan, *Austin Stack*, p. 214.

160. McKeon to C/S, 31 Jul. 1922. UCDA P7/B/145.

161. O'Donohue, *No Other Law*, p. 266.

162. A/G to A/C/S, 29 Jul. 1922. UCDA P69/38.

163. Memo from A/A/C/S to OCs N & E Command, 24 Jul. 1922. UCDA P17/A/54.

164. Anne Dolan, 'The Papers in Context', in Cormac O'Malley and Anne Dolan (eds.), *'No Surrender Here!' The Civil War Papers of Ernie O'Malley 1922–1924* (Dublin 2007), p. li.

165. C/S to A/A/C/S, 25 Jul. 1922. UCDA P17/A/60.

166. A/G to A/A/C/S, 25 Aug. 1922. UCDA P69/77.

167. John Borgonovo, *The Battle for Cork, July–August 1922* (Cork 2011), pp. 47–8.

168. GOC SW Command memo, UCDA P7/B/40.

169. C-in-C to W Command, 19 Oct. 1922. UCDA P7/B/74.

170. Collins to Griffith, 14 Jul. 1922. Copy in UCDA P151/106.

171. See John M. Regan, 'Michael Collins, General Commanding-in-Chief, as a Historiographical Problem', *History* 92 (2007), pp. 318–46.

172. James Mackay, *Michael Collins: A Life* (Edinburgh 1996), p. 256.

173. Hart, *Mick*, pp. 402–3.

174. McGarry, *Eoin O'Duffy*, pp. 107, 111.

175. Memo by Minister for Justice, 20 Jan. 1923. NAI D/T S3306.

176. *Irish Times*, 11 Oct. 1922.

177. Aodh de Blacam to Hanna Sheehy Skeffington, 27 Jul. 1922. NLI MS 33915.

178. Proclamation, May 1922. NAI D/T S1168.

179. Notes by General Michael Collins, 1922, in *The Path to Freedom* (Dublin 1922).

180. Ministry of Home Affairs report, Apr. 1922. NAI DE2/51.

181. Notes by Griffith, 1922. NAI DE2/355.

182. 'To all whom it may concern', memo by W. T. Cosgrave, Jul. 1922. UCDA P4/254.

183. Memo by Gen. C-in-C, 29 Jul.; Collins to Cosgrave, 6 Aug. 1922. UCDA P7/B/28,29. Regan, *Irish Counter-Revolution*, pp. 123–4.

184. C/S to C-in-C, 4 Aug. 1922. UCDA P7/B/143.

185. Béaslaí to Griffith, 10 Aug. 1922. NLI MS 33915.

186. W Command, Monthly operation report, Dec. 1922. UCDA P151/180.

187. William Sears note, 7 Oct. 1922. UCDA P8/7.

188. Comdt Gen. McKeon to C/S, 31 Jul. 1922. UCDA P7/B/145.

189. MAI CW/OPS/1/A, q. Clark, 'Fire, Boycott, Threat and Harm', p. 116.

190. OC 3rd WD to C/S, 10 Dec. 1922. UCDA P69/33.

191. OC 4th ND to M/D, 6 Jul. 1922. UCDA P104/1239.

192. 'Position of the 4th Northern Division from January 1922 to 17 July'; 4th ND declaration 17 Jul. 1922. UCDA P104/1240.

193. O'Duffy to Collins, 12 Aug. 1922. UCDA P7/B/39.

194. O'Higgins to Mulcahy, 1 Sep. 1922, q. McGarry, Eoin O'Duffy, p. 113.

195. Irish Independent, 7 Aug. 1922.

196. Separatist, 2 Sep. 1922, q. Kissane, Politics of the Irish Civil War, p. 157.

197. C/S to C-in-C, 4 Aug. 1922. UCDA P7/B/143.

198. James P. Casey, 'Republican Courts in Ireland 1919–1922', Irish Jurist 5 (1970), p. 332.

199. Kotsonouris, Retreat from Revolution, p. 37.

200. M/D to President, 7 Feb. 1922. NAI DE2/51.

201. Aire um Gnothai Duitche [Minister for Home Affairs], 25 Jul. 1922, q. Kotsonouris, Retreat from Revolution, p. 83.

202. BMH WS 1321 (Joseph Dennigan).

203. BMH WS 939 (Ernest Blythe).

204. Campbell, Emergency Law in Ireland, p. 164.

205. 2nd SD Intelligence report, 13 Oct. 1922. UCDA P8/7.

206. De Valera to McGarrity, 10 Sep. 1922. Cronin (ed.), McGarrity Papers, pp. 124–7.

207. Ibid., pp. 127–8.

208. C/S to A/A/C/S, 27 Aug.; Mellows to O'Malley, 29 Aug. 1922. UCDA P17/A/61.

209. For the editorial, see Greaves, Liam Mellows, p. 358.

210. Lynch to O'Malley, 30 Aug. 1922. UCDA P17/A/61.

211. Lynch to O'Malley, 18 Sep. 1922. Hopkinson, Green against Green, p. 186.

212. Adj. to OC N & E Command, 22 Sep. 1922. UCDA P17/A/63.

213. BMH WS 939 (Ernest Blythe).

214. Kissane, Politics of the Irish Civil War, pp. 147–8.

215. John Joe Sheehy in MacEoin (ed.), Survivors, p. 359.

216. Niall C. Harrington, Kerry Landing (Dublin 1992), p. 149.

217. BMH WS 939 (Ernest Blythe).

218. Kissane, Politics of the Irish Civil War, pp. 135–7.

219. O'Donoghue, No Other Law, p. 288.

220. Interview transcript, 27 Feb. 1923. UCDA P7/B/284, q. Regan, Irish Counter-Revolution, p. 122.

221. A/G to OC 2nd SD, 20 Feb. 1923. O'Malley MSS, NLI MS 10973/6.

222. O'Donoghue, No Other Law, p. 296.

223. Sean Dowling in MacEoin (ed.), Survivors, p. 412.

224. O'Donoghue, No Other Law, p. 305.

225. Andrews, Dublin Made Me, pp. 285–6.

CONCLUSION

1. Michael Noyk Statement, NLI MS 18975.
2. O'Connor, *The Big Fellow*, pp. 72, 69.
3. Stathis N. Kalyvas, *The Logic of Violence in Civil War* (Cambridge 2006), pp. 388–91.
4. R. F. Foster, *Modern Ireland 1600–1972* (London 1988), p. 506.
5. Hart, *IRA at War*, p. 30.
6. MCI (Michael O'Reilly), NA WO 35/158.
7. MCI, NA WO 35/147A.
8. MCI (Gilbert Potter), NA WO 35/158. Traynor had been captured in a fight with Auxiliaries in Dublin. Whether the Tipperary IRA's offer even reached the Castle is doubtful: Mark Sturgis seems not to have heard of it. After the execution he merely commented on Traynor's age (over forty) and the fact that he had left a wife and 'a pack of children, the poor deluded idiot'. Sturgis diary, 25 Apr. 1921. NA PRO 30/59/4.
9. Lee, *Ireland*, p. 125.

Bibliography

Aan de Wiel, Jérôme, *The Catholic Church in Ireland 1914–1918* (Dublin 2003)

Abbott, Richard, *Police Casualties in Ireland 1919–1922* (Cork 2000)

Akenson, Donald Harman, *Small Differences: Irish Catholics and Irish Protestants 1815–1922* (Montreal and Dublin 1988)

Andrews, C. S., *Dublin Made Me: An Autobiography* (Dublin 1979)

Augusteijn, Joost, *From Public Defiance to Guerrilla Warfare: The Experience of Ordinary Volunteers in the Irish War of Independence 1916–1921* (Dublin 1996)

Augusteijn, Joost (ed.), *The Irish Revolution 1913–1923* (Basingstoke 2002)

Augusteijn, Joost (ed.), *The Memoirs of John M. Regan: A Catholic Officer in the RIC and RUC, 1909–1948* (Dublin 2007)

Barry, Tom, *Guerilla Days in Ireland* (Dublin 1949, Tralee 1962)

Barry, Tom, *The Reality of the Anglo-Irish War 1920–21 in West Cork* (Tralee 1974)

Béaslaí, Piaras, *Michael Collins and the Making of a New Ireland*, 2 vols (Dublin 1926)

Bennett, Richard, *The Black and Tans* (London 1959)

Benton, Sarah, 'Women Disarmed: The Militarization of Politics in Ireland 1913–23', *Feminist Review* 50 (1995)

Berresford Ellis, Peter, *A History of the Irish Working Class* (London 1972)

Bew, Paul, *Ireland: The Politics of Enmity 1789–2006* (Oxford 2007)

Blythe, Ernest, 'Arthur Griffith', *Administration* VIII (1960)

Borgonovo, John (ed.), *Florence and Josephine O'Donoghue's War of Independence: A Destiny that Shapes our Ends* (Dublin 2006)

Borgonovo, John, *Spies, Informers and the 'Anti-Sinn Féin Society': The Intelligence War in Cork City 1920–1921* (Dublin 2007).

Borgonovo, John, *The Battle for Cork, July–August 1922* (Cork 2011)

Bowman, John, *De Valera and the Ulster Question 1917–1973* (Oxford 1982)

Bowman, Timothy, *Carson's Army: The Ulster Volunteer Force, 1910–22* (Manchester 2007)

Boyce, D. George, *Englishmen and Irish Troubles: British Public Opinion and the Making of Irish Policy 1918–22* (London 1972)

Boyce, D. George, *Nationalism in Ireland* (London 1982)

Boyce, D. George (ed.), *The Revolution in Ireland 1879–1923* (London 1988)

Boyce, D. George and Alan O'Day (eds.), *The Ulster Crisis 1885–1921* (Basingstoke 2006)

Boyle, Andrew, *The Riddle of Erskine Childers* (London 1977)

Breen, Dan, *My Fight for Irish Freedom* (Dublin 1924)

Brennan, Michael, *The War in Clare 1911–1921: Personal Memoirs of the War of Independence* (Dublin 1982)

Brewer, John D., *The Royal Irish Constabulary: An Oral History* (Belfast 1990)

Briollay, Sylvain, *Ireland in Rebellion* (Dublin 1922) (originally *L'Irlande Insurgée*, Paris 1921, based on articles written in 1920–21)

Butler, Ewan, *Barry's Flying Column: The Story of the IRA's Cork No. 3 Brigade 1919–21* (London 1971)

Campbell, Colm, *Emergency Law in Ireland 1918–1925* (Oxford 1994)

Campbell, Fergus, *Land and Revolution: Nationalist Politics in the West of Ireland 1891–1921* (Oxford 2005)

Canning, Paul, *British Policy towards Ireland 1921–1941* (Oxford 1985)

Carroll, Aideen, *Seán Moylan: Rebel Leader* (Cork 2010)

Carroll, F. M., *Money for Ireland: Finance, Diplomacy and the First Dáil Éireann Loans, 1919–1936* (Westport, Conn. 2002)

Clark, Gemma M., 'Fire, Boycott, Threat and Harm: Social and Political Violence within the Local Community: A Study of Three Munster Counties during the Irish Civil War, 1922–23', DPhil thesis, Oxford University 2010

Coldrey, Barry M., *Faith and Fatherland: The Christian Brothers and the Development of Irish Nationalism 1838–1921* (Dublin 1988)

Coleman, Marie, *County Longford and the Irish Revolution 1910–1923* (Dublin 2003)

Conlon, Lil, *Cumann na mBan and the Women of Ireland 1913–1925* (Kilkenny 1969)

Coogan, Oliver, *Politics and War in Meath 1913–23* (Dublin 1983)

Coogan, Tim Pat, *Michael Collins: A Biography* (London 1990)

Coogan, Tim Pat, *De Valera: Long Fellow, Long Shadow* (London 1993) (published as *Eamon de Valera: The Man Who Was Ireland* in New York 1993)

Costello, Francis J., *Enduring the Most: The Life and Death of Terence MacSwiney* (Dingle 1995)

Costello, Francis J., *The Irish Revolution and its Aftermath 1916–1923: Years of Revolt* (Dublin 2003)

Cottrell, Peter, *The Irish Civil War 1922–23* (Botley, Oxford 2008)

Coulter, Carol, *The Hidden Tradition: Feminism, Women and Nationalism in Ireland* (Cork 1993)

Crean, Tom, 'Crowds and the Labour Movement in the Southwest, 1914–23', in P. Jupp and E. Magennis (eds.), *Crowds in Ireland, c.1720–1920* (London 2000)

Cronin, Seán, *The Ideology of the IRA* (Ann Arbor 1972)

Cronin, Seán (ed.), *The McGarrity Papers* (Tralee 1972)

Crowley, Tony, *Wars of Words: The Politics of Language in Ireland 1537–2004* (Oxford 2005)

Curran, Joseph, *The Birth of the Irish Free State 1921–1923* (Tuscaloosa, Ala. 1980)

Dalton, Charles, *With the Dublin Brigade (1917–1921)* (London 1929)

Davis, Richard, *Arthur Griffith and Non-Violent Sinn Féin* (Dublin 1974)

Deasy, Liam, *Towards Ireland Free: The West Cork Brigade in the War of Independence 1917–1921*, ed. John E. Chisholm (Dublin and Cork 1973)

De Blacam, Aodh, *What Sinn Féin Stands For: The Irish Republican Movement, its History, Aims and Ideals* (Dublin 1921)

De Burca, Padraig and John F. Boyle, *Free State or Republic?* (Dublin 1922)

Delancy Ryan, Vincent J., *Ireland Restored: The New Self-Determination* (New York n.d.)

De Paor, Liam, *On the Easter Proclamation and Other Declarations* (Dublin 1997)

Desmond, Shaw, *The Drama of Sinn Féin* (London 1923)

De Vere White, Terence, *Kevin O'Higgins* (London 1948)

Doherty, Gabriel and Dermot Keogh (eds.), *Michael Collins and the Making of the Irish State* (Cork 1998)

Doherty, M. A., 'Kevin Barry and the Anglo-Irish Propaganda War', *Irish Historical Studies* 32 (Nov. 2000)

Dolan, Anne, *Commemorating the Irish Civil War: History and Memory, 1923–2000* (Cambridge 2003)

Dolan, Anne, 'Killing and Bloody Sunday, November 1920', *Historical Journal* 49 (2006)

Doyle, Tom, *The Summer Campaign in Kerry* (Cork 2010)

Dublin's Fighting Story (Tralee 1949)

Duff, Douglas V., *Sword for Hire* (London 1934)

Elliott, Marianne, *When God Took Sides: Religion and Identity in Ireland* (Oxford 2009)

English, Richard, 'Green on Red: Two Case Studies in Early Twentieth-Century Irish Republican Thought', in D. George Boyce et al. (eds.), *Political Thought in Ireland since the Seventeenth Century* (London 1993)

English, Richard, *Ernie O'Malley: IRA Intellectual* (Oxford 1998)

English, Richard, *Irish Freedom: The History of Nationalism in Ireland* (London 2006)

English, Richard and Cormac O'Malley (eds.), *Prisoners: The Civil War Letters of Ernie O'Malley* (Swords 1991)

English, Richard and Graham Walker (eds.), *Unionism in Modern Ireland* (London 1996)

Farrell, Brian, *The Founding of Dáil Éireann: Parliament and Nation Building* (Dublin 1971)

Farrell, Brian (ed.), *The Creation of the Dáil* (Dublin 1994)

Farry, Michael, *Sligo 1914–1921: A Chronicle of Conflict* (Trim 1992)

Farry, Michael, *The Aftermath of Revolution: Sligo 1921–23* (Dublin 2000)

Ferriter, Diarmaid, *Cuimhnigh Ar Luimneach: A History of Limerick County Council, 1898–1998* (Limerick 1999)

Ferriter, Diarmaid, *Lovers of Liberty? Local Government in 20th Century Ireland* (Dublin 2001)

Ferriter, Diarmaid, *The Transformation of Ireland 1900–2000* (London 2005)

Ferriter, Diarmaid, *Judging Dev: A Reassessment of the Life and Legacy of Eamon de Valera* (Dublin 2007)

Figgis, Darrell, *Recollections of the Irish War* (London 1927)

Fitzpatrick, David, *Politics and Irish Life: Provincial Experience of War and Revolution 1913–1921* (Dublin 1977)

Fitzpatrick, David (ed.), *Revolution? Ireland 1917–1923* (Dublin 1990)

Fitzpatrick, David, 'Militarism in Ireland 1900–1922', in T. Bartlett and K. Jeffery (eds.), *A Military History of Ireland* (Cambridge 1996)

Fitzpatrick, David, *The Two Irelands 1912–1939* (Oxford 1998)

Fitzpatrick, David, *Harry Boland's Irish Revolution* (Cork 2003)

Fitzpatrick, David (ed.), *Terror in Ireland 1916–1923* (Dublin 2012)

Follis, Bryan A., *A State under Siege: The Establishment of Northern Ireland 1920–1925* (Oxford 1995)

Forester, Margery, *Michael Collins: The Lost Leader* (London 1971)

Foster, R. F., *Modern Ireland 1600–1972* (London 1988)

Foster, R. F., *The Irish Story: Telling Tales and Making It Up in Ireland* (London 2001)

Foster, R. F., *W. B. Yeats: A Life*, 2 vols (Oxford 2003)

Fox, R. M., *Rebel Irishwomen* (Dublin 1935)

Foy, Michael T., *Michael Collins's Intelligence War: The Struggle between the British and the IRA 1919–1921* (Stroud 2006)

Garvin, Tom, *The Evolution of Irish Nationalist Politics* (Dublin 1981)

Garvin, Tom, *Nationalist Revolutionaries in Ireland 1858–1928* (Oxford 1987)

Garvin, Tom, *1922: The Birth of Irish Democracy* (Dublin 1996)

Gaughan, J. A. (ed.), *The Memoirs of Constable Jeremiah Mee RIC* (Dublin 1975)

Gaughan, J. A., *Austin Stack: Portrait of a Separatist* (Dublin 1977)

Gaughan, J. A., *Thomas Johnson 1872–1963: First Leader of the Labour Party in Dáil Éireann* (Mount Merrion 1980)

Glandon, Virginia E., *Arthur Griffith and the Advanced Nationalist Press in Ireland, 1900–1922* (New York 1985)

Grayson, Natasha, 'The Quality of Nationalism in Counties Cavan, Louth and Meath during the Irish Revolution', PhD thesis, Keele University 2008

Greaves, C. Desmond, *Liam Mellows and the Irish Revolution* (London 1971)

Gregory, Adrian and Senia Pašeta (eds.), *Ireland and the Great War: 'A War to Unite Us All'?* (Manchester 2002)

Gribbon, H. D., 'Economic and Social History, 1850–1921', in W. E. Vaughan (ed.), *Ireland under the Union 1870–1921*, vol. VI of *A New History of Ireland* (Oxford 1996)

Grob-Fitzgibbon, Benjamin, *Turning Points of the Irish Revolution: The British Government, Intelligence, and the Cost of Indifference, 1912–1921* (Basingstoke and New York 2007)

Harkness, David, *The Restless Dominion: The Irish Free State and the British Commonwealth 1921–31* (London 1969)

Harrington, Michael, *The Munster Republic: The Civil War in North Cork* (Cork 2009)

Harrington, Niall C., *Kerry Landing* (Dublin 1992)

Harris, Mary, *The Catholic Church and the Foundation of the Northern Irish State* (Cork 1993)

Hart, Peter, 'The Thompson Submachine Gun in Ireland Revisited', *Irish Sword* XIX (1995)

Hart, Peter, *The IRA and its Enemies: Violence and Community in Cork 1916–1923* (Oxford 1998)

Hart, Peter (ed.), *British Intelligence in Ireland, 1920–21: The Final Reports* (Cork 2002)

Hart, Peter, *The IRA at War 1916–1923* (Oxford 2003)

Hart, Peter, *Mick: The Real Michael Collins* (London 2005)

Healy, T. M., *Letters and Leaders of my Day*, 2 vols (London 1928)

Heffernan, Brian, 'Catholic Priests and Political Violence in Ireland, 1919–1921', PhD thesis, National University of Ireland, Maynooth 2010

Henry, Robert Mitchell, *The Evolution of Sinn Féin* (Dublin and London 1920)

Hepburn, A. C., *A Past Apart: Studies in the History of Catholic Belfast, 1850–1950* (Belfast 1996)

Hepburn, A. C., *Catholic Belfast and Nationalist Ireland in the Era of Joe Devlin 1871–1934* (Oxford 2008)

Herlihy, Jim, *The Royal Irish Constabulary* (Dublin 1997)

Hill, R. and M. Marsh (eds.), *Modern Irish Democracy* (Dublin 1993)

Holmes, Richard, *The Little Field-Marshal: Sir John French* (London 1981)

Hopkinson, Michael, *Green against Green: The Irish Civil War* (Dublin 1988)

Hopkinson, Michael (ed.), *The Last Days of Dublin Castle: The Diaries of Mark Sturgis* (Dublin 1999)

Hopkinson, Michael, *The Irish War of Independence* (Dublin and Montreal 2002)

Horne, John (ed.), *Our War: Ireland and the Great War* (Dublin 2008)

'I.O.' [C. J. C. Street], *The Administration of Ireland 1920* (London 1921)

Irish Labour Party and Trade Union Congress, *Who Burnt Cork City? A Tale of Arson, Loot and Murder: The Evidence of Over Seventy Witnesses* (Dublin 1921)

Jeffery, Keith, *Ireland and the Great War* (Cambridge 2000)

Jeffery, Keith, *Field Marshal Sir Henry Wilson* (Oxford 2006)

Johnson, D. S., 'The Belfast Boycott, 1920–1922', in J. M. Goldstrom and L. A. Clarkson (eds.), *Irish Population, Economy and Society* (Oxford 1981)

Jones, Thomas, *Whitehall Diary*, vol. III (Oxford 1971)

Joy, Sinéad, *The IRA in Kerry 1916–1921* (Cork 2005)

Kautt, William H., *Ambushes and Armour: The Irish Rebellion 1919–1921* (Dublin 2010)

Kee, Robert, *The Green Flag: A History of Irish Nationalism* (London 1972)

Kelly, Matthew, *The Fenian Ideal and Irish Nationalism 1882–1916* (Woodbridge 2006)

Kendle, John, *Walter Long, Ireland and the Union 1905–1920* (Montreal 1992)

Kennedy, D., *The Widening Gulf: Northern Attitudes to the Independent Irish State 1919–1949* (Belfast 1988)

Keogh, Dermot, *The Vatican, the Bishops and Irish Politics 1919–39* (Cambridge 1986)

Keogh, Dermot, *Ireland and Europe 1919–48* (Dublin 1988)

Keown, Gerard, 'The Ideas and Development of Irish Foreign Policy from the Origins of Sinn Féin to 1932', DPhil thesis, Oxford University 1997 (2010)

Kissane, Bill, *The Politics of the Irish Civil War* (Oxford 2003)

Knirck, Jason, 'Afterimage of the Revolution: Kevin O'Higgins and the Irish Revolution', *Eire-Ireland* 38 (2003)

Knirck, Jason, *Women of the Dáil: Gender, Republicanism and the Anglo-Irish Treaty* (Dublin 2006)

Kotsonouris, Mary, *Retreat from Revolution: The Dáil Courts, 1920–24* (Dublin 1994)

Laffan, Michael, *The Partition of Ireland 1911–1925* (Dublin 1983)

Laffan, Michael, "Labour Must Wait": Ireland's Conservative Revolution', in P. J. Corish (ed.), *Radicals, Rebels and Establishments* (Belfast 1985)

Laffan, Michael, *The Resurrection of Ireland: The Sinn Féin Party, 1916–1923* (Cambridge 1999)

Lawlor, Sheila, *Britain and Ireland 1914–23* (Dublin 1983)

Lee, J. J., *Ireland 1912–1985: Politics and Society* (Cambridge 1989)

Leeson, D. M., *The Black and Tans: British Police and Auxiliaries in the Irish War of Independence, 1920–1921* (Oxford 2011)

Lowe, W. J., 'The War against the RIC, 1919–21', *Eire-Ireland* 37 (2002)

Lowe, W. J. and E. L. Malcolm, 'The Domestication of the Royal Irish Constabulary, 1836–1922', *Irish Economic and Social History* 19 (1992)

Lynch, Robert, *The Northern IRA and the Early Years of Partition, 1920–1922* (Dublin 2006)

Lyons, F. S. L., *Ireland since the Famine* (London 1971)

Lyons, F. S. L., *Culture and Anarchy in Ireland 1890–1939* (Oxford 1979)

Macardle, Dorothy, *Tragedies of Kerry* (?Dublin 1923)

Macardle, Dorothy, *The Irish Republic 1911–1923* (London 1937)

McBride, Lawrence W., *The Greening of Dublin Castle: The Transformation of Bureaucratic and Judicial Personnel in Ireland 1892–1922* (Washington, DC 1991)

McCartan, Patrick, *With de Valera in America* (New York 1932)

McCarthy, Cal, *Cumann na mBan and the Irish Revolution* (Dublin 2007)

McCarthy, Col. J. M. (ed.), *Limerick's Fighting Story* (Tralee n.d.)

McColgan, John, *British Policy and the Irish Administration 1920–22* (London 1983)

McCoole, Sinéad, *No Ordinary Women: Irish Female Activists in the Revolutionary Years 1900–1923* (Dublin 2003)

Mc Cormack, W. J., *Dublin 1916: The French Connection* (Dublin 2012)

Mac Curtain, Margaret and Ó Corráin, Donncha (eds.), *Women in Irish Society* (Dublin 1978)

McDermott, Jim, *Northern Divisions: The Old IRA and the Belfast Pogroms 1920–22* (Belfast 2001)

McDonnell, Kathleen Keyes, *There is a Bridge at Bandon: A Personal Account of the Irish War of Independence* (Cork and Dublin 1972)

MacEoin, Uinseann (ed.), *Survivors* (Dublin 1980)

McGarry, Fearghal (ed.), *Republicanism in Modern Ireland* (Dublin 2003)

McGarry, Fearghal, *Eoin O'Duffy: A Self-Made Hero* (Oxford 2005)

McGarry, Fearghal and James McConnel (eds.), *The Black Hand of Republicanism: Fenianism in Modern Ireland* (Dublin 2009)

McGee, Owen, *The IRB: The Irish Republican Brotherhood from the Land League to Sinn Féin* (Dublin 2007)

Mackay, James, *Michael Collins: A Life* (Edinburgh 1996)

McKillen, Beth, 'Irish Feminism and National Separatism, 1914–23', *Eire-Ireland* 17 (1982)

MacSwiney, Terence, *Principles of Freedom* (Dublin 1921)

Maguire, Gloria, 'The Political and Military Causes of the Division in the Irish Nationalist Movement, January 1921 to August 1923', DPhil thesis, Oxford University 1985

Maher, Jim, *The Flying Column: West Kilkenny 1916–21* (Dublin 1987)

Maher, Jim, *Harry Boland: A Biography* (Cork 1998)

Malcolm, Elizabeth, *The Irish Policeman, 1822–1922: A Life* (Dublin 2006)

Mansergh, Nicholas, *The Irish Free State: Its Government and Politics* (London 1934)

Mansergh, Nicholas, *The Unresolved Question: The Anglo-Irish Settlement and its Undoing 1912–72* (New Haven and London 1991)

Markievicz, Constance de, *What Irish Republicans Stand For* (Dublin 1922)

Martin, F. X. (ed.), *Leaders and Men of the Easter Rising: Dublin 1916* (London 1967)

Martin, Hugh, *Ireland in Insurrection* (London 1921)

Matthews, Ann, *Renegades: Irish Republican Women 1900–1922* (Cork 2010)

Maume, Patrick, *The Long Gestation: Irish Nationalist Life 1891–1918* (Dublin 1999)

Maume, Patrick, 'Young Ireland, Arthur Griffith, and Republican Ideology: The Question of Continuity', *Eire-Ireland* 34 (1999)

Maye, Brian, *Arthur Griffith* (Dublin 1997)

Midleton, Earl of, *Records and Reactions* (London and New York 1939)

Miller, David W., *Church, State and Nation in Ireland 1898–1921* (Dublin 1973)

Mitchell, Arthur, *Labour in Irish Politics, 1890–1930: The Irish Labour Movement in an Age of Revolution* (Dublin 1974)

Mitchell, Arthur, *Revolutionary Government in Ireland: Dáil Éireann 1919–22* (Dublin 1995)

Morgan, Austen, *Labour and Partition: The Belfast Working Class 1905–23* (London 1990)

Morgan, Austen and Bob Purdie (eds.), *Ireland: Divided Nation, Divided Class* (London 1980)

Morris, Ewan, *Our Own Devices: National Symbols and Political Conflict in Twentieth-Century Ireland* (Dublin 2005)

Murphy, Brian P., *Patrick Pearse and the Lost Republican Ideal* (Dublin 1991)

Murphy, Brian P., *The Origins and Organisation of British Propaganda in Ireland 1920* (Aubane 2006)

Murphy, Desmond, *Derry, Donegal and Modern Ulster 1790–1921* (Londonderry 1981)

Murphy, Gerard, *The Year of Disappearances: Political Killings in Cork 1921–1922* (Dublin 2010)

Murray, Patrick, *Oracles of God: The Catholic Church and Irish Politics 1922–1937* (Dublin 2000)

Neeson, Eoin, *The Civil War in Ireland 1922–23* (Cork 1966)

Neeson, Eoin, *The Life and Death of Michael Collins* (Cork 1968)

Neeson, Eoin, *Birth of a Republic* (Dublin 1998)

Novick, Ben, *Conceiving Revolution: Irish Nationalist Propaganda during the First World War* (Dublin 2001)

Ó Broin, Leon, *Revolutionary Underground: The Story of the Irish Republican Brotherhood 1858–1924* (Dublin 1976)

O'Connor, Frank, *The Big Fellow: Michael Collins and the Irish Revolution* (London 1965)

O'Donoghue, Florence, *No Other Law* (Dublin 1954, 1986)

O'Donoghue, Florence, 'Guerrilla Warfare in Ireland 1919–1921', *An Cosantóir* XXIII (May 1963)

Ó Drisceoil, Donal, *Peadar O'Donnell* (Cork 2001)

O'Halpin, Eunan, *The Decline of the Union: British Government in Ireland 1892–1920* (Dublin 1987)

O'Halpin, Eunan, *Defending Ireland: The Irish State and its Enemies since 1922* (Oxford 1999)

O'Halpin, Eunan, 'Politics and the State, 1922–32', in J. R. Hill (ed.), *Ireland 1921–84*, vol. VII of *A New History of Ireland* (Oxford 2003)

O'Malley, Cormac and Anne Dolan (eds.), *'No Surrender Here!' The Civil War Papers of Ernie O'Malley 1922–1924* (Dublin 2007)

O'Malley, Ernie, *On Another Man's Wound* (London 1936, Dublin 1979)

O'Malley, Ernie, *The Singing Flame* (Dublin 1978)

O'Malley, Ernie, *Raids and Rallies* (Dublin 1982)

Ó Ruairc, Pádraig Óg, *Blood on the Banner: The Republican Struggle in Clare 1913–1923* (Cork 2009)

Ó Ruairc, Pádraig Óg, *The Battle for Limerick City* (Cork 2010)

O'Suilleabhain, Micheal, *Where Mountainy Men Have Sown* (Cork 1965)

Pakenham, Frank, *Peace by Ordeal* (London 1935, 1972)

Parkinson, Alan F., *Belfast's Unholy War: The Troubles of the 1920s* (Dublin 2004)

Pašeta, Senia, *Before the Revolution: Nationalism, Social Change and Ireland's Catholic Élite 1879–1922* (Cork 1999)

Phillips, Walter Alison, *The Revolution in Ireland* (London 1923)

Phoenix, Eamon, *Northern Nationalism: Nationalist Politics, Partition and the Catholic Minority in Northern Ireland, 1890–1940* (Belfast 1994)

Prager, Jeffrey, *Building Democracy in Ireland: Political Order and Cultural Integration in a Newly Independent Nation* (Cambridge 1986)

Regan, John M., *The Irish Counter-Revolution 1921–1936* (Dublin 1999)

Regan, John M., 'The "Bandon Valley Massacre" as a Historical Problem', *History* 97 (2012)

Ring, Jim, *Erskine Childers* (London 1996)

Roche, Desmond, *Local Government in Ireland* (Dublin 1975)

Rumpf, Erhard and A. C. Hepburn, *Nationalism and Socialism in Twentieth Century-Ireland* (Liverpool 1977)

Ryan, Desmond, *Seán Treacy and the Third Tipperary Brigade, IRA* (Tralee 1945)

Ryan, Louise, 'Drunken Tans: Representations of Sex and Violence in the Anglo-Irish War (1919–21)', *Feminist Review* 66 (2000)

Ryan, Meda, *The Real Chief: The Story of Liam Lynch* (Cork 1986)

Ryan, Meda, *Tom Barry: IRA Freedom Fighter* (Cork 2005)

Sceilg [J. J. O'Kelly], *A Trinity of Martyrs* (Dublin 1947)

Sheehan, Aideen, 'Cumann na mBan: Policies and Activities', in David Fitzpatrick (ed.), *Revolution? Ireland 1917–1923* (Dublin 1990)

Sheehan, William, *British Voices from the Irish War of Independence 1918–1921: The Words of British Servicemen Who Were There* (Cork 2007)

Sheehan, William, *Fighting for Dublin: The British Battle for Dublin 1919–1921* (Cork 2007)

Street, C. J. C., *Ireland in 1921* (London 1922)

Taylor, Rex, *Michael Collins* (London 1961)

Townshend, Charles, *The British Campaign in Ireland 1919–1921: The Development of Political and Military Policies* (Oxford 1975)

Townshend, Charles, 'The Irish Railway Strike of 1920: Industrial Action and Civil Resistance in the Struggle for Independence', *Irish Historical Studies* 21 (1979)

Townshend, Charles, *Political Violence in Ireland: Government and Resistance since 1848* (Oxford 1983)

Townshend, Charles, 'Civilization and "Frightfulness": Air Control in the Middle East between the Wars', in C. J. Wrigley (ed.), *Warfare, Diplomacy and Politics: Essays in Honour of A. J. P. Taylor* (London 1986)

Townshend, Charles (ed.), *The Oxford Illustrated History of Modern War* (Oxford 1997)

Townshend, Charles, *Ireland: The Twentieth Century* (London 1998)

Townshend, Charles, 'The Meaning of Irish Freedom: Constitutionalism in the Free State', *Transactions of the Royal Historical Society*, 6th series, vol. 8 (1998)

Townshend, Charles, 'Telling the Irish Revolution', in Joost Augusteijn (ed.), *The Irish Revolution 1913–1923* (Basingstoke 2002)

Townshend, Charles, *Easter 1916: The Irish Rebellion* (London 2005)

Urquhart, Diane, *Women in Ulster Politics 1890–1940* (Dublin 2000)

Valiulis, Maryann, *Almost a Rebellion: The Irish Army Mutiny of 1924* (Cork n.d.)

Valiulis, Maryann, *Portrait of a Revolutionary: General Richard Mulcahy and the Founding of the Irish Free State* (Dublin 1992)

Valiulis, Maryann (ed.), *Gender and Power in Irish History* (Dublin 2009)

Van Voris, Jacqueline, *Constance de Markievicz in the Cause of Ireland* (Amherst, Mass. 1967)

Walsh, Maurice, *The News from Ireland: Foreign Correspondents and the Irish Revolution* (London 2008)

Ward, Alan J., *Ireland and Anglo-American Relations 1899–1921* (London 1969)

Ward, Alan J., *The Irish Constitutional Tradition: Responsible Government in Modern Ireland* (Dublin 1994)

Ward, Margaret, 'Marginality and Militancy: Cumann na mBan, 1914–1936', in Austen Morgan and Bob Purdie (eds.), *Ireland: Divided Nation, Divided Class* (London 1980)

Ward, Margaret, *Unmanageable Revolutionaries: Women and Irish Nationalism* (Dingle 1983)

Williams, T. Desmond (ed.), *The Irish Struggle 1916–1926* (London 1966)

Wilson, Tim, 'Boundaries, Identity and Violence: Ulster and Upper Silesia in a Context of Partition 1918–1922', DPhil thesis, Oxford University 2007

With the IRA in the Fight for Freedom (Tralee 1955)

Younger, Calton, *Ireland's Civil War* (London 1968)

Acknowledgments

My thanks must in the first place go, once again, to the Leverhulme Trust. Without its award of a Major Research Fellowship in 2009–11 this book would quite simply not have been written. The Trust retains an understanding, now rare, of the working needs of researchers in the humanities. My colleagues in History at Keele University, besides providing an unfailingly stimulating scholarly atmosphere, were as always exceptionally co-operative in coping with the dislocation caused by my absence. An award from the British Academy under its late, lamented Small Grants scheme – likewise well adapted to humanities research – enabled me to commission Eve Morrison to produce a remarkable dataset from the Richard Mulcahy papers in University College Dublin Archives. Eve also generously shared her unique knowledge of the Bureau of Military History material in the Military Archives in Cathal Brugha Barracks, as well as other important archival sources. Professor Eunan O'Halpin kindly made office space available in Trinity College, which helped to advance my work considerably. The research for this book was carried out before the Witness Statements were made available (and searchable) online – an event which has transformed the utility of this remarkable source – and I am grateful for the assistance of Commandant Victor Laing and the staff of the Military Archives in making material available. Commandant Patrick Brennan and his team on the Military Service Pensions Archive Project were immensely helpful during the brief visit I was able to make as a historical adviser to the project; I regret that the Irish government has not permitted me to refer to the material in the Archive. I owe a particular debt of gratitude to Catriona Crowe of the National Archives, and I am grateful as ever to a number of outstanding scholars, especially Roy Foster, Richard

English and Senia Pašeta, for advice and support. Simon Winder at Penguin is a remarkable editor, and the book has benefited greatly from his careful critical reading, as it also has from the copyediting of Peter James. Without the assistance of Marina Kemp, few if any of the illustrations would have appeared.

Index

Figures in bold indicate entries in the biographical glossary

Abbey Theatre, Dublin, 196
Act of Union 1801, 3
Aghern, Co. Cork, 115
Ahane, Co. Limerick, 40
Aiken, Frank, 22, 32, 315, 320, 329,
    354, 377, 380, 391, 399, 424,
    431–2, 451, 446–7, **457**
aircraft, military use of, 11, 143,
    153–4
Allen, John, 227
Allihies, Co. Cork, 115
Amiens Street railway station,
    Dublin, 249
ambushes, 185, 187, 210–15, 246, 294
American Commission on Conditions
    in Ireland, 170
An tOglac, 75–8, 89, 94, 123, 124,
    130, 261, 292, 299, 300–301,
    351
    Republican IRA issue, 419–20
Anabla, Co. Kerry, 33
Ancient Order of Hibernians, 24,
    31, 172
Anderson, Sir John (Under Secretary,
    Dublin Castle), 138, 142,
    145, 149, 151, 154, 162, 224,
    227, 283
Andrews, C. S. (Todd), 19, 39, 57,
    203, 204, 205, 350, 358, 359,

    360, 390, 406, 408, 409,
    434, 447
Anglo-Irish Treaty 1921, 287, 334,
    335, 336, 339, 340, 344,
    347–52, 357, 358, 359, 360,
    376, 384, 404, 406, 449, 451,
    452, 454
    negotiations, 331–7, 339–44
anti-conscription movement, 8, 15,
    48, 91
Anti-Sinn Fein organisation, 155–7
Antrim, county, 61
Antrim Brigade, IV 383
arbitration courts, 125, 193
Archer, Liam, 36, 188, 356
Armagh, county, 45, 60,
    174, 378
Army Emergency Powers Resolution
    1922, 437, 441
Ashe, Thomas, 5, 6, 22, 23, 36, 42, 56,
    143, 194, **457**
Asquith, H. H., xvi, 99
Army of the Irish Republic, xv, 75, 77,
    89, 130, 386, 391, 393
Athlone, Co. Westmeath, 312
Athlone Brigade, IV 319
Australia, 335
Auxiliary Division, RIC *see* Royal
    Irish Constabulary

Balbriggan, Co. Dublin, 162, 163, 165
Balfour, Earl of, 155, 283, 303, 308
Ballina, Co. Mayo, 16, 169
Ballincollig, Co. Cork, 240
Ballinrobe, Co. Mayo, 127, 177
Ballyseedy Cross, Co. Kerry, 443, 450
Ballyshannon, 178
Ballytrain, Co. Monaghan, 114–15
Banbridge, Co. Down, 175
Bandon, Co. Cork, 19, 212
'Bandon Valley massacre', 370–73
Barraduff, Co. Kerry, 264
Barlow, Artie, 184
Barrett, Annie, 251
Barrett, Frank, 237
Barrett, Joe, 237
Barry, Dr Alice, 251
Barry, Kevin, 196–7, 203
Barry, Tom, 210–15, 245, 260, 265,
    279–80, 311–12, 375, 396, 403
Barton, Robert, 84, 85, 94, 127, 306,
    307, 308, 332, 324, 327–8, 334,
    347, 348, 349–50, 441, 450,
    457
Beal na mBlath, Co. Cork, 432–3
Béaslaí, Piaras, 65, 66, 75, 77, 89, 94,
    189, 190, 251, 300–301, 314,
    315, 350, 351, 353, 357, 384,
    421, 427, 428, **457–8**
Beaufort, Co. Kerry, 39
Beggars Bush barracks, Dublin,
    201, 291,
  HQ Free State army, 380,
    394, 431
Belfast, xii, 34, 39, 44, 45, 54, 58, 60,
    85, 138, 140, 145, 162, 163,
    172, 173, 174–6, 177, 376–7,
    380, 383, 405
  Belfast Boycott, 176–9, 313, 316,
    378, 379, 406
  Falls Division, 61
  East Belfast, 172

Belfast Telegraph, 380, 381, 383
Bell, Alan, 91, 192
Belmont, Co. Galway, 75
Belnadeega, Co. Kerry, 46
Bennett, Louie, 59
bicycles, use of, 258–9
Birkenhead, Viscount, 303, 339
Blessington, Co. Dublin, 411
Bloody Sunday (21 November 1920),
    200, 201–8, 210, 272
Blythe, Ernest, 12, 33, 34, 75, 84, 86,
    172, 177, 232, 250, 333, 334,
    387, 398, 433, 442, 444, 453,
    454, **458**
Boggeragh mountains, 290
Boland, Gerald, 411
Boland, Harry, 17, 58, 59, 62, 70, 71,
    72, 82, 92, 233, 326, 328,
    334, 335, 357, 359, 411, 415,
    441, **458**
Bonar Law, Andrew, 99, 144,
    339, 341
Borgonovo, John, 372–3
Borrisokane, Co. Tipperary, 119
Boundary commission, 378
Boyd, Maj. Gen. Gerald, 225
Brady, James Joseph (DI RIC), 166
Brailsford, H. N., 85
Breen, Dan, 73, 79, 81, 106, 107, 198,
    353
Brennan, Michael, 78, 151, 183,
    320–21, 325, 394–5, 422
Brennan, Robert, 58, 94
Brennan, Timothy, 158
British army, xiv, 4, 7, 14, 40, 41, 45,
    56, 116, 117, 158, 181, 187,
    212, 215, 224–5, 245, 256, 258,
    266, 271, 255, 371, 393, 452
  armoured vehicles, 153, 290
  counterinsurgency methods, 187–8,
    297–8
  motor transport, 153

recruitment, 4, 6, 7
strength, 224–5
Dublin District, 198, 224, 257,
    288, 291
5th Infantry Division, 153
6th Infantry Division, 218, 226,
    243, 288, 289, 311
36th (Ulster) Division, 182
14th Infantry Brigade, 187–8
16th Infantry Brigade, 106, 227
17th Infantry Brigade, 150,
    227, 311
Kerry Infantry Brigade, 242, 290
Dublin Fusiliers, 365
Duke of Wellington's
    Regiment, 393
East Kent Regiment, 105
Essex Regiment, 310
Lancashire Fusiliers, 206
Manchester Regiment, 240
see also Irish Command
British Commonwealth, 341,
    400–401
Broadstone railway station, Dublin,
    148, 249
Brooke, Basil, 181
Brotherton, C. H., 451
Brown (O'Donoghue), Josephine, 251
Brown, Walter, 105
Broy, Eamon (Ned), 190, 191
Brugha, Cathal, 6, 17, 24, 36, 53, 59,
    60, 66, 67, 82, 86, 87, 130, 198,
    203, 224, 234 267, 269, 300,
    308, 316, 320, 322, 323, 324,
    326–7, 330, 332, 367, 390, 398,
    409, 410, **458**
  Defence Minister, 84, 86–7, 106,
    131, 198, 267, 269, 293, 300,
    320, 322, 323, 326–7
  feud with Collins, 326–8
  New Army project, 329
  opposition to Treaty, 348, 360

Bryan, Dan, 207
Bureau of Military History, 214,
    215, 250
Busteed, Frank, 23, 57, 239, 240, 317,
    372
Buttimer, James, 370
by-elections
  East Clare 1917, 8, 20, 29
  North Roscommon 1917, 12
  East Cavan 1917, 17
Byrne, Sir Joseph (Inspector General,
    RIC), 8–9, 103, 161
Byrne, Vinnie, 433

Cabinet, British, 18, 99–103, 139,
    143, 146, 149, 152, 154, 194,
    217–18, 226, 228, 283, 301,
    303, 308, 310, 331, 405
  Irish Situation Committee,
    289, 302
Cabinet, Dáil Eireann, 84, 85, 128,
    286, 324, 329, 330–31, 332,
    336–7, 347–9, 350, 363, 368,
    386, 391, 396
Cabinet, Irish Free State/Provisional
    Government, 391–2, 395, 398,
    400, 433, 442, 444
Caherciveen, Co. Kerry, 443
Cahill, Paddy, 295–6
'Cairo Gang', 203–4
Campbell, Sir James (Irish Lord Chief
    Justice), 11, 197
Camlough, co. Armagh, 22, 32
Canada, 141, 335
Cannon, Paddy, 285
Carlow Brigade, IV 51
Carlyle, Thomas, 340
Carney, Winnie, 60
Carrick-on-Suir, Co. Tipperary, 22,
    146, 187, 361, 416
Carrigaholt, Co. Clare, 33
Carrigtwohill, Co. Cork, 108, 109, 114

Carson, Edward, xiv, 175
Carty, Frank, 360, 418
Casement, Sir Roger, 15–16, 72
Cashel, Co. Tipperary, 44
Castleconnell, Co. Limerick, 289
Castletownbere, Co. Cork, 30, 44
Catholic Bulletin, 12
Catholic Church, 11–12, 13, 14, 57,
    96–8, 270–73, 377, 417,
    425–6, 442
    hierarchy, 13, 15, 97, 108, 270, 427
    and Anglo-Irish Treaty, 358–9
Cavan Brigade IV, 147, 183, 282
Ceannt, Aine, 47
censorship, 428
Chamberlain, Austen, 164, 283, 339,
    344, 399, 400
Chauviré, Roger ('Sylvain Briollay'),
    20–21, 66, 70
Childers, Robert Erskine, 95–6, 124,
    252, 299, 324, 332, 341, 347,
    360, 379, 398, 420, 427, 441,
    442, **458**
Chisholm, Fr John, 214
Churchill, Winston, 139, 140, 150,
    154, 180, 219, 228, 283, 301,
    307, 308, 332, 339, 342, 343,
    377, 379, 380, 381, 386, 399,
    404, 405, 406, 407, 408
Civic Guard 1922 (Garda Siochana),
    388–9, 392, 428, 433
Clan na Gael, x, 71
Clancy, Joseph, 41, 123
Clancy, Peadar, 106, 143, 200, 201,
    202, 296
Clann na hEireann, 445
Clare, county, 11, 34, 41, 44,
    125, 130, 136, 149, 151,
    275, 337
Clare Brigade, IV 41, 255 West 33,
    122, 183, 187, 320
    Mid, 44, 236–8, 260–61

East, 41, 109, 123, 183, 257–8,
    259, 301, 320
Clarence Hotel, Dublin, 409
Clark, Sir Ernest (Under Secretary,
    Belfast 1920), 180, 226
Clarke, Basil, 298
Clarke, Kathleen, 47, 170
Clarke, Thomas, xv, xvi
Clemenceau, Georges, 68
Clogagh company IV, 88–9
Clonakilty, Co. Cork, 309, 402
Clonbannin, Co. Cork, 242–3
Clones, 354, 379
Clonmel, Co. Tipperary, 364, 447
Clonmult, Co. Cork, 227, 241
Clune, Conor, 202
Clune, Patrick Joseph (Archbishop of
    Perth), 223–4, 304
Cohalan, Daniel, 71, 72, 91
Cohalan, Daniel (Bishop of Cork),
    195, 270–72, 358
collective punishments, 163, 227,
    288
Colley, Harry, 203
Collins, Con, 23, 41, 92
Collins, Michael, 16, 17, 35, 56, 63,
    71, 72, 80, 81–3, 85, 96, 106,
    107, 126, 184, 194, 196, 208,
    223, 230, 231, 232–3, 234,
    251, 258, 259, 280, 286, 287,
    292, 299, 302, 304, 306, 308,
    309, 311, 312, 315, 319, 326,
    344, 358, 359, 360, 385, 387,
    388, 389, 397, 398, 402,
    404, 420, 421, 422, 426,
    427, 431, 432–3, 434–5,
    441, 449, 455, **459**
    acting president DE, 224
    and North, 177, 179, 284, 377–9,
    380, 381, 382
    Anglo-Irish Treaty negotiations,
    332, 336, 337, 339, 341–2, 344

Chairman of Provisional Government, 380, 386, 396, 405–7
Commander-in-Chief, 420, 421, 423–4, 428, 432
Director of Organisation IV, 6, 36–7, 182, 184, 198–9
Director of Information (Intelligence) IV, 189–92, 201, 202, 206, 207, 209, 326–7
feud with Brugha, 86, 87, 326–8
free state constitution, 399–402, 404, 405
Minister for Finance, 84, 85–6, 90–93, 321–2, 323, 324, 325, 386
President of IRB, xi, 87, 334, 367–8, 369
Treaty debate, 348, 354, 355, 356, 357, 368, 369, 384
Collinstown aerodrome, Co. Dublin, 105
Colonial Office, London, 378
Connachtman, 358
Congested Districts Board, 26, 128
Connolly Patrick, 326
Connolly, James, xi, xiv, xv, 19, 410
Connolly, Nora, 144, 332
Connolly, Sean, 293
conscription, 6, 11, 13, 14, 18, 30, 41, 42, 43, 48, 50, 56, 59, 75, 76, 77
constitutionalism, xiii
Cookstown, Co. Tyrone, 174
Coolavokig, Co. Cork, 106, 241–2
Cooney, Andy, 295
Cope, Andrew (Assistant Under Secretary, Dublin Castle), 138, 158, 163, 167, 304, 306, 331, 407, 408
Cork, county, 30, 37, 63, 108, 136, 147, 156, 218, 274, 280, 285, 298, 337, 375

Cork Brigade, IV 37–8, 39, 44, 46, 50, 81
Cork city, 195, 218, 270, 279, 309, 337, 350, 403, 413, 420
Cork County Club, 175
Cork Examiner, 91, 272
Cork gaol, 194
Cork No. 1 (Mid-Cork) Brigade IV, 51, 106, 108, 109–10, 156, 157, 179, 183, 193, 239, 240, 241, 260, 263, 265, 266, 268, 272, 273, 300, 372, 374, 382, 420
Cork No. 2 (North Cork) Brigade IV, 38, 105, 150, 183, 242, 259, 262–3, 279, 289, 290, 294
Cork No. 3 (West Cork) Brigade IV, 41, 106, 210, 241, 245, 260, 263, 266, 321
Corkery, Daniel, 285, 350
Cosgrave, William T., 24, 84, 120, 121, 123, 235, 236, 324, 332, 350, 381, 386, 426, 433, 434, 436–7, 445, 450, 453, **459**
Coughlan, F. X., 205
Council of Ireland, 141
Counter-state, 25, 27, 83–6, 90
Crake, Lt Col, 211
Craig, Sir James, 176, 306
Craig–Collins pacts, 377–9, 381
Crawford, Frederick, 179
creameries, cooperative, 166, 288
Crimes Act (Criminal Law and Procedure Act 1887), 151
Croke Park GAA stadium, Dublin, 35, 201, 208
Crossbarry, Co. Cork, 245
Crossmaglen, Co. Armagh, 280
Crozier, Brigadier Frank, 288
Crummey, Frank, 381
Culhane, Seán, 179
Cullen, Tom, 190, 202
Cumann na dTeachtaire, 47

Cumann na mBan, 15, 24, 30, 47–52, 61, 67, 170, 250, 256, 258, 282, 313, 408
  Convention 1918, 49, 52; 1921 52
  Executive, 51
  election work, 61, 62
  Treaty, 363–4
Cumann na Poblachta, 360–61
Cumming, Colonel Hanway, 242–4
Curragh camp, 388, 393, 417
Curragh mutiny 1914, xiv
Czira, Sidney, 33

Dáil Eireann, 64–6, 67, 69, 73, 76, 78, 79, 83, 90, 91, 96, 99, 120, 121, 122, 123, 124, 146, 149, 172, 176–7, 195, 231, 235, 261, 267, 268, 273–4, 285, 300, 304, 333, 337, 348, 349, 350, 360, 380, 384, 385, 386, 390, 391, 392, 398, 407, 431, 436
  and army, 86–9, 181, 231–2, 299, 329, 390, 391–2
  Commission of Inquiry into Resources and Industries, 93
  Constructive Work of Dail Eireann, 94, 324
  Department of Defence, 287
  Department of Home Affairs, 267, 268, 366, 435
  Department of Local Government, 120, 177, 326, 366
  Department of Propaganda (Ministry of Publicity), 94–6, 123–4, 130, 299–300, 324, 366
  emigration policy, 268
  Republican courts, 90, 124–30, 134, 266–7, 337–9, 435–6
  Republican loan, 71–2, 90–92, 96, 99
  Republican police, 128, 131–4, 149, 267–70

Ministry, 84–5, 86, 91, 120, 126, 129, 203, 283, 299, 307, 321–2, 324, 377, 386, 434
  Ministry of Fine Arts, 324
  proclaimed illegal, 93, 99, 100–101, 109, 141
  Treaty debate, 350–52, 360
  second Dáil, 285, 286–7, 333, 362, 434, 439, 440
Daily Mail, 156, 168
Daily News, 85, 129, 166, 168, 170, 195
Daily Telegraph, 218
Dalton, Charlie, 205, 292, 310, 365
Dalton, Emmet, 290, 315, 365, 393, 406, 407, 421–2, 433
Daly, Charlie, 382
Daly, Ned, 397
Daly, Paddy, 416
Davern, Mick, 80
Davitt, Michael, xiii
Deasy, Liam, 19, 41, 44, 46, 89, 106, 109, 214, 241, 403, 414, 415, 416, 444
Deasy, Patrick, 213, 215
De Blacam, Aodh, 15, 56, 274
Defence of the Realm Act, 15, 100, 101, 136, 142, 151, 227
  Special Military Areas, 100, 151
Declaration of Independence 1919, 66, 67
Democratic Programme 1919, 66, 144
Derby, Earl of, 305
Derrig, Tom, 285, 440
Derry battalion IV, 173
'Derry program', 173
Desmond, Shaw, 48
De Valera, Eamon, 5, 6, 13, 20, 24, 27, 29, 44, 52, 53, 58, 67, 70, 82–4, 87, 90, 96, 126, 172, 230, 255, 268, 284, 285, 299, 309, 312, 316, 327, 333, 337, 349,

350, 356, 358, 360, 367, 377,
384, 385, 386, 392, 398, 402,
409, 431, 433–4, 438, 441, 444,
446, 455, **459**
and republic, 53, 231, 284, 286,
305, 333, 335–6, 340, 341,
342–3, 347, 349
Anglo-Irish Treaty negotiations,
304–8, 331–7, 340, 341, 342,
343, 347–8
mission to USA, 70–72
as premier, 84, 126, 231–3, 272–3,
274–5, 286, 291–2, 321, 324,
327–8, 330, 332, 333, 334, 336,
384
opposes Treaty, 349, 350, 351,
356, 359, 360–61, 409–10
Relations with church, 97, 272–3
return from USA, 96, 97, 230–32,
277, 304
De Vere Hunt, Ada, 375
Devitt, Martin, 44
Devlin, Joseph, 32, 58, 172,
219, 223
Devoy, John, 71
Dillon, John, 16, 17, 172, **459**
Dingle peninsula, 295
Disposals Board, 153
Doherty, Brighid, 251
Donnelly, Simon, 204, 246, 255, 267,
268–9, 387
Dorr, James, 88
Dowling, Joseph, 16
Dowling, Sean, 328, 446
Drimoleague, Co. Cork, 241
Dripsey, Co. Cork, 239
Drishanebeg, Co. Cork, 241
Dublin Brigade IV
(1st), 38, 39, 44, 60, 120, 131, 143,
183, 188, 196, 199, 203, 206,
207, 208, 246–9, 291–2, 296,
314, 320, 394, 408
(2nd), 411
Active Service Unit, 247–8, 264,
394
2nd battalion, 292
5th Battalion, 188
Dublin Castle, 3, 8, 9, 11, 16, 107,
138, 153, 190, 197, 202, 223
Dublin city, xiv, 3, 5, 7, 11, 13, 19, 20,
36, 37, 43, 49, 59, 61, 66, 69,
72, 80, 81, 82, 87, 91, 93, 136,
252–3, 258, 267, 393, 403,
408–11, 414
Baggot Street Bridge, 415
Charlemont Bridge, 248
Church Street, 196
Custom House, 235, 236, 291–2,
305, 306, 365
Earlsfort Terrace, 364
Four Courts, 369, 388, 397, 405,
407, 408–9, 413, 414, 415,
425, 431
Grand Canal, 248
Great Brunswick Street, 259
Drumcondra, 248
Mespil Road, 248, 251
Mount Street Bridge, 82
North King Street, 203
O'Connell Street, 408, 410
Ormond Quay, 442
Parnell square, 190
Parnell street, 199
Phoenix Park, 107
Richmond Street, 248
Royal Canal, 248
St Stephen's Green, 433
South Dublin Union, 120
Upper Pembroke Street, 205, 206
Viceregal Lodge, 399
Dublin county, 38
Dublin Corporation, 68, 120, 235
Donegal, county, 259, 268, 281,
338, 384

Dublin Guards, 394, 443
Dublin Mansion House, 11, 13, 148, 307, 347
Dublin Metropolitan Police, 7, 31, 93, 100, 309, 387, 388, 389
    G Division, 25, 107, 190, 191, 199, 207
Dublin University, 285
Duff, Douglas, 161
Duggan, Edmund (Eamonn), 189, 307, 308, 347, 386
dugouts, 40, 254, 297, 443
Dundalk, 431
Dundalk Property Owners' Association, 179
Dundrum, Co. Tipperary, 46, 146
Dungannon Clubs, xii
Dunmanway, Co. Cork, 212, 219
Dunraven, Lord, 129
Duke, Henry (Chief Secretary for Ireland), 9–10

East Clare Brigade IV, 123
Easter rebellion 1916, xv–xvi, 4, 5, 7, 22, 36, 63, 82
electoral pact 1922, 398, 399–400, 402
Elphin, Co. Roscommon, 27
Ellis, John, 197
Elphin, Bishop of, 359
Emmet, Robert, 32, 91
Ennis, Co. Clare, 333
Ennis, Major General Tom, 406
Ennistymon, Co. Clare, 74, 164, 165, 187
external association, 335–6, 342, 349, 356
    neutrality see also
Eyeries, Co. Cork, 74

Farmers' Union, 444
Fenians see Irish Republican Brotherhood

Fenit, Co. Kerry, 416
Fermanagh, county, 61
Fermanagh Vigilance organization, 181
Fermoy, Co. Cork, 105–6, 164, 290, 416
Fethard, 42
Fianna Eireann, 23, 250, 317
Fianna Fáil, 455
Figgis, Darrell, 24, 33, 55, 58, 63, 64, 66, 67, 82, 93, 399, **460**
Fingal Brigade, IV 105, 131
Fintan Lalor, James, xii
Fisher, Sir Warren, 138, 139, 141, 152, 226, 229
FitzAlan, Viscount, 305, 336
FitzGerald, Desmond, 94–5, 177, 299, 324
Fitzpatrick, Thomas, 45, 173, 174, 376
Flanagan, Paddy, 205, 247
Fogarty, Bishop Michael, 304, 358
Forbes Patterson, William, 172–3
Forde, Liam, 325, 394
Forde, Sean (Tomas O Maoleoin), 119
Foreign Office, 273
Foster, R. F., 450
Four Courts garrison, 442
Fourmilewater, Co. Waterford, 23
Freeman's Journal, 94, 298, 358, 360, 397
French, Field-Marshal Viscount (Lord Lieutenant of Ireland), 11, 16, 18, 64, 99, 100–104, 107, 109, 135, 137, 140, 143, 144, 173, 197, 217, 218, 305
Frenchpark, Co. Roscommon, 160
Friends of Irish Freedom (New York), 71, 90
Frongoch internment camp, 57, 191
Furlong, Matt, 199–200

Gaelic Athletic Association, xiii
Gaelic League, xii, xv, 35, 54, 31, 445
    proclaimed illegal, 101

Gallagher, Frank, 24, 143, 299

Galway, county, 25, 27, 32, 104, 108, 125, 149, 164, 217, 229

Galway Brigade, IV 292, 320

Garda Siochana, 265

Garibaldi, Giuseppe, xiii

Gavan Duffy, George, 69, 82, 347, 349, 436, 441–2

Gaynor, Fr Patrick, 32, 133–4

Geddes, Eric, 147

General Council of County Councils, 122

general elections
1918, ix, 58–63
1921, 282–7
1922, 397–8, 402–3

George V, King, 301, 303, 306

'German Plot' 1918, 15–17, 58, 190

Gilmartin, Archbishop Thomas, 96–7

Ginnell, Laurence, 24, 26–7, 84, 436, **460**

Glasnevin cemetery, 5

Gleeson, Dan, 119

Gormanstown, Co. Dublin, 162, 163

Gough, Gen Sir Hubert, 218

Government of Ireland Act 1920, 120, 140–41, 177, 181, 223, 283, 285, 303, 385, 386

Grattan, Henry, 3

Gray, David, 370

Great Northern Railway, 146, 178

Great Southern and Western Railway, 148

Greaves, Desmond, 440

Greenwood, Sir Hamar (Chief Secretary for Ireland), 137, 142, 166–7, 168, 180, 217, 223, 225, 228, 229

Gregory, Augusta, Lady, 171, 195

Gresham Hotel, Dublin, 201, 396, 409, 410

Griffith, Arthur, xii–xiii, 5, 6, 17, 20, 24, 33, 53, 58, 64, 66, 67, 68–9, 83, 84, 91, 92, 93, 94, 96, 120, 126, 130, 177, 194, 196, 199, 208, 209, 223, 224, 231, 232, 267, 304, 306, 307, 324, 332, 344, 347, 348–9, 357, 360, 381, 397–8, 399, 404, 407, 422, **460**
Acting President, 199, 208
Anglo-Irish Treaty negotiations, 332, 336, 340, 341
President of Dáil 1922, 385, 386, 391–2, 395–6, 397, 406, 426–7, 435

guerrilla warfare, 39, 40, 52, 73, 78, 79, 83, 90, 104, 106, 109, 113–17, 134, 182, 185, 187–8, 230, 251, 253, 262, 279, 298, 301, 302, 408, 410, 416, 417–18, 420, 422, 425, 429

Guevara, Ernesto (Che), 113

Gwynn, Stephen, 129

Hacket Pain, Brigadier, 181

Hales, Seán, 46, 285, 351, 355, 442

Hales, Tom, 46, 375

Hammam Hotel, Dublin, 408, 410

Hargarden, Patrick, 131

Hart, Peter, 370–73, 452

Harte, Auxiliary Cadet, 219

Harty, Archbishop John, 97

Hassan, Fr John, 382

Hayes, Michael, 64

Healy, T. M., 15, 306

'hedge fighting', 39, 78

Henderson, Frank, 367

Henderson, Leo, 178, 406

Heuston, Sean, 317

Higgins, Michael, 42

Higginson, Colonel, 312

Hobson, Bulmer, xii, 83, 317
Hogan, Dan, 379
Hogan, J. J., 80–81
Hollyford, Co. Tipperary, 118
Home Office, 101, 341
Home Rule, xvi, 3–4, 10, 63, 98,
    99–100, 103, 140, 142, 171,
    173, 339, 454
  Bills (1886, 1893), ix, xii
  Act (1914), 99
  Dominion status, 151, 308, 343, 347
  see also Government of Ireland
    Act 1920
Horgan, John J., 121
House of Commons, Westminster,
    166, 386
House of Lords, ix, xiii, 289
Howth gunrunning, 1914, 317
Humphreys, Sheila, 47, 73, 85, 419
Hunt, [first name to come] (DI RIC),
    101, 105, 108
Hurley, Charlie, 44, 46, 245
Hyde, Douglas, xiii
Hynes, Frank, 37–8, 46

idealism, 21, 32, 52, 77, 89, 199,
    353–5, 357, 413, 427
Imperial Hotel, Killarney, 453
industrial unrest, 100
industrial action, xiv, 8–9, 15, 100,
    138, 143, 144–9, 173
intelligence services
  Irish Volunteers, 188–93, 201–7
  British, 13–16, 23, 52, 135, 136–7,
    191–2, 208, 209
Irish administration, 7, 8, 99
  see also Dublin Castle; Irish
    Executive
Irish Bulletin, 95–6, 124, 187, 298,
    299, 300, 309, 324
Irish Citizen Army, xiv, 47
Irish Command, 145, 288

Record of the Rebellion in
    Ireland, 371
  see also British army
Irish Convention 1917–18, 4
Irish courts system, 125–6
Irish Executive, 208
Irish Film Company, 93
Irish Food Council, 25
Irish Free State, 347, 355, 393, 412,
    424, 436, 443, 449
  Constitution (1922), 398–402, 454
    (1937) 455
  Executive Council, 434
  Home Affairs Ministry, 426
  policing, 386–9, 427
Irish Free State (Agreement) Act 1922,
    386, 397
Irish Independent, 94, 298
Irish-Ireland movement, 43
Irish Labour Party and TUC, 58–60,
    121, 144, 148, 175, 218–19,
    285–6, 403, 443
  Munitions of War Fund, 145, 146
Irish National Defence Fund, 14
Irish Parliamentary Party (United Irish
    League), ix, xvi, 4, 24, 285,
    286, 404
Irish Press, 71
Irish Republic, 47, 48, 52, 63, 64,
    66, 71, 76, 120, 124, 217,
    333, 384, 390, 431, 441,
    447, 449, 450
Irish Republican Army, 51, 84, 89,
    123, 133, 146, 150, 175, 181–2,
    189, 198, 199, 200, 202, 206,
    211, 212, 214, 229, 231–2,
    240–1, 246, 253, 258–60,
    262–4, 265, 267, 270, 274,
    276, 283, 285, 289, 290, 294,
    304, 310–12, 315–7, 319,
    325–6, 350–1, 353, 355, 358,
    359, 362, 366, 367, 369–75,

377, 379, 380–4, 387, 390,
392, 394, 399, 403–4, 405,
406, 413, 415–9, 421, 422,
430, 431, 439, 441, 442, 443,
445–7
IRA Convention 1922, 403
IRA Executive 1922, 392, 394,
397, 402, 404, 406, 413, 431,
438, 439, 441, 446
see also Irish Volunteers
Irish Republican Brotherhood, x–xi,
xiv, xvi, 24, 25, 44–6, 53, 57,
58, 70, 87, 328, 358, 362,
367–9, 382
Irish Self-Determination League of
Great Britain, 69
Irish Socialist Republican Party, xi
Irish Times, 121, 123, 129, 146, 451
Irish Trades Union Council,
14–15, 58
Irish Transport and General Workers'
Union, 144–5
Irish tricolour flag, 5, 31–3
Irish Volunteer, 40
Irish Volunteers, xiv–xv, 5, 6, 14, 28,
29, 31, 32, 33–46, 57, 73–82,
100, 113–19, 122, 128, 131,
136, 179–80, 223, 229–32, 285,
299, 317, 370, 373–4, 430–31,
449, 453
active service units ('flying
columns'), 109, 183–4, 238–9,
242, 292
arms, 104, 183, 316–17
Army Convention 1922, 362, 380,
382, 390, 391–2
battalions 44–6
brigades, 37–8
divisions, 275–80
intelligence, 188–92, 201, 238,
294, 326, 351
1st Eastern Division, 417

2nd Eastern Division, 406, 437
1st Midland Division, 418
1st Southern Division, 265, 273–4,
279, 320, 323, 350, 382, 392,
415, 419, 420, 446
2nd Southern Division, 44, 294–5,
393–4, 414, 437
3rd Southern Division, 313, 417
1st Northern Division, 281
2nd Northern Division, 278,
382, 383
3rd Northern Division, 282, 376,
377, 383
4th Northern Division, 281,
329, 431
5th Northern Division, 329,
379, 432
1st Western Division, 417
2nd Western Division, 418
3rd Western Division, 418
engineering department, 257
engineering sections, 77–8, 188
execution of spies and
informers, 262–6
Executive, 28, 75, 81–2, 87, 329,
390 [cf also IRA Executive]
General Headquarters, (GHQ) 17,
37, 38, 39, 60, 75, 78, 79, 83,
85, 88, 105, 106–7, 108, 114,
131, 132, 160, 165, 182, 184,
185, 186, 191, 192, 230,
236, 238, 242, 249, 252–3, 255,
256–7, 261, 263, 264, 267,
275–7, 279, 281, 287, 292–3,
295, 296, 297, 300, 310–11,
321, 328, 329, 353, 355, 362,
365, 366, 380; National Army
1922 395, 396
levies, 260, 321–3, 390, 394
munitions manufacture, 199–201,
296, 314, 323, 413
'new army', 328–31

Irish Volunteers, – *cont.*
    oath of allegiance to Republic,
        86–8
    'offensive against communica-
        tions', 256 in civil war 430
    officer corps, 44–6
    organizers, 116
    political activity, 122
    social composition, 43–4
    specialist services, 188, 255, 295
    The Squad, 106, 191–2, 203, 204,
        246, 247, 290, 388, 433
    training camps, 313
    truce liaison, 311–13
Irish Volunteers, (1782) 87
Irish Women's Franchise League, 15, 47
Irish Women's International
    League, 445
Irish Women Workers' Union, 47, 49
Irish World, 252

Jeudwine, Gen. Sir Hugh, 217,
    225–6, 228
Johnson, Thomas, 11, 59, 66, 144,
    148, **460**
Johnstone, Col William Edgeworth
    (Commissioner DMP),
    104, 135
Joint IRA offensive 1922, 382–4
Jones, Thomas, 308, 343, 401

Kanturk, Co. Cork, 23
Kearney, Leopold, 69
Kearney, Peadar, 73
Kehoe, Joe, 290
Kells, 264
Kelly, Tom (Alderman, Dublin), 58, 87
Kennedy, Hugh, 401
Kenure, John, 453
Kerry, county, 32, 33, 34, 116, 127,
    136, 218, 274, 280, 295, 320,
    363, 443

Kerry No. 1 Brigade IV, 295–6
    No. 2 Brigade, 104, 242, 264,
        295, 321
Kerryman, 250
Kettle, Thomas, 5, 165, 262, 365
Kiernan, Kitty, 356
Kilkenny, 415, 429
Kilkenny, county, 120, 218, 253–4,
    293, 294, 416
Kilkenny Brigade IV, 36
Killala, Bishop of, 359
Killaloe, Bishop of, 358
Killarney, Co. Kerry, 242, 264, 361,
    443, 453
Kilmallock, Co. Limerick, 119, 416
Kilmainham gaol, 412
Kilmaiham hospital, 308, 407
Kilmichael, Co. Cork, 210–15, 258
Kilmore, Co. Roscommon, 88
Kilmurry, Co. Cork, 109
Kilroy, Michael, 315
Kiltartan, Co. Galway, 169
Kilterna, Co. Galway, 186
King's Bench (Irish High Court), 227
Kingston, T. J., 265
Kingstown (Dun Laoghaire), 144
Kippagh, Co. Cork, 275
Knocklong, co. Tipperary, 80, 108
Knocknagoshel, Co. Kerry, 443
Ku Klux Klan, 156
Kut, siege of, 210

Labour Party (UK), ix, 141, 173, 219
Lacey, Dinny, 187, 294, 416, 446
Lahinch, Co. Clare, 165, 187
land question, ix, 22, 94, 25–9,
    127–9, 265
language question, 54
Land League, ix, xiii, 26, 28, 192
Land War, 25, 29, 124, 155
Langford, Riobard, 110
Lankford, Siobhan, 251

Lappinduff mountain, 282
Larne, Co. Down, 383
Lawlor, John, 264
Lawlor, Tony, 416, 429
Lawrence, T. E., 113, 230, 239
Leabhar na mBan, 50
Leahy, Mick, 108
League of Nations, 68
League of Women Delegates, 47
Lehane, James, 211
Lehane, Sean, 382
Leitrim, county, 39, 49, 51, 149, 158, 250, 293
Leitrim Brigade, IV 258
Lemass, Sean, 411, 415
liaison officers *see* Truce
Liberal Party, ix, 100
Liberty League, 20
Limerick IV, 263
    East Limerick Brigade, 266
    Mid-Limerick Brigade, 320, 325, 394
Limerick, city, 75, 100, 118, 217, 394–6, 415, 416, 422, 430, 431
Limerick, county, 30, 34, 91, 108, 136, 151, 156, 218, 263, 275, 337
Limerick Soviet, 100
Limerick, treaty of, 355
Lincoln gaol, 82
Lindsay, Mary, 240, 263, 300
Lisburn, Co. Down, 167, 178, 179
List, Friedrich, 93
Listowel, Co. Kerry, 158, 165
Lixnaw, 42
Lloyd George, David, xvi, 4, 7, 10, 40, 99, 102, 107, 153, 155, 163, 168, 208, 209, 219, 223, 224, 227, 301, 303, 304, 307, 310, 331, 333, 335, 336, 339, 340, 341, 342, 343, 349, 360, 400, 401–2, 405, 454

Local Government Board (UK), 121, 122, 235
local elections 1920, 119–23
Logue, Cardinal Michael (Primate of Ireland), 13–14, 97, 98, 272, 305, 306, 358
London Metropolitan Police, 138
Londonderry city (see also Derry city), 173
Londonderry, county, 115
Longford, county, 14, 42, 136, 182, 292, 337
Longford Brigade IV, 84, 182, North 244
Long, Walter, 10, 15, 16, 100, 102, 138
Lordan, John, 214
Loughnane, Harry, 170, 171
Louth, county, 123, 271
Louth Brigade IV, 123
Lucas, Brig Gen Cuthbert, 150–51
Luckie, Thomas, 280
Lyons, F. S. L., 371, 450
Lynch, Arthur, 40
Lynch, Diarmuid, 25, 70
Lynch, Liam, 54, 74, 81, 86, 105, 132, 150, 193, 244, 255, 261, 272, 273, 295, 296, 320, 321, 322–3, 354–5, 367, 368, 369, 382, 390, 391–2, 392, 396, 403, 409, 412, 413, 415, 416, 418, 419, 420, 431, 432, 434, 437, 439, 440, 441, 446–7, 449, **460**
Lynd, Robert, 85, 195
Lynn, Kathleen, 47

Macardle, Dorothy, 262, 331, 336, 357, 364, 403, 406, 443
MacBride, John, 113
MacBride, Sean, 403
MacBride, Joseph, 285
McCartan, Patrick, 70, 71
McConaill, Michael, 377

McCormack, Patrick, 75
McCormack, Captain, 205–6
McCorley, Roger, 39, 45, 54, 174–5, 179, 180, 376, 377, 380
Mac Curtain, Tomás, 37–8, 50, 107, 108, 109–10, 152, 179, 193, 270, 271, **461**
MacDermott, Sean, xv
McDonald, Rev Professor Walter, 98
McDonnell, Andy, 411
MacDonnell, Bob, 383
McDonnell, Kathleen Keyes, 375
McDonnell, Mick b, 191, 192
MacEoin (McKeon), Sean, 89, 182, 245, 290–91, 292, 312, 329, 334, 351, 353, 389, 395, 416, 421, 422, 429, 430, **461**
MacEntee, Sean, 87, 172, 176, 376, 378, **461**
McGarrity, Joseph, 71, 332, 337, 348, 359, 438–9, 441, 446
McGarry, Sean, 82, 107
McGrath, Frank, 119
machine guns, 242, 243, 423, 429
McHugh, Michael, 285
McHugh, Patrick, 200, 296, 413
McKee, Dick, 106, 190, 191, 196, 202, 203, 246
McKelvey, Joe, 354, 377, 392, 404, 409, 415
McKenna, Fr Michael, 28, 133–4
McKenna, Patrick b, 42
McKenna, Seamus, 45, 174, 180, 282, 368
MacLysaght, Edward, 202
McMahon family, killing of, 380–81
MacMahon, Sir James (Under Secretary, Dublin Castle), 138, 305
McMahon, Mick, 122
MacMahon, Sean, 233

MacNeill, Eoin, 19, 22, 24, 36, 84, 91, 171, 172, 173, **461**
Macpherson, Ian (Chief Secretary for Ireland), 99, 100, 101, 107
Macready, General Sir Nevil (GOC-in-C Irish Command), 137–9, 141, 144, 147, 150, 153–4, 155, 161, 162, 163, 167, 180, 181, 197, 209, 211, 217, 218, 219, 224, 225, 226, 227, 228, 245, 248, 283, 289, 297, 298, 301, 302, 308, 310, 337, 405, 407
Macroom, Co. Cork, 210, 211, 212, 242, 285
MacSwiney, Mary, 30, 252, 332, 334–5, 357–8, 363, 364, 368
MacSwiney, Terence, 55, 57, 92, 108, 110, 193–6, 226, 261, 271, 353, **461**
Maguire, Tom, 285, 293, 315, 359, 368, 445
Mahon, General Bryan (GOC Irish Command), 5, 6, 8–9
Mallow, Co. Cork, 243, 414
Manchester Guardian, 85, 99, 129, 161, 166
Markievicz, Constance, Countess, 15, 47, 60, 64, 84, 177, 317, 364, 387, 409, 410, **462**
martial law, 147, 153, 163, 168, 217–18, 223, 224, 225, 226–9, 289, 297, 302–3, 328, 437
Martial Law Area, 218, 227, 229, 243, 252, 288, 297, 311
Martin, Hugh, 166, 168, 169, 170
Maxwell, General Sir John, xvi, 9, 225
Maynooth, 98
Mayo, county, 16, 115, 125, 149, 285, 363
Mayo Brigade IV, South, 183, 293
Mayo County Council, 130

Mayobridge, Co. Down, 115
Mazzini, Guiseppe, xii, 453
Meath, county, 45, 123, 179, 319
Mee, Jeremiah, 27, 158
Mellows, Liam, 70–71, 355, 390, 391, 392, 393, 403, 409, 412, 415, 439, 440, 441, **462**
Mernin, Lily, 191, 251
Mesopotamia, 78, 210
Message to the Free Nations of the World 1919, 66
Midleton, Co. Cork, 228
Midleton, Earl of, 11, 229, 305, 306–8, 309, 315
Military Courts of Inquiry in Lieu of Inquest on Civilians, 152, 452–3
Military Service Act 1918, 7, 10, 13
    see also conscription
Millstreet, Co. Cork, 132
Milroy, Seán, 33, 82
Miltown Malbay, Co. Clare, 44, 165, 187
mines, 75, 77, 199, 213, 243–4, 245, 294, 296, 411
Mitchel, John, xii
Mitchell, Walter, 413–14
Moloney, Con, 393, 417, 419
Molony, Helena, 47
Monaghan, county, 35, 131, 149, 178, 278, 376
Monaghan, Philip, 123
Monaghan Brigade IV, 35
Monreal, Co. Clare, 237
Montagu, Edwin, 217
Monteagle, Lord, 129
Morrissey, Paddy, 293
Mountjoy gaol, 5, 194, 290–91, 439
    Republican hunger strike 1920, 142–3
Moy Hotel, Ballina, Co. Mayo, 169
Moylan, Seán, 38, 39, 40, 42, 44, 55–6, 74, 150, 241, 243–4, 279,

280, 285, 290, 318, 319, 359, 390, 403, 409
Mulcahy, Richard, 6, 17, 37, 76, 106, 107, 109, 114, 179, 182, 184, 188, 199, 203, 204, 208, 223, 231, 236, 237, 257, 261, 263, 267, 273, 275–6, 277, 278, 279, 280, 282, 287, 289, 290, 291, 293, 295, 296–7, 298, 300, 312, 313, 315, 316, 318, 320, 321, 322, 323, 325, 326, 327, 329, 330, 351–2, 363, 367, 369, 381, 388, 390, 391, 392, 394, 415, 416, **462**
military professionalization, 76, 109, 182, 186, 231, 255, 275, 295, 390
military strategy, 37, 109, 114, 184, 236, 275–80, 281, 313, 353
Minister for Defence 1922–3, 421, 427, 431, 433, 434, 435, 436, 437, 442, 443
Mulhern, Edward (Bishop of Dromore), 273
munitions embargo, 144–8, 178
Munster, 91, 150, 155, 159, 162, 175, 244, 257, 361, 373, 403, 414
'Munster Republic' 1922, 420–21
Murnaghan, James, 400
Murphy, Dick, 179
Murphy, Fintan, 82, 93, 183, 312, 313, 326
Murphy, Gerard, 374–6
Murphy, Mick, 374
Musgrace Street barracks, Belfast, 383

Naas barracks, 393
nationalism, xv, xvi 53–6, 76
    and Catholicism, 56–7
Nationality, 94

National Arbitration Courts
Committee, 125
National Army (Free State), 388, 391,
394, 406, 407, 415, 419,
422–3, 427, 429, 430,
437–8, 442–3
Army Council, 437
Eastern Command, 437
GHQ, 421
South-Western Command, 422
Western Command, 429
National Co-operative Mortgage
Bank, 94
National Guard, 387, 426
National Labour Conference
1920, 147–8
national self-determination, 3, 67
National Union of Railwaymen, 145
Neenan, Connie, 157, 272
Neutral IRA, 445
neutrality, 335, 342, 349, 455
New Ireland, 65, 66
New Statesman, 168, 195
New York Times, 150
New Zealand, 335
Newry Brigade IV, 281
Newtownbarry, Co. Wexford, 75
Neylon, Tosser, 237
Northcliffe, Baron, 94
Northern Ireland, 180, 347–8, 405–6
Special Powers Act 1922, 381
Northern Ireland Act 1949, 455
Northen Parliament (GIA 1920), 284,
286, 303, 306, 376, 381

O'Brien, Art, 56, 69, 299, 342, 378
O'Brien, Paddy, 213, 243, 244, 409,
412, 415
O'Brien, William, 53, 58–9, 144, **462–3**
Observer newspaper, 129, 168
O'Callaghan, Kathleen, 363
O'Connell, Daniel, 54, 90

O'Connell, J. J. (Ginger), 34, 39, 77,
255, 329, 393, 394, 395, 396,
406, 421
O'Connor, Art, 127
O'Connor, Batt, 351, 363, 419
O'Connor, Fr Dominic, 272
O'Connor, Frank, 353, 449, 451
O'Connor, Joseph, 39, 43, 44, 60, 83,
246, 247
O'Connor, Rory, 188, 356, 389, 391,
395, 396–7, 397, 403, 405, 409,
412, 415
O'Connor, T. P., 143
O'Daly, P. J., 131
O'Daly, Paddy, 394
O'Dempsey, T. J., 262
O'Doherty, Hugh, 173
O'Doherty, Bishop Thomas, 173
O'Donnell, Peadar, 412, 413
O'Donoghue, Florrie, 44, 46, 54, 81,
86, 88, 189, 193, 244, 272, 369,
375, 390, 391, 397, 403, 404,
413, 417, 445
O'Donoghue, Josephine (Brown), 375
O'Duffy, Eimar, 261
O'Duffy, Eoin, 35, 114, 178, 257, 278,
287, 298, 315, 320, 329–30,
351, 354, 367, 380, 381, 394,
396, 416, 421, 422, 424, 432,
433, **463**
O'Dwyer, Eamon, 30, 45, 125,
198–9, 230
O'Dwyer, George, 254
Offaly, county, 46, 264
Offaly No. 2 Brigade IV, 255
O'Farrelly, Agnes, 15, 49
O'Flanagan, Fr Michael, 12, 24, 58,
63, 65, 304, 451
O'Gorman, Patrick, 266
O'Hegarty, Diarmuid, 83–4, 93, 106,
128, 272, 276–7, 286, 299, 325,
334, 367

O'Hegarty, P. S., 57, 63, 362, 363, 445
O'Hegarty, Seán, 110, 156, 193, 241–2, 279, 285, 350, 403, 445
O'Higgins, Brian, 125
O'Higgins, Kevin, 21, 63, 121–2, 235, 381, 386, 424–5, 433, 437, 442, 445, 450, 451, 453, **463**
O'Keeffe, Paidin, 284
O'Kelly, J. J., 324, 441
O'Kelly, Seán T., 33, 64, 66, 68, 69, **463**
O'Leary, Jackie, 239–40
O'Leary, John, x
O'Leary, Thomas, 46
Omagh, Co. Tyrone, 31, 281
O'Malley, Ernie, 44, 46, 52–3, 73, 74, 113, 133, 184, 231, 257, 313, 315–16, 317, 320, 364, 374, 393, 395, 408, 409, 410, 412, 413, 414, 415, 417, 418–19, 439, 440, 441, **463–4**
   IV GHQ organizer, 106, 114–15, 116–19, 186, 253–4
   OC 2nd SD, 279–80, 287, 294, 298
O'Mullane, Brighid, 30, 49, 50
O Murthile, Seán, 106, 367, 368
O'Neill, Joseph, 374
O'Neill, Michael, 372
O'Neill, Sean, 45
O'Rahilly, Alfred, 400
'Orders of Frightfulness', 442
O'Shannon, Cathal, 144, 148
O'Shiel, Kevin, 12, 23, 31, 61, 63, 65, 91–2, 127, 130, 389
O'Sullivan, Gearoid, 106, 254, 315, 319, 367, 421
O'Sullivan, Seán, 73, 89
O'Rahilly, Michael, 31
Oriel House, Dublin (Criminal Investigation Department), 388
Ox Mountains, Co. Sligo, 418

Pakenham, Frank (Earl of Longford), 340, 341, 343
Paris Peace Conference 1919, 67–8
Parliament Act 1910, xiii
Parnell, Charles Stewart, ix, 63, 71, 90
partition, 141, 283, 285, 340, 347, 354, 368, 377, 451, 454–5
Passage East, Co. Cork, 320
Passage West, Co. Cork, 416
Pearse, Patrick, xv, 4, 19, 22, 37, 91
Peel, Sir Robert, 8
Peerless armoured cars, 153
People's Peace League, 445
Pilkington, Liam (Billy), 285, 315, 430
pikes and pike drill, 41–2
Plaza Hotel, Dublin, 36
Plunkett, George Noble, Count, 19–20, 23, 47, 65, 69, 324
Plunkett, Horace, 423
Plunkett, Joseph, 56
Polberg, 144
Portmagee, Co. Kerry, 160
Portobello barracks, Dublin, 304, 421
Potter, Gilbert (DI RIC), 453
Power, George, 105, 150, 294
Prescott Decie, Brigadier Cyril (RIC Divisional Commisioner, Munster), 155–6, 162, 218
press and public opinion, 358–9
Price, Eamon, 287
Price, Major Ivon, 16
Proclamation of the Irish Republic 1916, 19
Programme of Democratic Control, 439, 440
propaganda, 94–6, 251, 298–301, 324
proportional representation, 120–21, 403
Protestants, 452
Prout, General John T., 416, 421, 429, 446, 447

Provisional Government of the Irish Republic 1916, xv
Provisional Government (1922), 87, 359, 362, 378, 381, 382, 384, 385, 393, 394, 397, 399, 401, 404, 405, 406, 409, 412, 417, 421–5, 426, 434, 436
   Northern advisory committee, 381
   Ministry for Defence, 421
   War Council, 421, 433
Provisional IRA, 370, 374

Queen's University, Belfast, 377
Quilty, Co. Clare, 22, 28
Quinn, Ellen, 169, 171

Rabbitte, Roger, 186
railway embargo, 144–8, 178
Ranch War, 26
Rathkeale, Co. Cork, 23
Redmond, John, ix, 16, 21, 67
Redmond, William (Assistant Commissioner DMP), 104, 191
Representation of the People Act 1918, 60
reprisals, 105, 119, 161–8, 185, 202, 216, 218, 223, 227, 228–9, 231, 260, 270, 288–90, 305, 430, 433, 442
Republic of Ireland, 360
republican courts, 90, 124–30, 149, 150, 266–7, 310, 316, 337–9, 425, 435–6
republican police, 128, 131, 133, 148, 267–70, 376, 387, 420, 428
republicanism, ix, x–xi, xii, xiii, xvi, 4, 52–7, 58, 64, 76, 86–7, 172, 355, 373, 400, 403, 404, 454
Restoration of Order in Ireland Act 1920, 151–2, 153, 193, 196, 223, 227, 381
Rice, John Joe, 295

rifles, 40, 41, 183
Rineen, Co. Clare, 187, 237
Ring, Co. Waterford, 314
Riordan, Patrick, 114
Robertson, Field-Marshal Sir William, 301
Robinson, Sir Henry, 18, 43
Robinson, Seamus, 33, 34, 45, 57, 73, 74, 78–9, 106, 116, 198, 256, 287, 375, 390, 395, 409, **464**
Roiste, Liam de, 271, 285, 351
Rolls-Royce armoured cars, 153, 395, 408
Rosscarbery, Co. Cork, 265
Roscommon, county, 12, 42, 45, 49, 62, 118, 149, 156, 320
Roscommon Brigade IV
   North, 160, 183, 319
   South, 254, 262, 265
Royal Dublin Society, 388
Royal Irish Constabulary (RIC), 7–8, 17, 28, 49, 79, 103, 136–7, 139–40, 154–5, 157–9, 160–63, 216, 270, 387, 388, 389, 394
   Auxiliary Division, 140, 157–8, 168, 169, 170, 185, 198, 200, 201–2, 208, 210–11, 230, 241, 244, 249, 288–9, 292, 294, 319, 372, 394
   barracks attacked, 108–9, 114–16, 183, 281
   Black and Tans, 103–4, 148, 157–8, 163, 169–71, 217, 301, 319, 370, 394
   boycott of, 29–31, 48, 83–4, 101, 137, 160–61
   discipline, 288
   Listowel mutiny, 158–9
   militarization of, 137–40
   Weekly Summary, 161, 216
Rumpf, Erhard, 361, 362–3
Russell, George ('AE'), 379

Russell, Sean, 204, 296
Russia, 3, 70, 100
Ruttledge, P. J., 439
Ryan, John, 46
Ryan, Meda, 371–2
Ryan, Patrick, 23

St Enda's school, 91
Savage, Martin, 107, 354
Shaw, Lt Gen. Sir Frederick (GOC Irish Command), 135, 137
Sheehy Skeffington, Francis, 219
Sheehy Skeffington, Hanna, 47, 48, 67–8
Sheerin, Michael, 173
Shortt, Henry (Chief Secretary for Ireland), 11, 16, 99, 101, 102
Sinn Fèin, ix, xii, xvi, 4, 5, 11, 12, 13, 14, 15, 16, 17–25, 26–9, 30, 31–3, 37, 47, 49, 53, 54, 55, 57, 58–63, 64, 66, 67, 68, 69, 82, 83, 85, 87, 90, 91, 93, 94, 95, 104, 116, 120–23, 126, 127, 129, 140, 141, 146, 149, 150, 156, 157, 161, 162, 164, 165, 169, 171, 172, 173, 175, 188, 193, 194, 216–17, 218, 219, 228, 234, 261, 270, 271, 273, 283, 284–6, 304, 306, 325–6, 333, 341, 342, 343, 349, 360, 362, 364, 370, 377, 398, 403, 424, 438, 455
  Ard-fheis 1917, 5–6, 47
  Ard-fheis 1922, 364
  courts, 129–30, 193, 339; see also republican courts
  Executive, 13, 28, 47, 82
  Standing Committee, 17, 27
  MPs 1918, ix, 4, 61–2, 64, 91
  manifesto 1921, 284
  non-violence and civil resistance, 33, 83–5, 116
  Northern policy, 171–3
  proscription of, 100–101
Sirocco Engineering works, Belfast, 175
Sixmilebridge, Co. Clare, 41
Skibbereen, Co. Cork, 260
Slattery, Jim, 191
Sligo, county, 22, 32, 39, 49, 285, 296, 326, 358, 359, 430, 435, 451
Sligo Brigade, IV 267, 296, 326
Sligo Champion, 358
Sligo town, 166, 429
Smuts, Gen. Jan, 303, 307–8, 309–10
Smyth, Col Gerard, 175
Smyth, Patrick, 191
Solohead, Co. Tipperary, 34
Soloheadbeg ambush, 57, 78–9, 80, 98, 100, 108
Somme, battle 1916, 181
South Africa, 335
Southern Parliament (GIA 1920), 303, 385
Stack, Austin, 24, 42, 58, 126, 128, 224, 267, 269, 284, 324, 329–30, 332, 335, 337–8, 341, 348, 367, 409, 410, 415, 435, 441, 447, **464**
Staines, Michael, 388, 389
Standard Hotel, Dublin, 207
Stephens, James, x
Stokes mortar, 200
Stopford Green, Alice, 49, 308, 379
Strickland, Gen Sir Peter, 218, 224, 225, 240, 243, 288, 297, 310
Sturgis, Mark (Assistant Under Secretary, Dublin Castle), 142, 147, 152, 158, 162–3, 167–8, 169, 180, 197, 198, 205, 217, 219, 224, 226, 304, 305–6
Swanzy, Oswald (DI RIC), 156, 179
Sweetman, Roger, 304
Sweeney, John, 240
symbols, political, 19, 176, 340–42

Tegart, Charles, 209–10
terrorism, 155, 369–70, 381
The Times newspaper, 99, 130
Thomas Cook's agency, 269
Thompson submachine gun, 233–4,
    292, 314, 317, 328, 395
Thornton, Frank, 84, 190, 202, 203,
    204, 207, 297
'Three Judges Bill', 102
Thurles, Co. Tipperary, 40, 80, 98,
    100, 165, 167, 361
Tipperary, county, 30, 43, 45, 79, 84,
    98, 100, 101, 106, 108, 116,
    117, 119, 136, 146, 156, 218,
    235, 280, 297, 320, 376
Tipperary IV, 421
    No.2 Brigade IV, 298
    No.3 Brigade, 43, 186, 187, 198
    North Tipperary Brigade, 183, 418
Tobin, Liam, 190, 192, 202, 387
Tourmakeady, Co. Mayo, 293
Townshend, Caroline, 170
Tralee, Co. Kerry, 75, 416
Traynor, Oscar, 207, 251, 278, 395,
    408–9, 410, 411, 413, 415
Traynor, Thomas, 453
Treacy, Seán, 34, 45, 46, 79, 106,
    116, 198
Treaty see Anglo-Irish Treaty
Trenchard, Air Chief Marshal Sir
    Hugh, 154
Trim, Co. Dublin, 165, 288
Trinity College, Dublin, 32, 385
Troup, Sir Edward (Under Secretary,
    Home Office), 143, 194
Truce (July 1921), 51, 234, 269,
    283, 297, 300, 306–11, 318–19,
    321, 322, 326, 331, 337, 354,
    376, 453
    liaison arrangements, 311–13
Tuam, Co. Galway, 75, 162
Tuam, Archbishop of, 219

Tubbercurry, Co. Sligo, 165–7, 326, 418
Tudor, Maj. Gen. Hugh, 139–40, 155,
    156, 157, 159, 162, 163, 167,
    209, 218, 224, 248, 288, 301
Tulla, Co. Clare, 123
Twomey, Maurice (Moss), 409, 413, 439
Tyrone, county, 14, 45, 278
Tyrone Brigade IV, 384

United Irishmen, 373
Ulster, xiv, 41, 171–6, 181, 280–82,
    340
Ulster Council Command, 380
Ulster Covenant, xiv, 14
Ulster Imperial Guards, 181
Ulster Special Constabulary, 180–81,
    376, 379
Ulster Unionist Council, 378
Ulster Volunteer Force, xiv, 162, 175,
    180, 181, 383
Union 1801, 151
unionists, 4, 14, 54, 55, 80, 92, 142,
    145, 146, 171–2, 173, 223, 285,
    286, 289, 305, 378, 380
United Irish League, 24, 28
University College, Dublin, 360
Upton, Co. Cork, 241, 245
USA, 70, 90
US–Cuba treaty 1903, 335
USSR, 70

Victoria barracks, Cork, 218, 312
Viet Minh, 113
Virginia, Co. Cavan, 46

Walsh, J. J., 270, 285
Walsh, William (Archbishop of
    Dublin), 14, 96, 97, 195, 197
Wandsworth gaol, 34
Waterford, 415
Waterford, county, 62, 172, 218,
    274, 295

Waterford Brigade, IV 260, 322, 446
War Office, 228
Weber, Max, 24
Weekly Summary of Acts of Aggression by the Enemy, 95
West Clare Brigade, IV 122
Westmeath, county, 39
Westport, Co. Galway, 75
Wexford, Co. Wexford, 156
Wexford, county, 218, 304, 320
Wexford Brigade IV, 118
Whitechurch, Co. Cork, 260
Wicklow, county, 38, 269
Wilkinson, Ellen, 170
Wilson, Field-Marshal Sir Henry, 139, 141, 150, 152, 155, 162, 217, 224, 297, 301, 302, 404
Wilson, Woodrow, 3, 48, 67, 68
Winter, Ormonde, 209–10
Wolfe Tone, Theobald, xi, 22, 26, 373
Woodcock, Lt Col, 206

Woods, Seamus, 376, 381, 383
women, 10, 15, 17, 22, 24, 30, 47–52, 57, 60, 62, 143, 170–1, 191, 250–52, 258, 377
    and republicanism, 363–4
    as spies, 264
Women's International League, 170
Workers' Republic, xi, 439
Workman Clark shipyard, Belfast, 175
World War, ix, xiv, 113, 272
Worthington-Evans, Sir Laming, 301, 302
Wrett, Phil, 46
Wylie, William, 151
Wyndham-Quin, Richard, 305
Wyse Power, Jennie, 122, 363
Wyse Power, Nancy, 49

Yeats, Lily, 171
Yeats, William Butler, 195–6, 451, 452
Young, Ned, 214

ALLEN LANE
an imprint of
PENGUIN BOOKS

Recently Published

David Marquand, *Mammon's Kingdom: An Essay on Britain, Now*

Justin Marozzi, *Baghdad: City of Peace, City of Blood*

Adam Tooze, *The Deluge: The Great War and the Remaking of Global Order 1916-1931*

John Micklethwait and Adrian Wooldridge, *The Fourth Revolution: The Global Race to Reinvent the State*

Steven D. Levitt and Stephen J. Dubner, *Think Like a Freak: How to Solve Problems, Win Fights and Be a Slightly Better Person*

Alexander Monro, *The Paper Trail: An Unexpected History of the World's Greatest Invention*

Jacob Soll, *The Reckoning: Financial Accountability and the Making and Breaking of Nations*

Gerd Gigerenzer, *Risk Savvy: How to Make Good Decisions*

James Lovelock, *A Rough Ride to the Future*

Michael Lewis, *Flash Boys*

Hans Ulrich Obrist, *Ways of Curating*

Mai Jia, *Decoded: A Novel*

Richard Mabey, *Dreams of the Good Life: The Life of Flora Thompson and the Creation of* Lark Rise to Candleford

Danny Dorling, *All That Is Solid: The Great Housing Disaster*

Leonard Susskind and Art Friedman, *Quantum Mechanics: The Theoretical Minimum*

Michio Kaku, *The Future of the Mind: The Scientific Quest to Understand, Enhance and Empower the Mind*

Nicholas Epley, *Mindwise: How we Understand what others Think, Believe, Feel and Want*

Geoff Dyer, *Contest of the Century: The New Era of Competition with China*

Yaron Matras, *I Met Lucky People: The Story of the Romani Gypsies*

Larry Siedentop, *Inventing the Individual: The Origins of Western Liberalism*

Dick Swaab, *We Are Our Brains: A Neurobiography of the Brain, from the Womb to Alzheimer's*

Max Tegmark, *Our Mathematical Universe: My Quest for the Ultimate Nature of Reality*

David Pilling, *Bending Adversity: Japan and the Art of Survival*

Hooman Majd, *The Ministry of Guidance Invites You to Not Stay: An American Family in Iran*

Roger Knight, *Britain Against Napoleon: The Organisation of Victory, 1793-1815*

Alan Greenspan, *The Map and the Territory: Risk, Human Nature and the Future of Forecasting*

Daniel Lieberman, *Story of the Human Body: Evolution, Health and Disease*